This is Poetry

Theme

Typerbole
— Exaggerating

Emotive language

Metaphor

Onomatopoeia

Imagery

Sibilance/structure

Tone

Personification

Enjambment
— one line running into
the other

Assonance/Alliteration

Rhythm/Rhyme

Simile

Brian Forristal & Billy Ramsell

FORUM PUB

Published by
Forum Publications Ltd
Unit 1703, Euro Business Park,
Little Island, Cork
Tel: (021) 4232268 | Fax: (01) 6335347
www.forum-publications.com

Design & Layout: Faye Keegan
www.fayekeegandesign.com

Additional Layout: Gillian Quinn

ISBN: 978-1-906565-43-5

ACKNOWLEDGMENTS

Poems by Eavan Boland are published by Carcanet Press, reproduced by kind permission of Carcanet Press Ltd. Poems by
Paul Durcan have been reprinted from *Life Is A Dream: 40 Years Reading Poems 1967 – 2007*, published by Harvill Secker 2009.
The poems 'The Tuft of Flowers', 'Mending Wall', 'After Apple-Picking' are reproduced by kind permission from *The Poetry of
Robert Frost* edited by Edward Connery Lathem. Copyright 1916, 1928, 1930, 1934, 1939, 1969, by Henry Holt and Company,
copyright 1936, 1944, 1951, 1956, 1958 by Robert Frost, copyright 1964,1967 by Leslie Frost Ballantine. Poems by Sylvia Plath
are reproduced with permission from Faber and Faber Ltd; Poems by Elizabeth Bishop reprinted from The Complete Poems 1927-
1979; copyright © 1979, 1983 by Alice Helen Methfessel. Reprinted by permission of Farrar, Straus and Giroux, LLC; Poems by
Seamus Heaney are reprinted by kind permission of Faber and Faber Ltd.

Contents

Glossary of Poetry Ideas and Terms   **06**

Poems

Elizabeth Bishop   **8**
The Fish   10
The Bight   12
At The Fishhouses   14
The Prodigal   17
Questions of Travel   19
The Armadillo   22
Sestina   24
First Death in Nova Scotia   26
Filling Station   28
In the Waiting Room   30

Eavan Boland   **34**
The War Horse   36
The Famine Road   38
Child of Our Time   40
The Black Lace Fan My Mother Gave Me   41
The Shadow Doll   43
White Hawthorn in the West of Ireland   45
Outside History   47
This Moment   49
The Pomegranate   50
Love   52

Paul Durcan   **54**
Nessa   56
The Girl with the Keys to Pearse's Cottage   58
The Difficulty that is Marriage   60
Wife Who Smashed Television Gets Jail   61
Parents   63
En Famille, 1979   64
Madman   65
'Windfall', 8 Parnell Hill, Cork   66
Six Nuns Die in Convent Inferno   70
Sport   76
Father's Day, 21 June 1992   79
The Arnolfini Marriage   81
Ireland 2002   83
Rosie Joyce   84
The MacBride Dynasty   88

Robert Frost   **90**
The Tuft of Flowers   92
Mending Wall   94
After Apple-Picking   96
The Road Not Taken   98
Birches   100
'Out, Out –'   102
Spring Pools   104
Acquainted With The Night   106
Design   108
Provide, Provide   110

Seamus Heaney   **112**
The Forge   114
Bogland   116
The Tollund Man   118
Sunlight   122
A Constable Calls   124
The Skunk   126
The Harvest Bow   128
The Underground   130
The Pitchfork   132
Lightenings VIII   134
A Call   136
Postscript   138
Tate's Avenue   140

Gerard Manley Hopkins   **142**
God's Grandeur   144
As kingfishers catch fire, dragonflies draw flame   146
Spring   148
Pied Beauty   149
The Windhover   150
Inversnaid   152
Felix Randal   154
No worst, there is none. Pitched past pitch of grief   156
I wake and feel the fell of dark, not day   158
Thou art indeed just, Lord, if I contend   160

John Keats   **162**
To one who has been long in city pent   164
On First Looking into Chapman's Homer   166
When I have fears that I may cease to be   168
La Belle Dame Sans Merci   170
Ode To A Nightingale   172
Ode On A Grecian Urn   175
To Autumn   178
Bright star, would I were steadfast as thou art   180

Sylvia Plath   **182**
The Times Are Tidy   184
Black Rook In Rainy Weather   185
Morning Song   187
Mirror   189
Finisterre   191
Pheasant   193
Elm   195
The Arrival of the Bee Box   197
Poppies in July   199
Child   201

Poetry Notes

Elizabeth Bishop   202
The Fish   209
The Bight   212
At The Fishhouses   215
The Prodigal   219
Questions of Travel   222
The Armadillo   226
Sestina   229
First Death in Nova Scotia   231
Filling Station   234
In the Waiting Room   236

Eavan Boland   240
The War Horse   246
The Famine Road   248
Child of Our Time   252
The Black Lace Fan My Mother Gave Me   254
The Shadow Doll   257
White Hawthorn in the West of Ireland   260
Outside History   262
This Moment   265
The Pomegranate   266
Love   270

Paul Durcan   272
Nessa   275
The Girl with the Keys to Pearse's Cottage   277
The Difficulty that is Marriage   279
Wife Who Smashed Television Gets Jail   281
Parents   283
En Famille, 1979   285
Madman   285
'Windfall', 8 Parnell Hill, Cork   286
Six Nuns Die in Convent Inferno   289
Sport   294
Father's Day, 21 June 1992   296
The Arnolfini Marriage   299
Ireland 2002   301
Rosie Joyce   302
The MacBride Dynasty   306

Robert Frost   308
The Tuft of Flowers   311
Mending Wall   313
After Apple-Picking   315
The Road Not Taken   318
Birches   320
'Out, Out –'   323
Spring Pools   326
Acquainted With The Night   328
Design   330
Provide, Provide   332

Seamus Heaney   334
The Forge   338
Bogland   342
The Tollund Man   346
Sunlight   350
A Constable Calls   353
The Skunk   357
The Harvest Bow   361
The Underground   366
The Pitchfork   369
Lightenings VIII   372
A Call   374
Postscript   376
Tate's Avenue   379

Gerard Manley Hopkins   382
God's Grandeur   385
As kingfishers catch fire, dragonflies draw flame   388
Spring   391
Pied Beauty   394
The Windhover   396
Inversnaid   400
Felix Randal   403
No worst, there is none. Pitched past pitch of grief   405
I wake and feel the fell of dark, not day   409
Thou art indeed just, Lord, if I contend   412

John Keats   415
To one who has been long in city pent   418
On First Looking into Chapman's Homer   420
When I have fears that I may cease to be   423
La Belle Dame Sans Merci   426
Ode To A Nightingale   429
Ode On A Grecian Urn   436
To Autumn   440
Bright star, would I were steadfast as thou art   443

Sylvia Plath   445
The Times Are Tidy   448
Black Rook In Rainy Weather   450
Morning Song   453
Mirror   455
Finisterre   458
Pheasant   461
Elm   463
The Arrival of the Bee Box   467
Poppies in July   470
Child   471

How to Answer the Poetry Question   473

Rhyme

Rhyme Schemes

Since time immemorial, rhyme has been deeply associated with poetry. The poem's rhyme scheme describes how rhymes are arranged in each stanza. When we describe a rhyme scheme, we refer to lines that rhyme with one another by the same letter.

In 'Inversnaid' by Gerard Manley Hopkins, for example, the first line of each stanza rhymes with the second line and the third line rhymes with the fourth. We say, therefore, that the poem has an AABB rhyme scheme:

> This darksome burn, horseback brown, **A**
> His rollrock highroad roaring down, **A**
> In coop and in comb the fleece of his foam **B**
> Flutes and low to the lake falls home **B**

In 'Design' by Robert Frost, the first eight lines follow an ABBA rhyme scheme:

> I found a dimpled spider, fat and white, **A**
> On a white heal-all, holding up a moth **B**
> Like a white piece of rigid satin cloth – **B**
> Assorted characters of death and blight **A**
> Mixed ready to begin the morning right, **A**
> Like the ingredients of a witches' broth – **B**
> A snow-drop spider, a flower like a froth, **B**
> And dead wings carried like a paper kite. **A**

Half-rhyme

An important technique to watch out for is half-rhyme. This is where two lines end in words that almost rhyme.

In 'The War Horse' by Eavan Boland, for example, the poet rhymes 'death' with 'earth'.

Seamus Heaney makes use of half-rhyme in 'The Harvest Bow'. In the third stanza, the poet rhymes 'loops' and 'slopes', while in the second stanza he rhymes 'braille' and 'palpable'.

Metaphor and Simile

Metaphors and similes are incredibly common in poetry, and many poems owe their most vivid and memorable moments to these techniques.

A metaphor is when one thing is compared to something else. A simile is very similar to a metaphor in that it also compares one thing to something else. The big difference is that it uses the words 'like' or 'as'.

Each of the following phrases compares the hurler D.J. Carey to a lion:

- 'D.J. was like a lion in attack.'
- 'D.J. played as if he was a lion in attack.'
- 'D.J. was a lion in attack.'

The first two comparisons are similes because they use the words 'like' or 'as'. The third comparison is a metaphor because it does not feature the words 'like' or 'as'. Very often a metaphor is referred to as a 'strong' or 'direct' comparison, while a simile is referred to as a 'weak' or 'indirect' comparison. As a general rule, similes tend to occur more often than metaphors, especially in modern poetry.

Consider the following phrases, and in the case of each say whether it is a metaphor or a simile:

- *'The words are shadows'* (**Eavan Boland**)
- *'One tree is yellow as butter'* (**Eavan Boland**)
- *Suspicion climbed all over her face, like a kitten, but not so playfully'* (**Raymond Chandler**)
- *'A leaping tongue of bloom'* (**Robert Frost**)
- *'Love set you going like a fat gold watch'* (**Sylvia Plath**)
- *''a dump of rocks/ Leftover soldiers from old, messy wars'* (**Sylvia Plath**)
- *''The mists are … Souls'* (**Sylvia Plath**)
- *''He stumbles on like a rumour of war'* (**Eavan Boland**)
- *''My red filaments burn and stand, a hand of wires'* (**Sylvia Plath**)
- *'I thought of London spread out in the sun/ Its postal districts packed like squares of wheat'* (**Philip Larkin**)
- *''The sky is a torn sail'* (**Adrienne Rich**)

Personification

This is a technique whereby an inanimate object is described as if it had the qualities of a living thing. In 'Love', Eavan Boland personifies the emotion of love, depicting it as a winged cupid-like creature that came to live in her home: 'And we discovered there/ love had the feather and muscle of wings'.

Glossary of Poetry
Ideas & Terms

Hyperbole

This is where we deliberately exaggerate to make a point. For example:

- These books weigh a ton. (These books are heavy.)
- I could sleep for a year. (I could sleep for a long time.)
- The path went on forever. (The path was very long.)
- I'm doing a million things right now. (I'm busy.)
- I could eat a horse. (I'm hungry.)

Metonymy

This is a technique whereby we describe something without mentioning the thing itself; instead, we mention something closely associated with it.

For example, we use the phrase 'White House', to refer to the President of the US and his advisors, or 'Hollywood' to refer to the film industry.

Synecdoche

In this technique we identify something by referring to a part of the thing instead of naming the thing itself.

A good example is the phrase 'All hands on deck'. In this instance, the sailors are identified by a part of their bodies, i.e. their hands. Similarly, we might use the word 'wheels' to refer to a car or 'head' to refer to cattle.

Sound Effects

One of the features that most distinguishes poetry from ordinary language is its 'musical' quality. Much of this 'word music' is generated by assonance, alliteration and onomatopoeia.

Alliteration

Alliteration occurs when a number of words in close proximity start with the same sound.

We see this in the repeated 'l' sounds in line 2 of 'Spring' by Gerard Manley Hopkins: When weeds, in wheels, shoot long and lovely and lush'

Alliteration also occurs in 'The Difficulty That is Marriage' by Paul Durcan where the poet describes the arguments between him and his wife: 'We disagree to disagree, we divide, we differ'. The harsh, repeated 'd' sounds suggest the couple grating on each other's nerves as they work out their differences.

Assonance

Assonance occurs when a number of words in close proximity have similar vowel sounds.

John Keats uses assonance in 'On First looking into Chapman's Homer'. In line 4 he uses repeated 'o' sounds: 'Apollo hold'. A similar repetition of the 'o' sound is evident in line 11: 'stout Cortez'.

Onomatopoeia

Onomatopoeia occurs when a word or a group of words sounds like the noise it describes. Examples of onomatopoeic words include buzz, murmur and clang.

It features in 'Out, Out –' by Robert Frost where we are told 'The buzz-saw snarled and rattled in the yard'. In this phrase we can almost hear the growling of the saw as it cuts the wood.

Onomatopoeia is also a feature of 'Spring' by Gerard Manley Hopkins, where we can almost hear the hollow, echoing sounds of noises in the forest in the phrase 'echoing timber'.

Euphony and Cacophony

Euphony and cacophony are also important concepts. Euphony can be defined as any pleasing or agreeable combination of sounds. Cacophony, meanwhile, is a harsh, jarring or discordant combination of sounds.

Euphony features in 'This Moment' by Eavan Boland in the lines 'Stars and moths,/ And rinds slanting around fruit', where the soft 's' and 'r' sounds create a pleasant and soothing musical effect.

Cacophony features in 'Diving Into the Wreck' by Gerard Manley Hopkins. The harsh repeated consonants convey the poet's anguish and despair: 'Bones built in me, flesh filled, blood brimmed the curse'.

Other Useful Poetic Terms

Allegory A story in which the characters and events are symbols that stand for ideas about human life or for a political or historical situation.

Allusion Where a poem makes reference to another poem or text.

Anaphora The repetition of words or phrases at the beginning of lines.

Antithesis A figure of speech in which words and phrases with opposite meanings are balanced against each other. An example of antithesis is 'To err is human, to forgive, divine'.

Ballad A poem that tells a story. Ballads are traditionally rhymed ABAB.

Beat The rhythmic or musical quality of a poem. In metrical verse, this is determined by the regular pattern of stressed and unstressed syllables.

Couplet A unit comprising of two lines.

Elegy Poem written to lament the dead.

Ellipsis The omission of words whose absence does not impede the reader's ability to understand the expression.

Enjambment When a single sentence is spread across two or more lines of verse.

Form The structural components of a poem e.g. stanza pattern, metre, syllable count etc – as opposed to the content.

Free verse Verse without formal metre or rhyme patterns.

Imagery The mental pictures created by a piece of writing.

Internal rhyme Rhyme that occurs within a single line of verse. Also refers to rhyme between internal phrases across multiple lines.

Irony The expression of one's meaning by using language that normally signifies the opposite.

Neologism The coining of new words.

Oxymoron Figure of speech containing two seemingly contradictory expressions, e.g. a happy funeral.

Paradox Seemingly absurd or contradictory statement which, on closer examination, reveals an important truth e.g. Wordsworth's 'The child is father of the man'.

Pathetic Fallacy Occurs when human emotions or behaviours are attributed to the natural world.

Pun A humorous way of using a word or phrase so that more than one meaning is suggested. For example: 'She's a skilful pilot whose career has really taken off.'

Quatrain A stanza comprising of four lines.

Refrain A line or phrase that recurs throughout a poem – especially at the end of stanzas.

Sonnet A fourteen line poem usually in iambic pentameters. Typically it consists of an octave (eight lines) and a sestet (six lines). Usually the octave presents or outlines a problem, situation or dilemma. The sestet mediates on this issue or attempts to resolve it. There is usually a 'volta', a turn or change in tone or outlook, that occurs between the octave and the sestet.

- Italian or Petrarchan Sonnet The sonnet was originated by the Italian poet Guittone of Arezzo and then popularised by Petrarch (1304-74). The term sonnet derives from the Italian for 'little song'. The Italian sonnet has the following rhyme scheme: ABBA ABBA CDE CDE.

- Shakespearean or English Sonnet: The Shakespearean or English sonnet employs an ABAB CDCD EFEF GG rhyme scheme. Essentially, therefore, it consists of three quatrains and a final couplet. Sometimes the volta or change of direction only occurs in the last two lines. ●

Elizabeth Bishop

Elizabeth Bishop was born in 1911 in Worcester, Massachusetts. Her life was blighted by strife and tragedy from a very young age, starting with the death of her father, William Bishop, who passed away when Elizabeth was just eight months old. This loss had a catastrophic impact on her mother, Gertrude Bulmer Bishop, who suffered a series of breakdowns and was permanently institutionalised when Elizabeth was five. Elizabeth would never see her mother again.

Following her mother's hospitalisation, Bishop was initially raised in a loving environment by her maternal grandparents in Nova Scotia, until her paternal family brought her back to Worcester, Massachusetts. However, she was deeply unhappy with this turn of events, which she described as a 'kidnapping'. She later stated in a biographical piece: 'I had been brought back unconsulted and against my wishes to the house my father had been born in, to be saved from a life of poverty and provincialism ... I felt myself aging, even dying. I was bored and lonely.'

Bishop suffered from poor health from an early stage of life, a situation that resulted in a very fragmented educational experience. However, she attended Vassar College in the late 1920s, studying music at first, before settling on English. Bishop struggled with low self-esteem and depression throughout her university years, and she drank heavily. She battled ongoing ill health, including chronic asthma, which was far less manageable at the time. It was during this phase that Bishop's poetic talent began to blossom. The great American poet Marianne Moore became her friend and mentor. She took Bishop on as something of a poetic apprentice, and helped her to publish her first poems and stories. Bishop flirted briefly with the idea of pursuing medicine at Cornell, but in the end was dissuaded from this path by Moore.

After finishing her education, Bishop spent a great deal of time travelling. A small inheritance from her deceased father ensured she could satisfy this restlessness without worrying about employment. She spent many years shuttling on a shoestring between France, New York and Key West in Florida. In Florida, in particular, she cultivated an appreciation for fishing, which is reflected in a poem entitled 'The Fish'. However, it was also during these nomadic years that her alcoholism festered.

Some academics have suggested that Bishop's drinking stemmed from a desire to fill the parental void in her life as well as from her feelings of inadequacy. Surprisingly, given her obvious talent, Bishop had little confidence in her own artistic ability, and felt overwhelmed by her equally gifted contemporaries and the edgy New York literati. She binged destructively, and alcohol came to dominate her life, as indicated in the poem 'The Prodigal'. From 1945 to 1951, Bishop's personal life seemed to decline while her literary career took off on what would be a stellar trajectory. In 1946 she released her first collection of poetry, the award-winning *North and South*.

Feeling somewhat creatively and emotionally dissatisfied, Bishop sought to soothe herself with travel, and so, in 1951, she travelled by freight ship to Brazil. She intended to stay for two weeks, but instead settled there for almost two decades, during which time she won a Pulitzer Prize. She maintained a relationship with Lota Soares, a Brazilian woman she had known for many years. By all accounts, these were the most contented years of Bishop's life. Her lack of creative self-belief continued to cripple her, however, and she endured what could only have been excruciating bouts of writer's block. She sometimes spent months, or even years, attempting to finish a poem. She would write the poem out in big letters on cardboard sheets above her desk, leaving gaps for the perfect words that she struggled to pin down.

Bishop's final years were difficult. She was devastated by the suicide of her partner, Lota, in 1967. She had returned to the US and landed teaching positions at the University of Washington, Harvard University and Massachusetts Institute of Technology. She also supplemented her income by giving public readings of her work.

Bishop's literary celebrity increased, and her poetry was recognised with a glut of prestigious awards, including a National Book Award (1970), a Neustadt International Prize (1976) and a Guggenheim Fellowship (1978). Despite her success, these sometimes proved to be difficult and lonely years, as she continued to deal with alcoholism and depression. She died suddenly in 1979.

The tragedies that clouded Bishop's early life never truly left her. They contributed not only to her greatest personal battles but also to some of her most powerful poetry. Echoes of this formative trauma can be found in such poems as 'Sestina'. Her mother's absence left its mark and explains the prominence of motherhood or maternity that features in her work.

Although Gertrude Bulmer Bishop, the poet's mother, is explicitly referenced in only one poem ('First Death in Nova Scotia'), her life story also provided details for the disturbing short story called 'In the Village'. In this story, Bishop recalls how, when she was a five-year-old girl, her mother suffered her breakdown. The story provides an immense psychological insight into her life and work.

Bishop developed an enduring friendship with the esteemed poet Robert Lowell, to whom she was introduced in the late 1940s. They corresponded for years, right up until Lowell's death in 1977. They influenced one another's work in equal measure. After Lowell's death, Bishop remarked upon the warmth of their relationship: 'Our friendship was kept alive through years of separation only by letters, remained constant and affectionate, and I shall always be deeply grateful for it.' She wrote the poem 'North Haven' in Lowell's memory.

Bishop famously refused to appear in female-only anthologies, a fact that has been interpreted by some as an unspoken censure of the feminist movement, which gained significant traction in 1960s America – just when Bishop was reaching her literary zenith. However, in a 1978 interview, Bishop explicitly identified herself as a feminist and explained that her aversion to being included in women-only anthologies arose rather from a deeply held conviction that she should be judged purely as a writer, not according to gender.

The time that Bishop spent in Brazil also influenced her poetry. She became fascinated with Brazilian culture and translated many poems and stories from Portuguese into English. Her appreciation of Latin American literature is evident in 'Questions of Travel' and 'The Armadillo'.

While much of Bishop's personal life was marked with tragedy and personal torments, it was not the focal point of her work. She was not inclined to use writing to complain and was not drawn to the confessional style of her contemporaries, who laid bare many dark and sordid details from their personal lives. Instead, Bishop devoted her poetry to celebrating and exploring the terrors and beauties of the physical world, as well as the mystery and complexity of the human psyche. Her work seems to concentrate intensely on small details, possibly because she perceived such details to be the only concrete (and, therefore, most important) things in life. She explained this succinctly in one of her many letters to Robert Lowell: 'My passion for accuracy may strike you as old-maidish – but since we do float on an unknown sea I think we should examine the other floating things that come our way very carefully; who knows what might depend on it?'

The Fish

I caught a tremendous fish
and held him beside the boat
half out of water, with my hook
fast in a corner of his mouth.
He didn't fight.   [5]
He hadn't fought at all.
He hung a grunting weight,
battered and venerable
and homely. Here and there
his brown skin hung in strips   [10]
like ancient wallpaper,
and its pattern of darker brown
was like wallpaper:
shapes like full-blown roses
stained and lost through age.   [15]
He was speckled with barnacles,
fine rosettes of lime,
and infested
with tiny white sea-lice,
and underneath two or three   [20]
rags of green weed hung down.
While his gills were breathing in
the terrible oxygen
– the frightening gills,
fresh and crisp with blood,   [25]
that can cut so badly –
I thought of the coarse white flesh
packed in like feathers,
the big bones and the little bones,
the dramatic reds and blacks   [30]
of his shiny entrails,
and the pink swim-bladder
like a big peony.
I looked into his eyes
which were far larger than mine   [35]
but shallower, and yellowed,
the irises backed and packed
with tarnished tinfoil
seen through the lenses
of old scratched isinglass.   [40]

They shifted a little, but not
to return my stare.
– It was more like the tipping
of an object toward the light.
I admired his sullen face,   [45]
the mechanism of his jaw,
and then I saw
that from his lower lip
– if you could call it a lip –
grim, wet, and weaponlike,   [50]
hung five old pieces of fish-line,
or four and a wire leader
with the swivel still attached,
with all their five big hooks
grown firmly in his mouth.   [55]
A green line, frayed at the end
where he broke it, two heavier lines,
and a fine black thread
still crimped from the strain and snap
when it broke and he got away.   [60]
Like medals with their ribbons
frayed and wavering,
a five-haired beard of wisdom
trailing from his aching jaw.
I stared and stared   [65]
and victory filled up
the little rented boat,
from the pool of bilge
where oil had spread a rainbow
around the rusted engine   [70]
to the bailer rusted orange,
the sun-cracked thwarts,
the oarlocks on their strings,
the gunnels – until everything
was rainbow, rainbow, rainbow!   [75]
And I let the fish go.

[8] **venerable:** worthy of respect because of age or experience
[9] **homely:** plain, not particularly attractive
[32] **swim-bladder:** an organ that allows a fish to control buoyancy
[33] **peony:** bright red or pink flower
[40] **isinglass:** a gelatin-like substance obtained from the bladders of certain fish
[53] **swivel:** a circular fastening device that connects the fishing line to the hook
[68] **bilge:** dirty water that pools or gathers on the floor of a boat
[71] **bailer:** device used to bail out (remove) water from a boat
[73] **oarlocks:** supporting pivots for oars
[74] **gunnels:** the upper edges of the side of a boat

Tease It Out

1. Describe the manner in which the poet holds the fish while she observes it.
2. The fish did not put up any fight when it was caught. Why do you think it did not struggle or resist? Is the poet surprised at its behaviour? Give a reason for your answer.
3. The poet uses three adjectives to describe the fish: 'battered', 'venerable' and 'homely'. In pairs, discuss (with the aid of a dictionary) what each of these words means. What does each adjective suggest about the fish and the poet's feelings about the creature?
4. To what does the poet compare the patterns on the fish's skin?
5. How does the poet describe the condition of the fish's skin? What does the poet say has attached to the fish's skin?
6. Why do you think that the oxygen that the fish breathes is 'terrible' to him?
7. Lines 27 to 33: The poet imagines what the fish's flesh and internal organs must look like. To what does she compare the flesh? Why does she make this comparison?
8. How does the poet convey the vivid red colour of the fish's swim bladder?
9. In what ways are the fish's eyes different to the poet's?
10. The poet provides a detailed description of the fish's eye, comparing aspects of it to foil and isinglass. Can you describe the appearance of the eye in your own words?
11. The poet gazes into the fish's eye, seeming to hope for some response or reaction from the creature. How does the fish respond or react to her gaze? To what does she compare its movement? What does the description suggest about the fish's interest in the poet?
12. What it the first thing about the fish's jaw that the poet first finds fascinating? What does the term 'weaponlike' suggest about this aspect of the fish?
13. The poet suddenly notices five hooks lodged in the fish's lower lip. In what condition are the threads and wires connected to the hooks?
14. The poet compares the hooks and broken lines to medals and to a 'beard of wisdom'. What do these comparisons suggest about the fish's character?
15. The poet says that 'victory filled up' the boat. What do the presence of the hooks and the condition of the threads and wire tell the poet about the fish? What sort of 'victory' do you think the poet has in mind?
16. How does the poet describe the inside of the boat? What objects does she mention? What sort of condition is the boat in?
17. The poet says that 'oil had spread a rainbow/ Around the rusted engine'? What is she describing here?
18. Bishop says that suddenly 'everything/ was rainbow, rainbow, rainbow!' What do you understand her to mean by this? Are there different ways to interpret these lines?
19. Why do you think the poet repeats the word 'rainbow' in line 75? What effect does this have?
20. Why do you think the poet 'let the fish go'?

Think About Themes

1. Bishop has a remarkable talent for discovering beauty in the most unlikely places. How is this evident in her description of the fish?
2. The poet is determined to understand the fish that she has caught, but her efforts to do so are unsuccessful until she notices the hooks in the fish's lip. Making reference to the poem, write a response to this statement.
3. The poet is most excited to discover the hooks in the fish's lip because she suddenly sees that she and the fish are alike. Why is it, do you think, that the poet can suddenly relate to this creature? In what ways might they or their lives be similar?
4. What does the poem suggest to you about the poet's attitude to the natural world?

The Bight
(On my birthday)

At low tide like this how sheer the water is.
White, crumbling ribs of marl protrude and glare
and the boats are dry, the pilings dry as matches.
Absorbing, rather than being absorbed,
the water in the bight doesn't wet anything, [5]
the color of the gas flame turned as low as possible.
One can smell it turning to gas; if one were Baudelaire
one could probably hear it turning to marimba music.
The little ocher dredge at work off the end of the dock
already plays the dry perfectly off-beat claves. [10]
The birds are outsize. Pelicans crash
into this peculiar gas unnecessarily hard,
it seems to me, like pickaxes,
rarely coming up with anything to show for it,
and going off with humorous elbowings. [15]
Black-and-white man-of-war birds soar
on impalpable drafts
and open their tails like scissors on the curves
or tense them like wishbones, till they tremble.
The frowsy sponge boats keep coming in [20]
with the obliging air of retrievers,
bristling with jackstraw gaffs and hooks
and decorated with bobbles of sponges.
There is a fence of chicken wire along the dock
where, glinting like little plowshares, [25]
the blue-gray shark tails are hung up to dry
for the Chinese-restaurant trade.
Some of the little white boats are still piled up
against each other, or lie on their sides, stove in,
and not yet salvaged, if they ever will be, from the last bad storm, [30]
like torn-open, unanswered letters.
The bight is littered with old correspondences.
Click. Click. Goes the dredge,
and brings up a dripping jawful of marl.
All the untidy activity continues, [35]
awful but cheerful.

Bight: a large, curved and shallow bay
[1] **sheer:** thin, translucent
[2] **marl:** an earthy deposit that is rich in either lime or calcium
[3] **pilings:** structures, made from heavy beams called 'piles' that are used to support docks and piers.
[7] **Baudelaire:** Charles Baudelaire (1821–67), a French poet a poet who often used the sea as an image in his verse and who strongly emphasised the importance of sound in poetry.
[8] **marimba:** a xylophone-like musical instrument
[9] **ocher:** golden yellow or yellowish brown
[9] **dredge:** a machine used for dredging up or removing earth from the seabed
[10] **claves:** pairs of wooden blocks that are used as percussion instruments in tropical Latin music; they produce jazzy rhythmic patterns
[16] **man-of-war birds:** seabirds, similar to pelicans, that have long wings and tail
[17] **impalpable:** unable to be felt by touch; difficult to understand
[20] **frowsy:** untidy or dishevelled
[22] **jackstraw gaffs and hooks:** sticks with hooks; barbed spears
[25] **plowshares:** the cutting blades of a plough

Get In Gear

Watch Video 1 How would you describe Key West Harbour, which is shown in the video? What three adjectives would you use to describe it? Is it a place you would like to visit? Give a reason for your answer.

Tease It Out

1. What word does the poet use to convey the appearance of the water in the bay? Why do you think she chose this particular word?

2. What can the poet see emerging up through the shallow water? What colour is this material? How does the poet convey the manner in which this substance reflects the sun?

3. How does the poet say the water in the bay is behaving? What does she finds odd about this?

4. To what does the poet compare the colour of the water? What colour is being described here?

5. The poet says that 'One can smell [the water] turning to gas'. Do you think the poet can actually smell this happening, or is it just a trick of her mind? Give a reason for your answer.

6. Lines 9 to 10 describe the dredge that is 'at work off the end of the peer'. How does the poet characterise the sound it makes? Does the poet find this sound pleasant or unpleasant? Give a reason for your answer.

7. How does the poet describe the manner in which the pelicans enter the water? To what does she compare their actions?

8. What two similes does the poet use to describe how the tails of the man-of-war birds operate in flight? Why are the 'drafts' of air upon which they fly 'impalpable'?

9. The poet describes the sponge boats returning to the harbour. To what animal does she liken the boats to? What do you think it is about these boats that makes her think of this analogy?

10. What does the poet see protruding out of the sponge boats? To what does she compare these items?

11. What objects are 'hung up to dry' upon the 'chicken wire along the dock'? How does the poet describe the appearance of these?

12. The poet describes some of the 'little white boats' on the shore. What condition are these boats in? How did they end up like this?

13. To what does the poet compare the damaged boats? Why do you think she makes this comparison?

14. Class Discussion: The poet says that the 'bight is littered with old correspondences'. Consider the word 'correspondence'. What different meanings can this word have? How do you think the poet intends the word to be understood here?

15. In the closing lines, the poet sums up the activity that takes place in the bight. What adjectives does she use? Why do you think she uses each of these? What do they suggest about her mood and outlook on this particular day?

Think About Themes

1. What does the poet's descriptions of the sea and the birds suggest about her attitude to the natural world? Give reasons for your answer.

2. Bishop's poems often feature moments of awareness, where the poet suddenly gains an insight or understanding after carefully studying a scene or a particular object. Does such a moment occur in this poem? Give a reason for your answer.

3. The poem was written on the poet's birthday and the poet speaks of there being old 'correspondences' scattered around the bay. What does the poet's description of the bight tell us about the poet and how she is feeling on this occasion? How might the bight be said to resemble her life?

In Context

Bishop often adopts a neutral or detached tone in her poetry so that emotion will not interfere with her efforts to capture things as accurately as possible. Discuss this statement with reference to 'The Bight' and two other poems on the course.

At the Fishhouses

Although it is a cold evening,
down by one of the fishhouses
an old man sits netting,
his net, in the gloaming almost invisible
a dark purple-brown,   [5]
and his shuttle worn and polished.
The air smells so strong of codfish
it makes one's nose run and one's eyes water.
The five fishhouses have steeply peaked roofs
and narrow, cleated gangplanks slant up   [10]
to storerooms in the gables
for the wheelbarrows to be pushed up and down on.
All is silver: the heavy surface of the sea,
swelling slowly as if considering spilling over,
is opaque, but the silver of the benches,   [15]
the lobster pots, and masts, scattered
among the wild jagged rocks,
is of an apparent translucence
like the small old buildings with an emerald moss
growing on their shoreward walls.   [20]
The big fish tubs are completely lined
with layers of beautiful herring scales
and the wheelbarrows are similarly plastered
with creamy iridescent coats of mail,
with small iridescent flies crawling on them.   [25]
Up on the little slope behind the houses,
set in the sparse bright sprinkle of grass,
is an ancient wooden capstan,
cracked, with two long bleached handles
and some melancholy stains, like dried blood,   [30]
where the ironwork has rusted.
The old man accepts a Lucky Strike.
He was a friend of my grandfather.
We talk of the decline in the population
and of codfish and herring   [35]
while he waits for a herring boat to come in.
There are sequins on his vest and on his thumb.
He has scraped the scales, the principal beauty,
from unnumbered fish with that black old knife,
the blade of which is almost worn away.   [40]

Down at the water's edge, at the place
where they haul up the boats, up the long ramp
descending into the water, thin silver
tree trunks are laid horizontally
across the gray stones, down and down   [45]
at intervals of four or five feet.

Cold dark deep and absolutely clear,
element bearable to no mortal,
to fish and to seals … One seal particularly
I have seen here evening after evening. [50]
He was curious about me. He was interested in music;
like me a believer in total immersion,
so I used to sing him Baptist hymns.
I also sang 'A Mighty Fortress is Our God.'
He stood up in the water and regarded me [55]
steadily, moving his head a little.
Then he would disappear, then suddenly emerge
almost in the same spot, with a sort of shrug
as if it were against his better judgement.
Cold dark deep and absolutely clear, [60]
the clear gray icy water … Back, behind us,
the dignified tall firs begin.
Bluish, associating with their shadows,
a million Christmas trees stand
waiting for Christmas. The water seems suspended [65]
above the rounded gray and blue-gray stones.
I have seen it over and over, the same sea, the same,
slightly, indifferently swinging above the stones,
icily free above the stones,
above the stones and then the world. [70]
If you should dip your hand in,
your wrist would ache immediately,
your bones would begin to ache and your hand would burn
as if the water were a transmutation of fire
that feeds on stones and burns with a dark gray flame. [75]
If you tasted it, it would first taste bitter,
then briny, then surely burn your tongue.
It is like what we imagine knowledge to be:
dark, salt, clear, moving, utterly free,
drawn from the cold hard mouth [80]
of the world, derived from the rocky breasts
forever, flowing and drawn, and since
our knowledge is historical, flowing, and flown.

[4]	**gloaming:** dusk, twilight	
[6]	**shuttle:** tool used to repair nylon fishing nets	
[10]	**cleated gangplanks:** ridged wooden walkways with projecting strips of metal or rubber to provide traction	
[11]	**gables:** the triangular part of a wall that attaches to the roof	
[15]	**opaque:** not transparent	
[18]	**translucence:** having the quality of being semi-transparent	
[24]	**iridescent:** varying in colour when seen in different lights or from different angles	
[28]	**capstan:** a revolving cylinder around which rope or cable is wrapped. Used for hoisting heavy weights such as anchors	
[32]	**Lucky Strike:** a brand of cigarette	
[37]	**sequins:** small shiny discs used for ornamentation; in this case, the term is used as a metaphor for the fish scales that fall onto the old man's hands and clothes as he scrapes the fish with his knife.	
[53]	**Baptist:** a member of a Protestant Christian denomination that believes in baptising its adult members by total	
[54]	immersion	
[74]	**A Mighty Fortress Is Our God:** a popular Protestant hymn	
	transmutation: the process of changing from one form or state to another	

Tease It Out

Lines 1 to 40

1. What physical features of the fish-houses are mentioned by the poet?

2. How are fish transported into the storerooms in the fish houses' gables?

3. What task is the 'old man' performing? What instruments is he using? Why is he described as being 'almost invisible'?

4. What effect, in lines 13 to 17, does the twilight have on the landscape of Great Village?

5. Class Discussion: In what way does the sea differ from the other aspects of the landscape?

6. The poet describes the 'fish tubs' and the 'wheelbarrows'. Does she present these objects as ugly, as strangely beautiful or as banal and everyday? Give a reason for your answer?

7. What does the poet offer the old man? What personal connection do they establish? What do they talk about?

8. What is the old man waiting for as he sits outside the fish-houses?

9. What work does the old man do on a daily basis?

10. Which phrases suggest that he has been doing this work for a very long time?

11. What inventive metaphor does the poet use for the fish-scales on 'his vest and on his thumb'?

Lines 41 to 65

12. Describe, in your own words, the ramps used by the fishermen to 'haul up the boats'.

13. The poet has seen a seal that, she believe, is 'interested' in her. Suggest how the seal might convey this interest.

14. What songs does the poet sing to the seal? How does the seal respond to her singing?

15. The seal is presented as oddly human in its behaviour. Identify three words or phrases that convey this.

16. Look up the term 'total immersion'. What does it suggest about the poet's religious upbringing? How might the seal, in its own way, be described as 'a believer in total immersion'?

17. The poet uses personification to describe the forest of fir trees. Which phrases contribute to this effect? What are the trees portrayed as doing?

18. The trees seem to blend with their own shadows. What phrase does the poet use to describe this effect? Would you agree that this phrase, too, contains an element of personification?

Lines 65 to 83

19. The poet describes how the sea comes 'swinging'. What does this suggest about the movement of its waves?

20. True or false: The poet believes that the sea never changes.

21. The poet feels that the sea could flow anywhere, that it's un-bound by the laws of physics. Identify three different phrases that suggest this.

22. According to the poet, what would happen if you were to 'dip your hand in' the sea?

23. The poet compares the sea to a very strange form of fire. What features of this fire does she mention? What does this comparison suggest about her attitude to the ocean?

24. What does she imagine 'feeds' this fire?

25. 'The poet imagines that tasting the sea-water would be like ingesting acid'. Write three or four sentences in response to this statement.

26. The poet imagines the sea issuing from springs deep within the rocky sea-bed. What metaphors does she use to describe these springs?

Think About Themes

1. Would you agree that the poem's opening forty lines create an effective atmosphere? Which of our senses are appealed to in this rich descriptive passage?

2. Is Great Village portrayed as a thriving community or as one in decline? Gve a reason for your answer.

3. Twice the poet begins to describe the sea. (In lines 47 to 49 and in lines 60 and 61). And twice she allows herself to be distracted. How can we explain this reluctance to directly contemplate the ocean? Consider the following explanations and rank them in order of plausibility.
   - The poet is afraid of water.
   - The poet thinks the ocean looks menacing and unpleasant on this particular evening.
   - The poet associates the sea with her unconscious mind and traumatic self-knowledge.
   - The poet is bored of looking at the ocean.

4. The poet draws a comparison between the sea and 'what we imagine knowledge to be'. Is the poet referring a) to general knowledge, b) to a specific set of skills or c) to knowledge of the self and the unconscious mind.

5. Working in groups of four, take a large piece of paper and create a placemat like the one below The poet suggests that we imagine knowledge to be 'dark', 'salt', 'clear', 'moving' and 'utterly free'.

   Take each term in turn and, in your section of the placemat, jot down every association it has for you. Then, as a group, discuss each term. How might each be an accurate and effective description of self-knowledge?

6. Knowledge, the poet suggests, must be 'drawn' out of ourselves ,like water from the deepest rocky springs. Do you think that she views this as an easy process or as a difficult one? Give a reason for your answer.

7. 'The self, like the sea, is always in flux. Therefore our self-knowledge is always out of date. For no sooner have we understood ourselves than our minds and personalities have changed again'. Can you identify two phrases in the poem that support this statement?

The Prodigal

The brown enormous odor he lived by
was too close, with its breathing and thick hair,
for him to judge. The floor was rotten; the sty
was plastered halfway up with glass-smooth dung.
Light-lashed, self-righteous, above moving snouts,
the pigs' eyes followed him, a cheerful stare –
even to the sow that always ate her young –
till, sickening, he leaned to scratch her head.
But sometimes mornings after drinking bouts
(he hid the pints behind a two-by-four),   [10]
the sunrise glazed the barnyard mud with red;
the burning puddles seemed to reassure.
And then he thought he almost might endure
his exile yet another year or more.

But evenings the first star came to warn.   [15]
The farmer whom he worked for came at dark
to shut the cows and horses in the barn
beneath their overhanging clouds of hay,
with pitchforks, faint forked lightnings, catching light,
safe and companionable as in the Ark.   [20]
The pigs stuck out their little feet and snored.
The lantern – like the sun, going away –
laid on the mud a pacing aureole.
Carrying a bucket along a slimy board,
he felt the bats' uncertain staggering flight,   [25]
his shuddering insights, beyond his control,
touching him. But it took him a long time
finally to make his mind up to go home.

Prodigal: a spendthrift; someone who wastes his or her money in an extravagant fashion
Also refers to Jesus' parable of the Prodigal Son, which appears in the Gospel of Luke
[7] **sow:** a female pig
[10] **two-by-four:** a plank of wood
[20] **companionable:** sociable, suited to the company of others
[20] **Ark:** refers to the biblical tale of Noah's Ark
[23] **aureole:** a halo of light

[Handwritten annotations:]

Double Sonnet
12 Line stanzas
irregular
Rhyming scheme
follows a Rhyme

Rhyme in final
line emphasing
his feeliness of
isolation

Tone
loneliness
Darkness

knows better

believe you're right

his opinion of himself is very low

feels he is forced away out at times the beauty of morning sun returns him

metaphor
simile
simile

Even though he is unhappy it still took a long time to make a decision to go home – Loner

Bishop felt exile, isolated feels he's exanded

pigs

Precise images
– appauling conditions of pig sty are jouxtaposed contrasted with images of beauty

Tone
pessimistic, Bleak, disgusted, hope

synaesthesia – described as one thing eg. pig and smell

detail · metaphor – sight + touch
[5] powerful
vicious companions
cannabalistic
visual image

Alcoholic

– Note of hope – a world beyond pigsty
– visual image
– Redemption

night time is worst
– When first star appears its eerie
Assonance

Emphasise lonliness
Walking – light going away

envious of barn
– warm pleasant place
– Animals have eachother + Prodigal doesn't
– Homliness of cows + Horses emphasises isolation of prodigal

bats come out at night
– uncertain staggering of bats
– metaphor for prodigal

Get In Gear

Watch Video 2, which features the biblical story of the Prodigal Son. Were you familiar with this story? Do you think that the father's treatment of his two sons was fair and just? Give a reason for your answer.

Tease It Out

Stanza 1

1. In what type of building does the prodigal live and work?
2. What kind of work does he do there? Support your answer with reference to the poem.
3. The prodigal no longer notices the foul stench of the pigsty. Which lines indicate this?
4. We're told that the odour of the sty was 'enormous' and 'brown'. We're told that it was 'breathing' and had 'thick hair.' What do these phrases suggest about the nature of the odour? What kind of smell do you imagine when you read them?
5. Class Discussion: Which literary device is used in the description of this odour? (Hint: it starts with an 's').
6. Describe the condition of the sty's floor and walls.
7. Describe in your own words the pigs' facial expressions. How does the prodigal react to the way they stare at him?
8. Which lines indicate that the prodigal is an alcoholic?
9. What indication is there that the prodigal is ashamed of his drinking?
10. Where does he hide his pint bottles of gin or whiskey?
11. Class Discussion: Some mornings the sunrise has a particular effect upon the surface of the farmyard. Describe, in your own words, what the prodigal sees on these hung-over dawns.
12. Consider lines 13 to 14. What indications are there that the prodigal is unhappy with his current way of life, that he finds his existence in the pigsty something of a struggle?

Stanza 2

13. The prodigal feels a sense of dread as night approaches. Which line conveys this?
14. 'The lantern – like the sun, going away'. Who does this lantern belong to?
15. What does the prodigal's employer do each evening?
16. Describe in your own words the cows' and horses' sleeping conditions.
17. What indication is there that the pigs, too, sleep in a cosy and comfortable fashion?
18. While the animals sleep comfortably, the prodigal completes his work for the day. What task is depicted in line 24?

19. Can you suggest what 'insights' or moments of comprehension the prodigal might experience as night falls?
20. Why might these 'insights' cause him to shudder? What indication is there that he usually tries to suppress or ignore these insights?
21. Which phrase indicates that the bats are guided by instinct rather that sight?
22. Do the paths proceed in a smooth or jerky manner as they hover through the air? Give a reason for your answer.
23. Which phrase indicates that the prodigal identifies with the bats as he sees them hovering overhead?
24. In what sense is the prodigal, like the bats, guided by 'uncertain' instincts? Where are those instincts leading him?

Think About Themes

1. The second stanza creates an atmosphere of heart-breaking loneliness. Which lines and images contribute to this atmosphere?
2. "The Prodigal' provides a wonderfully grim depiction of the squalor and misery associated with addiction'. Would you agree with this interpretation of the poem? Give reasons for your answer.
3. Would you agree that the poem also highlights the comforts and consolations that addicts get from their addiction?
4. Group Discussion: 'But it took him a long time/ finally to make his mind up to go home'. The prodigal has a miserable existence in the pigsty. Yet he's reluctant or hesitant to change his life and return to his family. Suggest reasons why this might be the case.
5. Did your knowledge of the Gospel story affect your understanding of this piece? Do you think you'd have understood the poem differently without this background knowledge? Say why.
6. Elizabeth Bishop struggled with alcohol addiction throughout her life. Can 'The Prodigal', therefore, be considered a very personal poem? Give a reason for your answer.
7. Do you think that this poem is set in the past or in the present day? Support your answer with reference to the poem.

theme
Exile,
homelessness
Awareness,
Travel

Bishops Love for travel
- Explores nature of travel + what it means to her
- Travels to Brazil - what is the impact on the travel, why are we doing it?
- Climate change - impact on environment

Questions of Travel

handwritten: Time is passing

There are too many waterfalls here; the crowded streams
hurry too rapidly down to the sea,
and the pressure of so many clouds on the mountaintops
makes them spill over the sides in soft slow-motion,
turning to waterfalls under our very eyes. *metaphor*
– For if those streaks, those mile-long, shiny, tearstains,
aren't waterfalls yet,
in a quick age or so, as ages go here,
they probably will be.
But if the streams and clouds keep travelling, travelling,
the mountains look like the hulls of capsized ships,
slime-hung and barnacled.

Think of the long trip home.
Should we have stayed at home and thought of here?
Where should we be today?
Is it right to be watching strangers in a play
in this strangest of theaters?
What childishness is it that while there's a breath of life
in our bodies, we are determined to rush
to see the sun the other way around?
The tiniest green hummingbird in the world?
To stare at some inexplicable old stonework,
inexplicable and impenetrable,
at any view,
instantly seen and always, always delightful?
Oh, must we dream our dreams
and have them, too?
And have we room
for one more folded sunset, still quite warm?

TOO perfect
- sick of seeing them

Sibilance
- soft, comforting atmosphere

geographical changes
stream → waterfall
foliage, rock

metaphor

simile

bottom
sea, shells
negative aspects

bloated

Jondi's eye - point comes where you stop appreciating it
Paints a landscape picture
image of clouds, almost spilling down sides - streaks turning into waterfalls
negativity - sad, tearstains
mountain looks like an upside down ship

Questions?
Should she be somewhere else are
tourists, spying on people, watching natives of country, invading privacy
see sun from other side of equator
childishness, can't settle
tick off experiences
is it enjoyable?
why can't we be satisfied

[5]

[10]

[15]

[20]

[25]

But surely it would have been a pity
not to have seen the trees along this road,
really exaggerated in their beauty,
not to have seen them gesturing
like noble pantomimists, robed in pink.   [30]
– Not to have had to stop for gas and heard
the sad, two-noted, wooden tune
of disparate wooden clogs   [35]
carelessly clacking over
a grease-stained filling-station floor.
(In another country the clogs would all be tested.
Each pair there would have identical pitch.)   [40]
– A pity not to have heard
the other, less primitive music of the fat brown bird
who sings above the broken gasoline pump
in a bamboo church of Jesuit baroque: [45]
three towers, five silver crosses.

– Yes, a pity not to have pondered,
blurr'dly and inconclusively,
on what connection can exist for centuries
between the crudest wooden footwear   [50]
and, careful and finicky,
the whittled fantasies of wooden cages.
– Never to have studied history in
the weak calligraphy of songbirds' cages.
– And never to have had to listen to rain   [55]
so much like politicians' speeches:
two hours of unrelenting oratory
and then a sudden golden silence
in which the traveller takes a notebook, writes:

'Is it lack of imagination that makes us come   [60]
to imagined places, not just stay at home?
Or could Pascal have been not entirely right
about just sitting quietly in one's room?

Continent, city, country, society:
the choice is never wide and never free.   [65]
And here, or there … No. Should we have stayed at home,
wherever that may be?'

[22]	*inexplicable:*	can't be explained or accounted for
[23]	*impenetrable:*	can't be understood
[34]	*pantomimists:*	those who participate in or practise the exaggerated comedy of pantomime
[43]	*primitive:*	simple, unsophisticated or undeveloped
[45]	*Jesuit baroque:*	The baroque is a dramatic and complex style of architecture that was developed in 17th-century Europe; it was brought to South America by Jesuit priests
[52]	*whittled:*	wood that has been carved by repeatedly cutting small slices from it
[54]	*calligraphy:*	decorative writing
[57]	*oratory:*	formal speech
[62]	*Pascal:*	Blaise Pascal (1623–62) was a French mathematician, philosopher and inventor. He famously suggested: 'All human evil comes from a single cause, man's inability to sit quietly in a room'

Tease It Out

Lines 1 to 12

1. Would you agree that the speaker successfully creates a sense of hurry and pressure in the poem's opening three lines? Give a reason for your anwer.
2. The mountains are so high that their peaks breach the cloud cover. What metaphor does the speaker use to describe the clouds that go 'spilling' in this fashion?
3. The poet suggests that, in this part of Brazil, waterfalls will be formed 'in a quick age or so, as ages go here'. Does the speaker feel that time travels quickly in this location? Or does she feel that it travels slowly? Give a reason for your answer.
4. Group Discussion: Why does the poet repeat the word 'travelling' in line 10? What effect does this repetition create?
5. What simile does the speaker use to describe the mountains? Does it effectively capture their massiveness and stillness?

Lines 13 to 29

6. What negative aspect of travel does the speaker identify in line 13?
7. The speaker suggests that it might be better to imagine a place than to actually visit it. Which lines convey this? Do you think she has a point?
8. The poet compares travel and tourism to watching a play in a theatre. According to the poet, who are the performers and who are the audience members?
9. The speaker suggests that there's an element of 'childishness' in the behavior of tourists. Which words and phrases convey this? Would you agree that she has a point?
10. The poet believes that tourists engage with the things they see on only the most superficial level. Which phrase suggests this?
11. The poet suggests that tourism is a form of gluttonous consumption. What phrases suggest this?

Lines 30 to 66

12. In this section, the speaker mentions a number of experiences that it would have been 'a pity' to miss out on. List them. Which of these experiences seems most appealing to you? Which seems least appealing? Give reasons for your answers.
13. What simile does Bishop use to describe the trees?
14. Describe, in your own words, the sound produced by the man's clogs as he walks around the filling station.
15. Why do the clogs produce this musical effect?
16. Why, according to the speaker, would you not find this effect in 'another country'?

17. Which phrases indicate that the cage is a complex construction crafted from wood?
18. Why do you think the bird's music is described as being 'less primitive' than than that of the clogs? Do you find this assertion surprising?
19. Describe in your own words what the speaker 'ponders' as she waits in the filling station. Do her thoughts lead to any definite conclusion?
20. The cage is described as a form of 'weak calligraphy.' What visual similarity might exist between handwriting and this woven wooden object?
21. Class Discussion: The speaker claims that she is 'studying history' when she looks at the songbird's cage. What might she mean by this? What might the cages tell her about Brazil's past?
22. What simile does Bishop use to describe the sound of the tropical rain?
23. What do you understand by the speaker's suggestion that Pascal may not have been 'entirely right'?
24. Class Discussion: 'the choice is never wide and never free'. What does Bishop mean by this rather enigmatic pronouncement?

Think About Themes

1. Consider the poem's title. Can you list every question or issue surrounding travel that Bishop addresses in the poem?
2. 'This poem is an extremely balanced meditation on travel. Every experience Bishop describes is shown to have both a negative and positive aspect. The poem, therefore, simply does not make up its mind on the question of whether travel is a good thing or a bad thing.' Write a paragraph in response to this statement.

The Armadillo
for Robert Lowell

This is the time of year
when almost every night
the frail, illegal fire balloons appear.
Climbing the mountain height,

rising toward a saint   [5]
still honored in these parts,
the paper chambers flush and fill with light
that comes and goes, like hearts.

Once up against the sky it's hard
to tell them from the stars –   [10]
planets, that is – the tinted ones:
Venus going down, or Mars,

or the pale green one. With a wind,
they flare and falter, wobble and toss;
but if it's still they steer between   [15]
the kite sticks of the Southern Cross,

receding, dwindling, solemnly
and steadily forsaking us,
or, in the downdraft from a peak,
suddenly turning dangerous.   [20]

Last night another big one fell.
It splattered like an egg of fire
against the cliff behind the house.
The flame ran down. We saw the pair

of owls who nest there flying up   [25]
and up, their whirling black-and-white
stained bright pink underneath, until
they shrieked up out of sight.

The ancient owls' nest must have burned.
Hastily, all alone,   [30]
a glistening armadillo left the scene,
rose-flecked, head down, tail down,

and then a baby rabbit jumped out,
short-eared, to our surprise.
So soft! – a handful of intangible ash   [35]
with fixed, ignited eyes.

Too pretty, dreamlike mimicry!
O falling fire and piercing cry
and panic, and a weak mailed fist
clenched ignorant against the sky!   [40]

[3]   **fire balloon:** a balloon that rises when a
      small fire at its mouth heats and rarefies
      the air within it
[16] **Southern Cross:** a distinctive
      constellation visible in the southern
      hemisphere
[19] **downdraft:** downward current of air
[31] **armadillo:** a mammal with a protective
      leathery shell and long claws for digging
[35] **intangible:** something that cannot be
      touched; difficult to understand; vague
      and abstract

22

Get In Gear

1. In which country is this poem set? You may wish to research Bishop's biography online in order to answer this question.
2. Watch Video 3, which describes how to manufacture sky lanterns or fire balloons. Write a paragraph describing the main steps in this process.
3. The balloons, we're told, go 'rising toward a saint'. This is because they're released to celebrate St John, whose feast-day falls on the 24th of June. Have you heard of any other traditions that are celebrated, or rituals that are performed, around this date in Ireland or another country?

Tease It Out

1. The fire balloons are described as 'frail'. What does this suggest about the materials involved in their construction?
2. The fire balloons have been declared 'illegal'. Can you suggest why they might be banned by the authorities?
3. The balloon's flight-path follows the slope of a nearby mountain. Which phrase suggests this?
4. Class Discussion: The poet describes how light 'comes and goes' within the 'paper chambers' of the balloons as they drift upwards. Can you suggest what phenomenon is responsible for this effect?
5. What simile does the poet use to describe this effect? Is it a successful comparison?
6. True or false: According to the poet, the balloons resemble stars when they are 'up against the sky'.
7. Would you agree that the poet corrects herself when making this comparison?
8. Which four verbs does the poet use to describe the balloons' movement on a windy night? In each case, can you come up with an alternative verb of your own that has a similar meaning?
9. On 'still', windless nights the balloons move 'solemnly'. Working in pairs, consider this adverb and try to come up with three other words that it brings to mind.
10. Consider the phrase 'forsaking us'. Pick two adjectives of your won to describe the emotions felt by the spectators as they watch the balloons drift out of view.
11. The balloons, as they drift ever higher, seem to move among the stars themselves. What metaphor is used to describe this optical effect.
12. What's a 'downdraft'? What impact do such downdrafts have on the fire balloons?
13. Where did the fire balloon touch down on the previous night? What simile does the poet use to describe its impact?
14. What verbs are used to describe to the movement of the owls? Would you agree that these verbs convey a sense of panic and confusion?
15. Group Discussion: The owls are described as stained 'bright pink underneath'. What is the cause of this pinkness?
16. What has caused the armadillo to be 'rose-flecked'?
17. The armadillo's head and tail are 'down' as it flees. What does this suggest about its demeanour?
18. Which phrase indicates that the baby rabbit has been utterly incinerated by the flames?
19. The rabbit's remains are described as 'intangible'. What would happen if you touched this rabbit-shaped 'handful of ash'?
20. Group Discussion: Why did Bishop choose to print the final stanza in italics? Do these lines come from the poet's point of view or from some other viewpoint?
21. The final lines refer to a clenched fist that is described as 'mailed', 'weak' and 'ignorant'. Who or what does this fist belong to?
22. Why did Bishop choose to title this poem 'The Armadillo'?

Think About Themes

1. Class Discussion: What do you understand by the expression 'Too pretty, dreamlike mimicry'? What precisely do the fire balloons mimic? Consider the following possibilities and rank them in order of likelihood:
   - They resemble bombs, being launched upwards then crashing back down again.
   - They resemble prayers, drifting upwards towards the heavens.
   - They resemble spacecraft. (Remember that Bishop was writing at the dawn of the space age.)
   - They resemble love poems; after all, they're made out of paper, just like books of poetry.
2. Class Discussion: We can imagine how the sight of hundreds of floating fire balloons might be described as 'pretty' and 'dreamlike'. But in what sense might they be described as 'too pretty'?
3. Bishop is known as a poet with a measured, detached tone. Can you identify three phrases in this poem where this tone comes across?
4. Would you agree that the poem's last four lines are more directly emotional? What emotions, in your opinion, are expressed here?
5. 'Above all else, this poem is about the stupidity of men with regard to their environment'. Write a paragraph agreeing or disagreeing with this statement.
6. 'This poem is about things that are dangerous but that we can't stay away from. Things like war, love and art exude a glamorous attraction despite – or perhaps because of – their danger.' Write a paragraph in response to this statement.

Sestina

[handwritten: grief / family relationships / pathetic fallacy / About a child living with loss + her grandmother]

September rain falls on the house.
In the failing light, the old grandmother
sits in the kitchen with the child
beside the Little Marvel Stove,
reading the jokes from the almanac,   [5]
laughing and talking to hide her tears.

She thinks that her equinoctial tears
and the rain that beats on the roof of the house
were both foretold by the almanac,
but only known to a grandmother.   [10]
The iron kettle sings on the stove.
She cuts some bread and says to the child,

It's time for tea now; but the child
is watching the teakettle's small hard tears
dance like mad on the hot black stove,   [15]
the way the rain must dance on the house.
Tidying up, the old grandmother
hangs up the clever almanac

on its string. Birdlike, the almanac
hovers half open above the child,   [20]
hovers above the old grandmother
and her teacup full of dark brown tears.
She shivers and says she thinks the house
feels chilly, and puts more wood in the stove.

It was to be, says the Marvel Stove.   [25]
I know what I know, says the almanac.
With crayons the child draws a rigid house
and a winding pathway. Then the child
puts in a man with buttons like tears
and shows it proudly to the grandmother.   [30]

But secretly, while the grandmother
busies herself about the stove,
the little moons fall down like tears
from between the pages of the almanac
into the flower bed the child   [35]
has carefully placed in the front of the house.

Time to plant tears, says the almanac.
The grandmother sings to the marvellous stove
and the child draws another inscrutable house.

[handwritten annotations throughout: repressed emotion; moon changes; can't escape the sadness; predicted - lost someone; Child's imagination; normal life; Adjectives - Strassier; Mono-syllabic words; metaphor; personification/ominous; simile; predict; metaphor; Tight in - hold something; her father; sestina; contrast; simile; impossible to understand; 7 stanzas; dim, dark - negative; dark tone - secretive - mysterious - pessimistic centre of the child's world; weighing down impending doom; side/alone grandma; verb; enjambment; wants to carry on; monthly cycle; move on going to grow back sorrow could continue; Tears - hiding them - teakettle - teacup - man's buttons - moons; Repeated words Sestina - structure - 6 sestets (6 line stanza); Atmosphere; Pathetic fallacy; Sorrowful; bleak; Alienation from home; Anthropomorphism; Structure of the poem mirrors the repressed emotion, rain getting increasingly heavy; 3 line envoy]

---

[5] **almanac:** an annual publication containing tide tables, astronomical data, weather forecasts and important dates for agriculture as well as stories, jokes and trivia.

[7] **equinoctial:** occurring at an equinox (An equinox happens twice a year when day and night are equal in length.)

[39] **inscrutable:** impossible to interpret or understand

Get In Gear

1. Look up the poem's title. What is a 'sestina'? Can you work out how this poem follows the rules of the sestina form?
2. As a preparation for reading this poem, research Bishop's childhood online and write a brief paragraph describing the tragic events that she experienced.

Tease It Out

1. Describe the poem's setting in your own words. What time of day is it? What time of year? What is the weather like?
2. Where are the child and her grandmother? What is the grandmother doing at this moment?
3. What is the grandmother's emotional state? How does she attempt to conceal this from the child?
4. What is an almanac? What sort of content or information do such books usually contain?
5. What, according to the grandmother, did the almanac predict?
6. Class Discussion: Consider the expressions 'known to' and 'foretold'. Is it fair to say that they represent two different types of knowledge or experience? What are the differences between the two?
7. What does the grandmother offer the child? How does the child react to this offering?
8. Why is the almanac described as 'clever'? What does this suggest about the grandmother's attitude towards this book?
9. What does the almanac 'do' after it's been hung up on its string? How does the grandmother react?
10. Why is the almanac described as 'birdlike'? What might function as its wings?
11. What metaphor is used the describe both the beads of perspiration on the side of the kettle and the tea in the grandmother's cup? How does this metaphor fit the poem's overall mood?
12. Class Discussion: What tragic event is referred to in lines 25 to 26?
13. Describe in your own words what the child draws with her crayons.
14. What falls from the pages of the almanac? Where do these objects settle? Does the grandmother notice this happening?
15. The grandmother is depicted as singing to the stove. Describe in your own words what you visualise happening in these lines.

16. Group Discussion: Why does Bishop refer to the stove as the 'marvellous stove'?
17. The houses drawn by the child are described as 'inscrutable'. What might this suggest about the child's demeanour and psychological state at this moment?

Think About Themes

1. 'Sestina' has often been described as a poem where 'almost everything is left unsaid but where great feeling is conveyed indirectly'. Do you think this accurately describes the poem? Write a paragraph describing the emotions you experienced when you first read 'Sestina'.
2. 'In 'Sestina', Bishop uses an adult vocabulary but skilfully captures a child's point of view'. Would you agree with this statement? Which lines, phrases and images suggest that we're witnessing events at least partly from a child's point of view?
3. How would you describe the poem's atmosphere? Is it sad, menacing, cosy or depressing? Would you agree that the atmosphere changes throughout the poem? Give reasons for your answers.
4. Class Discussion: Certain images in this poem are dreamlike or surreal. List as many as you can. Are these images haunting and memorable or silly and over the top?
5. Pick three words that in your opinion best describe the 'character' of the almanac as depicted in the poem. In each case, write a brief paragraph explaining your choice.
6. 'The startling image of the almanac planting tears in the child's drawing is the poem's central image and emotional core'. Would you agree with this assessment, or is there another image that you found more memorable and effective? Say why.

In Context

Like 'First Death in Nova Scotia' and 'In the Waiting Room', 'Sestina' is a poem of childhood. Write a paragraph comparing and contrasting the depiction of childhood in these three poems.

First Death in Nova Scotia

In the cold, cold parlor
my mother laid out Arthur
beneath the chromographs:
Edward, Prince of Wales,
with Princess Alexandra,   [5]
and King George with Queen Mary.
Below them on the table
stood a stuffed loon
shot and stuffed by Uncle
Arthur, Arthur's father.   [10]

Since Uncle Arthur fired
a bullet into him,
he hadn't said a word.
He kept his own counsel
on his white, frozen lake,   [15]
the marble-topped table.
His breast was deep and white,
cold and caressable;
his eyes were red glass,
much to be desired.   [20]

'Come,' said my mother,
'Come and say good-bye
to your little cousin Arthur.'
I was lifted up and given
one lily of the valley   [25]
to put in Arthur's hand.
Arthur's coffin was
a little frosted cake,
and the red-eyed loon eyed it
from his white, frozen lake.   [30]

Arthur was very small.
He was all white, like a doll
that hadn't been painted yet.
Jack Frost had started to paint him
the way he always painted   [35]
the Maple Leaf (Forever).
He had just begun on his hair,
a few red strokes, and then
Jack Frost had dropped the brush
and left him white, forever.   [40]

The gracious royal couples
were warm in red and ermine;
their feet were well wrapped up
in the ladies' ermine trains.
They invited Arthur to be   [45]
the smallest page at court.
But how could Arthur go,
clutching his tiny lily,
with his eyes shut up so tight
and the roads deep in snow?   [50]

Nova Scotia: a province of Canada that lies on the country's rugged eastern coast
[3]   *chromograph:* an early form of colour photograph
[4]   *Edward, Prince of Wales:* The picture depicts King Edward VII back when he was still Prince of Wales.
That title is given to the heir apparent to the British throne.
[8]   *loon:* short-tailed birds that dive to catch fish; their cry is distinctive
[14] *He kept his own counsel:* he kept his thoughts and ideas to himself
[18] *caressable:* inviting to the touch
[25] *lily of the valley:* a plant with white, bell-shaped flowers
[36] *Maple Leaf:* the national emblem of Canada; 'The Maple Leaf Forever' was a popular patriotic song
[42] *ermine:* an expensive type of fur which comes from the rodent of the same name

Tease It Out

1. What has happened to Arthur? What family relationship does the speaker have with him?
2. Who has 'laid out' Arthur's body? What do you understand by the term 'laid out'?
3. Where has the body been placed?
4. Who is depicted in the images that hang on the wall?
5. 'Since Uncle Arthur fired/ a bullet into him'. Who or what had Uncle Arthur shot?
6. The speaker seems to find it noteworthy that the stuffed loon 'hadn't said a word'. Do you find this surprising? What does this suggest about the speaker's age?
7. What metaphor is used to describe the table on which the loon is situated?
8. Class Discussion: Does the phrase 'cold and caressable' refer to the stuffed loon or to little Arthur? Could it, on one level, refer to both?
9. What did Uncle Arthur use to replace the loon's dead eyes?
10. According to the speaker, these objects were 'much to be desired'. Do you think that they were really valuable?
11. What does the speaker's mother ask her to do?
12. What is the speaker then given? Why?
13. What metaphor is used to describe Arthur's coffin?
14. In lines 31 to 32, the speaker uses an unusual comparison to describe her dead cousin. How do these lines reinforce our sense of the speaker's age?
15. Google the folk character called 'Jack Frost'. According to legend, what does Jack Frost paint?
16. How much of Arthur's body had Jack Frost painted? Why, according to the speaker, had he failed to paint the rest?
17. The young speaker uses this little story to explain the whiteness of Arthur's body. Do you think she came up with this fantastic tale herself?
18. Class Discussion: Comment on the repetition of the word 'forever' in the fourth stanza. What does it indicate about the young speaker's understanding of death?
19. Describe in your own words the clothing worn by the royal couples depicted in the chromographs.
20. Where, according to the speaker, is little Arthur going? What job has been offered?
21. Who might have told the speaker this story? Why?
22. Why does she fear that Arthur might not be able to complete this trip?
23. Do you think the speaker really believes that Arthur has received such an invitation?

Think About Themes

1. 'This is a poem that creates a chilly, wintry atmosphere'. How many references to coldness can you identify? Can you identify any references to warmth and comfort? Would you agree that these, paradoxically, only increase the icy atmosphere of the poem as a whole?
2. 'This is a poem of white and reds'. Identify each reference to these colours. Are any other colours mentioned or referred to? How does this colour scheme contribute to the poem's atmosphere?
3. This poem attempts to capture a 'childhood mentality' and to depict the events it recounts from a child's point of view. Can you identify three phrases where such a mentality is conveyed?
4. 'This poem movingly recounts a child's first confrontation with death'. List the different ways in which the young speaker attempts to avoid thinking directly about Arthur's demise.
5. 'By the end of the poem, the young speaker is on the verge of coming to terms with death – this strange new concept – and with her cousin's alien, altered state.' In your opinion, does the young speaker, at the end of the poem, understand what has happened to her cousin? Write a paragraph explaining your answer.

In Context

'In the Waiting Room' is another poem that addresses Bishop's childhood. Write a short paragraph discussing the similarities and differences between these two poems. Would you agree that both poems deal with important moments of realisation?

Handwritten notes (left margin):
Language
- informal
- Conversational
- brackets (thought process)
- humour
- light hearted

Handwritten note (top right): Imagism — very percise visual images

Filling Station

Oh, but it is dirty!
– this little filling station,
oil-soaked, oil-permeated
to a disturbing, over-all
black translucency.
Be careful with that match! [5]

Handwritten: Sneering / disgusted / disdainful

Father wears a dirty,
oil-soaked monkey suit
that cuts him under the arms,
and several quick and saucy
and greasy sons assist him [10]
(it's a family filling station),
all quite thoroughly dirty.

Handwritten: Sibilance; contempt; dismissive; too small; masculine; cheeky, don't know what they are like

Do they live in the station?
It has a cement porch
behind the pumps, and on it [15]
a set of crushed and grease-
impregnated wickerwork;
on the wicker sofa
a dirty dog, quite comfy. [20]

Handwritten: saturated; Alliteration; Rhetorical question – curious; Curiosity; light furniture – dirty; homeliness

Some comic books provide
the only note of color –
of certain color. They lie
upon a big dim doily
draping a taboret [25]
(part of the set), beside
a big hirsute begonia.

Handwritten: domestic details; Alliteration; everything else dirty; oil / stool / Alliteration; hairy plant; masculine

Why the extraneous plant?
Why the taboret?
Why, oh why, the doily? [30]
(Embroidered in daisy stitch
with marguerites, I think,
and heavy with gray crochet.)

Handwritten: irrelevent; most unlikely element; baffled; Feminine touch

Somebody embroidered the doily.
Somebody waters the plant, [35]
or oils it, maybe. Somebody
arranges the rows of cans
so that they softly say:
ESSO–SO–SO–SO
to high-strung automobiles. [40]
Somebody loves us all.

Handwritten: sibilance; humour; soothing; sense of family

[3]	*permeated:* thoroughly saturated
[5]	*translucency:* clearness
[24]	*doily:* an ornamental mat, often made from cotton or linen — *cover*
[25]	*taboret:* a short stool without a back or arms
[27]	*hirsute:* hairy
[27]	*begonia:* a tropical plant, usually featuring waxy leaves and large flowers
[28]	*extraneous:* irrelevant or not belonging
[32]	*marguerites:* daisy-like flowers
[33]	*crochet:* form of needlework

28

Tease It Out

1. What is it about the filling station that immediately grabs the poet's attention?
2. How does the first stanza convey the degree to which the filling station is saturated in oil?
3. Does the layer of oil that coats the filling station blacken it in such a way that it is impossible to see what lies beneath? Explain your answer.
4. Why does the poet say 'Be careful with that match!' Do you think she is speaking aloud here? Is her remark addressed at someone? Give a reason for your answers.
5. What does the word 'disturbing' suggest about the level of dirt that is evident here and the poet's reaction to it?
6. The 'father' or owner of the filling station is wearing a 'monkey suit'. What is a 'monkey suit'? Why do you think the poet uses this term for his outfit?
7. Does the father's outfit fit him properly? Where is this evident in the poet's description?
8. Does the poet specify exactly how many of the owner's sons are working at the filling station? Why do you think this is the case?
9. The poet uses the terms 'saucy' and 'greasy' to describe the sons. What do each of these terms mean and what do they suggest about the young men?
10. Why do you think the poet mentions the fact that it is 'a family filling station'? Is she surprised at this? Give a reason for your answer.
11. Based on your reading of the first two stanzas, would you agree that the filling station is a very masculine environment? What features or details suggest this?
12. In the third stanza the poet discovers details that suggest the family live at the station. What does she observe that suggests this?
13. Where is the 'wickerwork' furniture located? What condition is this furniture in?
14. What word does the poet use to convey the fact that the wickerwork is also saturated in oil?
15. The poet observes some comic books lying on a table upon the porch. Why do you think these comics 'provide/ the only note of ... certain color' in the filling station? What does this suggest about the rest of the place?
16. What two decorative items does the poet identify in stanza four? Where are these items located?
17. How does the poet describe the 'doily' in stanza five? What does her description tell us about her?
18. Why is the poet so surprised and confused by the presence of the plant, the taboret and the doily in the filling station?
19. How are the cans of oil arranged? Does the speaker think that these were deliberately arranged in this manner?
20. What is the effect of this arrangement? How do they appear to the passing vehicles?
21. How does the speaker describe the 'automobiles' that pass the filling station? Why do you think she describes them in this manner?
22. The speaker sees that somebody is making an effort to make this filthy place nice and pretty. Do you think she has someone in mind, or is it a complete mystery who this person could be?
23. Class Discussion: 'Somebody loves us all'. What do you think the speaker means by this? Can this statement be understood to mean different things?

Think About Themes

1. The poem is essentially about the gender and the struggle for the feminine to survive or stand out in a male dominated world or environment. Write a paragraph discussing this statement.
2. Many of Bishop's poems feature a moment of insight or awareness that arises from the careful study or observation of a place or an object. Is this true of 'Filling Station'? Where does this moment occur in the poem and what does the poet suddenly come to realise?
3. What does the poem suggest are typical masculine values or characteristics? What does the poem suggest are typical feminine values or characteristics? Does the value one set over the other?

In Context

"Filling Station', like many Bishop poems, is a poem of place. And though it may be a more whimsical poem than 'At the Fishhouses' and 'The Bight', it nevertheless shares many characteristics with these poems.' Write a short essay based on this observation.

In the Waiting Room

In Worcester, Massachusetts,
I went with Aunt Consuelo
to keep her dentist's appointment
and sat and waited for her
in the dentist's waiting room. [5]
It was winter. It got dark
early. The waiting room
was full of grown-up people,
arctics and overcoats,
lamps and magazines. [10]
My aunt was inside
what seemed like a long time
and while I waited I read
the *National Geographic*
(I could read) and carefully [15]
studied the photographs:
the inside of a volcano,
black, and full of ashes;
then it was spilling over
in rivulets of fire. [20]
Osa and Martin Johnson
dressed in riding breeches,
laced boots, and pith helmets.
A dead man slung on a pole
– 'Long Pig,' the caption said. [25]
Babies with pointed heads
wound round and round with string;
black, naked women with necks
wound round and round with wire
like the necks of light bulbs. [30]
Their breasts were horrifying.
I read it right straight through.
I was too shy to stop.
And then I looked at the cover:
the yellow margins, the date. [35]

Suddenly, from inside,
came an *oh!* of pain
– Aunt Consuelo's voice –
not very loud or long.
I wasn't at all surprised; [40]
even then I knew she was
a foolish, timid woman.
I might have been embarrassed,
but wasn't. What took me
completely by surprise [45]
was that it was *me*:
my voice, in my mouth.
Without thinking at all
I was my foolish aunt,

I – we – were falling, falling,   [50]
our eyes glued to the cover
of the *National Geographic*,
February, 1918.

I said to myself: three days
and you'll be seven years old.   [55]
I was saying it to stop
the sensation of falling off
the round, turning world
into cold, blue-black space.
But I felt: you are an *I*,   [60]
you are an *Elizabeth*,
you are one of *them*.
Why should you be one, too?
I scarcely dared to look
to see what it was I was.   [65]
I gave a sidelong glance
– I couldn't look any higher –
at shadowy gray knees,
trousers and skirts and boots
and different pairs of hands   [70]
lying under the lamps.
I knew that nothing stranger
had ever happened, that nothing
stranger could ever happen.
Why should I be my aunt,   [75]
or me, or anyone?
What similarities –
boots, hands, the family voice
I felt in my throat, or even
the *National Geographic*   [80]
and those awful hanging breasts –
held us all together
or made us all just one?
How – I didn't know any
word for it – how 'unlikely' ...   [85]
How had I come to be here,
like them, and overhear
a cry of pain that could have
got loud and worse but hadn't?

The waiting room was bright   [90]
and too hot. It was sliding
beneath a big black wave,
another, and another.

Then I was back in it.
The War was on. Outside,   [95]
in Worcester, Massachusetts,
were night and slush and cold,
and it was still the fifth
of February, 1918.

[14] **National Geographic:** official magazine of the National Geographic Society; primarily contains articles about geography, history, and world culture

[20] **rivulets:** small streams

[21] **Osa and Martin Johnson:** an American couple who became famous in the early 20th century for their travels in Africa and other exotic locations; they wrote book and made films about their adventures.

[22] **riding breeches:** short trousers fastened just below the knee

[25] **Long Pig:** in certain Polynesian islands human flesh was referred to as 'long pig'

[95] **The War:** World War I

Tease It Out

Lines 1 to 35

1. What time of year is it? What is the weather like?

2. What age was the poet at the time?

3. The young poet waits for her aunt in the dentist's waiting room? How does she describe the other people in the waiting room? What do you imagine these people are doing while they wait?

4. How do you imagine the poet's younger self feeling, being the only child in the room?

5. The poet picks up a copy of National Geographic. Why do you think she does this? Is it because she is bored and wants to amuse herself? Or is it just a means of hiding her discomfort? Or both? Give a reason for your answer.

6. Why do you think the poet mentions the fact that she 'could read'? What does this suggest about the young poet's view of herself at the time?

7. The poet looks at pictures of a volcano in the magazine. What is happening in the first image of the volcano? What is happening in the second image?

8. How are the two explorers, Osa and Martin Johnson, dressed? Where do you imagine they are in the picture the poet describes?

9. The poet looks at images of cannibals preparing a dead man to be cooked, of 'Babies with pointed heads' and of 'black, naked women with necks/ wound round and round with wire'. What do you imagine is her reaction towards what she sees? How do you imagine each of these images makes her feel? Give reasons for your answers.

10. Why do you think the poet finds the women's breasts 'horrifying'? What is it, do you think, that fills the young poet with horror?

11. What does the poet do once she has read the magazine 'straight through'? Why do you think she does this?

Lines 36 to 53

12. What sound does the young poet suddenly hear? Where does she think this sound has come from?

13. Why does the poet say that she 'wasn't at all surprised' that her aunt might make such a sound?

14. Class Discussion: Although the noise surprises the poet, what takes her 'completely by surprise' is the fact that it came from her own mouth: 'it was me:/ my voice, in my mouth'. It was not the aunt, but the young poet who emitted a cry 'of pain'. What do you think caused this cry? Why did she not immediately realise that she herself had made it?

15. Why does the young poet suddenly think that she is her 'foolish aunt'?

16. What effect does the realisation that she and her aunt are in certain ways similar have on the young poet? How does she describe the sensation that she suddenly experiences?

17. What does the young poet do to try and control or compose herself at this terrifying moment?

Lines 54 to 74

18. Class Discussion: The poet tells herself that she is 'an I', but she must also acknowledge that she is 'one of them'. Who do you think the poet has in mind when she refers to 'them'? What sort of understanding is the young girl coming to here?

19. Who does the girl look at in order to get a sense of what being 'one of them' entails? What does she see when she looks?

20. Why do you think the girl cannot 'look any higher' than the 'knees' and 'hands'? What is she afraid of seeing or understanding?

21. When the poet first looked at the National Geographic, she saw pictures of women that seemed utterly alien to her. Now she suddenly sees that she is somewhat similar to these women. What sort of 'similarities' do you think the young poet has identified?

22. The poet describes a 'cry of pain that could have/ got loud and worse but hadn't'. Why do you think this cry could have 'got loud and worse'? Why do you think this did not happen?

23. How does the poet convey a sense that she is being over-whelmed by the thoughts she is experiencing and that she is about to pass out?

24. 'Then I was back in it'. What do you think the poet means by this? Are there different ways of understanding this statement? Give reasons for your answer.

25. To what do you think the 'War' that the poet mentions in line 95 is a reference?

3. Bishop's poems are marked by their attention to detail. We can see how, even as a young child, the poet was highly alert and interested in the world around her. How is this evident in 'In the Waiting Room'?

4. Is it just a single insight or understanding that troubles the young poet while she is in the waiting room, or does she come to a number of different, albeit related, understand-ings? Give reasons for your answer.

5. Why do you think the poet says that 'nothing/ stranger could ever happen'? What does this suggest about the nature or impact of what has just occurred?

Think About Themes

1. How would you characterise the poet's understanding of herself at the beginning of the poem? What does she come to suddenly realise or understand about herself as the poem progresses?

2. The young poet understands that she will one day grow up and be a woman. What do the images in the magazine, her aunt's behaviour and the presence of the other adults in the waiting room suggest to her about what this might entail? What do you think she finds most disturbing about this fact?

In Context

'Very few poets deal with childhood as sympathetically and as realistically as Elizabeth Bishop. In her poems, the child does not symbolise or represent some innocence that the older poet now desires to recapture. Instead, childhood is revealed as a troubled time of uncertainty when notions of innocence are constantly under threat.' In light of this statement, write an essay discussing three poems dealing with childhood by Bishop.

Eavan Boland

Eavan Boland was born in Dublin in 1944. Her father was a diplomat, and her mother was a well-known painter. At the age of six, Boland and her family moved to London, when her father was posted to the Irish diplomatic service there. Boland seems to have found it somewhat difficult growing up in the UK, where she experienced some of the anti-Irish prejudice that was common at the time. These experiences, expressed in her poem 'An Irish Childhood in England: 1951', made her keenly aware of her Irish heritage.

Boland later returned to Ireland, where she attended Trinity College and began writing poetry. She found 1960s Dublin a supportive and inspirational environment for a budding writer: 'The pubs were crowded. The cafés were full of apprentice writers like myself, some of them talking about literature, a very few talking intensely about poetry'. In this atmosphere of pints, coffee and literary chat, Boland's talent began to flourish, and she composed the poems that featured in her first book, *23 Poems*, which was published when she was only twenty-two.

Boland's life changed, however, when she married, had her first child, and moved to the Dublin suburb of Dundrum. Mundane suburban life was not fashionable literary subject matter in the 1960s, but Boland was now keenly aware of how art had neglected to engage with the very real and relevant landscape of domestic life. In an interview with *The Irish Examiner*, Boland reflected on this period: 'I was a woman in a house in the suburbs, married with two small children. It was a life lived by many women around me, but it was still not named in Irish poetry.'

Boland suddenly found herself occupying two very different roles: she was a poet, but she was also a wife and mother. Initially, Boland saw no contradiction between her duties as a mother and her aspirations as a poet: 'I wanted there to be no contradiction between the way I made an assonance fit a line and the way I lifted up a child at night'. She quickly discovered, however, that there was no real tradition of poetry about motherhood and the duties of the housewife: 'poetic conventions … whispered to me that the daily things I did, things which seemed to me important and human, were not fit material for poetry'.

No longer was she a part of Dublin's artistic society, frequenting the city's trendy bars and literary cafés.

Instead, she was confined to the comfortable safety of the suburbs. Though living only a few miles from the city centre, Boland felt half a world away from the vibrant artistic scene she had been part of as a student. To her literary friends who haunted the city centre, the suburbs might as well not have existed: 'Only a few miles away was the almost invisible world that everyone knew and no one referred to. Of suburbs and housing estates. Of children and women. Of fires lighted for the first winter chill; of food put on the table. The so-called ordinary world … was not even mentioned'.

Boland's new writing began to explore this 'ordinary world'. She turned away from the romantic and traditional poems she had written in college: 'The poems I had been writing no longer seemed necessary or true'. Her new work would focus on her life as a parent and spouse, dealing with such themes as love and marriage, children and motherhood, and the seemingly ordinary life of the suburbs. She began to write on 'rainy winter afternoons, with the dusk drawn in, the fire lighted and the child asleep upstairs'.

"Boland suddenly found herself occupying two very different roles: she was a poet, but she was also a wife and mother."

Boland's poetry gradually won her more and more attention. Books such as 1975's *The War Horse* (which contains 'The Famine Road' and 'Child of Our Time', as well as the famous poem which gave the collection its title), *In Her Own Image* and *Night Feed* established Boland as a woman writing about a woman's experiences – something that was extremely rare not just in Irish poetry, but in poetry generally: 'I know now that I began writing in a country where the word 'woman' and the word 'poet' were almost magnetically opposed'. These volumes staked out Boland's poetic territory, establishing the concerns that would dominate her poetic career: history and its victims, Ireland and Irishness, myth, and the beauty of the everyday.

From the late 1960s to the late 1980s, Boland worked as a freelance journalist and broadcaster, writing articles for *The Irish Times* and producing programmes for RTÉ. Since the mid 1980s, she has taught writing at several American colleges, including the prestigious International Writing Program at the University of Iowa. She is currently a professor of English at Stanford University and divides her time between Ireland and the US.

Boland's work is concerned with the forgotten voices of Ireland. The romanticised history of Ireland's independence – those heroic stories that have come to shape Irish society and our sense of nationhood – overshadowed the real stories of these people's lives and suffering.

Referring to the enormous social trauma of the Famine, Boland remarked 'I see that as a watershed: a powerful once-and-for-all disruption of any kind of heroic history. The most wrenching part of the story of the Famine is how utterly defenceless people were in the face of a disaster they couldn't control. It's also surprising to see how little the writing of that time actually turns to what was happening.

Looking at the nineteenth century was the first time I began to think that writing could add to a silence rather than break it. I was interested in turning a light on the silences and erasers that we learn to tolerate in the name of history.'

Boland's poetry also tends to expose and subvert the constructions of femininity and womanhood that have been so deeply rooted in Irish society and yet were omitted from Irish literature. As she put it, 'I couldn't accept the possibility that the life of the woman would not, or could not, be named in the poetry of my own nation.'

The experience of motherhood and the larger theme of violence against women is the focus of 'The Pomegranate', while 'The Shadow Doll' portrays the sense of suffocating limitations that traditional Irish life imposed on many women. In becoming a mother, Boland herself experienced the internalised restrictions that traditional Irish femininity enforced. For Boland the contradiction between being a woman and being a poet was never completely resolved: 'These, after all, are the two lives – a woman's and a poet's – that I have lived and understood. They are the lives whose aspirations I honour and they remain divided'. Instead of healing this division, Boland uses the tension it creates as the spur for poetic creativity, as the impetus to create a fresh style of writing with a radically different subject matter.

This is Poetry | 35

The War Horse

This dry night, nothing unusual
About the clip, clop, casual

Iron of his shoes as he stamps death
Like a mint on the innocent coinage of earth.

I lift the window, watch the ambling feather   [5]
Of hock and fetlock, loosed from its daily tether

In the tinker camp on the Enniskerry Road,
Pass, his breath hissing, his snuffling head

Down. He is gone. No great harm is done.
Only a leaf of our laurel hedge is torn –   [10]

Of distant interest like a maimed limb,
Only a rose which now will never climb

The stone of our house, expendable, a mere
Line of defence against him, a volunteer

You might say, only a crocus, its bulbous head   [15]
Blown from growth, one of the screamless dead.

But we, we are safe, our unformed fear
Of fierce commitment gone; why should we care

If a rose, a hedge, a crocus are uprooted
Like corpses, remote, crushed, mutilated?   [20]

He stumbles on like a rumour of war, huge,
Threatening; neighbours use the subterfuge

Of curtains; he stumbles down our short street
Thankfully passing us. I pause, wait,

Then to breathe relief lean on the sill   [25]
And for a second only my blood is still

With atavism. That rose he smashed frays
Ribboned across our hedge, recalling days

Of burned countryside, illicit braid:
A cause ruined before, a world betrayed.   [30]

[4] **mint:** place where coins are made

[6] **hock:** joint in the hind leg

[6] **fetlock:** joint of a horse's leg between the knee and the hoof

[6] **tether:** to tie; something that is used to tie

[15] **crocus:** a popular plant with a cup-shaped flower, often purple or yellow in colour.

[27] **atavism:** recurrence of an ancestral trait or character

[29] **illicit:** forbidden or illegal

[29] **braid:** ribbon; Boland is also using the phrase 'illicit braid' as an echo of the history of political agitation and sectarian violence in Ireland, where ribbons of various colours were often worn by the antagonists.

Tease It Out

Lines 1 to 16

1. Working in pairs, discuss the type of area the poet is living in. How do you imagine the street and the houses located here? What four adjectives would you use to describe this neighbourhood, based on your reading of these lines?

2. To whom does the horse belong? Where is the horse normally kept? How has the horse come to be in the poet's neighbourhood on this evening?

3. What sound draws the poet to her window? Why do you think the poet says that there is 'nothing unusual' about this sound?

4. What do the words 'ambling' and 'casual' suggest about the movements and the behaviour of the horse as it makes its way through the neighbourhood?

Lines 1 to 8:

5. Which words or phrases in these lines suggest that the poet finds the horse threatening or intimidating?

6. In what way do the horse's hooves resemble a 'mint', a place where coins are manufactured? What does the comparison suggest about the horse and its movements?

7. The horse causes some damage to the poet's garden. What are the three things that she says have been damaged?

8. Lines 11 to 16: The poet compares the damaged flowers and plants to casualties of war. What sort of injuries or effects does she describe? Who do you think she has in mind here: soldiers, civilians, or both? Give a reason for your answer.

9. Group Discussion: In what way might the horse represent or symbolise war and conflict?

10. The poet says that such casualties are of 'distant interest' and the victims 'expendable'. What sort of attitude is the poet displaying here towards conflict and war? Who do you think it is that, in the poet's view, may have such an attitude? Why do you think they feel this way about such atrocities?

Lines 18 to 30

11. Where does the poet say her neighbours have positioned themselves as the horse passes along the street? Is their behaviour the same as or different to that of the poet? Give a reason for your answer.

12. Lines 17 to 20: How would you characterise the attitude of the poet and her neighbours towards the horse and the threat it presented to them? What is their primary concern?

13. The horse is described as a 'rumour of war'. What is it about the horse and its behaviour that might bring war to mind?

14. Group Discussion: The poet says that the horse's presence causes her to experience a moment of 'atavism', a connection with her ancestors and what they might have felt or experienced. What events or moments from the past do you imagine the poet has in mind here? What sort of emotions does the contemplation of these events stir up within her?

Think About Themes

1. The poem was written during the Troubles, a period of great violence and conflict in Northern Ireland. What does the poem suggest about the violence that was taking place in the North at the time?

2. How would you characterise the poet's reaction to the horse as it makes its way down the street? What does this suggest about her attitude to the war and violence that is happening a relatively short distance away from her?

3. How does the poem present or characterise suburban life? Do you get a sense that the poet is happy to be living in the kind of neighbourhood she describes, or does she feels that she and her neighbours are too remote from the real world?

In Context

'Boland's poems reveal an enormous sensitivity towards the victims of violence. She is also very aware of the failures of others to respond and act appropriately.' Discuss this statement with regard to 'The War Horse', 'Child of Our Time' and 'Outside History'.

The Famine Road

'Idle as trout in light Colonel Jones,
these Irish, give them no coins at all; their bones
need toil, their characters no less.' Trevelyan's
seal blooded the deal table. The Relief
Committee deliberated: 'Might it be safe,   [5]
Colonel, to give them roads, roads to force
from nowhere, going nowhere of course?'

    'one out of every ten and then
    another third of those again
    women – in a case like yours.'   [10]

Sick, directionless they worked; fork, stick
were iron years away; after all could
they not blood their knuckles on rock, suck
April hailstones for water and for food?
Why for that, cunning as housewives, each eyed –   [15]
as if at a corner butcher – the other's buttock.

    'anything may have caused it, spores,
    a childhood accident; one sees
    day after day these mysteries.'

Dusk: they will work tomorrow without him.   [20]
They know it and walk clear; he has become
a typhoid pariah, his blood tainted, although
he shares it with some there. No more than snow
attends its own flakes where they settle
and melt, will they pray by his death rattle.   [25]

    'You never will, never you know
    but take it well woman, grow
    your garden, keep house, good-bye.'

'It has gone better than we expected, Lord
Trevelyan, sedition, idleness, cured   [30]
in one; from parish to parish, field to field,
the wretches work till they are quite worn,
then fester by their work; we march the corn
to the ships in peace; this Tuesday I saw bones
out of my carriage window, your servant Jones.'   [35]

    'Barren, never to know the load
    of his child in you, what is your body
    now if not a famine road?'

Famine Road: during the Famine the British government set up a relief scheme whereby people would be paid for the construction of roads. However, these roads were rarely meant to be used and often went nowhere, frequently ending in a bog or field.

[1] **Colonel Jones:** one of the British officers in charge of relief works around Newry

[3] **Trevelyan:** Charles Trevelyan was in charge of the whole relief project, operating out of London

[4] **Relief Committee:** one of the committees that organised local schemes to try and alleviate the starvation

[22] **typhoid:** bacterial disease transmitted by the ingestion of contaminated food or water

[22] **pariah:** a person who has been rejected by their society; outcast

[30] **sedition:** behaving or speaking in a way that encourages others to rebel against the state or monarchy

[33] **fester:** rot

Tease It Out

Lines 1 to 7

1. Sir Charles Trevelyan, the man in overall charge of Irish famine relief, has written a letter to the Relief Committee in Dublin, outlining what he thinks ought to be done about the starving Irish population. How does he characterise the Irish in the first three lines of the poem?

2. What sort of room do you imagine the Relief Committee have gathered in for this meeting? How do you imagine the table around which they sit?

3. The letter's seal is broken when the letter is opened and the poet describes how it 'blooded' the table. In what way might this broken seal resemble blood upon the table?

4. Colonel Jones, one of Trevelyan's deputies in Ireland, presides over the meeting. He reads Trevelyan's letter to the members of the committee sitting around the meeting. What does Trevelyan say he does not want to offer or give the starving Irish people? What does he say they ought to be given instead?

5. Having given careful consideration to Trevelyan's wishes, what solution does the committee propose? To what extent might this scheme aid the Irish while also carrying out Trevelyan's instructions?

Lines 11 to 16

6. The Relief Committee's plan is put into effect, and the poem now focuses on a group of starving famine victims working on one of the roads. What condition are these people in? What time of year is it, and what is the weather like?

7. What does the term 'directionless' suggest about the nature of their work and the manner in which they work?

8. The poet says that 'fork, stick/ were iron years away'. What does this suggest about the manner in which these people have been equipped to do their work?

9. What do the workers do to ease their thirst?

10. What do the starving workers contemplate doing in order to alleviate their hunger? To what are these workers compared as they contemplate doing this dreadful deed?

11. Whose thoughts about towards the starving Irish are presented in lines 12 to 16?

Lines 20 to 25

12. One of the workers in the group is sick with typhus. What does line 20 suggest will become of this man before the day is done?

13. Why do the other workers 'walk clear' of the man who is sick? How do they now view this man?

14. How does the poet suggest that the sick man is related to others in the group? Do these relatives treat the sick man any differently?

15. In pairs, consider the analogy that the poet draws between snow and the manner in which the workers treat the sick man. In what way are the two alike? What does the analogy suggest about these people's actions? Does it suggest that they are cruel and cold-hearted or just realistic and without any other option? Give a reason for your answer.

Lines 29 to 35

16. Colonel Jones writes to Trevelyan, letting him know how things have progressed. What reasons does he offer as evidence that the scheme has been a great success?

17. What does Colonel Jones's letter suggest or imply was the primary goal of the scheme all along?

18. What does the term 'sedition' mean? How has the scheme 'cured' the Irish of this?

19. What does Colonel Jones say that he saw out of his carriage window? Does this sight appal him or fill him with satisfaction? Give a reason for your answer.

Lines interspersed in italics

20. Do you think that the lines in italics relate to the period of the Irish famine or to a different period? Give a reason for your answer.

21. What possible reasons does the doctor offer the woman for her inability to conceive?

22. What statistics does the doctor quote in relation to infertility?

23. 'You never will, never you know'. What is the doctor telling the woman here? How would you characterise the manner in which he relates this news?

24. What does the doctor suggest the woman do to fill her time now that she can't have children? Is his advice practical and sympathetic or condescending and heartless? Give a reason for your answer.

25. Group Discussion: The poet says that the infertile woman's body is 'a famine road'. What does the analogy suggest about women who are unable to bear children? Whose attitude do you think is being expressed here?

Think About Themes

1. Do you think that the doctor in the poem is just a single uncaring individual in an otherwise caring society, or does he represent a greater aspect of society? Give reasons for your answer.

2. Write a paragraph about how the poem highlights the sufferings of the Famine and vividly portrays the ordeals that the starving Irish had to endure.

3. How does the poem highlight the British elite's perception of the Irish as inferior beings, undeserving of any care and help?

Child of Our Time
for Aengus

Yesterday I knew no lullaby
But you have taught me overnight to order
This song, which takes from your final cry
Its tune, from your unreasoned end its reason,
Its rhythm from the discord of your murder   [5]
Its motive from the fact you cannot listen.

We who should have known how to instruct
With rhymes for your waking, rhythms for your sleep,
Names for the animals you took to bed,
Tales to distract, legends to protect,   [10]
Later an idiom for you to keep
And living, learn, must learn from you, dead,

To make our broken images rebuild
Themselves around your limbs, your broken
Image, find for your sake whose life our idle   [15]
Talk has cost, a new language. Child
Of our time, our times have robbed your cradle.
Sleep in a world your final sleep has woken.

> [5] **discord:** disagreement between people; lack of harmony between things; lack of harmony between musical notes
> [6] **motive:** dominant idea or theme
> [11] **idiom:** a language, dialect, or style of speaking particular to a group of people

Tease It Out

1. What tragic event moved the poet to write this poem?
2. What particular aspect of this tragic event does the poet say she has decided to focus on in the poem? What could she have chosen to focus on or write about?
3. Who does the poet address in the poem?
4. Class Discussion: Boland says that the child 'taught' her to 'order/ This song'. Why do you think she describes the poem's inception and composition in this manner?
5. 'We who should have known how to instruct': Who do you think the poet has in mind when she says 'We'?
6. What sort of 'rhymes' does the poet have in mind in line 8? What purpose do these 'rhymes' serve? What are the 'rhythms' that she mentions? Again, what purpose do such 'rhythms' serve?
7. The poet identifies two different types of story in line 10. What different stories does the poet have in mind here, and what are their different functions?
8. Class Discussion: The poet says that, as children grow up, they must be taught 'an idiom' that they will 'keep'. What do you think the poet means by 'idiom' here? How is such an 'idiom' taught, and who is responsible for doing this?
9. Consider lines 8 to 13. Does the poet suggest that 'We' have succeeded or failed in instructing this child in the appropriate way? Give a reason for your answer?

10. The poet suggests that the role of adult and child been reversed in the case of this child's death. How?
11. The poet suggests that society has certain 'images' or values that define what it is and how it should be. Why does the poet think that this tragic event has led to the 'breaking' of such images?
12. The poet says that we must 'learn' from the child to 'rebuild' our 'broken images'. What do you think might be involved in such a process?
13. Around what does the poet suggest our 'images' ought to be rebuilt?
14. The poet suggests that the language that has been used over the course of the conflict has failed and that a 'new language' is needed. What sort of change in society, and in how we think about and relate to one another, might bring about this 'new language'?

Think About Themes

The poem seems to offer a way forward or, at least, a different path that we might follow if we are to finally escape the conflict and violence that have played a major role in Ireland over the years. What does the poem suggest needs to happen in order for this become a reality?

The Black Lace Fan
My Mother Gave Me

It was the first gift he ever gave her,
buying it for five francs in the Galeries
in pre-war Paris. It was stifling.
A starless drought made the nights stormy.

They stayed in the city for the summer.   [5]
They met in cafés. She was always early.
He was late. That evening he was later.
They wrapped the fan. He looked at his watch.

She looked down the Boulevard des Capucines.
She ordered more coffee. She stood up.   [10]
The streets were emptying. The heat was killing.
She thought the distance smelled of rain and lightning.

These are wild roses, appliquéd on silk by hand,
darkly picked, stitched boldly, quickly.
The rest is tortoiseshell and has the reticent,   [15]
clear patience of its element. It is

a worn-out, underwater bullion and it keeps,
even now, an inference of its violation.
The lace is overcast as if the weather
it opened for and offset had entered it.   [20]

The past is an empty café terrace.
An airless dusk before thunder. A man running.
And no way now to know what happened then –
none at all – unless, of course, you improvise:

The blackbird on this first sultry morning,   [25]
in summer, finding buds, worms, fruit,
feels the heat. Suddenly she puts out her wing –
the whole, full, flirtatious span of it.

[2]   *francs:* the currency used in France up until the introduction of the euro
[2]   *Galeries:* refers to the Galeries Lafayette, a famous department store
[13]   *appliquéd:* applied using decorative needlework
[17]   *bullion:* a heavy lace trimming made of gold or silver threads
[18]   *inference:* a conclusion reached through reasoning and evidence; a sign; an indication
[25]   *sultry:* a word used to describe hot and humid weather

Tease It Out

1.   'It was the first gift he ever gave her'. In this poem the poet writes about a black lace fan. It was given by the poet's father to her mother many years ago and has since been passed on to the poet herself. Think of an item that you received as a gift (it needn't be a family heirloom!) and write a detailed description of its physical appearance.

2.   Watch Video 4 which is about the material known as 'tortoise shell'. Why, according to the filmmaker, should we avoid purchasing products manufactured from this substance?

Stanzas 1 to 3

3.   In what city are the poem's opening stanzas set?

4.   What time period does the phrase 'pre-war' suggest to you?

5.   Where did the couple meet for their dates during that long-ago summer?

6.   What was the name of the store where the poet's father bought the fan? How much did it cost?

7.   Consider the words 'drought' and 'stifling'. What do they suggest about the weather conditions in the city during that long ago summer?

8.   The nights were 'starless'. Can you suggest what might have been responsible for this lack of star-light?

9.   What phrase suggests that the weather was even more oppressive on the evening the poet's father purchased the black lace fan?

10.   There are signs, however, that the weather is going to break. What suggests this?

11.   That evening he was later'. What phrases suggest the man's sense of hurry or tension as he rushes to make his date?

12.   What phrases suggest the mother's tension or agitation as she waits for him?

Stanzas 4 to 5

13.   True or False: When the poet extends the fan, its lace is practically transparent.

14.   What ingenious metaphor, relating to that long ago Paris evening, does Boland use to convey this?

15.   Roses have been stitched or appliquéd on to the lace. Do they strike the poet as pleasant and attractive or as unsettling and off-putting? Give a reason for your answer.

16.   From what material has the fan's frame or 'rest' been manufactured?

17.   What phrase indicates that this a precious and expensive material?

18.   Group Discussion: Consider the terms 'reticent', 'clear' and 'patience'. What does each term suggest about the frame's appearance, or about its origins?

19.   Class Discussion: When the poet looks at the frame she gets an 'inference' or suggestion of some 'violation' that took place. Who or what was violated in the frame's manufacture?

Stanzas 6 to 7

20.   The poet thinks once more about that long-ago evening in Paris. What is her father doing?

21.   'The past is an empty café terrace'. Suggest why the Parisian streets have suddenly become empty.

22.   Has the poet been told all the details of what happened on that long-ago evening?

23.   Is it possible for her now to discover any details of which she was not made aware? Suggest why this might be the case.

24.   What kind of weather conditions is described in the poem's final stanza?

25.   Is this stanza set in the past or in the present day?

26.   What is the blackbird doing? Why does it extend its wing?

Think About Themes

1.   Would you agree that the poet's depiction of the weather conditions contributes to the poem's tense atmosphere?

2.   Group Discussion: 'Each aspect of the fan suggests both a positive and a negative aspect of the parents' relationship'. Working together, attempt to tease out how each aspect of the fan represents not only love's rewards but also its stresses and pressures.

3.   'This poem emphasises the mystery of the past. We can never really know what happened or why, not even to our closest relatives. All we can do is "improvise', reconstruct the past as best we can in our imaginations'. Would you agree with this assessment?

4.   Do you think that in this poem Boland creates a successful 'reconstruction' of past events?

5.   The poet presents the blackbird's wing as a symbol of her parents' marriage: 'the whole, full, flirtatious span of it'. What does it suggest about their relationship?

6.   Class Discussion: Consider the move from the symbol of the fan to the symbol of the blackbird. What physical similarities are there between these two items? And what differences?

7.   Would you agree that the blackbird's wing represents a more positive view of her parents' relationship?

8.   Imagine you are either the woman or the man on that long ago night in Paris. Write a diary entry describing your experience.

In Context

Marriage is a theme that preoccupies Boland in much of her work. Compare her depiction of marriage in this poem to that in 'Love' and 'The Shadow Doll'. Which of these poems do you find most realistic in its approach to marriage?

The Shadow Doll

They stitched blooms from ivory tulle
to hem the oyster gleam of the veil.
They made hoops for the crinoline.

Now, in summary and neatly sewn –
a porcelain bride in an airless glamour –   [5]
the shadow doll survives its occasion.

Under glass, under wraps, it stays
even now, after all, discreet about
visits, fevers, quickenings and lusts

and just how, when she looked at   [10]
the shell-tone spray of seed pearls,
the bisque features, she could see herself

inside it all, holding less than real
stephanotis, rose petals, never feeling
satin rise and fall with the vows   [15]

I kept repeating on the night before –
astray among the cards and wedding gifts –
the coffee pots and the clocks and

the battered tan case full of cotton
lace and tissue-paper, pressing down, then   [20]
pressing down again. And then, locks.

Shadow Doll: In the 19th century porcelain dolls were used to help brides choose
an appropriate gown. Miniature gowns would be manufactured and placed on the dolls,
allowing brides to evaluate gowns without the expense of having a full-sized dress made.

[1]   *tulle:* a fine silk netting used in dress-making
[2]   *hem:* turn under and sew the edge of a piece of fabric
[2]   *oyster:* an off-white colour
[3]   *crinoline:* a stiff fabric used to line clothes or to shape petticoats and dresses
[5]   *porcelain:* a delicate, white and semi-transparent ceramic
[9]   *quickenings:* fluttering heartbeats
[11] *seed pearls:* small pearls found in the shells of oysters or other molluscs
[12] *bisque:* a type of unglazed porcelain
[14] *stephanotis:* a tropical plant

Get In Gear

Class Discussion: This poem was inspired by a doll Boland saw in an American museum. Based on your reading of the poem, can you suggest what was the doll's 'purpose' or 'occasion'? In what sense might the doll be said to have 'survived' this occasion?

Tease It Out

1. The poet mentions 'stitched blooms'. From what material have these flowers been manufactured?
2. Where on the doll's veil have they been placed?
3. What phrase, in line 2, indicates the veil's intense and glowing whiteness?
4. The doll's dress is manufactured from 'crinoline'. What kind of material is this? And why might hoops be added to such a bridal gown? (Google it if necessary!)
5. From what material is the doll itself manufactured?
6. Working in pairs, consider the phrase 'airless glamour'. In what sense is the doll associated with 'glamour'? In what sense might its situation be described as 'airless'?
7. Consider the phrases 'airless', 'Under glass', 'under wraps'. What do they suggest about the poet's view of women in society, especially in the 19th Century and early part of the 20th Century?
8. Stanza 3 features the literary device known as personification. In what different ways is the doll personified, or presented as if it were a living, flesh-and-blood person?
9. Working in groups of four, take a large piece of paper and create a placemat like the one below.

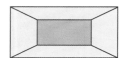

The doll, we're told, has experienced 'visits, fevers, quickenings and lusts'. How are we to understand each of these terms? Take each term in turn and, in your section of the placemat, jot down every association it has for you. Then, as a group, discuss each term. Can you agree on what type of human experience each term represents?

10. When she examined the doll, the young bride-to-be could 'see herself/ inside' its glass case. What does this suggest about her state of mind? Rank the following options in order of plausibility.
    - She was delighted about her upcoming wedding.
    - She felt trapped, like the doll in its glass case.
    - She was delighted with the miniature dress and was eager to wear the full-size version.
    - The thought of marriage filled her with dread.
11. In lines 14 to 15, the young bride-to-be felt as if she were transforming into the porcelain doll. What phrases indicate this?
12. The porcelain seems to have been an incredibly detailed model. What two of its details are mentioned in lines 10 to 15?
13. The poet 'kept repeating' her marriage vows on the night before her wedding. What does this suggest about her state of mind? Once again, rank the following options in order of plausibility:
    - She was uncomfortable with the meaning of these words.
    - She was filled with nervous excitement.
    - She wanted to practice her vows so she wouldn't forget them during the ceremony.
14. The poet describes herself as having been 'astray among the cards and wedding gifts' on the night before her wedding. What does the term 'astray' suggest about her state of mind on this ostensibly happy occasion?
15. The poem's conclusion features a 'battered tan case'. Does the case contain a) her wedding dress, b) the various items she's taking on honeymoon or c) a selection of the presents that she and her fiancé have received? Give a reason for your answer.
16. Class Discussion: The poem concludes with the case being 'locked'. Would you agree that the word 'locks', in this line, serves a symbolic function? Who or what is about to be locked in? And what might the locks themselves represent?

Think About Themes

1. The doll, we're told, has remained 'discrete' about such experiences. What does this suggest about women's freedom to express themselves, especially when it comes to their own bodies?
2. Class Discussion: 'This poem suggests that, beneath the surface, not much has changed for women since the 19th Century'. Would you agree with this reading?
3. Group Discussion: 'This poem moves through three different focuses or perspectives'. Can you identify them? Would you agree that these shifts add to the power of the poem?
4. 'The Shadow Doll' presents a negative view of marriage. Can you identify three negative aspects of marriage at which it hints? Do you find its view of marriage reasonable or overly negative?

In Context

How does Boland's attitude to marriage in 'The Shadow Doll' compare to her approach to the same topic in 'The Black Lace Fan My Mother Gave Me'? Would you agree that both poems depict marriage in a negative light? Give reasons for your answer.

White Hawthorn in the West of Ireland

I drove West
in the season between seasons.
I left behind suburban gardens.
Lawnmowers. Small talk.

Under low skies, past splashes of coltsfoot,   [5]
I assumed
the hard shyness of Atlantic light
and the superstitious aura of hawthorn.

All I wanted then was to fill my arms with
sharp flowers,   [10]
to seem, from a distance, to be part of
that ivory, downhill rush. But I knew,

I had always known
the custom was
not to touch hawthorn.   [15]
Not to bring it indoors for the sake of

the luck
such constraint would forfeit –
a child might die, perhaps, or an unexplained
fever speckle heifers. So I left it   [20]

stirring on those hills
with a fluency
only water has. And, like water, able
to re-define land. And free to seem to be –

for anglers,   [25]
and for travellers astray in
the unmarked lights of a May dusk –
the only language spoken in those parts.

---

[5] **coltsfoot:** a wild plant with yellow flowers
[20] **speckle:** to mark something with spots or patches
[20] **heifers:** a cow that has not yet borne a calf

Note on the Hawthorn and Irish Folklore: In Ireland a number of superstitions are traditionally associated with the hawthorn bush, which is sometimes described as a 'fairy tree' and is associated with supernatural forces. It was widely believed that uprooting a hawthorn bush would bring bad luck and that anyone who brought hawthorn flowers into their house risked the possibility of a death in the family. It has been suggested that this superstition arises from the flower's unpleasant smell, which is eerily like that of decaying flesh.

Get In Gear

Watch Video 5, which features a reading of the poem by Boland herself. Consider the West of Ireland as it is portrayed in this footage. Does it strike you as an attractive and inviting landscape or as a bleak and forbidding one? Give a reason for your answer.

Tease It Out

1. The poet 'drove West' at a time when the weather was in transition, when it wasn't really spring anymore but summer had yet to arrive. What phrase conveys this?
2. The poet presents the suburbs as a dull and tame environment. Identify two phrases that suggest this.
3. Consider the phrase 'small talk'. Does it suggest a) that the speaker enjoys chatting with her neighbours in the suburbs or b) that the speaker views suburbia as a place of shallow and frivolous conversation?
4. What wild flower does the speaker see on her way to the West of Ireland?
5. The poet declares that she sees 'splashes' of this flower? Would you agree that this is an effective metaphor for the flower's appearance on fields and hillsides?
6. Class Discussion: What does the phrase 'hard shyness' suggest about the light on Ireland's western coast? What does it mean for this light to be described as 'hard'?
7. Look up the verb 'assume' online or in your dictionary. Can you identify at least two different meanings of this word? How might each meaning be relevant to line 6?
8. Group Discussion: The speaker claims that the hawthorn plant is surrounded by an 'aura'. What's an aura? Does the speaker literally mean that she sees such an aura around the plant, or is she being metaphorical? What might she be implying?
9. Having reached the West, what does the speaker want to do?
10. The speaker imagines wandering on a hawthorn-covered hill. What phrase suggests this?
11. What custom prevents her from doing this?
12. Consider the term 'constraint' in line 18. Who or what does the poet imagine being constrained? How would they or it be constrained?
13. According to tradition, what would happen to the 'luck' of those who were responsible for such constraint?
14. What specifically did people fear might happen if they brought hawthorn flowers into their homes?
15. What does the speaker decide to do in relation to the hawthorn plants?
16. Towards the poem's conclusion, the hawthorn is compared to water. What similarities, according to the speaker, exist between these substances? Do you find this comparison reasonable or outlandish?

17. In the poem's final lines, the poet imagines a situation involving 'travellers' and 'anglers'.
    • Where do these individuals find themselves?
    • What time of day is it?
    • Are they disorientated, or are they confident of where they are and where they're going?
18. What phrase suggests that the anglers and travellers are in a very remote and isolated setting?
19. The poet suggests that these travellers and anglers smight regard the hawthorn as 'the only language spoken in these parts'. What do you think Boland has in mind here? Consider the following options and rank them in order of plausibility:
    • The flickering glow of the twilight on the hawthorn flowers would resemble a visual form of communication, like Morse code.
    • The travellers and anglers might hallucinate and believe that voices were coming from the hawthorn bushes.
    • The wind whispering through the hawthorn bushes would sound like human voices.
20. Group Discussion: What atmosphere is produced by the poem's last four lines? Pick three adjectives that in your opinion best describe it, and in each case give a reason for your answer.

Think About Themes

1. In this poem, the speaker contrasts two very different worlds, a world of suburban gardens, on the one hand and a world of fields and wild flowers on the other. Which of these worlds does the speaker seem to prefer? Give a reason for your answer.
2. 'In the suburbs of the East, everything is fixed and solid, while in the West, everything is flowing and unstable'. Would you agree with this assessment? Write a paragraph explaining your answer.
3. Would you agree that the speaker sees the West of Ireland as a place of great beauty but also as somewhat threatening and menacing? Write a paragraph explaining your answer.
4. Class Discussion: Would you agree that the speaker travels West in an attempt to reconnect with her roots and heritage as an Irish woman? Is her journey a successful one? Does she end up feeling at home in the West or ill at ease?
5. Group Discussion: 'This poem stresses how fragile our control of nature can sometimes seem. It reminds us how easy it would be for wilderness to reclaim the entire countryside and sweep human settlement aside'. Discuss this statement and together come up with a paragraph in response.
6. What do you know about the West of Ireland today? Do you think that this poem provides a reasonable and realistic view of the West's landscape, atmosphere and people?

Outside History

There are outsiders, always. These stars –
these iron inklings of an Irish January,
whose light happened

thousands of years before
our pain did: they are, they have always been   [5]
outside history.

They keep their distance. Under them remains
a place where you found
you were human and

a landscape in which you know you are mortal.   [10]
And a time to choose between them.
I have chosen:

out of myth into history I move to be
part of that ordeal
whose darkness is   [15]

only now reaching me from those fields,
those rivers, those roads clotted as
firmaments with the dead.

How slowly they die
as we kneel beside them, whisper in their ear.   [20]
And we are too late. We are always too late.

[2]   *inklings:* suggestions, hints or intimations; a sense that something may be about to take place
[17] *clotted:* clogged, blocked up
[18] *firmaments:* heavens or skies

Get In Gear

Watch Video 6. What do you know about stars and their distance from Earth? Approximately how long does it take the light of a star to reach us?

Tease It Out

1. Class Discussion: The poem deals with 'history' and 'our pain'. What do you think the poet means by 'history' in this context, and why does she characterise it as painful?

2. The poet gazes up at the night sky and views the stars. Where do you imagine she is as she does this? What time of year is it?

3. The poet says that the stars are 'outsiders'. What is it that the stars are not a part of? Why, according to the poem, is this the case?

4. The poet describes the stars that she views in the night sky as 'iron inklings'. What does this phrase suggest about the stars' appearance and their distance from earth?

5. In what way does the poet suggest the stars resemble hermits and recluses? What do both have in common?

6. Based on your reading of the first seven lines, what do you think the poet finds attractive about the stars? What is it that she finds problematic?

7. The poet contrasts the stars with Earth – especially with the Irish landscape. What do you think the poet means when she says that Earth is a place where 'you found you were human'? What else does the poet say we come to 'know' from living on Earth?

9. Class Discussion: The poet associates stars with myth, fictional stories handed down from one generation to the next. Why do you think she compares the stars to myth? What does she suggest both of these have in common?

10. The poet speaks about an 'ordeal' and a 'darkness' that she has become acquainted with. What 'ordeal' or struggle do you think she has in mind here? Why do you think that this 'ordeal' is associated with 'darkness'? What do you think is concealed or lost in this darkness?

11. The poet can sense the 'ordeal' and its darkness in the 'fields', 'rivers' and 'roads' that surround her. What do you think it is that the poet is beginning to sense in the Irish landscape? What is she starting to become more conscious or aware of?

12. According to the poet, the Irish landscape is 'clotted' with 'the dead'.

13. The poet imagines kneeling down beside the dead and whispering in their ear. What do you think these imagined actions represent? What do you think the poet is striving to accomplish here?

14. Why are we 'always too late' when we make the gesture or effort that the poet has in mind?

Think About Themes

1. How does the poet characterise or describe Irish history?

2. The poem is concerned with Irish myth and history, and with the role that women have played in both. Women are powerful presences in Irish myth but they are absent from Irish history. Do you agree that this is the case? If so, why?

3. The poet feels that she must 'choose between' myth and history. Why do you think she feels compelled to make this choice? What do you think she hopes to achieve by doing so?

In Context

'The poetry of Eavan Boland reveals a deep sense of compassion and understanding when it comes to those who have suffered in the past'. Write an essay responding to this statement. Refer to at least three poems by Boland on the course.

This Moment

A neighbourhood.
At dusk.

Things are getting ready
to happen
out of sight.   [5]

Stars and moths.
And rinds slanting around fruit.

But not yet.

One tree is black.
One window is yellow as butter.   [10]

A woman leans down to catch a child
who has run into her arms
this moment.

Stars rise.
Moths flutter.   [15]
Apples sweeten in the dark.

Tease It Out

1. This poem is set in a 'neighbourhood'. Having read the poem carefully, what do you imagine this neighbourhood looks like? Take a moment to picture this setting in your own mind. Then, write down its main features as you imagine them.
2. What time of day is it?
3. Lines 6 to 7 mention three things that are 'out of sight'. Can you identify them? How, in their different ways, are they 'out of sight'?
4. Can you suggest why the tree might appear 'black'?
5. What simile is used to describe the window? What is the basis for this comparison? Is it an effective one, in your opinion?
6. Class Discussion: 'Things are getting ready to happen ... But not yet'. What in your opinion are these 'things' waiting for? What event seems to permit or trigger these occurrences?
7. Group Discussion: In line 15 we're told that 'Stars rise'. What is happening here? How might stars be said to 'rise' in the evening sky?
8. Consider the verb 'flutter'. What does it suggest about the moths' flight?
9. What is happening to the apples in the poem's last line?

Think About Themes

1. 'This is a poem in which nothing really happens'. Would you agree with this assessment? Read the poem carefully again, and provide reasons for your answer.
2. It has been suggested that this poem is 'a feast for the senses'. Which of our senses are appealed to in this poem, and in which lines does this happen?
3. Would you agree that the poet creates an atmosphere of mystery and suspense in the poem's first five lines? Which words and phrases contribute to this atmosphere?
4. 'This poem describes a world with motherhood at its centre'. Would you agree that 'This Moment' is in some sense a celebration of the relationship that exists between a mother and her child?
5. 'This poem is a celebration of the ordinary and the everyday. It slows time to show us the hidden magic and mystery that occurs out of sight in a single, seemingly ordinary moment.' Would you agree with this assessment? Give reasons for your answer.

The Pomegranate

The only legend I have ever loved is
the story of a daughter lost in hell.
And found and rescued there.
Love and blackmail are the gist of it.
Ceres and Persephone the names.   [5]
And the best thing about the legend is
I can enter it anywhere. And have.
As a child in exile in
a city of fogs and strange consonants,
I read it first and at first I was   [10]
an exiled child in the crackling dusk of
the underworld, the stars blighted. Later
I walked out in a summer twilight
searching for my daughter at bed-time.
When she came running I was ready   [15]
to make any bargain to keep her.
I carried her back past whitebeams
and wasps and honey-scented buddleias.
But I was Ceres then and I knew
winter was in store for every leaf   [20]
on every tree on that road.
Was inescapable for each one we passed.
And for me.
   It is winter
and the stars are hidden.   [25]
I climb the stairs and stand where I can see
my child asleep beside her teen magazines,
her can of Coke, her plate of uncut fruit.
The pomegranate! How did I forget it?
She could have come home and been safe   [30]
and ended the story and all
our heart-broken searching but she reached
out a hand and plucked a pomegranate.
She put out her hand and pulled down
the French sound for apple and   [35]
the noise of stone and the proof
that even in the place of death,
at the heart of legend, in the midst
of rocks full of unshed tears
ready to be diamonds by the time   [40]
the story was told, a child can be
hungry. I could warn her. There is still a chance.
The rain is cold. The road is flint-coloured.
The suburb has cars and cable television.
The veiled stars are above ground.   [45]
It is another world. But what else
can a mother give her daughter but such
beautiful rifts in time?
If I defer the grief I will diminish the gift.
The legend will be hers as well as mine.   [50]
She will enter it. As I have.
She will wake up. She will hold
the papery flushed skin in her hand.
And to her lips. I will say nothing.

Note: The 'legend' refers to an ancient Greek myth that tells of the abduction of Persephone by the god of the underworld. Persephone's mother was Ceres, the goddess of agriculture. Persephone was eventually found and rescued but because she had eaten six pomegranate seeds while in captivity, she was condemned to spend six months each year in the underworld

[12] **blighted:** spoiled or obscured, in this case by the fog and smog of the city

[18] **buddleias:** shrubs with lilac, pink or cream flowers

[43] **flint-coloured:** grey

[48] **rifts:** breaks or intervals

Get In Gear

Google the myth of Ceres and her daughter, Persephone. How does the story explain the seasonal division of the year?

Tease It Out

Lines 1 to 23

1. The poet describes how she moved to London when she was a child. How does she characterise her move there? What term does she use to suggest that this move was a deeply unwelcome one?

2. At that time, what did Boland think of London? What two features stand out in her memory?

3. It was while living in London as a child that the poet first became acquainted with the myth of Ceres and Persephone. Which character did she identify with at the time? Why do you think she identified with her?

4. Why might London have seemed like the 'underworld' to the young poet?

5. Lines 12 to 19: When did the poet next strongly identify with the myth of Ceres and Persephone? With which character did she identify on this occasion?

6. The poet describes the Dublin suburban neighbourhood that she was living in at the time. What features or aspects of the place stand out in her mind?

7. Who was the poet looking for on this occasion? How did she feel when she finally found her?

8. Lines 19 to 23: What sort of knowledge or understanding does the poet suggest she had acquired by this point in her life?

Lines 24 to 54

9. The poem shifts to the present day. What time of year is it now? Where is the poet? Where is her daughter?

10. What objects are next to the daughter's bed?

11. Why does the pomegranate remind the poet of the myth of Ceres and Persephone? What is the significance of this fruit in the story?

12. How does the poet describe the underworld in lines 37 to 40?

13. What does Boland say that Persephone did in lines 32 to 35? Why did she do this?

14. Look again at lines 34 to 42. Of what simple fact does Persephone's action remind the poet?

15. Lines 43 to 46: How does the poet describe the area in which she and her daughter are living? Why does she say that this is 'another world'?

16. Boland says that there is 'still a chance' for her to 'warn' her daughter. What do you think she might want to warn her about?

17. Class Discussion: What do you think is the 'grief' that the poet mentions in line 49? In what way might the poet 'defer' this grief? Does she think it would be a good idea to do this?

18. Lines 46 to 48: Boland says that a mother can only give her daughter 'beautiful rifts in time'. What do you think she means by this?

19. The poet says that her daughter will eventually 'enter' the myth and that the legend 'will be hers'. What do you think she means by this?

20. What does the poet say that her daughter will do when she wakes up? What do you think that this act represents or symbolises for the poet? Why do you think that the poet has decided to 'say nothing'?

Think About Themes

1. In what way, do you think, has the legend of Ceres and Persephone helped the poet deal with difficult moments in her life? What does the poem suggest about the importance of myths and legends in our lives?

2. What does the poem suggest about motherhood? Does the poem suggest that it is easy to be a mother?

3. Although the poet and her daughter live in 'another world,' there are aspects of the myth of Ceres and Persephone that are as true today as they were when the story was first told. What truths or details of the story remain permanently true?

4. The poem suggests that in order to fully live and enjoy life, we must experience the bad as well as the good. Would you agree with this statement?

In Context

How does Boland's depiction of suburban life in 'The Pomegranate' compare with her handling of the same theme in 'The War Horse' and 'This Moment'?

Love

Dark falls on this mid-western town
where we once lived when myths collided.
Dusk has hidden the bridge in the river
which slides and deepens
to become the water   [5]
the hero crossed on his way to hell.

Not far from here is our old apartment.
We had a kitchen and an Amish table.
We had a view. And we discovered there
love had the feather and muscle of wings   [10]
and had come to live with us,
a brother of fire and air.

We had two infant children one of whom
was touched by death in this town
and spared: and when the hero   [15]
was hailed by his comrades in hell
their mouths opened and their voices failed and
there is no knowing what they would have asked
about a life they had shared and lost.

I am your wife.   [20]
It was years ago.
Our child is healed. We love each other still.
Across our day-to-day and ordinary distances
we speak plainly. We hear each other clearly.

And yet I want to return to you   [25]
on the bridge of the Iowa river as you were,
with snow on the shoulders of your coat
and a car passing with its headlights on:

I see you as a hero in a text –
the image blazing and the edges gilded –   [30]
and I long to cry out the epic question
my dear companion:

Will we ever live so intensely again?
Will love come to us again and be
so formidable at rest it offered us ascension   [35]
even to look at him?

But the words are shadows and you cannot hear me.
You walk away and I cannot follow.

This poem refers to the ancient Roman legend of Aeneas, a Trojan hero who ventured into the land of the dead (here referred to as 'hell'). To do so, he crossed the terrifying River Styx. On the other side, he met the souls of his dead companions, who approached him, eager for news of the world above. However, they were unable to communicate with this living intruder in the realm of the dead; their mouths opened, but no words came out.

[8] **an Amish table:** a table manufactured in the reclusive Amish communities of North America, who are known for their craftsmanship.

[30] **gilded:** covered in a thin layer of gold

[31] **epic question:** a great question, one of overwhelming importance

[35] **ascension:** rising or moving upwards, also suggests entering a higher spiritual or psychological state

Get In Gear

1. The speaker is revisiting Iowa, a town in America where she once lived with her husband. Try to think of a place that you fondly remember, a place you lived or visited or where you went on holiday. Write a paragraph in which you record at least three memories associated with that location.

2. Watch Video 7, which recounts Aeneas's journey into the underworld, a story referenced by Boland throughout the poem.

Tease It Out

1. What time of day is it? Why is it difficult for the poet to see the bridge across the Iowa River?

2. Group Discussion: According to the speaker, the river 'slides and deepens'. What do you imagine happening here? In your own words, try to describe what it would be like for a river to suddenly shift in this fashion.

3. The poet compares the Iowa River to another, very different, river. Which river does she have in mind?

4. The poet remembers that she and her husband lived in an apartment in this part of town. Do you think that she remembers this apartment fondly? Give a reason for your answer.

5. When the poet and her husband lived in Iowa, the love between them was at its height. The poet uses personification to illustrate the intensity of this emotion. How is love personified in these lines?

6. Do you think that this personification is effective? Or is it silly and over the top? Give a reason for your answer.

7. The couple also endured a traumatic and frightening event during this period. What was it?

8. When Aeneas met the ghosts of his fallen comrades in the underworld, they were unable to speak to him. What phrases convey this aspect of the legend?

9. True or False: In the years since they lived in Iowa, the poet has fallen out of love with her husband.

10. Does the poet feel that she and her husband enjoy good communication in their relationship? Give a reason for your answer.

11. The poet focuses on one specific memory of her husband from their long-ago stay in Iowa. Where was he in this particular memory? What was he wearing? What was the weather like?

12. What desire does the speaker express in lines 25 to 26? Is it a realistic one?

13. 'I see you as a hero in a text'. What kind of document does the poet have in mind here? Rank the following options in order of plausibility:
    *   She's thinking of a text message.
    *   She's thinking of a decorated scroll.
    *   She's thinking of a text-based video game.
    *   She's thinking of an ordinary printed book.

14. What 'epic question' does the speaker long to ask this remembered version of her husband? Rewrite it as best you can in your own words.

15. Do you think the speaker already knows or suspects the answer to this question?

16. Group Discussion: Consider the question 'Will love come to us again and be so formidable [?]' What does it suggest about the poet's attitude to her relationship? Is she happy or unhappy?

17. Class Discussion: Consider the use of the word 'ascension' in line 35. What does this word mean, and what associations does it have? What does it suggest about the intense emotions experienced by the speaker and her husband when they lived in Iowa?

18. 'The words are shadows'. Do you agree that this is an effective metaphor? In what sense might the poet's words be described as shadowy and insubstantial?

19. 'You walk away and I cannot follow'. Where does the poet want to go? Why is it impossible for her to make this journey?

Think About Themes

1. 'In the poem's final lines, the poet's husband resembles Aeneas, while the poet herself resembles the dead companions that Aeneas encountered in the underworld'. Write a paragraph in response to this statement. Try to identify at least two ways in which this parallel holds true and one way in which it doesn't.

2. 'This poem celebrates the ability of love to survive the ups and downs of a long-term relationship'. Do you agree with this statement? Or do you get the impression that the poet is bored and disappointed with the current state of her marriage?

3. 'This is a powerful poem of nostalgia, in which the speaker wants to somehow meet once again a long-ago version of her husband. Although we may all experience them at one time or another, such desires can never be fulfilled'. Do you agree with this assessment? Do you find the poet's desire to revisit the past moving or ridiculous and over-the-top? Write a paragraph outlining your answer.

In Context

Consider the phrase, 'when myths collided'. What two myths are being referred to here? Is it possible that one relates to the couple's relationship while the other relates to their daughter's illness? Consider this in light of 'The Pomegranate', another poem that makes extensive use of mythological material. In which poem is myth most effectively deployed? Give reasons for your answer.

Paul Durcan

Paul Durcan was born into a period in Irish history that was – relatively speaking – both socially and culturally bleak. Events such as mass emigration damaged the national psyche, and the gulf between the country's early political ambitions and its profoundly disappointing results was demoralising for the nation at large. Durcan captures this sentiment in 'The Girl with the Keys to Pearse's Cottage': 'Our world was strange because it had no future;/ She was America-bound at summer's end. She had no choice but to leave her home …'

Also at this time, the Catholic Church had significant sway over Irish society, particularly in health and education. This created a conservative society where divorce, contraception, abortion and pornography were banned, and a large number of books and films were censored. Durcan is highly critical of this abuse of power, and hints at the conjoined nature of Church and state in the poems 'Rosie Joyce' and 'Wife Who Smashed Television Gets Jail'. Many other poems, not included on this course, reveal Durcan levelling his incisive poetic aim at the Catholic Church with satirical pieces entitled 'Cardinal Dies of Heart Attack in Dublin Brothel' or 'Priest Accused of Not Wearing a Condom'.

Durcan was born in Dublin in 1944. His childhood was divided between Dublin and the village of Turlough in Co. Mayo, where his father, John James Durcan, worked as a Circuit Court judge, and his mother, Sheila MacBride, was trained as a solicitor. Durcan attended Gonzaga College and later studied law and economics at University College. His childhood was characterised by a fraught relationship with his father, who subjected Durcan to regular beatings, often for trivial reasons such as his academic performance or for a perceived lack of masculinity. Durcan enjoyed a much warmer dynamic with his mother, and memorialised her in his 2007 collection *The Laughter of Mothers*. The hostility his father harboured came to a peak when Durcan, aged just nineteen, was forcibly committed to a psychiatric hospital by his family. Over the course of nearly three years in different facilities, he was needlessly exposed to dozens of electroconvulsive-therapy (ECT) sessions.

His experiences of the Irish psychiatric system in the early 1960s left a scar that he carried for much of his life and led to bouts of depression. He fled hospital in 1965 and made his way to London. Here, he spent some time working in a planetarium and at the North Thames Gas Board. Along with Martin Green, he helped to establish a quarterly literary journal called *Two Rivers*. His first collection of poetry, *Endsville*, which he co-authored with fellow writer Brian Lynch, was published in 1967.

Soon after, Durcan met Nessa O'Neill at a wedding that Patrick Kavanagh had invited him to. He wrote the poem 'Nessa' about her, describing how he first met her and what appears to have been a slightly overwhelming romance. In 1968 Durcan spent three months living in Barcelona with Brian Lynch and Nessa. He later married Nessa and they had two daughters together. Durcan, Nessa and their children returned to Ireland in 1970. Durcan went back to education, studying archaeology and medieval history at University College Cork after reportedly being informed by figures in the English department that he did not understand English or poetry and 'had no future in it'. He graduated in 1973 with first-class honours, and in 1974, some seven years after he had published his first collection of poetry, he won the Patrick Kavanagh Poetry Award.

His second book of poetry (arguably his first solo effort), *O Westport in the Light of Asia Minor*, was published in 1975. This marked the beginning of a period of rich creativity for Durcan. Between 1976 and 1978 he published two more collections, *Teresa's Bar* and *Sam's Cross*. Throughout the 1970s he also wrote extensively on the Troubles in Northern Ireland, often berating key

"His experiences of the Irish psychiatric system in the early 1960s left a scar that he carried for much of his life and led to bouts of depression. He fled hospital in 1965 and made his way to London."

political groups on both sides for allowing their agendas to aggravate a conflict where countless civilian lives were being lost. In 1980 he released *Jesus, Break His Fall*, and in 1982 *The Selected Paul Durcan*.

His marriage to Nessa Durcan ended in 1984, after sixteen years. *The Berlin Wall Café*, which was published just one year later, reflected much of the emotional fallout of this event and received unprecedented attention as a result. However, Durcan's breakthrough came when his father passed away in 1988. It brought out some of his most potent writing, and the ensuing volume of poetry, entitled *Daddy, Daddy*, won the prestigious Whitbread Award for poetry in 1990.

Durcan continued to publish poetry and collaborate creatively with other artists and musicians (including Van Morrison). In addition to writing poetry, he wrote a weekly column for the *Irish Examiner* and was a regular contributor to RTÉ radio. Durcan was a writer in residence at both Frost Place in New Hampshire and in Trinity College, Dublin. Having lived in London, Cork, Mayo and New Hampshire, Durcan settled in Dublin, where he currently lives.

Durcan counts Patrick Kavanagh and T.S. Eliot among his literary muses, and has said in interviews that Eliot's epic poem *The Waste Land* was the first book he borrowed from the library as a child. Durcan first met Kavanagh in the 1960s and his work shares much of Kavanagh's love/hate view of Ireland. Many critics have drawn comparisons between Durcan's and Kavanagh's poetry.

Durcan is a master of satire and his sharp, wry humour is evident in much of his poetry. Some of his material can be deeply personal, focusing on intimate biographical events such as his romantic travails, his time in psychiatric hospitals, or the destructive influence his father had on him. For example, he explores the complexity of romantic relationships in 'The Difficulty That is Marriage', and illustrates the concurrent affection and strife that characterised his marriage in the poem 'Nessa'. Elsewhere, we can see streaks of anger and emotional turmoil in the likes of 'Mad Man', 'Sport' and '"WindFall", 8 Parnell Hill, Cork'.

However, Durcan ocassionally ventures into far more public subject matter. He has used his writing to launch searing criticisms of traditional Irish society, particularly the culture of hypocrisy and corruption among Ireland's untouchables – doctors, judges and politicians – which had a huge, negative influence on his own life and the lives of others. One of his favourite targets is the Catholic Church and the malign power it held over Irish people throughout the 20th century. Durcan's time in journalism for newspapers influenced this type of social poetry. Certain poems are titled like newspaper headlines, such as 'Eight Nuns Die in Convent Inferno' and 'Wife Who Smashed Television Gets Jail'. These poems are also written in a slightly journalistic style. This style often serves to enhance the satirical intensity of Durcan's social commentary and highlights the absurdity of Ireland's conservative social mores.

Closely tied to this is his more political poetry. He revisits with a critical eye the country's historical origins in a number of poems. The names and faces that defined and masterminded the country's independence weighed heavily on Durcan's mind. His mother, Sheila MacBride Durcan, was the niece of Irish republican soldier, Major John MacBride. He explores this connection in 'The MacBride Dynasty', where he recalls satirically a childhood memory of visiting his grand-aunt – MacBride's former wife and Yeats' literary muse – the famous Maud Gonne. There is also a strong sense of political disillusionment in 'The Girl with the Keys to Pearse's Cottage'.

Handwritten annotations:

- Anecdotal
- Clear structure
- 2 stanzas of 6, 1 of 8
- No clear rhyming
- Conversational
- Repitition to emphasise key moments
First encounter of wife

- Powerful women
- Nessas Red hair - irish goddess
+ Ballad/lyrical feel

Nessa

→ The dominant partner, carefree
1st of August connected to whirlpools

paradise, -Exotic, completley intoxicating

I met her on the first of August
In the Shangri-La Hotel, — At a wedding
metaphor - captivated by her
She took me by the index finger
And dropped me in her well. *— Exciting Mysterious, dangerous*
And that was a whirlpool, that was a whirlpool, [5]
And I very nearly drowned. *risk*

direct language
Take off your pants, she said to me, *Humour*
And I very nearly didn't; *Confident, Alluring*
Would you care to swim? she said to me,
And I hopped into the Irish Sea. [10]
And that was a whirlpool, that was a whirlpool, *lively, unformal language*
And I very nearly drowned. 'Refrain'

soft tone -invitation *image*
On the way back I fell in the field *Fell for her*
And she fell down beside me. *— comfort in her presence*
I'd have lain in the grass with her all my life [15]
With Nessa: *— pause - emphasises her centrality to poem* *relaxed*
She was a whirlpool, she was a whirlpool,
And I very nearly drowned. *essential*

suggest he would've laid here but she mightn't have

captivated by her
Oh Nessa my dear, Nessa my dear, *Metaphors* *constantly moving*
Will you stay with me on the rocks? [20] *Asking her to hang on*
Will you come for me into the Irish Sea *Senses he is out of control*
And for me let your red hair down? *Present tense*
And then we will ride into Dublin City
In a taxi-cab wrapped up in dust. *darker [25] image*
Oh you are a whirlpool, you are a whirlpool, *-Sense of doom*
And I am very nearly drowned. *-uncertain -mysterious*

Tender, exciting *self deprecating*

[2] *Shangri-La Hotel:* a hotel that was located in Dalkey, Co. Dublin

56

Tease It Out

1. Where did the poet first meet Nessa? What time of year was it?
2. Group Discussion: Consider the line 'She took me by the index finger'. What does this suggest about the budding relationship between Nessa and the poet? Who seems to occupy the dominant role in this new affair?
3. Class Discussion: The poet compares Nessa to a 'well' and to a 'whirlpool'. What impression does this provide of her character and personality? Is it a positive or a negative one?
4. What did Nessa suggest that they do in the second stanza?
5. How did the poet respond to this suggestion? Give a reason for your answer.
6. The poet compares the Irish Sea to a whirlpool in which he nearly drowned. Did he actually get into difficulty while swimming or is he speaking metaphorically? Give a reason for your answer.
7. What happened to the poet on the way back to the hotel after their swim?
8. What did Nessa do in response? Do you think this was accidental or deliberate?
9. How did this occurrence make the poet feel?
10. What three words would you use to describe Nessa's personality based on your reading of the first three stanzas? What three words would you use to characterise the poet?
11. The poet repeatedly states that he 'nearly drowned' on the day of that first meeting. What does this suggest about his emotional state?
12. Is the poem's final stanza set on that first day or sometime in the future? Give a reason for your answer.
13. Is there a difference in tone between this stanza and the first three? If so how would you characterise this difference?
14. Where is the poet in the fourth stanza? Do you think he is really in this location or is it only his imagination?
15. What does the poet call on Nessa to do for him? What do his pleas suggest about their relationship?
16. Class Discussion: Consider the image of the 'taxi-cab wrapped up in dust'. Is this a surreal or a realistic image? How could a taxi become covered in dust in such a way? How does this image contribute to the stanza's atmosphere?
17. Consider the last lines of each of the stanzas. How does the last line of the fourth differ from the first three?

Think About Themes

1. What do the first three stanzas suggest about infatuation and the beginning of a new relationship? Try to write four sentences describing the poem's take on these matters in your own words.
2. Which of the poem's images and phrases capture the headiness of a new relationship?
3. Consider the various images and metaphors associated with the sea and water. Why do you think the poet decided to use these? What do they suggest both about the relationship and his state of mind?
4. Count how many of the poem's lines begin with the word 'And'. What effect does this have on our reading of the poem?
5. 'Many of Durcan's poems celebrate powerful women'. Write three paragraphs discussing this statement in relation to 'Nessa'.
6. Would you consider this to be ultimately a joyous or a sorrowful piece of writing? Write a paragraph saying why.
7. Do you think 'Nessa' is a fitting title for this poem? If you were asked to come up with an alternative title what would you suggest?

In Context

Compare the relationship in 'Nessa' with that depicted in 'Father's Day, 21 June 1992'. Identify one similarity and one difference between the relationships depicted in each poem.

The Girl with the Keys to Pearse's Cottage

to John and Judith Meagher

When I was sixteen I met a dark girl;
Her dark hair was darker because her smile was so bright;
She was the girl with the keys to Pearse's Cottage;
And her name was Cáit Killann.

The cottage was built into the side of a hill; [5]
I recall two windows and cosmic peace
Of bare brown rooms and on whitewashed walls
Photographs of the passionate and pale Pearse.

I recall wet thatch and peeling jambs
And how all was best seen from below in the field; [10]
I used sit in the rushes with ledger-book and pencil
Compiling poems of passion for Cáit Killann.

Often she used linger on the sill of a window;
Hands by her side and brown legs akimbo;
In sun-red skirt and moon-black blazer; [15]
Looking toward our strange world wide-eyed.

Our world was strange because it had no future;
She was America-bound at summer's end.
She had no choice but to leave her home –
The girl with the keys to Pearse's Cottage. [20]

O Cáit Killann, O Cáit Killann,
You have gone with your keys from your own native place.
Yet here in this dark – El Greco eyes blaze back
From your Connemara postman's daughter's proudly mortal face.

Pearse's Cottage: Patrick Pearse (1879-1916) was an Irish nationalist, poet and writer who was one of the leaders of the 1916 rebellion against British rule in Ireland. The cottage, where he wrote many of his poems and plays, is located in Rosmuc, Co. Galway.

[7] **whitewashed:** painted in a low-cost white paint
[9] **jamb:** side post or frame of a door
[11] **rushes:** flowering, grassy plants
[11] **ledger-book:** used by shop-keepers for recording transactions
[14] **akimbo:** with legs open
[23] **El Greco:** a Spanish painter of Greek origin. The women in his paintings are known for their brown eyes and Mediterranean beauty.

Get In Gear

What do you know about Patrick Pearse? Research him online and find out what association he had with Rosmuc in Connemara. What hope or vision did he have for Ireland?

Tease It Out

1. How does the poet describe Cáit Killann's appearance? What colour was her hair?
2. How did Cáit's smile accentuate the colour of her hair?
3. Why do you think the poet describes her as a 'dark girl'?
4. Class Discussion: Although the poet does not tell us, why do you think that Cáit possesses the keys to Pearse's cottage?
5. Describe the cottage. Where is it located? What sort of condition is it in? How is it furnished?
6. How does the poet characterise the atmosphere of the location? Why do you think he describes it in this manner?
7. How does Durcan describe Pearse's appearance in the photographs on the wall? What does each adjective suggest about Pearse?
8. Why do you think that the poet says the cottage was 'best seen from below in the field'?
9. Where used the young poet sit? What used he do here?
10. Where would Cáit often 'linger'? How would she sit? What does the poet recall her wearing on these occasions?
11. The poet says that their 'world was strange because it had no future'. What do you think he means by this?
12. Where was Cáit set to travel at the end of the summer? Why do you think she 'had no choice but to leave her home'?
13. The poet says that Cáit has gone with her 'keys from [her] own native place'. What keys do you think he has in mind here? Are they the 'keys to Pearse's Cottage' or do they represent something else?
14. What 'dark' is the poet referring to in the second-last line of the poem?
15. How does the poet describe Cáit's face in the final lines? Why do you think he describes her face as 'proudly mortal'? What do you think the poet is contrasting her face with here?

Think About Themes

1. What impression does the poem give of Ireland at the time?
2. How would you describe the tone and atmosphere in the first five stanzas? Is there a significant change in the final stanza?
3. Pearse imagined that Ireland would become a perfect place once the country had gained independence from Britain. What does the poem suggest has become of his dream? How might Pearse's cottage function as a symbol for this idea?
4. What picture does this poem paint of teenage love and infatuation?
5. How do you think Cáit felt about Ireland? Do you imagine that she was happy or sad to be leaving the country and travelling to America?
6. Would you agree that the poem captures the passion and intensity of teenage love?

In Context

1. Compare and contrast this poem's depiction of romantic love with 'Nessa' and 'The Difficulty that is Marriage'.
2. Write a short essay in which you discuss Durcan's view of Ireland based on your reading of the poems on the course.

[handwritten: Theme - Marraige   Form - somet]

The Difficulty that is Marriage

[handwritten annotations surrounding poem: Speaking about his own marriage - 80 years into marriage; day to day; can't come to an arrangement; self depricating tone of Durcan; Alliteration/Assonance cannot sleep die + buried - end of it mental health; metaphorical distance - can't reach out to her; No belief; image created using small tiles; image to illustrate that self depricating; He would stay on earth forever if he was with her [10] NO JJ 4; sum up what love means to him; doesn't think one is perfect he sees her for who one is; Nobody is perfect   Staccato rhythm - Aggetation]

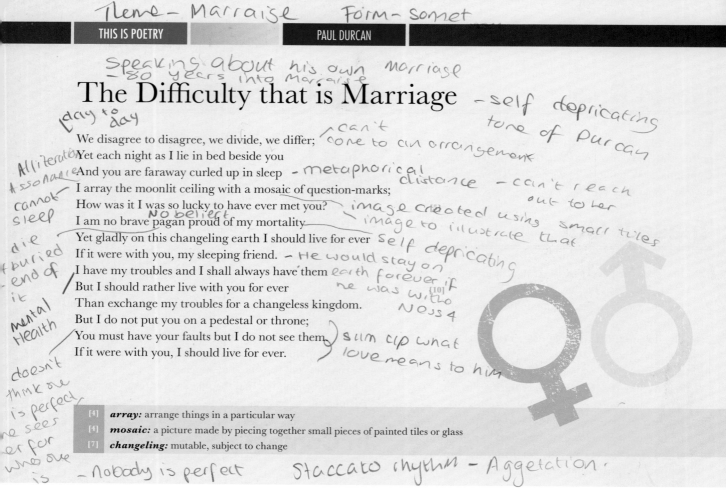

We disagree to disagree, we divide, we differ;
Yet each night as I lie in bed beside you
And you are faraway curled up in sleep
I array the moonlit ceiling with a mosaic of question-marks;
How was it I was so lucky to have ever met you?
I am no brave pagan proud of my mortality
Yet gladly on this changeling earth I should live for ever
If it were with you, my sleeping friend.
I have my troubles and I shall always have them
But I should rather live with you for ever
Than exchange my troubles for a changeless kingdom.
But I do not put you on a pedestal or throne;
You must have your faults but I do not see them
If it were with you, I should live for ever.

[4] **array:** arrange things in a particular way
[4] **mosaic:** a picture made by piecing together small pieces of painted tiles or glass
[7] **changeling:** mutable, subject to change

Tease It Out

1. How does the poet characterise the relationship with his wife in the poem's opening line?
2. What common expression does the poet play with in the opening line? What does his way of putting it suggest about their relationship?
3. What does the poet say he does each night as he lies beside his sleeping wife? What image does he use to illustrate the thoughts that run through his mind? What is it that he thinks about?
4. What is it about 'pagans' that the poet admires? Why is he not like such people?
5. Why do you think the poet describes the earth as 'changeling'? Is this a good or a bad thing?
6. How does the poet characterise his life in line 9?
7. What do you think the poet has in mind when he refers to 'a changeless kingdom'?
8. Under what condition would the poet favour living for ever on earth over an eternity in a 'changeless kingdom'?
9. Having read the poem, what do you think is the 'difficulty' that the poet mentions in the title?

Think About Themes

1. Do you think the poem presents marriage in a favourable or unfavourable light?
2. What do you think the poem has to say about religion? Based on your reading of the poem, do you think that the poet is a religious man?
3. Do you think that this is a romantic poem? Give reasons for your answer.
4. 'I do not put you on a pedestal'. Do you think that the poet is being honest with himself when he says that he does not idolise his wife?
5. How does the poet characterise (a) life on earth and (b) the afterlife? Would you, like the poet, favour living for ever on earth?

In Context

1. Compare and contrast Durcan's treatment of marriage in this poem with that in 'Wife Who Smashed Television Gets Jail'.
2. 'Durcan's poems celebrate romantic love but do not shy away from the difficulties and problems that all couples experience'. Discuss this statement in light of your reading of this poem and 'Father's Day, 21 June 1992'.

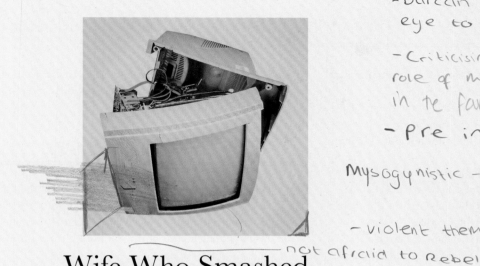

Wife Who Smashed Television Gets Jail

'She came home, my Lord, and smashed in the television;
Me and the kids were peaceably watching *Kojak*
When she marched into the living room and declared
That if I didn't turn off the television immediately
She'd put her boot through the screen;   [5]
I didn't turn it off, so instead she turned it off –
I remember the moment exactly because Kojak
After shooting a dame with the same name as my wife
Snarled at the corpse – Goodnight, Queen Maeve –
And then she took off her boots and smashed in the television;   [10]
I had to bring the kids round to my mother's place;
We got there just before the finish of *Kojak*;
(My mother has a fondness for *Kojak*, my Lord);
When I returned home my wife had deposited
What was left of the television into the dustbin,   [15]
Saying – I didn't get married to a television
And I don't see why my kids or anybody else's kids
Should have a television for a father or mother,
We'd be much better off all down in the pub talking
Or playing bar-billiards –   [20]
Whereupon she disappeared off back down again to the pub.'
Justice O'Brádaigh said wives who preferred bar-billiards to family
   television
Were a threat to the family which was the basic unit of society
As indeed the television itself could be said to be a basic unit of   [25]
   the family
And when as in this case wives expressed their preference in forms
   of violence
Jail was the only place for them. Leave to appeal was refused.

[2] **Kojak:** American detective series popular in the 1970s
[20] **bar-billiards:** a form of billiards played on a small table, typically in a public bar, in which balls are struck into holes guarded by pegs

Handwritten annotations:

- Durcan took a clinical eye to Irish society
- Criticising the central role of media + television in the family - central
- Pre internet (takes away from fam time)
- Mysogynistic - prejudice against women
- violent themes
- not afraid to Rebel

Feels the TV has destroyed her family life
- what her husband said in court
- detective/violence
Aggressive/Violent

Trying to suck up to the judge

engrossed

inequality

Pool

Judge reinforcing the idea that the TV should have a central role

This is Poetry 61

Tease It Out

1. Consider the poem's title. What form of very popular writing does a title like this bring to mind?

2. Who is speaking at the beginning of the poem? To whom is he speaking?

3. What was he doing when his wife came into the living room?

4. Who was present with him at the time?

5. Class Discussion: What does the word 'peaceably' mean? Why do you think the speaker uses this word? What impression is he trying to create?

6. Consider the words 'marched' and 'declared'. What impression do they create of the wife's attitude and demeanour?

7. What did his wife demand? What threat did she make?

8. How did he respond to this unexpected development?

9. How exactly did the wife make good on her threat?

10. What was the television depicting at this moment?

11. Comment on the use of the word 'dame' in line 8. Why do you think the speaker uses this term?

12. Where did the speaker and his children go in the wake of this event?

13. Why did he take them to this particular venue?

14. What did the wife do with the remnants of the television set?

15. 'I didn't get married to a television'. In what tone of voice do you imagine this line being spoken? Give a reason for your answer.

16. The wife speaks about televisions serving as fathers and mothers. Describe in your own words what you understand by this statement. Does the wife believe that this is a positive development?

17. What according to the wife is a preferable activity to watching television? Where does she go having made this claim?

18. Who seems to be speaking (or writing) in the poem's final lines? And whose speech is being reported?

19. According to the judge, what 'preference' did the wife express?

20. What, according to the judge, is threatened by such a preference?

21. What surprising claim does the judge make about televisions and the family unit?

22. The judge refers to the wife's actions as a 'form of violence'. Do you think this is fair?

23. What punishment did the wife receive for her actions?

24. Class Discussion: How would you characterise the tone of these last five line? What specific words and phrases contribute to this tone?

Think About Themes

1. 'television itself could be said to be a basic unit of the family' How does the judge's attitude toward television differ from that of the wife's? How are they strangely similar? Which attitude do you think the poet himself finds most agreeable?

2. 'An interesting aspect of this poem is how it reverses our usual expectations of gender'. Do you think this is a fair comment? In what sense might the wife's behaviour be considered untypical of her gender? In what sense might the husband's?

3. Is this a realistic portrait of society or is it more a zany and surrealistic narrative? Could it be both? Write a paragraph giving the reasons for your answer.

4. The wife feels that it's better for a family to drink in the pub together than watch television together. Why do you think she believes this? Do you feel that she has a point?

5. 'This poem depicts a nightmare reality where screens are more important than people and where each human being is lost in his or her personal technology'. Write a couple of paragraphs responding to this statement.

6. Given that this poem was written in the 1970s is it still relevant to the Ireland of today? Give a reason for your answer.

7. Class Discussion: In this poem Durcan uses the language and techniques of newspaper journalism. Why do you think he made this choice? Is it an effective one?

In Context

Durcan's poetry frequently celebrates strong women. In light of this statement compare and contrast 'Wife Who Smashed Television Gets Jail' with 'The MacBride Dynasty', 'Nessa' or 'Six Nuns Die in Convent Inferno'.

Parents

A child's face is a drowned face:
Her parents stare down at her asleep
Estranged from her by a sea:
She is under the sea
And they are above the sea: [5]
If she looked up she would see them
As if locked out of their own home,
Their mouths open,
Their foreheads furrowed –
Pursed-up orifices of fearful fish –   [10]
Their big ears are fins behind glass,
And in her sleep she is calling out to them
   Father, Father
   Mother, Mother
But they cannot hear her: [15]
She is inside the sea
And they are outside the sea.
Through the night, stranded, they stare
At the drowned, drowned face of their child.

> [3] *estranged:* distant, separated
> [9] *furrowed:* lined, wrinkled
> [10] *orifices:* bodily opening, such as a mouth, gill, etc.

Tease It Out

1. Where is the child? Where are the parents? What is the child doing? What are the parents doing?
2. What do you think of when you imagine a 'drowned face'? How might a child's face resemble such a face?
3. What does it mean to be 'Estranged' from someone? Why might the child and the parents be estranged?
4. The poet uses the sea as a metaphor to describe the distance that exists between the parents and the sleeping child. What does the metaphor suggest about this distance?
5. The poet imagines how the parents would appear to the child if she were to awake. What does he compare them to? What does the image suggest about the parents' feelings as they watch their sleeping child?
6. What does the poet imagine the sleeping child is 'calling out' to her parents in her sleep?
7. 'But they cannot hear her:/ She is inside the sea'. What does the sea represent? Is this gulf only present when the child sleeps?

Think About Themes

1. Were you surprised by the poem's opening line? Why do you think the poet chose this particular image to describe the face of a child?
2. What does the poem suggest about what it is like to be a parent?
3. How would you describe the atmosphere of this poem? How did reading the poem make you feel?
4. Do you think that this poem describes something universal or do you think that this is more about the poet's personal experience of being a parent?
5. The poem features a number of similes and metaphors. Identify three and say which one you found most effective.

In Context

Write a short essay in which you discuss the securities and insecurities that accompany family life based on your reading of the poetry of Paul Durcan.

En Famille, 1979

Bring me back to the dark school – to the dark school of childhood:
To where tiny is tiny, and massive is massive.

En Famille: with one's family; at home

Think About Themes

1. This poem was written in 1979. What age was Paul Durcan at that time?
2. Consider the phrase 'dark school'. What images or phrases come to mind when you think about this concept?
3. Is this 'dark school' a specific place or building? Or does it refer to a more general state of mind?
4. Does the phrase 'dark school of childhood' have positive or negative association for you? Give a reason for your answer.
5. The poet considers childhood a 'dark school'. What does this immediately suggest to you about his own childhood experiences?
6. We sometimes associate darkness with ignorance and light with understanding. Could these ways of using the terms be relevant to this poem?
7. Consider the words 'tiny' and 'massive'. Are these words you especially associate with being used by children?
8. 'Line 2 conveys a sense of childhood's comforting certainty'. Write a few sentences responding to this statement.
9. 'There's also a sense in which line 2 conveys something of childhood's threat and menace'. Write a sentence or two in response to this statement as well.

10. Why do you think the poet wishes to return to the 'dark school of childhood'? In what sense might he view this dark place or state of mind as a desirable one to inhabit?
11. What does his need to go there suggest about his state of mind when writing the poem?
12. Class Discussion: How do you imagine the poet's tone? Does he really want to make such a return or is he speaking sarcastically?
13. Consider the poem's title. Is the poet referring to the family he grew up in or to the family he himself started as an adult? Give reason for your answer.

In Context

'For Durcan, the family is a sacred unit, an oasis from the troubles and dangers that lurk in the world beyond the family home.' Discuss this statement based on your reading of this poem and 'Windfall'.

Madman

Every child has a madman on their street:
The only trouble about our madman is that he's our father.

Think About Themes

1. With who or what do you associate the term 'madman'?
2. What do you think the poet means when he says that 'Every child has a madman on their street'?
3. What does the first line of the poem suggest about the way children view the world?
4. Who do you imagine is speaking these lines? What age do you imagine the speaker to be?
5. Read the poem aloud. Does the impact of the poem change depending on the tone in which it is read – for instance, a serious tone, a humorous tone, a sad tone, and so on?
6. Do you think a poem as short as this is capable of dealing with complex themes?
7. What emotions are conveyed in the poem? Do we get any sense of how the speaker feels about his situation?

In Context

Write a short essay discussing the way Durcan depicts childhood in his poems. Make reference to at least three poems on the course in your answer.

'Windfall', 8 Parnell Hill, Cork

But, then, at the end of day I could always say –
Well, now, I am going home.
I felt elected, steeped, sovereign to be able to say –
I am going home.
When I was at home I liked to stay at home;   [5]
At home I stayed at home for weeks;
At home I used sit in a winged chair by the window
Overlooking the river and the factory chimneys,
The electricity power station and the car assembly works,
The fleets of trawlers and the pilot tugs,   [10]
Dreaming that life is a dream which is real,
The river a reflection of itself in its own waters,
Goya sketching Goya among the smoky mirrors.
The industrial vista was my Mont Sainte-Victoire.
While my children sat on my knees watching TV   [15]
Their mother, my wife, reclined on the couch
Knitting a bright-coloured scarf, drinking a cup of black coffee,
Smoking a cigarette – one of her own roll-ups.
I closed my eyes and breathed in and breathed out.

It is ecstasy to breathe if you are at home in the world.   [20]
What a windfall! A home of our own!
Our neighbours' houses had names like 'Con Amore',
'Sans Souci', 'Pacelli', 'Montini', 'Homesville'.
But we called our home 'Windfall'.
'Windfall', 8 Parnell Hill, Cork.   [25]
In the gut of my head coursed the leaf of tranquillity
Which I dreamed was known only to Buddhist Monks
In lotus monasteries high up in the Hindu Kush.
Down here in the dark depths of Ireland,
Below sea level in the city of Cork,   [30]
In a city as intimate and homicidal as a Little Marseilles,
In a country where all the children of the nation
Are not cherished equally
And where the best go homeless, while the worst
Erect block-house palaces – self-regardingly ugly –   [35]
Having a home of your own can give to a family
A chance in a lifetime to transcend death.

At the high window, shipping from all over the world
Being borne up and down the busy, yet contemplative, river;
Skylines drifting in and out of skylines in the cloudy valley;   [40]
Firelight at dusk, and city lights;
Beyond them the control tower of the airport on the hill –
A lighthouse in the sky flashing green to white to green;
Our black-and-white cat snoozing in the corner of a chair;
Pastels and etchings on the four walls, and over the mantelpiece   [45]
'Van Gogh's Grave' and 'Lovers in Water';
A room wallpapered in books and family photograph albums
Chronicling the adventures and metamorphoses of family life:
In swaddling clothes in Mammy's arms on baptism day;

[3]   *steeped:* elevated
[3]   *sovereign:* independent, possessing supreme power
[13] *Goya:* Spanish painter
[14] *vista:* distant view
[14] *Mont Sainte-Victoire:* mountain in southern France, the subject of a number of Cézanne's paintings
[28] *Hindu Kush:* mountain range that stretches between central Afghanistan and northern Pakistan
[31] *Marseilles:* second largest city in France, with a reputation for being a violent and seedy port
[34] *where the best go homeless, while the worst ...:* reference to Yeats' 'The Second Coming': 'The best lack all conviction, while the worst/ Are full of passionate intensity'
[48] *metamorphoses:* changes or transformations
[49] *swaddling clothes:* clothes for wrapping an infant

Being a baby of nine months and not remembering it;   [50]
Face-down in a pram, incarcerated in a high chair;
Everybody, including strangers, wearing shop-window smiles;
With Granny in Felixstowe, with Granny in Ballymaloe;
In a group photo in First Infants, on a bike at thirteen;
In the back garden in London, in the back garden in Cork;   [55]
Performing a headstand after First Holy Communion;
Getting a kiss from the Bishop on Confirmation Day;
Straw hats in the Bois de Boulougne, wearing wings at the seaside;
Mammy and Daddy holding hands on the Normandy Beaches;
Mammy and Daddy at the wedding of Jeremiah and Margot;   [60]
Mammy and Daddy queuing up for *Last Tango in Paris*;
Boating on the Shannon, climbing mountains in Kerry;
Building sandcastles in Killala, camping in Barley Cove;
Picnicking in Moone, hide-and-go-seek in Clonmacnoise;
Riding horses, cantering, jumping fences;   [65]
Pushing out toy yachts in the pond in the Tuileries;
The Irish College revisited in the Rue des Irlandais;
Sipping on *orangé* presse through a straw on the roof of the Beaubourg;
Dancing in Père Lachaise, weeping at Auvers.
Year in, year out, I pored over these albums accumulating,   [70]
My children looking over my shoulder, exhilarated as I was,
Their mother presiding at our ritual from a distance –
The far side of the hearthrug, diffidently, proudly.
Schoolbooks on the floor and pyjamas on the couch –
Whose turn is it tonight to put the children to bed?   [75]

Our children swam about our home
As if it was their private sea,
Their own unique, symbiotic fluid
Of which their parents also partook.
Such is home – a sea of your own –   [80]
In which you hang upside down from the ceiling
With equanimity, while postcards from Thailand on the mantelpiece
Are raising their eyebrow markings benignly:
Your hands dangling their prayers to the floorboards of your home,
Sifting the sands underneath the surfaces of conversations,   [85]
The marine insect life of the family psyche.
A home of your own – or a sea of your own –
In which climbing the walls is as natural
As making love on the stairs;
In which when the telephone rings   [90]
Husband and wife are metamorphosed into smiling accomplices,
Both declining to answer it;
Initiating, instead, a yet more subversive kiss –
A kiss they have perhaps never attempted before –
And might never have dreamed of attempting   [95]
Were it not for the telephone belling.
Through the bannisters or along the bannister rails
The pyjama-clad children solemnly watching
Their parents at play, jumping up and down in support,
Race back to bed, gesticulating wordlessly: [100]

The most subversive unit in society is the human family.
We're almost home, pet, almost home . . .
Our home is at . . .
I'll be home . . .
I have to go home now . . .   [105]
I want to go home now . . .
Are you feeling homesick?
Are you anxious to get home? . . .
I can't wait to get home . . .
Let's stay at home to tonight and . . .   [110]
What time will you be coming home at? . . .
If I'm not home by six at the latest, I'll phone . . .
We're nearly home, don't worry, we're nearly home . . .

But then with good reason
I was put out of my home: [115]
By a keen wind felled.
I find myself now without a home
Having to live homeless in the alien, foreign city of Dublin.
It is an eerie enough feeling to be homesick
Yet knowing you will be going home next week;   [120]
It is an eerie feeling beyond all ornithological analysis
To be homesick knowing that there is no home to go home to:
Day by day, creeping, crawling,
Moonlighting, escaping,
Bed-and-breakfast to bed-and-breakfast;   [125]
Hostels, centres, one-night hotels.

Homeless in Dublin,
Blown about the suburban streets at evening,
Peering in the windows of other people's homes,
Wondering what it must feel like   [130]
To be sitting around a fire –
Apache or Cherokee or Bourgeoisie –
Beholding the firelit faces of your family,
Beholding their starry or their TV gaze:
Windfall to Windfall – can you hear me?   [135]
Windfall to Windfall . . .
We're almost home, pet, don't worry anymore, we're almost home.

[51]   *incarcerated:* imprisoned, confined
[58]   ***Bois de Boulougne:*** large public park in Paris
[61]   ***Last Tango in Paris:*** 1970s movie set in Paris, starring Marlon Brando
[66]   ***Tuileries:*** public garden in Paris
[67]   ***Rue des Irlandais:*** street in Paris where the Centre for Irish Culture is located
[68]   ***Beaubourg:*** area in Paris
[69]   ***Père Lachaise:*** Large cemetery in Paris
[69]   ***Auvers:*** Paris suburb in which Vincent Van Gogh is buried
[78]   *symbiotic:* having an interdependent relationship
[82]   *equanimity:* evenness of mind especially under stress
[93]   *subversive:* seeking or intended to subvert an established system or institution
[121]   *ornithological:* branch of zoology that concerns the study of birds
[124]   ***Moonlighting:*** having a second job, typically secretly and at night
[132]   ***Apache:*** a member of an American Indian people living chiefly in New Mexico and Arizona
[132]   ***Cherokee:*** a member of an American Indian people formerly inhabiting much of the southern US
[132]   ***Bourgeoisie:*** member of the middle classes

Tease It Out

Lines 1 to 19

1. Where would the poet sit when he was 'at home' in 8 Parnell Hill? What could he see from his window?

2. How does he describe his wife and children? What are they doing? How would you describe the atmosphere in the family home?

3. Durcan says that he felt 'elected, steeped' and 'sovereign' to be able to say 'I am going home'. What do each of these words mean? What does each of these words suggest about the way the poet felt?

Lines 20 to 37

4. What does the word 'windfall' mean? Why do you think that the family decided to use this as the name of their house?

5. Lines 26 to 28: How does the poet describe his state of mind during this period of his life? What image does he use to convey this?

6. How does the poet describe the city of Cork in line 31? To what city does he compare Cork?

7. How does the poet describe or characterise Ireland in lines 32 to 35?

Lines 38 to 75

8. The poet describes what he could see from the 'high window' in the house. List the various sights he describes.

9. What do you think the poet means when he describes 'Skylines drifting in and out of skylines in the cloudy valley'? How do you picture this?

10. What is the 'lighthouse in the sky' that the poet mentions in line 43?

11. Lines 45 to 48: What does the poet say adorned the walls of some of the rooms in the house? What sort of atmosphere is evident in these lines?

12. In lines 49 to 69, the poet describes some of the family photographs in the albums that he loved to pore over. What aspects of family life does he describe in these lines? What picture do these photographs paint of the family?

13. What 'ritual' does the poet describe himself and his children enjoying in line 72? How did his wife respond to this?

Lines 76 to 101

14. The poet compares the family home to a 'private sea'. What is it about the family home that the poet is seeking to express here?

15. How does the poet convey the sense of freedom he felt when at home in lines 80 to 83 and lines 88 to 89?

16. Class Discussion: Durcan speaks of the 'marine insect life of the family psyche'. What do you think he is describing here?

17. What does the ringing telephone encourage the poet and his wife to initiate or attempt? What does this moment suggest about their relationship? What does the word 'subversive' mean?

18. Why do you think that Durcan considers the 'human family' to be the 'most subversive unit in society'?

Lines 102 to 137

19. The poet lists a number of expressions that feature the word 'home' in lines 102 to 113. Who do you imagine speaking each of them? What do these expressions suggest about the importance of home?

20. What does the poet say happened to him in lines 114 to 115? To what does he compare this moment in line 116?

21. How does the poet describe the city of Dublin in line 118? Why do you think he describes it in this manner?

22. Durcan describes two forms of homesickness. What is the difference between them?

23. 'It is an eerie feeling beyond all ornithological analysis'. Why do you think the poet describes the feeling in this unusual manner?

24. How does the poet describe his daily routine in lines 123 to 134? To what does he compare himself in line 128?

Think About Themes

1. The poem describes how wonderful having a home can be. List the different benefits that the poet mentions in lines 1 to 89.

2. What sort of picture does the poem present of married life?

3. How did reading this poem make you feel? Did you find that the poet's light-hearted and humorous tone in the early parts of the poem served to heighten the sadness in the final section?

4. What picture of family life does the poem present? Would you agree that the 'human family' can be the 'most subversive unit in society'?

In Context

Paula Meehan said that Durcan writes poems 'for the befuddled, the disorganised, the demented, the muddling through, the most of us'. Discuss three of the poems on the course in light of this statement.

Six Nuns Die in Convent Inferno

*To the
happy memory of six Loreto nuns
who died
between midnight and morning of
2 June 1986*

I

We resided in a Loreto convent in the centre of Dublin city
On the east side of a public gardens, St Stephen's Green.
Grafton Street – the *paseo*
Where everybody *paseo*'d, including even ourselves –
Debouched on the north side, and at the top of Grafton Street,   [5]
Or round the base of the great patriotic pebble of O'Donovan Rossa,
Knelt tableaus of punk girls and punk boys.
When I used pass them – scurrying as I went –
Often as not to catch a mass in Clarendon Street,
The Carmelite Church in Clarendon Street   [10]
(Myself, I never used the Clarendon Street entrance,
I always slipped in by way of Johnson's Court,
Opposite the side entrance to Bewley's Oriental Café),
I could not help but smile, as I sucked on a Fox's mint,
That for all the half-shaven heads and the martial garb   [15]
And the dyed hair-dos and the nappy pins
They looked so conventional really, and vulnerable,
Clinging to warpaint and to uniforms and to one another.
I knew it was myself who was the ultimate drop-out,
The delinquent, the recidivist, the vagabond,   [20]
The wild woman, the subversive, the original punk.
Yet, although I confess I was smiling, I was also afraid,
Appalled by my own nerve, my own fervour,
My apocalyptic enthusiasm, my other-worldly hubris:
To opt out of the world and to   [25]
Choose such exotic loneliness,
Such terrestrial abandonment,
A lifetime of bicycle lamps and bicycle pumps,
A lifetime of galoshes stowed under the stairs,
A lifetime of umbrellas drying out in the kitchens.   [30]

I was an old nun – an agèd beadswoman –
But I was no daw.
I knew what a weird bird I was, I knew that when we
Went to bed we were as eerie an aviary as you'd find
In all the blown-off rooftops of the city: [35]
Scuttling about our dorm, wheezing, shrieking, croaking,
In our yellow corsets, wonky suspenders, strung-out garters,
A bony crew in the gods of the sleeping city.
Many's the night I lay awake in bed
Dreaming what would befall us if there were a fire: [40]
No fire-escapes outside, no fire-extinguishers inside;

[3] *paseo:* Spanish word meaning promenade
[4] *paseo'd:* play on the Spanish verb *paseo*, which means to stroll in a leisurely manner
[7] *tableaus:* groups of models depicting scenes from history
[15] *martial garb:* military-style clothing
[20] *delinquent:* young, petty criminal
[20] *recidivist:* criminal who reoffends
[20] *vagabond:* someone who wanders from one place to another without a home or job
[21] *subversive:* one who undermines the establishment
[24] *hubris:* excessive pride
[29] *galoshes:* waterproof overshoes, typically made of rubber
[32] *daw:* fool
[34] *aviary:* an enclosure for birds
[37] *garters:* bands worn around the leg to keep stockings up

To coin a Dublin saying,
We'd not stand a snowball's chance in hell. Fancy that!
It seemed too good to be true:
Happy death vouchsafed only to the few.   [45]
Sleeping up there was like sleeping at the top of the mast
Of a nineteenth-century schooner, and in the daytime
We old nuns were the ones who crawled out on the yardarms
To stitch and sew the rigging and the canvas.
To be sure we were weird birds, oddballs, Christniks,   [50]
For we had done the weirdest thing a woman can do –
Surrendered the marvellous passions of girlhood,
The innocent dreams of childhood,
Not for a night or a weekend or even a Lent or a season,
But for a lifetime.   [55]
Never to know the love of a man or a woman;
Never to have children of our own;
Never to have a home of our own;
All for why and for what?
To follow a young man – would you believe it –   [60]
Who lived two thousand years ago in Palestine
And who died a common criminal strung up on a tree.

As we stood there in the disintegrating dormitory
Burning to death in the arms of Christ –
O Christ, Christ, come quickly, quickly –   [65]
Fluttering about in our tight, gold bodices,
Beating our wings in vain,
It reminded me of the snaps one of the sisters took
When we took a seaside holiday in 1956
(The year Cardinal Mindszenty went into hiding   [70]
In the US legation in Budapest.
He was a great hero of ours, Cardinal Mindszenty,
Any of us would have given our right arm
To have been his nun – darning his socks, cooking his meals,
Making his bed, doing his washing and ironing.)   [75]
Somebody – an affluent buddy of the bishop's repenting his affluence –
Loaned Mother Superior a secluded beach in Co. Waterford –
Ardmore, along the coast from Tramore –
A cove with palm trees, no less, well off the main road.
There we were, fluttering up and down the beach,   [80]
Scampering hither and thither in our starched bathing-costumes.
Tonight, expiring in the fire, was quite much like that,
Only instead of scampering into the waves of the sea,
Now we were scampering into the flames of the fire.

That was one of the gayest days of my life,   [85]
The day the sisters went swimming.
Often in the silent darkness of the chapel after Benediction,
During the Exposition of the Blessed Sacrament,
I glimpsed the sea again as it was that day.
Praying – daydreaming really –   [90]
I became aware that Christ is the ocean
Forever rising and falling on the world's shore.

Now tonight in the convent Christ is the fire in whose waves
We are doomed but delighted to drown.
And, darting in and out of the flames of the dormitory,   [95]
Gabriel, with that extraordinary message of his on his boyish lips,
Frenetically pedalling his skybike.
He whispers into my ear what I must do
And I do it – and die.
Each of us in our own tiny, frail, furtive way   [100]
Was a Mother of God, mothering forth illegitimate Christs
In the street life of Dublin city.
God have mercy on our whirring souls –
Wild women were we all –
And on the misfortunate, poor fire-brigade men   [105]
Whose task it will be to shovel up our ashes and shovel
What is left of us into black plastic refuse sacks.
Fire-brigade men are the salt of the earth.

Isn't it a marvellous thing how your hour comes
When you least expect it? When you lose a thing,   [110]
Not to know about it until it actually happens?
How, in so many ways, losing things is such a refreshing experience,
Giving you a sense of freedom you've not often experienced?
How lucky I was to lose – I say, lose – lose my life.
It was a Sunday night, and after vespers   [115]
I skipped bathroom so that I could hop straight into bed
And get in a bit of a read before lights out:
Conor Cruise O'Brien's new book *The Siege*,
All about Israel and superlatively insightful
For a man who they say is reputedly an agnostic –   [120]
I got a loan of it from the brother-in-law's married niece –
But I was tired out and I fell asleep with the book open
Face down across my breast and I woke
To the racket of bellowing flame and snarling glass.
The first thing I thought was that the brother-in-law's married niece   [125]
Would never again get her Conor Cruise O'Brien back
And I had seen on the price-tag that it cost £23.00:
Small wonder that the custom of snipping off the price
As an exercise in social deportment has simply died out;
Indeed a book today is almost worth buying for its price,   [130]
Its price frequently being more remarkable than its contents.

The strange Eucharist of my death –
To be eaten alive by fire and smoke.
I clasped the dragon to my breast
And stroked his red-hot ears.   [135]
Strange! There we were, all sleeping molecules,
Suddenly all giving birth to our deaths,
All frantically in labour.
Doctors and midwives weaved in and out
In gowns of smoke and gloves of fire.   [140]
Christ, like an Orthodox patriarch in his dressing gown,
Flew up and down the dormitory, splashing water on our souls:
Sister Eucharia; Sister Seraphia; Sister Rosario;
Sister Gonzaga; Sister Margaret; Sister Edith.

If you will remember us – six nuns burnt to death – [145]
Remember us for the frisky girls that we were,
Now more than ever kittens in the sun.

II

When Jesus heard these words at the top of Grafton Street
Uttered by a small, agèd, emaciated, female punk
Clad all in mourning black, and grieving like an alley cat, [150]
He was annulled with astonishment, and turning round
He declared to the gangs of teenagers and dicemen following him:
'I tell you, not even in New York City
Have I found faith like this.'

That night in St Stephen's Green, [155]
After the keepers had locked the gates,
And the courting couples had found cinemas themselves to die in,
The six nuns who had died in the convent inferno,
From the bandstand they'd been hiding under, crept out
And knelt together by the Fountain of the Three Fates, [160]
Reciting the Agnus Dei: reciting it as if it were the torch song
Of all aid – Live Aid, Self Aid, Aids, and All Aid –
Lord, I am not worthy
That thou should'st enter under my roof;
Say but the word and my soul shall be healed. [165]

[45]	***vouchsafed:*** granted
[47]	***schooner:*** a sailing ship
[70]	***Cardinal Mindszenty:*** Hungarian Catholic cardinal who defied Communist rules banning religious freedom
[87]	***Benediction:*** prayer asking for divine blessing
[88]	***Exposition of the Blessed Sacrament:*** the displaying and adoration of Holy Communion
[96]	***Gabriel:*** an angel who typically serves as a messenger sent by God
[97]	***Frenetically:*** frantically
[118]	***Conor Cruise O'Brien:*** Irish politician, writer, historian and academic
[119]	***superlatively:*** excellently, magnificently
[120]	***agnostic:*** one who believes that nothing is known or can be known of the existence of God
[129]	***deportment:*** etiquette; polite behaviour
[132]	***Eucharist:*** the Christian ceremony in which bread and wine are consecrated and consumed
[141]	***Orthodox patriarch:*** bishop of an Eastern Orthodox church
[151]	***annulled:*** obliterated, wiped out
[152]	***dicemen:*** street performers
[160]	***The Fountain of the Three Fates:*** fountain with statue in St Stephen's Green
[161]	***Agnus Dei:*** traditional prayer recited during mass
[162]	***Live Aid:*** concert held in 1985 to raise funds for victims of famine in Africa
[162]	***Self Aid:*** benefit concert for the unemployed, held in Dublin in 1986
[163-5]	***Lord, I am not worthy …:*** Prayer of Humble Access, recited before Holy Communion

Tease It Out

Lines 1 to 62

1. Where was the convent located? How does the speaker describe the area?

2. Where does the speaker recall seeing groups of 'punk girls and punk boys'? Where would she often be heading when she would pass these punks?

3. What was it about these punks that would make the nun smile?

4. Lines 19 to 21: How does the speaker describe herself in these lines? List the words that she uses and say what each of them mean.

5. Lines 22 to 24: 'I was also afraid'. What was it about her vocation or herself that caused the speaker to feel afraid?

6. In lines 25 to 30, the speaker sums up the religious life. How does she characterise this? What objects does she mention? Why do you think she associates these items in particular with a nun's life?

7. To what does the speaker compare the nuns and their convent in lines 33 and 34? Why do you think she makes this comparison?

8. Lines 36 to 38: The speaker imagines how she and the other nuns would have appeared if the roof was torn off the building and someone peered inside. What does she describe them doing? To what does she compare the nuns and the convent in line 38?

9. What did the speaker sometimes contemplate when lying in bed at night? Why do you think she considers such a fate a 'Happy death'?

10. The speaker compares the nuns' existence to life aboard an old ship in lines 46 to 49. What similarities does she find between the two?

11. 'For we had done the weirdest thing a woman can do'. What does the speaker consider to be the 'weirdest thing a woman can do'?

12. How does the nun describe Christ in lines 60 to 62?

Lines 63 to 108

13. How does the speaker describe the scene in the convent during the fire in lines 63 to 67? What was she reminded of at this moment? Why?

14. Why was Cardinal Mindszenty a 'great hero' to the speaker?

15. What would the nun sometimes 'daydream' about when she was praying during the Exposition of the Blessed Sacrament? How would she imagine Christ on these occasions? Why do you think she thought about Him in this manner?

16. In lines 93 to 94 the speaker says that she can feel Christ's presence in the burning room. How does she consider Him to be present?

17. Who else does the speaker say is present in the burning room? What do you think this person whispers in the speaker's ear?

18. How does the speaker characterise the nuns and their work in lines 100 to 104? Why does the speaker think that she and the other nuns were 'Wild women'?

Lines 109 to 147

19. How does the speaker think about her moment of death in lines 109 and 114? Why does she consider herself to be so 'lucky'?

20. What was the speaker doing the evening that the fire broke out?

21. What is the speaker's view of Conor Cruise O'Brien and his book?

22. What was the first thing that the speaker thought about when she woke to the noise of the fire?

23. Class Discussion: The speaker considers her death to be a 'strange Eucharist'. What do Catholics believe takes place during the Eucharist? Why do you think the speaker thinks of her death as a form of Eucharist?

24. How does the speaker describe herself and the other nuns in lines 136 to 140? To what does she compare the process of dying? Why do you think she makes this comparison?

25. How does the speaker say she would like herself and her fellow nuns to be remembered?

Lines 148 to 165

26. Who do you think speaks these lines?

27. Where does the poet imagine Jesus to be? Who is Jesus listening to?

28. How does Jesus respond? Why do you think He says that He has not found faith such as this 'even in New York City'? Why do you think New York is considered a place of faith?

29. What does the poet imagine happening in St. Stephen's Green after the gates have been locked for the night?

30. Where do the six nuns kneel? What prayer do they recite?

31. What is a 'torch song'? Why do you think the nuns recite their prayer 'as if it were the torch song/ Of all aid'?

32. How would you characterise the atmosphere and the events described in this part of the poem?

Think About Themes

1. Do you think that the poem offers us an interesting insight into the life of a nun? What impression did it give you of such a life?

2. The poet seems to consider the nun's life to be both admirable and ridiculous. Would you agree with this? What do you think the poet most admires about the nun? What do you think he finds most ridiculous?

3. What view of organised religion does the poem present? Do you think that the poet is a religious man, based on your reading of this poem?

4. 'They looked so conventional, really, and vulnerable'. What did you make of the nun's reaction to the punks she sees on the street? Do you think that she is right when she says that she is the 'ultimate drop-out'?

5. The poem is based on a real event. Do you think that the poet's reimagining of this event is in good taste? What do you think motivated or inspired him to write the poem?

6. What images in the poem did you find particularly memorable?

7. What impression does the poem offer of Ireland? Does the poet present Dublin as an attractive city to live in?

8. Did you find the ending of the poem satisfying? Do you think that it adds an interesting twist to the narrative?

9. Discuss the poet's use of simile and metaphor. Which did you find most effective?

In Context

The humour in Durcan's poetry has been described as 'savage and satirical'. Do you agree with this statement? Refer to at least three of Durcan's poems in your answer.

word I is used 13 times - deeply personal

Humour

Physco institituion
- His father came to watch him play a match
- He wanted to play well

Theme
family

Autobiographical / conversational language - disspasionate

irregular stanzas, loose lies - things in his life were staggard

Sport

Area - Pun

There were not many fields
In which you had hopes for me *— his father didn't have high hopes for him*
But sport was one of them.
Pride On my twenty-first birthday *— He celebrated his 21st B-day playing for mental hospital*
I was selected to play
For Grangegorman Mental Hospital   [5]
In an away game
Against Mullingar Mental Hospital.
I was a patient
In B Wing. *— Anxious + Hopeful to impress his father*   [10]
You drove all the way down, *— Occasion*
Fifty miles,
To Mullingar to stand *— Judgement*
insecure On the sidelines and observe me.

I was fearful I would let down   [15]
Not only my team but you. *Worried*
It was Gaelic football.
I was selected as goalkeeper.
There were big country men
Surreal image On the Mullingar Mental Hospital team,   [20]
Men with gapped teeth, red faces, *— Picture he paints — Bizzare*
Oily, frizzy hair, bushy eyebrows. *— intimidating / humorous*
concious thats how people looked at him Their full forward line *stereotypical image*
Were over six foot tall
Fifteen stone in weight.   [25]
All three of them, I was informed,
Cases of schizophrenia.

Light-hearted language

humour fine Big strong +heavy men

Anecdote

There was a rumour
That their centre-half forward
Was an alcoholic solicitor   [30]
Who, in a lounge bar misunderstanding,
Had castrated his best friend
But that he had no memory of it.
He had meant well – it was said.
His best friend had had to emigrate   [35]
To Nigeria.

To my surprise,
I did not flinch in the goals.
I made three or four spectacular saves,
Diving full stretch to turn   [40]
A certain goal around the corner,
Leaping high to tip another certain goal
Over the bar for a point.
It was my knowing
That you were standing on the sideline   [45]
That gave me the necessary motivation –
That will to die
That is as essential to sportsmen as to artists.
More than anybody it was you
I wanted to mesmerise, and after the game –   [50]
Grangegorman Mental Hospital
Having defeated Mullingar Mental Hospital
By 14 goals and 38 points to 3 goals and 10 points –
Sniffing your approval, you shook hands with me.
'Well played, son.'   [55]

I may not have been mesmeric
But I had not been mediocre.
In your eyes I had achieved something at last.
On my twenty-first birthday I had played on a winning team
The Grangegorman Mental Hospital team.   [60]
Seldom if ever again in your eyes
Was I to rise to these heights.

Handwritten annotations:

remove testicles

– humour
'individual meant well
– humerow approach

self-depricating

played his heart out   live action in the game

Other team were sure they were going to score

Dynamic verbs

The reason he tried so hard – motivated him

who is he doing it for?

father disapproved of him as a poet - wasn't manly enough
→ work as hard in sport as it is to be a poet
– make yourself vulnerable

wasn't wholehearted

– Fathers voice
– means so much to Durcan

Average - happy he wasn't average
– All he wanted

wasn't worthy for his father

On a day many people wouldn't think its a real success to spend your 21st in a mental hospital - for Durcan it was the best day of his life

Tinge of sadness lonliness

Tease It Out

1. Who is the poet addressing in this poem?
2. 'There were not many fields/ In which you had hopes for me'. What do these lines suggest about the father's attitude toward his son?
3. Where was the poet residing on his twenty-first birthday?
4. In what sport did the poet participate on that day?
5. In what position did he play?
6. Where did the match take place?
7. What did the poet's father do on the day of the match?
8. What made the poet 'fearful' before the match?
9. The poet vividly describes the opposing Mullingar team. Based on your reading of lines 19 to 22, come up with three words of your own to describe this group of men.
10. What condition affected all three members of the opposition's full-forward line?
11. Describe in your own words the rumours surrounding the Mullingar centre-half forward.
12. How did the poet perform in the game? Mention two of the feats he pulled off during the match.
13. What motivated him to play in this manner? Who did he want to impress with his performance?
14. Class Discussion: What does the poet say is 'essential' to sportsmen and artists? What similarities can you think of between sportsmen and artists? Why do you think the members of these two professions might have such a 'will' in common?
15. What was the final score? Do you think this is a realistic scoreline?
16. 'In your eyes I had achieved something at last'. How did the father react to his son's performance?
17. How do you imagine the father expressing this reaction? Do you visualise him as being loud or quiet, jolly or reserved?
18. What do the closing lines suggest about the poet's relationship with his father in the subsequent years?

Think About Themes

1. Did the poem surprise you? Were you expecting something different from a poem entitled 'Sport'? Do you think it was the poet's intention to play with our expectations?
2. Did you find this poem amusing? If so, identify the lines you found entertaining and say why.
3. Do you think Durcan really experienced the events the poem describes? Is he being truthful or is he exaggerating? Give a reason for your answer.
4. What impression does the poem give us of the poet's father? Read the poem again carefully and take a moment to visualise him. Write a paragraph describing how you imagine him looking, speaking and acting.
5. Do you think the father loves his son? Write a paragraph outlining the reasons for your answer.
6. The poet wrote this poem some years after the events it describes. Do you think he looks back on that day with bitterness or with forgiveness and understanding?
7. How would you characterise the tone of this poem? Is it serious or light-hearted? Do you think it shifts at any point?
8. Consider again the phrase 'will to die'. Try to think of a moment when you witnessed a sportsman exhibit the 'will to die'. Have you ever heard of an artist or musician exhibiting such a will? Try to think of at least one example.
9. Imagine you are the poet's father. Write a diary entry describing your experience at the match.

In Context

'Durcan's poems often deal with painful personal experiences, but never in a self-pitying manner'. Write a short essay discussing this statement and refer to at least three poems by Durcan on your course.

Father's Day, 21 June 1992

Just as I was dashing to catch the Dublin–Cork train,
Dashing up and down the stairs, searching my pockets,
She told me that her sister in Cork wanted a loan of the axe;
It was late June and
The buddleia tree in the backyard [5]
Had grown out of control.
The taxi was ticking over outside in the street,
All the neighbours noticing it.
'You mean that you want me to bring her down the axe?'
'Yes, if you wouldn't mind, that is –' [10]
'A simple saw would do the job, surely to God
She could borrow a simple saw.'
'She said that she'd like the axe.'
'OK. There is a Blue Cabs taxi ticking over outside
And the whole world inspecting it, [15]
I'll bring her down the axe.'
The axe – all four-and-a-half feet of it –
Was leaning up against the wall behind the settee –
The fold-up settee that doubles as a bed.
She handed the axe to me just as it was, [20]
As neat as a newborn babe,
All in the bare buff.
You'd think she'd have swaddled it up
In something – if not a blanket, an old newspaper,
But no, not even a token hanky [25]
Tied in a bow round its head.
I decided not to argue the toss. I kissed her goodbye.

The whole long way down to Cork
I felt uneasy. Guilt feelings.
It's a killer, this guilt. [30]
I always feel bad leaving her
But this time it was the worst.
I could see that she was glad
To see me go away for a while,
Glad at the prospect of being [35]
Two weeks on her own,
Two weeks of having the bed to herself,
Two weeks of not having to be pestered
By my coarse advances,
Two weeks of not having to look up from her plate [40]
And behold me eating spaghetti with a knife and fork.
Our daughters are all grown up and gone away.
Once when she was sitting pregnant on the settee
It snapped shut with herself inside it,
But not a bother on her. I nearly died. [45]

As the train slowed down approaching Portarlington
I overheard myself say to the passenger sitting opposite me:
'I am feeling guilty because she does not love me
As much as she used to, can you explain that?'

Handwritten annotations:

Theme: marraige, Family, Powerful women = Axe

He feels separated from his family

fathers day

disintergration of his marraige
– wife asked him to bring Axe

repitition

Lilac shrub

sisters house

→ wife is acting reasonable

flustered, disorganised

Metaphor → things gone out of control, parts need to be cut

→ self conscious / anxiety — tension

dialogue Nessa

reason, not to bring the axe

→ reasonable tone

'pause

Axe – key symbol

→ agrees + gives in

couch / in sitting room

somebody has had to use it as a bed

Simile – compare
Alliteration
wrap something up

Axe is ready to make the split

conflict

baby image

Happier times when kids were babies / they were more connected

Humerous image

short sentences – he feels responsible

come + go a bit for work – feels guilty

feel for him

repitition

→ she is happy → issues with sexual relationship

reasons
what made their relationship nessecary
– children kept them together

Anecdote

Metaphor

confident she felt trapped

– funny memory

anxiety

– sudden outpour of grief

– tragic

Humerous

This is Poetry | 79

Hillarious

Aware of Axe

The passenger's eyes were on the axe on the seat beside me. [50]
'Her sister wants a loan of the axe . . .' — *Alliteration*
As the train threaded itself into Portarlington — *Portarlington*
I nodded to the passenger 'Cúl an tSúdaire!'
The passenger stood up, lifted down a case from the rack,
Walked out of the coach, but did not get off the train. *didn't want to sit beside him*
For the remainder of the journey, we sat alone, [55]
The axe and I, — *Personification*
All the green fields running away from us, *emphasises his isolation*
All our daughters grown up and gone away.

Pace slows down

tragedy he feels so lonely.
metaphor distance growing from him & his family

[5] **buddleia:** shrubs with lilac, pink or cream flowers
[18] **settee:** sofa
[39] **coarse:** vulgar
[53] **Cúl an tSúdaire:** the Irish name for Portarlington in County Laois

Tease It Out

1. Where is the poet 'dashing' to? Is he composed and organised or rushed and hurried?
2. Who does he speak to before he leaves the house?
3. Who has requested the axe and why?
4. What is the poet's immediate reaction to the request?
5. What makes the poet ultimately agree to what's being asked of him?
6. How do you imagine lines 9 to 16 being spoken? What tone of voice do you imagine the poet using in such a situation? What tone of voice might his wife use?
7. Where was the axe leaning?
8. What surprised the poet about how the axe was presented to him by his wife? Why might he be uneasy or uncomfortable about this state of affairs?
9. 'I decided not to argue the toss'. Why do you think the poet chooses not to argue about this issue? Could there be more than one reason for this decision?
10. What emotion does the poet experience while sitting on the train to Cork?
11. 'But this time it was the worst'. Why do you think the poet felt worse on this occasion than on previous trips away?
12. The poet reckons his wife will be glad to get a break from him for two weeks. He mentions four reasons for this. Describe each of them in your own words.
13. What mishap befell the poet's wife when she was pregnant? How did she react? How did the poet react? What does this little episode suggest to us about her personality?
14. What expression does the poet use to indicate that he found himself speaking out loud almost absentmindedly?
15. What question does he ask the passenger opposite him? What does this question reveal about the state of his marriage?
16. How does the passenger opposite react to the poet's words?
17. Why do you think the poet gives the Irish name for Portarlington as they pull into the station? What do you think he hoped his fellow passenger's reaction would be to this?
18. 'All the green fields running away from us'. What perception or experience does this line describe?
19. How would you characterise the mood of the poem's ending?

Think About Themes

1. Were there any aspects of this poem you found amusing or entertaining? If so, list them and in the case of each say why.
2. Would you agree that in this piece the poet offers a self-deprecating or self-mocking portrayal of his life and personality? Give a reason for your answer.
3. What impression does the poem offer us of the poet's wife? Based on what we learn in this poem, do you think the poet and his wife are similar or different in their outlooks?
4. In the final lines the poet seems to view the axe as a symbol or metaphor for the wife he's left behind. Do you think his wife would be happy to read these lines? Is there any way such a comparison could actually be viewed as flattering? Think carefully before answering.
5. Try to describe in your own words the reasons for the guilt the poet feels when on the train. Would you agree that he's experiencing a complex set of emotions?
6. 'This poem presents a moving and realistic depiction of the difficulties and challenges faced by any marriage or long-term relationship'. Do you think this is a reasonable assessment?
7. Write a paragraph outlining why you think Durcan chose the title 'Father's Day' for this poem. You might also want to consider how the line 'Our daughters are all grown up and gone away' is repeated almost exactly.

The Arnolfini Marriage

after Jan Van Eyck

We are the Arnolfinis.
Do not think you may invade
Our privacy because you may not.

We are standing to our portrait,
The most erotic portrait ever made,
Because we have faith in the artist

To do justice to the plurality,
Fertility, domesticity, barefootedness
Of a man and a woman saying 'we':

To do justice to our bed
As being our most necessary furniture;
To do justice to our life as a reflection.

Our brains spill out upon the floor
And the terrier at our feet sniffs
The minutiae of our magnitude.

The most relaxing word in our vocabulary is 'we'.
Imagine being able to say 'we'.
Most people are in no position to say 'we'.

Are you? Who eat alone? Sleep alone?
And at dawn cycle to work
With an Alsatian shepherd dog tied to your handlebars?

We will pause now for the Angelus.
Here you have it:
The two halves of the coconut.

Jan Van Eyck: a Flemish painter (1390–1441). His most famous work is 'The Arnolfini Wedding' (1432), a portrait of the wealthy Italian merchant Giovanni di Nicolao Arnolfini and his wife. It is now housed in the National Gallery of London

[7] **plurality:** the state of being plural; more than one
[8] **domesticity:** home or family life
[8] **barefootedness:** referring to the fact that Arnolfini appears to be barefoot
[15] **minutiae:** small details; trifles
[22] **the Angelus:** a Catholic devotion to commemorate the Incarnation of Jesus, signalled by the daily ringing of church bells at noon and 6pm

---

Handwritten annotations:

1994 After breakup of Duncan's marriage

confident / v. important

Ekphrasis - poem written in response to a painting

Located in Bedroom - Private / erotic because it's in their bedroom

in authority

repitition

standing for attention

nothing erotic or sexual in a modern day but are erotic in 15th century [5]

paying tribute to artists

we'

create in bedroom

Trust that the artist will capture

Exposing themselves / humbling

smug

To do justice to our bed [10]

To reproduce

Mirror

EGOS

A good match

bizzare image / there of them being smug / superior / intelligent [15]

A loyal follower faithfulness

Arrogant

confidence

Together not alone

sense of importance

Duncans demons

Taunting the portrait [20]

getting Judged

nobody to mind the dog

bizzare note

Arnolfini + wife? They are one way + he's the other half

religious

odd / unusual

glim / dissmissive throw away ending

isolated poet

Contrast

our - 8 Times
we - 7 Times

Get In Gear

1. Google the painting that inspired this poem. It is famous for the richness of its brushwork, the complexity of its arrangement and the intensity of the emotions it captures. Some critics claim that the painting depicts the wedding day of Giovanni Arnolfini, an Italian merchant. Others argue that in the painting Arnolfini and his wife are already married. What message do you think the painting is trying to convey?

Tease It Out

1. Who is speaking in this poem?
2. Who are they speaking to? Is it the poet, the reader or the patrons of the art gallery?
3. Class Discussion: They say this person cannot 'invade' their privacy. Why do you think they are so confident that this is the case?
4. The Arnolfinis describe their portrait as the 'most erotic' ever painted. Do you find this statement convincing? In what sense might the painting be described as an erotic one?
5. The couple say they 'have faith in the artist.' What are they confident the artist will do?
6. Class Discussion: The Arnolfinis associate marriage with four different ideas or concepts. What are they? Why do you think they highlight these four things especially?
7. The Arnolfinis describe the bed as 'our most necessary furniture', as the most important thing in their house. What different things is a bed necessary for?
8. Group Discussion: Consider the painting carefully. Why do the Arnolfinis describe their life as a 'reflection'? What might make it so?
9. What does the terrier seem to be sniffing in the painting? What, according to the Arnolfinis, is he actually sniffing? What are we to understand by this unusual phrase?
10. Class Discussion: 'Our brains spill upon the floor'. Why do the couple say this when it's not apparent in the painting?
11. What short and simple word do the Arnolfinis use to celebrate their togetherness?
12. Who do you think is the 'you' referred to in lines 19 to 21? What type of life does this person lead?
13. Class Discussion: Who is speaking in the last three lines of the poem? Is it still the Arnolfinis or does it make more sense to imagine these lines spoken by the poet himself?

14. 'We will pause now for the Angelus.' What associations does this phrase have for you? Why is such a pause inserted into the poem at this point?
15. Group Discussion: What might the coconut symbolise? What in your opinion might be represented by the coconut's two halves?

Think About Themes

1. How do you imagine the tone of voice in which the Arnolfinis speak? Do you imagine it to be confident, smug, accusing, insecure or something else entirely?
2. This poem features several vivid images. Identify one that appealed to you and say why.
3. 'This poem contrasts the unity, strength and security of marriage with the loneliness of the single life.' Write a couple of paragraphs agreeing or disagreeing with this statement.
4. Class Discussion: 'This poem celebrates the power of a great artist to capture not only the physical, but also the emotional world in all its complexity and detail.' Do you agree with this statement?
5. Consider once again the painting on which the poem is based. Has Durcan, in your opinion, managed to do justice to Van Eyck's work? Write a paragraph giving the reasons for your answer.
6. Imagine for a moment that you are Jan Van Eyck and have just completed the painting of the Arnolfinis. Write a couple of paragraphs outlining your impression of the couple and the life they live.

In Context

1. Compare and contrast the treatment of romantic love in this poem with that in 'Nessa'.
2. Compare and contrast the treatment of marriage in this poem with that in 'Wife Who Smashed Television Gets Jail'.

Ireland 2002

Do you ever take a holiday abroad?
No, we always go to America.

Get In Gear

What do you know about Ireland in 2002? Use the Internet to learn something about the state of the Irish economy and society at that time.

Think About Themes

1. 'No, we always go to America'. This Irish speaker doesn't consider America to be 'abroad'. Why do you think this is? What differences might he or she perceive between America and other foreign parts?
2. Do you think this piece of writing deserves to be called a poem? Give reasons for your answer.
3. 'This poem celebrates the wealth and freedom enjoyed by even ordinary Irish people in 2002. They travel so frequently to America it doesn't seem like 'abroad' to them anymore'. Do you think such a positive reading of the poem is reasonable?
4. 'This poem laments the dominance of Hollywood and American culture generally. The whole world in a sense is America now'. Do you find this interpretation convincing? Is it more plausible than the interpretation given in question 3?
5. 'In only two lines this poem conveys a lot'. Would you agree with this statement? What does the poem suggest about the Irish attitude towards America in 2002?

In Context

Compare this poem to 'Madman'. Which of these two-line pieces is more effective in your opinion? Which has the better 'punchline'? In each case write a few sentences supporting your answer.

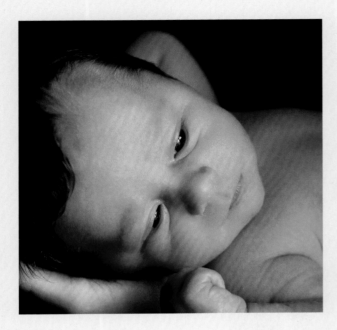

Rosie Joyce

I

That was that Sunday afternoon in May
When a hot sun pushed through the clouds
And you were born!

I was driving the two hundred miles from west to east,
The sky blue-and-white china in the fields   [5]
In impromptu picnics of tartan rugs;

When neither words nor I
Could have known that you had been named already
And that your name was Rosie –

Rosie Joyce! May you some day in May   [10]
Fifty-six years from today be as lucky
As I was when you were born that Sunday:

To drive such side-roads, such main roads, such ramps, such roundabouts,
To cross such bridges, to by-pass such villages, such towns
As I did on your Incarnation Day.   [15]

By-passing Swinford – Croagh Patrick in my rear-view mirror –
My mobile phone rang and, stopping on the hard edge of P. Flynn's highway,
I heard Mark your father say:

'A baby girl was born at 3:33p.m.
Weighing 7 and a ½ lbs in Holles Street.   [20]
Tough work, all well.'

[6] **impromptu:** spontaneous, unplanned

[15] **Incarnation:** the process by which a soul acquires a body and enters the world

[16] **Croagh Patrick:** a mountain in Co. Mayo that is a well-known pilgrimage site

[17] **P. Flynn:** Pádraig Flynn, a former Fianna Fáil TD, minister and EU commissioner

[20] **Holles Street:** a maternity hospital in Dublin

II
That Sunday in May before daybreak
Night had pushed up through the slopes of Achill
Yellow forefingers of Arum Lily – the first of the year;

Down at the Sound the first rhododendrons   [25]
Purpling the golden camps of whins;
The first hawthorns powdering white the mainland;

The first yellow irises flagging roadside streams;
Quills of bog-cotton skimming the bogs;
Burrishoole cemetery shin-deep in forget-me-nots;   [30]

The first sea pinks speckling the seashore;
Cliffs of London Pride, groves of bluebell,
First fuchsia, Queen Anne's Lace, primrose.

I drove the Old Turlough Road, past Walter Durcan's Farm,
Umbrella'd in the joined handwriting of its ash trees;   [35]
I drove Tulsk, Kilmainham, the Grand Canal.

Never before had I felt so fortunate
To be driving back into Dublin city;
Each canal bridge an old pewter brooch.

I rode the waters and the roads of Ireland,   [40]
Rosie, to be with you, seashell at my ear!
How I laughed when I cradled you in my hand.

Only at Tarmonbarry did I slow down,
As in my father's Ford Anglia half a century ago
He slowed down also, as across the River Shannon   [45]

We crashed, rattled, bounced on a Bailey bridge;
Daddy relishing his role as Moses,
Enunciating the name of the Great Divide

Between the East and the West!
We are the people of the West,   [50]
Our fate to go East.

No such thing, Rosie, as a Uniform Ireland
And please God there never will be;
There is only the River Shannon and all her sister rivers

And all her brother mountains and their family prospects.   [55]
There are higher powers than politics
And these we call wildflowers or, geologically, people.

Rosie Joyce – that Sunday in May
Not alone did you make my day, my week, my year
To the prescription of Jonathan Philbin Bowman –   [60]

Daymaker!
Daymaker!
Daymaker!

Popping out of my daughter, your mother –
Changing the expressions on the faces all around you –   [65]
All of them looking like blue hills in a heat haze –

But you saved my life. For three years
I had been subsisting in the slums of despair,
Unable to distinguish one day from the next.

III
On the return journey from Dublin to Mayo   [70]
In Charlestown on Main Street
I meet John Normanly, organic farmer from Curry.

He is driving home to his wife Caroline
From a Mountbellew meeting of the Western Development Commission
Of Dillon House in Ballaghadereen.   [75]

He crouches in his car, I waver in the street,
As we exchange lullabies of expectancy;
We wet our foreheads in John Moriarty's autobiography.

The following Sunday is the Feast of the Ascension
Of Our Lord into Heaven: [80]
Thank You, O Lord, for the Descent of Rosie onto Earth.

[60] **Jonathan Philbin Bowman (1969–2000):** was a well-known broadcaster, journalist and TV personality. *Daymaker* was a slot where listeners sent him details of an event or person that had 'made their day', that had brought hope and positivity into their lives

[74] **Western Development Commission:** an organisation dedicated to fostering growth, jobs and enterprise in the West of Ireland

[78] **we wet our foreheads:** this probably refers to the practice of crossing one's forehead with holy water as one enters a Catholic church

[78] **John Moriarty:** John Moriarty (1938–2007) was a writer, philosopher and poet. Among his themes are the materialism, corruption and greed that have gripped Irish society

[79] **Feast of the Ascension:** a Christian feast day celebrating how Jesus ascended bodily into heaven

Tease It Out

Part I

1. Where in Ireland was the poet when Rosie was born? What was he doing?
2. What was the weather like?
3. What, according to the poet, does the sky resemble? What do the fields resemble?
4. What does the poet wish for Rosie to have? Why do you think he wishes her this?
5. Consider the phrase 'your Incarnation Day'. What does the word 'incarnation' mean? What is the poet attempting to convey here?
6. Why do you think the poet describes the road as 'P. Flynn's highway'?

Part II

7. Where was the poet when he awoke that morning?
8. What species of flower had appeared overnight and for the first time that year?
9. List the other species of flower the poet saw that morning.
10. How does the poet feel when he re-enters Dublin city? How does he convey this emotion? How does he convey the tiny size of newborn Rosie?
11. He claims to have slowed down only once on his journey. Where was this and why?
12. What according to the poet is the special significance of the River Shannon?
13. What memories come to the poet as he crosses this river?
14. The poet refers to the Shannon's 'sister rivers' and 'brother mountains'. What does this suggest about the unity of nature?
15. Class Discussion: What are we to make of the word 'geologically' in line 57? It has been suggested that it refers to the evolution of the human race over millions of years. Is this plausible?
16. What comparison does the poet make to describe the joy on the faces of those present when Rosie was born? Do you consider this comparison to be effective?
17. List the different phrases the poet uses to convey his own joy at Rosie's birth.
18. What state of mind had the poet been in for the previous three years?
19. He claims that Rosie's birth saved his life. What does he mean by this?

Part III

20. Who does the poet meet on his return journey to Mayo? What trip is this man making?
21. Class Discussion: The poet says that he and this other man exchange 'lullabies of expectancy'. What does this suggest about the way in which they reacted to one another?

22. The poet and his friend are said to 'wet their foreheads' or cross themselves using John Moriarty's autobiography. Would you agree that this is a metaphor? What do you think they actually did? What does this line suggest about their attitude to Moriarty and his writing?
23. The poet's final expression of gratitude for Rosie's birth involves an unexpected or ironic reversal. What is this?

Think About Themes

1. Pick three words that in your opinion best describe the tone and atmosphere of this piece.
2. 'There are higher powers than politics': What is the poet referring to here? In what way might these things be said to be above and beyond politics?
3. Class Discussion: What does the poet mean by the phrase 'Uniform Ireland'? Do you think he regards such an Ireland as an appealing or an appalling prospect? What according to the poet prevents Ireland being such a 'Uniform' place?
4. 'This poem captures not only the beauty but also the tragedy and poverty of the West of Ireland.' Do you think this is a reasonable assessment of the poem? In your reply, consider the references to the River Shannon, 'P. Flynn's highway' and the Western Development Commission.
5. This poem features many metaphors, similes and other instances of descriptive language. Identify three such comparisons that you found to be particularly effective and say why. Are there any you found ineffective?
6. Many readers have suggested that this poem has the tone and atmosphere of prayer, specifically a prayer of thanksgiving and celebration. Read it carefully again. Do you think it's fair to describe it as a religious or spiritual piece of writing?
7. This poem deals powerfully with the topic of depression. Write a paragraph describing how it illustrates the passage from one emotional state to another.
8. Class Discussion: 'This poem is ruined by sentimentality, consisting chiefly of the over-emotional gushing of a doting grandfather.' Do you think this is a fair assessment? Write a paragraph saying why.

In Context

Write a couple of paragraphs on the importance of family in Paul Durcan's poetry. Compare this poem to two of the following: 'Father's Day, 21 June 1992', 'The Arnolfini Marriage', 'The MacBride Dynasty'.

The MacBride Dynasty

What young mother is not a vengeful goddess
Spitting dynastic as well as motherly pride?
In 1949 in the black Ford Anglia,
Now that I had become a walking, talking little boy,
Mummy drove me out to visit my grand-aunt Maud Gonne   [5]
In Roebuck House in the countryside near Dublin,
To show off to the servant of the Queen
The latest addition to the extended family.
Although the eighty-year-old Cathleen Ní Houlihan had taken to her bed
She was keen as ever to receive admirers,   [10]
Especially the children of the family.
Only the previous week the actor Mac Liammóir
Had been kneeling at her bedside reciting Yeats to her,
His hand on his heart, clutching a red rose.
Cousin Séan and his wife Kid led the way up the stairs,   [15]
Séan opening the door and announcing my mother.
Mummy lifted me up in her arms as she approached the bed
And Maud leaned forward, sticking out her claws
To embrace me, her lizards of eyes darting about
In the rubble of the ruins of her beautiful face.   [20]
Terrified, I recoiled from her embrace
And, fleeing her bedroom, ran down the stairs
Out onto the wrought-iron balcony
Until Séan caught up with me and quieted me
And took me for a walk in the walled orchard.   [25]
Mummy was a little but not totally mortified:
She had never liked Maud Gonne because of Maud's
Betrayal of her husband, Mummy's Uncle John,
Major John, most ordinary of men, most
Humorous, courageous of soldiers,   [30]
The pride of our family,
Whose memory always brought laughter
To my grandmother Eileen's lips. 'John,'
She used cry, 'John was such a gay man.'
Mummy set great store by loyalty; loyalty   [35]
In Mummy's eyes was the cardinal virtue.
Maud Gonne was a disloyal wife
And, therefore, not worthy of Mummy's love.
For dynastic reasons we would tolerate Maud,
But we would always see through her.   [40]

Dynasty: a familial line or succession of rulers

[2] **dynastic:** related to a dynasty

[5] **Maud Gonne:** Irish nationalist, activist and actress. Famed for her great beauty

[7] **the servant of the Queen:** the title of Maud Gonne's autobiography. The 'Queen' in question is the land of Ireland rather than the Queen of England

[9] **Cathleen Ní Houlihan:** a mythical personification of Irish nationalism, similar to America's Uncle Sam. W.B. Yeats also wrote a play called *Cathleen Ní Houlihan* in which Maud Gonne played the title role

[12] **Mícheál Mac Liammóir:** Alfred Willmore, an English-born actor, writer and painter, who became enthralled by Irish culture. He learned to speak Irish fluently, changed his name to Mícheál Mac Liammóir and founded the Gate Theatre

[28] **Uncle John:** Maud Gonne married Major John MacBride, who was executed for his part in the 1916 Rising. Their relationship ended badly and Gonne accused him of child abuse, allegations almost universally believed to be false

Get In Gear

Do some brief research online about Maud Gonne and her husband Major John MacBride. Write a brief paragraph about each of their lives.

Tease It Out

1. The poet describes young mothers as 'vengeful goddesses' who 'spit' pride. What image does such a description conjure up? Would you agree that this is an unusual way to describe young mothers? Do you think it's an effective one?
2. Group Discussion: What do you understand by the phrase 'dynastic pride'? What do you understand by the concept of motherly pride? In what way are these concepts different?
3. 'I had become a walking talking little boy'. What age was the poet when the events of the poem took place?
4. Why did his mother take him to visit Maud Gonne?
5. Where was Maud living at the time? How did they travel there?
6. Class Discussion: In lines 7 to 9 why does the poet describe Maud Gonne as 'the servant of the Queen' and as 'Cathleen Ní Houlihan'?
7. How old was Maud at this time?
8. In lines 10 to 14 what indications are there that Maud was a famous and respected person?
9. Who meets the poet and his mother when they arrive at Roebuck House?
10. Describe in your own words Maud's appearance as she reaches out to embrace the young poet.
11. What metaphor does the poet use to describe Maud's aged eyes and face? Do you think it is an effective one?
12. What is the poet's emotional response to Maud's greeting? What does he do?
13. How did he spend the rest of the visit?
14. How did the poet's mother respond to her son's retreat?
15. Why had the mother 'never liked' Maud?
16. What kind of man, according to the poet's family, was Major John MacBride, Maud's former husband?
17. John MacBride is described as an 'ordinary man'. In what sense might the word ordinary be intended as compliment?
18. How did the poet's grandmother Eileen feel about John?
19. John MacBride is described as a 'gay man'. In this context, what does the word gay suggest about his personality?
20. According to the poet, Maud 'betrayed' John. What form do you think this betrayal might have taken?
21. What, according to the poet's mother, is the greatest virtue a person can possess?
22. Why would Maud always be unworthy of her love?
23. Try to describe in your own words why the poet's family would always 'tolerate' Maud.
24. Class Discussion: The poet claims that his immediate family would always be able to 'see through' Maud Gonne. What does this suggest about Maud's personality? What does it suggest about their attitude toward her?

Think About Themes

1. 'She was keen as ever to receive admirers.' What does the poem say to you about the elderly Maud Gonne's personality? Consider the above line and the other evidence scattered throughout the piece.
2. Would you agree that this poem powerfully portrays the passage of time, especially the ruin time brings even to the beautiful and powerful? Write a paragraph giving reasons for your answer.
3. What is the exact familial relationship between the poet and Maud Gonne?
4. Class Discussion: What is a dynasty? According to the poet, his immediate family tolerated Maud for 'dynastic reasons'. What do you think he means by this?
5. Consider the events of the poem and especially its title. How do you think the poet's immediate family felt about their connection to Maud Gonne and Major John MacBride? Do you think they were proud, ashamed, indifferent or something else entirely? Write a paragraph giving the reasons for your answer.
6. 'This poem highlights the darker side of family life, the resentment and bitterness that all too often lurks behind the polite and civil exterior relatives adopt toward one another.' Write a paragraph responding to this statement.

In Context

'Again and again, Paul Durcan's poetry deals with the difficulties and consolations of family life.' Write a couple of paragraphs that compare and contrast 'The MacBride Dynasty' with two other poems on the course in light of the above statement.

Robert Frost

Robert Frost was born in San Francisco, California on 26 March 1874. His father, a journalist, died of tuberculosis when Frost was eleven. Soon after, Frost moved with his mother and his sister Jeanie to Lawrence, Massachusetts, to live with his grandparents. Frost excelled at school, sharing high school valedictory honours with classmate Elinor White, with whom he became romantically involved.

Frost quickly proposed marriage, but the level-headed Elinor suggested that they wait until they were both finished college and able to make a living. They went to separate universities – Elinor to St Lawrence and Frost to Dartmouth. Frost studied the classics, Greek and Latin, and joined a fraternity. However, he did not settle well, often going on hikes by himself along the river and venturing into the woods alone at night. This solitary aspect to his character was later reflected in poems such as 'The Tuft of Flowers' and 'Acquainted With the Night'.

Frost was unable to tolerate college beyond the first year. The experience of being a college dropout perhaps influenced his poetry; he was keen to remove elitism from his work, and make it accessible to those from unprivileged backgrounds like his own. His first published poem, 'My Butterfly: An Elegy', appeared in a New York literary journal in 1894. He was paid $15 – over $400 in today's money. Buoyed by this success, and worried that Elinor was seeing other men, Frost arrived unannounced at her university to propose. When Elinor refused him, wanting to complete her education first, he was driven to despair. In his gloom, he went wandering for three weeks in Dismal Swamp, Virginia, fully embracing his inner turmoil. This theme of setting out into the unknown, of casting free from the bonds of society, is revisited in poems such as 'The Road Not Taken', 'Acquainted With the Night' and 'Birches'.

Robert and Elinor were eventually married in 1895 and welcomed their first child, Elliot, in 1896. Frost tried academia again, enrolling at Harvard in 1897 to study liberal arts, but had to drop out after two years due to health concerns. In 1900 the family moved to a farm in New Hampshire, where they would live for the next twelve years. That same year, Elliot died of cholera, two months shy of his fourth birthday. In all, the Frosts had five more children: Lesley (born 1899), Carol (1902), Irma (1903), Marjorie (1905) and finally Elinor (1907), who died three days after her birth. Frost suffered much loss in his family life; of his six children, only Lesley and Irma would outlive him.

Besides farming, Frost also supported his family by teaching English at various New Hampshire high schools. As a teacher he was very fair-minded, valuing critical thinking over learning by rote. He described his teaching philosophy as 'freedom', saying: 'You might define a schoolboy as one who could recite to you everything he read last night, in the order in which he read it. That's just the opposite of what I mean by a free person. The person who has the freedom of his material is the person who puts two and two together, and the two and two are anywhere out of space and time, and brought together. One little thing mentioned, perhaps, reminds him of something he couldn't have thought of for twenty years.'

Though Frost had some success with his poetry during the years on the farm, publishing 'The Tuft of Flowers' in 1906, he couldn't find a publisher for his book. In 1912 the family sold the farm and moved to England, where they felt there would be more publishing opportunities. At the age of 38, Frost was finally able to devote himself fulltime to writing. Within a few months, Frost had found a publisher in London. He also made many influential friendships, such as with the poet Ezra Pound, who would become a strong advocate of his work. Frost's

> "In his work, he found greatest meaning in the natural world. Shunning the modern landscape of the city, and all the existential angst that the poets after the First World War sought to articulate, Frost relied on his natural surroundings to provide him with inspiration."

first book, *A Boy's Will,* was brought out in 1913, and followed a year later by *North of Boston.* Favourable reviews resulted in American publication of the books, and in the establishment of Frost's reputation on both sides of the Atlantic.

The Frosts returned to America in February 1915, soon after the breakout of World War I. Once again they settled on a farm, this time in Franconia, New Hampshire. *North of Boston* was published by Frost's American publisher Henry Holt – who would remain with him for the rest of his life – and was followed by *Mountain Interval* in 1916. The following year, Frost began lecturing at Amherst College. This marked the beginning of a long career as a teacher at various colleges, including the University of Michigan and his alma maters Dartmouth and Harvard. Though Frost never graduated from college, more than forty universities awarded him honorary degrees throughout his life.

By 1920, the Frosts were well off enough to purchase a second home in Shaftsbury, Vermont. In 1924 he received his first Pulitzer Prize in poetry for *New Hampshire.* In total he won the Pulitzer a record four times, for *Collected Poems* (1931), *Further Range* (1937) and *A Witness Tree* (1943). The Pulitzers cemented Frost's status as a national treasure. However, during this period he also endured a terrible series of family disasters. His sister Jeanie died in 1929 in a mental institution, having suffered from depression. In 1934 his youngest daughter, Marjorie, died a slow death from puerperal fever contracted after giving birth to her first child. In 1938 his wife Elinor died suddenly of a heart attack, followed by the suicide of his son Carol two years later. Another daughter, Irma, suffered from mental disorders and was finally institutionalised. In 1941, in what must have been a very lonely time for the

poet, Frost moved to Cambridge, Massachusetts, where he would live for the rest of his life; he spent his winters at another home in South Miami, Florida.

Frost served as US Poet Laureate from 1958-9. In 1961 he was asked to recite a poem at the inauguration of President John F. Kennedy. Though he had written a poem, 'Dedication', especially for the occasion, the bright sunshine on the day made it difficult for the eighty-seven year-old Frost to read the poem, and he recited 'The Gift Outright' from memory instead. In 1962, Frost added the Congressional Gold Medal to his long list of accolades. He died of complications from surgery in 1963, aged eighty-eight. He is buried in the family plot in Bennington, Vermont. His epitaph reads 'I had a lover's quarrel with the world' – a line from his poem 'The Lesson for Today'.

Frost's style married the poetry of the 19th and 20th centuries. Like the 19th-century poets, he used formal structure and meter and never wrote in free verse, saying 'I would as soon play tennis without a net.' However, his use of everyday, colloquial language and the rhythms of American speech give his work a 20th-century edge. In his work, he found greatest meaning in the natural world. Shunning the modern landscape of the city, and all the existential angst that the poets after the First World War sought to articulate, Frost relied on his natural surroundings to provide him with inspiration, celebrating both the beauty and darkness in nature. Part of his work's appeal is that it provides readers with a connection to nature in an urbanised, industrial society. However, Frost himself always refused classification as a `nature poet', insisting that his poems contained so much more. His ambition is reflected in his famous words: 'If poetry isn't understanding all, the whole world, then it isn't worth anything.'

The Tuft of Flowers

I went to turn the grass once after one
Who mowed it in the dew before the sun.

The dew was gone that made his blade so keen
Before I came to view the leveled scene.

I looked for him behind an isle of trees;   [5]
I listened for his whetstone on the breeze.

But he had gone his way, the grass all mown,
And I must be, as he had been – alone,

'As all must be,' I said within my heart,
'Whether they work together or apart.'   [10]

But as I said it, swift there passed me by
On noiseless wing a bewildered butterfly,

Seeking with memories grown dim o'er night
Some resting flower of yesterday's delight.

And once I marked his flight go round and round,   [15]
As where some flower lay withering on the ground.

And then he flew as far as eye could see,
And then on tremulous wing came back to me.

I thought of questions that have no reply,
And would have turned to toss the grass to dry;   [20]

But he turned first, and led my eye to look
At a tall tuft of flowers beside a brook,

A leaping tongue of bloom the scythe had spared
Beside a reedy brook the scythe had bared.

I left my place to know them by their name,   [25]
Finding them butterfly weed when I came.

The mower in the dew had loved them thus,
By leaving them to flourish, not for us,

Nor yet to draw one thought of ours to him.
But from sheer morning gladness at the brim.   [30]

The butterfly and I had lit upon,
Nevertheless, a message from the dawn,

That made me hear the wakening birds around,
And hear his long scythe whispering to the ground,

And feel a spirit kindred to my own;   [35]
So that henceforth I worked no more alone;

But glad with him, I worked as with his aid,
And weary, sought at noon with him the shade;

And dreaming, as it were, held brotherly speech
With one whose thought I had not hoped to reach.   [40]

'Men work together,' I told him from the heart
'Whether they work together or apart.'

[1] **turn the grass:** grass cut early in the morning, being wet from the dew, needs to be turned later in the day to allow it to dry in the sun
[3] **keen:** sharp
[6] **whetstone:** stone tool for sharpening blades
[12] **bewildered:** puzzled, confused
[18] **tremulous:** trembling, quivering
[23] **scythe:** a long, curved blade for cutting grass
[35] **kindred:** likeminded, similar, connected
[36] **henceforth:** from then on

Tease It Out

Lines 1 to 20

1. The speaker has come to 'turn the grass' in a field. What does it mean to 'turn' grass? Why is this done?
2. Who had been working in the field before the speaker arrived? What did this person do?
3. What tool did the mower use for his work?
4. Where does the speaker look for the mower? What sound does he listen for? Is the mower anywhere to be seen?
5. How does the speaker feel when he realises that the mower is not around?
6. Class Discussion: The speaker says that 'all must be [alone] ... Whether they work together or apart.' What do you think he means by this?
7. The speaker is suddenly distracted by a butterfly that flies past him. What is the butterfly looking for? Does it find it?
8. The poet uses the terms 'bewildered' and 'tremulous' when describing the butterfly. What do these words mean? What do they suggest about the way that the butterfly is feeling?
9. Class Discussion: For a moment the speaker thinks of 'questions that have no reply'. What sort of questions do you think he means?

Lines 20 to 42

10. To what does the butterfly draw the speaker's attention in lines 21 to 22?
11. The speaker says that these flowers had been 'spared' by 'the scythe'. Whose scythe was it that spared these flowers?
12. Where exactly are the flowers located?
13. The speaker describes the flowers as a 'leaping tongue of bloom'. With what would you ordinarily associate the term 'leaping tongue'?
14. What type of flowers does the speaker discover them to be when he takes a closer look?
15. Class Discussion: Read lines 27 to 30. Why does the speaker think that the mower spared these flowers?
16. 'By leaving them to flourish, not for us,// Nor yet to draw one thought of ours to him.' What two reasons for sparing the flowers does the speaker rule out here?
17. Lines 33 to 34: The flowers inspire the speaker to hear certain sounds. What does he hear?
18. Seeing the flowers makes the speaker 'feel a spirit kindred to my own'. What does it mean to have a kindred spirit? Who is the kindred spirit that the speaker has in mind here?
19. 'I worked no more alone ... I worked as with his aid'. What does the speaker mean by this? Is someone now working with him?
20. What does the speaker do at noon when he is feeling 'weary'?
21. Who does the speaker seek the 'shade' with?
22. Who or what does the speaker hold 'brotherly speech' with? What do you think he means by 'brotherly speech'? Can you think of another way of expressing this idea?
23. How does the speaker's view of life differ at the end of the poem to the view he expressed early on?

Think About Themes

1. Do you agree that it is possible to experience a connection with someone that we have never met? Can you think of examples in your own life of such instances?
2. What does the poem suggest about the natural world? In what ways can it benefit our lives?
3. 'Men work together ... Whether they work together or apart.' In what way can people be said to be working together when they are 'apart'? What do you understand the poet to mean by this?
4. What do you think the flowers in the poem might symbolise? Are there other things that have a similar effect or impact on our lives?
5. Did you find this poem inspiring? What do you think is the poem's central message?
6. Can you identify two examples of assonance and two examples of alliteration in the poem? What effect did these have on the mood or atmosphere of the lines in which they feature?

In Context

'Frost uses simple, everyday language to convey complex truths about our lives.' Write a short essay in response to this statement, referring to 'The Tuft of Flowers' and at least two other poems by Frost on your course.

[handwritten: written in 1914]

Mending Wall

Something there is that doesn't love a wall,
That sends the frozen-ground-swell under it,
And spills the upper boulders in the sun,
And makes gaps even two can pass abreast.
The work of hunters is another thing: [5]
I have come after them and made repair
Where they have left not one stone on a stone,
But they would have the rabbit out of hiding,
To please the yelping dogs. The gaps I mean,
No one has seen them made or heard them made,   [10]
But at spring mending-time we find them there.
I let my neighbor know beyond the hill;
And on a day we meet to walk the line
And set the wall between us once again.
We keep the wall between us as we go.   [15]
To each the boulders that have fallen to each.
And some are loaves and some so nearly balls
We have to use a spell to make them balance:
'Stay where you are until our backs are turned!'
We wear our fingers rough with handling them.   [20]
Oh, just another kind of outdoor game,
One on a side. It comes to little more:
There where it is we do not need the wall:
He is all pine and I am apple orchard.
My apple trees will never get across   [25]
And eat the cones under his pines, I tell him.
He only says, 'Good fences make good neighbors.'
Spring is the mischief in me, and I wonder
If I could put a notion in his head:
'Why do they make good neighbors? Isn't it   [30]
Where there are cows? But here there are no cows.
Before I built a wall I'd ask to know
What I was walling in or walling out,
And to whom I was like to give offence.
Something there is that doesn't love a wall,   [35]
That wants it down.' I could say 'Elves' to him,
But it's not elves exactly, and I'd rather
He said it for himself. I see him there,
Bringing a stone grasped firmly by the top
In each hand, like an old-stone savage armed.   [40]
He moves in darkness as it seems to me,
Not of woods only and the shade of trees.
He will not go behind his father's saying,
And he likes having thought of it so well
He says again, 'Good fences make good neighbors.'   [45]

Handwritten annotations:

- Iambic pentametre – 5 beats for line
- super natural forces – mysterious force of nature / force of nature / mother nature
- 10 syllables in most lines
- descriptive
- gaps in the wall
- Theme 1 Division
- Wall - visual
- Berlin wall - separating societies
- natural occurrence
- Determined
- -05
- creating division
- Repetition - between them
- 1 stanza / 45 lines
- Far away
- Half rhyme
- (physical barrier)
- metaphors
- describing the shape
- mysterious
- building the wall
- doesn't need a wall there
- personification
- Humor
- (metaphor) doesn't believe barriers are needed
- couldn't be more different
- questioning?
- What's the point.
- metaphorically - If they didn't have a wall it would be chaos
- Berlin wall - neccessary to divide (super natural event)
- Excludes and includes people
- Image
- Simile
- stuck in time - not open minded
- Passing tradition to his son
- Refrain 'Good fences make good neighbours'

94

Tease It Out

Lines 1 to 11

1. The poet refers to the 'work of hunters'. What effect do hunters have on the wall?
2. What type of animal do these hunters pursue?
3. Read lines 7 to 8 carefully. Do you think the hunters damage the wall deliberately or merely through carelessness?
4. What does the poet do in response to the hunters' activities?
5. What line indicates that the poet isn't referring to the damage caused by these hunters but to a different phenomenon?
6. The poet refers to 'Something' that dislikes walls. What do you think this something might be? *Elves*
7. What does this 'Something' do to the ground on which the wall is built?
8. What effect does this have on the wall's components?
9. How large, according to the poet, are the gaps created by this process?
10. Are there ever any witnesses to this process?

Lines 12 to 22

11. What does the speaker tell his neighbour? What do they arrange to do?
12. Is this a dry stone wall or is cement used to hold its stones and boulders together?
13. Frost compares some of these stones to 'loaves'. What does this suggest about their shape?
14. Some of the boulders present the men with a particular difficulty. What is this?
15. Describe in your own words the little superstition or ritual they use in response to this problem.
16. The two men are careful to stay on their own side of this boundary between their two properties. Why do you think this is?
17. What phrase indicates that this is difficult work?
18. The speaker describes their work as an 'outdoor game'. Why do you think he makes this comparison? What similarity might be drawn between their labours and an outdoor sport or activity?

Lines 23 to 35

19. The two men come to a section of land where the speaker believes a wall is not necessary. Why does the speaker believe this?
20. What witty comment does he use to make this point to his neighbour?
21. What is the neighbour's response to this suggestion?
22. Describe the speaker's mood in your own words as suggested by lines 28 to 29.
23. In lines 31 to 36, the speaker mentions several reasons why he's reluctant to build the wall in this area. What are they?

Lines 36 to 45

24. Class Discussion: 'But it's not elves exactly'. What force or presence do you think the speaker has in mind here?
25. 'I'd rather/ He said it for himself.' What does the speaker want his neighbour to admit?
26. At the poem's conclusion the speaker presents his neighbour in an unflattering light. In what terms does he describe him?
27. Why does he claim the neighbour 'moves in darkness'?
28. 'He will not go behind his father's saying'. What does Frost mean by this?

Think About Themes

1. 'Mending Wall' is often described as a mysterious poem. How is this sense of mystery created? What words or phrases give the poem a somewhat eerie, supernatural or otherworldly atmosphere?
2. 'The speaker of the poem is opposed to the building of walls.' Write a few lines detailing the arguments both in favour of and against this statement.
3. In what ways do the speaker and his neighbour have a different view of the world? Which worldview do you find more attractive? Why?
4. Repetition is an important feature of this poem. Identify the examples of repetition and suggest why Frost chooses to repeat these words or phrases.
5. Make a list of the main images in the poem. Which of these did you find most effective and why?
6. "Mending Wall" is ultimately a poem about how boundaries are necessary for society to function. It shows how walls unite as well as divide.' Write a few paragraphs in response to this statement, arguing for or against it.

In Context

1. Work is an important theme in Frost's writing, featuring in 'A Tuft of Flowers', 'After Apple-Picking' and "Out, Out—". Write a paragraph outlining how Frost's depiction of work differs in each of these three poems.
2. How does the depiction of community and isolation in 'Mending Wall' differ from Frost's treatment of these themes in 'A Tuft of Flowers'?
3. Would you agree that nature is depicted as a menacing force in 'Mending Wall'? Compare the poem to 'Spring Pools' and 'Design' in your answer.

After Apple-Picking

My long two-pointed ladder's sticking through a tree
Toward heaven still,
And there's a barrel that I didn't fill
Beside it, and there may be two or three
Apples I didn't pick upon some bough.   [5]
But I am done with apple-picking now.
Essence of winter sleep is on the night,
The scent of apples: I am drowsing off.
I cannot rub the strangeness from my sight
I got from looking through a pane of glass   [10]
I skimmed this morning from the drinking trough
And held against the world of hoary grass.
It melted, and I let it fall and break.
But I was well
Upon my way to sleep before it fell,   [15]
And I could tell
What form my dreaming was about to take.
Magnified apples appear and disappear,
Stem end and blossom end,
And every fleck of russet showing clear.   [20]
My instep arch not only keeps the ache,
It keeps the pressure of a ladder-round.
I feel the ladder sway as the boughs bend.
And I keep hearing from the cellar bin
The rumbling sound   [25]
Of load on load of apples coming in.
For I have had too much
Of apple-picking: I am overtired
Of the great harvest I myself desired.
There were ten thousand thousand fruit to touch,   [30]
Cherish in hand, lift down, and not let fall.
For all
That struck the earth,
No matter if not bruised or spiked with stubble,
Went surely to the cider-apple heap   [35]
As of no worth.
One can see what will trouble
This sleep of mine, whatever sleep it is.
Were he not gone,
The woodchuck could say whether it's like his   [40]
Long sleep, as I describe its coming on,
Or just some human sleep.

[5]	**bough:** branch
[7]	**Essence:** scent
[12]	**hoary:** greyish white, in this case a reference to the frost on the ground
[20]	**russet:** reddish brown
[21]	**instep:** part of the foot between the toes and the ankle
[40]	**woodchuck:** groundhog; a North American mammal

Tease It Out

Lines 1 to 24

1. Lines 6 to 7: What time of day is it? Where is the speaker? What is he doing?
2. What was the speaker doing all day?
3. Where is the speaker's ladder? How does the speaker describe the ladder's position?
4. Did the speaker fill his last barrel before he finished for the day?
5. What is the 'Essence of winter sleep' that the speaker describes? Does this suggest that winter has arrived or that winter is soon to arrive?
6. The speaker describes something that happened in the morning when he went to get a drink of water from the 'drinking trough'. What is the 'pane of glass' that he 'skimmed' from this trough?
7. What did the speaker do with the 'pane of glass'? What effect do you imagine this had on what he viewed?
8. How has what the speaker did with the 'pane of glass' in the morning affected him since?
9. What sort of condition was the speaker in when he commenced his work in the morning?
10. 'I could tell/ What form my dreaming was about to take'. What is it that the poet will be dreaming about when he sleeps?
11. How does the speaker describe the apples in lines 18 to 20? Why do you think he describes them in this manner?
12. The speaker is still experiencing certain sensations or physical effects from the work he has completed. What are these?
13. What sounds does the speaker 'keep hearing' as he lies in bed?

Lines 25 to 42

14. Lines 27 to 31: How does the speaker characterise the way he felt about the harvest when the work was just commencing? How does he feel about it now that it is done?
15. What does the speaker say became of the apples that fell to the ground when they were being picked? Did the apples need to be badly damaged in order to be treated in this manner?
16. 'One can see what will trouble/ This sleep of mine'. Is it clear what will trouble the speaker when he sleeps? What do you think will preoccupy him?

17. The speaker says that he is unsure what kind of sleep he is about to experience. What different types of sleep does he describe? What do you understand each type of sleep to represent?

Think About Themes

1. The poem captures the way our minds sometimes operate just before we fall asleep, when we are not quite fully awake or asleep. Discuss the ways in which the poem conveys this sensation.
2. Where do you imagine the speaker is located? How long has it been, do you think, since he finished his day's work?
3. What does the poem suggest about the way we feel at the beginning of a long project and the way we inevitably feel at the end?
4. The poem describes the effects that repetitive work has on not only our bodies but our minds. What sorts of effects does the poem describe?
5. Do you think that the apple harvest works as a metaphor for other human endeavours? Is there a way that the apple harvest might represent the poet's own work?
6. Do you think that there might be a religious or spiritual overtone to the poem? What images or objects in the poem might be said to have religious significance?
7. How does the poet use assonance and alliteration to create a sleepy, dreamy atmosphere?

In Context

1. Discuss the representation of physical work in the poetry of Frost. Do his poems celebrate such work or is it characterised as a burden on some of our lives?
2. 'Frost often expresses a desire to get away from life for a while, but he is never so weary of life that he wishes it to end'. Discuss this statement making reference to three poems by Frost on your course.
3. 'Frost's poems describe not only the beauty of the natural world, but also the strangeness and darkness that we discover there'. Write a short essay in response to this statement.

[handwritten notes: 4 stanzas / 5 lines each]

[handwritten notes: Rhyming ABAAB]

*[handwritten notes top right:
Theme
Nature
Decision making
consequences of decisions
Regret
Sorrow
despair
Transcience]*

The Road Not Taken

[handwritten: decisions in life]

Two roads diverged in a yellow wood,
And sorry I could not travel both
And be one traveler, long I stood   *[weighing up his options]*
And looked down one as far as I could
To where it bent in the undergrowth;   [5]

Then took the other, as just as fair,
And having perhaps the better claim,   *[think it might be better   Adventerous]*
Because it was grassy and wanted wear;   *[Alliteration]*
Though as for that the passing there
Had worn them really about the same,   [10]

And both that morning equally lay   *[Alliteration]*
In leaves no step had trodden black.
Oh, I kept the first for another day!   *[promised himself he would explore the other road]*
Yet knowing how way leads on to way,
I doubted if I should ever come back.   [15]

[once you make a choice you can't go back]

I shall be telling this with a sigh
Somewhere ages and ages hence: *[Alliteration   He will be telling people]*
Two roads diverged in a wood, and I –
I took the one less traveled by,
And that has made all the difference.   [20]

[Hardly/sad sigh]

[1]	*diverged:*	split
[6]	*fair:*	promising, suitable
[8]	*wanted:*	lacked
[9]	*passing:*	traffic
[17]	*hence:*	from now

Tease It Out

Stanza 1

1. Where is the speaker at the beginning of the poem? *wood*
2. Why does the speaker describe the wood as 'yellow'? What time of year is it? *Autumn / happy*
3. 'Two roads diverged': The speaker has come to a fork in the road. What is he immediately 'sorry' that he cannot do? Why is it not possible for him to do this? *choose both*
4. Lines 3 to 5: The speaker 'stood' for a 'long' time before the roads. What does he say he did during this time?
5. Does the speaker inspect both roads carefully?
6. What prevents the poet from seeing too far down one of the roads?

Stanza 2

7. 'Then took the other'. Does the speaker give the impression that he has carefully considered or examined this 'other' road?
8. How does the poet say the road he takes compares to the other road?
9. What do you think the poet means by the term 'fair' in line 6?
10. The poet goes on to say that the road he took had 'perhaps the better claim'. Why does he think it had the 'better claim'?
11. What is the 'passing' that the speaker mentions in line 9? What effect has this 'passing' had on both roads?

Stanza 3

12. The poet describes the leaves that cover both roads. What condition are the leaves in?
13. Is there a difference in the amount of leaves that cover the individual roads?
14. Line 13: Having made up his mind to take one road, what does the speaker propose to do with the other? Is the speaker confident that he will be able to achieve what he proposes?
15. The speaker says that 'knowing how way leads on to way' makes him doubt he 'should ever come back'. Explain in your own words what the speaker is describing here.

Stanza 4

16. When does the speaker imagine he will be 'telling this' story of encountering two roads?
17. Why do you think the speaker will be telling the story 'with a sigh'? Are there different ways to understand such a 'sigh'?
18. Who do you imagine the speaker might be telling his story to?
19. Lines 18 to 19: How does the speaker imagine he will tell the story? Does his account of what happened correspond with or differ from what we learnt from the first three stanzas?
20. 'And that has made all the difference.' What is it that the speaker considers has 'made all the difference'? What do you think the 'difference' is?

Think About Themes

1. The poem describes moments that everyone encounters in life, moments when we are faced with different options and have to make a difficult decision. What does the poem suggest about such moments and the decisions that we ultimately make?
2. The speaker says that he took the road 'less traveled by'. What does taking such a road suggest or imply? Is the speaker being honest with himself when he says that he took the 'one less traveled'? Give reasons for your answer.
3. What does the poem suggest about missed or lost opportunities? Does the poem suggest that it is the roads we don't take that end up troubling us more than the roads we do take in life?
4. The poem is often mistakenly referred to as 'The Road Less Traveled'. Why do you think this might be the case? What does it suggest about the way that many people read the poem?
5. How would you describe the poet's tone in this poem? Do you think that this is an uplifting poem? Give reasons for your answer.

[handwritten annotations throughout]

Structure   1916

1 stanza
59 lines

Theme
Nostalgia
Childhood Memories
escape
Isolation

Metaphor
Swinging on branches -
escaping life

10 syllables
Iambic pentametre

(Tree)

Birches

When I see birches bend to left and right
Across the lines of straighter darker trees,
I like to think some boy's been swinging them.
But swinging doesn't bend them down to stay. *Mother nature*
Ice storms do that. Often you must have seen them   [5]
Loaded with ice a sunny winter morning
After a rain. They click upon themselves
As the breeze rises, and turn many-colored
As the stir cracks and crazes their enamel. *Alliteration, onomatopoeic, metaphor*
Soon the sun's warmth makes them shed crystal shells *sibilance*   [10] *Alliteration*
Shattering and avalanching on the snow crust —
Such heaps of broken glass to sweep away *Frost shatters*
You'd think the inner dome of heaven had fallen.
They are dragged to the withered bracken by the load,
And they seem not to break; though once they are bowed   [15]
So low for long, they never right themselves: *metaphor put down by others*
You may see their trunks arching in the woods
Years afterwards, trailing their leaves on the ground,
Like girls on hands and knees that throw their hair *Simile + image*
Before them over their heads to dry in the sun.   [20]
But I was going to say when Truth broke in *personification (reality)*
With all her matter-of-fact about the ice storm,
I should prefer to have some boy bend them *conversational*
As he went out and in to fetch the cows —
Some boy too far from town to learn baseball, *(rural) isolated*   [25]
Whose only play was what he found himself,
Summer or winter, and could play alone.
One by one he subdued his father's trees
By riding them down over and over again
Until he took the stiffness out of them,   [30]
And not one but hung limp, not one was left
For him to conquer. He learned all there was
To learn about not launching out too soon *doesn't let go to early*
And so not carrying the tree away
Clear to the ground. He always kept his poise *determined to climb to the top* [35]
To the top branches, climbing carefully
With the same pains you use to fill a cup *value of patience*
Up to the brim, and even above the brim. *+ composure*

Alliteration   *burst of energy*
Then he flung outward, feet first, with a swish, *Onomatopoeia*
Kicking his way down through the air to the ground.   [40]
So was I once myself a swinger of birches.
And so I dream of going back to be. *go back to childhood*
It's when I'm weary of considerations, *tired of problems*
And life is too much like a pathless wood *how old he is*
Where your face burns and tickles with the cobwebs *point wrinkles/senses* [45]
Broken across it, and one eye is weeping
From a twig's having lashed across it open. *metaphor - damaged by life*
I'd like to get away from earth awhile
And then come back to it and begin over. *escape*
May no fate wilfully misunderstand me *take a break*   [50]
And half grant what I wish and snatch me away
Not to return. Earth's the right place for love:
I don't know where it's likely to go better.
I'd like to go by climbing a birch tree, *getting away from struggles*
And climb black branches up a snow-white trunk   [55]
Toward heaven, till the tree could bear no more,
But dipped its top and set me down again.
That would be good both going and coming back.
One could do worse than be a swinger of birches.

you could do worse than fantisise your childhood dreams

metaphor - life - getting over troubles

[9]	**enamel:** a glossy protective layer – in this case, ice
[14]	**bracken:** a type of fern
[28]	**subdued:** overpowered
[50]	**wilfully:** intentionally

Tease It Out

Lines 1 to 20

1. Lines 1 to 5: The poet sometimes comes across birch trees that are bent 'to left and right'. What does he 'like to think' has caused the trees to bend in this manner? *boy playing on it* What has actually caused the trees to bend? *mother nature*

2. How do such birch trees compare with the 'darker trees' in the forest? *bent left + right trees are straight + darker*

3. The poet describes the process that causes the birches to bend. How do the trees appear on a 'winter morning/ After a rain'? *loaded with ice*

4. Lines 7 to 9: To what is the poet referring when he speaks of the birches' 'enamel'? *the ice* What happens to this 'enamel' as the 'breeze rises'? *cracks* Why do the birches 'turn many-colored' when this is happening? *the breeze moves the ice*

5. What effect does the 'sun's warmth' have on the birches? *makes them shed*

6. Consider the poet's description of the ice falling to the snow-crusted forest floor. How does he convey the drama and magnitude of this occurrence?

7. What does the poet say you might imagine had happened if you saw 'Such heaps of broken glass'?

8. Line 14: What effect does the weight of the ice have on the birches?

9. Do the birches ever return to their original position after such ice storms?

10. The poet describes the birches that are arched or bent, 'trailing their leaves on the ground'. To what does he compare the appearance of such trees?

Lines 21 to 40

11. Lines 23 to 24: The poet has just described how ice storms cause the birches to bend 'down to stay'. What does he say he'd prefer to imagine caused the birches to bend in this manner?

12. What does the poet say interrupted his initial attempt to talk about a boy 'swinging' the birches?

13. The poet imagines 'some boy' swinging the birches as he passes through the woods. Where does he imagine this boy is going?

14. Why would such a boy not spend his time learning baseball with the other boys his age?

15. What sort of 'play' does the poet say is left to someone like this boy?

16. Lines 28 to 31: Explain in your own words what the poet imagines the boy doing to his father's trees. What effect do the boy's activities have on the birches?

17. Lines 32 to 35: What did the boy 'learn about' by engaging in this activity? What would have been the consequence or effect of him 'launching out too soon'?

18. Lines 35 to 38: The poet describes how the boy 'always kept his poise/ To the top branches'. To what does he compare the care that the boy took when climbing to the top of the trees?

19. What does the poet describe the boy doing in lines 39 to 40? How does the boy behave as he does this? How does the poet convey the sounds and the thrill of this moment?

Lines 41 to 59

20. The poet says that he was once a 'swinger of birches' and that he dreams 'of going back to be'. On what occasions does he say he dreams of 'going back'.

21. The poet describes how life can sometimes be 'too much like a pathless wood'. What do you understand him to mean by this?

22. The poet describes the experience of making your way through a pathless wood. What difficulties and irritations does he describe encountering on such a journey?

23. What do the irritations described in lines 45 to 47 represent?

24. What does the poet say he'd like to do in lines 48 to 49?

25. Lines 50 to 52: The poet is concerned that some 'fate' might misunderstand his desire to 'get away from earth awhile'. In what way might his wish be misunderstood? What would be the consequence of such a misunderstanding?

26. How does the poet characterise Earth in lines 52 to 53?

27. Lines 54 to 57: The poet describes the manner in which he would like to 'get away from earth awhile'. How would he like to do this?

28. Why do you think the poet has italicised the word 'Toward'?

Think About Themes

1. What do you think the swinging of birches represents for the poet now that he is an older man? What did it represent for him when he was a young boy?

2. What does the poem suggest about the importance of the imagination?

3. Write a paragraph discussing the poet's use of assonance and alliteration to convey sound in the poem? Can you identify at least two instances of onomatopoeia in the poem?

4. How would you describe the mood of this poem? Does it alter or change as the poem progresses?

5. Identify two similes and say which one you found most effective.

In Context

Isolation is a recurring theme in the Robert Frost's poetry. Compare and contrast his treatment of this theme in 'Birches' with at least two other poems on your course.

Handwritten annotations (left margin):
Theme
Nature
Death
sadness
family
Pain
Childhood
Tragedy

Handwritten (top right): 1 stanza / 34 lines / Iambic Pentrameter

'Out, Out –'

The buzz-saw snarled and rattled in the yard
And made dust and dropped stove-length sticks of wood,
Sweet-scented stuff when the breeze drew across it.
And from there those that lifted eyes could count
Five mountain ranges one behind the other [5]
Under the sunset far into Vermont.
And the saw snarled and rattled, snarled and rattled,
As it ran light, or had to bear a load.
And nothing happened: day was all but done.
Call it a day, I wish they might have said [10]
To please the boy by giving him the half hour
That a boy counts so much when saved from work.
His sister stood beside them in her apron
To tell them 'Supper'. At the word, the saw,
As if to prove saws knew what supper meant, [15]
Leaped out at the boy's hand, or seemed to leap –
He must have given the hand. However it was,
Neither refused the meeting. But the hand!
The boy's first outcry was a rueful laugh.
As he swung toward them holding up the hand, [20]
Half in appeal, but half as if to keep
The life from spilling. Then the boy saw all –
Since he was old enough to know, big boy
Doing a man's work, though a child at heart –
He saw all spoiled. 'Don't let him cut my hand off – [25]
The doctor, when he comes. Don't let him, sister!'
So. But the hand was gone already.
The doctor put him in the dark of ether.
He lay and puffed his lips out with his breath.
And then – the watcher at his pulse took fright. [30]
No one believed. They listened at his heart.
Little – less – nothing! – and that ended it.
No more to build on there. And they, since they
Were not the one dead, turned to their affairs.

Handwritten annotations (right of poem):
onanatopoeia
personification – threatening
everyday life
Alliteration
hyperbole – exaggeration
Tranquility
Repitition – saw cut his hand
Change of Tone
Wishing they called him in half hour earlier
Personification / own fault
Shock
cut his hand off – realised what happened him
anasthetic / put to sleep
life goes on.

Handwritten (left of poem): He did something
doesn't want to spill blood

Handwritten (bottom left):
Tone
realistic
Starts - Dark
Changes - lighthearted
End - sad
realistic

'**Out, Out –**': The title is taken from William Shakespeare's *Macbeth*. The words occur in a speech made by Macbeth when reflecting upon the brevity and futility of life: 'Out, out, brief candle!/ Life's but a waking shadow, a poor player/ That struts and frets his hour upon the stage/ And then is heard no more. It is a tale/ Told by an idiot, full of sound and fury,/ Signifying nothing.'

[1] **buzz-saw:** a circular saw often used for cutting lumber, can be hand-held or stationary
[6] **Vermont:** a state in the north-eastern USA
[19] **rueful:** expressing sorrow and regret, especially in a wry or humorous way
[28] **ether:** chemical used as an early form of anaesthetic

Tease It Out

Lines 1 to 12

1. In what environment do you imagine the boy to be working? Is it a lumberyard, a factory of some kind or a family farm? Give a reason for your answer. *From farm*
2. What time of day is it? *evening*
3. What does the boy's work with the saw produce? *wood*
4. For what purpose are these lengths of wood intended?
5. What does the freshly cut wood smell like? *sweet*
6. Describe in your own words the main features of this New England landscape. *countryside/farm mountain ranges*
7. Consider the use of the word 'snarl' in relation to the buzz-saw. What usually snarls? What effect does the image of the snarling saw create? *animal – personification*
8. Group Discussion: Identify an example of repetition in these opening twelve lines. What effect does this have on the poem's atmosphere? *Saw – engages reader*
9. Has this been an eventful or an uneventful day?
10. Why does Frost wish the workers had finished early on this particular evening? Do you think there is more than one reason for this? *so the child wouldn't*

Lines 13 to 18

11. Why does the boy's sister enter the yard? *supper*
12. Describe in your own words how the saw is personified in these lines. *leaps*
13. Does the speaker really believe that the saw 'leaped out' at the boy's hand? *No*
14. 'He must have given the hand.' What does the speaker mean by this? *He must've done something*
15. 'But the hand!' Identify three different emotions conveyed by this simple phrase.

Lines 19 to 25

16. What is the boy's first reaction to the accident? Does this reaction surprise you?
17. Why, according to the speaker, does he hold his hand up?
18. Consider the phrase 'Half in appeal'. What does the speaker mean by this? What is the boy appealing against?
19. What does he quickly realise?
20. Why, according to the speaker, is he capable of realising this?
21. What does he ask his sister to do? Is this request in vain?

Lines 26 to 34

22. What action does the doctor take when he arrives?
23. What brings 'fright' to the person watching over the anesthetised boy?
24. What happens to the boy's pulse and heartbeat?
25. How do the others respond to this development?
26. Describe in your own words how they respond to the boy's eventual death.

Think About Themes

1. Sound is very important in this poem, and Frost uses a mixture of lines filled with pleasant word music and lines that are characterised by a harsh combination of sounds. Read the poem aloud and find one example of euphony *– pleasant* and one example of cacophony. *– harsh*
2. How would you describe the atmosphere of the poem's opening lines? Is it an atmosphere of ease or one of building menace? Give a reason for your answer.
3. Frost depicts the boy's saw as a living thing, as a hungry and dangerous animal. What poetic techniques does he use to achieve this? Do you find his depiction of the saw effective?
4. What is your reaction to the behaviour of the boy's family after the accident? Do you find their response to the boy's death cold and unsympathetic or merely realistic?
5. How would you describe the speaker's tone: is he a detached or a sympathetic observer of the boy's plight?
6. Do you like or dislike this poem? Write a few lines saying why.
7. Read the speech from *Macbeth* that gives the poem its title. How does it relate to the poem's themes and concerns?
8. Could this poem be taken as a comment on the issue of child labour? Give a reason for your answer.

In Context

'This poem presents the view that life is nasty, brutish and short, showing the world to be a cold and uncaring place.' Would you agree with this statement? Answer by comparing 'Out, Out –' to at least two other poems by Frost.

Spring Pools

These pools that, though in forests, still reflect
The total sky almost without defect,
And like the flowers beside them, chill and shiver,
Will like the flowers beside them soon be gone,
And yet not out by any brook or river,   [5]
But up by roots to bring dark foliage on.

The trees that have it in their pent-up buds
To darken nature and be summer woods –
Let them think twice before they use their powers
To blot out and drink up and sweep away   [10]
These flowery waters and these watery flowers
From snow that melted only yesterday.

[2]   ***without defect:*** perfectly, flawlessly
[5]   ***brook:*** a small stream
[6]   ***foliage:*** clusters of leaves, flowers and branches
[7]   ***pent-up:*** bottled up, held in or held back

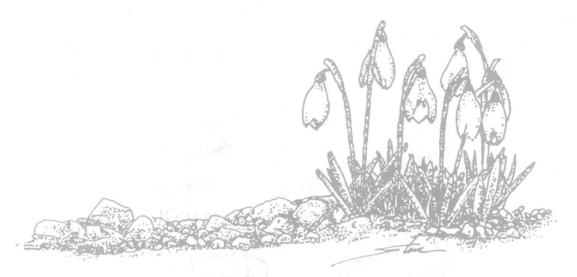

Tease It Out

1. Where are the pools located? What is reflected on their surfaces?
2. What phrase indicates that these reflected images are extremely clear and detailed?
3. Is the water in the pools warm or cold?
4. How do you visualise the flowers that grow beside the pools?
5. The pools will 'soon be gone'. Describe in your own words the process of their disappearance.
6. The water now in the pools will contribute to a great change in the forest. What is this?
7. Why do you think the flowers will also disappear?
8. Consider the meanings and associations of the word 'pent-up'. What does its use here suggest about the buds on the barren trees?
9. What are these buds capable of producing? What effect will this have on the other aspects of 'nature' that exist within the forest?
10. According to the poet, what 'powers' do the trees possess?
11. The poet asks the trees to 'think twice' before using these powers. What does this suggest about the winter scene he's observing in the forest?
12. How do you imagine the tone of this line? Is it a request, a plea, a threat or a demand?
13. The pools are described as 'flowery'. What aspect of their appearance is being referred to here?
14. What does the description 'watery' suggest about the flowers? Does this adjective refer to their appearance or to another aspect of these blooms?
15. What is the origin of the spring pools, as described in the last line? Does this add anything to your visual image of the pools?

Think About Themes

1. In poetry and song 'summer' usually has positive associations. Would you agree that in this poem it has negative ones? Give a reason for your answer.
2. Describe the poem's atmosphere in your own words. What literary devices does the poet use to convey this atmosphere?
3. 'The fact that these icy and pristine pools will "soon be gone" contributes greatly to the effect they have on the poet.' Write a paragraph responding to this statement.
4. Class Discussion: The poet addresses the trees directly. What is the name of this literary technique? Would you agree that it's effective in this instance?
5. 'In the natural world, one phenomenon passes away so another can exist.' Write a paragraph describing the cycle of nature as outlined in 'Spring Pools'.

In Context

1. In a speech at Frost's eighty-fifth birthday party, the critic Lionel Trilling said he regarded Frost as 'a terrifying poet.' Do you find the parasitic depiction of 'summer woods' in 'Spring Pools' unsettling? Are there any 'terrifying' moments in the other poems by Frost you have studied?
2. A major theme of this poem is transience: the changes that occur with the passing of time. Bearing this theme in mind, compare 'Spring Pools' to 'Provide, Provide' and 'After Apple-picking'.
3. Discuss how 'Spring Pools' deals with the themes of death and fate. Compare the poem's treatment of this theme with that of 'Out, Out –'.

Theme   written in 1928

- mental health, depression + anxiety
- grief
- isolation

Tone
lonely
dark
poignant
gloomy

10 syllables -
Iambic pentrameter
structure
5 Stanzas
14 lines
- refrain

inner or external conflict

Pathetic Fallacy — weather reflects mood

Dante - first to use 3 line rhyming stanza in his work 'Dante Inferno'

metaphor his thoughts are going around + around

Acquainted With The Night

dark, eerie, Alone in a city   slightly depression

Fiat NOX - let there be Light
Fiat lux - let there by night

I have been one acquainted with the night.
I have walked out in rain – and back in rain.   plodding along,
I have outwalked the furthest city light   exploring

Superlative emphasises   Traveler Exploring all realm of depression

I have looked down the saddest city lane.
I have passed by the watchman on his beat   [5]
And dropped my eyes, unwilling to explain.   isolation - doesn't want to make eye contact.

I have stood still and stopped the sound of feet   Silence
When far away an interrupted cry   — Violent world - hand over mouth   - trouble to communicate
Came over houses from another street,

not for him, he's alone separate from him

But not to call me back or say good-bye;   [10]
And further still at an unearthly height —
One luminary clock against the sky   doesn't matter if its day or night he still feels the same
moon

Proclaimed the time was neither wrong nor right.
I have been one acquainted with the night.

relapse

     Acquainted: familiar
[3]   ***outwalked:*** walked beyond
[5]   ***beat:*** patrol, route, circuit
[12]   ***luminary:*** a natural light-giving body, in this case the moon

Tease It Out

1. What does the speaker mean when he claims to be 'acquainted with the night'? *so dark trought*
2. What does he spend his nights doing? *walking*
3. What is the weather like on these occasions? *rain*
4. The speaker feels compelled to keep walking, even when he passes beyond the lights of the city. What does this suggest about his mood or temperament? *determined*
5. The speaker mentions the 'saddest city lane'. Take a moment to visualise this environment. Write a short paragraph describing how you imagine this lane's atmosphere and appearance.
6. Class Discussion: Are all lanes sad in the city through which the speaker walks? Or does he perceive these streets as sad because of his tortured mental state? Or is he drawn only to the more depressed and depressing quarters of his city?
7. Who does the speaker encounter in line 5? How does he react to this person?
8. Class Discussion: What is the speaker 'unwilling to explain'? Is there more than one possible answer to this question?
9. What phrase indicates that the speaker is often utterly alone on these occasions?
10. What sound does he hear coming from 'another' street?
11. This sound is described as being 'interrupted'. What do you imagine happening here? Would you agree that there's something sinister – or even violent – about the interruption of this sound?
12. 'But not to call me back or say good-bye'. What does this line suggest about the speaker's mood and frame of mind?
13. The speaker mentions a 'luminary clock' at an 'unearthly height'. What is he referring to here?
14. Group Discussion: 'Proclaimed the time was neither wrong nor right'. Many people find this line puzzling and mysterious. We can imagine how the time might be right for something. We can imagine how it might be wrong. But how can the time be neither? Discuss this line as a group and reach a possible interpretation of its meaning.

Think About Themes

1. 'Acquainted With the Night' describes an individual who takes late-night walks through the city streets. Do you think he goes out walking every night? Do you feel that this behaviour has been going on for a long time? Is it likely to continue into the future? Give reasons for your answers.

2. How would you describe the mental state of the speaker in the poem? Pick three adjectives that in your opinion best describe his state of mind. In each case support your answer with reference to the text.
3. Now pick three adjectives that in your opinion describe the atmosphere of the physical environment through which he wanders. In each case give a reason for your answer.
4. '"Acquainted With the Night" describes a speaker searching desperately for an escape that never comes.' Write a paragraph in response to this statement. What is the speaker looking to escape from? How could such an escape occur?
5. Consider the poem's opening and closing lines. In what sense might it be described as a kind of loop? Now consider its rhyme scheme. How might this also be said to possess a kind of looping quality? Would you agree that this contributes to the poem's atmosphere and themes?
6. 'This is a poem in which much is left unsaid. The poet is "unwilling to explain" to his readers, just as the speaker is "unwilling to explain" to the watchman'. Write a paragraph in response to this statement.
7. "The time was neither wrong nor right". Based on your reading of the poem, do you think the speaker is referring only to his own life here? Or does he have in mind the entire society in which he lives?
8. Class Discussion: At the end of the poem, the speaker seems to be looking to the moon for answers. What is Frost attempting to convey here? Is there a religious or philosophical point being made? Are we to take these lines in a literal or metaphorical sense?

In Context

1. 'Acquainted With the Night' is often compared to 'The Tuft of Flowers'. Both poems deal with the topic of isolation. Write a few lines comparing Frost's treatment of this theme in each of these poems.
2. 'Both "Acquainted With the Night" and "Design" present a rather dark view of the world.' Would you agree with this statement? Write a paragraph exploring the similarities and differences between them.

Design

I found a dimpled spider, fat and white,
On a white heal-all, holding up a moth
Like a white piece of rigid satin cloth –
Assorted characters of death and blight
Mixed ready to begin the morning right,   [5]
Like the ingredients of a witches' broth –
A snow-drop spider, a flower like a froth,
And dead wings carried like a paper kite.

What had that flower to do with being white,
The wayside blue and innocent heal-all?   [10]
What brought the kindred spider to that height,
Then steered the white moth thither in the night?
What but design of darkness to appall? –
If design govern in a thing so small.

[1]	**dimpled:** flesh marked by a series of small depressions
[2]	**heal-all:** a blue herbaceous plant, often used for medicinal purposes
[4]	**blight:** a particular type of plant disease, but also disease in general
[6]	**broth:** soup, brew, concoction
[10]	**wayside:** side of a road
[11]	**kindred:** related, alike, comparable
[12]	**thither:** to that point or place
[13]	**appall:** shock, horrify

Tease It Out

Lines 1 to 8

1. List the three adjectives used to describe the spider. What impression of this creature do they create? Is it a pleasant or unpleasant one?
2. Where was the spider located? What was startling or unusual about this flower?
3. What was the spider 'holding up' between its legs?
4. What simile is used to describe the spider's prey? Is it an effective comparison in your opinion? Explain your answer.
5. Group Discussion: What rather sinister association might we have with a 'white piece of rigid satin cloth'?
6. Consider the poet's choice of the word 'rigid' in line 3. What does it tell us about the unfortunate moth?
7. In line 4, what associations do the spider, moth and flower have for the poet?
8. Look up the word 'character' in your dictionary. Does it have more than one meaning? How might each different meaning be relevant to this description?
9. In lines 5 to 6 what simile is used to describe the combination of spider, moth and flower?
10. Would you agree that this comparison is unusual and unexpected? Do you find it interesting and unsettling? Or silly and over the top?
11. Class Discussion: What is a homonym? What homonyms exist for the word 'right'? Might any of those homonyms be relevant to line 5?
12. What simile is used to describe the heal-all in line 7? How does it contribute to your sense of the flower's visual appearance?
13. What simile is used to describe the moth in line 8? Is this a reasonable comparison in your opinion?

Lines 9 to 14

14. Where, according to the poet, do heal-all flowers normally grow? And what colour are they usually?
15. According to the poet, these are usually 'innocent' flowers. Why do you think he chooses this adjective to describe them?
16. The poet seems upset or perturbed that this particular heal-all is white rather than blue. What phrase indicates this?
17. Why does the poet refer to the spider as the heal-all's 'kindred' or relation? What physical feature do they have in common?
18. According to the poet, 'design of darkness' brought the flower, moth and spider together. What different meanings does the word 'design' have? What does it mean for something to be designed by darkness?
19. Why according to line 13 might 'design of darkness' have arranged this combination of creatures?
20. Class Discussion: 'If design govern in a thing so small.' Does the poet believe this combination of creatures is random rather than the product of design? Give a reason for your answer.
21. In these lines the poet asks three questions. Rewrite them as best you can in your own words.

Think About Themes

1. The poet has a particular reaction to the flower, moth and spider. Pick two adjectives that in your opinion best characterise his reaction and in each case give the reason for your choice. Do you think his reaction is reasonable or over the top?
2. Class Discussion: Consider once more the phrase 'design of darkness'. What associations do this concept have for you? What type of force, entity or power is Frost referring to here?
3. Group Discussion: Consider the following three statements:
   - Forces of darkness govern the entire universe.
   - Forces of darkness govern much of the universe, but ignore certain 'small' or irrelevant things.
   - The universe consists of a series of random events; it is governed by nothing at all.
   Which in your opinion best describes the vision of the world articulated by 'Design'?
4. Would you agree that there is a shift between the octet and sestet of this poem? Describe this shift in your own words.
5. There are four similes in the poem's octave. Identify them. Which one, in your opinion, is most effective? Give a reason for your answer.
6. Identify three examples of sound effects in these lines (for example, assonance and alliteration) and say how they contribute to the poem's atmosphere.
7. Class Discussion: Do you think the poem's last line is effective? Does it strenghten or undermine the vision of the poem up to that point?
8. What is your personal reaction to 'Design'? Did you find it pleasant or unpleasant to read, boring or compelling? Mention the poem's imagery and sound effects, and say whether you find its arguments silly or convincing.

In Context

1. In 'Design', 'After Apple-Picking' and 'The Tuft of Flowers', a scene from the natural world inspires Frost to ask serious questions about human existence. Write a paragraph comparing the three poems in light of this statement.
2. Would you agree that the view of life presented in 'Design' is similar to that put forward in 'Provide, Provide' and 'Out, Out –'? Give a reason for your answer.

1930

Beauty is ephemeral (it lasts a short time)

Tercet (3 lines per stanza)

Rhyme

7 Stanzas 21 lines

Tone Lighhearted Simple beat

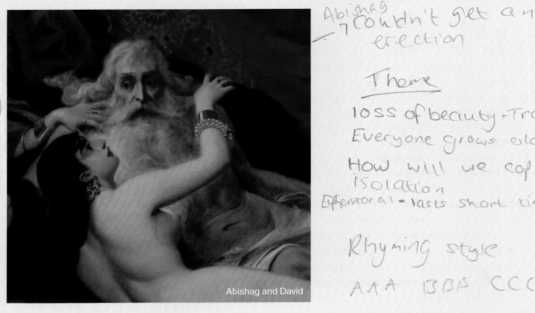
Abishag and David

Abishag → couldn't get an erection

Theme
loss of beauty - Transience
Everyone grows old
How will we cope
Isolation
Ephemoral - lasts short time

Rhyming style
AAA BBB CCC

Provide, Provide

The witch that came (the withered hag) *looks no good to her now*
To wash the steps with pail and rag
Was once the beauty Abishag,

The picture pride of Hollywood. *Alliteration*
Too many fall from great and good *If hollywood stars loose beauty we have no chance*
For you to doubt the likelihood. [5]

Die early and avoid the fate.
Or if predestined to die late, *die accepting your old + wirured*
Make up your mind to die in state.

Make the whole stock exchange your own! [10] *live by yourself you don't have to worry about anyone else*
If need be occupy a throne,
Where nobody can call you crone.

Some have relied on what they knew, *Accept your fate*
Others on being simply true.
What worked for them might work for you. [15]

No memory of having starred *popular* *Despite being a hollywood beauty doesn't make a difference*
Atones for later disregard
Or keeps the end from being hard. *fake friend*

Better to go down dignified
With boughten friendship at your side [20]
Than none at all. Provide, provide! *repitition*

[3]	***Abishag:*** a biblical figure renowned for her beauty
[8]	***predestined:*** fated
[9]	***in state:*** as a public figure
[12]	***crone:*** an ugly old woman
[20]	***boughten:*** shop-bought (as opposed to homemade)

Tease It Out

1. Lines 1 to 4: What work did the woman come to do?
2. How does the poet characterise this woman in the opening line? Why do you think he describes her in this manner? What does it suggest about her appearance and the kind of person she is?
3. The poet says that this woman was once 'the beauty Abishag'. Who was Abishag?
4. The poet says that the woman was once the 'picture pride of Hollywood'. What does this description suggest about who the woman once was?
5. Why do you think the poet says that this woman was once 'Abishag' and the 'picture pride of Hollywood'?
6. What does the fact that such a person has come to 'wash the steps with pail and rag' tell us about their lives? What do you imagine might have happened to this woman?
7. How does the poet characterise the woman's fate in the fifth line?
8. Why does the poet say that we should not doubt the possibility that something similar could happen to us?
9. The poet gives us some advice to ensure that we 'avoid the fate' of this old woman. How does he suggest that some people will avoid this fate in line 7?
10. What do you think it means to be 'predestined to die late'? What does the poet recommend that people who are 'predestined to die late' do?
11. Lines 10 to 12: Describe the sort of person the poet has in mind in line 10. What sort of person does he describe in line 11? Why would such a person not have to worry about being called a 'crone'?
12. What does the poet say has enabled certain people to avoid the old woman's fate in line 13? What sort of person do you think the poet has in mind here?
13. What does the poet say has enabled certain people to avoid the old woman's fate in line 14? What sort of person is the poet describing?
14. Lines 16 to 18: The poet describes people who have memories 'of having starred?' What sort of person is he describing here? What does the poet say such memories will not safeguard against?
15. What sort of 'disregard' do you think the poet means in line 17?
16. What do you think the poet means by 'to go down'?
17. How does the poet recommend we 'go down' in line 19? What do you think he means by this?
18. What do you understand 'boughten friendship' to be? How might this differ from ordinary friendship?
19. Why does the poet say that it is better to have 'boughten friendship at your side/ Than none at all'?
20. The poem finishes with the poet calling on us to 'Provide, provide'. What is it that he is calling on us to do?

Think About Themes

1. How would you characterise the poet's tone in this poem? Do you think he is being serious or light-hearted? Give reasons for your answer.
2. Who do you think the poet is addressing in this poem? Do you think that the poem is directed at people involved in the 'fame game' especially, or do you think that the poem offers prudent advice to us all?
3. Do you agree with the poem's central point that we ought to 'provide' now for when we are old?
4. How does the poem's structure and rhyme contribute to its impact or effect?
5. Does the poem suggest that money and power are important in life? Does the poem suggest that they are essential if we wish to avoid the old woman's fate?
6. Were you surprised that Frost wrote this poem? What do you imagine compelled or inspired him to compose 'Provide, Provide'?

In Context

Frost has often been described as a 'philosopher-poet'. Compare the outlook on life expressed in 'Provide, Provide' with that of at least two other poems on your course. Which outlook do you find most appealing?

Seamus Heaney

William Butler Yeats was born in Sandymount, Dublin on Seamus Heaney was born on 13 April 1939, the eldest of nine children. He grew up on the family farm, Mossbawn, near Castledawson in Co. Derry. His father, Patrick, worked as a cattle dealer as well as a farmer. Patrick was a man of few words, while Heaney's mother, Margaret, was articulate and outspoken. Heaney inherited both of these traits, and believed this to be fundamental to the 'quarrel with himself' from which his poetry arises.

At age twelve, Heaney won a scholarship to St Columb's College, a Catholic boarding school in Derry city. Heaney's family, meanwhile, moved from Mossbawn to the nearby village of Bellaghy. Though they left the farm where Heaney was reared in 1953, Mossbawn looms large in his work, and rural Co. Derry is the 'country of the mind' where much of his poetry is grounded.

While Heaney was studying at St Columb's, his brother Christopher was killed in a road accident at the age of four. Christopher's death had a profound effect on the young Heaney, and he would write extensively about it in later years, most notably in his famous poem 'Mid-Term Break'.

In 1957, Heaney left school and began studying English literature at Queen's University Belfast. He developed an interest in poetry during his college years, particularly that of Ted Hughes. He graduated in 1961 with a first class honours degree and went on to teacher training college at St Joseph's in Belfast.

While on teaching placement, Heaney met the writer Michael McLaverty, who became a mentor to the young poet, introducing him to the work of Patrick Kavanagh and encouraging Heaney to publish his work. After graduating from St Joseph's, Heaney became a lecturer there in 1963. Under the guidance of the poet Philip Hobsbaum, he joined a writing workshop with Derek Mahon, Michael Longley and others.

In 1965 he married Marie Devlin, a teacher from Co. Tyrone. The following year, just before Marie gave birth to Michael, the first of their three children, Heaney's first collection of poetry was published. *Death of a Naturalist* dealt primarily with Heaney's childhood experiences of growing up in rural Co. Derry. It won several awards, including the Geoffrey Faber Prize. Heaney's reputation grew, and he was appointed a lecturer in Modern English Literature at Queen's that same year.

Another son, Christopher, was born in 1968. Heaney's second collection, *Door into the Dark*, was published in 1969. It includes the poems 'The Forge' and 'Bogland' and was well-received, becoming the Poetry Book Society Choice for the year. In 1970 he taught for a year at the University of California, Berkeley, before returning to Belfast.

In 1972 he published *Wintering Out*, in which he continued his exploration of landscape, and in particular boglands, in poems such as 'The Tollund Man'. He resigned his lectureship at Queen's University and moved his family to Glanmore, Co. Wicklow. By moving to Wicklow he wanted, as he put it later, 'to put the practice of poetry more deliberately at the centre of my life'. He also wanted to escape the pressures he felt as a Catholic writer working in the North: 'In the

> "Though they left the farm where Heaney was reared in 1953, Mossbawn looms large in his work, and rural Co. Derry is the 'country of the mind' where much of his poetry is grounded"

late sixties and early seventies the world was changing for the Catholic imagination. I felt I was compromising some part of myself by staying in a situation where socially and, indeed, imaginatively, there were pressures against regarding the moment as critical. Going to the South was perhaps emblematic for me and was certainly so for some of the people I knew. To the Unionists it looked like a betrayal of the Northern thing.'

For the next three years, Heaney made his living as a full-time writer. Then, in 1975, he resumed lecturing at Carysfort, a teacher-training college in Dublin. Heaney moved to Sandymount, Dublin shortly afterwards, and it remained his home for the rest of his life. 1975 also saw the publication of *North*, arguably his most political collection, which juxtaposes imagery of bog bodies and Vikings with violence in Northern Ireland. The book won the W.H. Smith Award, the Duff Cooper Memorial Prize and was a Poetry Book Society Choice. 'The Skunk' and 'Harvest Bow' were among the poems included in *Field Work* (1979), and his first volume of *Selected Poems* followed in 1980.

When Aosdána, the association of Irish artists, was formed in 1981, Heaney was one of the first artists to be made a member. That same year, Heaney left his lectureship at Carysfort to become a visiting professor at Harvard University. By 1984 he was elected Boylston Professor of Rhetoric and Oratory at Harvard. 1984 also saw the publication of *Station Island*, and the death of his mother, Margaret. Heaney's father Patrick died in 1986, and the loss of both parents within two years affected Heaney deeply. He explored his grief in the sonnet cycle 'Clearances', which appeared in the 1987 collection *The Haw Lantern*.

In 1989, Heaney was elected professor of poetry at Oxford, a position which he held for a five-year term until 1994. Throughout this period, he continued to divide his time between Ireland and the United States. *Seeing Things* (1991), his ninth collection of poetry, included such poems as 'The Pitchfork' and 'Lightenings'.

Heaney was awarded the Nobel Prize for Literature in 1995 for what the Nobel committee described as 'works of lyrical beauty and ethical depth, which exalt everyday miracles and the living past.' He was the fourth Irishman to receive the honour, after William Butler Yeats, George Bernard Shaw and Samuel Beckett. His 1996 collection *The Spirit Level*, which includes the poem 'Postscript', won the Whitbread Book of the Year Award, as did his 1999 translation of Beowulf.

In 2003, the Seamus Heaney Centre for Poetry was opened in Queen's University Belfast. Today, it houses the Heaney Media Centre – a record of all his writings, TV and radio appearances – and also serves as a creative writing school for postgraduate students.

He suffered a stroke in August 2006, from which he recovered. That same year, his collection *District and Circle*, which includes 'Tate's Avenue', won the T.S. Eliot Prize. In 2008, the poet Dennis O'Driscoll published a series of interviews with Heaney in the book *Stepping Stones*, which is regarded as the closest Heaney ever came to an autobiography.

2010 saw the publication of Heaney's twelfth and final collection, *Human Chain*. It was inspired in part by his stroke and was critically acclaimed, winning the Forward Poetry Prize. In 2011, he donated his personal literary papers to the National Library of Ireland.

Heaney died on 30 August 2013 in hospital after a short illness. He was seventy-four years old. His funeral Mass was held in Donnybrook, Dublin and was broadcast live on RTE. He was buried in his home village of Bellaghy, Co. Derry, in the same graveyard as his parents and brother Christopher. His epitaph is taken from his poem 'The Gravel Walks', and reads 'Walk On Air Against Your Better Judgement'.
'

[handwritten: Thinking about a blacksmith]

[handwritten: (Allegory - one story represents another story)]

[handwritten: Poetic inspiration]
[handwritten: change of time]
[handwritten: Theme]
[handwritten: Skills + crafts]
[handwritten: (Mysterious) don't know where your next poem is coming from]
[handwritten: - Extended Metaphor]

The Forge *[handwritten: - where blacksmith works]*

All I know is a door into the dark.
Outside, old axles and iron hoops rusting;
Inside, the hammered anvil's short-pitched ring,
The unpredictable fantail of sparks
Or hiss when a new shoe toughens in water.
The anvil must be somewhere in the centre,
Horned as a unicorn, at one end square,
Set there immoveable: an altar
Where he expends himself in shape and music.
Sometimes, leather-aproned, hairs in his nose,
He leans out on the jamb, recalls a clatter
Of hoofs where traffic is flashing in rows;
Then grunts and goes in, with a slam and flick
To beat real iron out, to work the bellows.

[handwritten annotations: poetic inspiration; onomatopoeia; Simile; Horses; metaphor of wheel; poetic ideas; discarded metal; Harsh consonant sounds; Assonance; onomatopoeia; imagery - metaphor; poetic [5] inspiration; metaphor → The clock for the poet; musicality - the noises are a type of energy to create poems; Music; onomatopoeia; period of change - remembering Horses not cars; metonymy; cigarette; 1 stanza 14 lines; cars aren't real iron; real work]

Forge: a blacksmith's workshop where metal is heated and shaped
[2] **axles**: bars or shafts on which wheels revolve
[3] **anvil**: a heavy block of iron with a smooth face on which heated metals are hammered into desired shapes
[4] **fantail**: a fan-shaped tail or end
[11] **jamb**: vertical side of a doorframe
[14] **bellows**: device used to pump oxygen into a furnace to increase the temperature of the fire inside

Get in Gear

Watch Video 8 of a blacksmith at work in Bunratty Castle, Co. Clare. Then answer the following questions:

- What is he making?
- Name the different pieces of equipment he uses.
- Choose three adjectives that best describe the sounds of the forge and three adjectives that best describe the colours and visuals of the forge.

Tease it Out

1. The poet has never actually been inside the forge. What phrase indicates this? Do you think the poet finds this 'door into the dark' fascinating or intimidating or a mixture of both? Explain your answer.
2. What can the poet see outside the door of the forge?
3. Has the blacksmith been based here for a long time or is this a relatively new business? Give a reason for your answer.
4. What one sight can the poet make out when he peers through the forge's door? What might cause this phenomenon? Suggest why it appears at 'unpredictable' intervals.
5. The blacksmith's labour produces two sounds that can be heard outside the forge. What qualities does each sound possess? What activity is responsible for each one?
6. Why according to the poet does the blacksmith place freshly fashioned horseshoes in cold water? Can you describe the scientific process at work here?
7. The poet imagines the blacksmith's anvil. In what part of the forge does he envisage it being located?
8. The poet mentions two aspects of the anvil's shape, as he imagines it. What are these? What verb suggests that the blacksmith's work leaves him exhausted?
9. What can the blacksmith see passing by outside his forge? What used to travel along this roadway years ago?
10. What implication might this change have for the blacksmith and his livelihood?
11. Read line 13 carefully. What three things does the blacksmith do before returning to his forge? What does his behaviour suggest about his attitude to modernity and the changes in society he has witnessed?

Think About Themes

1. What hints are there that the poet holds the blacksmith and his craft in high esteem?
2. Class Discussion: The blacksmith, we're told, re-enters his forge in order to work with 'real iron'. Can you identify where fake or counterfeit iron might be said to appear in the poem? Is it possible that there's more than one type of fake iron present?

3. Think about the questions below on your own for a few minutes. Then compare your ideas with the person beside you. Together formulate answers, supporting your conclusions with evidence from the poem.
The poet's describes the blacksmith's craft as one of 'shape and music'.
   - In what way do the blacksmith's endeavours involve shaping various items?
   - How might they produce music of a kind?
   - In what way does poetry also involve shape and music?
   - Does the poem suggest any other links between these two seemingly very different pursuits?

In Context

1. 'This is a great poem of imagination. The poet himself never crosses the door into the darkness of the blacksmith's workspace. Only his imagination makes this transition'. Identify two other poems by Heaney where the power of imagination is celebrated.
2. 'This poem expresses the joy we find when we do what we want with our lives'. Discuss how Heaney explores this theme in 'The Forge' and at least two other poems on your course.
3. 'Throughout his work, Heaney shows a captivation with the symbols of a traditional way of life that is fast disappearing in our modern world'. Discuss this statement with reference to 'The Forge' and at least one other poem on your course.

Language Lab

1. The sonnet is an elegant and tightly structured poetic form, typically associated with love poetry. Is there an interesting contrast between this refined form of poetry and the elemental, chaotic, physical world of the forge? Why do you think Heaney chose to make this poem a sonnet?
2. This poem is full of memorable descriptions of sound. Pick out the description you find most effective and explain your choice.

Bogland

for T.P. Flanagan

We have no prairies
To slice a big sun at evening –
Everywhere the eye concedes to
Encroaching horizon,

Is wooed into the cyclops' eye   [5]
Of a tarn. Our unfenced country
Is bog that keeps crusting
Between the sights of the sun.

They've taken the skeleton
Of the Great Irish Elk   [10]
Out of the peat, set it up,
An astounding crate full of air.

Butter sunk under
More than a hundred years
Was recovered salty and white.   [15]
The ground itself is kind, black butter

Melting and opening underfoot,
Missing its last definition
By millions of years.
They'll never dig coal here,   [20]

Only the waterlogged trunks
Of great firs, soft as pulp.
Our pioneers keep striking
Inwards and downwards,

Every layer they strip   [25]
Seems camped on before.
The bogholes might be Atlantic seepage.
The wet centre is bottomless.

[1]   *prairie*: an extensive stretch of flat land without trees, especially in North America
[5]   *wooed*: to be won over; seduced; attracted to
[5]   *cyclops*: in myth, a one-eyed giant
[6]   *tarn*: a small mountain lake
[10] *the Great Irish Elk*: extinct species of giant deer; Heaney's neighbours dug the skeleton of one from a bog when he was a child
[12] *An astounding crate full of air*: refers to the Elk's huge skeleton
[18] *definition*: meaning or significance; having a definite shape or outline
[23] *pioneers*: explorers; discoverers of a new landscape
[27] *Atlantic seepage*: the poet imagines that water from the Atlantic seeps through the bedrock of the country and up through the bog's layers until it reaches the surface

Get In Gear

Watch Video 9. What impression does this video give you of the Irish bogland and its ability to tell us about our past?

Tease It Out

1. The poet mentions the American prairies. What comes to mind when you think of prairies? What two adjectives would you use to describe such landscapes?
2. The poet describes how the prairie slices the 'big sun at evening'. Imagine sunset on a prairie. In what manner might the landscape be said to 'slice' the sun?
3. Why do you think the poet describes the sun setting over the prairie as 'big'? What is it about such a landscape that makes the sun appear this way?
4. 'We have no prairies'. Think about the Irish landscape. How does it compare or contrast with the American prairie?
5. 'Everywhere the eye concedes to/ Encroaching horizon'. What is it about the Irish landscape that the poet is describing here? What is it that the eye must concede to when we attempt to look into the distance?
6. What is a 'tarn'? Why do you think the poet compares it to a 'cyclops' eye'? In what way might they be considered similar?
7. The poet says that our eye is 'wooed' by the tarns that are a feature of the Irish landscape. What does the term 'wooed' suggest about the appearance of these tarns?
8. Some of the Irish landscape is 'unfenced', just like the American prairie. However, the Irish 'unfenced country' is very different in composition and texture to the American prairie. What does the poet say our 'unfenced country' is comprised of?
9. How does the poet describe the cycle of day and night in line 8? What does he say happens to the bog each night and day?
10. To what does the poet compare the texture of the surface of the bog in lines 16 to 17? What does the comparison suggest about the boggy ground?
11. Why do you think the poet describes the boggy ground as 'kind'?
12. The poet makes reference to the bog's incredible powers of preservation. What items or things does he describe emerging intact from the bog? State why each discovery was remarkable.
13. What 'last definition' is the bog 'Missing'? Why is it missing this 'By millions of years'?
14. The bog is made up of layers that when stripped away reveal more layers beneath. What do you think the poet means when he says that 'Every layer... Seems camped on before'? What does the word 'camped' suggest about the nature of each occupation of the land?
15. Referring to the last two lines of the poem, how does the poet convey or suggest that there might be no end to this voyage of discovery into the bogs?
16. The poet mentions 'pioneers', 19th century explorers who journeyed across the prairies, charting the new lands of America. He suggests that in Ireland we have our own 'pioneers' who 'keep striking/ Inwards and downwards'. Consider the following questions on your own for five minutes:
    *   What sort of people does the poet have in mind here?
    *   What sort of activity involves going 'Inwards and downwards'?
    *   In what way might these people be compared with the American pioneers?
    Now pair with the person next to you and compare answers. Can you agree on your answers?

Think About Themes

1. The poem draws an interesting contrast between the Irish landscape and the American prairie. Consider the following list of adjectives: expansive; varied; soft; beautiful; unfenced; rugged; featureless; mutable; flat; awe-inspiring.
    Draw a Venn diagram, labelling one circle 'The American prairie' and the other 'The Irish landscape'. Now categorise the adjectives, placing those that correspond with both categories in the centre where the circles overlap.
3. In what way might the Irish bog be considered the memory of the landscape?
4. 'Inwards and downwards'. Do you think that these terms might be applied to the Irish race and their outlook on life? Give reasons for your answer.
5. How does the poem capture or describe the manner in which the world is constantly changing?
6. Watch Video 10. Why do you think the poet dedicated the poem to the artist T.P. Flanagan?

Language Lab

1. The poem features a number of fine metaphors. In each case state what is being described, what it is being compared to, and what the comparison suggests about it.
    *   'We have no prairies/ To slice a big sun at evening'
    *   'the cyclops' eye/ Of a tarn'
    *   'An astounding crate full of air'
    *   'The ground itself is kind, black butter'
2. The poem makes repeated references to the wet, soggy texture of the bog. Identify as many references as you can. Would you agree that the poet identifies a special kind of beauty in these descriptions of the bog? Give reasons for your answer.
3. Describe and comment on the poet's use of alliteration and assonance in lines 3 to 6.

The Tollund Man

(handwritten) Trubles - catholic v protestans

(handwritten) Tone — reverent - respectful tone towards religious

(handwritten) Denmark simple, clear, language

(handwritten) metaphor — Pees in a pod - curved, soft

(handwritten) metaphor

(handwritten) Pagan — Quiet mood - gentle description — slow pace - reflect — VS personification

I

Some day I will go to Aarhus
To see his peat-brown head,
The mild pods of his eyelids,
His pointed skin cap.

(handwritten) museum Denmark — seen something about Tollund Man

(handwritten) describing - gentle laungase

In the flat country nearby   [5]
Where they dug him out,
His last gruel of winter seeds
Caked in his stomach,

(handwritten) - last thing he ate

Naked except for
The cap, noose and girdle,   [10]
I will stand a long time.
Bridegroom to the goddess,
She tightened her torc on him
And opened her fen,
Those dark juices working   [15]
Him to a saint's kept body,

(handwritten) leater skin

(handwritten) bog → bog needs a man to reproduce - stays fertile

(handwritten) Necklace

(handwritten) Marsh

(handwritten) Moisture / sexual imagery - preserve him

Trove of the turfcutters'
Honeycombed workings.
Now his stained face
Reposes at Aarhus.   [20]

(handwritten) - Alliteration — Metaphor — metaphor — poetic imagery

(handwritten) something valuable — shape of it — Assonance - o - soft language

II

I could risk blasphemy,
Consecrate the cauldron bog
Our holy ground and pray
Him to make germinate

(handwritten) something offence to church — pay their respects — Northern Ireland

(handwritten) ground of catholics — Multiple - flourish

The scattered, ambushed   [25]
Flesh of labourers,
Stockinged corpses
Laid out in the farmyards,

(handwritten) 4 catholic brothers were killed — 1920s — Hursh sounds consonant

(handwritten) Harster sounds — unpleasant image

Tell-tale skin and teeth
Flecking the sleepers   [30]
Of four young brothers, trailed
For miles along the lines.

(handwritten) Pulled along - Traintrack — 'dragging - Assonance

(handwritten) in contrast to 1st part.

(handwritten) Sectarian violence - Religion

Tollund Man: the well-preserved body of a man who lived during the fourth century BC. He was found in 1950 on the Jutland Peninsula in Denmark, buried in a peat bog near the village of Tollund. He was discovered with a pointed leather cap on his head, a belt or 'girdle' around his waist and a noose around his neck. He'd been hanged and afterward had his body carefully placed in the bog. It's believed he died as a human sacrifice in an ancient fertility rite.

[1] **Aarhus:** city in Denmark (the Tollund Man is on display near here at a museum in Silkeborg)

[13] **torc:** a collar or necklace consisting of a twisted narrow band, in this case the rope around the Tollund Man's neck

[14] **fen:** boggy land

[16] **saint's kept body:** reference to the Catholic belief that saints' bodies do not decompose after death as a sign of their holiness

[17] **Trove:** treasure found hidden in the earth

[17] **turfcutters:** men who cut the turf from the bogs

[22] **Consecrate:** to make or declare sacred

[22] **cauldron bog:** the poet likens the bog to a pot used to brew or mix magic potions, suggesting the bog's magical ability to preserve bodies

[24] **germinate:** to cause a seed to sprout

[25-29] **Stockinged corpses ... in the farmyards:** description of the remains of farm workers executed by the Black and Tans

[30] **sleepers:** wooden beams supporting the rails on a railway track

[31] **four young brothers:** reference to the killing of four Catholic brothers by Protestant paramilitaries. Their bodies had been trailed along the railway lines, over the sleepers, as a kind of mutilation.

Heaney imagining he's the Tollund Man (handwritten)

III

Something of his sad freedom   [35]
As he rode the tumbril— *sad* (handwritten)
Should come to me, driving,
Saying the names

— mournful tone (handwritten)

— where bog men have been found (handwritten)

Tollund, Grauballe, Nebelgard,
Watching the pointing hands   [40]
Of country people,
Not knowing their tongue.

Synecdoche (handwritten)

metonymy (handwritten)

Pointing + talking about him, he doesn't speak their language (handwritten)

Out there in Jutland
In the old man-killing parishes   [45]
I will feel lost,
Unhappy and at home.

— because Heaney was from N.I (handwritten)
— 4 brothers were killed in N.I because of their religion. (handwritten)
— This place people are killed because of their religion (handwritten)
he understands it (handwritten)

> [34] **tumbril:** two-wheeled, open cart
> [37] **Tollund, Grauballe, Nebelgard:** Sites on the Jutland Peninsula in Denmark where bog bodies were discovered

Get In Gear

Watch Video 11. Why does the presenter consider the Tollund Man's death to have been a sacrificial killing rather than an execution?

Tease It Out

Section I

1. How does the poet characterise the colour of the Tollund Man's head? Why is the head this colour?
2. The poet describes the Tollund Man's eyelids as 'mild pods'. Are the Tollund Man's eyes open or shut? Why do you think the poet compares the eyelids to pods? What do 'pods' normally contain? Why do you think he describes the pods as 'mild'?
3. The Tollund Man was 'Naked except for/ The cap, noose and girdle'. What shape was the cap and what was it made from? What is a 'girdle'? Where is it worn and what purpose does it serve?
4. Around the Tollund Man's neck was a braided leather rope tightened in a noose. What does this tell us about the manner in which he died?
5. What did the Tollund Man eat before he died?
6. How does the poet describe the countryside near Aarhus, where the Tollund Man was discovered?
7. Who discovered the Tollund Man? What work were they doing when they came across the well-preserved body?
8. The poet describes the 'workings' of the men who discovered the body as 'Honeycombed'. What aspect of their work is he describing here?
9. It is believed that the Tollund Man's death was sacrificial, that his life was offered up to appease some god or goddess in order to ensure that the land remained fertile. How does the poet's description of the relationship between the bog and the Tollund Man in line 12 allude to or suggest this aspect of the Tollund Man's death?
10. Lines 12 to 16: The poet personifies the bog, describing it as a 'goddess'. How does he describe the manner in which the bog grasped or took hold of the Tollund Man? To what does the poet compare the noose that was used for the hanging?
11. The bog then 'opened her fen' and used her 'dark juices' to preserve him. What is a 'fen'? What are the 'dark juices' that the poet mentions?
12. What sort of wedding ritual or ceremony do lines 13 to 15 call to mind? Would you consider these lines to be in any way sensual or erotic? Give reasons for your answer.
13. The bog worked the Tollund Man's body to 'a saint's kept body'. Why does the poet compare the Tollund Man's body to a 'saint's' body? What is said to happen to or become of saints' bodies when they die?
14. Where does the poet say he will go 'Some day'? What will he do when he arrives at this place?

Section II

15. The poet shifts his attention or focus to Northern Ireland, where he lives, and thinks about the violence happening here. In lines 25 to 26 he describes what became of a group of 'labourers'. How did these men die? What became of their bodies after they died? How does the poet suggest that these men suffered horrifically violent deaths?

16. The poet describes how 'four young brothers' were brutally murdered and how their bodies were dragged for 'miles along' the train lines. What image does he present us with to convey their terrible fates?

17. Lines 21 to 24: The poet considers conducting some form of ritual upon the bog of his native land. What does he imagine doing? To whom does he imagine praying?

18. How does the poet characterise the Irish bog in line 22? Why do you think he describes it in this manner? How does the image correspond with what the poet is considering doing?

19. The poet hopes that his prayers will somehow 'make germinate' the terrible deaths that he describes in lines 25 to 32. What does it mean for something to 'germinate'? What do you think the poet is hoping for here?

20. Why might it be considered 'blasphemy' for the poet to 'pray' to the Tollund Man? Who would consider such an act blasphemous?

21. Contrast the manner in which the Tollund Man's body was treated after he died with the bodies of the victims Heaney describes in lines 25 to 32. Take five minutes to think about this. Write down some ideas. Now pair with the person beside you and chat about this for another five minutes. Share your ideas with the class!

Section III

22. The poet imagines himself being in Denmark, driving through the different places where bog bodies have been discovered. What does he imagine himself saying as he drives? Why do you think he might repeat these words?

23. The poet describes the 'sad freedom' that he imagines the Tollund Man would have felt as he was being brought to the place where he was to be killed or sacrificed. In what way might he have experienced a sense of 'freedom'? Why would this freedom be tinged with sadness?

24. What sort of vehicle was used to transport the Tollund Man?

25. Why do you think the poet imagines a similar sense of 'sad freedom' should come to him as he drives through Denmark?

26. Why does the poet picture or imagine the local Danish people 'pointing' their hands? What might the poet be asking for that would require such pointing?

27. How does the poet characterise the 'parishes' through which he imagines himself passing through? Why do you think he describes them in this manner?

28. 'I will feel lost,/ Unhappy and at home'. Why will the poet feel 'lost'? Why will he feel 'unhappy'? Why will he feel 'at home' in this place?

Think About Themes

1. How would you characterise the poet's attitude towards the Tollund Man's sacrificial death? Consider the following statements and say whether you consider them to be true or false. Give reasons for your answers.
   - He is outraged that a man was killed by members of his own community in this manner. Such ritual killings are no better than the brutal murders taking place in the Northern Ireland.
   - He has mixed feelings about the killing. On the one hand it is sad that someone lost their life in this manner, but the Tollund Man's death was no tragedy – this is someone who would have prepared for death and died in the belief it was for the greater good of the community.
   - He is fascinated and inspired by the manner of the Tollund Man's death and burial.
2. Why do you think the poet draws comparisons between the Tollund Man and the murdered men in Northern Ireland? What is he seeking to highlight about the violence and conflict in the North? Do you think that the comparison succeeds?
3. Why do you think the poet is drawn to the Tollund Man? What is it about this body discovered in the bog that so enthralls or interests him?
4. Consider lines 21 to 24. What does the poet's desire to pray to the Tollund Man suggest about his attitude towards the established religions in the Northern Ireland? Do you think he considers religion to be a force for good or evil? Give reasons for your answer.
5. 'Heaney's fascination with and love for the natural world is evident in 'The Tollund Man''. Write a short essay responding to this statement.

Language Lab

1. 'Trove of the turfcutters'/ Honeycombed workings'. These lines are richly poetic. Write a short paragraph discussing the poet's use of assonance, alliteration and metaphor and state what effect or impact each device has. Can you identify other instances of assonance, alliteration and metaphor in the poem?
2. 'Tell-tale skin and teeth/ Flecking the sleepers'. Discuss the poet's use of cacophony in these lines. Where in the poem can you find examples of euphony?
3. How would you characterise the mood and atmosphere of the third section of the poem? What is it that creates or determines this mood and atmosphere?

In Context

'Heaney's poems demonstrate a great admiration and respect for ritual but seem sceptical or critical of religion'. Discuss this statement making reference to at least three poems on your course.

[Handwritten annotations:]

Themes
Memory
Conflict + violence
Landscapes

Mossbawn - farmhouse
sunny days of his
childhood

Sunlight

[Handwritten annotations around title: Mossbawn, pathetic fallacy, stresses outside world c place of comfort, metaphor]

There was a sunlit absence.
The helmeted pump in the yard
heated its iron,
water honeyed

in the slung bucket   [5]
and the sun stood
like a griddle cooling
against the wall

of each long afternoon.
So, her hands scuffled   [10]
over the bakeboard,
the reddening stove

sent its plaque of heat
against her where she stood
in a floury apron   [15]
by the window.

Now she dusts the board
with a goose's wing,
now sits, broad-lapped,
with whitened nails   [20]

and measling shins:
here is a space
again, the scone rising
to the tick of two clocks.

And here is love   [25]
like a tinsmith's scoop
sunk past its gleam
in the meal-bin.

[Handwritten annotations: Alliteration, personification, Assonance, sibilance, simile, memory, Admires her skill and ability, onomatopoeia, honey, warming up, metaphor, Enjambment, metaphor, Image of Aunt, Admires her skill + abilities, flour, Alliteration - sibilance, passage of time, oven + life, simile, Assonance, Embodiment of love, passage of time, be himself]

[2] **helmeted pump:** describes how the protective iron cladding on the pump resembled a helmet, especially the bulbous part on the top

[4] **honeyed:** describes how sunlight lends the water a golden appearance resembling honey

[5] **slung:** describes how the bucket's handle is hung from the top of the pump so it can be filled

[7] **griddle:** a circular, flat iron plate that is heated and used for cooking food

[10] **scuffled:** describes how her fingers interlocked and rubbed against one another as she kneaded the dough

[11] **bakeboard:** a wooden board on which dough is kneaded and rolled

[13] **plaque of heat:** the poet imagines heat emanating from the oven door in an intangible plaque or square of warmth

[18] **goose's wing:** a feather used as a duster

[21] **measling:** having or developing red spots

[26] **tinsmith's scoop:** a scoop or spoon made of tin

[28] **meal-bin:** a container for storing flour or animal feed

Get in Gear

Do a Google image search for the following terms: 'cast iron water pump'; 'goose-wing duster'; 'tinsmith's scoop'; 'meal-bin'. Print off or save your favourite picture for each item, then answer the following questions. Are you familiar with any of these items? In what context or environment would you expect to see them?

Tease it Out

1. Where is the poem set?
2. What time of year do you imagine it is? Give a reason for your answer.
3. Heaney introduces the figure of his aunt in stanza 3. What is the aunt doing? What does the word 'scuffled' suggest about the way she works?
4. The speaker describes his aunt as 'broad-lapped'. What does this suggest about her, and about the speaker's perception of her? Is she maternal or girlish, strong or dainty? Explain your answer.
5. To what does the poet compare the surge of heat that comes out of the oven door? Why do you think he makes this comparison? What does it suggest about the manner in which the heat is radiated?
6. Consider the poet's description of the yard outside the kitchen in the first two stanzas. From what vantage point do you imagine the yard is being viewed?
7. What springs to mind when you think of a 'sunlit absence'? What 'absence' might the sun be highlighting?
8. Describe in your own words the effect that the sunlight has on the pump and the water coming out of it.
9. To what does the poet compare the sun in stanza 2? What similarities can this item be said to have to the sun?
10. Consider the phrase 'the wall// of each long afternoon.' What 'wall' can the sun be said to be 'cooling/ against' on a long afternoon? What does the word 'wall' suggest about the force of the afternoon's heat?
11. What does the speaker's aunt use to clean up after her work?
15. Why do you think that the tinsmith's scoop, symbolising love, is 'sunk past its gleam'? Pair with a classmate and consider the following possibilities, ranking them in order of likelihood:
    The love between them is 'sunk past its gleam' be cause it's past its best.
    • It represents how firmly this familial love is embed ded in both of them.
    • The love between them is 'sunk past its gleam' because although they don't verbalise it with fancy words ('gleam'), they both still know it's there.
12. The speaker notes three ways that his aunt's work has temporarily altered her appearance. Describe each in your own words.

13. Line 22: 'here is a space'. What does it say about the poet's aunt that she only allows herself to sit down after the scones are put in the oven and the workspace cleared up?
14. Line 24: 'to the tick of two clocks.' Why do you think the poet specifically mentions two clocks? What might the two clocks ticking in harmony together symbolise?

Think About Themes

1. 'Nearly every image in this poem is tinged with a sense of the marvellous. A scoop in a meal-bin comes to symbolise love; a griddle pan becomes the sun itself'. Write a short essay in response to this statement.
2. 'In phrases such as "sunlit absence" and "water honeyed", we can sense Heaney's deep nostalgia. He is looking at his childhood through rose-tinted glasses'. Do you agree or disagree with this statement? Write a few paragraphs in response.

Language Lab

1. In line 2, why do you think the speaker describes the pump as 'helmeted'? What literary device is the poet using here? Do you find this a humorous or a slightly threatening image? Explain your answer.
2. Heaney compares the heat that emerges from the heating oven to a 'plaque'. Do you find this to be an effective metaphor? Can you identify another moment in the poem where Heaney compares heat to a tangible, solid structure?
3. • Do you find the images of the cast iron water pump, goose-wing duster, tinsmith's scoop and meal-bin to be striking images or are they humble and everyday? What do you think Heaney saw in them that led him to highlight them in the poem?
4. Imagine you have been asked to make a video accompanying a reading of 'Sunlight'. What sort of lighting would you use? How would you film it – in close-ups or wider shots? Would you use music and if so, what kind? Jot down at least five bullet points describing how you would replicate the poem's tone and atmosphere on-screen.

In Context

1. 'In several of his poems, Heaney celebrates ordinary, everyday physical work and the quiet mastery of older men and women'. Discuss this statement with reference to 'Sunlight' and at least two other poems on your course.
2. 'In Heaney's work, familial love is often unspoken. If love is expressed at all, it's usually though gestures rather than words'. Do you agree with this statement? Write a short essay in response, referring to 'Sunlight' and at least one other poem on your course.

A Constable Calls

His bicycle stood at the window-sill,
The rubber cowl of a mud-splasher
Skirting the front mudguard,
Its fat black handlegrips

Heating in sunlight, the 'spud'
Of the dynamo gleaming and cocked back,   [5]
The pedal treads hanging relieved
Of the boot of the law.

His cap was upside down
On the floor, next his chair.   [10]
The line of its pressure ran like a bevel
In his slightly sweating hair.

He had unstrapped
The heavy ledger, and my father
Was making tillage returns   [15]
In acres, roods, and perches.

Arithmetic and fear.
I sat staring at the polished holster
With its buttoned flap, the braid cord
Looped into the revolver butt.   [20]

'Any other root crops?
Mangolds? Marrowstems? Anything like that?'
'No.' But was there not a line
Of turnips where the seed ran out

In the potato field? I assumed   [25]
Small guilts and sat
Imagining the black hole in the barracks.
He stood up, shifted the baton-case

Further round on his belt,
Closed the domesday book,   [30]
Fitted his cap back with two hands,
And looked at me as he said goodbye.

A shadow bobbed in the window.
He was snapping the carrier spring
Over the ledger. His boot pushed off   [35]
And the bicycle ticked, ticked, ticked.

Handwritten annotations:

Precise cold
Adjective — mudguard
Light
metal — shape of spud
Metonymy
Sibilance — notebook
Short sentence
Area
Sibilance
highly detailed description
Alliteration
weapon
intimidating
onomatopoeia
Threat + danger

personification
metaphor
↓ onomatopoeia
↓ Harsh consonant sounds
metaphor
metaphor (a gun) → harsh consonant sounds
Personification
synecdoche
→ simile
Alliteration
Crops
→ holds a gun
→ full stop
cacophony
Questions
→ childs thought
→ took them on
Imagery
imagery
metaphor
imagery
onomatopoeia
Metonymy
bomb
↓ Harsh consonant sound eg. ck, k, T

Themes
Conflict
Violence

[2] **cowl:** hood-shaped covering
[2] **mud-splasher:** cover draped over or around the mudguard
[5] **spud:** Heaney compares the dynamo's shape to a potato or 'spud'
[6] **dynamo:** a type of generator attached to a bicycle to produce electricity for the its lights
[7] **pedal treads:** the upper surface of the pedal, on which the foot is placed
[11] **bevel:** the weight of the constable's helmet produces a slanted ridge in his hair
[15] **making tillage returns:** calculating the profits arising from the production of different crops
[16] **roods:** a measure of land area, equal to a quarter of an acre
[16] **perches:** another measurement of land
[22] **Mangolds:** a variety of beet
[22] **Marrowstems:** a root vegetable, also known as kale
[30] **domesday book:** Heaney compares the constable's ledger to the record of a survey of the lands of England made by William the Conqueror in 1086

Tease It Out

The Constable's Visit

1. A police constable has come to visit the farm. How does the constable arrive?
2. The speaker says that 'my father/ Was making tillage returns'. What are tillage returns? How are these returns measured?
3. Where does the constable record this information?
4. The constable, as an agent of the state, has been sent to gather this data. Why might it be of value to the government?
5. Do you think this is a routine visit, or something out of the ordinary?

The Constable's Bicycle

6. Where does the constable park his bicycle?
7. Based on the detailed description given in lines 2 to 8, divide into pairs and discuss the different features of the bicycle. When you think you have a good understanding of what the poet is describing, attempt to sketch the bicycle that the constable rides.

The Constable

8. The constable is associated with an almost oppressive weight. He has a heavy hat, heavy boots and a heavy book. Identify the lines or images where each of these appears.
9. Line 12: The speaker takes note of the constable's 'slightly sweating hair'. How do you visualise the constable's appearance? Is he a big man or small? Do you imagine him as friendly or reserved?
10. The constable has one item of equipment in particular that fascinates the young poet. What is it?
11. 'Arithmetic and fear'. What precise arithmetic is being conducted by the constable?
12. Line 17 describes an atmosphere of 'fear'. In your opinion, who or what is generating this fear? Consider the following possibilities and rank them in order of likelihood, giving reasons for your decisions:
    - The child is afraid
    - The child detects fear coming from his father
    - The constable is nervous
    - The line refers to a broader fear in society
13. What last question does the constable ask before he leaves? What is the father's response? According to the young poet, does his father answer truthfully? What precisely is the father concealing from the constable?
14. Which do you think is the most likely reason for why the father might conceal information from the constable? As a class, discuss each of the below possibilities and then vote on the one you consider most likely.
    - He doesn't want to pay tax on this secret row of crops
    - He resents the state poking around his farm
    - He regards the constable as representative of a hated and oppressive Protestant regime

15. 'No' is the only word of the father quoted in the poem. What does this suggest about his attitude to the constable?
16. 'But was there not a line/ Of turnips where the seed ran out// In the potato field?' Can you suggest a reason why the turnips might have been planted in this location on the farm?

The Child's Reaction to the Constable

17. Look up the word 'assume' and write down its different meanings. Which meaning is intended here? Is it possible that more than one meaning is intended?
18. 'I assumed/ Small guilts'. The child feels guilty over the lie his father has told. In what way has he been party to this deception?
19. Consider the word 'small'. Did the young poet think this was a small matter at the time, or did he consider it a big deal? Give a reason for your answer.
20. What did the young poet fear might happen to him because of his part in this minor fraud?
21. Has the young poet actually seen the barracks, or is he imagining it?
22. List the different things that the constable does as he prepares to leave the house.
23. 'And looked at me as he said goodbye'. What kind of look do you imagine the constable giving the poet as he departs? Is it affectionate, suspicious or indifferent?
24. What does the poet imagine is on the constable's mind as he 'looked at [him]'?

Think About Themes

1. 'In 'A Constable Calls', Heaney vividly captures the experience of being forced to comply with a regime that treats you as a number rather than a person'. Write a short essay in response to this statement.
2. Heaney is a poet well known for his ability to capture a child's point of view. Can you identify three or four phrases or lines in the poem where a child's outlook and concerns are accurately conveyed?
3. Watch Video 12, which depicts a series of events that took place twenty years after those described in this poem. What is ticking at the conclusion of the poem? What other devices are known for producing a ticking sound? Do these lines anticipate the Troubles depicted in the video?

In Context

'The tension between two different communities that bubbles beneath the surface in 'A Constable Calls' explodes into violence in 'The Tollund Man'.' Write two paragraphs comparing the poems in light of this statement.

The Skunk

Up, black, striped and damasked like the chasuble
At a funeral Mass, the skunk's tail
Paraded the skunk. Night after night
I expected her like a visitor.

The refrigerator whinnied into silence.   [5]
My desk light softened beyond the verandah.
Small oranges loomed in the orange tree.
I began to be tense as a voyeur.

After eleven years I was composing
Love-letters again, broaching the word 'wife'   [10]
Like a stored cask, as if its slender vowel
Had mutated into the night earth and air

Of California. The beautiful, useless
Tang of eucalyptus spelt your absence.
The aftermath of a mouthful of wine   [15]
Was like inhaling you off a cold pillow.

And there she was, the intent and glamorous,
Ordinary, mysterious skunk,
Mythologised, demythologised,
Snuffing the boards five feet beyond me.   [20]

It all came back to me last night, stirred
By the sootfall of your things at bedtime,
Your head-down, tail-up hunt in a bottom drawer
For the black plunge-line nightdress.

[1]	**damasked:**	damask is a heavy patterned fabric made of linen or silk
[1]	**chasuble:**	a long sleeveless vestment worn by a priest; for funerals, a black and white chasuble is worn
[3]	**Paraded the skunk:**	the skunk's tail is so lavish and prominent that, to the poet, it seems to be leading the skunk rather than the other way around
[5]	**whinnied:**	describes how the sound of the refrigerator resembles the neighing of a horse
[6]	**verandah:**	a large open porch across the front of a house
[8]	**voyeur:**	person who gains sexual pleasure and excitement from watching others
[10]	**broaching:**	to broach is to mention a subject; also to pierce a cask in order to draw out the liquid within
[12]	**mutate:**	to change; in linguistics, a mutation is a change in the sound of a vowel
[14]	**eucalyptus:**	a type of gum tree with aromatic leaves
[20]	**Snuffing:**	the sniffing sounds made by an animal as it investigates an object's scent
[22]	**sootfall:**	the soft sound of soot falling down the inside of a chimney

Tease It Out

Stanza 1

1. What is a 'chasuble' and what colour is the chasuble worn at a funeral Mass? Do you think that it's reasonable to compare the skunk's tail to this garment? Would you agree that it's a surprising comparison?
2. '[T]he skunk's tail/ Paraded the skunk'. What might we consider surprising about this statement?
3. Consider the verb 'parade'. What does it suggest about the manner in which the skunk moved? Does it creep about stealthily or strut in a confident and carefree fashion?
4. How often does the poet see the skunk?
5. Based on your reading of the first stanza, do you think the poet looked forward to seeing this 'visitor', actively disliked its appearances or was indifferent to them? Give a reason for your answer.
6. The poet refers to the skunk as 'she'. Why do you think he assumes it's a female? It isn't easy, after all, to tell male and female skunks apart.

Stanza 2

7. The poet describes himself writing in the evening. What phrase indicates that his desk is positioned near the back door of his house?
8. Can his desk light illuminate much of the yard outside? What species of tree grows there?
9. What animals typically produce a whinnying sound? Do you think this is a good comparison for the humming produced by a refrigerator? Was anything else audible in the house?
10. What kind of behaviour do voyeurs typically engage in? Why might this make them tense?
11. Why might the poet describe himself as a voyeur? What does he long to see on this particular evening?

Stanzas 3 and 4

12. In what part of the world were these events taking place? What phrase indicates that the poet's wife didn't accompany him on this stay?
13. The poet claims that he hadn't written his wife any love letters over the previous eleven years. Can you suggest two different reasons why this might have been the case?
14. In a most unusual metaphor, the poet compares the word 'wife' to a cask or barrel of wine. Break into pairs and answer the following questions:
    - Is he thinking of a new vintage or an aged one? Give a reason for your answer.
    - How does one broach a cask of wine? (Google it!) The poet describes himself broaching the word 'wife'. But how can you broach a word in this way? What precisely does the poet have in mind here?
    - The poet imagines this vowel spreading into the 'night earth and air' like the scent from a just-broached barrel. What does this suggest about his feelings toward his absent wife?

15. The poet describes how the 'Tang' or scent of the ucalyptus trees seems almost to communicate with him. What does it 'spell' out or remind him of?
16. The poet remembers 'inhaling' his wife's scent. From what surface did he breathe it in? Do you think his wife was present when he did this?
17. What taste, now that he's far away from her in California, reminds him of this aroma?

Stanza 5

18. What phrase indicates the suddenness with which the skunk makes its appearance in the poet's yard?
19. Consider the adjectives 'ordinary', 'mysterious', 'intent' and 'glamorous'. Working in pairs, describe in your own words what each suggests about the skunk's demeanour and behaviour. Is it possible for something to be both 'ordinary' and 'mysterious' at the same time?
20. What does the skunk do to the boards of the poet's verandah?
21. At this moment how far is the skunk from the poet's writing desk?

Stanza 6

22. This stanza takes place some years after the poet's stay in California. What phrase indicates this jump forward in time?
23. What are the 'things' referred to in line 22?
24. What kind of sound does soot make when it falls down a chimney? What reminds the poet of this sound now?
25. The poet describes how he's 'stirred' by the sound he's hearing. What do you think he means by this?
26. What is his wife looking for in the bottom drawer?
27. 'It all came back to me'. Why do you think this incident reminds the poet of his stay in California?

Think About Themes

1. The poet clearly misses his wife while he's in California. List the different ways in which he expresses this.
2. Would you agree that there's a sense in which the poet has taken his wife ever-so-slightly for granted? That he only appreciates how wonderful she is when he's far away from her?
3. For the poet, the skunk becomes 'Mythologised'. He starts to think of it as something greater than it really is, its nightly visits somehow coming to stand in for the wife he misses so much. Write two paragraphs in response to this statement, in which you refer to each of the following words or phrases: 'I expected her'; 'there she was'; 'demythologised'; 'tense as a voyeur'; 'glamorous'; 'ordinary'; 'mysterious'.
4. 'This poem's final stanza celebrates how erotic love continues even in marriages and long-term relationships'. Write a paragraph in response to this statement.

The Harvest Bow

As you plaited the harvest bow
You implicated the mellowed silence in you
In wheat that does not rust
But brightens as it tightens twist by twist
Into a knowable corona,
A throwaway love-knot of straw.

Hands that aged round ashplants and cane sticks
And lapped the spurs on a lifetime of gamecocks
Harked to their gift and worked with fine intent
Until your fingers moved somnambulant: [10]
I tell and finger it like braille,
Gleaning the unsaid off the palpable,

And if I spy into its golden loops
I see us walk between the railway slopes
Into an evening of long grass and midges,   [15]
Blue smoke straight up, old beds and ploughs in hedges,
An auction notice on an outhouse wall –
You with a harvest bow in your lapel,

Me with the fishing rod, already homesick
For the big lift of these evenings, as your stick   [20]
Whacking the tips off weeds and bushes
Beats out of time, and beats, but flushes
Nothing: that original townland
Still tongue-tied in the straw tied by your hand.

The end of art is peace   [25]
Could be the motto of this frail device
That I have pinned up on our deal dresser –
Like a drawn snare
Slipped lately by the spirit of the corn
Yet burnished by its passage, and still warm.   [30]

Harvest Bow: a bow that was traditionally woven from fresh straw at harvest time; worn to celebrate a fruitful harvest and sometimes given as a token of affection

[2] **implicated:** to convey or suggest; to be held responsible for something; to weave or entwine. All three meanings are relevant here, as the poet describes how his relationship with his father is expressed through the harvest bow

[4] **brightens as it tightens:** tightening the straw dries it out and prevents it from rotting so it retains its golden colour

[5] **corona:** a circle of light surrounding a moon or planetary body; a crown or crown-like structure

[7] **ashplants:** walking sticks made from ash

[7] **cane sticks:** walking canes

[8] **lapped the spurs:** spurs are the sharp protrusions of bone at the sides of the cock's claws. These were 'lapped' or covered with pieces of cloth in order to prevent injury

[8] **game cocks:** a type of rooster bred for fighting

[9] **Harked:** listened to

[10] **somnambulant:** as if sleepwalking; describes how the father's fingers moved with an absentminded ease

[11] **braille:** a system of writing designed for use by the blind and visually impaired in which words are read by touch

[12] **Gleaning:** to obtain information; to reap or gather (both meanings are relevant here)

[12] **palpable:** tangible, capable of being touched

[18] **lapel:** the fold on each side of a coat or jacket just below the collar

[22] **flushes:** in this instance, refers to beating bushes to scare out any birds that might be hiding in them

[25] **The end of art is peace:** a quote from the English writer Coventry Patmore

[26] **device:** an implement or tool, but also a symbol or emblem

[27] **dresser:** a piece of furniture with drawers and shelves, used for displaying kitchenware

[28] **snare:** a trap set for capturing birds

[30] **burnished:** polished

Get In Gear

Watch Video 13 of Seamus Heaney reading 'The Harvest Bow' and 'A Call'. Describe in your own words how these bows were manufactured. Why, according to the poet, did this tradition originate?

Tease It Out

Stanza 1

1. The poet describes his father making a harvest bow. From what substance is it manufactured?
2. Consider the words 'plaited', 'tightens' and 'twists'. What do they suggest about the process by which the bow was created?
3. Class Discussion: The poet describes the bow as 'knowable'. What does he learn or know through contemplating the harvest bow? And is this knowledge gained by touching it, by looking at it or through both senses? Give a reason for your answer.
4. A 'corona' can be defined as a) the glow around the edge of the sun or b) a crown or crown-like structure. Which definition do you think Heaney has in mind here? Do you think both definitions could be relevant? Give a reason for your answer.
5. What word suggests that the harvest bow wasn't intended to last for a very long time, that it was created as a disposable piece of decoration?
6. The bow is described as a 'love-knot' or love token. For whom, do you think, was this token of love intended?

Stanza 2

7. Throughout his life, the poet's father handled 'ashplants' and 'cane sticks'. Suggest several different uses the father, as a farmer, might have made of these implements.
8. Roosters and cockerels are born with 'spurs' of bone that protrude from their claws. What do you think the word 'lapped' means, in the context of these spurs? Suggest why farmers might carry out such a procedure on their male poultry.
9. Consider the questions below on your own for five minutes and jot down some ideas, before comparing notes with the person beside you. Finally, share your ideas with the class.
   - What phrase suggests that in making the harvest bow the father is responding to some impulse, talent or calling that lay deep within his psyche?
   - What phrase suggests that the poet's father initially worked with intense concentration?
   - What phrase suggests that after a while the father didn't even need to concentrate anymore, that his fingers seemed to be moving automatically?

Stanzas 3 and 4

10. The poet remembers taking a stroll with his father. At what time of day did this take place?
11. Identify three hints that suggest that this walk took place at harvest time, toward the end of summer or in early autumn.
12. What phrase indicates that it was a still and windless evening? What indications are there that this was a rural, farming environment?
13. What was the poet carrying?
14. Consider the phrase 'big lift'. What does it suggest about the evening sky? Have you personally ever experienced the optical illusion that makes the sky seem bigger or higher at certain times of the year?
15. What was the father doing as they walked along the country road?
16. Did the rhythm of his stick match the rhythm of their footsteps?
17. Class Discussion: What other meaning might the phrase 'out of time' have? What does it suggest about the father and his ways in the modern world?
18. The father, we're told, 'flushes nothing' as he beats the bushes with his stick. What might he have been attempting to flush or scare from the hedgerows?

Stanza 5

19. The poet has kept one of the bows made by his father. Where exactly in his house has he positioned it?
20. 'The end of art is peace'. Write a few lines describing what you understand by this statement.
21. The poet declares that this phrase could be the 'motto' of the harvest bow. What does this suggest about his attitude toward this object?
22. Using a simile, the poet compares the harvest bow to a snare used for trapping animals. Is this a valid or accurate visual comparison in your opinion? Give a reason for your answer.
23. What, according to the poet, has recently been trapped by this snare? Has this object or entity managed to escape? What two traces has it left on the bow?

Think About Themes

1. The poet suggests that certain things were 'unsaid' between himself and his father. Suggest two different topics or areas of conversation they might have avoided. Would you agree that such reluctance or difficulty in communication is relatively common among Irish fathers and sons?
2. Would you agree that the memory depicted in stanzas 4 and 5 is presented in an especially vivid fashion? What images or details create this effect?
3. 'This poem highlights Heaney's great respect for and interest in traditional craft'. Write a short paragraph in response to this statement.

Honeymoon with his wife.

The Underground

tmase - High Arched

There we were in the vaulted tunnel running,   *special coat*
You in your going-away coat speeding ahead   *greek god pan*
And me, me then like a fleet god gaining
Upon you before you turned to a reed

carefree simile - light hearted

metaphor   *splash of beetroot on her coat*
Or some new white flower japped with crimson   *tmase [5] - loss of virginity*
As the coat flapped wild and button after button
Sprang off and fell in a trail   *Allusion - Alluding to mythology / fairytales.*
Between the Underground and the Albert Hall.

Alliteration, Assonance

Honeymooning, mooning around, late for the Proms,   *him to follow*
Our echoes die in that corridor and now   *trail for [10]*
I come as Hansel came on the moonlit stones
Retracing the path back, lifting the buttons   *eerie, Thrilling*

sense of chase or sense of following each other + chasing eachother

cold, unwelcoming   *way back - retracing path back*

To end up in a draughty lamplit station
After the trains have gone, the wet track   *Train track*
Bared and tensed as I am, all attention   *[15]*
For your step following and damned if I look back.

personified combined with Simile

responsibility   *loose her forever, nice ending*

[1] **vaulted:** arched
[3] **fleet god:** the Greek god Pan, who was half-man, half-goat, associated with great sexual prowess
[4] **before you turned to a reed:** a reference to the myth of Syrinx: she ran away from Pan in order to escape his sexual attentions. As Pan was about to catch her she prayed to the gods for help. They responded by transforming her into a reed, thereby allowing her to escape Pan's clutches
[5] **japped:** spattered or stained
[7] **the Albert Hall:** a concert hall in South Kensington, London
[8] **the Proms:** a series of classical music concerts presented each summer by the BBC
[11] **Hansel:** The young boy from the fairytale 'Hansel and Gretel'. Hansel leaves a trail of breadcrumbs behind them as they trek through the woods in order to later find their way back home
[16] **damned if I look back:** a reference to the Greek myth of Orpheus and Eurydice. When Eurydice died, her husband, Orpheus, freed her from the Underworld on the condition that he could not look back at his wife until they reached the earth. Just as they were about to return to the land of the living, Orpheus glanced back. Eurydice vanished and Orpheus lost her forever

Get in Gear

Watch Video 14 of Seamus Heaney speaking about and reading this poem. What feelings or emotions come across from his performance of the poem? Does his reading style convey regret, anger, fondness, nostalgia, or something else entirely?

Tease It Out

1. The poet remembers the honeymoon he took with his wife. Which city did they visit?

2. What does the phrase 'going-away coat' suggest – do you think this was a special coat? Why might the wife have worn it on this occasion?

3. What does the word 'vaulted' suggest about the size and structure of the tunnel in which they find themselves? Do you envisage this as a tunnel containing the train platforms or one leading from the platforms to the road above?

4. The couple are 'running' through this tunnel. Suggest two or three reasons why they might be in such a hurry.

5. The wife is running ahead of the husband. What phrase indicates this?

6. The wife's coat 'flapped wild' as they exited the Underground. Write a couple of lines describing what you visualise happening to the coat. Suggest what might have been responsible for the coat's flapping motion.

7. What happened to the buttons of the coat as the couple moved through the city streets?

8. Toward what venue were they headed, and what event were they due to attend there?

9. Consider the phrase 'mooning around'. What does it mean? Can you think of any other colloquial expressions that mean the same thing? What does this phrase suggest about the behaviour or demeanour of the couple before leaving for the Albert Hall?

10. 'Our echoes die in that corridor'. What corridor is the poet referring to? Is it the Underground station, or a tunnel leading from the station, or a corridor in the Albert Hall? Give a reason for your answer.

11. '[A]nd now'. The poem's last six lines take place in the present tense, sometime after the concert in the Albert Hall. How much time do you imagine has transpired between the concert and what the poet is now experiencing? Is it later in the same night, some days later at the end of the honeymoon, or even months or years later?

12. The poet finds himself walking the cobbled streets of the city. What phrase indicates that darkness has fallen and it is now night-time?

13. Is the poet alone? Give a reason for your answer.

14. What does he use to retrace his steps back to the station?

15. To what fairytale character does he compare himself?

16. What is the station like when he gets there? What information do we glean about the weather from his description?

17. What phrase indicates that the trains have stopped running for the night?

18. The poet describes himself as being 'Bared and tensed'. What does this suggest about his state of mind as he moves through the empty station? How do we usually use the word 'bared'? What might its use in this context suggest about the poet's feelings of vulnerability?

19. '[Y]our step following'. Who do you think was walking behind the poet?

20. What phrase indicates the poet's intense focus on the sound of this person's steps?

21. '[D]amned if I look back'. Why do you think the poet was unwilling to look behind at the person following him? In what other ways do we use the word 'damned'? How might they be relevant in this context?

22. Reread lines 11 to 16. Write a paragraph in your own words describing what occurs.

23. Do you think these events, or anything like them, ever really happened? Or is this simply a story that Heaney invented? Give a reason for your answer.

Think About Themes

1. Read the myth of Orpheus and Eurydice. In what ways does the last stanza of the poem resemble this myth? In what ways does it differ?

2. The last six lines of the poem present a bizarre situation where the poet walks through the streets and the underground station, followed by his wife. He listens intently for her every step behind him, but like Orpheus believes that if he looks back something terrible will happen. Pair with a classmate and consider the following possibilities, ranking them in order of likelihood:
   - The poet has fallen out of love with his wife
   - The poet worries that she has fallen out of love with him
   - One of them is moving to another country, forcing them to have a long-distance relationship
   - Nothing at all – these are just a series of cool images that the poet came up with

3. 'The poem's opening ten lines capture the energy and excitement of young love'. Write a paragraph in response to this statement.

4. Atmosphere is a very important feature of this poem. Pick three words that best capture the atmosphere of a) its first ten lines and b) its second ten lines.

5. Would you agree that each of these two sections of the poem represents a very different moment in a relationship?

6. Read the story of Pan and Syrinx. Why does the poet describe himself and his wife in these terms? Is the idea of virginity important here? Remember, the poem is set in a honeymoon in 1965, a time when sex before marriage was relatively uncommon.

The Pitchfork

Of all implements, the pitchfork was the one
That came near to an imagined perfection:
When he tightened his raised hand and aimed with it,
It felt like a javelin, accurate and light. [5]

So whether he played the warrior or the athlete
Or worked in earnest in the chaff and sweat,
He loved its grain of tapering, dark-flecked ash
Grown satiny from its own natural polish. [10]

Riveted steel, turned timber, burnish, grain,
Smoothness, straightness, roundness, length and sheen. [15]
Sweat-cured, sharpened, balanced, tested, fitted.
The springiness, the clip and dart of it.

And then when he thought of probes that reached the farthest,
He would see the shaft of a pitchfork sailing past [20]
Evenly, imperturbably through space,
Its prongs starlit and absolutely soundless –

But has learned at last to follow that simple lead
Past its own aim, out to an other side
Where perfection – or nearness to it – is imagined
Not in the aiming but the opening hand.

[6] *in earnest:* in a serious manner, with determination
[6] *chaff:* husks separated from seeds during threshing
[7] *tapering:* gradually becoming thinner toward one end
[8] *satiny:* smooth and silky to the touch
[9] *Riveted:* a rivet is a metal bolt or pin; in this instance, rivets bind the pitchfork's metal teeth to its wooden handle
[9] *burnish:* polish
[11] *cured:* preserved, usually by salting
[15] *imperturbably:* calmly and in an untroubled fashion; describes how the probe moves steadily through the vastness of space

Get In Gear

Video 15: This video contains a news item on NASA's space probe Juno. Watch the video carefully, then answer the following questions:

- How long has Juno been flying through space? What was the probe's destination?
- Describe in your own words the shape and movement of the probe.
- List three aspects of the planet investigated by Juno.
- What eventually happened to Juno?

Tease It Out

1. 'The farmer thinks of his pitchfork as a perfect implement'. Is this statement true or false? Write a few lines explaining your answer.
2. The farmer makes believe that the pitchfork is a different type of implement. What does he pretend it is?
3. Both warriors and athletes use this other implement, but in very different ways. What does each do with it?
4. What does the farmer do with the pitchfork during these moments of play-acting?
5. The farmer, of course, also uses the pitchfork 'in earnest', for serious work. Based on your reading of the poem, can you determine what task he performs with it?
6. From what type of wood is the pitchfork's handle manufactured? Read lines 7 to 10 carefully. List everything we learn about the handle's shape.
7. From what substance are its prongs manufactured? How are they secured to its handle?
8. Consider the words 'satiny', 'burnish', 'smoothness' and 'sheen'. What feature of the pitchfork do they emphasise?
9. How is wood usually cured? What effect does this produce? (Google it!) How has the pitchfork's handle been cured?
10. What words or phrases suggest that the farmer cares for and maintains this implement?
11. What line suggests the light and nimble nature of the pitchfork?
12. What technological wonder reminds the farmer of his pitchfork? Does this comparison surprise you? What visual similarities might exist between these two very different objects?
13. Line 13: To what does 'the farthest' refer? Is the poet referring to 'the farthest' reaches of space or does he simply mean the probes that can travel 'the farthest'? Could it be both? Give a reason for your answer.
14. What illuminates these reaches of space, as the farmer imagines them? What noise conditions does he imagine prevailing here? Is this scientifically accurate?

15. Line 17: Who or what has 'learned' to follow a 'simple lead'? What do you understand by the term to 'follow your own lead'? How might this phrase apply to the trajectory of a space probe or a pitchfork?
16. According to the poet, the pitchfork-probe travels 'Past its own aim'? Has it a) overshot and missed its target or b) travelled farther than was ever intended or envisaged? Give a reason for your answer.
17. The poet refers to 'an other side' in line 18. Where might this 'other side' be located?
18. Think about throwing a ball or a javelin. What associations do the phrases 'aiming hand' and 'opening hand' have for you? How might 'perfection' be imagined in each of these? Which is most important to get right?

Think About Themes

1. In pairs, give some thought to the following statements and discuss and record your responses:
   - Perfection, according to the poet, can only be 'imagined'. It can never actually be attained.
   - The farmer finds something approaching perfection in the pitchfork, an implement superbly suited to its purpose.
   - The poem suggests two different understandings of perfection. There's one 'on this side' associated with the 'aiming hand' and one on 'the other side' associated with the 'opening hand'.

   Share your thoughts with the rest of the class.
2. 'Heaney is well known as a poet of the marvellous and in this poem he finds it in both the most traditional of tools and the most futuristic of technology'. Write a paragraph in response to this statement.
3. 'Heaney's celebration of craftsmanship is nowhere more evident than in 'The Pitchfork', where he lavishes praise on this humblest of instruments, reminding us of its everyday beauty and its fitness for purpose'. Write a paragraph in response to this statement.

Language Lab

1. The rich detail and imagery in this poem is a source of pleasure for the reader. Would you agree with this statement? Explain your answer.
2. Discuss the use of punctuation in 'The Pitchfork'. Over the course of this poem, commas gradually give way to dashes. What effect do the dashes have on the pace and rhythm of the final two stanzas?
3. Describe how the closing lines refer back to the opening stanza. What effect does this have on the tone and atmosphere of the poem?

Lightenings VIII

The annals say: when the monks of Clonmacnoise
Were all at prayers inside the oratory
A ship appeared above them in the air.

The anchor dragged along behind so deep
It hooked itself into the altar rails   [5]
And then, as the big hull rocked to a standstill,

A crewman shinned and grappled down the rope
And struggled to release it. But in vain.
'This man can't bear our life here and will drown,'

The abbot said, 'unless we help him.' So   [10]
They did, the freed ship sailed, and the man climbed back
Out of the marvellous as he had known it.

Lightening: becoming lighter or less dark

[1]   *annals:* the Annals of Clonmacnoise, a seventeenth-century translation of chronicles or historical records thought to be based on materials gathered at the monastery of Clonmacnoise

[1]   *Clonmacnoise:* monastery situated in County Offaly on the River Shannon, founded in the sixth century AD

[2]   *oratory*: small chapel or room used for prayers

[6]   *hull*: the main body of a ship including the bottom, sides and deck

[7]   *shinned:* to shin or 'shinny' is to climb a rope by gripping it with the arms and legs

[10]   *abbot*: the head of a monastery

Get In Gear

This poem is set in Clonmacnoise, a monastery in Co. Offaly. Search online for information about Clonmacnoise and write a paragraph summarising your research.

Tease It Out

1. What are the 'annals'? Would you expect the annals to have authority and be accurate in their information? Explain your answer.
2. The poem describes the monks at Clonmacnoise monastery. What do you imagine life was like in this monastery? What adjectives would you use to describe the atmosphere at such a place?
3. The monks were at prayer in the oratory, which we might imagine was open-roofed. What enormous object appeared above them?
4. How do you imagine the monks responding to the appearance of this vessel?
5. The ship appears to sail on the earth's atmosphere, just as our ships sail on the surface of the ocean. How do you imagine the crewmen, therefore, view the earth's surface? Do you think that they would be able to survive if they descended to this level? Give a reason for your answer.
6. What drags behind the ship and gets caught in the 'altar rails'? What effect does this have?
7. What sounds do you imagine can be heard as the enormous ship comes to a halt?
8. Try to visualise the manner in which one of the ship's crewmen descends the rope. Describe in your own words the technique he uses to descend.
9. Why do you think the crewman struggles to release the anchor?
10. How do you imagine the monks are behaving as they witness this man coming down the rope to free his ship?
11. What is it that the abbot suddenly realises as he watches the crewman struggle to release the anchor?
12. How do the monks help the crewman? What does the crewman then do?
13. What do you think the poet means by 'the marvellous as he had known it'? How might the monks and the oratory have appeared to the crewman?

Think About Themes

1. 'The poem makes the point that the marvellous is to a large extent a matter of perspective. What is ordinary and mundane to one person will be extraordinary and marvellous to another'. Write a few short paragraphs outlining your response to this statement.
2. Do you think that the poet is suggesting that the marvellous is a rare phenomenon, something that we hardly ever experience in our lives, or do you think he is suggesting that the everyday world around us can be considered marvellous if we just take the time to view it in the right way?

Language Lab

1. How would you describe the tone and atmosphere of this piece? For a poem that describes an extraordinary event, does the language present a contrast to this marvellous occurrence? Why might Heaney have made this stylistic choice?
2. What image in the poem had the biggest impact on you? Give a reason for your choice.

[handwritten: Phone call with his father.]

A Call

[handwritten: nothing specifically special]

[handwritten left margin: deeper meaning - called from life]

[handwritten: Dialogue / conversational everyday speech]

'Hold on,' she said, 'I'll just run out and get him.
The weather here's so good, he took the chance
To do a bit of weeding.'

[handwritten: monosyllabic]

        So I saw him

[handwritten: monosyllabic]

Down on his hands and knees beside the leek rig, [5]
Touching, inspecting, separating one
Stalk from the other, gently pulling up
Everything not tapered, frail and leafless,
Pleased to feel each little weed-root break,
But rueful also … [10]

[handwritten: Verbs / Highlights the craft]
[handwritten: gentle, careful, kind man / onomatopoeia]
[handwritten: Active]
[handwritten: Admiration for a skill - fathers craft in the garden.]
[handwritten: image]
[handwritten: ruefully ending weeds life]

[handwritten left margin: father is aging]

            Then found myself listening to
The amplified grave ticking of hall clocks
Where the phone lay unattended in a calm
Of mirror glass and sunstruck pendulums …

[handwritten: empty hall]
[handwritten: metaphor - passage of time + aging.]
[handwritten: Assonance]
[handwritten: ellipsis - punctuation mark - something yet to come]

[handwritten left margin: conscious]

And found myself then thinking: if it were nowadays, [15]
This is how Death would summon Everyman.

Next thing he spoke and I nearly said I loved him.

[handwritten: monosyllabic]
[handwritten left margin: complex]

[5] **leek rig:** a structure around the plot where the leeks are growing
[8] **tapered:** becoming thinner towards one end
[10] **rueful:** sad, regretful
[14] **pendulum:** a swinging weight that regulates the mechanism of a clock
[16] **Death would summon Everyman:** refers to a 15th century play with a Christian message. A character called Everyman, representing all mankind, is summoned by Death. Everyman is permitted to take one companion with him to the next world. Characters called Fellowship, Knowledge, Goods, Strength and Beauty are all either unwilling or unable to accompany him. In the end it is only Good Deeds who can travel with him to the afterlife and final judgment

[handwritten: Meticulously]

Get In Gear

1. Watch Video 16, which is based on the medieval play called *Everyman*. What in your opinion are the three or four main things this story says about death and dying?
2. The play was written for a Christian audience. Do you believe its message is relevant to believers and non-believers alike?

Tease It Out

1. The poet has called his father but somebody else answers. Who might this person be who answers the phone? Bear in mind that the poem describes a period when the poet's father was quite old.
2. Do you think the poet has called a mobile phone or a landline?
3. 'I'll just run out and get him'. Where was the poet's father and what was he doing?
4. 'So I saw him'. Is the poet imagining his father, or is he actually seeing him over Skype or Facetime, or some other videocall application?
5. What is a 'leek rig' and how does it function?
6. The poet's father is surveying his crop of leeks with great focus and attention. Identify the words and phrases that suggest this.
7. What is the father 'pulling up' out of the soil?
8. The poet envisages the leeks as being 'tapered, frail and leafless'. The weeds on the other hand are the opposite of this. Pick three words that in your opinion best describe the weeds.
9. The father plucks each weed individually. What does he feel break each time he does this?
10. Why might this sensation please the father?
11. What does the word 'rueful' mean?
12. Why might the father feel rueful each time he plucks a weed?
13. In what part of the house is the father's phone located?
14. As the poet waits for his father to come to the phone, what can he hear?
15. Class Discussion: Suggest why there might be more than one clock in the hallway. What type of clocks do you imagine? What might have caused the clocks to sound 'amplified'?
16. In lines 13 to 14 the poet visualises the hallway in some detail. Write a short paragraph describing this scene in your own words, noting its atmosphere, the light, and the different objects present.
17. Do you think the poet is very familiar with this house and this particular room?
18. Who was Everyman? How did Death summon him? What did this summons by Death mean?
19. The poet imagines the story of Everyman taking place today. What technology would Death use to summon Everyman in today's modern world?
20. What do these thoughts suggest about the father's physical and mental state?
21. What does the poet want to say to his father when he comes to the phone? Does he actually say this? Suggest why.

Think About Themes

1. Lines 6 to 10 suggest a great deal about the character of the poet's father. Consider the following traits or characteristics. Which of the following traits is suggested most strongly in the text? Rank them in order.
   - Pride in his work
   - Good with his hands
   - Attention to detail
   - Kind-hearted
   - Practical or pragmatic
   - Sensitive to nature's beauty
   - Loves working with the natural world
2. The poet's father is in his latter years. How does the poet feel about the fact that his father might soon be dead? Does he clearly state how he feels?
3. Death all too often strikes when we least expect it. In the Bible, for instance, there is a saying that death comes like a thief in the night. In the medieval play death interrupts Everyman as he is busy with his affairs. How does Heaney update this personification for the modern age?
4. Would you agree that the poet's affection and admiration for his father are obvious throughout the poem?
5. Why is he unwilling or unable to express this affection in the poem's final line? What does this suggest about the relationship between the two men?
6. Class Discussion: Do you think this father-son relationship is typical of Irish men? Would you classify it as a healthy or dysfunctional relationship?

Language Lab

1. This is a poem about death and frailty. How might the following contribute: the leeks, the weeds, the clocks?
2. Comment on the word 'grave' in line 12. What two meanings of this word might be intended here?
3. The description of the hall is richly atmospheric. How would you characterise this atmosphere? Is it sombre and forbidding, or peaceful and soothing?
4. Imagine it was Death on the phone, rather than the poet. How would the father react to being summoned into the afterlife? Would he respond with calmness and acceptance, or disbelief and rage? Would he bargain and plead as Everyman did in the video?
5. 'I nearly said I loved him'. Write the dialogue that you think actually occurred between the poet and his father.

Postscript

And some time make the time to drive out west
Into County Clare, along the Flaggy Shore,
In September or October, when the wind
And the light are working off each other
So that the ocean on one side is wild   [5]
With foam and glitter, and inland among stones
The surface of a slate-grey lake is lit
By the earthed lightning of a flock of swans,
Their feathers roughed and ruffling, white on white,
Their fully grown headstrong-looking heads   [10]
Tucked or cresting or busy underwater.
Useless to think you'll park and capture it
More thoroughly. You are neither here nor there,
A hurry through which known and strange things pass
As big soft buffetings come at the car sideways   [15]
And catch the heart off guard and blow it open.

Postscript: last-minute addition to a letter, often written quickly and casually and added after the letter has been signed. Can also refer to a section added to a book at the last minute, often between the completion of the main work and its publication

[2] **Flaggy Shore:** beautiful stony beach on one of the most northerly parts of Co. Clare, in the Burren. The stones here have been worn flat by the sea, resembling 'flag stones'

[8] **earthed lightning:** the swans are so brilliantly bright that they resemble bolts of lightning that have been attracted by some kind of earthing device and anchored to the ground

[9] **ruffling:** to ruffle is to make the feathers stand erect

[10] **headstrong:** proud, stubborn

[11] **cresting:** describes the swans' heads when they are level with the water's surface

[15] **buffetings**: to buffet is to batter or strike repeatedly

Get In Gear

Have you visited or are you familiar with the coast of Co Clare, where this poem is set? Do a Google search for 'the Flaggy Shore' and write a short paragraph describing your impressions. What geological features is it famous for?

Tease It Out

1. Class Discussion: Who is the 'you' referred to in this poem? Is the speaker addressing a specific person, such as a friend or acquaintance? Or is it possible that he's even addressing himself?
2. What trip does the speaker recommend in the opening lines?
3. When, according to the speaker, is the best time to visit this location?
4. Read lines 5 to 7, where the speaker remembers or visualises driving along the Clare coastline. What can be seen on each side of the car as he drives by?
5. Class Discussion: The speaker claims that the wind and light are 'working off each other'. Does it suggest that these forces are working together or are they in conflict? How is it possible for these two intangible elements to interact at all? How do you visualise the effect they have on the landscape and on the surface of the ocean?
6. Is the ocean calm or stormy or somewhere in between? What causes the appearance of 'glitter' on its surface?
7. What phrase indicates that this is a rough and rugged landscape? What colour is the lake the poet passes by? What might have lent it this shade?
8. What might be responsible for roughing up and ruffling the feathers of the swans?
9. What human emotion does the speaker attribute to the swans? Have you ever personally observed swans at rest on water? If so would you agree that this description seems accurate and appropriate?
10. Describe in your own words the three different ways the swans position their heads. Why might their heads be 'Tucked'? What might they be 'busy' doing 'underwater'?
11. 'The speaker feels it'd be a good idea to park, step out of the car and take a moment to more fully appreciate the scene'. Is this statement true or false? Give a reason for your answer.
12. The speaker imagines being 'A hurry' that things pass through. Consider this unusual turn of phrase. Have you ever heard a person described as a 'hurry' before? What does it suggest about the pace at which the speaker is travelling this beautiful landscape?
13. Line 15 describes the wind's impact on the speaker's car as he drives along the coast. Is the wind closer in force to a mild breeze or a howling gale? Does its impact on the car make the speaker uneasy or is he quite comfortable being buffeted by these gusts?
14. What does the speaker mean by the phrase 'You are neither here nor there'? Consider the following possibilities and rank them in order of likelihood, giving reasons for your decisions:

    - He is referring to the car journey: he's between his starting point and his destination
    - The scene before him is so magical that he feels suspended between the real world and a mysterious, dreamlike world
    - The speaker, because he's sealed within a car, is somehow both present and not present in the landscape that surrounds him
    - He is referring to the contrast between the 'wild' ocean and the more tranquil lake

Think About Themes

1. "Some time make the time' is not only the opening phrase but also the most important message of this poem. It's a work that urges us to find a space for beauty and contemplation amid the stresses and strains of modern life'. Write a paragraph in response to this statement.
2. "Postscript' is an ode to driving, capturing how settling into a long car journey can be a pleasantly meditative experience, allowing both expected and unfamiliar thoughts to pass through the mind'. Would you agree with this interpretation of the poem's conclusion? Give a reason for your answer.

Language Lab

1. Consider the questions below on your own for five minutes and jot down some ideas, before comparing notes with the person beside you. Finally, share your ideas with the class.
    - What does it mean for a bolt of lightning to be 'earthed'? What device is used in this process and how does it work?
    - The poet compares the floating swans to such 'earthed' lightning. Do you find this metaphor an effective one? What similarity, if any, allows the comparison these two very different things?
    - According to the speaker, this 'flock of swans' illuminates the lake on which they float. Describe in your own words what you visualise here. Does the speaker mean this in a metaphorical or in a literal fashion?
2. Can you suggest why Heaney might have chosen the title 'Postscript' for his poem? What features of a typical postscript does it possess or not possess? (It's worth noting that this was the final poem in his collection *The Spirit Level*).

Tate's Avenue

Not the brown and fawn car rug, that first one
Spread on sand by the sea but breathing land-breaths,
Its vestal folds unfolded, its comfort zone
Edged with a fringe of sepia-coloured wool tails.

Not the one scraggy with crusts and eggshells   [5]
And olive stones and cheese and salami rinds
Laid out by the torrents of the Guadalquivir
Where we got drunk before the corrida.

Instead, again, it's locked-park Sunday Belfast,
A walled back yard, the dust-bins high and silent   [10]
As a page is turned, a finger twirls warm hair
And nothing gives on the rug or the ground beneath it.

I lay at my length and felt the lumpy earth,
Keen-sensed more than ever through discomfort,
But never shifted off the plaid square once.   [15]
When we moved I had your measure and you had mine.

[1]   *fawn:* a light brown colour
[3]   *vestal:* virginal; chaste, pure
[4]   *sepia:* a dark reddish-brown colour
[7]   *Guadalquivir:* a river in Spain
[8]   *corrida:* a bullfight

Tease It Out

Memory 1

1. Read the first stanza carefully. Think about the questions below on your own a few minutes before comparing your ideas with the person beside you. Together formulate answers, supporting your conclusions with evidence from the poem.
   - Why does the poet describe this rug as the 'first rug'?
   - Where was this rug stowed when not in use?
   - What phrase suggests that the rug emits a stale or musty odour, especially in comparison with the freshness of the sea air?
   - The rug is described as 'vestal'. What does this suggest about the sexual relationship between the poet and his wife during the period they owned this rug?

Memory 2

2. What event were the poet due to attend after their picnic of Spanish delicacies. Does their trip strike you as a typical Spanish holiday? Give a reason for your answer.

3. 'In this stanza the popping language captures the excitement the poet must have felt as he experienced the smells and tastes of Spain'. Identify three examples of assonance or alliteration in these lines.

Memory 3

4. Now let's turn to the third memory. Does it surprise you that in Belfast public parks were once locked on Sundays? Google the reason for this policy. When was it abolished?

5. Class Discussion: Did the event the poet remembers here take place:
   a) before the poet and his wife had gotten together as a couple?
   b) shortly after they had gotten together as a couple?
   c) a relatively long time before they had gotten together as a couple?

6. With no access to the parks, where, on this particular Sunday, did the poet and his future wife decide to sit out and enjoy the warm weather?

7. Does this strike you as a pleasant or unpleasant location? Give a reason for your answer.

8. What was the poet's future wife doing as she lay on the rug?

9. The poet lay down on the rug beside his future wife. What phrase indicates that his whole body was pressed against hers?

10. 'Nothing gives'. What response, if any, did his future wife give to the poet lying down beside her? What response do you think the poet might have been hoping for?

11. What phrases indicate that the poet was physically uncomfortable as he lay on the rug? Did this discomfort cause him to move? Why do you think this was?

12. The poet describes how he was 'Keen-sensed' at this moment. Suggest two different reasons his senses might have heightened as he lay beside his future wife.

13. What does the phrase 'to have someone's measure' mean? What had the poet and his future wife learned about each other's feelings by the time they finally moved from the rug? How had this knowledge been conveyed?

Think About Themes

1. In this poem the poet considers three different memories. Break into groups of four. Place a large sheet of paper on your table, divided like this placemat diagram.

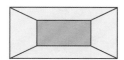

   On your section of the placemat jot down everything that occurs to you in response to the following statements:
   - Which memory has the most pleasant setting? Which has the most unpleasant?
   - What phrase suggests that the third memory is the one the poet holds most dear?
   - What phrases suggest that the other memories are rejected or passed over in its favour?
   - What phrase suggests that the poet returns to this memory again and again?
   - Suggest why this memory might be so important to him.
   Share your ideas with the group, writing in the centre the answers you can all agree on.

2. 'Perhaps more than anything else, this poem captures the intense excitement of a budding relationship, of that moment when you suspect, but are not certain, that the object of your affection likes you back'. Write a paragraph in response to this statement.

3. Class Discussion: 'This poem celebrates the longevity of a couple's enduring love, describing how over the years different rugs, like their relationship itself, have proved a "comfort zone", a place where the outside world can't reach them'. In what ways might a rug serve as a compelling and powerful metaphor for a relationship? In what ways might it be considered an ineffective metaphor?

In Context

'This poem sees the poet swiping through an interior instagram of memories, before settling on the recollection he loves most'. Write a paragraph comparing 'Tate's Avenue' to 'The Skunk', another poem that deals with the process of memory.

Gerard Manley Hopkins

Hopkins was born in Stratford, Essex, on 28 July 1844, to a wealthy and cultured family. His father was a businessman and diplomat who dabbled in literature, writing books and articles on a variety of subjects, including several books of poetry. His mother, Catherine, was the daughter of a physician and was noted for her love of philosophy and literature. Hopkins, it seems, had a relatively happy childhood. His education began at home and was influenced by his father's literary interests.

He attended the prestigious Highgate School, where he received a classical Victorian education, focusing on subjects such as history, Greek and Latin. He was a reasonably sociable and outgoing boy, one who by all accounts got on quite well with his fellow schoolmates. Though Hopkins was slight and physically unimposing, he was surprisingly tough and athletic, managing to hold his own on the vicious playing pitches of a Victorian public school.

However, there were signs that he was not an average schoolboy. Even at Highgate he began to exhibit a strong inclination toward an ascetic or self-punishing lifestyle – a quality that in later life would lead him to pursue a vocation as a Jesuit priest. On one occasion, he theorised that people consumed more liquids than they needed and, to prove himself right, abstained from drinking water and other liquids for three days before he began to suffer from dehydration. He also exhibited a stubborn nature that often caused him to run afoul of the school authorities, and he was once whipped and threatened with expulsion. However, it was also at Highgate that Hopkins' poetic instincts began to stir, and he won a prize for writing a long poem.

After school, Hopkins went to Oxford University, where he continued to write poetry. Though he could be stubborn, touchy and arrogant, he was popular with his fellow students and enjoyed the university's social life, especially boating with friends on the River Cherwell. At the time, Oxford was buzzing with theological debate. Many young students of an artistic bent, including Hopkins, were unhappy with their own Protestant religion. They were also unwilling to contemplate the possibility of atheism.

Beguiled by what they regarded as the drama and mystery of Mass and confession, many of these Protestant men found themselves drawn to the Catholic religion. They regarded Catholic rituals as a kind of theatre, and its rich symbolism appealed to their artistic nature. Their interest in Catholicism was a form of rebellion, since at the time the Roman Catholic Church was held in deep suspicion by the majority of English people. Protestants who adopted the ceremonies and rituals of the Catholic Church while retaining their Protestant beliefs were known as 'Anglo-Catholics'.

Throughout his time at Oxford, Hopkins – like many young students – was an Anglo-Catholic. More and more, however, he drifted toward Catholicism proper. He adopted Catholic customs, such as going to confession and not eating meat on Fridays. He would even chastise himself with a whip during Lent. Hopkins, it seems, was attracted to Catholicism not only because of its symbolism and mystery but also because of its rigour and severity. He eventually took the leap and converted to the faith in 1866, at the age of twenty-two.

Much has been made of Hopkins' sexuality. At Oxford he opted for a celibate life, which has prompted many critics to suggest that Hopkins was deeply uncomfortable with his sexual orientation. There is evidence to suggest he was attracted to a young poet called Digby Dolben, who drowned in 1865, shortly before Hopkins' conversion. Several critics maintain that it was Hopkins' discomfort with his own sexuality that led to his decision to join the priesthood. It also, perhaps, gave rise to the feelings of self-loathing expressed in poems such as 'No worst, there is none' and his notorious tendency toward self-punishment. Throughout his life Hopkins was to dwell on his own faults with an almost painful attention to detail. He would be overcome with remorse for even the tiniest failing or transgression.

Having graduated from Oxford, Hopkins taught for nine months at the Oratory school founded by John Henry Newman, one of England's leading Catholics. While there he decided to become a priest. His decision to join the Jesuit order – known as the 'spiritual army' of the Church – shows his desire for rigorous order and soldierly discipline. Life as a Jesuit was incredibly demanding and austere – an endless succession of fasting, praying and penance. Throughout this time Hopkins studied at Manresa House, which is the Jesuit school in London, and also at Stonyhurst, near Blackburn in Lancashire.

Hopkins' health was consistently poor, however, and the order sent him to St Bueno's in Wales to recuperate. The period in Wales was one of the happiest in Hopkins' life. He fell in love with the Welsh countryside, and – prompted by the rector at St Bueno's – began writing poetry again. Many of Hopkins' best-known poems date from this period, including 'Spring', 'The Windhover' and 'God's Grandeur'.

From 1877 onwards Hopkins spent much of his time in the bleak slums of industrialised northern Britain. He spent several periods at Stonyhurst, a few months in Glasgow and a particularly dismal time in Liverpool. The bleakness of urban industrialised life did not agree with Hopkins and he struggled to find inspiration for his poetry ('Felix Randal' – written during his Liverpool period – was inspired by the death of one of his parishioners).

In 1884 the Jesuits moved Hopkins to Dublin to teach at the newly formed Catholic university. This was a particularly unhappy period in Hopkins' life. He felt out of place in Ireland, deeply missing the friends and acquaintances he had left behind in Britain. To him the Irish seemed an alien and incomprehensible race and he found it difficult to relate to his students, colleagues and indeed to Dublin life in general. His Irish co-workers, for their part, didn't know what to make of this intense and eccentric Englishman had been thrust into their midst. He despised the grimy slums that had overtaken the once grand city, and to make matters worse, he was massively overworked at the university.

Under these conditions Hopkins' physical health, always fragile, became very poor. His mental well-being also deteriorated and he was overcome by feelings of depression, frustration and religious doubt. Hopkins' 'terrible sonnets' – including 'No worst, there is none' and 'I wake and feel the fell of dark' – stem from this bleak period. As one critic put it, he was a 'sensitive, over-scrupulous and unusual man who had been formed with too little capacity for human happiness'. Hopkins spent five years in Dublin, until his poor health, exacerbated by the filth and squalor of the city, finally got the better of him. He died, harassed and exhausted, from typhoid fever in 1889. His last words were 'I am so happy, I am so happy'.

God's Grandeur

The world is charged with the grandeur of God.
    It will flame out, like shining from shook foil;
    It gathers to a greatness, like the ooze of oil
Crushed. Why do men then now not reck his rod?
Generations have trod, have trod, have trod;   [5]
    And all is seared with trade; bleared, smeared with toil;
    And wears man's smudge and shares man's smell: the soil
Is bare now, nor can foot feel, being shod.

And for all this, nature is never spent;
    There lives the dearest freshness deep down things;   [10]
And though the last lights off the black West went
    Oh, morning, at the brown brink eastward, springs –
Because the Holy Ghost over the bent
    World broods with warm breast and with ah! bright wings.

[1]	*charged:*	suggests the charge of an electrical current
[1]	*grandeur:*	splendour, majesty
[4]	*reck:*	acknowledge, recognise, pay heed to
[6]	*seared:*	parched, dry
[6]	*bleared:*	blurred, reddened
[6]	*smeared:*	soiled, tarnished
[12]	*brink:*	edge, precipice
[14]	*broods:*	suggests how birds sit on eggs to warm them and encourage them to hatch

Tease It Out

Lines 1 to 3

1. Think about the word 'charged'. What generally happens when something is charged?
2. What do you think the poet means by the 'grandeur of God'? Where does the poet say that God's 'grandeur' is evident?
3. Why do you think the poet chose to use the verb 'charged' to describe the presence of God's grandeur in the world? What does the verb suggest about the 'grandeur of God'?
4. In what way do you imagine God's grandeur might 'flame out' from the world? To what does the poet compare the way that God's grandeur emanates from the world?
5. What do you think Hopkins means when he says that God's grandeur 'gathers to a greatness'?
6. The poet imagines something being crushed to produce oil (olives, perhaps). How does this image illustrate the idea of God's grandeur combining into a single 'greatness'?

Lines 4 to 8

7. The poet imagines that God possesses a 'rod'. What do you think this 'rod' symbolises?
8. Hopkins says that people no longer 'reck' or notice this 'rod'. What is the poet suggesting about human beings here?
9. Class Discussion: Read lines 5 to 8. How does the poet characterise and describe the way people have treated the earth for generations?
10. Why do you think the poet repeats the word 'trod' in line 5? What effect does this repetition have?
11. The poet says that 'all is seared with trade'. What do you understand the word 'seared' to mean? In what way might 'trade' result in a searing of the world?
12. What sort of 'toil' do you imagine the poet has in mind in line 6? How might such 'toil' result in the world being 'bleared' and 'smeared'?
13. Why do you think the poet says that the 'soil/ Is bare now'? What do you imagine has made the soil 'bare'?
14. Hopkins laments the fact that we now wear shoes. Why does he lament this fact? What do you think our wearing shoes symbolises for the poet?

Lines 9 to 14

15. The poet says that 'nature is never spent'. What do you think he means by this?
16. Class Discussion: Discuss the way in which the poet uses the sunset and sunrise to illustrate nature's power.

17. Comment on the change of tone in the sestet or last six lines of the poem.
18. How does the poet describe the presence of the Holy Ghost in the world? What does the word 'brood' call to mind?
19. What does the image in the last two lines suggest about God's relationship with man?
20. Why do you think the poet chose to use the expression 'ah' in the final line? What effect does this have?

Think About Themes

1. The poem was written around the time of the industrial revolution, when cities were growing and many factories were being built. Do you think that the way the poet characterises man's relationship with the world is still relevant today?
2. Hopkins says that the whole earth now 'wears man's smudge and shares man's smell'. What do you think he is suggesting here about the way humans treat the planet? Do you think that the poet's view of mankind is too negative?
3. How does the poem characterise God? Is He described as a caring and benevolent being?
4. Discuss the different images that the poet presents us with in the poem. Which did you find most memorable and effective?
5. Do you think that this can be read as an environmental poem before its time?
6. Would you agree that this is ultimately a poem of hope?

In Context

The idea that God is present in the natural world is a theme of many of Hopkins' poems. Discuss this theme with reference to 'God's Grandeur' and two other Hopkins poems on your course.

As Kingfishers Catch Fire, Dragonflies Draw Flame

As kingfishers catch fire, dragonflies draw flame;
 As tumbled over rim in roundy wells
 Stones ring; like each tucked string tells, each hung bell's
Bow swung finds tongue to fling out broad its name;
Each mortal thing does one thing and the same: [5]
 Deals out that being indoors each one dwells;
 Selves – goes itself; *myself* it speaks and spells,
Crying *What I do is me: for that I came.*

Í say more: the just man justices;
 Keeps gráce: that keeps all his goings graces;   [10]
Acts in God's eye what in God's eye he is –
 Chríst. For Christ plays in ten thousand places,
Lovely in limbs, and lovely in eyes not his
 To the Father through the features of men's faces.

---

[3] **tucked:** plucked
[9] **justices:** lives a just life; acts in a just manner
[10] **Keeps gráce:** lives in accordance with God's law and stays free of sin
[10] **goings:** activities or actions

Get In Gear

Look up kingfishers and dragonflies. What physical characteristics do these two species have in common?

Tease It Out

Lines 1 to 4

1. What is happening to the kingfishers in line 1?
2. Why does Hopkins say that they 'catch fire'? Is this an effective metaphor in your opinion?
3. Class Discussion: Consider the word 'draw' in line 1. Could it have different meanings? How might each of these meanings apply to the dragonflies?
4. What is an adjective? The entire phrase 'tumbled over rim in roundy wells' could be thought of as a single adjective. What object or set of objects does it describe?
5. What happens to the stones in lines 2 to 3? What kind of sound do they produce when this happens?
6. What phrase describes the sound produced by the vibrating string?
7. Consider the phrase 'hung bell's'. Where do you imagine the bells to be hanging?
8. Class Discussion: What is the bell's 'bow'? When might this bow be 'swung'? Who might swing it?
9. Consider the phrase 'finds tongue'. What do we mean by this? When and how might a bell be said to 'find tongue' in this way? When does this happen?
10. How does Hopkins indicate that the sound of the bell travels a great distance?

Lines 5 to 8

11. Group Discussion: According to line 6 something dwells 'indoors' or within each aspect of God's creation. What does Hopkins have in mind here?
12. Class Discussion: In line 7 Hopkins uses the noun 'self' as a verb. What might it mean in this context to 'self'? What kind of behaviour does this freshly coined verb suggest?
13. According to Hopkins, the behaviour of each living thing resembles a 'cry': 'myself it speaks and spells'. What do they use this 'cry' to express or reveal?
14. According to line 8 every aspect of God's creation has a purpose. What do you understand this purpose to be?
15. 'Each mortal thing does one thing and the same'. What are 'mortal things'? Having read lines 5 to 8 carefully write a short paragraph describing what every mortal thing does.

Lines 9 to 14

16. In line 9 Hopkins again uses a noun as a verb. Which one? What kind of behaviour might this freshly coined verb describe?
17. What do we understand by the word 'goings': 'keeps all his goings graces'? What kind of behaviour keeps or maintains the grace or goodness of these goings?
18. Who according to lines 11 to 12 does the just man resemble in his behaviour?
19. Consider lines 12 to 13. What does Hopkins mean by this? How can Christ be present in all these different places, limbs and eyes?
20. What words and phrases indicate God's appreciation of the just man's behaviour?

Think About Themes

1. 'This poem celebrates how each aspect of God's creation is unique with its own particular colours and sounds.' Write a few lines in response to this statement.
2. 'However, it paradoxically also shows how each aspect of God's creation has something in common.' Write a few lines in response to this statement.
3. The sestet (final six lines) deals with humanity while the octet (first eight lines) deals with other aspects of God's creation. What differences are there between the two?
4. Hopkins' poetry has been described as 'a sequence of alliteration, internal rhymes and crisp consonants wrapped around closely packed contrasting vowel sounds'. Discuss this statement with detailed reference to the poem.
5. Read this poem aloud a number of times. Identify two or more internal rhymes in this poem. Do you find this intense sound-patterning pleasant or disconcerting?
6. 'This poem initially seems complex and off-putting but actually has a fairly simple message.' Does this sum up your experience of the poem? Write a paragraph or two saying why.

In Context

1. This poem, like 'The Windhover' and 'I wake and feel the fell of dark', makes explicit reference to Christ. Write three paragraphs describing the differences in how Christ is portrayed in each one.

2. This poem is often compared to 'God's Grandeur'. Write one paragraph describing a few similarities between the two poems and another commenting on the differences.

Spring

Nothing is so beautiful as Spring –
   When weeds, in wheels, shoot long and lovely and lush;
   Thrush's eggs look little low heavens, and thrush
Through the echoing timber does so rinse and wring
The ear, it strikes like lightnings to hear him sing;   [5]
   The glassy peartree leaves and blooms, they brush
   The descending blue; that blue is all in a rush
With richness; the racing lambs too have fair their fling.

What is all this juice and all this joy?
   A strain of the earth's sweet being in the beginning   [10]
In Eden garden. – Have, get, before it cloy,

Before it cloud, Christ, lord, and sour with sinning,
   Innocent mind and Mayday in girl and boy,
Most, O maid's child, thy choice and worthy the winning.

[4] **wring:** to twist or squeeze (as with a damp cloth)
[11] **cloy:** to become distasteful or sickening
[13] **Mayday:** The first day of May, traditionally associated with the Virgin Mary
[14] **maid's child:** Jesus, who was born of a maid or virgin

Tease It Out

1. What, according to the poet, compares to the beauty of spring?
2. Group Discussion: The poet refers to 'weeds'. What has he got in mind here? In what sense might these 'weeds' resemble 'wheels'?
3. Group Discussion: Can you imagine how 'thrush's eggs' might resemble 'little low heavens'?
4. According to the poet the thrush's singing has a cleansing effect on the ear and mind. What words and phrases does he use to suggest this?
5. How does the poet indicate the exhilarating effect of the thrush's song?
6. What happens to the pear tree? Why do you think Hopkins refers to it as 'glassy'? What part or parts of the tree does Hopkins have in mind here?
7. How does Hopkins indicate the intense blueness of the sky?
8. How do you picture the lambs' behaviour as described in line 8?
9. What Bible story is Hopkins reminded of when he considers the spring time? Why do you think this is?
10. What view of children is put forward in line 13?
11. Class Discussion: What does the poet fear will happen to the children of the world? What does he call on God to do about this?
12. Who is the 'maid's child'? Why does Hopkins use this term?
13. What does Hopkins want the maid's child to do in relation to the children of the world?

Think About Themes

1. 'This poem celebrates the freshness, newness and energy of the springtime.' Write a paragraph or two in response to this statement.
2. 'Hopkins' writing skilfully captures this energy and freshness.' Identify three or four lines or phrases in the poem that support this point. In each case give the reason for your selection.
3. The sonnet's sestet begins with the question 'What is all this juice and joy?' Do you think that it provides an answer to this question? If so, what is it?
4. Do you think the comparison between springtime and the Garden of Eden is a reasonable one? Is there more than one similarity between these two concepts? What are the differences between the two?
5. Group Discussion: Is Hopkins' view of childhood innocence accurate or idealistic? In your opinion does he feel that the innocence of each child will inevitably be clouded and soured by sin?
6. Class Discussion: Hopkins calls on Christ to 'get' and 'have' the children of the world before their innocence is destroyed. Is this a reasonable or realistic request? How might such a task be accomplished?

In Context

How does Hopkins combine the subjects of nature and religion in his poetry? Discuss with reference to 'Spring' and two other poems on your course.

Pied Beauty

Glory be to God for dappled things –
   For skies of couple-colour as a brinded cow;
   For rose-moles all in stipple upon trout that swim;
Fresh-firecoal chestnut-falls; finches' wings;
   Landscape plotted and pieced – fold, fallow, and plough; [5]
   And all trades, their gear and tackle and trim.

All things counter, original, spare, strange;
   Whatever is fickle, freckled (who knows how?)
   With swift, slow; sweet, sour; adazzle, dim;
He fathers-forth whose beauty is past change: [10]
   Praise Him.

Pied: having two or more different colours
[1] **dappled:** spotted
[2] **brinded:** grey or tawny with darker streaks or spots
[3] **rose-moles:** marks on the scales of trout that resemble roses
[3] **stipple:** dotted or speckled
[4] **firecoal:** coal that is turned the colour of fire
[5] **fallow:** land that is ploughed but left idle so that the soil can replenish itself
[8] **fickle:** prone to change

Tease It Out

1. What is the simile in line 2? Have you ever come across this comparison before? Is it an effective simile?
2. Hopkins coins the compound word 'couple-colour' in line 2. How effective is this term as a description of the sky?
3. What does Hopkins compare the inside of the fallen chestnuts to?
4. Why do you think that the poet mentions the wings of finches?
5. List the several examples of 'dappled things' that Hopkins mentions. How many of these are natural and how many are man-made?
6. What is the poet's attitude towards trades in this poem?
7. Note the beginning and ending of this poem. Do you think that this poem has a traditional religious framework? What is the subject of the poem?
8. What do you think attracts the poet to diversity and variety?
9. Comment on the form of this poem. Why do you think Hopkins has shortened the sonnet?
10. Does Hopkins attach moral qualities to the 'dappled things' he mentions? Discuss with detailed reference to the poem.
11. Why do you think Hopkins chooses to commend 'dappled things' in particular?
12. Whose 'beauty is past change' in this poem?
13. Do you think there's irony in the notion that the great variety in the natural world is a testimony to the perfect unity of God?
14. Comment on the poet's use of alliteration.
15. What is the poem's rhyme scheme? Is it regular or irregular? Why do you think the poet chose this particular rhyming scheme?
16. Comment on the praise of God as He who 'fathers-forth'. Do you think the poet's role can be compared to God's in terms of creation?

Think About Themes

1. Do you think the 'dappled things' Hopkins praises God for are traditionally considered to be praiseworthy? Or is Hopkins being unconventional in what he considers to be beautiful?
2. Read this poem aloud a couple of times. Do you think that Hopkins successfully approximates the rhythms and style of normal speech, as was his aim?
3. Would you agree that diversity increases the richness of our surroundings?

In Context

1. Discuss the importance of reading Hopkins' poems aloud. Detail your answer with reference to at least three poems on your course.
2. 'For Hopkins, the role of the poet is to show how God is reflected in nature.' Do you agree with this statement? Detail your answer with reference to at least three poems on your course.

The Windhover

To Christ our Lord

I caught this morning morning's minion, king-
   dom of daylight's dauphin, dapple-dawn-drawn Falcon, in his riding
   Of the rolling level underneath him steady air, and striding
High there, how he rung upon the rein of a wimpling wing
In his ecstasy! then off, off forth on swing,
   As a skate's heel sweeps smooth on a bow-bend: the hurl and gliding   [5]
   Rebuffed the big wind. My heart in hiding
Stirred for a bird, – the achieve of, the mastery of the thing!

Brute beauty and valour and act, oh, air, pride, plume, here
   Buckle! AND the fire that breaks from thee then, a billion
Times told lovelier, more dangerous, O my chevalier!   [10]

No wonder of it: shéer plód makes plough down sillion
   Shine, and blue-bleak embers, ah my dear,
Fall, gall themselves, and gash gold-vermilion.

Windhover: a falcon
[1] **minion:** favourite
[2] **dauphin:** crown prince
[4] **wimpling:** rippling; undulating
[9] **valour:** courage in the face of battle
[11] **chevalier:** a mounted soldier or knight
[12] **shéer plód:** sheer hard work or plodding labour
[12] **sillion:** a word coined by Hopkins to describe furrows of cut earth
[14] **gash:** cut, bleed
[14] **vermilion:** red, the colour of nobility and royalty

Tease It Out

Lines 1 to 4

1. What time of day is it? Where is the poet? What does he observe in the sky?

2. What does the word 'minion' mean? Why do you think the poet considers the falcon to be the 'morning's minion'?

3. What does the word 'dauphin' mean? What does it suggest about the falcon that it is considered 'daylight's dauphin'?

4. Class Discussion: The falcon is described as 'dapple-dawn-drawn'. In what way might the bird be 'drawn'? What is it that draws the falcon? Does the word 'dapple' apply to the dawn or the falcon or both?

5. Consider the words 'riding', 'striding' and 'rein'. With what animal might you normally associate these words?

6. The falcon is said to be 'riding' upon something. What is it that he rides upon?

7. Class Discussion: Consider the phrase 'rolling level underneath him steady' as pertaining to the word 'air'. What does this phrase suggest about the air beneath the bird?

8. What is the bird's controlled hovering movement compared to in the phrase: 'he rung upon the rein of a wimpling wing'? Look particularly at his choice of verbs and adjectives.

Lines 5 to 8

9. The falcon suddenly flies off on a swinging arc over the landscape. To what does the poet compare its flight? What does the comparison suggest about the bird's movements?

10. The falcon flies directly into a 'big wind'. How does it react or respond to the force of the breeze?

11. What do the words 'hurl' and 'gliding' suggest about the bird?

12. The poet tells us that his heart has been 'in hiding'. What do you think he means by this? What does it suggest about the way he has been feeling recently?

13. What effect does seeing the falcon in flight have upon the poet's 'heart'?

14. The poet associates the falcon with achievement ('achieve') and 'mastery'. What is it that the falcon achieves and masters?

Lines 9 to 14

15. In line 9 the poet lists the things that he finds most extraordinary about the bird. List the words that he uses and say what each suggests about the falcon's character, movement and appearance.

16. What might it mean to say that all the things mentioned in line 9 'Buckle'?

17. Class Discussion: In line 10 the poem seems to shift focus from the falcon to Christ. Why do you think the falcon's struggle with the wind reminds the poet of Christ?

18. Why do you think the poet considers Christ to be his 'chevalier'?

19. Why do you think the poet considers Christ's actions to be a 'billion/ times' more beautiful and dangerous than the falcon's?

20. It is likely that the poet has Christ's crucifixion in mind in the line: 'AND the fire that breaks from thee then'. Why do you think he says that a 'fire' burst forth from Christ on the cross?

21. Class Discussion: In the final lines of the poem the poet compares the magnificence that Christ displayed on the cross to two things: the earth that is broken and exposed by a ploughman's labour, and a dying ember that falls to the ground and breaks open. Why do you think he makes these comparisons?

Think About Themes

1. What words or phrases do you think best capture the falcon's appearance and movements?

2. Read the poem aloud. How does the poet's use of punctuation contribute to the mood and energy of the poem?

3. Did you find this poem inspiring? What was it that most inspired you? The description of the bird? The poet's use of language? The description of Christ?

4. Do you agree with the sentiment expressed at the end of the poem, that things are at their most beautiful when they are broken and exposed?

5. The word 'Buckle' has a number of different meanings. Identify as many meanings of the word as you can and say how each might be applied to the falcon and Christ as the poet describes them.

6. How does the poem characterise Christ?

7. 'However the poem is read, it's quite a trick of metaphor-magic to turn a hungry bird looking for breakfast into, among much else, a prince, a horseman, a knight, a plough, a fire's embers, and eventually Christ himself.' Discuss this statement with detailed reference to the poem.

In Context

'This poem follows the pattern of so many of Hopkins' sonnets, in that a sensuous experience or description leads to a set of moral reflections.' Discuss this statement with reference to three poems on your course.

Inversnaid

This darksome burn, horseback brown,
His rollrock highroad roaring down,
In coop and in comb the fleece of his foam
Flutes and low to the lake falls home.

A windpuff-bonnet of fáwn-fróth   [5]
Turns and twindles over the broth
Of a pool so pitchblack, féll-fŕowning,
It rounds and rounds Despair to drowning.

Degged with dew, dappled with dew
Are the groins of the braes that the brook treads through,   [10]
Wiry heathpacks, flitches of fern,
And the beadbonny ash that sits over the burn.

What would the world be, once bereft
Of wet and of wilderness? Let them be left,
O let them be left, wildness and wet;   [15]
Long live the weeds and the wilderness yet.

      Inversnaid: place in the Scottish Highlands
[1] *darksome:* dark, sombre
[1] *burn:* small stream
[3] *coop:* 'enclosed hollow' (definition from Hopkins' notebook)
[3] *comb:* rippling stretch of water
[4] *Flutes:* brings to mind both the musical instrument and a long-stemmed glass
[5] *bonnet:* hat
[5] *fáwn-fróth:* the fawn-coloured foam that is sometimes generated by the motion of water in streams and rivers
[6] *twindles:* a mixture of 'twists', 'twitches' and 'dwindles'
[7] *féll:* evil, dark and menacing
[9] *Degged:* sprinkled (Scots dialect)
[10] *braes:* steep bank or hillside (Scots dialect)
[11] *heathpacks:* heather clumps
[11] *flitches:* strands, branches
[12] *beadbonny:* one of the many phrases Hopkins invented, with 'bonny' meaning beautiful and 'bead' possibly a reference to berries

Get In Gear

Take a moment and try to identify your favourite place in Ireland. Write a couple of paragraphs describing its sights and sounds as you remember them. Try to capture something of why this location appeals to you.

Tease It Out

Stanza 1

1. What colour is the water in the 'burn' or stream?
2. The poet compares the stream to which animal?
3. What might this suggest about the stream's movement down the hill?
4. Consider the words 'roaring' and 'rollrock'. How do they further reinforce our sense of the stream's power?
5. The poet describes the physical features that the stream passes through in the words 'highroad', 'coop' and 'comb'. Describe these in your own words.
6. What metaphor is used to describe the foam that forms on the stream as it rushes downhill?
7. What is the stream's 'home' referred to in line 4?

Stanza 2

8. The stream encounters a hollow on its journey downhill and forms a little swirling pool. The poet finds this miniature whirlpool somewhat sinister or depressing. What words and phrases convey this response?
9. Class Discussion: The poet uses the word 'drowning' in connection with this little pool. Is he speaking literally or metaphorically? What thoughts or emotions is he trying to convey?
10. Consider the words 'Turns' and 'twindles'. What do they suggest about the movement of the water on the surface of this pool?
11. In line 5 what metaphors are used to describe the froth that forms on the pool's surface?

Stanza 3

12. What damp substance is sprinkled on the 'braes' or hillside that the stream flows down?
13. Name the different plants that Hopkins mentions growing there.
14. Class Discussion: List the compound words in this stanza. Do you think that they effectively add to the descriptive quality of the poem?

Stanza 4

15. What worry does the poet express in lines 13 to 14?
16. What hope or prayer does he express?
17. Class Discussion: What is the effect of repetition in these lines?
18. What does the word 'weeds' refer to in the poem's last line? Would you agree that Hopkins is using this word in a somewhat unusual way?

Think About Themes

1. In your own words, and with as much detail as possible, describe the landscape that Hopkins depicts in this poem.
2. What do you think the world would be like if there were only towns, and no countryside left?
3. In your opinion, is Hopkins despairing or hopeful about the future of nature in this poem? Refer to the text in your answer.
4. Can you identify two rhyming couplets and two internal rhymes in this poem?
5. Would you agree that the mood or tone of this piece shifts several times? Can you identify where the tone is happy and full of celebration, and where it is darker and more anxious?
6. Identify each of the coinages or new words that Hopkins invents throughout this poem. Working within a group, try to make up three new words to describe some object of your choice.

In Context

'Hopkins put a lot of sound effects into his poetry. He uses a lot of unusual rhyming, alliteration and compound words to add to both the descriptive and lyrical quality of his verse.' Discuss this statement with reference to 'Inversnaid' and two other Hopkins poems on your course.

Felix Randal

Felix Randal the farrier, O is he dead then? my duty all ended,
Who have watched his mould of man, big-boned and hardy-handsome
Pining, pining, till time when reason rambled in it and some
Fatal four disorders, fleshed there, all contended?

Sickness broke him. Impatient, he cursed at first, but mended   [5]
Being anointed and all; though a heavenlier heart began some
Months earlier, since I had our sweet reprieve and ransom
Tendered to him. Ah well, God rest him all road ever he offended!

This seeing the sick endears them to us, us too it endears.
My tongue had taught thee comfort, touch had quenched thy tears,   [10]
Thy tears that touched my heart, child, Felix, poor Felix Randal;

How far from then forethought of, all thy more boisterous years,
When thou at the random grim forge, powerful amidst peers,
Didst fettle for the great grey drayhorse his bright and battering sandal!

[1] *farrier:* a blacksmith
[3] *pining:* wasting away
[4] *contended:* fought, struggled, competed
[6] *anointed:* rubbed with oil as part of a religious ceremony; in this instance refers to the last rites administered to the dying by a Catholic priest
[7] *sweet reprieve and ransom:* Holy Communion
[8] *tendered:* administered
[8] *all road ever:* whoever (dialect expression)
[9] *endears:* causes a feeling of fondness or love
[10] *quenched:* extinguished, quelled
[12] *forethought of:* imagined in advance, anticipated
[12] *boisterous:* lively, energetic
[13] *random:* made from rough uneven stones
[13] *forge:* a blacksmith's workshop
[14] *fettle:* fix
[14] *drayhorse:* a work horse used to pull ploughs, carts, etc.
[14] *sandal:* horseshoe

Tease It Out

Lines 1 to 8

1. What was Felix's job?
2. What has happened to him?
3. The poet says his duty toward Felix Randal is 'all ended'. Why would the poet have a duty toward this man?
4. Group Discussion: Hopkins refers to Felix's 'mould of man'. What does he mean by this?
5. What were Felix's physical characteristics before he became ill? Describe them in your own words.
6. What does the word 'pining' mean? Why do you think Hopkins repeats this word?
7. The phrase 'till time when' in line 3 is an example of Hopkins' compression of language. Rewrite this phrase in your own words.
8. What happened to Felix's sanity, to his powers of reason?
9. How many disorders or ailments did Felix suffer from?
10. The phrase 'fleshed there' is another example of Hopkins' unusual use of language. Rewrite this phrase in your own words.
11. The poet suggests that Felix's various illnesses 'contended' with one another. What are we to make of these lines? What do they suggest about his condition?
12. What was Felix's attitude toward God when he first became ill?
13. What phrase suggests that Hopkins gave Felix the last rites on his deathbed?
14. According to Hopkins these last rites 'mended' Felix. What do you think he means by this?
15. What had Hopkins done for Felix 'some/ Months earlier', i.e. some months before he died?
16. What effect did this have on the grievously ill blacksmith?
17. Hopkins coins a brand new adjective: 'heavenlier'. Describe what this means in your own words.
18. What prayer does Hopkins say for the recently deceased Felix?

Lines 9 to 14

19. One of a priest's duties is tending to the sick. What effect does this duty have on the sick person? What effect does it have on the priest?
20. How did the poet attempt to comfort Felix?
21. What phrase indicates that Felix's suffering affected the poet deeply?
22. Why do you think the poet refers to Felix as a 'child'? What might this suggest about the nature of their relationship?

23. What do you understand when the poet refers to Felix's 'more boisterous years'?
24. Where is Felix depicted working in the poem's final lines?
25. What phrase indicates that his physicality made him stand out from other workers?
26. What task does the poet imagine Felix performing?

Think About Themes

1. 'This poem is a powerful study of the consolations brought by faith and religion.' Write a paragraph in response to this statement.
2. Do you think a religious person would get more from this poem than someone with no religious belief? Give a reason for your answer.
3. Group Discussion: Line 12 is an example of Hopkins' experimentation with and compression of language. Rewrite the meaning of this line, as you understand it, in your own words.
4. Would you agree that there are two different portrayals of Felix in this poem? Describe them. How do you think Felix would like to be remembered?
5. Alliteration plays a very important part throughout this poem. Choose the two lines that you feel give the best example of the poet's use of alliteration. How does the use of alliteration contribute to the meaning and atmosphere in these lines?
6. The poem is set in Lancashire. Can you identify the different colloquial expressions Hopkins uses throughout the piece? Why do you think he makes this choice? What effect do they have on the poem's tone?
7. 'This poem highlights how quickly and suddenly health and good looks can be snatched away.' Write a paragraph outlining your response to this statement.
8. How would you describe the poem's overall tone? Is it despairing and angry or resigned and accepting?
9. Imagine you are Felix Randal. Write two paragraphs describing your interactions with and reaction to the poet and his priestly duties.

In Context

Both 'Felix Randal' and 'No worst, there is none' deal with the notion of religious doubt. Write a couple of paragraphs describing one similarity and one difference in their approach to this theme.

No worst, there is none

No worst, there is none. Pitched past pitch of grief,
More pangs will, schooled at forepangs, wilder wring.
Comforter, where, where is your comforting?
Mary, mother of us, where is your relief?
My cries heave, herds-long; huddle in a main, a chief   [5]
Woe, world-sorrow; on an age-old anvil wince and sing –
Then lull, then leave off. Fury had shrieked 'No ling-
ering! Let me be fell: force I must be brief.'
O the mind, mind has mountains; cliffs of fall
Frightful, sheer, no-man-fathomed. Hold them cheap   [10]
May who ne'er hung there. Nor does long our small
Durance deal with that steep or deep. Here! creep,
Wretch, under a comfort serves in a whirlwind: all
Life death does end and each day dies with sleep.

[1]   *pitch:* to throw; a musical note or tone; a tar-like substance
[2]   *forepangs:* earlier pangs
[2]   *wring:* squeeze, twist, torture
[6]   *wince:* grimace or hiss in pain
[7]   *Fury:* in Greek mythology the furies were demons who relentlessly persecuted their prey
[8]   *force:* perforce, of necessity, it is essential
[8]   *fell:* evil, wicked
[8]   *brief:* quick
[12] *Durance:* endurance

Tease It Out

Lines 1 to 4

1. Consider the phrase 'No worst'. What does it mean for there to be no 'worst' state of affairs?

2. What different meanings does the word 'pitch' have? List them.

3. Class Discussion: Bearing the above answer in mind what do you think Hopkins means by the 'pitch of grief'?

4. What might it mean to be past this pitch? What emotional state does this phrase suggest?

5. What are 'forepangs'?

6. What according to Hopkins will these 'forepangs' teach the pangs that come after them?

7. Group Discussion: Consider the verb 'wring' as used in line 2. What different meanings of this word might be relevant here?

8. Who do you think is the 'comforter' referred to in line 3?

9. The poet cries out for 'relief'. Do you think he has spiritual, physical or psychological relief in mind here? Support your answer with reference to the text.

10. What lines or phrases indicate that the poet feels abandoned by God?

Lines 5 to 8

11. Group Discussion: What does the speaker compare his cries to in line 5? Is this a surprising metaphor? Do you think it is effective?

12. According to the poet his suffering is part of 'chief-woe' or 'world-sorrow'. What great evil or difficulty might Hopkins be referring to in this line?

13. Class Discussion: In line 6, the poet refers to an 'anvil'. Who or what is being beaten on this anvil? Why do you think the anvil is described as being 'age-old'? In each case give reasons for your answer.

14. What line indicates that the poet enjoys a brief moment of relief or respite?

15. What effect does the splitting of the word 'ling-/ering' have?

16. What is a Fury? What does Hopkins intend the Fury to symbolise or personify?

17. Describe in your own words what the Fury demands.

Lines 9 to 14

18. In lines 9 to 10 the poet compares his mind to a landscape. Describe this landscape's features in your own words.

19. Class Discussion: What metaphor for the mind does the poet introduce in the sestet? How is this metaphor developed over the next few lines?

20. In line 10, the poet states that the mind's mountains are 'no-man-fathomed'. What do you understand by this phrase?

21. Group Discussion: The phrase: 'Hold them cheap/ May who ne'er hung there' is a classic example of how Hopkins squeezes and compresses language. Together write a couple of lines in which you try to 'unpack' this phrase.

22. In line 12 Hopkins refers to things that are 'steep' and 'deep'. What aspects of human existence does he have in mind here?

23. Why according to the poet are human beings ill-equipped to deal with such things?

24. What does the image of the 'whirlwind' suggest to you?

25. What two forms of 'comfort' does Hopkins offer to miserable wretches like himself who suffer in this whirlwind?

26. Do you think that the poem's last lines are effective as a form of consolation?

Think About Themes

1. Write a paragraph describing the poet's state of mind in your own words.

2. In your opinion, does Hopkins employ hyperbole or deliberate exaggeration in this poem?

3. Comment on the poet's use of punctuation. What effect does this unusual punctuation have?

4. How does the poet's use of alliteration and repetition contribute to the meaning and the atmosphere of the poem?

5. Would you agree that this is a difficult poem to like? Write a couple of paragraphs giving the reason for your answer.

In Context

Discuss the theme of mental anguish in 'No worst, there is none' and 'I wake and feel the fell of dark'. List two similarities and two differences between these poems.

I wake and feel the fell of dark

I wake and feel the fell of dark, not day.
What hours, O what black hours we have spent
This night! what sights you, heart, saw; ways you went!
And more must, in yet longer light's delay.
   With witness I speak this. But where I say   [5]
Hours I mean years, mean life. And my lament
Is cries countless, cries like dead letters sent
To dearest him that lives alas! away.

   I am gall, I am heartburn. God's most deep decree
Bitter would have me taste: my taste was me;   [10]
Bones built in me, flesh filled, blood brimmed the curse.
   Selfyeast of spirit a dull dough sours. I see
The lost are like this, and their scourge to be
As I am mine, their sweating selves; but worse.

[1]   **fell:** wickedness or ferocity
[5]   **with witness:** from personal experience
[7]   **dead letters:** letters that cannot be delivered because the recipient has moved away
[9]   **gall:** bitter fluid secreted by the liver
[9]   **decree:** official order or ruling
[12]   **Selfyeast:** coined by Hopkins from the words self and yeast. Yeast is what causes bread to rise
[13]   **The lost:** those without religious faith
[13]   **scourge:** pain, whip, or something that causes suffering

Get In Gear

Think about what it is like to wake in the middle of the night and not be able to go back to sleep. What sorts of thoughts go through your head? How would you characterise your mood when this occurs?

Tease It Out

Lines 1 to 8

1. What does the poet expect to see or experience when he wakes? What does he actually experience or 'feel'?
2. The poet describes the 'dark' as something tangible – it is something that he can 'feel'. To what does he compare the dark? Does the comparison suggest a number of different meanings?
3. The poet speaks of having to endure 'black hours'. What different meanings might the word 'black' have here?
4. The poet addresses his 'heart' and says that it is 'we' who have suffered on these occasions. Why do you think he does this? What do you think his 'heart' represents?
5. What sort of 'sights' do you think the poet has in mind in line 3? How did the poet's 'heart' react to the events of the night?
6. The poet says that he speaks 'With witness'. What do you think it means to speak with witness?
7. What does the fact that the poet speaks 'With witness' suggest about his familiarity with such anguish?
8. How long does the poet say he has been enduring these terrible nights?
9. What do you think the speaker's 'lament' might be?
10. To whom has the speaker been addressing his 'lament'?
11. Why does the poet compare his 'cries' to 'dead letters'? What does this suggest about the kind of response his cries for help have been receiving?
12. Who do you think 'dearest him' refers to? What does it mean that this person has been living 'away'?

Lines 9 to 14

13. With what do you associate the terms 'gall' and 'heartburn'?
14. What do you think the poet is trying to convey when he says that he is 'gall' and 'heartburn'?
15. Do you think that lines 9 to 11 describe mental or physical pain?

16. What do you think the poet is describing when he says that his 'taste' is 'Bitter'?
17. What do you understand the word 'decree' to mean? Why do you think that poet says that it was God's decree that he would 'taste' bitter?
18. What process does the poet describe in line 11? Why do you think he describes this as a 'curse'?
19. How does the poet characterise his 'spirit' or soul in line 12? How does the poet characterise the relationship between his body and his 'spirit'?
20. How does the poet convey a sense of being trapped or confined in lines 11 to 12?
21. Who do you think the 'lost' are? What do you think their 'scourge' or punishment is? Does the poet suffer the same 'scourge' or affliction?
22. In what way do you think the 'lost' might be 'worse' off than the poet?

Think About Themes

1. Is it one thing in particular that is causing the poet to suffer so much, or are there multiple reasons for his anguish? What do you think his chief 'lament' might be?
2. How does this poem present the relationship between God and man? How does the poem portray God?
3. What is the poet's attitude to his physical self? Why do you think he holds this view?
4. Is there any evidence in this poem that Hopkins was quite ill at the time? What effect do you think this may have had on the poet's outlook on life?
5. Hopkins often uses unusual syntax in his poems, ordering or arranging the words in ways that differ significantly from normal or everyday speech. Can you identify instances of this in 'I wake and feel'? Why do you think the poet chooses to use such syntax?
6. Discuss the poet's use of assonance and alliteration. How do these devices contribute to the impact of the poem?

In Context

Making reference to at least three poems by Hopkins on the course, discuss the poet's references to light and darkness in his poetry. What different things do light and darkness symbolise?

Thou art indeed just, Lord

*Justus quidem tu es, Domine, si disputem tecum: verumtamen
justa loquar ad te: Quare via impiorum prosperatur? &c. (Jerem xii 1)*

Thou art indeed just, Lord, if I contend
With thee; but, sir, so what I plead is just.
Why do sinners' ways prosper? and why must
Disappointment all I endeavour end?

Wert thou my enemy, O thou my friend,   [5]
How wouldst thou worse, I wonder, than thou dost
Defeat, thwart me? Oh, the sots and thralls of lust
Do in spare hours more thrive than I that spend,

Sir, life upon thy cause. See, banks and brakes
Now, leavèd how thick! lacèd they are again   [10]
With fretty chervil, look, and fresh wind shakes

Them; birds build – but not I build; no, but strain,
Time's eunuch, and not breed one work that wakes.
Mine, O thou lord of life, send my roots rain.

This sonnet is based upon the following extract from the scriptures:
*You are righteous, O LORD,
when I bring a case before you.
Yet I would speak with you about your justice:
Why does the way of the wicked prosper?
Why do all the faithless live at ease?
(Jeremiah xii 1)*

[1]   ***contend:*** argue
[2]   ***plead:*** make an appeal
[4]   ***endeavour:*** strive
[7]   ***thwart:*** frustrate, prevent
[7]   ***sots:*** in this instance, those who are controlled by lust
[7]   ***thralls:*** in this instance those who are hypnotised, enthralled or enslaved by lust
[8]   ***spend:*** exhaust, wear out
[11]   ***fretty:*** adorned with interlaced design
[11]   ***chervil:*** fragile herb
[13]   ***eunuch:*** castrated man, lacking virility or power

Get In Gear

Group Discussion: 'All too often in life wrongdoers get ahead while good people suffer'. Identify three instances from history, news or current affairs where this might be said to hold true.

Tease It Out

Lines 1 to 8

1. In what very formal setting might you expect to hear terms such as 'contend', 'plead' and 'sir'? How do these terms contribute to the tone and atmosphere of the first eight lines?
2. In the opening lines Hopkins launches a plea or complaint against God. However, he is careful to do so in a most respectful manner. What words or phrases indicate this respect?
3. According to the poet, do sinners typically suffer for their wrongdoings? Or do they get ahead in life despite their misdeeds? How do you think the speaker feels about this?
4. According to lines 3 to 4, do the poet's various projects typically end in success or failure?
5. In line 5 the poet is careful to stress that he regards God as his 'friend'. However, does he feel that God is actually treating him like a friend?
6. The poet feels that God couldn't really be treating him any worse. What lines or phrases convey this?
7. Group Discussion: What do you understand by the phrase 'sots and thralls of lust'? What kind of people does this highly expressive phrase refer to?
8. What contrast does the poet draw between himself and these people?
9. What cause has the poet 'spent' his life serving? Consider the word 'spend'. Could it have more than one meaning in this context?

Lines 9 to 14

10. Describe in your own words the riverbank as Hopkins depicts it in lines 9 to 11.
11. What are the birds doing in line 12?
12. What contrast is there between Hopkins' life and the riverbank?
13. What contrast is there between his existence and the activity of the birds?
14. What words or phrases indicate the poet's unsuccessful efforts to bring his projects to completion?

15. The poet claims that he is unable to 'breed one work that wakes'. What different types of 'work' might he be referring to here?
16. What might be the difference between a work that 'wakes' and a work that doesn't wake?
17. Consider the phrase 'Time's eunuch'. What might this mean in the context of Hopkins' life choices and vocation? What has he denied himself by choosing such a path?
18. How do you imagine Hopkins felt about such self-denial when he wrote this poem?
19. What does the poet ask God to do in the final line? What might he mean by this?
20. There are several instances in these lines where the normal order of words in a sentence is reversed. Identify these instances. What effect do these reversals have on our reading of the poem?

Think About Themes

1. Do you think that deep down the poet actually considers God to be 'just' and to be his 'friend'? Pay close attention to the text when developing your answer to this question.
2. Consider the tone of this piece. Would you have an actor read it in aloud in a tone of anger, frustration, bafflement, humility or despair? Would you agree that the tone changes over the course of the poem? Write a paragraph or two explaining your answer.
3. Do you think that in this poem Hopkins regrets his priestly vocation and envies the 'sots and thralls of lust'? Support your answer with reference to the text.
4. Class Discussion: This poem touches on several different notions of fertility and productivity. It also touches on several notions of infertility. Can you identify examples of each?
5. Would you agree that there is shift in focus or point of view between the octet and the sestet?
6. Write a paragraph discussing the poet's use of alliteration, and its effect on the poem's atmosphere and meaning.

In Context

1. 'In both 'God's Grandeur' and 'Thou art indeed just, Lord' nature is used to describe man's relationship with God.'Write a couple of paragraphs discussing both poems in the light of the above statement.
2. Both 'Thou art indeed just, Lord' and 'No worst, there is none' are considered among Hopkins' so-called 'terrible' sonnets. What similarities are there between these poems? How do they differ in tone?

John Keats

John Keats was born in London on 31 October 1795. The eldest son of a stable-keeper, he had one sister and three brothers. When Keats was eight years old, his father was killed in a riding accident. In 1810 his mother died from tuberculosis, leaving the children in the care of their grandmother. Although an inheritance was granted to the children, due to legal complications they never saw too much of this money in their lifetimes.

Though of small stature, as a young boy Keats was fond of cricket and fighting. He was a diligent student. According to a friend, 'He was at work before the first school hour began, and that was at seven'. He attended John Clarke's school in Enfield and it was here that he developed a passion for history, the classics and Renaissance literature, all of which would later influence his own poetic endeavours.

Keats was not university educated. Under his guardian's guidance, he left school at the age of fifteen and embarked on a five-year apprenticeship under a chemist and surgeon in London. He was, initially at least, a good student, and his commitment to his career in medicine was such that in 1816 he began to study further to qualify as a surgeon. However, his interest in poetry never waned and it vied constantly with the demands of his career.

In 1817 he chose not to sit his surgical examinations so that he could be present when his first collection of poetry was being printed. He finally abandoned his studies, sacrificing his medical ambitions in the pursuit of a literary life. According to his friend Charles Brown, 'he ascribed his inability [to be a surgeon] to an overwrought apprehension of every possible chance of doing evil in the wrong direction of the instrument. 'My last operation,' he told me, 'was the opening of a man's temporal artery. I did it with the utmost nicety; but, reflecting on what passed through my mind at the time, my dexterity seemed a miracle, and I never took up the lancet again.' His first book, *Poems*, was published in March 1817. It contained thirty-one poems, including 'On First Looking into Chapman's Homer'.

Keats, like many of his contemporaries, felt that he couldn't really be a poet unless he composed a long poem, and so set about writing the 4,000 line 'Endymion'. Though it deals with many of the themes that occur throughout the later writings, such as the imagination, love and beauty, the poem lacked cohesion and was widely criticised. Blackwood's Magazine described 'Endymion' as 'imperturbable drivelling idiocy'. The poet Shelley – who was a friend of Keats and convinced of his literary genius – wrote that 'no person should possibly get to the end of it'.

He began working on an epic poem called 'Hyperion' around this time, but it became too unwieldy and he abandoned it so that he could tend to his brother, Tom, who had become gravely ill with tuberculosis. It was also during this period that Keats met, and fell in love with, a young woman named Frances (Fanny) Brawne. She, too, had lost family to tuberculosis and the pair became close when his brother was sick. Following Tom's death in December 1818, Fanny became an important element in Keats' life.

In late April 1819, Keats began composing one of his best-loved works, 'La Belle Dame Sans Merci'. But even this popular poem did not hint at the great works yet to come. Keats himself considered it mere light verse and, in a letter to his younger brother George, dismissed it with a joke. Then, in the space of a few weeks, he composed three of the most beautiful works of poetry ever written – 'Ode on a Grecian Urn', 'Ode to a Nightingale' and 'Ode on Melancholy'. Later that August he wrote 'To Autumn'. Keats was just twenty-three at this time.

He wanted to marry Fanny but his financial situation was difficult. He met with his publishers in November and plans were made for another book of poems. In January, his brother George returned from America to borrow more money from Keats, who could ill afford it. He came to an agreement with their guardian over the final settlement of his grandmother's estate. It was a small sum of money in the end, and Keats decided to give most of it to George. Though younger, George was married and settling into his own business while Keats could not afford to marry Fanny. 'George ought not to have done this,' Keats remarked to Fanny about the loan, 'he should have reflected that I wish to marry myself – but I suppose having a family to provide for makes a man selfish.' His letters to George, both before and after George's January 1820 visit to England, are wonderful documents – engaging, witty, profound; but rarely does Keats admit to any depression and worry. His protective instinct towards his siblings would never disappear.

On 3 February 1820 Keats began to cough blood. Over subsequent months his health grew worse. It soon became apparent that he was suffering from Tuberculosis. Though his spirits were low he managed to make the final corrections to his third collection of poetry, which was entitled *Lamia, Isabella, The Eve of St Agnes, and other Poems*. It contained thirteen poems, including the great odes of 1819 and 'Hyperion'.

The book was published in June and received positively by critics. The good reviews lifted Keats' mood, but his ill health prevented any real celebration. His friends suggested a trip to Italy to recover his health, a trip he undertook with his friend, the artist Joseph Severn, in August. Such trips to warmer climates were common for tubercular patients. However, he did not recover. Keats died in Rome the following February at the age of twenty-five. Upon his tombstone, by request, was inscribed nothing more than the words, 'Here lies one whose name was writ in water'.

Remarkably Keats' poetic career spanned less than four years. It began in 1816, when he decided that he did not wish to be a surgeon, and lasted until late 1819. In all, Keats wrote about 150 poems, but many of his best remembered works, and those upon which his reputation rests, were written in 1819.

Keats was born at a time of great social and political change. The French Revolution of 1798 was a momentous event that led to people questioning established values and beliefs. The idea that a king or an institution such as the Church ought to dictate what people should think or believe was suddenly called into question. People began to trust in the power of human reason to create values and define how society should be structured and governed. Advances in science inspired a growing confidence in man's ability to control the environment in which he lived. It was also a time of revolution in industry, with the development of machines and factories that led to increased productivity and a move away from traditional trades and work practices. Cities began to grow in size and there was a rapid shift in population from the rural to the urban.

The works of many early 18th century poets celebrated the power of reason and rational thought over emotion and imagination. Their works embraced the notion that scientific understanding would ultimately lead to a better world where order might triumph over chaos. But as the century progressed and the negative effects of the industrial revolution on the lives of ordinary people became clearer, some poets began to question the direction in which society was heading and the values now being embraced. These poets wanted to restore faith in the power of human imagination and give greater emphasis to passion and emotion. They considered the city to be an ugly, soul-destroying environment and celebrated instead the beauty and power of nature. Such poets came to be known as the Romantics and Keats is considered one of the greatest of these. His poems are full of lush and sensuous descriptions of the natural world and they celebrate the power of the imagination over reason.

To one who has been long in city pent

To one who has been long in city pent,
   'Tis very sweet to look into the fair
   And open face of heaven,– to breathe a prayer
Full in the smile of the blue firmament.   [5]
Who is more happy, when, with heart's content,
   Fatigued he sinks into some pleasant lair
   Of wavy grass, and reads a debonair
And gentle tale of love and languishment?
Returning home at evening, with an ear   [10]
   Catching the notes of Philomel, – an eye
Watching the sailing cloudlet's bright career,
   He mourns that day so soon has glided by:
E'en like the passage of an angel's tear
   That falls through the clear ether silently.

[1]   **pent:** confined, shut up in a small place
[4]   **blue firmament:** the vault of heaven; sky
[7]   **debonair:** carefree, stylish, charming, sophisticated
[8]   **languishment:** romantic longing
[10] **Philomel:** daughter of the king of Athens whom the gods turned into a nightingale for her own protection; a nightingale
[14] **ether:** the sky or heavens; the element once believed to fill the upper regions of space

Pre-Reading

The poem is addressed to those who have 'been long in city pent'. What does it mean to be pent up somewhere? Have you ever felt this way about a certain place?

Comprehension

Lines 1 to 8

1. The poem describes the benefits of getting away from the city for a while. What sort of place does the poet recommend escaping to?

2. Lines 1 to 3: The poet describes the pleasure of gazing up at the sky. To what does he compare the sky? What adjectives does he use to describe the sky? How would you describe the poet's characterisation of the sky?

3. What does the poet recommend that someone do when they are looking up at the sky? What sort of 'prayer' do you think he has in mind?

4. Lines 5 to 7: What does the word 'lair' mean? How do you think the poet intends the word to be understood in these lines?

5. How does Keats describe the 'lair' in line 6? What does he imagine someone doing here? How does he imagine this person feeling when they do this?

6. Lines 7 and 8: The poet imagines the person lying upon a bed of grass reading a book. What sort of book does he imagine them reading? Why do you think this book would suit someone who has been 'long in city pent'?

Lines 9 to14

7. Lines 9 and 10: What does the poet imagine someone might hear in the evening as they return home? How does he describe this sound?

8. Lines 10 and 11: What does the poet imagine this person might see as they make the journey home in the evening?

9. What do the words 'sailing' and 'career' suggest about the 'cloudlet's' movements in the sky?

10. What sort of mood or atmosphere do the words 'sailing' and 'bright' create?

11. What does the poet imagine someone might 'mourn' as they return home after the day he has just described in the poem?

12. What does the phrase 'glided by' suggest about the manner in which time passes?

13. Lines 13 and 14: To what does the poet compare the passage of time in the last two lines of the poem?

14. What does the comparison made in the final lines suggest about the passage of time?

Personal Response

1. Based on your reading of this poem, what sort of person do you think Keats was?

2. Although the poem describes a 'happy' retreat from the stresses of city life, there is a certain sadness at its core. Comment on the different moods that are evident in the poem.

3. Did you enjoy reading this sonnet? Do you think that Keats' advice is still as apt today as it was when the poem was written?

4. Comment on the poet's use of assonance and alliteration and say how these contribute to the poem's atmosphere.

In Context

'Like many of Keats' poems, 'To one who has been long in city pent' acknowledges the pains of living without lapsing into despair. At the heart of the poem is a realisation of the beauty that the natural world holds and the joy it can bring.'= Compare three poems by Keats in light of these comments.

On First Looking into Chapman's Homer

Much have I travell'd in the realms of gold,
   And many goodly states and kingdoms seen;
   Round many western islands have I been
Which bards in fealty to Apollo hold.
Oft of one wide expanse had I been told   [5]
   That deep-brow'd Homer ruled as his demesne;
   Yet did I never breathe its pure serene
Till I heard Chapman speak out loud and bold:
Then felt I like some watcher of the skies
   When a new planet swims into his ken;   [10]
Or like stout Cortez when with eagle eyes
   He star'd at the Pacific – and all his men
Look'd at each other with a wild surmise –
   Silent, upon a peak in Darien.

Chapman: George Chapman (1559–1634), writer who translated works by Homer

Homer: Ancient Greek poet who wrote epic poems called the *Iliad* and the *Odyssey* and is widely considered to be the greatest poet in Europe's history

[1] **realms of gold:** refers to the experience of reading poetry

[4] **bards:** poets

[4] **fealty:** loyalty sworn by a servant to a king, in this case loyalty sworn by the bards to Apollo, the god of poetry and song

[6] **deep-brow'd:** may refer to Homer's lined forehead or to the depth of thought that lay behind his brow

[6] **demesne:** dominion, territory

[7] **serene:** air

[10] **ken:** knowledge, range of vision, sight

[11] **Cortez:** explorer, one of the first Europeans to see Mexico City. Keats confuses him with another man, Bilboa, who was the first European to reach the Pacific Ocean

[13] **wild surmise:** wildly speculating about this new body of water and what its discovery might mean

[14] **Darien:** an old name for the Panama isthmus, the neck of land joining North and South America

Pre-Reading:

1. Look up the Greek poet Homer. List three facts that are known about his life and work. List three things that are not known about this great writer.
2. Look up the *Iliad* and the *Odyssey*, Homer's two epic poems. What role do travel and discovery play in these stories?

Comprehension

1. Class Discussion: In this poem Keats compares reading to a very different activity. What is it?
2. The poet mentions many different countries he has visited, referring to 'realms', 'states' and 'kingdoms'. What does each individual country represent?
3. Consider the phrase 'realms of gold'. What does this suggest about the poet's attitude towards, and appreciation of, poetry as an art form?
4. Class Discussion: Some poets are described as 'bards' and their writings are compared to 'western islands'. What poets in particular might Keats be referring to here? Why are they set apart from the poets referred to in the first two lines?
5. Who was Apollo? What does Keats mean when he says that these poets were loyal to Apollo? What is he suggesting about these poets' attitude towards their craft?
6. Why do you think Homer is described as being 'deep-brow'd'? Write a few lines describing how you visualise this. What does this phrase suggest about Homer's mind and personality?
7. List, in your own words, the characteristics of Homer's realm or 'demesne', as Keats describes it.
8. Why has the poet been unable to enter Homer's realm and breathe its 'pure serene'?
9. Why is he now capable of doing this?
10. In line 8 what metaphor does the poet use to describe the power and clarity of Chapman's translation?
11. What's another word for a 'watcher of the skies'?
12. What does this watcher notice or discover?
13. The poet describes how the explorer Cortez discovered the Pacific. Look up Darien and describe where exactly in the world this discovery took place.
14. The poet describes Cortez as 'stout' and eagle-eyed. How do you visualise this intrepid explorer? What actor would you cast to play him in a movie? Why?
15. Where were Cortez and his men standing when this discovery took place?
16. What does the phrase 'wild surmise' suggest about the men's reaction to this discovery? What did they do? Did they say anything?

Personal Response

1. Based on your reading of this poem write a paragraph describing your impression of the role poetry must have played in John Keats' life.
2. 'This poem skilfully uses images of travel and discovery to convey the pleasure and excitement of reading poetry'. List the different images of travel and discovery used throughout the poem. Do you think the comparison between reading and travelling is an effective one?
3. Consider the two comparisons the poet uses in order to convey his excited reaction to Chapman's translations. In your opinion are they reasonable or over the top? Which do you think is more effective? Why?
4. In this poem Keats makes a factual error. What is it? In your opinion does this mistake lessen the quality of the poem or does it simply not matter?
5. 'This is a poem about freshness and newness.' List the lines, images and phrases that support this point of view.
6. How would you characterise the tone of this sonnet? Would you describe it as urgent, mournful, energised or depressed? Support your answer with quotations.

In Context

'Poetry and art were at the centre of Keats' life.' In light of this statement write three paragraphs comparing 'On First Looking into Chapman's Homer' to two other poems by Keats on the Leaving Cert course.

When I have fears that I may cease to be

When I have fears that I may cease to be
  Before my pen has glean'd my teeming brain,
Before high-piled books, in charactery,
  Hold like rich garners the full ripen'd grain;
When I behold, upon the night's starr'd face,   [5]
  Huge cloudy symbols of a high romance,
And think that I may never live to trace
  Their shadows with the magic hand of chance;
And when I feel, fair creature of an hour,
  That I shall never look upon thee more,   [10]
Never have relish in the faery power
  Of unreflecting love; – then on the shore
Of the wide world I stand alone, and think
Till love and fame to nothingness do sink.

[2]	***teeming:***	stocked to overflowing, abundant, prolific
[3]	***charactery:***	print or writing
[4]	***garners:***	storehouses for corn, granaries
[11]	***relish:***	delight, joy
[11]	***faery:***	fairy
[12]	***unreflecting:***	unthinking, irrational

Comprehension

Lines 1 to 4

1. In lines 2 to 4 the poet uses the metaphor of harvesting grain to describe the creative process. What features do these two very different activities have in common?

2. The poet refers to his 'teeming brain'. What do you understand by the word 'teeming'? What, according to the poet, is 'teeming' in his mind?

3. Through what process does the poet intend to 'glean' or harvest his ideas?

4. What does the metaphor of the 'full ripen'd grain' refer to?

5. The poet compares books to 'garners' or storehouses for grain. Do you think this is a reasonable comparison?

6. What, according to the first four lines, is Keats desperate to accomplish before he dies?

Lines 5 to 8

7. What metaphor does the poet use to describe the night sky?

8. What, according to the poet, do the clouds drifting across the night sky symbolise?

9. Class Discussion: Consider the phrase 'high romance'. What images, ideas or associations does this phrase bring to mind?

10. The poet wishes to 'trace' the 'shadows' of these clouds. What are we to understand by this?

11. Class Discussion: He says that he will do so with the 'magic hand of chance'. What does he mean by this? What force or energy does he envisage coming to his aid? Why do you think he describes this as a form of 'magic'?

Lines 9 to 14

12. In line 9 the poet mentions a 'fair creature'. Who or what is he referring to here? What fear or anxiety grips him in relation to this creature?

13. Group Discussion: Consider the phrase 'of an hour'. What might this suggest about the poet's attitude towards the 'fair creature' and indeed towards love in general?

14. The poet refers to love as a 'faery power'. What might this suggest about his attitude towards relationships and romance?

15. Class Discussion: The poet also describes love as 'unreflecting'. List the different ways in which this might be interpreted.

16. What is the poet's response to the various fears he outlines in lines 1 to 12? Where does he go? What does he do?

17. In the final line the poet describes how love and fame sink into 'nothingness'. What is happening here? What mental process might this line describe?

Personal Response

1. How would you describe the tone or atmosphere of this poem? Would you say it is solemn, urgent, despairing or hopeful?

2. Class Discussion: What view of romantic love is put forward by this sonnet? How does it differ from the view of love put forward in other Keats poems?

3. This poem is about fear. Would you agree that it also contains hope? Give reasons for your answer, focusing especially on the poem's conclusion.

4. The poem contains several images of plenty, vastness and abundance. Read it carefully once more and list them.

5. This poem is especially well known for its comparison between writing and harvesting. Would you agree that this is a reasonable metaphor? Give a reason for your answer.

6. Based on your reading of this poem what would you say are Keats' hopes, fears, dreams and obsessions? How do his concerns and priorities in life differ from your own?

In Context

'Keats regards writing not as a craft or a science but as an almost supernatural or magical activity.' Write two paragraphs comparing 'When I have fears' to another poem by Keats in light of this statement.

La Belle Dame Sans Merci

O what can ail thee knight at arms,
   Alone and palely loitering?
The sedge has withered from the Lake
   And no birds sing!

O what can ail thee, knight at arms! [5]
   So haggard and so woe-begone?
The squirrel's granary is full
   And the harvest's done.

I see a lily on thy brow
   With anguish moist and fever dew, [10]
And on thy cheeks a fading rose
   Fast withereth too –

I met a Lady in the Meads,
   Full beautiful a faery's child
Her hair was long, her foot was light [15]
   And her eyes were wild –

I made a Garland for her head,
   And bracelets too, and fragrant Zone;
She look'd at me as she did love,
   And made sweet moan – [20]

I set her on my pacing steed,
   And nothing else saw all day long
For sidelong would she bend and sing
   A faery's song –

She found me roots of relish sweet [25]
   And honey wild, and manna dew
And sure in language strange she said
   'I love thee true' –

She took me to her elfin grot
   And there she wept and sigh'd fill sore [30]
And there I shut her wild wild eyes
   With kisses four.

And there she lulled me asleep,
   And there I dream'd – Ah! Woe betide!
The latest dream I ever dreamt [35]
   On the cold hill side.

I saw pale kings and Princes too,
   Pale warriors, death pale were they all;
They cried – 'La Belle Dame sans Merci
   Hath thee in thrall' [40]

I saw their starv'd lips in the gloam
   With horrid warning gaped wide,
And I awoke and found me here
   On the cold hill's side.

And this is why I sojourn here [45]
   Alone and palely loitering;
Though the sedge is wither'd from the Lake
   And no birds sing –

La Belle Dame Sans Merci: the title of the poem is borrowed from Alain Chartier's poem of the same name. It means 'the beautiful lady without mercy'

[3] **sedge:** coarse grass

[6] **woe-begone:** sad or miserable looking

[7] **granary:** a storehouse for grain; in this instance refers to the squirrel's store of nuts for winter

[12] **withereth:** withers

[13] **Meads:** meadows

[17] **Garland:** wreath

[18] **Zone:** girdle or ornate belt

[19] **as she did love:** as though she did love me

[26] **manna:** a miraculous foodstuff that appears with the dew each morning; in the Bible manna was given to the Israelites while they travelled through the desert

[29] **elfin:** having to do with fairies, elves or similar supernatural beings

[29] **grot:** grotto, cave

[30] **sigh'd full sore:** sighed in great pain or sadness

[34] **Woe betide:** an exclamation of warning

[35] **latest:** last, most recent

[40] **thrall:** a state of submission or enslavement

[41] **gloam:** twilight

[45] **sojourn:** to stay, in this case meaning to linger

Comprehension

Stanzas 1 to 3

1. Who do you think is speaking in the first three stanzas?
2. What is a 'knight at arms'? With what period of history would you associate such a person?
3. What is the knight doing when the speaker encounters him?
4. What does the speaker ask the knight?
5. What other lines indicate the knight's weary and distressed appearance?
6. What is a 'granary'? What does the metaphor 'squirrel's granary' refer to? At what time of year might the 'squirrel's granary' be full?
7. The poem is set in a barren winter landscape. What lines indicate this?
8. What line indicates that the knight is sweating?
9. What does the third stanza tell us about the knight's complexion? Would you describe it as healthy or unhealthy?

Stanzas 4 to 7

10. Who is speaking in these stanzas?
11. According to the knight what was unusual or even supernatural about the woman he encountered?
12. Where was the knight when he met the Lady?
13. According to the knight the Lady was 'full beautiful'. What lines or phrases suggest her attractive appearance?
14. Class Discussion: The Lady's eyes were 'wild'. What might this suggest about her temperament and personality?
15. What did the knight make for the Lady? From what were these items manufactured?
16. The knight felt that the Lady was falling in love with him. What gave him this idea?
17. What did the Lady do as they rode through the meadow?
18. Class Discussion: The knight says that he saw 'nothing else' besides the Lady as they rode through the meadow. What do we understand by this claim? Could it be interpreted in more than one way?
19. What did the Lady give the knight to eat and drink?
20. Why do you think the Lady speaks in a 'strange' language?
21. What did the knight think the Lady was saying?
22. Is it possible that she was saying something else?

Stanzas 8 to 12

23. Where do the knight and the Lady go that evening?
24. Take a moment to visualise this location in your own mind. What do you imagine? Write a paragraph describing this place in your own words.
25. What lines indicate that the Lady becomes distressed? Can you suggest a reason for this sudden unhappiness?
26. What does the knight do to comfort the Lady?
27. What types of people appear in the knight's dream?
28. What phrases indicate their sickly and distressed appearance?
29. What 'horrid warning' do they give the knight?
30. What do you think happened to these people?
31. Group Discussion: What phrase indicates this was the last dream the knight had? Why do you think he hasn't dreamed since this moment?
32. Where is the knight when he wakes up? Is he in the same place where he fell asleep? Give a reason for your answer.
33. 'And this is why I sojourn here'. Write a paragraph describing the knight's present situation.
34. What do you think has condemned him to this plight?
35. What do you think will happen to him now?

Personal Response

1. Would you agree that this poem could be described as a 'fairy story'? Do you think its use of supernatural elements is effective? In both cases give a reason for your answer.
2. Why do you think Keats uses two different voices in this poem? Would you agree that the knight's tale is actually a story within a story? What effect did this structure have on your reading of the poem?
3. Do you think the knight is a trustworthy or reliable narrator? Can we simply believe his version of events?
4. Consider the poem's title. Do you think it effectively encapsulates the piece?
5. Would you agree that this poem serves as an effective metaphor for love? What warning does it issue with regard to romance and relationships?
6. Many female critics have expressed unhappiness with this poem. Could you suggest why this might be the case?
7. Write a paragraph commenting on Keats' use of repetition in this poem.
8. What kind of mood or atmosphere is created by this poem? Would you agree that the atmosphere changes throughout the poem? Write a short paragraph giving the reasons for your answer.

Ode to a Nightingale

I

My heart aches, and a drowsy numbness pains
    My sense, as though of hemlock I had drunk,
Or emptied some dull opiate to the drains
    One minute past, and Lethe-wards had sunk: [5]
'Tis not through envy of thy happy lot,
    But being too happy in thine happiness, –
        That thou, light-winged Dryad of the trees,
           In some melodious plot
Of beechen green, and shadows numberless, [10]
        Singest of summer in full-throated ease.

II

O, for a draught of vintage! that hath been
    Cool'd a long age in the deep-delved earth,
Tasting of Flora and the country green,
    Dance, and Provencal song, and sunburnt mirth! [15]
O for a beaker full of the warm South,
    Full of the true, the blushful Hippocrene,
        With beaded bubbles winking at the brim,
           And purple-stained mouth;
That I might drink, and leave the world unseen, [20]
    And with thee fade away into the forest dim:

III

Fade far away, dissolve, and quite forget
    What thou among the leaves hast never known,
The weariness, the fever, and the fret
    Here, where men sit and hear each other groan; [25]
Where palsy shakes a few, sad, last gray hairs,
    Where youth grows pale, and spectre-thin, and dies;
        Where but to think is to be full of sorrow
           And leaden-eyed despairs,
Where Beauty cannot keep her lustrous eyes, [30]
        Or new Love pine at them beyond tomorrow.

IV

Away! away! for I will fly to thee,
    Not charioted by Bacchus and his pards,
But on the viewless wings of Poesy,
    Though the dull brain perplexes and retards: [35]
Already with thee! tender is the night,
    And haply the Queen-Moon is on her throne,
        Cluster'd around by all her starry Fays;
           But here there is no light,
Save what from heaven is with the breezes blown [40]
    Through verdurous glooms and winding mossy ways.

[2] **hemlock:** a poison derived from the herbaceous plant of the same name
[3] **opiate:** a family of drugs including morphine and codeine; they reduce pain and induce sleep
[3] **drains:** dregs
[4] **Lethe:** in Greek mythology Lethe was a river in the underworld. Its waters made the souls of the dead forget their lives on Earth
[7] **Dryad:** in Greek mythology dryads were tree spirits; here it is a poetic reference to the nightingale
[8] **melodious:** musical
[9] **beechen:** composed of beech trees
[9] **numberless:** countless, without number
[11] **draught:** a drink or measure
[12] **deep-delved:** deeply dug or excavated; in this case refers to caves beneath the earth
[13] **Flora:** the Roman goddess of flowers
[14] **Provencal song:** Provence is a region in the south of France famous for music
[15] **warm South:** in this instance refers to wine from the south
[16] **Hippocrene:** a spring that was sacred to the Muses; drinking from it brought poetic inspiration
[25] **palsy:** sickness
[29] **lustrous:** shining
[32] **Bacchus:** Roman god of wine
[32] **pards:** leopards; according to tradition Bacchus's chariot was driven by leopards
[33] **viewless:** invisible
[33] **Poesy:** poetry
[36] **Queen-Moon:** Diana, the moon-goddess
[37] **starry Fays:** the stars are compared to fairies that serve or attend the moon
[40] **verdurous:** lush green growth

V

I cannot see what flowers are at my feet,
    Nor what soft incense hangs upon the boughs,
But, in embalmed darkness, guess each sweet
    Wherewith the seasonable month endows   [45]
The grass, the thicket, and the fruit-tree wild;
    White hawthorn, and the pastoral eglantine;
        Fast fading violets cover'd up in leaves;
        And mid-May's eldest child,
    The coming musk-rose, full of dewy wine,   [50]
        The murmurous haunt of flies on summer eves.

VI

Darkling I listen; and, for many a time
    I have been half in love with easeful Death,
Call'd him soft names in many a mused rhyme,
    To take into the air my quiet breath;   [55]
Now more than ever seems it rich to die,
    To cease upon the midnight with no pain,
        While thou art pouring forth thy soul abroad
        In such an ecstasy!
        Still wouldst thou sing, and I have ears in vain –   [60]
        To thy high requiem become a sod.

VII

Thou wast not born for death, immortal Bird!
    No hungry generations tread thee down;
The voice I hear this passing night was heard
    In ancient days by emperor and clown: [65]
Perhaps the self-same song that found a path
    Through the sad heart of Ruth, when, sick for home,
        She stood in tears amid the alien corn;
        The same that oft-times hath
    Charm'd magic casements, opening on the foam   [70]
        Of perilous seas, in faery lands forlorn.

VIII

Forlorn! the very word is like a bell
    To toll me back from thee to my sole self!
Adieu! the fancy cannot cheat so well
    As she is fam'd to do, deceiving elf.   [75]
Adieu! adieu! thy plaintive anthem fades
    Past the near meadows, over the still stream,
        Up the hill-side; and now 'tis buried deep
        In the next valley-glades:
    Was it a vision, or a waking dream?   [80]
        Fled is that music: – Do I wake or sleep?

[42] **boughs:** branches
[43] **embalmed darkness:** darkness steeped in scent, but also suggesting the concern with death in the following stanza
[46] **eglantine:** the sweetbriar, a wild rose
[50] **murmurous:** filled with a murmuring sound
[51] **Darkling:** in darkness
[60] **requiem:** music played at a funeral
[66] **Ruth:** in the Bible Ruth is forced by circumstance to work in foreign fields (see Ruth 2:3)
[67] **alien:** foreign
[69] **casements:** a type of window
[73] **fancy:** imagination
[75] **plaintive:** sad, melancholy

Comprehension

1. Class Discussion: Describe in your own words the poet's reaction to the nightingale's song. Would you agree that it is a complex reaction, one of mixed emotions?
2. What words or phrases indicate the poet's relaxed, numb or drowsy state of mind?
3. Consider the phrase 'being too happy in thine happiness'. Try to puzzle out what it suggests about the poet's response to this music.
4. Where is the nightingale located as it sings?
5. Is its song happy or melancholic, loud or quiet?
6. What does Keats want to drink?
7. What does this liquid look like?
8. Where does it come from?
9. What comparisons does Keats use to convey its wonderful taste?
10. What effect does he believe this magical substance will have on his imaginative powers?
11. Why does Keats want to 'Fade far away, dissolve, and quite forget'?
12. What is it that the nightingale has 'never known'?
13. Make a list of the different woes Keats mentions in stanza 3.
14. What do you understand by the expression 'where but to think is to be full of sorrow'?
15. How will the poet 'fly' to the nightingale?
16. What challenge must the poet overcome to accomplish this flight?
17. How does the poet indicate that alcohol will not assist him in this imaginative feat?
18. What literary device does the poet use to describe the moon and stars?
19. Is the woodland plot dark or relatively bright? Give a reason for your answer.
20. What effect does this 'seasonable month' have on the plants and flowers in this woodland plot?
21. What is the 'incense' referred to in line 42?
22. What is referred to as 'mid-May's eldest child'?
23. What creatures hang around this flower?
24. Describe in your own words the sound they produce.
25. What desire does the poet express in stanza 6?
26. Describe in your own words the relationship with death outlined in this stanza.
27. Class Discussion: What literary devices does the poet use to convey this relationship?
28. Why does this particular evening strike the poet as a fitting one on which to die?
29. What does he imagine happening after his death?
30. What does the speaker mean when he declares that the nightingale was 'not born for death'?
31. What effect do 'generations' or the passing of time have on the nightingale?

32. How does the poet indicate that the nightingale has existed for centuries? In stanza 7 the speaker mentions a number of places where the nightingale's song has been heard. List them.
33. Read lines 68 to 70 and describe in your own words the landscape you envisage.
34. What happens at the beginning of stanza 8?
35. What is the poet's reaction to this occurrence?
36. How doe he indicate that the power of 'fancy' or imagination has its limits?
37. Where does the nightingale go?
38. What confusion does the poet experience at the end of the poem?

Personal Response

1. Write a brief paragraph describing the atmosphere created by this poem. Would you agree that the atmosphere shifts from stanza to stanza?
2. Class Discussion: Several critics have suggested that the nightingale in this poem functions as a symbol. What might it symbolise?
3. Identify the three images in the poem that most appealed to you and say why you like them.
4. Write a paragraph describing Keats' use of assonance and alliteration in this poem. How does it contribute to the poem's atmosphere?
5. On balance would you consider this to be a sad or a happy poem? Give reasons for your answer.

In Context

Write a brief paragraph comparing and contrasting the depiction of nature in this poem with that in 'To Autumn'.

Ode on a Grecian Urn

I

Thou still unravish'd bride of quietness,
    Thou foster-child of silence and slow time,
Sylvan historian, who canst thus express
    A flowery tale more sweetly than our rhyme:
What leaf-fring'd legend haunts about thy shape   [5]
    Of deities or mortals, or of both,
        In Tempe or the dales of Arcady?
    What men or gods are these? What maidens loth?
What mad pursuit? What struggle to escape?
        What pipes and timbrels? What wild ecstasy?   [10]

II

Heard melodies are sweet, but those unheard
    Are sweeter; therefore, ye soft pipes, play on;
Not to the sensual ear, but, more endear'd,
    Pipe to the spirit ditties of no tone:
Fair youth, beneath the trees, thou canst not leave   [15]
    Thy song, nor ever can those trees be bare;
        Bold Lover, never, never canst thou kiss,
Though winning near the goal – yet, do not grieve;
    She cannot fade, though thou hast not thy bliss,
        For ever wilt thou love, and she be fair!   [20]

[1] **unravish'd:** untouched, virginal
[3] **Sylvan:** of the woods
[5] **leaf-fring'd:** surrounded or decorated with leaves
[5] **legend:** inscription; story handed down from earlier times
[6] **deities:** gods
[7] **Tempe:** a valley in Ancient Greece, celebrated for its beauty and the happiness of its inhabitants
[7] **dales:** valleys
[7] **Arcady:** a region in southern Greece; the ideal pastoral world
[8] **loth:** unwilling
[10] **timbrels:** percussion instruments resembling tambourines
[14] **ditties:** short songs

continued overleaf

III

Ah, happy, happy boughs! that cannot shed
    Your leaves, nor ever bid the Spring adieu;
And, happy melodist, unwearied,
    For ever piping songs for ever new;
More happy love! more happy, happy love!   [25]
    For ever warm and still to be enjoy'd,
        For ever panting, and for ever young;
All breathing human passion far above,
    That leaves a heart high-sorrowful and cloy'd,
        A burning forehead, and a parching tongue.   [30]

IV

Who are these coming to the sacrifice?
    To what green altar, O mysterious priest,
Lead'st thou that heifer lowing at the skies,
    And all her silken flanks with garlands drest?
What little town by river or sea shore,   [35]
    Or mountain-built with peaceful citadel,
        Is emptied of this folk, this pious morn?
And, little town, thy streets for evermore
    Will silent be; and not a soul to tell
        Why thou art desolate, can e'er return.   [40]

V

O Attic shape! Fair attitude! with brede
    Of marble men and maidens overwrought,
With forest branches and the trodden weed;
    Thou, silent form, dost tease us out of thought
As doth eternity: Cold Pastoral!   [45]
    When old age shall this generation waste,
        Thou shalt remain, in midst of other woe
Than ours, a friend to man, to whom thou say'st,
    'Beauty is truth, truth beauty,' – that is all
        Ye know on earth, and all ye need to know.   [50]

[21]   *boughs:* branches of a tree
[29]   *cloy'd:* wearied by excessive sweetness
[30]   *parching:* drying, thirsting
[33]   *heifer:* a cow that has not yet borne calves
[36]   *citadel:* fortress city
[41]   *Attic:* relating to Attica, a region in Greece
[41]   *brede:* braiding or embroidery
[42]   *overwrought:* the design of the artwork on the surface of the urn; to be overcome emotionally
[45]   *Pastoral:* art dealing with the countryside

Comprehension

Stanza 1

1. Read the first stanza carefully. What sort of characters and objects seem to be depicted on the urn's surface?

2. What sort of landscape is illustrated on the urn? Where does the poet imagine this place might be?

3. Is it clear or not whether the people depicted on the urn are gods or human?

4. The poet associates the urn with 'quietness', 'silence' and 'slow time' in the first two lines. Why do you think he associates the urn with these things?

5. What does the word 'Sylvan' mean? Why do you think the poet considers the urn to be a 'Sylvan historian'?

6. Class Discussion: The poet mentions 'pipes and timbrels', a 'mad pursuit' and a 'struggle to escape'. What sort of events or activities do you think are being depicted?

Stanza 2

7. Lines 11 to 14: How does he describe the music that the 'pipes' make?

8. The poet distinguishes between melodies that are played for the 'sensual ear' and those that appeal to the 'spirit'. Is it to the 'sensual ear' or the 'spirit' that the urn's pipes appeal?

9. Lines 15 to 16: The poet describes a young man or 'Fair youth' singing as he sits 'beneath the trees'. Why do you think the poet says that this youth can never 'leave [his] song'? Why can the trees never 'be bare'?

10. In lines 17 to 20 the poet describes a 'Bold Lover'. What is it that this person is trying to do? Will he never achieve this 'bliss'?

11. Why does the poet tell the 'Bold Lover' to 'not grieve'? What does he tell the 'Bold Lover' to console him?

Stanza 3

12. In the third stanza the poet considers the trees, the musician and the lovers he mentioned in the second stanza. Why does he say that the branches or 'boughs' of the tree are 'happy'? Why will they never 'bid the Spring adieu'?

13. How does the poet describe the musician or 'melodist'? Why will he be 'For ever piping songs for ever new'?

14. Class Discussion: In lines 26 to 27 the poet describes the love that the 'Bold Lover' and his beloved share. Read these two lines carefully. How does the poet characterise their love?

15. Class Discussion: 28 to 30: The poet contrasts the love that the couple depicted on the urn share with the love or 'passion' that living people experience. How does he describe 'breathing human passion'?

Stanza 4

16. The poet shifts his attention to a scene depicting a procession of people bringing a heifer to be sacrificed. How does the poet describe the heifer?

17. Who is leading the cow? Why do you think the poet uses the word 'mysterious' to describe this person?

18. Keats imagines the 'little town' that is empty now because all the townspeople have gone to attend the religious sacrifice. What different locations does the poet imagine for this town?

Stanza 5

19. Class Discussion: In the final stanza the poet addresses the urn in four different ways: 'Attic shape', 'Fair attitude', 'silent form' and 'Cold Pastoral'. Why does he use these terms of address and what do each of them say or suggest about the urn?

20. What do you think the poet means when he says to the urn 'Thou dost tease us out of thought'? Why do you think that contemplating 'eternity' has the same effect on us?

21. What will happen to the urn when the poet and his generations have passed away?

22. What sort of 'woe' do you think the poet has in mind in line 47?

23. Class Discussion: Keats says that the urn conveys the following message or lesson to man – 'Beauty is truth, truth beauty'. What do you think he means by 'beauty' and by 'truth'? Why do you think he equates the two? What does it mean to say that 'beauty' and 'truth' are the same thing?

24. The poet says that 'that is all' that we 'know on earth' and 'all [we] need to know'. Why do you think he says this?

Personal Response

1. The poem presents the reader with a number of oppositions. For example: mortality and immortality; silence and noise; the physical and the spiritual. Identify as many of these as you can and in each case say which the poet seems to value or favour most.

2. Did you find the descriptions of the scenes depicted on the urn appealing? Write a short paragraph describing each of the different scenes the poet describes throughout the poem.

3. In the third stanza the poet compares the 'happy love' of the couple depicted on the urn with 'breathing human passion'. What does he say about each? Do you think that his assessment of real human love is fair?

4. What does this poem suggest about the power and significance of art?

5. What do the last two lines mean to you?

To Autumn

I

Season of mists and mellow fruitfulness,
   Close bosom-friend of the maturing sun;
Conspiring with him how to load and bless
   With fruit the vines that round the thatch-eves run;
To bend with apples the moss'd cottage-trees,   [5]
   And fill all fruit with ripeness to the core;
     To swell the gourd, and plump the hazel shells
   With a sweet kernel; to set budding more,
And still more, later flowers for the bees,
Until they think warm days will never cease,   [10]
     For Summer has o'er-brimm'd their clammy cells.

II

Who hath not seen thee oft amid thy store?
   Sometimes whoever seeks abroad may find
Thee sitting careless on a granary floor,
   Thy hair soft-lifted by the winnowing wind;   [15]
Or on a half-reap'd furrow sound asleep,
   Drows'd with the fume of poppies, while thy hook
     Spares the next swath and all its twined flowers:
And sometimes like a gleaner thou dost keep
   Steady thy laden head across a brook;   [20]
   Or by a cider-press, with patient look,
     Thou watchest the last oozings hours by hours.

III

Where are the songs of Spring? Ay, where are they?
   Think not of them, thou hast thy music too, –
While barred clouds bloom the soft-dying day,   [25]
   And touch the stubble plains with rosy hue;
Then in a wailful choir the small gnats mourn
   Among the river sallows, borne aloft
     Or sinking as the light wind lives or dies;
And full-grown lambs loud bleat from hilly bourn;   [30]
   Hedge-crickets sing; and now with treble soft
   The red-breast whistles from a garden-croft;
     And gathering swallows twitter in the skies.

[7] *gourd:* the hard shell of various fruits

[15] *winnowing:* the process of separating the grain from the chaff at harvest time. The beaten corn was thrown in the air and the wind blew off the lighter chaff

[18] *swath:* a row of corn as it falls when reaped

[19] *gleaner:* person gathering ears of corn left by the reapers

[25] *barred:* of varying colour

[28] *sallows:* low-growing willow trees

[30] *bourn:* stream

[32] *croft:* small agricultural holding

Pre-Reading

1. Class Activity: Create a list of ten words that you associate with autumn. Is autumn anybody's favourite time of year? What is it about this time of the year that is appealing?

2. Think about the crops and fruits that are grown on farms. What usually happens to these during autumn?

Comprehension

Stanza 1

1. How does the poet describe autumn in the opening line? Why do you think he considers the 'fruitfulness' to be 'mellow' at this time of year?

2. The poet says that autumn and the sun work together as a team. What is it that they plan to do in lines 3 and 4?

3. What sort of fruit do you imagine grows on the 'vines' mentioned in line 4? Where do these vines grow?

4. What will autumn and the sun do to the 'moss'd cottage-trees'?

5. Lines 6 to 8 focus on the ripening of fruit and nuts that occurs at this time of year. What verbs does the poet use to describe this process?

6. What do you think the poet means by 'later flowers' in line 9? What will autumn and the sun do to these flowers?

7. What effect will the continuous budding of flowers have on the bees?

8. What are the 'clammy cells' that Keats mentions in line 11? What condition are these cells in after the summer months?

Stanza 2

9. How does Keats allude to autumn's harvest in the opening line of the second stanza?

10. The poet personifies the season in this stanza and imagines her being in different locations. Where does he imagine her being in lines 13 to 15?

11. The poet mentions the 'winnowing wind' in line 15. What is this 'wind'? What is happening in the granary where autumn sits? What effect does the wind have on her?

12. How does Keats describe the season's demeanour in line 14?

13. Where does the poet imagine the season to be in lines 16 to 18? What activity has been taking place here?

14. What does the poet say has caused autumn to fall asleep? What is the 'hook' that lies beside her? What has she been doing with this?

15. What is a 'gleaner'? In what way does the poet say that autumn is like a gleaner?

16. Keats describes how autumn keeps her 'laden' head 'Steady' as she crosses a brook or stream. What do you imagine autumn is carrying here?

17. Where does the poet imagine autumn to be in lines 21 to 22: ? What is she watching happen here?

Stanza 3

18. Class Discussion: What do you think Keats means by the 'songs of Spring'? Why do you think he asks where these 'songs' are?

19. Lines 25 and 26: What time of day is the poet describing here? How does he describe the sky? What effect does the sun's light have on the fields? What are the 'stubble plains' mentioned in line 26?

20. In lines 27 to 33 the poet describes the different sounds that contribute to the 'music' of autumn. What is the 'wailful choir' that he mentions in line 27? Why do you think the poet describes the sound as 'wailful'? What do you think it is that the gnats 'mourn'?

21. Where are the gnats located? How does the poet describe their movements? What is it that raises them up and lowers them down again?

22. What sounds does the poet describe in lines 30 to 33? What verbs does Keats use to describe these different sounds?

23. How does the poet characterise the whistling of the red-breast?

Personal Response

1. Did this poem make you think or feel differently about autumn?

2. How would you describe the mood and atmosphere in each of the poem's three stanzas? Do the mood and atmosphere change as the poem progresses?

3. The poem is full of wonderful sounds and a number of words and phrases have an onomatopoeic quality, i.e., they sound like the very thing they are describing. Identify as many instances of onomatopoeia as you can in the poem.

4. Keats uses plenty of tactile imagery throughout the poem and there are times when you can almost feel what he is describing. Can you identify any such instances in the poem? Which image is your favourite?

5. The three stanzas of the poem seem to correspond not only with three distinct stages of the season but three stages of the day. Write a short essay in which you discuss these two progressions.

In Context

'The poetry of John Keats celebrates the solitary individual and considers the world to be most pleasant when there is no one around to spoil its beauty.' Discuss this statement, making reference to three poems by Keats on your course.

Bright star

Bright star, would I were stedfast as thou art –
   Not in lone splendour hung aloft the night
And watching, with eternal lids apart,
   Like nature's patient, sleepless Eremite,
The moving waters at their priestlike task   [5]
   Of pure ablution round earth's human shores,
Or gazing on the new soft-fallen mask
   Of snow upon the mountains and the moors –
No – yet still stedfast, still unchangeable,
   Pillow'd upon my fair love's ripening breast,   [10]
To feel for ever its soft fall and swell,
   Awake for ever in a sweet unrest,
Still, still to hear her tender-taken breath,
And so live ever – or else swoon in death.

[1]   **stedfast:** unchanging, fixed in position
[4]   **Eremite:** a hermit, recluse
[6]   **ablution:** washing, sometimes in a ceremonious manner

Pre-Reading

What does it mean to be 'stedfast'? In what way might a star be considered 'stedfast'?

Comprehension

Lines 1 to 8

1. Can you re-write the first line in your own words?
2. Line 2: The poet does not wish to be 'stedfast' like the star in one respect. What is it about the star's existence that he finds unappealing?
3. What two things does the poet imagine the star sees from its high vantage?
4. What is an 'Eremite'? Why do you think the poet considers the star to be 'nature's ... Eremite'?
5. What two adjectives does Keats use in line 4 to describe the star? Why do you think he uses these?
6. What are the 'moving waters' that the poet mentions in line 5?
7. What does the word 'ablution' mean? What priestly activity involves 'ablution'?
8. Keats says that the 'moving waters' perform a 'task/ Of pure ablution round earth's human shores'. What phenomenon do you think he has in mind here?
9. What do you think the poet means by 'earth's human shores'?
10. What sort of snow does the poet describe in lines 7 and 8? Where does he imagine this snow resting? What word does Keats use to describe the way the snow covers these places?

Lines 9 to 14

11. Why does the poet begin the ninth line of the poem with the word 'No'? To what is he saying 'No'?
12. In lines 1 to 8 the poet outlines the way in which he does not wish to be 'stedfast'. In the last six lines of the poem he states how he wishes to be 'stedfast'. What sort of steadfastness is he describing in line 9?
13. Where would the poet like to rest his head?
14. Why do you think the poet uses the word 'ripening' to describe his beloved's breast?
15. What does the poet describe feeling in line 11?
16. Class Discussion: Keats says that he would like to 'Awake forever in a sweet unrest'? What do you think he means by 'sweet unrest'?
17. The poet repeats the word 'still' in line 13. Are there different ways that this word can be understood in this context? Do you think the poet intended for the word to have different meanings?

18. List the different adjectives and adverbs that the poet uses to describe his beloved and her movements. What sort of picture do they present?
19. 'And so live for ever'. How would the poet like to live forever?
20. If the poet cannot live forever in the way he describes he would prefer to 'swoon in death'. What do you think he means by this? Why do you think he chose the word 'swoon'? What sort of death do you think he has in mind here?

Personal Response

1. Many of Keats' poems deal with the theme of timelessness and immortality. Based on your reading of the poem, what is it that appeals to the poet about living forever?
2. Consider the description of Earth contained within the poem. Is there a suggestion that the world is only beautiful seen from a very great distance?
3. What does the poem suggest to you about the poet's views on love? Do you think that Keats is a realist or idealist when it comes to affairs of the heart?
4. There are numerous references to motion and stillness in the poem. What objects remain static and what things move?

In Context

Discuss how Keats links love and death in both 'Bright Star' and 'When I have fears that I may cease to be'. How do the poems compare and differ?

Sylvia Plath

Sylvia Plath was born in Boston, Massachusetts in October 1932. Her father, Otto Plath, was a professor of entomology, the study of insects, and published an important scientific book entitled *Bumblebees and Their Ways* (a specialisation, perhaps, that influenced Plath's later interest in bee-keeping and poems such as 'The Arrival of the Bee Box'.) Plath seems to have had a happy childhood, and from the beginning it was clear that she was extremely bright and academically gifted. When she was eight years old, however, her father developed diabetes and died from complications during a surgery to amputate his foot. Plath experienced a loss of faith as a result of this tragedy.

Plath's interest in literature began at an early age and she published her first poem in the *Boston Herald* when she was just eight years old. At high school, Plath excelled academically and by then had set her sights on becoming a writer. She devoted much of her spare time to reading and to writing poems and stories, a number of which were published in the school magazine.

It was around this time that Plath was rejected for a creative-writing class she had applied for, conducted by the Irish writer Frank O'Connor. The rejection sent her into a black depression. She underwent a course of electroconvulsive therapy, attempted suicide by overdosing on sleeping pills, and spent several months thereafter in a psychiatric institution. Plath recovered from this setback, however, and returned to Smith College, from where she graduated in 1955. Her academic performance, as usual, was exceptional, and earned her a two-year Fulbright scholarship to Cambridge University.

Plath loved Cambridge but continued to endure bouts of depression and self-loathing. In January 1956 she met Ted Hughes, a young poet who shared her hunger for literary success. The two fell in love and were married four months later. The young couple spent 1957–59 in the US. She taught for a while at Smith College and later did part-time secretarial work.

Her marriage to Hughes was turbulent. She struggled with depression and fits of writer's block, but continued to produce powerful poetry, including 'The Times Are Tidy' and 'Black Rook in Rainy Weather'. In 1959 she attended a writing class with the highly respected American poet Robert Lowell and, with Hughes, spent time at the famous artists' colony at Yaddo in New York State, two developments that greatly contributed to her maturation as a writer.

Plath and Hughes returned to England at the end of 1959 and moved to London, where Plath gave birth to her first child, Frieda. 'Morning Song' dates from this period. In the autumn of 1961 the family relocated to what Plath described as her 'dream house' in the Devon countryside. Here, the couple wrote and shared the responsibility of looking after their baby daughter. Many of Plath's most important poems were written in Devon. That autumn she wrote 'Finisterre' and 'Mirror'. The following spring brought 'Elm' and 'Pheasant'.

Plath gave birth to a second child, Nicholas, in January 1962, but by that summer her marriage had started to collapse. Hughes became involved with another woman. Plath's anguish at this development is evident in 'Poppies in July'. The two separated that autumn, leaving Plath alone in Devon with her two children. This was an extremely difficult period in Plath's life and she became profoundly depressed. She continued to

> **"She had continued to write up until the very end. 'Child', for example, was written on 28 January, just two weeks before her death."**

write powerful poetry, however, including 'The Arrival of the Bee Box'. In December, Plath left behind the isolation of Devon and returned to London with her children. Her famous, semi-autobiographical novel, *The Bell Jar*, which offers a fictionalised retelling of her summer at *Mademoiselle* magazine, was published in 1963. However, the strain of a failed marriage and the weariness of a lifelong battle with depression simply became too much for Plath. In February 1963 – just a month after *The Bell Jar* was published – Plath took her own life. She was thirty years old.

For many readers, the poetry of Sylvia Plath will always be overshadowed by the tragedy of her suicide. It is tempting to view Plath's work as a protracted suicide note, a record of her psychological and spiritual decline. Much of Plath's mental anguish stemmed from the fear that her poetic gifts would desert her, that she would never again feel sufficiently inspired to write another poem. It is perhaps ironic, therefore, that she produced the majority of her most famous poems when she was at her lowest psychological ebb. In the weeks and months before her suicide, in particular, she was extremely prolific, writing a poem, or even two, a day.

A key observation of the body of Plath's writing is the transition toward an intense confessional style of poetry. *The Colossus* – Plath's first collection, comprising some forty poems – was published in 1960. This included works such as 'The Times are Tidy' and 'Black Rook in Rainy Weather'. The British scholar, Bernard Bergonzi, described it as an 'outstanding technical accomplishment'. However, *Ariel*, her most celebrated collection – and arguably the poetry upon which most of her literary status rests – was not published until 1965, two years after her death. It featured pieces that would go on to become some of Plath's best-known poems, such as 'Poppies in July', 'Elm' and 'Morning Song'.

Ariel received rave reviews, partly because it offered a powerful insight into Plath's darkening depression and despair. There was a marked change in Plath's output after her split from Hughes. In the aftermath of their separation, Plath penned dozens of poems that were ripe with anger and inexorable sadness. This was almost certainly inspired in part by Hughes's infidelity. The highly personal poems in *Ariel* reveal the extent of the psychological toll that Plath experienced as a result of the break-up. Her renewed industry in the wake of the separation has led some academics to suggest that Plath was (or felt) subordinated to Hughes's own literary endeavour while they were married.

She had continued to write up until the very end. 'Child', for example, was written on 28 January, just two weeks before her death. She was buried in the church of St Thomas the Apostle in Heptonstall, Yorkshire, and her headstone is inscribed with the phrase 'Even amidst fierce flames the golden lotus can be planted'.

The Times Are Tidy

Unlucky the hero born
In this province of the stuck record
Where the most watchful cooks go jobless
And the mayor's rôtisserie turns
Round of its own accord.   [5]

There's no career in the venture
Of riding against the lizard,
Himself withered these latter-days
To leaf-size from lack of action:
History's beaten the hazard.   [10]

The last crone got burnt up
More than eight decades back
With the love-hot herb, the talking cat,
But the children are better for it,
The cow milks cream an inch thick.   [15]

[4] *rôtisserie:* a rotating spit used for cooking whole animals
[8] *latter-days:* in recent times
[11] *crone:* witch

Tease It Out

1. What do you associate the word 'tidy' with? Do you think that times being 'tidy' is a positive or a negative thing?

2. The poet describes a certain place as the 'province of the stuck record'. What do you associate a 'stuck record' with? What does the description suggest about the place that the poet has in mind?

3. Plath says that the 'most watchful cooks go jobless' in this place. What do you imagine she means by 'watchful'? What does the fact that such people cannot find work tell us about the times or place that the poem describes? What has replaced the people with such skills?

4. What sort of person do you imagine the poet has in mind when she mentions 'the hero' in the opening line? Why do you think that the poet says such a person would be 'Unlucky' to be born in these times?

5. The poem mentions lizards, 'talking' cats and witches ('crone'). What sort of place or time do you think the poet has in mind when she mentions these things? How does this place or time compare with the times that the poet is living in?

6. Plath says that there is no longer a 'career' in 'riding against the lizard'. What do you think the 'lizard' represents? What sort of person would ride out against such a creature?

7. The poet says that the 'lizard' has 'withered' in recent times from 'lack of action'. What do you think the poet is suggesting about modern times when she says this?

8. Lines 11 to 13: Plath says that the 'last crone' got 'burnt up' more than 'eight decades back'. What sort of people does the poet have in mind here? Why were these people 'burnt'?

9. In the second last line of the poem Plath says that the 'children are better for it' because the 'cow' now 'milks cream an inch thick'. Do you think she is being serious or sarcastic here?

Think About Themes

1. What does the poem suggest about the times in which the poet is living? What do you think it is that bothers her most about these times?

2. What do you think the poem has to say about modern scientific and technological advances? Is the poet entirely negative about such things?

3. Why, in your opinion, might the poet pine for the times when witches were burnt at the stake?

4. The poem contrasts two very different times or worlds. Write a paragraph describing each. Which time period is more appealing to you?

5. Is the modern world as predictable as the poem makes out? Have we 'beaten the hazard?'

In Context

Write an essay discussing how the poems 'The Times Are Tidy', 'Black Rook in Rainy Weather', and 'Child' celebrate the importance and value of the imagination.

Black Rook in Rainy Weather

On the stiff twig up there
Hunches a wet black rook
Arranging and rearranging its feathers in the rain.
I do not expect a miracle
Or an accident   [5]

To set the sight on fire
In my eye, nor seek
Any more in the desultory weather some design,
But let spotted leaves fall as they fall,
Without ceremony, or portent.   [10]

Although, I admit, I desire,
Occasionally, some backtalk
From the mute sky, I can't honestly complain:
A certain minor light may still
Leap incandescent   [15]

Out of kitchen table or chair
As if a celestial burning took
Possession of the most obtuse objects now and then –
Thus hallowing an interval
Otherwise inconsequent   [20]

By bestowing largesse, honor,
One might say love. At any rate, I now walk
Wary (for it could happen
Even in this dull, ruinous landscape); skeptical,
Yet politic; ignorant   [25]

Of whatever angel may choose to flare
Suddenly at my elbow. I only know that a rook
Ordering its black feathers can so shine
As to seize my senses, haul
My eyelids up, and grant   [30]

A brief respite from fear
Of total neutrality. With luck,
Trekking stubborn through this season
Of fatigue, I shall
Patch together a content   [35]

Of sorts. Miracles occur,
If you care to call those spasmodic
Tricks of radiance miracles. The wait's begun again,
The long wait for the angel,
For that rare, random descent.   [40]

[2]	**rook:** a type of crow
[8]	**desultory:** haphazardly; randomly
[10]	**portent:** omen, a sign of things to come
[15]	**incandescent:** glowing, incredibly bright
[18]	**obtuse:** physically blunt or lacking sharp edges, stupid or slow to understand
[19]	**hallowing:** making holy or sacred
[19]	**interval:** a period of time
[20]	**inconsequent:** unimportant
[21]	**largesse:** generosity
[23]	**wary:** cautious
[25]	**politic:** prudent, crafty, sensible
[31]	**respite:** a period of relief
[37]	**spasmodic:** fitful, occasional, unpredictable

Tease It Out

1. Look up the species of bird popularly known as the 'rook'. What are the main physical features of this species? Describe its appearance in your own words.

2. Read the first two stanzas carefully. Describe in your own words the landscape through which the speaker is walking. What time of year is it? What is the weather like?

3. Why do you think the leaves are described as 'spotted'? Could the spots that mark them be caused by more than one thing?

4. Where is the rook situated? What is it doing?

5. 'The speaker believes that there is some pattern or design to falling leaves, that they might reveal some meaning or message'. Is this statement true or false? Give reasons for your answer.

6. Class Discussion: In lines 3 to 18 the speaker uses three different metaphors to describe poetic inspiration. She refers to something that would 'set the sight on fire/ In [her] eye'. She refers to backtalk coming from the sky. She refers to an 'incandescent' light that might 'leap' out of ordinary objects. Which of these strikes you as the most imaginative? Which makes most sense to you? Which strikes you as the least logical or reasonable?

7. The speaker also describes inspiration as a 'miracle' or 'accident'. Take each of these words and write down five other words associated with it. What does your list suggest about poetic inspiration as the speaker has presented it?

8. Based on your reading of lines 1 to 13, does the speaker expect such a 'miracle' or 'accident' to occur as she walks through this landscape?

9. The speaker says she 'can't honestly complain'. Why is this?

10. 'As if a celestial burning took/ Possession of the most obtuse objects now and then'. Why do you think the speaker refers to these objects as 'obtuse'? Is more than one meaning of obtuse involved here?

11. Try to describe in your own words what the speaker perceives happening to these objects in lines 19 and 20. Do you consider this an effective metaphor for poetic inspiration?

12. What effect does this 'celestial burning' have on periods of time that would otherwise be 'inconsequent' or totally unimportant?

13. The speaker claims to have been granted 'largesse', 'honor' and 'love' during such moments. What does this suggest about her attitude towards poetic inspiration?

14. The speaker walks 'wary' through the landscape. What is the reason for this wariness? What does she think 'could happen' at any moment?

15. Yet another metaphor is used for poetic inspiration in lines 26 and 27. What is it?

16. Group Discussion: Consider the words 'skeptical' and 'politic'. What do these terms mean? What do they suggest about the speaker's attitude to the possibility of inspiration in this 'dull' place?

17. What sudden impact does the sight of the rook have on the speaker?

18. According to the speaker, this experience staves off the threat of 'total neutrality'. What do you think she means by 'total neutrality'? What kind of mental state is being referred to here? Do you think it is a pleasant or unpleasant one?

19. Read stanza 7 carefully and pick three words that, in your opinion, best describe the speaker's state of mind as she 'treks' along.

20. What do you think is the 'content' the speaker aims to patch together?

21. 'The wait's begun again'. What is the speaker waiting for?

22. Class Discussion: This poem has a hidden rhyme scheme. Can you identify it?

Think About Themes

1. List the many metaphors for poetic inspiration in this poem. Based on your list try to write out the five main features of poetic inspiration as viewed by Plath.

2. Sylvia Plath viewed the ability to write poetry as being essential to her mental well-being. Identify three instances where the poem communicates this view.

3. Pick three adjectives that, in your opinion, best describe the speaker of this poem and in each case write a brief paragraph explaining your choice. (Suggestions: determined, hysterical, hopeful, despairing, focused, self-absorbed, nature-loving).

4. Group Discussion: 'This poem is structured around the opposition between heat and light on one hand and coldness and darkness on the other'. Discuss this issue with your group and write a few lines listing where these opposites appear throughout the course of the poem.

In Context

Plath once said: 'Oh, satisfaction! I don't think I could live without it. It's like water or bread, or something absolutely essential to me. I find myself absolutely fulfilled when I have written a poem, when I'm writing one. Having written one, then you fall away very rapidly from having been a poet to becoming a sort of poet in rest, which isn't the same thing at all. But I think the actual experience of writing a poem is a magnificent one'. Write a few lines relating these comments to 'Black Rook in Rainy Weather'.

Morning Song

Love set you going like a fat gold watch.
The midwife slapped your footsoles, and your bald cry
Took its place among the elements.

Our voices echo, magnifying your arrival. New statue.
In a drafty museum, your nakedness
Shadows our safety. We stand round blankly as walls. [5]

I'm no more your mother
Than the cloud that distils a mirror to reflect its own slow
Effacement at the wind's hand.

All night your moth-breath
Flickers among the flat pink roses. I wake to listen: [10]
A far sea moves in my ear.

One cry, and I stumble from bed, cow-heavy and floral
In my Victorian nightgown.
Your mouth opens clean as a cat's. The window square [14]

Whitens and swallows its dull stars. And now you try [15]
Your handful of notes;
The clear vowels rise like balloons.

---

[9]   *effacement:* the process of being erased or obliterated
[14] *Victorian:* having characteristics commonly associated with the Victorians; unglamorous and conventional

Tease It Out

Lines 1 to 9

1. Read the first six lines of the poem. How would you describe the atmosphere in these lines?

2. The poet compares the baby to a 'fat gold watch'. Why do you think she makes this comparison?

3. How does the poet describe the baby's arrival in lines 2 and 3? What is the first thing that it receives?

4. Why do you think that the poet uses the word 'bald' to describe its cry?

5. What do you understand 'the elements' to be a reference to? Do these lines suggest that the world is a warm and welcoming place?

6. The poet says that the baby 'Took its place among the elements'. What does this line suggest about the position that the baby occupies in the world?

7. Why do you think the poet says that their voices 'echo'? What is she describing here? What do you imagine the poet and her husband say?

8. The poet compares the baby to a 'New statue'. What does this suggest about both the baby and the parents' reaction to its arrival?

9. Class Discussion: 'your nakedness/ Shadows our safety'. What do you think the poet means by this?

10. 'We stand round blankly as walls'. What does this comparison suggest about the way the parents are feeling about the arrival of their child?

11. In line 8 the poet describes a cloud distilling 'a mirror'. What do you think she has in mind here? In what way might a cloud distil a mirror?

12. Plath says that the mirror that the cloud distils 'reflect[s] its own slow/ Effacement at the wind's hand'. What does the word 'effacement' mean? How might the wind efface a cloud? What is it that reflects this effacement?

13. To what is Plath comparing the baby in lines 7 to 9? To what is she comparing herself in these lines? What is the nature of the relationship suggested in these lines?

Lines 10 to 18

14. Consider the comparisons that the poet makes in the fourth stanza ('moth-breath', 'flat pink roses', 'far sea'). How do these differ from the ones used in the first two stanzas? How would you describe the atmosphere in the fourth stanza?

15. What does the term 'moth-breath' suggest about the child's breathing?

16. What do you think the 'flat pink roses' are a reference to?

17. What is the 'far sea' that the poet listens to when she wakes during the night? Why do you think she uses this comparison?

18. How does the poet describe herself and her newfound role as mother in the fifth stanza?

19. 'The window square/ Whitens and swallows its dull stars'. What is being described here?

20. How does the poet describe the sounds that the baby makes after it has been fed?

Think About Themes

1. Were you surprised by the first three stanzas? Do you think that the lines describe the way many parents feel when their child is born?

2. Class Discussion: What three words would you use to describe the poet's reaction to the birth of her child?

3. Why do you think that the poet chose the title 'Morning Song' for this poem? What does it suggest that the poem is ultimately about?

4. How would you characterise the world presented in the first six lines? How does it differ from the world presented in the second half of the poem?

5. The poem contains numerous images from the natural world. List as many as you can and say which ones you found most effective.

In Context

1. Compare this poem with 'Child'. What do each of these poems suggest about the emotional stresses of parenthood?

2. In the poetry of Sylvia Plath the natural world often serves as a metaphor or a mirror for her inner emotions. Discuss this statement with reference to at least three poems by Plath on the course.

Mirror

I am silver and exact. I have no preconceptions.
Whatever I see I swallow immediately
Just as it is, unmisted by love or dislike.
I am not cruel, only truthful
The eye of a little god, four-cornered.
Most of the time I meditate on the opposite wall.   [5]
It is pink, with speckles. I have looked at it so long
I think it is a part of my heart. But it flickers.
Faces and darkness separate us over and over.

Now I am a lake. A woman bends over me,
Searching my reaches for what she really is.   [10]
Then she turns to those liars, the candles or the moon.
I see her back, and reflect it faithfully.
She rewards me with tears and an agitation of hands.
I am important to her. She comes and goes.
Each morning it is her face that replaces the darkness.   [15]
In me she has drowned a young girl, and in me an old woman
Rises toward her day after day, like a terrible fish.

Handwritten annotations: personification, personification, metaphor, metaphor, image, onomatopoeia, repitition, metaphor, image, personification, repitition, image, image, repitition, image, simile, Themes, Passage of time, Anxiety

Tease It Out

Stanza 1

1. Class Discussion: What does the mirror mean by the word 'exact'? Do you think more than one meaning of this word might be intended here?

2. The mirror emphasises how it reflects an accurate and unbiased image of anyone who looks into it. What words and phrases convey this message?

3. The mirror says that it 'swallows' whatever it sees. What do you think it means by this? Do you think it is fair to say that in this context the word 'swallow' has negative or sinister connotations?

4. Class Discussion: In line 5 the mirror describes itself as a kind of god-like being. In what sense might mirrors be said to function like gods in our everyday lives?

5. What does the mirror spend its days doing?

6. Write a short paragraph describing, in your own words the mirror's feelings toward the speckled wall.

7. What repeatedly 'separates' the mirror from the wall?

8. The mirror stresses that it is 'not cruel'. Based on your reading of the first stanza do you think this is a fair statement?

Stanza 2

9. The mirror compares itself to a lake. Do you think this is a good or accurate comparison? What similarities, if any, are there between a mirror and a lake?

10. The mirror's owner is described as 'searching' in the mirror. What is she searching for? Are these lines literal or metaphorical? Write a short paragraph describing the woman's behaviour in your own words.

11. Class Discussion: According to the mirror, the candles and the moon are merely 'liars'. What might the mirror mean by this? In what sense might these sources of light be considered misleading or untruthful?

12. What do lines 13 and 14 suggest about the mirror's relationship with its owner? In what tone of voice do you imagine these lines being spoken? Are they sad or angry, pleading or sarcastic?

13. What does line 14 suggest about the owner's state of mind? Pick three words that, in your opinion, best describe her mental state and in each case give reasons for your choice.

14. The mirror claims it is 'important' to the woman. In what ways might a mirror be important to an individual? Consider here psychological as well as purely practical factors.

15. Line 16 suggests that the opposite is also true; that the woman is also important to the mirror. How does it do this?

16. Group Discussion: The poem's final two lines provide a powerful metaphor for the aging process. Read them carefully and write a paragraph describing in your own words the various comparisons present in these lines.

Think About Themes

1. This poem is unusual in that it is spoken by an inanimate object. What is the technical term for this poetic technique? Do you think this literary device is successful or silly in 'Mirror'? Give a reason for your answer.

2. Class Discussion: Do you imagine the mirror as a male or female character? Or do you think of it as somehow 'gender neutral'? Why?

3. ''Mirror' is not a poem with a sustained argument. Instead, it communicates its meaning by a dreamlike movement from image to image'. Do you agree with this statement? Write a paragraph outlining the reason for your answer.

4. Pick out two different images from the poem. In the case of each image, say whether or not you think it is convincing and effective.

5. 'Mirror' is commonly regarded as a poem of despair and desperation. How did reading it make you feel? Do you think the poem features any hope?

6. Imagine you are the woman in the poem. Write a few lines describing your daily routine, your mental state and your attitude towards the mirror.

In Context

Mirror is similar to 'Elm' in that both seem to be spoken by inanimate objects. Write a paragraph in which you identify three other similarities between these two poems. You might think of mood, atmosphere, tone, images and so on.

Finisterre

This was the land's end: the last fingers, knuckled and rheumatic,
Cramped on nothing. Black
Admonitory cliffs, and the sea exploding
With no bottom, or anything on the other side of it,
Whitened by the faces of the drowned.   [5]
Now it is only gloomy, a dump of rocks –
Leftover soldiers from old, messy wars.
The sea cannons into their ear, but they don't budge.
Other rocks hide their grudges under the water.

The cliffs are edged with trefoils, stars and bells   [10]
Such as fingers might embroider, close to death,
Almost too small for the mists to bother with.
The mists are part of the ancient paraphernalia –
Souls, rolled in the doom-noise of the sea.
They bruise the rocks out of existence, then resurrect them.   [15]
They go up without hope, like sighs.
I walk among them, and they stuff my mouth with cotton.
When they free me, I am beaded with tears.

Our Lady of the Shipwrecked is striding toward the horizon,
Her marble skirts blown back in two pink wings.   [20]
A marble sailor kneels at her foot distractedly, and at his foot
A peasant woman in black
Is praying to the monument of the sailor praying.
Our Lady of the Shipwrecked is three times life size,
Her lips sweet with divinity.   [25]
She does not hear what the sailor or the peasant is saying –
She is in love with the beautiful formlessness of the sea.

Gull-colored laces flap in the sea drafts
Beside the postcard stalls.
The peasants anchor them with conches. One is told: [30]
'These are the pretty trinkets the sea hides,
Little shells made up into necklaces and toy ladies.
They do not come from the Bay of the Dead down there,
But from another place, tropical and blue,
We have never been to.   [35]
These are our crêpes. Eat them before they blow cold.'

Finisterre: a reference to Finistère, a region in the far edge of Brittany in north-western France. The name comes from the Latin 'finis terræ', meaning 'end of the earth', hence the reference in the first line to 'land's end' [1]

rheumatic: suffering from rheumatism; sore, stiff and immobile [3]

Admonitory: warning [10]

trefoils: a three-leafed plant, such as clover [13]

paraphernalia: stuff, bits and pieces, miscellaneous gear [19]

Our Lady of the Shipwrecked: a large statue of the Virgin Mary is located on Pointe du Raz, a rocky and isolated headland in the Finistère region [25]

divinity: holiness [30]

conches: snail-shaped sea shells [33]

Bay of the Dead: the bay overlooked by the cliffs of Finistère [36]

crêpes: a light, thin pancake, especially popular in the Brittany region

Tease It Out

Stanza 1

1. The poet describes rocky outcrops jutting from the sea. What do the phrases 'knuckled and rheumatic' and 'cramped on nothing' suggest about the appearance of these geographical features? (Look these words up in a dictionary if necessary.)

2. Describe the cliffs in your own words. Are they pleasant and inviting or dark and threatening?

3. The speaker suggests that the ocean has 'no bottom' or 'anything on the other side' of it. Does she really think that this is the case? Why does she make this outlandish claim?

4. What metaphor does the poet use to describe patches of foam on the ocean's surface? Do you think it is an effective comparison?

5. What phrase indicates that the water is dark and opaque rather than shimmering and transparent?

6. The bay is littered with small rocks that protrude through the water's surface. What metaphor does the poet use to describe these?

7. Consider the words 'cannons' and 'exploding'. What do they suggest about the manner in which the waves roll in?

8. 'Other rocks hide their grudges under the water'. What does Plath mean by this metaphor? What does the use of the word 'grudges' suggest about these rocks' physical features and the danger they might pose?

9. What 'war' does the poet refer to in this stanza? Identify all the words and phrases and images she uses that are associated with war and combat.

Stanza 2

10. Flowers grow around the cliff edge. What phrases indicate their intricate and complex patterns?

11. What phrases indicate the flowers' weakness and fragility?

12. Group Discussion: What metaphor is used to describe the mists that drift up from the sea? Is it an effective one?

13. The speaker claims that the mists briefly 'bruise the rocks out of existence'. What does she mean by this?

14. What happens to the speaker when she enters the mist?

15. Group Discussion: Why does the speaker claim to be beaded with tears when she exits the mist? Is this phrase open to more than one interpretation?

Stanza 3

16. Describe in your own words the monument on the cliff-side. What figures does it depict? What size is it? What colours have been used?

17. 'Her lips sweet with divinity'. What does this suggest about the statue's facial expression?

18. Who is praying at the monument?

19. Why, according to the speaker, does Our Lady of the Shipwrecked ignore the sailor and the peasant woman?

20. Group Discussion: Read the lines about Our Lady carefully. What poetic device does Plath use in her depiction of this inanimate object?

21. Class Discussion: The peasant woman's prayers seem directed at the statue of the sailor rather than at the statue of the virgin herself. Is this significant? Taken as a whole, what does this stanza suggest about Plath's attitude toward religion?

Stanza 4

22. The speaker visits nearby 'postcard stalls' where little trinkets are for sale. How are these fragile souvenirs created?

23. Where do the shells used in their manufacture originate?

24. How do the peasants prevent these objects from blowing away in the 'sea drafts'?

25. What type of food do the peasants offer the speaker?

Think About Themes

1. While composing 'Finisterre', Plath was deeply concerned about the possibility of a global nuclear conflict that would destroy the human race. How does this concern colour her description of the personal experience of visiting Finisterre?

2. Examine each of the poem's four stanzas. In the case of each, list the adjectives that in your opinion best describe the stanza's atmosphere and the speaker's tone of voice.

3. Based on your reading of the poem as a whole, what do you think is the poet's attitude towards religion? Does the poem suggest that she believes in God? Does it suggest that she regards religion as a positive force in the world?

4. 'In 'Finsiterre', Plath uses the physical description of a landscape to illustrate her own state of mind'. Do you think this is a reasonable understanding of the poem? What might the poem's detailed physical descriptions suggest about Plath's state of mind when she composed them?

5. Class Discussion: In what ways does the final stanza differ from the rest of the poem? How, if at all, does it alter your response to what has gone before?

In Context

The sea is a regular presence throughout Plath's work. In 'Elm', too, it has dark associations. In 'Morning Song', however, the mention of a gentle 'far sea' echoes the peasants' comments about the tropical and blue waters that exist far from the Bay of the Dead. Write a short essay about the depiction of the sea in Plath's poetry.

Pheasant

You said you would kill it this morning.
Do not kill it. It startles me still,
The jut of that odd, dark head, pacing

Through the uncut grass on the elm's hill.
It is something to own a pheasant,   [5]
Or just to be visited at all.

I am not mystical: it isn't
As if I thought it had a spirit.
It is simply in its element.

That gives it a kingliness, a right.   [10]
The print of its big foot last winter,
The tail-track, on the snow in our court –

The wonder of it, in that pallor,
Through crosshatch of sparrow and starling.
Is it its rareness, then? It is rare.   [15]

But a dozen would be worth having,
A hundred, on that hill – green and red,
Crossing and recrossing: a fine thing!

It is such a good shape, so vivid.
It's a little cornucopia.   [20]
It unclaps, brown as a leaf, and loud,

Settles in the elm, and is easy.
It was sunning in the narcissi.
I trespass stupidly. Let be, let be.

[3]   *jut:* protrusion
[7]   *mystical:* holding beliefs in
      things beyond normal human
      understanding
[14] *crosshatch:* criss-cross pattern
[20] *cornucopia:* a mythical horn,
      perpetually full of flowers and
      fruit; a symbol of abundance
[23] *narcissi:* white and yellow flowers
      that blossom in spring.

Tease It Out

1. Where is the pheasant that the poet describes? What details does the poet give about this location in the second stanza?
2. Who do you imagine the poet is addressing in the opening lines of the poem? What does this person intend to do to the pheasant?
3. 'It startles me still'. What is it about the pheasant that 'startles' the poet?
4. What word does the poet use to describe the movements of the pheasant's head? What does this word suggest about the way the bird's head moves as it walks?
5. 'I am not mystical'. Why do you think the poet mentions this? How does the fact that she is not 'mystical' influence the way she values or appreciates the pheasant?
6. This is not the first time that the pheasant has appeared on the poet's land. When does the poet say the bird first appeared? How was the poet aware that the pheasant had been in their garden on that occasion?
7. What is it that the poet considers gives the pheasant a 'right' to be where it is?
8. Consider the references that the poet makes to royalty in the fourth stanza. Why do you think she makes such references?
9. What is the 'pallor' a reference to in line 13? What effect does this 'pallor' have on the pheasant's appearance?
10. 'Through crosshatch of sparrow and starling'. What is a 'crosshatch'? What exactly is the poet describing here?
11. Why do you think the poet considers the pheasant to be 'rare'?
12. What does the poet imagine in stanza 6? Why does this idea appeal to her?
13. What does the word 'cornucopia' mean? Why do you think Plath describes the pheasant as a 'little cornucopia'?
14. 'It unclaps'. What action or movement by the pheasant is the poet describing here?
15. Where was the pheasant before it settled in the elm?
16. Why does the poet feel that she is trespassing? What does this suggest about the pheasant's right to be where it is?
17. What is it that the poet wishes to 'let be' at the end of the poem? Who do you think she is addressing here?

Think About Themes

1. Class Discussion: Identify the different reasons the poet gives for not interfering with the pheasant. What is it about the bird that she most values?
2. What does the poem suggest about the right of people and other creatures to dwell in certain places?
3. The life of the pheasant is held in balance throughout the poem. Do you think that the poet succeeded in convincing the person she addresses in the opening lines not to kill it?
4. What do we learn about the poet from reading this poem?
5. Like many of Plath's poems, 'Pheasant' is full of rich, vivid images. Which ones did you find particularly pleasing and memorable?
6. Do you think that the poet values the bird for what it is or simply for the pleasure it offers her?

In Context

'I am not mystical'. Plath was very sensitive to the natural world without being sentimental about it. Compare and contrast her descriptions of the natural world in such poems as 'Pheasant', 'Black Rook in Rainy Weather' and 'Poppies in July'.

Elm

I know the bottom, she says. I know it with my great tap root:
It is what you fear.
I do not fear it: I have been there.

Is it the sea you hear in me,
Its dissatisfactions?
Or the voice of nothing, that was your madness?   [5]

Love is a shadow.
How you lie and cry after it
Listen: these are its hooves: it has gone off, like a horse.

All night I shall gallop thus, impetuously,   [10]
Till your head is a stone, your pillow a little turf,
Echoing, echoing.

Or shall I bring you the sound of poisons?
This is rain now, this big hush.
And this is the fruit of it: tin-white, like arsenic.   [15]

I have suffered the atrocity of sunsets.
Scorched to the root
My red filaments burn and stand, a hand of wires.

Now I break up in pieces that fly about like clubs.
A wind of such violence   [20]
Will tolerate no bystanding: I must shriek.

The moon, also, is merciless: she would drag me
Cruelly, being barren.
Her radiance scathes me. Or perhaps I have caught her.

I let her go. I let her go   [25]
Diminished and flat, as after radical surgery.
How your bad dreams possess and endow me.

I am inhabited by a cry.
Nightly it flaps out
Looking, with its hooks, for something to love.   [30]

I am terrified by this dark thing
That sleeps in me;
All day I feel its soft, feathery turnings, its malignity.

Clouds pass and disperse.
Are those the faces of love, those pale irretrievables?   [35]
Is it for such I agitate my heart?

I am incapable of more knowledge.
What is this, this face
So murderous in its strangle of branches?—

Its snaky acids hiss.   [40]
It petrifies the will. These are the isolate, slow faults
That kill, that kill, that kill.

[1]   *tap root:* a central root that grows vertically downwards and provides a tree with much of its nourishment

[10] *impetuously:* unthinkingly

[15] *arsenic:* a deadly poison, often in the form of a white powder

[18] *filament:* a thread of fibre or wire

[24] *scathe:* to harm or injure, especially by fire

[27] *endow:* to give something a quality or asset

[33] *malignity:* evil, wickedness

[35] *irretrievables:* things that can never be regained

[36] *agitate:* trouble, bother

Tease It Out

1. What is a tree's 'tap root'? What does the elm tree mean when it says this root 'knows the bottom'?

2. Can this claim to 'know the bottom' be understood in more than one way?

3. According to the elm, what is the woman afraid of? Describe this fear in your own words.

4. The elm suggests that it's producing a sound similar to the sea. How is this possible? What very common thing is happening to the elm to make it produce such a swirling sound?

5. Group Discussion: Think about the sounds made by the sea. In what sense might they resemble the cries of a distressed or dissatisfied person?

6. Class Discussion: 'Love is a shadow'. How do we understand this phrase? What does it suggest about the elm's attitude toward love?

7. What do lines 7 to 9 suggest about the poet's present difficulties?

8. What metaphor does the elm use to describe the sound made by its branches in lines 9 and 10?

9. 'Till your head is a stone, your pillow a little turf/ Echoing, echoing'. What do you understand by these lines? What will have happened to the woman to make her head a 'stone'?

10. In stanza 5 the elm describes how it has been tortured by a particular type of rain. Describe this rainfall and its consequences in your own words. What form of pollution might it remind us of?

11. What impact have 'sunsets' had on the elm tree?

12. These are clearly no ordinary sunsets. What terrible events from history do they recall?

13. What causes the elm tree to 'break up in pieces'?

14. What two torments does the moon visit upon the elm tree?

15. Why, according to the elm tree, does the moon act in such a cruel manner?

16. Group Discussion: What is 'radical surgery'? In what sense might such surgery be said to have occurred in lines 28 and 29?

17. 'Diminished and flat'. Is this phrase used to describe the moon or the elm tree? Give a reason for your answer.

18. 'How your bad dreams possess and endow me'. What does this suggest about the relationship between the elm and the woman to whom it speaks?

19. Would you agree that in stanzas 10 and 11 it is difficult to determine who is speaking – that these lines could be spoken either by the elm or by the woman? Give a reason for your answer.

20. 'I am inhabited by a cry … I am terrified by this dark thing/ That sleeps in me'. Assume that these lines are spoken by the elm tree. What might the 'dark thing' be? Now assume they are spoken by a human being. What 'dark thing' might it now be?

21. Would you agree that the poem's last three stanzas seem to be spoken by the woman rather than by the elm tree? Again give a reason for your answer.

22. In stanza 12 love is compared to clouds passing and dispersing about the sky. What does this comparison suggest about the nature of love and romance?

23. 'I am incapable of more knowledge'. What mental state does this phrase suggest? Pick three words that in your opinion best capture the speaker's state of mind.

24. The poem's final lines describe a 'face' that seems to appear among the elm's branches. What are the physical features of this face? What impact does it have on the speaker? Do you think the speaker really sees such a face in the bark?

25. Class Discussion: 'These are the isolate, slow faults/ That kill, that kill, that kill'. Based on your reading of the poem what faults or failings do you think are being referred to here?

Think About Themes

1. 'Elm' is an intensely visual poem and contains many powerful images. Identify one image from the poem that you found memorable or vivid, and explain why you found it compelling.

2. In 'Elm', Plath's mastery of sound effects is at its greatest. Read the poem again and identify one example of each of the following: assonance, alliteration, cacophony, rhyme and repetition. Say how each contributes to the poem's mood , atmosphere or meaning.

3. When Plath was composing 'Elm', she was very concerned about the possibility of a nuclear conflict between Russia and the United States. How is this fear of impending apocalypse evident in the poem?

4. Choose three words that best describe the poem's atmosphere.

5. Read the poem aloud. How would you describe its tone? Describe how the tone alters as the poem progresses.

6. 'This poem has elements of a horror or fantasy story, featuring a bizarre 'psychic link' between a woman and an elm tree growing in her garden. The elm somehow shares the woman's bad dreams. It seems to be the woman's 'dark double', embodying the unpleasant, dangerous and hidden aspects of her personality.' Do you find this reading persuasive? Give reasons for your answer.

The Arrival of the Bee Box

I ordered this, this clean wood box
Square as a chair and almost too heavy to lift.
I would say it was the coffin of a midget
Or a square baby
Were there not such a din in it.   [5]

The box is locked, it is dangerous.
I have to live with it overnight
And I can't keep away from it.
There are no windows, so I can't see what is in there.
There is only a little grid, no exit.   [10]

I put my eye to the grid.
It is dark, dark,
With the swarmy feeling of African hands
Minute and shrunk for export,
Black on black, angrily clambering.   [15]

How can I let them out?
It is the noise that appals me most of all,
The unintelligible syllables.
It is like a Roman mob,
Small, taken one by one, but my god, together!   [20]

I lay my ear to furious Latin.
I am not a Caesar.
I have simply ordered a box of maniacs.
They can be sent back.
They can die, I need feed them nothing, I am the owner. [25]

I wonder how hungry they are.
I wonder if they would forget me
If I just undid the locks and stood back and turned into a tree.
There is the laburnum, its blond colonnades,
And the petticoats of the cherry.   [30]

They might ignore me immediately
In my moon suit and funeral veil.
I am no source of honey
So why should they turn on me?
Tomorrow I will be sweet God, I will set them free. [35]

The box is only temporary.

Get In Gear

1. Take a moment to think about bees. List the things that come to mind. Group these associations into two groups: positive and negative. On the whole do you think of bees in a positive light?

2. The Greek myth of Daphne and Apollo is referred to in the poem's sixth stanza. Research this ancient tale and write a paragraph describing the story in your own words.

Tease It Out

Stanzas 1 to 2

1. What physical features of the bee box are mentioned in these two stanzas? List them. Then take a moment to visualise this object and briefly describe its appearance in your own words.

2. Why does the box make such a 'din'?

3. The speaker compares the bee box to a coffin. What does this suggest about her attitude toward it?

4. The speaker describes the box as 'dangerous'. What danger might the box pose?

5. Class Discussion: Though the speaker thinks the box is 'dangerous', she is unable to 'keep away from it'. Why do you think this is?

6. What line indicates that the speaker can't immediately get rid of the box?

7. 'I ordered this'. Based on your reading of stanzas one and two, describe the speaker's initial response to the box's arrival. Is she delighted, worried, horrified, or perhaps even surprised at her own decision?

Stanzas 3 to 5

8. Can the speaker see much when she puts her eye to the box's grid? Give a reason for your answer. What most striking and unusual comparison does she use to describe the bees' appearance through the grid?

9. 'angrily clambering'. The speaker watches the bees moving around inside the box. Describe in your own words what she sees.

10. Pick two words that in your opinion best describe the speaker's reaction to the sound emanating from the box.

11. What historical comparison does the speaker use to describe the bees and their buzzing?

12. To the speaker the bees resemble 'maniacs'. What associations does the term 'maniac' have for you? Write down three other words that come to mind.

13. Class Discussion: 'I am not a Caesar ... I am the owner'. In your opinion, does the speaker feel in control of the situation she has created by ordering the box?

14. 'How can I let them out?' Why do you think the speaker is reluctant to release the bees? What options does she feel she has in relation to this box that frightens her so much?

Stanzas 6 to 7

15. In what strange way does the speaker imagine evading the bees in the case that they attack her?

16. Group Discussion: 'colonnades ... petticoats'. The speaker uses a metaphor to describe the laburnum tree, another to describe the cherry tree. Outline as best you can the comparisons she makes in these lines.

17. 'my moon suit and funeral veil'. What is the speaker referring to here?

18. 'They might ignore me'. Why does she feel the bees won't 'turn on' her if she releases them?

19. What does she finally decide to do with the box and the bees it contains?

Think About Themes

1. Like much of Plath's best work, this poem is intensely visual. Identify two images from the poem that struck you as vivid or memorable, and say why.

2. How would you characterise the tone of the poem? Is it happy or sad? On the whole, would you describe it as an optimistic or pessimistic piece?

3. 'In this poem, Plath seems to forecast her own tragic death. She envisages herself slipping away from this human life, transforming into a tree, wearing a funeral veil like a mourner, or a 'moon suit' like an astronaut ready to depart this world'. Do you agree with this reading? Give reasons for your answer.

4. Consider the following phrases: 'I am not a Caesar ... I will be sweet God'. Do you think it's fair to say that this poem is about confronting and mastering one's fears? Write a paragraph giving reasons for your answer.

5. Class Discussion: It has often been suggested that in this poem the bee box functions as a symbol or metaphor for the poet's own mind. Do you think this is a reasonable view? What features of the box might be said to resemble or represent the human mind's deepest aspects?

In Context

Plath once said: 'I believe that one should be able to control and manipulate experiences, even the most terrific, like madness, being tortured, this sort of experience, and one should be able to manipulate these experiences with an informed and an intelligent mind'. Write three paragraphs comparing this poem to 'Elm' and/or 'Poppies in July' in light of this statement.

(handwritten annotations: Lots of images / Mental anguish / physic psychic landscape)

(handwritten: benign / opens)

Poppies in July

(handwritten: →metaphor / →Rhetorical Questions / she is locked into emotional pain)

(handwritten: Alliteration / onomatopoeia)

Little poppies, little hell flames,
Do you do no harm?

(handwritten: Rhyme)

You flicker. I cannot touch you.
I put my hands among the flames. Nothing burns.

(handwritten: onomatopoeia / →imagery / enjambment / image)

And it exhausts me to watch you   [5]
Flickering like that, wrinkly and clear red, like the skin of a mouth.

(handwritten: Simile / →metaphor / →Simile)

A mouth just bloodied.
Little bloody skirts!

(handwritten: metaphor / period / image / →repetition)

There are fumes that I cannot touch.
Where are your opiates, your nauseous capsules?   [10]

(handwritten: Assonance / Rhetorical Questions)

If I could bleed, or sleep! –
If my mouth could marry a hurt like that!

(handwritten: broad vowel sounds / Alliteration / →metaphor)

Or your liquors seep to me, in this glass capsule,
Dulling and stilling.

(handwritten: Assonance / drug - opiates)

But colorless. Colorless.   [15]

(handwritten: Repetition)

[10] **opiates:** narcotic drugs extracted from seed capsules of the opium poppy

Get In Gear

Do some quick research on the internet to learn about poppies. What colour are they? How would you describe their appearance? What are poppies traditionally used for and associated with?

Tease It Out

1. What sort of tone or mood is established in the opening lines?
2. The speaker compares the poppies to 'little hell flames'. What does the comparison suggest about *(a)* the flowers' appearance and *(b)* the poet's mood or state of mind?
3. What does the speaker hope will happen when she reaches out her hand? What actually happens when she does so?
4. What is it about the flowers that 'exhausts' the speaker?
5. The poet describes the flowers as 'wrinkly and clear red'. What two things do they remind her of?
6. What does the speaker imagine rising from the flowers in line 9? What effect do you think she expects these to have on her?
7. Class Discussion: The speaker mentions 'opiates' and 'nauseous capsules' in line 10. Why does she associate these things with the poppies? What do you think she has in mind when she mentions 'capsules'? Why might these make her feel sick or 'nauseous'?
8. Class Discussion: 'If I could bleed, or sleep!' The speaker longs for one of two very different experiences. What is it about each, do you think, that appeals to her?
9. What do you think the speaker means when she expresses a desire to 'marry a hurt'? Why do you think she uses the word 'marry'? What different meanings or connotations does this word have?
10. The poet suggests that she is living in a 'glass capsule'. What does this image call to mind? Can you think of any story or fairy tale that features a female character sleeping in such a capsule?
11. What do you think the 'glass capsule' represents for the speaker? Why do you think she feels like she is living inside such a capsule?
12. The speaker imagines 'liquors' from the poppies seeping into the 'glass capsule'. What does she imagine these liquors will do?
13. What do you think the poet hopes the liquors will dull and still?
14. The final line repeats the word 'colorless'. Why do you think the speaker wishes to be 'colorless'? Why do you think she repeats the word?

Think About Themes

1. What was your reaction to this poem? Were you shocked or surprised at the poet's choice of imagery? Which of the poem's images did you find most powerful?
2. Would you agree that this poem is a powerful description of intense mental anguish and suffering? What do you think is making the poet feel the way she does?
3. How does the poem convey a sense of emotional and physical numbness?
4. Discuss the role that colour or the absence of colour plays in the poem.

In Context

1. 'Plath often uses the natural world to illustrate or represent her own emotions and feelings. Discuss this statement, making reference to at least three poems by Sylvia Plath on the course.
2. 'Plath's poetry often presents the world as a cold and terrifying place'. Do you agree? Refer to at least three poems by Plath in your answer.

[handwritten top right:] 2 weeks before death

Child

Your clear eye is the one absolutely beautiful thing.
I want to fill it with color and ducks, *— ASSONANCE*
The zoo of the new *— ASSONANCE*

Whose names you meditate –   [5]
April snowdrop, Indian pipe,
Little

Stalk without wrinkle, *— Alliteration*
Pool in which images
Should be grand and classical

[10]

Not this troublous
Wringing of hands, this dark
Ceiling without a star. *metaphor* *what she represents* *loss of hope*

> [5] **April snowdrop:** white flower that blossoms in late spring
> [5] **Indian pipe:** plant native to temperate regions of Asia and America
> [10] **troublous:** agitated
> [11] **wringing of hands:** clasping and twisting of hands, indicating anxiety and distress

Tease It Out

1. How does the poet describe her child's eye in the first line?
2. Read lines 6 to 8. What two things does the poet compare her child to? What does each comparison suggest about the child? How do these descriptions compare to the opening line?
3. What does the poet want to 'fill' her child's eye with?
4. In lines 8 and 9 the poet describes the kinds of 'images' she wishes her child to see. What two words does she use to describe them? What sorts of images do you think she has in mind?
5. Class Discussion: The poet wishes to expose her child to the 'zoo of the new'. What do you think the poet has in mind here?
6. The poet mentions two types of flower in line 5. What does the poet wish her child to do with the 'names' of these flowers? Where do you think the child might find these names?
7. If the child's eye is the 'one absolutely beautiful thing', what does this suggest about everything else that exists?
8. In the last three lines the poet mentions two things that her child should not experience or see. The first concerns the poet's hands. What is she doing with her hands? What does this action suggest about the poet's mood and state of mind?
9. The second thing that the poet says her child should not see or experience is 'this dark/ Ceiling without a star'. What do you think the poet is describing here? Do you think that the 'dark ceiling' could be a metaphor for something?
10. How would you describe the mood and atmosphere of the last three lines?

Think About Themes

1. List as many images as you can find in the poem and arrange them under two headings – happy and sad. What image do you find most effective?
2. Class Discussion: Discuss the way colour and light, and the absence of colour and light, play a significant part in this poem. Why do you think the poet uses images of light and dark to describe herself and her child?
3. Do you think that the poet expects too much of herself as a parent? Is her view of childhood and what a child ought to receive realistic or idealistic?
4. How did you feel when you read this poem? Do you find it tragic?

Elizabeth Bishop

Themes

Love and Respect for the Natural World

Bishop's love and respect for the natural world comes across in her careful, detailed descriptions of birds, animals and other wildlife. In 'The Bight', for example, she takes great care to describe the birds that soar above her head and dive into the sea, capturing their movements in vivid detail.

In 'At the Fishhouses', meanwhile, Bishop provides lovingly detailed depictions of the sea and the fir trees. But her love of nature is especially evident in her description of the seal, and in her account of the 'relationship' that she cultivates by singing to him each evening. There is something light-hearted, perhaps almost comical, about this depiction of the poet singing to an uncomprehending animal, who looks at her with a strange mix of curiosity and indifference.

Bishop's fascination with nature is especially evident in 'The Fish', where she examines the titular creature in loving, exhaustive detail. No aspect of the fish's appearance is considered to be merely ugly or repulsive. She is intrigued by the dull brown shapes on the fish's skin, by its 'sullen face' and by the 'mechanism of his jaw'.

'The Armadillo' also deepens our sense of Bishop as someone with a keen awareness of her environment. She's aware for instance that there's an 'ancient nest' at the back of her property where a 'pair of owls' have nested. She even notices, in the middle of the chaotic inferno caused by the crashed balloon, that the baby rabbit is of the 'short-eared' South American variety.

'The Armadillo', then, can be read as an environmentalist poem, as a protest against mankind's careless indifference to nature. Bishop gives voice to the armadillo's rage, condemning on its behalf the annual ritual that visits such destruction on the local wildlife: 'Too pretty, dreamlike mimicry!/ O falling fire and piercing cry/ and panic'.

Unfortunately, the local people seem utterly indifferent to the 'falling fire and piercing cry/ and panic' that their tradition all too often produces. In one sense, then, the

poem can be read as an attack on human selfishness and short-sightedness, a condemnation of our continuing indulgence in unnecessary activities even though we know that they damage the natural world.

Moments of Awareness

Many of Bishop's poems are marked by moments of epiphany, moments when a person suddenly realises something profound and important about themselves and the world.

In 'First Death in Nova Scotia', for instance, the narrator is a very young girl who has little or no understanding of death. No doubt, she has heard the words 'death' and 'dead' being mentioned by the adults around her, but she doesn't fully grasp what death is, or what it actually means for someone to die.

Now, however, her young cousin Arthur has passed away and his body has been laid out in the parlour of the house. This compels the young poet, for the first time, to encounter death directly. She is forced into a terrible moment of awareness, one in which she must come to terms with this strange and unsettling concept.

Throughout the poem, however, the young poet attempts to shut out this uncomfortable new reality, to avoid thinking about death directly. In stanza 2, for instance, she focuses on the stuffed loon, rather than on her cousin's body. While in stanza 5, she tells herself that Arthur won't be around anymore, not because he is dead, but because he is heading off to the court of King George in London, where he will work as the 'smallest page'.

But the poem concludes with the young poet on the cusp of awareness. She is about to realise that death is something permanent and scary and unalterable. Such knowledge will forever change how she views the world.

'Sestina' is similar in this regard. It is difficult not to read the poem terms of Bishop's biography. We can't help but recall that Bishop's father died when she was only eight months old and that, when Bishop was five years old, her mother suffered a mental collapse and was institutionalised.

Thes tragedy that has struck the family in the poem is 'known only to a grandmother'. The child is still too young to fully comprehend the terrible events that have occurred. Nevertheless, we get the impression that awareness of this tragedy is slowly dawning on her. She thinks of 'tears' running down the tea-kettle and filling the grandmother's cup. The drops from the kettle seem to dance 'like mad', an image that may well have been evoked by the poet's recollection of her mother's mental breakdown. Furthermore, she imagines the stove and the almanac talking about the tragedy: 'It was to be, says the Marvel Stove./ I know what I know, says the almanac'.

We get an impression that the child attempts to shield herself from sorrow by drawing houses. It's as if she tries to create in her imagination an ideal house, an alternative world where the tragedy that struck her never occurred. But this defence will only last for so long. The almanac seems to symbolise an unspoken awareness of the tragedy that is waiting to descend upon the child. It hovers above her in an ominous fashion and 'plants tears' in the child's drawing. We get the impression that tears have also been 'planted' in the child's life and will soon bear fruit when she becomes fully aware of the tragic events that have unfolded.

'In the Waiting Room' also features such a moment of epiphany. At the poem's conclusion, the poet realises that that she is just one more member of the vast human race that populates the planet – and that there is more that unites her with every other human being (especially the female members of the population) than sets her apart. At the start of the poem the young poet focused on what she believed made her unique, but she now realises that she has more in common with everyone else. It is as if she has undergone a procedure – something far more distressing than a filling or a root canal – that has altered her outlook and the way she thinks about herself. It is as if a door within her mind has been thrown open and can never be shut again.

When Bishop wrote 'At the Fishhouses', she was undergoing psychoanalysis in order to come to terms with her various childhood traumas. The poet uses an extraordinary simile to describe the waters off Great Village, depicting them as a vast and all-consuming sea of fire. But this is fire that's been 'transmuted' or transformed, so that it 'burns with a dark gray flame'. The poet describes it as a blaze so intense that it could burn through rock, consuming the 'blue-gray stones' of the seabed.

This bizarre depiction of the sea wonderfully suggests the treacherous nature of the unconscious mind. The sea is depicted as being filled with tormenting slate-grey flames, just as the unconscious mind is filled with potentially dangerous memories and emotions. To enter or even touch the sea is to risk physical pain. To confront the unconscious mind, similarly, is to risk psychological pain.

But confront it, the poet must. For these burning waters represent not only the dangers and traumas that lurk within the unconscious but also the self-knowledge that can be found there: 'It's like what we imagine knowledge to be'. Like someone wading into a sea of flames, then, the poet must enter and explore her own unconscious mind. For it's only by doing so that she can gain the self-knowledge she so desperately craves.

In 'The Fish', the poet experiences a brighter and more hopeful insight. She realises that the old fish that she has snared is a survivor, a creature who has had to constantly fight to stay alive and has somehow managed to persevere.

For a brief moment, the world around the poet seems beautiful and joyous, and the rainbow colours in the oily water suddenly seem to filter or flood into everything around her: 'everything/ was rainbow, rainbow, rainbow!' For the poet is suddenly aware that the fish, like the poet herself, is a stubborn survivor and deserves to be set free: 'And I let the fish go'.

Oblique Self-Revelation

Bishop's poems tend to look outwards, focusing on and describing the external world in careful and minute detail. Rarely does the poet draw the reader's attention directly to herself by describing or discussing her own thoughts and feelings. Yet, despite this, the poet is very much present in her poems. We get a sense of her personality through her descriptions of her physical environment, and through her reactions to particular objects and events.

In 'The Bight', for instance, it's possible to see the bay, with all its messy activity, as a metaphor for the poet's own life on this particular birthday. Perhaps she feels that her-life is unfruitful or unproductive, that she's like the man-of-war birds that dive into the water but rarely come up with anything to show for their efforts. The 'torn-open, unanswered letters' might be a reference to the poet's own desk and her neglect of certain affairs, while the broken boats that have yet to be salvaged 'from the last bad storm' could also represent emotional or psychological damage from which the poet is still recovering.

'Filling Station' is another poem where the poet's observations of the external world reveal her inner life. Bishop was a rather fastidious person who appreciated neatness and order. No wonder, then, that the filling station that she comes across here appals and offends her – shocking her with its absolute filth.

'The Fish' features similarly oblique self-revelation. The poet doesn't directly reveal anything about her past predicaments or her present emotional state. And yet, through the poet's identification with the fish, we get a sense of the kind of person she must be.

The five hooks lodged in the fish's lower lip tell us that it has faced great adversity and survived, that it has been hooked again and again, only to struggle and free itself each time.

The poet's bond with the fish, then, suggests that she too is someone who has displayed great resilience, who has struggled and survived. Bishop, after all, lost her father at a very young age and was separated from her mother when she was five. She also battled alcoholism and suffered from chronic illness most of her life. Survival, then, is the 'victory' that the poem celebrates in its thrilling, elated conclusion. Like the fish, the poet has suffered greatly and has survived against the odds.

Childhood

'First Death in Nova Scotia' is one of several poems in which Bishop wonderfully captures the mentality of childhood. The speaker's childlike innocence comes across when she compares Arthur's corpse to a doll 'that hadn't been painted yet' and his coffin to 'a little frosted cake'. The same innocence is evident in her readiness to believe, or almost believe, the story about Arthur bring summoned to serve as the 'smallest page at court'.

The young poet thinks of Jack Frost painting Arthur's corpse, which makes her think of him painting the maple leaves, which in turn makes her think of a song titled 'Maple Leaf (Forever)'. This popular song, written in 1867, served as one of Canada's unofficial national anthems. It has been suggested that in this phrase, the young poet exhibits a childlike logic, her mind flitting unpredictably from one topic to the next.

Throughout 'Sestina', too, there are moments when Bishop skilfully inhabits a child's point of view. The phrase 'clever almanac', for instance, has a distinctly childish ring to it. The child, presumably, is aware from observing the adults around her that the almanac contains predictions and folk wisdom. Therefore, in an amusingly babyish phrase, she refers to it as 'clever'. Similarly effective is the description of the stove as 'marvellous'. We can imagine that this is how the granddaughter might refer to the stove. To this innocent and childish girl, the stove is a wondrous and fascinating object.

She therefore confuses the brand name 'Marvel' with the word 'marvellous'

The second half of the poem, in particular, is full of strange and bizarre occurrences. We get the impression, though, that these weird events are not 'real' but merely take place in the granddaughter's imagination. She imagines that the almanac hovers around the kitchen with a mind of its own and sends a rain of moons into her picture, that her grandmother's cup contains tears rather than tea and that the stove and the almanac have a brief conversation. With its extremely creative use of such images, the poem wonderfully captures how a child's imagination can run riot, viewing even simple household objects as living things and as a source of fear and wonder.

'In the Waiting Room' is another poem that artfully conveys a child's sense of the world. But it doesn't trivialise or romanticise childhood. On the contrary, it demonstrates that although childhood is a time of innocence, it can also involve trauma, stress and uncertainty.

Exile and Homelessness

Bishop's father, we remind ourselves, died when she was only eight months old and her mother was institutionalised when she was five. In the years that followed, she was shunted from guardian to guardian in both Canada and the United States.

Because her childhood had been spent in so many different locations, Bishop felt that she didn't really come from anywhere. She didn't have a 'home' in the sense of a point of origin, a native place that she and her family hailed from and to which she could, return. This sense of what we might call 'homelessness' is indicated by the final enigmatic lines in 'Questions of Travel': 'Should we have stayed at home,/ wherever that may be?' Not only is she uncertain about where her 'home' might be, she's not even sure that she has one.

A similar sense of exile and homelessness is evident in 'At the Fishhouses'. In returning to Great Village, the fishing community that was the site of her earliest memories, the poet has found something resembling home. By reconnecting with her roots on her mother's side of the family, she has rediscovered a place that feels like her own point of origin, one that she feels she could return to again and again.

And yet we sense that this newly rediscovered 'home' is very much under threat. The fact that the poet sees only an old man on her evening walk suggests that this is an aging community. Indeed, the poet and the old man talk about how the population of Great Village is 'declining'. The young, no doubt, are keen to leave behind the hard life of this fishing community for the bright lights of the major cities. Consequently, as the elder generation die off, there is no one to take their place on the fishing boats. Great Village, it seems, is a community threatened with extinction.

Perhaps the old man's 'worn' shuttle and his old knife, which is 'almost worn away', serve as metaphors for a way of life that is in decline as fewer and fewer people enter the fishing industry. Even the fact that the poem is set at evening, just as darkness falls, reinforces our sense that Great Village might well be a community nearing its end.

The notions of exile and homelessness also feature prominently in 'The Prodigal'. The prodigal lives and works in absolutely miserable conditions. He could end his suffering simply by returning home. For a very long time he refuses to do so, however, deciding to 'endure' his self-imposed 'exile' instead of returning to his family. We get a sense, then, that the prodigal feels that he does not really have a home to go to anymore, that he is simply not welcome any longer in his father's house. The word 'home', it should be noted, is the only end-word in the poem that does not have a full rhyme, perhaps suggesting the difficulty that the 'concept' of home causes to the prodigal. As is so often the case in Bishop's poetry, the journey 'home' is not an easy one to make.

There are several poems in which Bishop presents herself as a detached, neutral observer of a community to which she doesn't belong and that she can't really understand. In 'Questions of Travel', for instance, the phrase 'as ages go here' suggests that she is a visitor rather than a native inhabitant of the environment that she is describing. She ponders what the clogs and cage might tell her about Brazilian history, but can do so only in a blurred and inconclusive manner.

'The Armadillo' is similar in this regard. The phrase 'in these parts', for instance, suggests that this is a community that the poet is still attempting to make sense of, rather than one in which she feels completely at home. Significantly, she takes no part in the ritual of the fire balloons that so engages the local population. Perhaps, as a visitor from a richer, more advanced country, she regards such rituals and beliefs as primitive and backward.

To the poet, then, the fire balloons are a strange local custom, one that is not only quaint and beautiful but also senseless and dangerous. She acknowledges the beauty that the fire balloons possess as they drift smoothly into the distance, but she also condemns the damage that they all-too-often cause when they fall earthwards.

Addiction

'The Prodigal' is a moving and honest portrayal of an addict. The prodigal suffers from severe alcohol addiction. He drinks even in the mornings, hiding bottles behind planks of wood. Like the character in the Bible story, the prodigal's vices have brought him to a terrible situation. He spends his days amid the filth and squalor of the pigsty. Even worse, he spends his nights there, too. He also suffers from terrible loneliness. Furthermore, we get the impression that his nights are racked by guilt and self-loathing.

The poem also emphasises how difficult it is for an addict to leave addiction behind, even when he realises the damage it is causing to his life. In the evenings, there are moments of 'shuddering insight' when the prodigal realises the full horror of his situation. However, in the mornings – as he drunkenly watches a sunrise – he feels 'reassured' that he can endure his miserable way of life for at least another year. In the end, it takes the prodigal 'a long time' to finally decide to give up his addictions and return to his father's house.

'The Armadillo' is another poem in which Bishop describes people who are caught up in what can only be described as compulsive behaviour. Of course, the local population are aware of the risks posed by the balloons that they release each June. They know that the fire balloons all too often destroy wildlife when they come crashing down to earth. They also know that the balloons are 'illegal'.

Yet their devotion to their local saint compels them to continue observing this dangerous ritual. Perhaps they are motivated by devotion to their local saint, by the desire to uphold a tradition, or by a strangely misguided sense of community spirit. Whatever the motivation, it is perhaps not too outlandish to regard this religious impulse as a form of addiction, a compulsion that people brought up in this tradition are powerless to resist or control.

Language

Attention to Detail

The poetry of Elizabeth Bishop is marked by its extraordinary attention to detail. This is especially evident in 'The Fish', where the poet paints a vivid picture not only of the fish's external appearance but also of its imagined inner organs. She focuses on every little detail, describing each one as clearly and as vividly as possible, until a very clear picture of the creature begins to form in the reader's mind.

The description of the fish's eye is particularly impressive. Bishop captures the off-silver colour that surrounds the iris, comparing it to 'tarnished tinfoil'. It is as if this tainted or dulled material has been packed in tightly around and behind the iris. The poet also describes how the eye's jelly-like lens, which the poet compares to 'isinglass', a layer of hardened gelatin, obscures the view of the iris. It is as if there is a layer of 'scratched isinglass' coating the fish's eye.

'The Bight' works in a similar fashion. The poet focuses on different aspects or features of the bight, describing each in great detail. The descriptions and details gradually acumulate until we have a complete picture of the landscape as it appears on this one particular day.

The description of the sponge boats returning to the harbour is particularly impressive. The poet compares them to 'obliging' retriever dogs bounding back to their master. She compares the rods that stick up out of the boats to 'jackstraws' that have been decorated with 'bobbles of sponges'. The description seems to perfectly capture not only the appearance of these vessels, but also something of the mood and atmosphere on this particular day in Key West.

'At the Fishhouses', yet another sea-themed poem, is arguably even more detailed. We see Bishop go into descriptive overdrive in her depiction of the five fish houses ,with their angular roofs, for instance, and in her equally memorable depiction of the fir forest. In her depiction of the fish tubs and wheelbarrows Bishop appeals not only to our sense of vision, by describing how they are 'lined' or 'plastered' with scales that shimmer as they catch they light, but also to our sense of touch, by noting the 'creamy texture' of the accumulated scales. She even notes the flies that rest upon these objects, observing that they, like scales they crawl upon, are also iridescent.

This tendency is also evident in 'The Prodigal', where the poet describes the world that the prodigal inhabits in vivid

and memorable detail, appealing to a number of our senses in the process. Interestingly, Bishop describes the pigsty's smell in visual terms, telling us that the odour is 'brown' and 'enormous'. She also appeals to our senses of hearing and of touch in depicting this stink, referring to the odour's 'breathing' and its 'thick hair'.

Here, Bishop uses a poetic technique known as synaesthesia, whereby an experience associated with one sense is described in terms of another. In her description of the dung on the pigsty's walls, Bishop skillfully appeals to the sense of touch, describing it as 'glass-smooth'. Another fine piece of description occurs in lines 22 to 23, which describes how the reflection of the farmer's lantern 'paces' alongside him as he returns to the farmhouse.

The poems set in Brazil, 'Questions of Travel' and 'The Armadillo', also feature exquisitely detailed descriptive passages. In 'The Armadillo', for instance, Bishop wonderfully captures the drifting fire balloons, focusing especially on the flaring candles within these delicate structures: 'the paper chambers flush and fill with light'.

In 'Questions of Travel', meanwhile, Bishop provides an equally vivid depiction of the mountainous landscape, with its streams, clouds and waterfalls. The crowded streams resemble 'slowmotion' waterfalls as they flow down the mountain: 'turning to waterfalls under our very eyes'. The poet imagines that over time these streams will turn into actual waterfalls through some unspecified geological process: 'For if those streaks … aren't waterfalls yet,/ in a quick age or so, as ages go here,/ they probably will be'.

Bishop is also known as a poet who typically zooms in on one specific detail that reveals the truth about an entire location or situation.

- We see this in 'Questions of Travel' when she focuses on the 'sad, two-noted, wooden tune' produced by the filling station owner as he walks around his premises, which wonderfully captures the air of desperation that clings to him and to his business. (The word 'disparate', so close to 'desperate', suggests this in a sly and brilliant fashion).
- In 'Filling Station', for instance, she focuses on the owner's ill-fitting overalls, describing them as 'a dirty,/ oil-soaked monkey suit/ that cuts him under the arms'. But these few short lines deftly captures the character and appearance of the filling station's owner. We can almost picture him in this filthy gear, his body hunched

and rendered comical by the tightness of the overalls. The term 'monkey-suit' also makes us think of someone moving in an inelegant, ape-like manner.

- 'First Death in Nova Scotia', too, features several telling details that really bring the scene to life. Among these are the loon with its fake red eyes and the royal couples in the chronographs, with their feet snugly wrapped by the furred trains of the ladies' gowns.

- We also see this in 'The Armadillo' when the poet declares that the balloons resemble 'stars' as they drift across the sky: 'Once up against the sky it's hard/ to tell them from the stars'. However she corrects herself, declaring that the balloons in fact resemble not stars, but celestial bodies – Venus, Mars and the Moon – that are far closer than the stars and therefore seem far brighter and bigger in the night sky.

A similar focus on precision is evident in line 29 of the same poem, where the poet stresses that she didn't actually see the nest burn. She only assumed it was destroyed because she saw the owls flying away: 'The ancient owls' nest must have burned'.

Similar precision is evident in 'At the Fishhouses':

- She notes for instance, the 'steeply peaked roofs' of the fish houses and that the gangways that lad up them are 'cleated' to prevent the wheelbarrows slipping.

- She notes that the buildings near the waterfront have moss growing only on their 'shoreward walls'.

- She notes that the tree trunks on the boat ramps are laid at 'intervals of four or five feet'.

- Such precision is even evident when she discusses the hymns she sings to the seal each evening. She's careful to distinguish the Baptist hymns from 'A Mighty Fortress Is Our God', which is a hymn associated with the Lutheran tradition.

A Detached and Neutral Tone

Bishop's poetry tends to focuses outwards rather than inwards. Her poems typically adopt a detached or neutral tone, as the poet patiently and carefully contemplates a scene or topic. In Bishop's work, emotion tends not be expressed directly. But we can detect it, sometimes, lurking beneath the serene surface of her meticulous descriptions.

A similar tone dominates 'The Bight'. Bishop takes in the somewhat messy and chaotic scene before her in a casual, objective manner'. She never expresses or registers any intense emotion at what she sees on this occasion. There

is a matter-of-factness about the descriptions she offers, no matter how odd or strange the scene before her might appear.

'Filling Station', too, is dominated by detached neutrality. The poem's opening ('Oh, but it is dirty!') betrays a sense of disgust. But this quickly gives way to a tone of neutral description and idle curiosity. Bishop wittily asks whether the plants have been oiled, and suggests that the plant on the porch resembles the filling station's workers: 'a big hirsute begonia'. She comes across as poet interested in registering the smallest details than she is in directly expressing her inner life.

Both the 'The Fish' and 'The Armadillo' open with Bishop's signature detachment but evolve into a very different, more expressive tonality. 'The Fish' is neutral, almost emotionless, for most of its length, with the poet focusing on the myriad details of the fish's appearance, rather than on her own thoughts and feelings. (We might, however, detect a faint hint of pride and excitement when the poet declares that she caught a 'tremendous fish'). The tone changes towards the end of the poem when the poet realises just how much the fish has struggled throughout its long life. The poem closes with a sense of joy, one might almost say, elation.

'The Armadillo', too, sees Bishop's usual detached tone prevail for most of its length. For the first nine of its ten stanzas the poet functions as a kind of neutral observer While she describes the ritual of the fire-balloons, she does not directly reveal her feelings on the matter.

In sharp contrast, the final stanza is a direct outpouring of emotion. The poet's distress at the plight of the armadillo (as well as the sufferings of the baby rabbit and the owls) prompts an emotional outburst of anger and condemnation, an outburst that shatters the normally serene surface of her verse. The poet not only reveals her own anger but also, as we've seen, gives voice to the voiceless creatures that have seen their habitat destroyed.

It might be argued that 'In the Waiting Room' functions in a similar fashion. The beginning of the poem is characterised by almost banal observations, as the poet describes events in the waiting room in a flat, emotionless fashion : 'My aunt was inside/ what seemed like a long time'. By the conclusion of the poem, however, this flatness has disappeared, and Bishop skilfully changes the atmosphere from one of self-satisfied certainty to terrified disorientation. Bishop uses repetition and images of things spinning out of control to convey the child's sudden loss of equilibrium: 'I – we – were falling,

falling'; 'the sensation of falling off/ the round, turning world'.

'Questions of Travel' is very much a poem of anxiety and unease, with the poet wondering where she should be and what, exactly, she should be doing with her life. As is so often the case with Bishop, however, the emotion is contained beneath the poem's rather serene surface. On the surface, the poet's tone throughout is relaxed, almost cheerful, as she probes the issues surrounding travel with a series of rhetorical questions (questions that require no answer). One might argue, however, that the poet's emotions are more directly expressed in the notebook entry with which the poem concludes.

'At the Fishhouses' is similar in this regard. This is a poem that deals with profoundly personal truths, with a poet's search to embrace and overcome long-buried trauma. The poem, however, features few expressions of direct emotion. And there is no direct reference to the painful childhood memories that the poet associates with Great Village.

It's only at the poem's conclusion, with its increasingly unrealistic depiction of the water, that we sense the painful and powerful emotions that lie beneath the seemingly serene surface of the verse. But even here Bishop operates indirectly, using the sea as a symbol of trauma and its uncovering, instead of tackling such concepts in a blunt and straightforward fashion.

Metaphor and Simile

'The Fish' features a number of striking similes. The fish's skin is compared to peeling wallpaper decorated with roses: the shapes on the fish's skin are 'like fullblown roses/ stained and lost through age'. The fish's flesh is 'packed in like feathers'. It has a 'pink swim-bladder/ like a peony'. The eyes move 'like the tipping/ of an object toward light.' The lines attached to the fish's jaw are 'Like medals with their ribbons/ frayed and wavering'. The fish's jaw is 'weaponlike'.

The poet also uses effective metaphors to describe the fish's appearance: the irises are 'backed and packed/ with tarnished tinfoil', and the lenses are 'old scratched isinglass'. The lines that hang from the fish's jaw resemble 'a five-haired beard of wisdom'.

Effective metaphors are also used in 'The Bight'. Bishop compares the marl protruding through the water to 'ribs'. The sponge boats are compared to 'obliging' dogs. The poet uses a striking simile when she compares the pilings to matches: 'the pilings dry as matches'. The pelicans are 'like pickaxes' when they dive 'unnecessarily hard' into the water. The man-of-war birds' tails are compared to scissors and wishbones. The shark tails shine like 'little plowshares' in the sun. The broken boats are 'like torn-open, unanswered letters'.

Bishop also uses persuasive similes and metaphors in 'Sestina'.

- In a fine metaphor, the drops of moisture on the kettle's side are compared to tears.
- In an equally fine simile, the buttons on the man in the child's drawing are compared to tears.
- In another effective simile, the moons falling from the almanac's pages are compared to tears, and we can imagine how the full, half and quarter moons depicted on the almanac's pages might resemble tears.
- In another striking simile, the almanac is compared to a bird: 'Birdlike, the almanac/ hovers half open above the child/ hovers above the old grandmother'. We can imagine the half-open pages acting like wings as the almanac flies around about the kitchen.

Personification occurs in lines 15 to 16, where both the rain falling on the roof and the droplets falling on the stove are depicted as dancing (Personification occurs when a non-human object is described as having human characteristics; in this instance, both the rain and the droplets are described as dancing, a very human activity.)

There are also several fine metaphors in 'The Prodigal'. The hay packed above the animals in the barn's hayloft is compared to 'clouds', and we can imagine it as cloudy golden puffs above the sleeping cows and horses. In line 11 the red light of sunrise is compared to a 'glaze' that is spread over the mud of the farmyard. The red glow of its reflection on the puddles is compared to fire: 'the burning puddles'.

In 'First Death in Nova Scotia', Bishop uses several convincing metaphors and similes in her description of the parlour in which the poem is set. In a memorable metaphor, the table on which the loon rests is compared to a frozen lake: 'He kept his own counsel/ on his white frozen lake,/ the marble-topped table'. In an equally fine simile, the young speaker compares Arthur's corpse to a little doll: 'He was all white, like a doll/ that hadn't been painted yet.' In another metaphor, Arthur's coffin is compared to a 'little frosted cake'.

The Fish

INTRODUCTION

Bishop moved to Key West, one of a string of tropical islands stretching about 120 miles off the southern tip of the U.S. state of Florida, in 1937 and made it her home for the next ten years. It was here that she developed a love for fishing. The poem is based on actual experience of fishing in Key West in 1938. In an interview, Bishop once said: 'I always tell the truth in my poems. With "The Fish", that's exactly how it happened. It was in Key West, and I did catch it just as the poem says. That was 1938. Oh, but I did change one thing; the poem says he had five hooks hanging from his mouth, but actually he only had three. Sometimes a poem makes its own demands. But I always try to stick as much as possible to what really happened when I describe something in a poem'.

LINE BY LINE

The poet is out on the water in a 'little rented boat'. The little boat that she sits in is old, worn and dirty. The boat's engine and bailer are rusty, and the 'thwarts', the crosspieces of timber used for seats, are cracked from being exposed to the sun. A pool of water and engine oil has gathered on the floor of the boat.

The poet has just caught an enormous or 'tremendous' fish. We get a sense of the fish's size when the poet tells us that she holds him 'beside the boat/ half out of the water' so that she can observe him. This is not a fish that she can dangle on the line

> The Atlantic goliath grouper, also known as the Caribbean jewfish, is a large saltwater fish common to the Florida Keys. It is found primarily in shallow tropical waters among coral reefs. These massive creatures can reach lengths of up to eight feet and can weigh more than 700 pounds.

before her in order to get a better look at it – its sheer mass means that it remains not only outside the boat, but half submerged in the water: 'held him beside the boat/ half out of the water.

We might imagine that such an enormous fish would have put up a considerable fight. But this fish 'didn't fight' and 'hadn't fought at all'. This, of course, surprises the poet. And it is perhaps for this very reason that she decides to hold the creature beside the boat and observe it rather than bring it into the boat and commence her journey back to land. She wishes to observe this anomaly – a creature of 'tremendous' size that did not put up any kind of fight whatsoever.

The fish hangs from the hook that is lodged 'fast in a corner of his mouth'. It is obviously feeling threatened and produces a 'grunting' sound to signal its distress. The poet observes that the fish is old and that it bears the marks and signs of having lived. It is 'battered' or damaged, its skin hanging from its body in places, like very old wallpaper peeling off a wall. And yet, because of its age and the wear and tear that its body exhibits, the creature is accorded a certain amount of respect by the poet, who describes it as 'venerable'.

The poet observes that the fish is not a beautiful creature. She uses the term 'homely', which means unattractive, but does not imply ugliness. The fish is rather plain and unadorned with pretty colours. Its skin is brown, and the patterns upon the skin a 'darker' shade of brown. The patterns form shapes on the skin that resemble roses: 'shapes like full-blown roses'. But these patterns are no longer as vivid as they once might have been, having faded and become 'stained' over the years. The colour and the shapes on the fish's skin again make the poet think of wallpaper.

The fish is 'speckled with barnacles', small, shelled creatures that have attached themselves to its body. These barnacles form white, intricate, rose-shaped patterns: 'fine rosettes of lime'. The fish's skin is also 'infested with .... sea-lice'. Seaweed adheres to its body, and 'two or three' pieces hang from the underside of the fish. The seaweed is like some old, tattered, green coat that hangs off the fish in 'rags'.

The poet again draws our attention to the fact that the fish is out of its element and far from comfortable. Its gills were designed to extract oxygen from the water, rather than inhale it from the air. To the fish, therefore, the air is repellent or 'terrible': 'his gills were breathing in/ the terrible oxygen'. The poet also finds the fish's gills unsettling and 'frightening'. They are firm or 'fresh' and 'crisp with blood'. The poet knows how sharp these gills can be and how easily they 'can cut so badly'.

The poet imagines the fish's insides:
- She thinks of the 'coarse white flesh' tightly packed and overlapping like a bird's 'feathers'.
- She thinks of the fish's 'big bones and the little bones'.
- She imagines the 'dramatic reds and blacks/ of his shiny' inner organs or entrails.
- She pictures the 'pink swim-bladder', the fish's internal gas-filled organ that helps it to control its buoyancy. The poet imagines this looking like a 'big peony', a vivid red flower.

The fish's eyes are 'far larger' than the poet's, but they are 'shallower', suggesting that they are flatter and not as deep set. There is a yellow tint to the eyes, and it is as if dulled tinfoil has been packed in behind and around the irises: 'the irises backed and packed/ with tarnished tinfoil'. The lenses covering the eye look like they are made from some jellied substance that has become worn and scratched: 'lenses/ of old scratched isinglass'. Isinglass is a transparent gelatin prepared from the inner membrane of the swim bladder of certain fish and used to make jellies and glue.

As the poet stared at the fish's eyes, they 'shifted a little', but they do not move to look at her. It is as if the eyes are drawn or tilt naturally towards the light: 'like the tipping/ of an object toward the light'. The fish's face is gloomy, or 'sullen'. The poet admires the structure and arrangement of the parts of the fish's jaw: 'the mechanism of his jaw'. The fish's 'lower lip' is described as uninviting and forbidding or 'grim'. It strikes the poet as threatening and 'weaponlike', something that can be used to inflict considerable damage.

It is while she is examining the fish's jaw that the poet suddenly notices that there are 'five big hooks' lodged firmly in the fish's 'lower lip'. The hooks have been lodged there for some time and have 'grown firmly into his mouth'. Attached to the hooks are tattered and frayed pieces of line and wire that would once have connected the hooks to a rod. One of the lines is green and 'frayed' or ravelled 'at the end/ where he broke it'. Two of the lines are 'heavier', and one is 'a fine black thread/ still crimped', or curled, 'from the strain and the snap/when it broke and he got away'.

The hooks with their ragged lines and wire are like 'medals' that might adorn an old soldier's uniform. The tattered pieces of line hang down like the ribbons attached to such medals. The hooks and ragged lines also resemble a 'five-haired beard of wisdom', making the fish seem like some tribal elder or noble old warrior.

THEMES

MOMENTS OF AWARENESS

Many of Bishop's poems are marked by moments of awareness or epiphany – moments when a person suddenly realises something profound and important about themselves or about the world. But these epiphanies do not happen spontaneously or immediately – they result from the poet's patient and careful observation of what stands before her.

Seeing the hooks with their broken lines lodged in the fish's jaw has a profound effect on the poet. She realises that she is looking at something remarkable, a creature that has been caught five times but each time has fought hard for and won his freedom. She stares at the fish and gets an overwhelming sense of 'victory'.

She has suddenly been granted an insight or an understanding, an epiphany of sorts. She realises that this old fish is a survivor,

a creature who has had to fight for survival again and again and has somehow managed to persevere. She now knows something about the fish and can, therefore, relate to it, whereas prior to this moment the fish was a somewhat strange and alien creature.

The world around the poet suddenly seems transformed by this fact. She says that 'victory filled up/ the little rented boat'. The sense that something marvellous has just occurred is heightened by the colours that surround the poet in the boat. Oil has seeped into the pool of water that lies at the bottom of the boat ('the pool of bilge'), and this has created a multico-loured effect around the engine of the boat that resembles a rainbow. The poet says that the 'oil had spread a rainbow/ around the rusted engine'. The 'rusted engine' and the 'bailer rusted orange' add to the vivid colours that surround the poet, and they seem to somehow enhance the sense of 'victory' that the fish has inspired.

For a brief moment the world around the poet seems beautiful and joyous, and the rainbow colours in the oily water suddenly seem to filter or flood into everything around her: 'everything/ was rainbow, rainbow, rainbow!' What the poet's intentions were when she initially caught the fish was never made clear, but having seen how he has repeatedly fought for his freedom and won, the poet decides that he deserves to be set free and she returns him to the water: 'And I let the fish go'.

LOVE AND RESPECT FOR THE NATURAL WORLD

Bishop's fascination with and respect for the natural world is very evident in this poem. She is intrigued by the fish that she has caught, examining and studying it closely, observing every little detail. She considers the fish to be 'venerable' or worthy of respect because of its age.

The poet does not find any aspect of the fish repulsive. Every feature intrigues her, and she seeks to describe it as accurately as she possibly can. In the process, she discovers forms of beauty – the dull, brown shapes upon the fish's skin remind her of 'full-blown roses', as do the barnacles that speckle the fish's body. She admires the fish's 'sullen face' and the 'mechanism of his jaw', even as she finds it threatening and 'weaponlike'.

The poet remains conscious of the otherness of the fish and the fact that it is out of its natural element and far from comfortable. Although she seems to want to establish some sort of connection with the fish, she acknowledges that the fish has no interest in her. She remarks on how the fish's eyes do not return her 'stare', but rather roll away 'toward the light'.

FINDING WONDER IN THE EVERYDAY

The poet takes the time to study the creature very closely and, in the process, finds many of the details fascinating and even beautiful. She considers how the barnacles form rose-like patterns upon the fish's body. She even imagines the insides of the fish, thinking how its 'swim-bladder' would resemble a peony and the flesh would be packed in layers like a bird's feathers.

OBLIQUE SELF-REVELATION

Although the focus of the poem is very much on the fish, the poem's speaker, the 'I', is a constant and significant presence. As we read the poem, we begin to get a sense of what the speaker must be like. As one critic put it, '[The poem's] main character is the enormous Caribbean jewfish that Elizabeth caught at Key West, but it shares top billing with the fisher, the 'I' of the poem.'

The poet's careful eye eventually finds the detail that allows her to understand something about the fish and the life it has lived – the five hooks lodged in the fish's lower lip. The hooks tell us that this fish has been caught five times before, and that each time he has managed to break the line and free himself. The fish has faced great adversity, but on each occasion he has fought back hard and survived.

Suddenly, the poet's observation at the beginning of the poem that the fish 'didn't fight', that he 'hadn't fought at all', has to be revisited. This fish has fought and fought all his life – he did not fight when the poet caught him because he was old and worn out from fighting – he no longer had the energy to fight. But the poet's careful consideration and imagination enables her to see not only the fish's insides but also what he has had to endure and overcome.

The poet suddenly feels a bond with the fish. She can identify with him as she, too, has struggled and survived. Perhaps the five hooks represent or symbolise five occasions in her life when she has had to overcome great adversity or trauma. This, after all, is someone who lost her father at a very young age and was separated from her mother when she was five, someone who battled alcoholism and suffered from chronic illness most of her life. (The reference to isinglass in line 40 might indeed be an oblique reference to the poet's struggles with alcohol, as this substance is also used as a fining agent in certain alcoholic drinks). Like the fish, however, the poet has fought and survived.

The 'victory', therefore, that the poet celebrates is just this – an ability to endure and survive. And the elation that Bishop feels when she contemplates the fish's victory stems from her own victory as a survivor, her ability to triumph over adversity. The fish may now be exhausted from the battles he has had to fight, but the poet is not exhausted yet, and the fish has inspired to fight on.

The Bight

INTRODUCTION

This poem was written in 1948. The poet was 37 at the time – in fact, the poem is set on her birthday – and she was living in Key West, a small U.S. island city that is part of the Florida Keys archipelago. A bend in the shoreline on the northwest side of the island creates the 'bight' that the poem describes, a wide bay and naturally protected harbour. The Key West harbour was a busy fishing port when Bishop lived there. When the poem was written sponge harvesting was a major industry in Key West, and there would have been well over one hundred boats operating out of the bay.

LINE BY LINE

THE WATER

The poet is standing on the bight's dock or pier. She looks out at the water in the bay. It is low tide, so the water is not very deep. In fact, the water seems to be barely covering the seabed. The poet uses the word 'sheer' to describe the meagre presence of the water in the bay. The word 'sheer', which means transparently thin, is often used to describe fabric or clothing that is so fine that you can almost see through it. Here, it suggests that the water is barely concealing the seabed beneath. The still water, in the bright sunshine, has a light blue colour. The poet compares this colour to 'the gas flame' of a lantern or a stove 'turned as low as possible'.

Aspects of the seabed are exposed, emerging up through the thin layer of

Sea sponges are aquatic animals that cling to hard surfaces on the sea floor. Natural sea sponges are harvested from the bottom of the ocean by fishing boats that specialise in sponge fishing. Sea sponges are harvested by divers using specially designed cutting hooks or knives. When the sponges have been cut, the divers gently squeeze the entrails out of the sponges and take them back to the boats. The sponges are then pounded to clean them and covered with wet canvas sacks on the deck of the ship, where the heat from the sun releases a gas that rots the sponges' skins so that they can be more easily removed.

water in the bay. The poet describes how ridges of 'marl' or silt 'protrude' above the water's surface. They are like 'ribs' that poke through or are visible beneath the surface of the skin. These white mounds reflect the sun's intense light, dazzling the speaker: 'White, crumbling ribs of marl protrude and glare'. The word 'glare' can also mean to stare in an angry or fierce way. It is as if the marl is staring right back at the poet, returning her gaze.

The water in the bight doesn't seem to be behaving as water ought to behave: it 'doesn't wet anything'. The timber boats that float upon its surface are 'dry', as are the timber 'pilings', the long wooden poles driven into the seabed to support and secure the pier or dock. To the poet, the pale blue substance that coats the bay seems more like a strange form of gas ('peculiar gas') than a liquid. In fact, as she stands on the dock, she feels as if she 'can smell it turning to gas'. There is a hint of danger here. The combination of gas, matches and dry timber means that the whole bay can be seen as ready or set to ignite.

THE BIRDS

The poet describes the pelicans and the man-of-war birds that are present in the bay. Both are very large seabirds, and the poet is struck by their great size, describing them as 'outsize' or enormous. The poet observes the pelicans diving into the sea to catch fish. They 'crash' into the water in a manner that she considers 'unnecessarily hard'. They behave like 'pickaxes' striking down on rock. Despite their intense efforts, they rarely emerge from the sea 'with anything to show'. The poet describes how they fly away in an amusing manner, jostling and shoving each other: 'going off with humorous elbowings'.

The man-of-war birds don't dive, but stay aloft, soaring on drafts of air that are not visible or evident to the poet on the ground. The poet describes how, as they fly, they use their long forked tails to steer. When they wish to swerve, they 'open their tails like scissors'. On other occasions, they 'tense' their tails, hardening them to create lift. When the tails are tensed in this manner they 'tremble' with the effort to hold hard against the drafts of air upon which they ride. Bishop likens the rigid tails to 'wishbones', the forked bone found between the neck and breast of a bird.

THE BOATS

The poet observes the sponge boats returning to the harbour. She observes that these boats are continuously 'coming in'. To her, they seem like 'retrievers', dogs that are trained to go and retrieve game for hunters. The boats seem to have the 'obliging air' of these animals, a sort of good-natured willingness or eagerness to help or please.

The boats are untidy and scruffy. The numerous poles and hooks that the fishermen use to gather the sponge are standing up and sticking out of the boats at different angles. They resemble the small rods of wood that are used in the game 'jackstraw', a game in which players try to remove one slim rod or 'jackstraw' at a time without disturbing the others. The poles sticking up out of the boats also resemble the bristles, or spiky hairs, on an animal's back, again calling to mind the image of dogs. The boats, the poet says, are 'bristling with jackstraw gaffs and hooks'.

Hanging off the top of the poles and hooks are some of the sponges that the fishermen have harvested. The sponge is hung up to dry in the sun as the boats return to the harbour and the poet observes how they resemble 'bobbles', small balls of material, usually made of wool, used for decorating clothes.

The poet observes the 'fence of chicken wire' – wire consisting of thin, flexible, steel wire with hexagonal gaps – that runs along the dock. The fence is used by the local fishermen to hang the severed tails of sharks up to dry. These shark tails will later be sold to Chinese restaurant owners and used to make soup. The poet describes the 'blue-gray' colour of the tails and the manner in which their smooth surfaces glisten in the sun. To the poet, these tails resemble the sharp, smooth, metallic blades of a plough: 'glinting like little ploughshares'.

At the end of the dock, a small yellow or reddish brown ('ocher') dredge is at work. A dredge is a machine, like a digger or excavator, used to remove material from a seabed or riverbed. The poet hears the constant clicking sound that the machine makes as it works. The rhythm of this clicking sound reminds her of the 'off-beat' rhythm of 'marimba' music. (The marimba is a percussion instrument consisting of a set of wooden bars that are struck with rubber mallets to produce musical tones.)

Key West is a place that experiences regular tropical storms. In fact, in the year that the poem was written, Key West experienced the most intense tropical cyclone that had been seen in the area in over a decade, the September 1948 Florida Hurricane. The poet observes that there are still a number of small boats 'piled up/ against each other' or lying on their sides 'from the last bad storm'. Many of these boats have been badly damaged by the storm, their sides smashed or 'stove' in. Nobody has bothered to come and retrieve these boats, and the poet wonders if they will ever be 'salvaged'. These small white boats remind the poet of letters that have been torn open, tossed to one side and left unanswered on someone's desk.

The poet says that the bight is 'littered with old correspondences'. This is a place that the poet has visited often and has come to identify with. There is something very familiar about it – it is a place that she can readily relate to. It is as if she has been interacting with the harbour, communicating with it, even, for such a period of time that a whole pile of 'correspondence' has gathered and accumulated. We can imagine that the poet has come here on different occasions and in different moods and found some solace or comfort in it all. Here is a place that seems to correspond with her own messy and disorganised life.

As the poet listens to the mechanical dredge going about its business at the end of the pier, she reflects upon the happenings in the bight. There is much activity 'here', but it is an 'untidy' activity, and there is little order to the place. The sponge boats are 'frowsy', which means scruffy and unkempt, shark tails are hanging on the wire fence and the boats damaged by the recent storm have been left where the storm tossed them. Yet everyone goes about their business, and 'All the untidy activity continues'. There is something horrid and unpleasant about all of this. But there is something 'cheerful' about it all as well. As Bishop wrote to a friend shortly after: 'I wrote ['The Bight'] last year but I still think if I can just keep the last line in mind ('all the untidy activity continues, awful but cheerful'), everything may still turn out all right'.

BAUDELAIRE

The French poet Charles Baudelaire (1821-1867) had a theory that it was possible to discover correspondences, or analogies, between the external world and the soul. For Baudelaire, the natural world was a special place full of symbols or messages.

He believed that the natural world was in communication with man. Baudelaire also claimed to have a synaesthetic ability (synaesthesia occurs when one type of stimulation evokes the sensation of another, as when the hearing of a sound produces the visualisation of a colour). Bishop makes a humorous reference to the French poet's special talent: 'if one were Baudelaire/ one could probably hear it turning to

THEMES

LOVE AND RESPECT FOR THE NATURAL WORLD

Bishop's love and respect for the natural world is evident in her careful, detailed description of the Key West harbour. She takes great care to describe the birds that soar above her head and dive into the sea, capturing their movements in vivid detail. The poem also registers the poet's fascination with the sea. She is intrigued by the water, which on this particular day, which does not seem to be acting as it ought to.

Bishop does not glorify or idealise the natural world, however. She is simply fascinated by its every detail, no matter how strange or unpleasant. The water is like 'peculiar gas' that is 'Absorbing, rather than being absorbed'. The birds and fish seem to resemble tools or implements that are used by humans: the pelicans are 'like pickaxes', the man-of-war birds are like 'scissors' and the shark tails are 'like little plowshares'.

MOMENTS OF AWARENESS

Bishop's poetry is marked by its extraordinary attention to detail. Whenever she was fascinated by something, she would strive to describe it as accurately and clearly as possible. This is again evident in 'The Bight' where the poet describes the coastal scene before her with great precision, focusing on its every aspect.

In many of Bishop's poems, such careful focus and description leads to some important insight or revelation. In 'The Bight', the poet does not experience a startling or sudden epiphany, but the messy bay area that she observes seems to gradually make some kind of sense to her. It suggests that life is anything but neat and orderly. On the contrary, life is an 'untidy' affair that we can never wrap up definitively. But the poet seems to accept this fact. She is content to observe and record all the 'untidy activity' – in fact, she is, on the whole, rather 'cheerful' about the need to do so.

OBLIQUE SELF-REVELATION

Bishop's poems tend to look outwards, focusing on and describing the external world in careful and minute detail. Rarely does she turn the attention directly on herself and discuss or describe how she is feeling or what she is thinking. Yet, despite this, the poet is very much present in many of her poems, and we get a sense of the type of person she is and what she is feeling through her descriptions and from her reactions to particular objects and events.

Perhaps the bight, with all its messy activity, strikes the poet as a perfect metaphor for her own life at this moment in time or on this particular occasion. Perhaps she considers her life to be a somewhat messy affair, disorganised and not quite coming together in any harmonious manner. And like the man-of-war birds that dive into the water but rarely come up with anything to show for their efforts, the poet feels that her life is unfruitful, or not as productive as it ought to be.

The 'torn-open, unanswered letters' might be a reference to the poet's own desk and her neglect of certain affairs. Perhaps there are many people who have written to her to whom she has yet to reply. The broken boats that have yet to be salvaged 'from the last bad storm' could also represent emotional or psychological hurt that the poet has suffered and that has never properly healed. These damaged boats could also represent drafts of poems that the poet has neglected or never gotten around to finishing.

At The Fishhouses

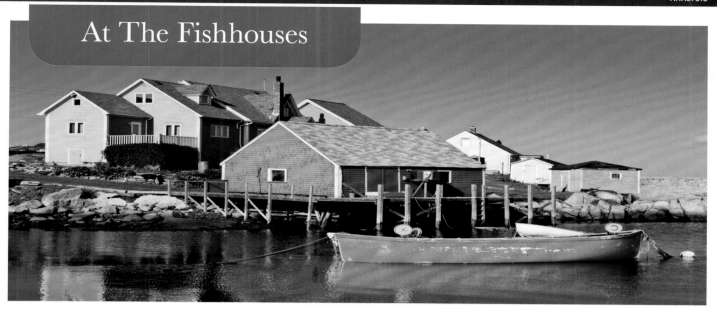

INTRODUCTION

This poem is set in Great Village, Nova Scotia, the Canadian fishing community where Bishop lived between the ages of three and six. Bishop always bore a great fondness for Nova Scotia and its landscape, and for her maternal grandparents, with whom she and her mother lived during this time. But Great Village was also associated with traumatic events in the poet's life:

- Elizabeth and her mother moved there shortly after her father's tragically early death.
- While Elizabeth was living in Great Village, her mother was committed to a mental hospital, and Elizabeth never saw her again.
- Eventually, at the age of six, Elizabeth was taken away to Massachusetts in the United States, to live with her dead father's parents. Elizabeth found this change especially jolting, referring to it, with only slight exaggeration, as a 'kidnapping'.

These events, then, were a source of terrible childhood trauma and of the emotional instability that haunted the poet as an adult. Many years after the events had taken place, Bishop's therapist suggested that she return to Great Village in an effort to come to terms with these terrible memories.

For many years, then, Bishop made regular trips back to Great Village. These return visits were made not only out of love for the bleakly beautiful Nova Scotia landscape, but also in an effort to confront her childhood traumas and heal herself on a psychic and emotional level.

SETTING THE SCENE

The poet is taking an evening stroll along the Great Village coastline by Nova Scotia. She nears the village's fish houses. These are buildings where each day's catch of cod and herring is brought ashore. The area around the fish houses, unsurprisingly, stinks of fish, of cod especially. The smell, according to the poet, is strong enough to make 'one's nose run and one's eyes water'.

The fish houses have 'steeply peaked roofs' that allow for attic storage space, or 'storerooms in the gables'. These storerooms are accessed by means of wooden ramps or gangplanks. Having first been descaled and gutted, the filleted fish would be carried up these ramps in wheelbarrows. (The ramps are 'cleated', meaning they had strips of wood running across them to prevent the wheelbarrows rolling back down). Once in the storehouses, the precious fillets would be packed in salt or ice for preservation, until they could be transported to the markets of the towns and cities.

The poet notices an old man sitting by one of the fish houses. It is 'a cold evening' and, as we've seen, it's beginning to get dark. But the old man continues to sit there, nevertheless, busily repairing one of his fishing nets: 'an old man sits netting'. In the failing light, the poet can hardly make out the net itself: 'his net, in the gloaming almost invisible'. It strikes her as no more than a blob of colour, of 'dark purple-brown' in the fast descending-darkness.

The poet was raised in the Baptist tradition. To become a Baptist, you must be baptised by 'total immersion', by having your body completely covered with water.

The poet wittily declares that the seal must also be a believer in total immersion. After all, doesn't it spend all day completely immersed in the water? But another, more serious, sense of total immersion will emerge as the poem goes on, with the poet determined to immerse herself in her own unconscious mind.

THE POET TALKS TO THE OLD MAN

The poet decides to go and talk to the old man. She strolls in his direction, passing the 'fish tubs' and wheel-barrows that sit outside the fish houses. As each fish was filleted, guts and scales would be cast into the 'huge' tubs. The wheel-barrows, meanwhile, would be used to cart the fillets of fish into the storage areas within the fish-houses themselves.

The poet approaches the old man and offers him a cigarette, which he accepts: 'The old man accepts a Lucky Strike'. The old man, it turns out, was a friend of the poet's grandfather, who has long since passed away. The poet and the old man make small talk in the dusk. Naturally, they discuss fish and the business of fishing. (Bishop, we remember, was herself very keen on fishing).

The poet is keenly aware that this is a hard-working man, one who has spent a life-time engaged in this difficult, unpleasant work. He has scraped, she realises, the scales off countless or 'unnumbered' fish. He has used the same old 'black old knife' for year after year of work at the fish houses, so much so that its blade is 'almost worn away'.

The old man is waiting 'for a herring boat to come in'. For now, he's happy to sit and chat, or to almost idly repair his netting. When the herring boat arrives, however, he will spring into action, gutting and descaling with his worn black knife until the 'huge tubs' are brimming with fish guts, until he's busy pushing wheelbarrows of freshly-gutted herring up the 'gangplanks' into the store rooms of the fish-houses.

THE POET AND THE SEAL

The poet tells us about the seal that she encountered regularly during her evening walks: 'One seal particularly/ I have seen here evening after evening'. Eventually, the poet found herself attributing human emotions and motivations to this creature. She sensed that the seal 'was curious about [her]'. She also got the feeling that the seal 'was interested in music'. She indulged this apparent interest by singing to him.

THE FIR TREES

The poem's landscape also features a large forest. The poet uses hyperbole, or deliberate poetic exaggeration, to emphasise the forest's size, declaring that it consists of a million fir trees. The fir trees, of course, are green. But in the twilight they seem to have a 'Bluish' glow. These trees run right down to the water's edge, where poet sits chatting with the old man.

THE SEA

The poet contemplates the shallows, watching the waves ebb and flow above a bed of 'gray and blue-gray stones'. The stones have been eroded by the water's ceaseless passage, each one caressed by the waves into a 'rounded' shape. And beneath the stones there is 'the world', the layers of shingle, clay and rock leading down all the way to the earth's crust. The water, as the poet so memorably puts it, moves 'above the stones and then the world'.

The poet, in an inspired turn of phrase, describes how the waves go 'swinging above the stones', wonderfully capturing the regular, almost pendulum-like movement of each wave as it surges inward and drains away again.

The sea, the poet maintains, is always the same but always different. The poet, as we noted, takes a walk each evening around the harbour of Great Village and finds herself looking at the ocean. Each evening, the ocean seems to be the same mass of 'clear dark' water, 'swinging' inward and outward in the very same fashion: 'I have seen it over and over, the same sea'. Yet the poet also realises that each evening the waters off Great Village are only 'slightly' the same; each evening finds their depths subject to different flows and currents, their surfaces agitated by different winds.

The poet's description of the water moving 'Indifferently' over the rocks powerfully captures the unthinking nature of the sea. It reminds us that we're dealing with an inhuman force of nature, one that swings relentlessly inward and outward, utterly oblivious to the destruction it causes through storms, riptides and erosion.

To the poet, then, the icy water exhibits total freedom as it moves 'icily free above the stones'. The ocean, she says, 'seems suspended', as if this great body of water were not actually resting on the stones but was somehow hovering above them: 'The water seems suspended/ above the rounded gray and blue-gray stones'. It's as if the water were immune to the laws of physics and no longer constrained by currents and weather conditions, but could flow anywhere at any time.

MOMENTS OF REVELATION

When Bishop wrote the poem, she was undergoing psychoanalysis in order to come to terms with her various childhood traumas. Indeed, as we noted above, it was her therapist who first suggested that she return to Great Village, a location associated with some of the events that scarred her childhood. Psychoanalysis involves exploring the unconscious mind and bringing to light various traumatic memories and emotions.

Throughout the poem, then, the sea serves as a symbol for the unconscious mind. The sea, according to the poet, is 'opaque', meaning that we cannot see down through the seawater. And the depths of the self, of the unconscious mind, are similarly obscure and are extremely difficult to experience or understand.

The sea, according to the poet, is 'swelling' or expanding and looks as if it is 'considering spilling over', as if it might come bursting across the jagged rocks, flooding the entire village. This reflects how unconscious trauma can spill over into our conscious lives, often resulting in poor decisions and erratic behaviour. Such trauma can threaten to overwhelm our lives ,just as the sea, during a flood, threatens to overwhelm the land.

Perhaps it's not too fanciful to imagine that the boat ramp also has a symbolic function: 'the long ramp leading into the water'. Perhaps the ramp represents the techniques of psychoanalysis. For just as the ramp allows us to move from the land to the ocean, so psychoanalysis allows us to move from the conscious to the unconscious mind.

The poet twice begins to contemplate the ocean, declaring that it is 'Cold dark deep and absolutely clear'. But she twice allows herself to be distracted. On the first occasion, she finds her focus switching from ocean to the seal that she encounters on her evening walks. On the second occasion, she finds her focus switching to the forest of fir trees behind her.

It's as if the poet can't bear to look at this 'dark deep' mass of water, this vast intimidating presence. And this, of course, reflects her unwillingness to engage with her own unconscious mind and to confront the various traumas that lurk within it.

Finally, the begins to confront the ocean directly. Its waters are presented as strange and highly dangerous:

*   They are described as being 'bearable to no mortal', suggesting that no human being could stand to be immersed in them for very long.
*   Even touching the water, according to the poet, would cause you great pain. Your wrist, she claims, would begin to 'ache immediately', the discomfort spreading inward until it penetrated your very bones.
*   And 'your hand would burn' if you immersed it in the waves, as if you'd thrust it into a raging fire.
*   Tasting the water, too, is highly dangerous. You'd experience bitterness, she claims, followed by an intense saltiness. And then your tongue would 'surely burn', as if you'd accidentally ingested acid.

The poet uses an extraordinary simile to describe the waters off Great Village, depicting them as a vast and all-consuming sea of fire. But this is fire that's been 'transmuted' or transformed, so that it 'burns with a dark gray flame'. The poet describes it as a blaze so intense that it could burn through rock, consuming the 'blue-gray stones' of the seabed

This bizarre depiction of the sea wonderfully suggests the treacherous nature of the unconscious mind. The sea is depicted as being filled with tormenting slate-grey flames, just as the unconscious mind is filled with potentially dangerous memories and emotions. To enter or even touch the sea is to risk tremendous physical pain. To confront the unconscious mind, similarly, is to risk tremendous psychological pain.

But the poet must confront it. For these burning waters represent not only the dangers and traumas that lurk within the unconscious, but also the self-knowledge that can be found there: 'It's like what we imagine knowledge to be'. Like someone wading into a sea of flames, then, the poet must enter and explore her own unconscious mind. For it's only by doing so that she can gain the self-knowledge she so desperately craves.

She imagines what such self-knowledge would feel like, were she to successfully acquire it. Such knowledge would be 'dark', like deep waters impenetrable to the sun. This image suggests the trauma's and horrors of the poet's childhood. Such knowledge would be clear, like water that is free from all pollutants and particulates, reflecting the new sense of clarity and self-awareness that the poet would gain. In another sense, self-knowledge would be 'salt', it would be difficult and abrasive to absorb but ultimately cleansing. Like waters that seem to swirl with a mind of their own, such knowledge would be 'free', reflecting the intense liberty that the poet will experience when she is finally unburdened of her past.

The sea-bed's rocky springs, from which the burning water issues are compared to breasts and mouths, to the 'cold hard mouth of the world', to 'rocky breasts'. The burning water, then, is 'drawn' or 'derived' from these springs like milk issuing from the breast of a nursing mother.

Bishop tells us that this image had its origins in a dream she had about Ruth Foster, her psychoanalyst. The dream featured a 'wild & dark' storm in which Bishop imagined a 'baby size' version of herself feeding at Foster's breast. Bishop reassured herself that this must be 'a common dream about a woman analyst'.

Psychoanalysis emphasises early childhood trauma, especially trauma relating to one's parents. Perhaps the dream about 'breasts', therefore, mixes up trauma relating to Bishop's loss of her mother with the analyst who was helping her come to terms with that trauma.

The poet imagines this strange burning water flowing out from springs within the rocks of the sea-bed. Once again, then, the burning water serves as a metaphor for self-understanding. Self-understanding must come from the very depths of the psyche, just as the watery fire comes from the very bedrock of the world. And it can only be 'drawn' or 'derived' from the depths of the unconscious with the greatest of mental efforts.

The burning water, the poet insists, is not only 'flowing' but also 'flown'. It flows or circulates like any normal liquid. But then it flies away, evaporating into the air.

*   We can, if we're focused and determined, acquire the self-knowledge that the poet speaks about. This might be represented by cupping some of the seawater in our outstretched hands.
*   By the time you come to an understanding of your psyche, your psyche will already have changed. For the subject of such knowledge is not stable, since it is a constantly shifting personality.
*   Any self-knowledge we acquire, therefore, while valuable, will always be slightly out of date. This is represented by the water evaporating or flying away before our very eyes.

We can understand ourselves fully, therefore, for only the briefest moment, before our knowledge becomes 'historical', relating as it does at each point to a slightly earlier version of our constantly shifting personality.

A LOVE AND RESPECT FOR THE NATURAL WORLD

In 'At the Fishhouses' as in so many of her poems, we get a sense of Bishop as someone with a keen awareness of her environment, someone who notices the birds, animals and other wildlife that surround her. This comes across in Bishop's lovingly detailed depictions of the sea and of the fir trees. But it's especially evident in her description of the seal, and in the 'relationship' she cultivates by singing to him each evening.

The seal's response to her singing is oddly human-like; he stares at her and shakes his head as if he was wondering what on earth this strange, singing woman was up to. 'He stood up in the water and regarded me/ steadily, moving his head a little'.

The seal seemed to exhibit human-like indecision when he 'disappeared', only to quickly reappear again 'almost in the same spot'. He would shrug as if he were bored with this singing human but had nothing better to do than listen to her songs: 'then suddenly emerge with a sort of shrug/ as if it were against his better judgment'. The poet, then, captures how uncannily human seals can appear. Anyone who has observed these creatures at close quarters knows how oddly human their eyes and faces can appear, how they seem to mimic and exhibit human behaviours and emotions.

There is something light-hearted, perhaps almost comical, about this depiction of the poet singing to an uncomprehending mammal, who looks at her with a strange mix of curiosity and indifference.

EXILE AND HOMELESSNESS

Bishop, as we've already noted, had a traumatic childhood that involved her being moved between several different locations in Canada and the United States. As a result, she felt 'rootless', as if she didn't really come from anywhere.

In returning to Great Village, however, the poet has found something resembling home. She has reconnected with her roots on her mother's side of the family. Here she inhabits a community of which her extended family is very much a part. (The old man, for instance, 'was a friend of [her] grandfather'.) The poet, then, has rediscovered a place that feels like her own point of origin, one that she could return to again and again.

And yet we sense that this newly rediscovered 'home' is very much under threat. Indeed, the poet and the old man talk about how the population of Great Village is 'declining'. The young, no doubt, are keen to leave the hard life of this fishing community behind, and set off for the bright lights of the major cities. As the elder generation die off, therefore, there is no one to take their place on the fishing boats. Great Village, it seems, is a community threatened with extinction.

The fact that, when she is on her evening walk, the poet sees only an old man adds to our impression of an aging community. Perhaps the old man's 'worn' shuttle and his old knife, which is 'almost worn away', serve as metaphors for a way of life that is in decline as fewer and fewer people enter the fishing industry. Even the fact that the poem is set at evening, just as darkness falls, reinforces our sense that Great Village might well be a community nearing its end.

The Prodigal

LINE BY LINE

This poem can be read as an updating of the well-known parable from the Gospel of St Luke. Jesus tells us about a son who asks for his inheritance from his wealthy father and then heads off to a foreign country, where he squanders his money on drink, gambling and other vices. Eventually, his funds run out, and he ends up working in a pigsty. For a long time, he endures labouring in the muck and dung, as he is too ashamed to return home with his money spent and in such a lowly condition. Eventually, he can take no more, and he returns to his father, who forgives him and welcomes him with open arms.

There is a strong autobiographical element to this poem. Since her college days, Bishop had been a problem drinker. After leaving college, she spent a period attempting to break into New York's literary scene, during which she quickly developed into a full-blown alcoholic. According to her biographers, Bishop drank to combat feelings of low self-esteem and depression. As is so often the case, however, drinking only made these feelings worse. Her struggle with alcohol was lifelong, and was fought with varying degrees of success.

STANZA 1

Inspired by this parable, Bishop's poem describes an alcoholic farm labourer who not only works in but also sleeps in a pigsty. He is employed on a farm that is a long way from home. He is a voluntary 'exile', who would rather work in the pigsty than return to where he came from. The pigsty is described as unpleasant:

• The floor is 'rotten'.

• The walls are covered with dung: 'The sty was plastered halfway up with glass-smooth dung'.

• One female pig, we are told, consistently devours her own children: 'the sow that always ate her young'.

- There is something unpleasant or even slightly sinister about how the pigs' eyes follow the prodigal around the barn: 'the pigs' eyes followed him, a cheerful stare'.
- The foul stench of the place closes in around the prodigal in a way that is swamping and claustrophobic.

The odour has so overpowered the prodigal's sense of smell that he can no longer 'judge' it; he no longer notices its foulness: It 'was too close … for him to judge'. Unsurprisingly, the prodigal finds himself disgusted, or 'sickening', in this foul environment.

Like many alcoholics, the prodigal is secretive about his drinking, hiding pint bottles of liquor behind the pigsty's planks of wood: 'he hid the pints behind a two-by-four'.

'On mornings after drinking bouts', the prodigal is struck by the beauty that the sunrise brings to the farmyard. The mud and puddles of the yard reflect the colour of the sunrise. The puddles seem to 'burn', and the mud is described as being 'glazed' with red. This beautiful sight seems to 'reassure' the prodigal, making him feel that his life in the barn is worth living: 'the burning puddles seemed to reassure'. In such moments, he feels he can continue to put up with the filth and squalor of the pigsty for at least another year instead of returning home: 'And then he thought he almost might endure/ his exile yet another year or more'. (Of course, this sense of 'reassurance' might also stem from the alcohol he has just consumed.)

STANZA 2

This stanza describes an evening in the farmyard. It is getting dark. The sun is 'going away', and the 'first star' has appeared in the sky. The prodigal completes what are presumably his last tasks of the day: 'Carrying a bucket along a slimy board'. His employer 'shuts the cows and horses in the barn' and returns to his farmhouse by the light of a lantern. As he walks away, his lantern casts an 'aureole', or halo of light, on the farmyard's mud. This aureole seems to 'pace' along with him as he returns to the farmhouse: 'The lantern – like the sun, going going away –/ Laid on the mud a pacing aureole'.

If the prodigal's mornings are sometimes filled with hope and reassurance, then his nights seem truly miserable. He views the 'first star' as a warning to him that night is on its way, which suggests that his nighttime hours are highly unpleasant. We can imagine his nights being filled with guilt and self-loathing caused by his addiction and by the fact that he has ended up living and working in such a squalid environment.

The prodigal's circumstances are contrasted to those of the farmer and the farm animals. Each evening, the cows and horses are 'shut up' snugly in their barn, 'safe and companionable' like the animals in Noah's Ark. The pigs, meanwhile, snore contentedly: 'the pigs stuck out their little feet and snored'. Having seen to the cows and horses, the farmer returns to the warmth and comfort of his farmhouse.

The image of the farmer's lantern receding into the distance is almost unbearably sad; it powerfully emphasises the prodigal's isolation. These lines emphasise the intense loneliness of the prodigal's nights. On evenings like this – as darkness is drawing in and he prepares for another night alone in the barn – the prodigal's mind is struck by moments of insight: 'He felt … shuddering insights, beyond his control,/ touching him'. He becomes aware of the full grimness of his situation, and shudders in horror at the awfulness of his life in the pigsty. These moments of horrified insight are 'beyond his control'. He may find these thoughts unwelcome or unpleasant but there is nothing he can do to avoid them. He cannot fend them off with drink, or with reassuring thoughts about the sunrise.

These 'shuddering insights' seem related to the prodigal's awareness of the bats that fly above the barn: 'he felt the bats' uncertain staggering flight'. It has been suggested that these bats flying blindly through the night serve as a metaphor for the prodigal's situation. Just as they stumble and fumble through the air, so the prodigal staggers and lurches through life, uncertain as to how he should live. Yet the bats, though blind, possess a 'homing instinct' that allows them to navigate safely. The prodigal, too – it is implied – possesses such a 'homing instinct', some inner drive or intuition that will eventually cause him to leave the pigsty and return to his father's house.

Surprisingly, however, these moments of 'shuddering insight' do not cause the prodigal to immediately change his life. Although he realises the misery of his situation, it is a long time before he can find it in himself to leave the pigsty behind and return home: 'But it took him a long time/ finally to make his mind up to go home'.

The misery of the prodigal's sleeping arrangements is emphasised. While the farmer and his animals are comfortable, he must sleep amid the filth and discomfort of the pigsty. We also see the intense loneliness of his situation. The animals sleep in a 'companionable' togetherness, whereas the prodigal is completely alone. Our sense of his loneliness is reinforced when the farmer returns to his farmhouse for the night, leaving the prodigal behind in the pigsty.

THEMES

ADDICTION

'The Prodigal' is a moving and honest portrayal of an addict. The prodigal, as we have seen, suffers from severe alcohol addiction. He drinks even in the mornings, hiding his bottles of spirits behind planks of wood. Like the character in the Bible story, his vices have brought him to a terrible situation. He spends his days amid the filth and squalor of the pigsty. Even worse, he spends his nights there, too. He also suffers from terrible loneliness. Furthermore, we get the impression that his nights are racked by guilt and self-loathing.

The poem, then, paints an unflinching picture of the misery addiction brings. Yet it also highlights how addicts take comfort and solace in their own condition. Addiction may be a miserable way of life, but it is one they understand and are familiar with. This is presumably why the pigsty's foul odour no longer offends the prodigal. Even the 'glass-smooth' dung caked on the walls is presented as being somewhat attractive. The pigs, too, are depicted as having a certain curious attraction with their 'light-lashed' eyes and 'cheerful stare'. They offer the prodigal a strange kind of companionship, which is evident when he leans down to scratch the sow's head.

The poem also emphasises how difficult it is for an addict to leave addiction behind, even when he realises the damage it is causing to his life. The prodigal seems torn about changing his life. In the evenings, there are moments of 'shuddering insight' when he realises the full horror of his situation. His awareness of the bats flying through the sky reminds him that he could follow his instincts and return home, leaving his addiction and the pigsty behind. However, in the mornings – as he drunkenly watches a sunrise – the prodigal feels 'reassured' that he can endure his miserable way of life for at least another year. In the end, it takes the prodigal 'a long time' to finally decide to give up his addictions and return to his father's house.

EXILE AND HOMELESSNESS

Throughout her life, Bishop was something of a wanderer, dogged by feelings of restlessness and rootlessness. This notion of 'homelessness' is one that occurs several times in Bishop's poetry, including 'The Prodigal'. The prodigal lives and works in absolutely miserable conditions. He could end all this simply by returning home. Yet for a very long time, he refuses to do so, deciding to 'endure' his self-imposed 'exile' rather than return to his family. We get a sense, then, that the prodigal feels he does not really have a home to go to anymore, that he is simply not welcome any longer in his father's house. The word 'home' is the only end-word in the poem that does not have a full rhyme, which may suggest how difficult the 'concept' of home has become for the prodigal. As is so often the case in Bishop's poetry, the journey 'home' is not an easy one to make.

Questions of Travel

1

This poem describes events that occurred during a trip through Brazil the poet took in 1951, along with her companion Lota de Macedo Soares. The poem is set in the mountains near Petrópolis, the town near Rio de Janeiro where Bishop lived for a time with her lover Lota de Macedo Soares.

The poet looks out at this extraordinary vista of enormous peaks, with waterfalls running down their sides. Some of the mountains are so high that their summits breach the cloud cover, causing tendrils of cloud to drift down across their upper slopes.

According to the poet, however, this landscape is unpleasantly cluttered. There are 'so many clouds', she declares, and 'too many waterfalls'. In fact there are so many waterfalls that their streams seem 'crowded' together as they rush down the slopes to the ocean below: 'There are too many waterfalls here; the crowded streams'.

Pressure, too, is a feature of this landscape. According to the poet, the weight of the cloud-mass forces it onto the peaks, pushing billows of cloud down the mountains' upper slopes: 'the pressure of so many clouds on the mountain tops/ makes them spill over the sides'. The cloud-mass, then, is pressed down upon the mountaintops like a lemon on a juicer.

The poet also associates this landscape with haste and hurry. The waterfalls, we're told, 'hurry too rapidly down to the sea'. Both the clouds and streams are described as always 'traveling, traveling' – the repetition emphasising the pace and relentlessness of their movement. Even time itself seems to be in a hurry. The age it takes for the cloud streams to become waterfalls will be a 'quick' one.

All in all, then, when the poet looks out at this seemingly spectacular landscape, she experiences stress rather than relaxation, anxiety rather than awe. The whole scene puts her in mind of pressure, haste and crowdedness. There is a note, too of weariness and indifference here, as if the poet has seen and experienced too much on her travels. We see this in the rather unpleasant images she uses. In a wonderful metaphor, the clouds spilling down the mountainside are described as 'streaks' and 'tearstains'. In an equally vivid simile, the mountains themselves are compared to the slimy hulls of capsized ships. We get the impression that Bishop is bored by sights like this one, that no mountain range, no matter how spectacular, can thrill her now.

2

Issues with travel

The poet, as she looks out over the mountains, meditates on the question of travel, highlighting several problems associated with travel and tourism. The first issue she raises is a very practical one, relating to the inconvenience of going abroad. 'Think of the long trip home', Bishop declares, suggesting that any experiences we might have in a foreign country aren't worth the sheer hassle of travelling there and back again.

Ethical issues

The poet also raises the various ethical problems that surround tourism. She wonders where, from a moral point of view, 'should we be today?' Should be travelling, or should we stay at home? Tourism can contribute not only to global warming but also to economic and environmental problems in popular destinations. Perhaps, then, we really ought to cancel our travel plans and remain in our home countries?

The poet uses a wonderful metaphor to highlight one particular ethical issue, comparing the act of travelling abroad to that of going to the theatre. The foreign locations that we visit are compared to the theatre's stage, while the local people that we see on our travels are compared to its actors. We, the tourists who gaze at the locals as they go about their daily lives, are compared to the theatre's audience.

The poet wonders if it is right to watch these strangers in the hope that we will be entertained or will get an exotic photo for our Instagrams. Perhaps our touristic gaze is a kind of voyeurism, an invasion of the local people's privacy and an unwelcome intrusion into their lives.

Shallowness

Human beings, according to the poet, are always eager to see new things and sample new cultural attractions. Sometimes we're eager to see remarkable species of animal, such as 'the tiniest green hummingbird in the world'. Sometimes we're more interested in buildings and monuments and are keen to visit the 'old stonework' of a French cathedral or an ancient Brazilian temple.

We engage with such sights on only the shallowest level, however. They are, as the poet memorably puts it, 'instantly seen'. We spend only a second or two examining each one, perhaps posing for a photo to post on social media. Then we declare it to be 'delightful' (or cool or lovely or whatever) and move on to the next attraction: 'instantly seen and always, always delightful?'

Furthermore, many aspects of a foreign country, like the temple's old 'stonework', simply can't be understood by people from outside the culture that created them. To visitors, then, they will always remain 'inexplicable' and 'impenetrable', utterly impossible to understand. (To emphasise this point, Bishop repeats the word 'inexplicable'). Perhaps, therefore, the only way to know or understand a country is by actually living there.

Childish Consumerism

The poet suggest that the impulse to travel and be a tourist, which so many of us experience, is a childish one. In her view, when we engage in tourism, we behave in a rather silly or hyperactive fashion, being 'determined to rush' from sight to sight, from attraction to attraction. And this childish impulse doesn't diminish with age. Instead, those who experience this impulse when young continue to do so until they very day they die: 'while there's a breath of life/ in our bodies'.

Bishop presents tourism as a form of gluttonous consumption. We fill our memories with mental images, or our Instagram accounts with digital ones, just as we might fill our bellies with treats from a food stall. In a wonderful metaphor, tourist's experiences are compared to 'folded' foodstuffs like crepes or tacos. From the poet's viewpoint, tourists mindlessly consume such experiences, just as they might consume such tasty treats: 'And have we room/ for one more folded sunset, still quite warm?'

Imagination

The poet's final objection to travel is particularly unusual: she suggests that we're better off not visiting our dream destinations. Maybe she's suggesting that the reality of such destinations can never live up to the expectations we have for them, that it's better to stick with our imagined idea of a place, than to experience the disappointing reality.

The poet, it seems, has often dreamed of visiting this part of Brazil and has fantasised about the mountains that form such an impressive part of its lush landscape. Now that she's actually there, however, a part of her wishes that she'd stayed at home. To some extent, the poet now wishes that, instead of actually visiting this spectacular location, she had continued to see it only in her imagination: 'Should we have stayed at home and thought of here?'

Each of us has dreams and ambitions. And we live in a society that emphasises the fulfilment of such goals. The poet, however, resists this pressure to make our every dream a reality: 'Oh, must

we dream our dreams/ and have them, too?' This even applies to dream destinations, which the poet feels we might be better off imagining than visiting.

3

The Trees

The poet thinks about the journey she made in order to reach this part of Brazil, recalling how she and her companion drove along one particular tree-lined road. Using a wonderful simile, she compares the trees to performers in a pantomime. Their blossom is compared to the performers' costumes, while the movement of their branches is compared to the gestures that the performers might make during a show.

'It would have been a pity', the poet says, to have missed out on this experience, 'not to have seen the trees along this road'. After all, the pink blossom lends the trees a great 'beauty'. There was something 'noble', she feels, something both imposing and uplifting about the sight of this tree-lined highway.

But Bishop's experience of the trees wasn't entirely positive. She describes their appearance as 'really exaggerated' and compares them to performers in a pantomime, which suggests that there was something silly or over the top about their appearance.

The filling station

While the poet and her companion were on their way to their destination in Brazil they 'had to stop for gas' at a filling station. This seems to have been in an extremely remote and poverty-stricken area. Its inhabitants were so poor that they even made their own shoes, carving crude wooden clogs from blocks of wood. While the poet and her companion were refuelling, a particularly heavy rain-storm arrived. They ended up staying in the filling station for several hours while the storm blew itself out.

The poet recalls the owner of the filling station. Because they were homemade, his two clogs were 'disparate' or unalike. Each was distinct in terms of weight and shape. Each made a different sound when it struck the filling-station floor, producing a 'two-noted wooden tune' as the owner walked around his premises.

'It would have been a pity', the poet feels, not to have experienced this 'clacking' sound. She notes that in another country, perhaps a more developed one, shoes would be mass-produced and 'tested' in a factory. Each individual shoe would be identical in terms of weight and shape, producing a similar 'pitch' or note when impacting the floor.

Perhaps the poet felt, therefore, that she was experiencing something fun and quirky. Or perhaps she felt as if she were experiencing the 'real Brazil', that she had, at least for a moment, left the commercialised modern world behind.

At the same time, however, the poet is forced to acknowledge that the filling station is a depressing environment. An air of desperation clings to its owner, as if he's been ground down by poverty. He takes little pride in his premises; the floor is 'grease-stained' and at least one of the pumps is 'broken'. He moves in a sloppy fashion, 'carelessly clacking' across the dirty floor.

The Bird

The poet recalls the filling station owner's pet, a 'fat brown bird' that he kept in a cage above the broken petrol pump. It would have been a pity, she feels, not to have heard this brown bird's song. For the poet, the sound of its singing was more complicated, and no doubt more pleasant, than the clacking sound of the owner's clogs: 'A pity not to have heard/ the other, less primitive music of the fat brown bird'.

The poet is forced to acknowledge, however, that this memory also has a negative aspect. Although the bird might sing sweetly, it is still a prisoner, caged in this miserable filling station with its broken pump and its grease-stained floor.

The cage

The bird's cage, like the clogs, was homemade. The poet was struck by the contrast between these two items. The clogs, being the 'crudest wooden footwear', were carved in a rough and ready fashion. The cage, on the other hand, was created in a fashion that was both 'careful' and 'finicky' or fussy. According to the poet, it was 'whittled' from bamboo, which suggests that it was carved in a slow, deliberate and repetitive fashion.

The clogs were created purely with function in mind, with no hint of style or decoration. The cage, on the other hand, was highly decorative. The fact that it's described as being 'of Jesuit baroque' suggests that it was a complex and elaborate structure. In fact, the poet describes it as a 'fantasy', suggesting that it was the product of real creativity and imagination.

As she sat in the filling station, the poet found herself wondering what possible 'connection' could exist between these two pieces of woodwork. Why, 'for centuries', have the people of rural Brazil produced elaborate cages for their birds, while continuing to make only the most basic footwear for themselves?

Why do they spend hour after hour carving complex birdcages, while spending so little time making shoes?   Do they simply not care about style or even comfort when it comes to footwear? What are we to make of such strange priorities?

The poet feels that it would have been 'a pity' to miss out on this experience. If she hadn't stopped in the filling station, she wouldn't have had the opportunity to 'ponder' these questions. Once again, however, she stresses that her experience wasn't an entirely positive one, because her thoughts were vague and imprecise and led to no real answers or conclusions.

History

The poet studied the birdcage, wondering what it might tell her about Brazilian history. The cage's elaborately woven bars, she felt, were a type of 'calligraphy' She studied those bamboo loops and squiggles just as one would study words and letters in a historical document.

Ultimately, however, studying the birdcage told the poet little or nothing about Brazil's troubled past. The cage's patterns, therefore, are compared to 'weak calligraphy'. Perhaps the poet has in mind a document whose letters have faded over the years, or maybe one that was poorly written to begin with.

Silence

The poet recalls the rain that fell while she was in the filling station, waiting for the storm to pass by. She uses a wonderful simile to capture this dull, monotonous sound, comparing it to 'politicians' speeches'. The sound of the rain, she declares, was 'unrelenting'. For 'two hours' it never paused or altered or diminished in intensity.

The poet, therefore, took special pleasure in the silence that she experienced when the rain suddenly stopped. This, she says, was a 'sudden golden silence', which suggests her intense relief that the rain had passed and she no longer had to endure its monotonous drumming. As she sat in the suddenly silent filling station, the poet jotted a few lines in her notebook, and it's those notes – set apart by being printed in italics – that conclude the poem.

THEMES

TRAVEL

The poem, it must be said, takes a rather dim view of the whole area of travel and tourism. Its opening shows how even the keenest travellers and tourists can become jaded from sightseeing. The poet responds to a spectacular landscape with weariness, almost with disgust, referring to the streams of cloud as 'streaks' and 'tearstains' and to the mountains as 'slime-hung'. She describes this vista in terms of pressure, haste and crowdedness, which suggests that the landscape brings her stress rather than happiness or relaxation.

As we've seen, this poem criticises travel and tourism in both practical and moral terms. Tourism is presented as a vulgar form of consumerism, whereby we rush around 'doing' as many sights as possible as quickly as possible. The poet even suggests that, instead of actually visiting our dream destinations, we should stay at home and see them only in our imaginations.

The poem especially emphasises how difficult it is to really know or understand a foreign country. We see this in the filling station when the poet attempts to understand Brazil's past but can only do so only in the feeblest and most uncertain manner. The point is that, as tourists, we engage with foreign countries on only the most superficial level. What we witness will always be as artificial as a performance in a theatre. The 'old stonework' of monuments and other attractions will always remain 'inexplicable' and 'impenetrable'.

Such negativity is also present in her description of the journey to Petrópolis. The poet mentions six experiences she had in or around the filling station that she visited while en route, declaring that 'surely it would have been a pity' to miss out on each one of them.

As we have seen, however, the poet's description of each experience is highly qualified – each is depicted as having a negative as well as a positive aspect. Would the poet really have regretted missing out on these experiences? Or is she merely trying to convince herself that her journey to Petrópolis was worthwhile?

This negative attitude to travel continues in the notebook entry that concludes the poem. The poet wonders why we can't 'just stay at home?' She even refers to the 17th-century French theologian Blaise Pascal's famous suggestion that 'all the evil in the world comes from man's inability to sit quietly in his room'.

Yet despite all these objections and criticisms, Bishop can't help wondering if travel might still be justifiable or even necessary. She can't help hoping that Pascal might have been wrong, or at least 'not entirely right' when he gave his famous advice.

So finally, then, does the poet feel that travel is a good or a bad thing? Should we be 'here, or there'? Should we be travelling, or should we have 'stayed at home'? Ultimately, Bishop refuses to answer. For it's a question that, given her own particular background and psychology, she feels unable to address in any definitive fashion.

EXILE AND HOMELESSNESS

Bishop's father, we remind ourselves, died when she was only eight months old and her mother was institutionalised when she was only four. In the years that followed, Bishop was shunted from guardian to guardian in both Canada and the United States.

Because her childhood was spent in so many different locations, Bishop felt that she didn't really come from anywhere. She didn't have a 'home' in the sense of a point of origin, a native place that she and her family hailed from and to which she could return. This sense of what we might call 'homelessness' is indicated by the poem's final enigmatic question: 'Should we have stayed at home,/ wherever that may be?' The poet is uncertain, therefore, as to where her 'home' might be, and whether she even has one.

The poem also highlights Bishop's acute sense of restlessness. During her adult years Bishop regularly changed her place of residence. And when she did settle in one place, she experienced what we might describe as 'itchy feet', embarking on regular trips and excursions. Bishop's traumatic and unsettled childhood, no doubt, contributed greatly to this restlessness.

The poem suggests that Bishop dislikes her own inability to settle down. She's one of those people who, until the day they die, will be 'determined to rush' about the place, visiting and revisiting various locales. She simply can't help it, but she views this impulse as one of utter 'childishness'.

The poet's restlessness makes her agitated and uneasy. This is suggested by the sense of haste and pressure in the poem's opening, with its streams and clouds that 'keep travelling, travelling', its waterfalls that 'hurry too rapidly'.

The poet doesn't want to keep 'travelling, travelling', but neither does she want to stay in one place. She'd find it unbearable to be static and unmoving, like the mountains she's come to visit. This is why she compares them to the ugly, sunken hulls of 'capsized ships', which are covered with slime and barnacles.

The poet seems to view her urge to travel as a failure of imagination. She sits at home and contemplates 'imagined places', places she's never been. She suggests that if her powers of imagination were greater, she'd be able to visualise such locations in extraordinary detail. Her mental image of these 'imagined places' would be so rich that she'd never actually feel the urge to visit them: 'Is it lack of imagination that makes us come/ to imagined places, not just stay at home?'

For most of her adult life, Bishop had a modest independent income and no regular job. If she wished, therefore, she could live in or visit any 'Continent, city, country, society'. And yet she feels no sense of freedom: 'The choice is never wide and never free'.

Perhaps Bishop experiences no sense of 'choice' because, like an addict, she feels compelled by urges that she can't control and doesn't fully understand. Or perhaps she thinks that everywhere she visits is ultimately the same. No matter where she goes, she's dogged by the same feelings of restlessness, the same sense of never truly being at home.

This is one of several poems in which Bishop presents herself as a detached, neutral observer of a community to which she doesn't belong and can't really understand. The phrase 'as ages go here' suggests that she is a visitor rather than a native inhabitant. As we've seen, she ponders what the clogs and cage might tell her about Brazilian history, but can do so only in a blurred and inconclusive manner.

The Armadillo

'The Armadillo' is set in Petrópolis, Brazil, where Bishop lived with her partner Lota Soares for many years.

Armadillos are medium-sized animals, about 150 centimetres long, that are native to Brazil and elsewhere in South America. They are distinguished by their long narrow snouts, their short legs and, especially by the leathery armour shell that covers their bodies. This protective covering is composed of overlapping plates that resemble the mail armour worn by medieval warriors. (This is why the armadillo's fist is described as 'mailed').

The feast day of Saint John, which falls on the 24th of June, was marked by a carnival in Rio and in other Brazilian cities. In the weeks leading up to this celebration, the local people would release fire balloons 'almost every night'. The community would gather and watch hundreds, maybe thousands, of these balloons drifting into the night sky: 'This is the time of year when … the frail, illegal fire balloons appear'.

Bishop describes these fire balloons as 'frail', suggesting their delicate design. Each balloon consisted of a thin paper shell, with an opening at the bottom. At the centre of the shell was placed a 'candle' made from paraffin wax. When the candle was ignited ,it heated the air inside the balloon, causing it to rise. Eventually, however, the candle would go out and the balloon would drift to earth again.

Like many fireworks, the balloons were declared 'illegal' by the authorities. This is because fire balloons tended to fall to earth with their candles still smouldering. Sometimes, on impact, the balloon's paper shell would go up in flames. This could lead to wildfires that consumed everything in the crashed balloon's vicinity: wooden houses, crops, cliffs or dried-out scrubland. Bishop even installed a sprinkler system on her own property as a precaution against the destruction that the fire balloons might cause.

But neither the risk of such environmental damage nor the threat of prosecution prevented the local population from indulging in this ritual celebration of Saint John. On most June nights, the fire balloons continued to fill the sky.

2

The poet clearly appreciates the balloons' mysterious beauty. From time to time, the paraffin in each 'paper chamber' flares, causing the flame to grow bigger and brighter. Then it dies down again. Bishop wonderfully captures this flickering effect, observing that each balloon seems to 'flush and fill with light/ that comes and goes'.

We can imagine that such a vast flotilla of flickering spheres would indeed make a sight to remember. We can imagine hundreds, or even thousands of balloons drifting upwards, each one flickering on and off according to its own irregular rhythm.

The poet watches the balloons floating into the night sky:
- The balloons float upwards at an angle, their flight-path tracking the slope of the mountain: 'Climbing the mountain height'.
- A statue of Saint John, the saint that the fire balloons were designed to honour, sits on the mountain peak. The balloon float upwards toward his likeness: 'rising toward a saint/ still honored in these parts'.
- The balloons keep rising – higher than the statue, higher than the mountain peak – until they are 'up against the sky'.
- On a 'still' night, the balloons rise 'steadily', drifting upwards in an even fashion, untroubled by any winds. According to the poet, there is something 'solemn' about their movement. We can imagine how the sight of hundreds, or even thousands, of such balloons drifting slowly upwards might strike us not only as dignified and ceremonial but also as awe-inspiring and majestic.
- On such a windless night, the balloons rise so high that they seem to merge with the great mass of stars overhead. Bishop uses a wonderful metaphor to capture this optical effect, telling us that the balloons seem to 'steer between' the constellations.
- Finally, the balloons disappear from view altogether. They keep 'receding' or moving away. Their light keeps 'dwindling', becoming fainter and fainter as they rise so high that they are no longer visible.
- The poet tells us that observers on the ground feel forsaken by the fire balloons as they float out of sight. The observers feel dejected and abandoned now that they can no longer see the fire balloons' grace and beauty.

3

On windy nights however, the movement of the balloons is not so graceful. Gusts of air cause them to stall or 'falter' in their gentle upward movement. They 'wobble' awkwardly in the breeze. Their movement becomes erratic and unpredictable, as they are tossed around by the wind. They 'flare and falter, wobble and toss'.

Sometimes, the balloons are caught by a 'downdraft', a sudden current of air gusting down the mountain-side. Such gusts can carry the balloons dangerously close to people and to buildings: 'in the downdraft from a peak,/ suddenly turning dangerous'.

The previous night, a large fire balloon crashed into the ground behind the poet's property: 'Last night another big one fell'. The poet tells us that this balloon 'splattered like an egg of fire against the cliff behind the house'. And we can indeed visualise the spherical balloon as a kind of egg, but one that spills fire, rather than yolk and egg-white, on impact with the ground.

The poet observes how the crashed balloon set fire to the vegetation on the cliff side, causing great destruction. The flames consumed an 'ancient' nest where 'a pair of owls' had resided for years or even decades. The poet watched as these terrified birds fled the conflagration, flying 'up and up' into the night sky.

The owls, it seems, were on fire as they fled. The poet, in a brilliant descriptive touch, describes the flames as a pink stain on their 'black-and-white' feathers. She describes how they went 'whirling' through the sky: 'whirling black-and-white/ stained bright pink underneath'. We can imagine them wheeling about in confusion, but also, no doubt, striving to quench the flames that were consuming them. Finally, they disappeared from view, 'shrieking' in pain and terror as they did so.

The poet observes a rabbit leaping from the burning vegetation on the cliff-side: 'And then a baby rabbit jumped out'. It stared directly ahead in a 'fixed' fashion, as rabbits often do when in a panicked state. We can imagine that it was almost hypnotised by the inferno that suddenly surrounded it.

This 'baby' rabbit, it seems, was absolutely tiny, so small that it might fit in the palm of one's hand. The poet watched as it was consumed by the flames. She watched as it was reduced, before her very eyes, to a tiny a rabbit-shaped heap of ashes. This pile of ash is described as 'intangible', because if it was touched, it would crumble, losing its rabbit shape: 'So soft! – a handful of intangible ash'.

A single armadillo also attempted to flee the chaos. Its leathery armoured shell was 'rose-flecked' from the flames. It is unclear whether the armadillo is actually on fire or whether its shell is simply speckled with little pieces of burning material. Its head and tail are described as being 'down', as if it were cowering in fear in a desperate attempt to protect itself.

4

A notable feature of the poem is the fact that the final stanza is printed in italics. This is because the poet is speaking for the armadillo, attempting to articulate this poor animal's reaction to the human carelessness that has destroyed its home.

- She expresses the armadillo's feelings of terror and incomprehension as it flees this chaotic scene where flame has suddenly started 'falling' from the sky, a scene filled with panicking animals and their ear-splitting cries: 'O falling fire and piercing cry and panic'.
- She expresses the armadillo's anger at the destruction visited upon its habitat when she condemns the fire balloons for their 'Too pretty, dreamlike mimicry!'
- She observes how the armadillo raises its clenched fist against the sky, in a traditional gesture of anger and defiance. It's as if the armadillo is cursing or condemning the fire balloons and their creators.

The creature's rage is futile, however. It is too 'ignorant' to understand the destruction that has occurred and too weak to repair the damage or exact revenge.

THEMES

TRAVEL AND EXILE

The speaker presents herself as something of an outsider in the Brazilian community in which she lives. Her position as an immigrant, or a long-term visitor, rather than a native inhabitant, is one that really comes across throughout the poem.

The phrase 'in these parts', for instance, suggests that this is a community the poet is still attempting to make sense of, rather than one in which she feels completely at home. It is significant that she takes no part in the ritual of the fire balloons that so engages the local population. Perhaps, as a visitor from a richer, more advanced country, she regards such rituals and beliefs as primitive and backward.

To the poet, then, the fire balloons are a strange local custom, one that is not only quaint and beautiful but also senseless and dangerous. She acknowledges the beauty of the fire balloons as they drift smoothly into the distance, but condemns the damage they all too often cause when they fall earthwards.

A LOVE AND RESPECT FOR THE NATURAL WORLD

In 'The Armadillo', as in so many of her poems, we get a sense of Bishop as someone with a keen awareness of her environment, someone who notices the birds, animals and other wildlife that surround her. She's aware for instance that there's an 'ancient nest' at the back of her property where a 'pair of owls' have nested. She even notices, in the middle of the chaotic inferno caused by the crashed balloon, that the baby rabbit is of the 'short-eared' South American variety.

'The Armadillo', then, can be read as an environmentalist poem, as a lament for mankind's careless indifference to nature. The poet's perspective contrasts strongly with that of the local people, who seem utterly indifferent to the 'falling fire and piercing cry/ and panic' that their tradition all too often produces. In one sense, then, the poem can be read as an attack on human selfishness and short sightedness, condemning our continuing engagement in unnecessary activities even when we know they damage the natural world.

The poet's love and respect for the natural world are especially palpable in the final stanza. Here, as we've noted, she seeks to speak on behalf of the armadillo, and on behalf of the other creatures affected by the 'falling fire'. Here, Bishop seeks to expresses these creatures' feelings of anger and incomprehension, their reaction to the human carelessness and selfishness that have caused them so much harm. She gives voice to the armadillo's rage, condemning on its behalf the annual ritual that visits such destruction on the local wildlife: 'Too pretty, dreamlike mimicry!/ O falling fire and piercing cry/ and panic'.

ADDICTION

Despite all this, however, the local people continue to celebrate their ritual. And 'almost every night', the fire balloons throng the sky.

This is one of several poems where Bishop describes people who are caught up in what can only be described as compulsive behaviour. The local population – of course – are aware of the risks posed by the balloons they release each June. They know that the fire balloons all too often destroy wildlife when they come crashing down to earth. They know that these balloons are 'illegal'.

Yet their devotion to their local saint makes them want to persist with this dangerous activity. They may also be motivated by the desire to uphold a tradition or by a strangely misguided sense of community spirit. Whatever the motivation, it is perhaps not too outlandish to regard this religious impulse as a form of addiction, a compulsion that people brought up in this tradition are powerless to resist or control. In this regard, the poem resembles 'The Prodigal', with its portrayal of a chronic alcoholic, and 'Questions of Travel', which touches on the notion of the compulsive traveller.

WAR

The Armadillo' was published in 1957, a year when Bishop, like the rest of the world, was concerned about the possibility of a catastrophic conflict between the United States and the Soviet Union. At the end of World War II, the United States had dropped atomic bombs on the Japanese cities of Hiroshima and Nagasaki. The Soviet Union had responded by testing its own atomic bomb in 1949. The 1950s, meanwhile, saw both sides developing vastly more destructive hydrogen bombs. Such weapons meant that any

conflict between these two superpowers could spell the end of life on planet earth.

Anxiety about bombs, then, was much in the air when Bishop composed 'The Armadillo'. The balloons, as Bishop sees them, resemble such weapons in important respects. They are bomb-like because they are launched from a specific point on earth, only to come crashing down elsewhere, bringing great destruction. In their 'mimicry' of bombs, then, the balloons cause great destruction, bringing 'falling fire' wherever they descend.

In the face of such destructive forces, of course, the ordinary citizen can do little. We are as vulnerable as the immolated baby rabbit or the owls that wheel away, terrified, into the sky. We can, if we wish, protest against the proliferation and use of nuclear weapons. But our complaints will be as futile as those of the armadillo uselessly shaking his fist against the sky. (Bishop, it's worth noting, eventually dedicated 'The Armadillo' to her long-term friend and fellow poet Robert Lowell. Lowell had gone to jail rather than fight in World War II and throughout the 1950s campaigned vigorously for nuclear disarmament).

To Bishop, then, it seemed that the world was locked on a course that would lead to an apocalyptic nuclear confrontation. This is symbolised by the relationship between the planets. The planet Venus, named after the Roman god of love, is in retrograde, meaning that it appears to be sinking from the sky. The planet Mars, named after the Roman God of War, is in the ascendant. This, then, is an era of conflict rather than love and togetherness.

The launching of the fire balloons is a religious act, designed to honour Saint John. It is also an act of community and national solidarity, the celebration of an ancient Brazilian ritual. But just as the fire balloons cause damage to local property, so nationalism and religious fervour all too often lead to disaster on a global scale, giving rise to one war after another.

The balloons are said to be 'pretty' and 'dreamlike' as they float up against the sky. And we can imagine how such a sight might resemble something from a beautiful dream. This suggests how religious and national solidarity can be a beautiful thing, bringing communities together and giving meaning to peoples' lives.

Yet the poet also suggests that the balloons are 'too pretty'. This suggests how people can become hypnotised by love of their own nation or religion, losing sight of what unites all human beings. Lost in such a beautiful, dangerous dream, they can all too easily be led down the path of violence.

Sestina

LINE BY LINE

The poem is set in the kitchen of what might be a farmhouse. It is a rainy evening in September. The kitchen is occupied by a grandmother and her granddaughter. They sit by the stove on which a kettle is boiling, the grandmother reading jokes aloud from an almanac. Almanacs, once extremely popular in rural America, were like diaries in that they had a page for every day of the year. Each page contained jokes and folk sayings, as well as horoscopes, weather predictions and agricultural advice. Almanacs were often attached to a piece of string that would be looped around a hook on the farmhouse wall.

It seems that the family has been struck by some terrible sorrow. In line 6, we are told that, while the grandmother might laugh at the jokes in the almanac, she does so only 'to hide her tears'. This great sorrow is 'known only to a grandmother'. The child's mental capacity is not developed enough for her to fully grasp or comprehend the tragedy that has taken place. We get the impression that the grandmother 'hides her tears' in an attempt to shield the child from awareness of this terrible event.

The kettle makes a whistling noise as its water reaches boiling point: 'The iron kettle sings on the stove'. The grandmother declares that tea is ready, and she begins to slice some bread. The granddaughter, however, is distracted by the moisture running down the kettle's sides: 'but the child/ is watching the teakettle's small hard tears/ dance like mad on the hot black stove'. To the granddaughter, the moisture on the kettle resembles 'small hard tears'. Perhaps this indicates that on some level she is aware that a great sorrow has struck her family, though she may be too young to fully grasp the tragedy that has taken place.

The grandmother clears up after tea and returns the almanac to its hook. At this point, the poem becomes bizarre, dreamlike and sinister. The almanac begins to fly around the kitchen, like a kite on the end of its string: 'Birdlike, the almanac/ hovers half open above the child/ hovers above the old grandmother'. In line 22, we are presented with the strange and haunting image of the grandmother's teacup being 'full of dark brown tears' rather than tea. The stove and the almanac are depicted as having a conversation about the tragedy that has struck the family: 'It was to be, says the Marvel Stove./ I know what I know, says the almanac'.

Throughout the poem, the almanac is presented in a distinctly sinister light. The grandmother believes that the family tragedy was somehow 'foretold' by its horoscopes and predictions. There is something almost conceited about the almanac's declaration, 'I know what I know', as if it is proud of the fact that it predicted the family's loss. Furthermore, there is something ominous about the way it hovers above the child and her grandmother. Tellingly, at this point, the grandmother 'shivers'.

THE POEM'S FORM

The 'sestina' is a notoriously difficult poetic form, one that few English-language writers have been able to employ successfully. In this poem, however, Bishop displays consummate command of the form, perhaps using its intense difficulty and rigid structure to contain the difficult childhood emotions she feels compelled to explore. The sestina consists of six six-line stanzas and a three-line section called an envoi.

The sestina employs six 'end-words' instead of rhymes – in this case 'house', 'grandmother', 'child', 'stove', 'almanac' and 'tears'. The same six end-words must be used in each stanza. The position of each end-word shifts from stanza to stanza. 'Home', for example, concludes the first line of stanza 1, the second line of stanza 2, the fourth line of stanza 3, the fifth line of stanza 4, the third line of stanza 5 and the last line of stanza 6. The other end-words shift in a similar fashion. The envoi must contain all six end-words: three at the end of its lines and three in the middle.

The granddaughter draws a house with her crayons. We can imagine this as a typically happy and simple, childish drawing, one composed of 'rigid' lines featuring a flower bed, a winding path and a man standing in the garden. The child shows this drawing 'proudly' to her grandmother.

Once again, however, the almanac is depicted in a sinister light. It hovers above the child's drawing. Little moons fall out of its pages, presumably from its star charts and horoscopes, and tumble into the child's picture. These little moons 'fall like tears', dropping into the flower bed that the child has drawn. The almanac declares that it is 'Time to plant tears'. There is something unsettling about the notion of these tears somehow taking root among the flower beds of the granddaughter's drawing.

THEMES

CHILDHOOD

Like 'First Death in Nova Scotia' and 'In the Waiting Room', 'Sestina' wonderfully depicts the mentality of childhood. We see this in the description of the granddaughter staring at the kettle as it comes to boil and ignoring her grandmother's declaration that it is time for tea. We can imagine a young girl being mesmerised by the sight of 'tears' running down the kettle's side, and thinking how these drops resemble the rain on the farmhouse roof.

Childhood mentality is also artfully portrayed in the depiction of the granddaughter drawing a house with her crayons. She draws in the typically 'rigid', over-deliberate fashion of children everywhere. She approaches the task with an innocent and childish dedication, 'carefully' sketching a flower bed and showing the finished picture 'proudly' to the grandmother.

Throughout the poem, there are moments when Bishop skilfully inhabits a child's point of view. The phrase 'clever almanac', for instance, has a distinctly childish ring to it. The child, presumably, is aware from observing the adults around her that the almanac contains predictions and folk wisdom. Therefore, in an amusingly babyish phrase, she refers to it as 'clever'. Similarly effective is the description of the stove as 'marvellous'. We can imagine that this is how the granddaughter might refer to the stove. To this innocent and childish girl, the stove is a wondrous and fascinating object. No wonder, then, that at the end of the poem, the Little Marvel stove is explicitly said to be 'marvellous', just as its name promises.

As we have seen, the poem's second half is full of strange and bizarre occurrences. We get the impression, however, that these weird events are not 'real' and merely take place in the granddaughter's imagination. She imagines that the almanac hovers around the kitchen with a mind of its own and sends a rain of moons into her picture, that her grandmother's cup contains tears rather than tea, that the stove and the almanac have a brief conversation.

The grandmother notices none of these events. She goes about her business as if nothing strange is happening, reinforcing our sense that these bizarre occurrences take place only in the imagination of the child. This sense is further reinforced when the almanac 'secretly' plants moons in the child's drawing, somehow unnoticed by the grandmother as she 'busies herself about the stove'. The poem then wonderfully captures how a child's imagination can run riot, viewing even simple household objects as living things and as sources of fear and wonder.

MOMENTS OF AWARENESS

Many of Bishop's poems are marked by moments of awareness or epiphany, moments when a person suddenly or gradually realises something profound and important about themselves or about the world.

It is difficult not to interpret 'Sestina' in terms of Bishop's biography. Bishop's father died when she was only eight months old, and when she was eight years old her mother suffered a mental collapse and was institutionalised. Following these tragic events, Bishop went to live with her maternal grandparents.

Turning back to 'Sestina' with these real-life tragedies in mind, the first thing we note is that the tragedy that has struck the family in the poem is 'known only to a grandmother'. The child is still too young to fully comprehend the terrible events that have occurred. Yet we get the impression that awareness of this tragedy is slowly dawning on her. She thinks of 'tears' running down the tea-kettle and filling the grandmother's cup. The drops from the kettle seem to dance 'like mad', perhaps suggesting the mental breakdown of the poet's mother. Furthermore, the poet imagines the stove and the almanac talking about the tragedy: 'It was to be, says the Marvel Stove./ I know what I know, says the almanac'.

We get an impression that the child attempts to shield herself from sorrow by drawing houses. It's as if she tries to create in her imagination an ideal house, an alternative world where the tragedy that struck her never occurred. The house she draws is described as 'rigid', which suggests that it is a tough and solid safe haven. The man in the drawing presumably represents the father that the young Bishop so tragically lost. Yet the fact that the man's buttons are like 'tears' suggests that, even in the idealised world of her drawing, the child cannot escape the dawning awareness of sorrow.

The child is protected from sorrow by her inability to understand. But this defence will only last for so long. The almanac seems to represent awareness of the tragedy that is waiting to descend upon the child. It hovers above her in an ominous fashion and 'plants tears' in the child's drawing. We get the impression that tears have also been 'planted' in the child's life and will soon bear fruit in the form of the terrible sorrow that will overcome her.

First Death in Nova Scotia

J for Jack Frost,
a plump little fellow.
He's painting the leaves
all scarlet and yellow.

LINE BY LINE

In 1915, when Elizabeth Bishop was four years old, her mother took her to live in Nova Scotia, a province in northwestern Canada. They moved in with her mother's parents in Great Village, a fishing community on the bleak but beautiful Nova Scotia coast.

The following year, Elizabeth's little cousin Arthur tragically passed. This was the young poet's 'first death', her first proper encounter with loss and dying. The poem powerfully describes her reaction to these strange, unsettling concepts and experiences.

1

The poet remembers how her mother 'laid out' Arthur's body, dressing the little boy's corpse and presenting it in a dignified fashion. Arthur's body is laid out in the house's 'parlour' or sitting room. We might think of this as the house's 'good room', one that sees little everyday use and is reserved for special occasions. We can imagine how this seldom-utilised space might be colder than the rest of the house during the Nova Scotia winter: 'In the cold, cold parlour, my mother laid out Arthur'.

The parlour features several ornaments. There are two chromographs which depicts King George V of England, who was then Canada's head of state, and other members of the royal family.

(Chromographs were an early type of colour photograph). One chromograph shows King George and Queen Mary. The other shows George's father, Edward VII, back when he was Prince of Wales. He is depicted alongside his wife, the then Princess Alexandra.

There is also a stuffed loon, which is a species of lake-dwelling bird distinguished by its white chest feathers and its black and white wings. This particular loon had been 'shot and stuffed' by the young poet's Uncle, who is the father of the dead little boy: 'by Uncle/ Arthur, Arthur's father'.

No doubt, friends and neighbours would be calling by to commiserate with the family following their loss. We can imagine how these visitors might first pay their respects to Arthur in the relatively formal environment of the parlour, before retiring to the kitchen for refreshments.

2

The four year old Elizabeth enters the parlour. But her attention, at first, is drawn to the stuffed loon, rather than to her cousin's body. She focuses especially on the plumage around the dead bird's breast, noting its intense whiteness. These feathers, she says, look 'deep', so fluffy that you could sink your hand into their yielding mass. They also look 'caressable'; they seem so soft that, when you see them, you want to reach out and touch them.

She notes the marble table on which the dead bird rests, comparing it to a frozen lake: 'his white frozen lake,/ the marble-topped table'. She describes how, as part of the taxidermy process, the bird's eyes have been replaced with pieces of red glass. To the young speaker, these pieces of glass resemble gems or precious stones: 'his eyes were red glass/ Much to be desired'.

3

The young poet's mother is also present in the parlour. She urges Elizabeth to bid her cousin a final farewell, lifting her up so that she is face to face with Arthur's body. She gives Eliazbeth a flower and instructs her to place it in the dead boy's hands: 'I was lifted up and given/ one lily of the valley/ to put in Arthur's hand'.

The young Elizabeth still doesn't directly contemplate her cousin's body, however. Instead, her attention is drawn to the coffin, which she compares to 'a little frosted cake'. We can imagine how the white coffin might strike the child as cake-like, how its puffy lining might resemble a cake's frosted topping. She also finds herself thinking, once more, about the stuffed loon, which seems to watch the coffin from the table on which it rests nearby.

4

Only now does the young poet begin to focus on Arthur's body. She is taken aback by the intense whiteness of the corpse, which leads her to compare the body to an unpainted doll: 'He was all white/ like a doll/ that hadn't been painted yet'. How could Arthur be so white? The young poet explains this paleness to herself by referring to the legendary figure of Jack Frost:

- Jack Frost, she tells herself, had been given the task of painting Arthur's body, restoring it to its normal, colourful state: 'Jack Frost had started to paint him/ the way he always painted/ the Maple Leaf (Forever)'.
- Jack Frost, she tells herself, had set about his task. He had started by painting Arthur's hair: 'He had just begun on his hair, a few red strokes'.
- But then Jack Frost's work was interrupted, causing him to drop his paintbrush and run away.

As a result, Arthur's little body will never be restored to its normal, colourful state. It will remain forever deathly pale: 'Jack Frost had dropped the brush/ and left him white, forever'.

Jack Frost is a character from folk tales and popular culture. Often depicted as a mischievous little boy, he is a personification of winter, ice and snow. According to tradition, he paints windows with frosty, fern-like patterns during winter. He is also said to paint leaves and foliage red when autumn comes around. He is often, therefore, depicted with a brush and a paint-pot. The young poet, it seems, must have come across such an image in one of her picture books.

5

The young poet's attention is now drawn to the two 'gracious royal couples' depicted in the chromographs that hang on the parlour wall. The royal couples, she feels, look extremely cosy. They are dressed in the red often used by members of the British royal Family and wear 'warm' clothing that happens to be appropriate to the current winter weather.

The Queen and Princess wear dresses with 'ermine trains' that are designed to trail along behind them as they walk. ('Ermine' is in an expensive type of white fur that is derived from stoats). In the pictures, these trains are draped around the feet of the royal couples, making the royals seem even cosier: 'their feet were well wrapped up/ in the ladies' ermine trains'.

The young poet imagines that the royals have summoned Arthur to their court in London, where he will serve them as one of their pageboys: 'They invited Arthur to be/ the smallest page at court'. This could be a childish fantasy concocted by the speaker herself. However, it could also be the kind of gentle lie that an adult might tell a child to shield her from the truth about death. Perhaps Bishop's mother told her this fantastic story, wanting her to understand that Arthur will not be around anymore but also desiring to shield her from the harsh reality of death.

MOMENTS OF AWARENESS

Many of Bishop's poems are marked by moments of epiphany, moments when a person suddenly or gradually realises something profound and important about themselves and about the world.

In this poem, for instance, the narrator is a very young girl who has little or no understanding of death. No doubt, she has heard the words 'death' and 'dead' mentioned by the adults around her. But she doesn't fully grasp what death is, or what it actually means for someone to die.

We see this in her description of the stuffed loon. The poet describes how the loon has been silent since it was shot by her uncle: 'Since Uncle Arthur fired/ a bullet into him,/ he hadn't said a word'. The fact that this surprises the child, that she even considers it worth remarking on, indicates her lack of comprehension of the reality of death.

The loon, she declares, has 'kept its own counsel' where it sits on the marble-topped table. To keep one's own counsel means to keep one's thoughts to oneself. The young Elizabeth, then, seems to think that the stuffed loon could at any moment choose to break its silence, could burst into song or even speech. She seems to have no understanding, then, of what it means for something to die. She doesn't quite realise that the dead no longer go around talking and walking.

Now, however, her young cousin Arthur has passed away, and his body has been laid out in the parlour of the house. This forces the young poet, for the first time, to encounter death directly. She is forced into a terrible moment of awareness, one in which she must come to terms with this strange and unsettling concept.

Throughout the poem, however, the young poet attempts to shut out this uncomfortable new reality, to avoid thinking about death directly:

- In Stanza 2, for instance, she focuses on the stuffed loon, rather than on her cousin's body.
- Even when she is lifted up to place a flower in Arthur's hands, she tries to avoid contemplating his strange new state. She prefers to focus instead on the stuffed loon opposite him, on even on the coffin in which he lies.
- She notices the extreme whiteness of Arthur's corpse, but uses fantasy to explain away this pallor. She tells herself that Arthur is so white only because Jack Frost failed to paint him properly.
- In Stanza 5, she tells herself that Arthur won't be around anymore, not because he is dead, but because he is heading off to the court of King George in London, where he will work as the 'smallest page'.

Yet the young poet can't shut out death completely. For even as she considers the loon, Arthur seems to be at the back of her mind. For she describes the bird in terms more appropriate to her human cousin, telling us that he was 'caressable' and 'kept his own counsel'. It is also significant that the poet always refers to the dead bird as a 'he', rather than an 'it'.

We should also note how the word 'forever' is emphasised: by being bracketed off in line 33 and by being repeated in line 38. Despite the speaker's attempts to avoid thinking about death, she is becoming aware, on some level, that a final, irreversible change has taken place, that Arthur's eyes, 'shut up so tight', will never again be open.

At the poem's conclusion, however, the narrator seems to realise that this story just doesn't make sense: 'But how could Arthur go,/ clutching his tiny lily ... ?' Why was this obscure Canadian boy chosen for such an honour? And why is he required to undertake the journey to London alone, especially at this time of year when the roads are 'deep in snow'?

We get the impression that the fantastic stories she tells herself, about Jack Frost and about King George, aren't capable of shielding her from the truth. She seems to know, deep down, that the story about Arthur going off to be a page at court simply can't be true.

The poem concludes, then, with the young poet on the cusp of awareness. She is about to realise that death is something permanent and scary and unalterable. And such knowledge will change forever how she views the world.

CHILDHOOD

This is one of several poems where Bishop wonderfully captures the mentality of childhood.

- The speaker's childlike innocence comes across when she compares Arthur's corpse to a doll 'that hadn't been painted yet', and his coffin to 'a little frosted cake'.
- Her innocence comes across when she thinks of the loon's eyes as precious gemstones, 'much to be desired'. In reality, of course, they are only cheap pieces of glass that are used in taxidermy.
- The speaker's childhood innocence is also evident in how she believes, or almost believes, the story about Arthur bring summoned to serve as the 'smallest page at court'.
- We see the speaker's childlike imagination at work when she struggles to explain the whiteness of Arthur's corpse, and comes up with a vivid fantasy about Jack Frost and his paint brush.

The young poet thinks of Jack Frost painting Arthur's corpse, which makes her think of him painting the maple leaves, which in turn makes her think of a song entitled 'Maple Leaf (Forever)'. This popular song, written in 1867, served as one of Canada's unofficial national anthems. It has been suggested that in this phrase the young poet exhibits a childlike logic, her mind flitting unpredictably from one topic to the next.

Filling Station

LINE BY LINE

The poet is travelling and has come across a filling station that grabs her attention. This is a small, family-run station, a place where you can purchase fuel, top up on oil and perhaps get some basic repair work done. The poet can see the owner and his sons at work on the premises.

A VERY MASCULINE ENVIRONMENT

The filling station strikes her as a stereotypical masculine environment. There is an utter lack of regard for the aesthetic appearance of the place. The filling station is absolutely filthy. It seems that the place hasn't been cleaned for years, if indeed it ever was, and that a shocking level of filth and grime has accumulated.

Over the years, oil has seeped into every nook and cranny, gradually permeating every surface. Even the wicker furniture on the concrete porch to the rear of the filling station is saturated with oil: 'grease-impregnated'. This furniture has also been badly damaged or 'crushed' over the years. The poet sees a 'dirty dog' resting on the sofa and looking 'quite comfy' there.

Because everything is coated in grime and oil, there is a distinct lack of colour to the place. The only objects in the filling station that have not been coated in oil are some comic books that lie upon a small table on the porch. The comics, likely purchased by one of the young men working in the filling station, have not been around long enough to become so filthy. They, therefore, stand out and 'provide/ the only note of color - / of certain color' in the filling

The fact that the poet says 'several' sons, rather than giving a specific number, suggests that the exact number is not entirely clear, that she can't quite make out how many are working there. Perhaps the sons are not easily distinguishable from one another, or there is so much bustling activity going on that those working are never still enough for the poet to make a count. Bishop describes the sons as 'quick', suggesting that they are going about their work with great alacrity.

station. Everything else is glazed in black, making it hard to say what colour the object beneath might be.

An obvious lack of concern for appearance evident in the men that working. Like everything else around them in the filling station, the sons are 'greasy', coated in grime and oil. The owner also seems to pay scant regard to his appearance. He wears a pair of dirty overalls that are a size too small for him and, therefore, catch him tight under the arms: 'cuts him under the arms'. The poet refers to the owner's overalls as a 'monkey-suit', a slang term for such an outfit. The use of this term implies that the man wearing the suit is rather primitive or ape-like in his manner and behaviour.

In keeping with the particular stereotype to which the men seem to conform, the sons are described as being 'saucy', which suggests that they are cheeky and brash in their manner and fond of making sexually suggestive jokes. We can imagine them as boisterous, jokey lads who are very much at ease with each other and the tools and machines that they use. We get the impression that these are not men who like to devote themselves to intellectual matters. No books, magazines or even newspapers can be seen around the place. A few comics on the table were the only reading materials that the poet could see.

FEMININE TOUCHES

Beyond the pumps is a concrete porch, a raised platform that probably leads into the family home. On the porch is a 'begonia', a garden plant with brightly coloured leaves that is native to moist subtropical and tropical climates. There is also a set of wicker furniture. The poet mentions a 'wicker sofa' and a 'taboret' or small table.

The poet's observant eye notices an embroidered mat or 'doily' draped over the taboret. She even knows the exact stitch or pattern used in the doily: 'Embroidered in daisy stitch/ with marguerites, I think,/ and heavy with gray crochet'. A 'daisy stitch' is an embroidery stitch formed by an elongated loop held down at the free end by a small stitch. 'Marguerites' are a variety of daisy. So the person who created the doily used a particular kind of stitch to create daisy-like patterns in the fabric.

The poet observes how the cans of oil to the front of the station have been lined up in a particular and deliberate manner. The word 'ESSO' is visible on the first, but the word is semi-obscured on the cans that follow, so that you can only see the '–SO'. As such, the text running along the row of cans reads 'ESSO-SO-SO-SO'.

The oil does not form an opaque or impenetrable layer of grime – it blackens the various surfaces and soaks into the different materials, obscuring but not entirely concealing what lies beneath. The layer of grime remains at least partially transparent. The poet describes how the oil lends the place an 'over-all/ black translucency'.

The poet considers the soft, sibilant sound of this text and how it forms a rather soothing message for the passing motorists to read.

The oil contained within the cans is designed to 'soothe' the engines of these cars and make them run smoothly. Bishop imagines that the cans are speaking to the cars that pass, cars that she characterises as 'high strung'. But the term 'high strung' also relates to the stressed-out, hurried drivers of the automobiles. The poet imagines the text on the lined-up oil cans delivering a soothing message, almost a lullaby to calm and soothe these drivers' nerves.

The poet does not say who is responsible for the aesthetic, homely touches that she observes, but the implication here is that it is a woman – most likely the mother of the 'saucy' boys and the wife of the badly dressed owner. And if someone can love these men and is willing to make an effort to add a touch of beauty and homeliness to this filthy place, then surely anyone and any place can be loved: 'Someone loves us all'.

THEMES

MOMENTS OF AWARENESS

The poet is struck by the squalor and filth of a little filling station that she encounters somewhere on her travels. But she is also intrigued by the place and stops to take a close look at it. Although the filth preoccupies her at the beginning, she takes the time to notice subtle details that give the place its unique character.

The poet's careful observations ultimately lead to a a moment of awareness. She suddenly realises that somebody cared enough to try to make this filthy place homely and attractive: 'Somebody embroidered the doily./ Somebody waters the plant'. They even arranged the cans of oil so that they deliver a soothing message to the passing motorists. Operating out of sight is someone – most likely the mother of the 'saucy boys' – who cares not only about this wretched place, but also the unsophisticated men who work there. In even the filthiest environments, the poem suggests, a woman's touch can reveal itself.

But these feminine touches struggle to survive or stand out in such a masculine environment, a place where even the plant has acquired a manly appearance, which inspires the poet to describe it as 'a big hirsute begonia'.

The men dominate the place, coating everything in oil and filth and not caring about how the filling station looks. They mistreat the wicker furniture and could not care less that the sofa is serving now as a bed for the dog.

The oil that coats the entire place and all but obscures such feminine touches seems like a very masculine substance. The poet describes how the wicker furniture has been 'impregnated' with oil. The term 'impregnated' means saturated or soaked, but it also

means inseminated. It is as if these feminine features have been sexually dominated by the masculine.

In spite of all this, the feminine dimension holds out and survives in this most unlikely of places. It might be more subtle than the crude masculine elements that dominate the filling station, but it is there, nevertheless, and can be seen by the observant and sensitive eye.

OBLIQUE SELF-REVELATION

Bishop's poems tend to look outwards, focusing on and describing the external world in careful and minute detail. Rarely does the poet turn the reader's attention to herself by saying how she is feeling or thinking. Despite this, however, the poet is very much present in her poems, and something of her personality comes across.

The poet's presence is especially evident in her poetry's obvious attention to detail. We are dealing here with someone who was fascinated by the world around her and took the time to make sense of places and observe every little detail. In this poem, for instance, we get a clear sense of the poet's dislike of mess and untidiness. Bishop was a rather fastidious person who appreciated neatness and order. It is no wonder, then, that this filling station appals and offends her – shocking her with its absolute filth.

Bishop was always alert to pockets of beauty, wherever they might be found. She had a talent for finding beautiful or aesthetically pleasing details in the most unlikely places. Here, she notices the fine embroidery in the fabric that covers the taboret, and she appreciates the fact that the oil cans have been set up in such a way that they display a soothing message to the passing motorists.

In the Waiting Room

BACKGROUND

The poem is set in Worcester, Massachusetts on the fifth of February, 1918. The young poet was six at the time and just three days away from her seventh birthday. America had joined the First World War in the previous year, and fighting would continue in Europe until the end of 1918. The winter of 1917 to 1918 was the coldest in Boston's weather history. According to weather records it stayed below 20 degrees from 29 December 1917 to 4 January 1918.

Bishop was living with her paternal grandparents in Worcester at the time when the poem is set. Although she was born in Worcester and spent the earliest years of her life there, she never felt at home in that city. She developed both asthma and eczema sores, which became so severe that she was confined to bed. 'In the Waiting Room' is set during this very unhappy and traumatic period in the young poet's life.

LINE BY LINE

It is winter in Worcester, Massachusetts. The poet is aged six. She accompanies her Aunt Consuelo on a visit to the dentist. While her aunt is in with the dentist, the young poet sits quietly in the waiting room.

The young poet is the only child in the room: the waiting room was 'full of grown-up people'. Everyone is wearing enormous winter coats, 'arctics and overcoats' to keep warm on this freezing cold winter evening. Lamps have been lit to brighten the room and magazines are stacked on a table to keep people amused or distracted while they wait.

To the child, who must wait uncomfortably in a room full of 'grown-up people', the aunt seems to be in with the dentist for a very long time. In order to pass the time and feel less self-conscious the young poet takes a copy of National Geographic, and reads it. Bishop emphasises the fact that she 'could read' at this age. We get a sense of the child's pride at being able to do so. This poet also wishes us to know that when she says she 'read' the magazine, she means that she actually read all the words in the magazine.

National Geographic is a magazine that contains articles about science, geography, history and world culture. It features stunning pictures from places near and far, capturing the remarkable, beautiful and exotic features of the planet and the different peoples who inhabit it. Unsurprisingly, it's the photographs that really grab the young poet's attention and captures her imagination. She describes some of the pictures featured in the magazine:

- There is a series of images of a volcano, at various stages of erupting. The first image shows the 'inside of a volcano' just as the eruption is commencing. Thick ash gathers inside the volcano as the pressure builds up in the magma chambers beneath. Bishop describes how the volcano is 'black and full of ashes' – we can imagine an aerial shot of the volcano, looking down into the dark vault at its centre. In the next image, the volcano is erupting; lava is spilling out over the top and running down the sides of the volcano in streams: 'then it was spilling over/ in rivulets of fire'.

- There is a picture of 'Osa and Martin Johnson'. Martin Elmer Johnson and his wife Osa Helen Johnson were American adventurers and documentary filmmakers. In the first half of the 20th century, they captured the public's imagination through their films and books of adventure set in exotic lands. In the photograph that the young poet looks at, the couple are 'dressed in riding breeches,/ laced boots, and pith helmets'. We can imagine that they are on safari in Africa. The 'pith' helmet, also known as the 'safari' helmet, is a lightweight sun helmet made from the dried pith of a tropical plant.

- The young poet is also exposed to shocking images of cannibals preparing a dead human body for consumption. The dead man is 'slung on a pole', ready to be suspended over a fire and cooked. A caption beneath the photograph refers to the dead man as 'Long Pig', a term used by a tribe in the Polynesian islands in the South Pacific for human flesh.

- The young poet sees images of the Mangbetu people of the Democratic Republic of Congo. The babies in the photographs have 'pointed heads' that are 'wound round and round with string'. Members of the Mangbetu tribe considered the elongated skull to be a sign of higher intelligence and a status symbol among the ruling class. To ensure that their children developed the desired shape as they grew up, women in the community wrapped their babies' heads with tight cloths at birth.

- The women in the Mangbetu tride also have wire wrapped around their necks, forcing their shoulders down and their heads up and giving the impression that their necks are considerably longer than normal. Stretching the neck in this manner was considered beautiful or desirable to the male members of the tribe. The young poet thinks how they resemble 'the necks of light bulbs'.

Although the stories and images she encounters are strange, frightening and disturbing, the young poet reads the magazine 'straight through'. She tells us that she is 'too shy to stop'. She is self-conscious, being the only child in a room full of adults. If she stops reading, she might have to engage with others in the room, they might talk to her out of politeness, but the young girl does not want this to happen. If she continues to read, just as we imagine all the other people in the room are doing, no one will bother with her. And so, even when she has read the magazine right through, the young poet studies 'the cover:/ the yellow margins, the date' – that will save her from looking at the other people around her.

Suddenly she hears 'an oh! of pain' coming 'from inside'. It is her 'Aunt Consuelo's voice'. The cry of pain is brief and almost inaudible: 'not very long or loud'. The young poet is not 'at all surprised' that her aunt would make this noise. She says that, even at this young age, she knew that her aunt ' was/ a foolish, timid woman'.

But it was not the aunt who cried out in pain; it was the young poet, and this realisation startles the young girl: 'What took me/ completely by surprise/ was that it was me:/ my voice, in my mouth'. An involuntary cry has just erupted within her. The sound that has emerged which sounds exactly like her aunt's voice. This is why the girl immediately assumes that it is the aunt she has heard. But she quickly realises that it was her own voice that produced the sound, and is shocked to learn that her voice sounds just like her aunt's.

Why does the cry occur?

In order to understand why an involuntary cry of pain erupts within the young girl, we must remind ourselves of what she had recently endured.

She has had a traumatic childhood. Her father died before her first birthday, and her mother was committed to a mental hospital when she was five. She has been living with her grandparents in Worcester, but her health is rapidly deteriorating. She has developed asthma and severe eczema. There is a world war in progress, and the young girl, no doubt, is hearing reports about this each day. It is the worst winter on record. With all this going on, she finds herself alone in a room full of strange 'grown-ups'. And to top it all off, she has just been looking closely at some very disturbing and unsettling images. No wonder, it all gets to be too much for her. She has been trying desperately hard to hold it all in, to keep it all together, but it is too much for her body (or, indeed, her psyche, to take).

What surprises the young poet towards the end of the poem is that this cry of pain 'could have/ got loud and worse but hadn't'. With all that she has had to endure, and with the magnitude of the thoughts and questions that have been assaulting her mind, it would be understandable if the young girl had let out a loud scream and suffered some kind of breakdown or collapse.

REALISATIONS

The fact that the sound of the young poet's voice resembles her aunt's triggers a number of unsettling thoughts and feelings.

The young poet suddenly realises that she is not entirely unique. She shares a family voice with her aunt. In certain ways, therefore, she and her aunt are the same. This is the aunt that the young girl had just defined herself against. Her aunt is a 'foolish, timid' woman, whereas she is a bright, brave young girl. But now she has to identify with her aunt. It is as if they are both one, or that her sense of self has become fused with that of her aunt: 'Without thinking at all/ I was my foolish aunt'.

The poet is troubled by the notion that she is similar to her 'foolish' aunt and tries to focus on what it is that makes her unique. She is an 'I', an 'Elizabeth'. But she suddenly realises that everyone is an 'I', everyone has the individuality and the rich inner experience that she has. And the fact that she is an 'Elzabeth' offers little consolation, because of course there are many, many Elizabeths in the world.

The young poet realises that, if she is like her aunt, she is also similar to the other people in the waiting room, members of the wider community to which she belongs. She must also share traits, customs and characteristics with these people: 'you are one of them'. This thought frightens and perplexes the young girl. Why should she be just like them and not entirely unique and different? 'Why should you be one, too?' She does not even want to see what this entails or means: 'I scarcely dared to look/ to see what it was I was'. The young poet is tempted to raise her eyes and to look directly at or gaze upon that which she is destined to become – but she cannot bring herself to do so and instead casts a furtive 'sidelong glance'. Even then, she cannot lift her eyes higher than the knees of the people sitting close by.

The realisation that she is somehow similar to the strangers in the waiting room leads to the notion that she must also share somethings with the rest of humanity. It is as if the poet is suddenly seeing a web of connection that unites us all. Every person in the world is an 'I' and experiences the world just as the poet experiences it. Every person has similar needs and experiences the same emotions.

The young poet suddenly realises that she is in some ways the same as all the strange and alien people she saw in the magazine. This is expecially true perhaps of the women with the 'awful hanging breasts'. The poet realises that she will grow up to become a woman. Her body will mature and change and she too will make efforts – albeit different ones from those made by the women in the magazine – to conform to the required standards of beauty. It turns out, then, that she has more in common with these women than she could ever than she could have ever imagined only a few short moments ago.

THE PANIC

The realisation that she shares traits with her 'foolish aunt' and with everyone else who inhabits the planet has a dramatic effect on the young poet. She is overwhelmed by the thoughts and questions that flood her mind, and things suddenly seem to be spinning out of control. She describes feeling as if she is suddenly 'falling off/ the round, turning world/ into cold, blue black space'.

The 'turning world' represents the normal, everyday world that the young poet inhabits. In that world she is sure of the facts and knows what to do. But 'blue, black space' represents the vast unknown and the unknowable. This is where human understanding and reason falter and fail. The young poet feels as if she is about to fall from a place of certainty into this other, terrifying realm of uncertainty.

The young poet also describes what we might consider a panic attack. Suddenly, the light in the room seems too intense, and she begins to feel feverish, or 'too hot'. It is as if she is going to black out. Bishop describes the sensation of one enormous black wave after another crashing down upon the waiting room.

In order to arrest or control this – and perhaps to disguise the fact that she is experiencing such anxiety – the young poet keeps her eyes 'glued to the cover' of the magazine, focusing intently on the name and date. She also tries to steady herself by reminding herself that her birthday will be in three days. She latches on to this fact in an effort to 'stop/ the sensation of falling off/ the round, turning world'. But thoughts about her identity keep coming, and she tries desperately to make sense of it all.

The young poet realises that she will probably never have a stranger or more profound realisation than this in her life. She will never experience anything else that will so profoundly alter the way she thinks about herself and her place in the world: 'I knew that nothing stranger/ had ever happened, that nothing/ stranger could ever happen'.

BACK IN IT

And just as suddenly as the whole ordeal began, it ends. The poet somehow calms or steadies herself – or perhaps, the moment just passes naturally. It is as if her mind has refocused, has snapped out of one mode of thinking and resumed normal thought.

The poet says that she was 'back in it'. She is back in the room, and the spinning and falling sensations have ceased. The poet re-orientates herself quickly. She remembers that the 'War is on'; that is is 'still the fifth/ of February, 1918'; that she is in 'Worcester, Massachusetts'; and that outside the warm and lamp-lit waiting room it is night and cold, and there is 'slush' on the ground.

The statement that 'The War was on' refers to the fact that World War I was still going on. But it can also be understood to mean that the young poet has now engaged with the world in a very different way. She has undergone a profound, life-changing experience and has been transformed by it. She leaves the waiting room a different person. She is no longer the innocent child who entered the room and and thought she was unique and special. She realises that she is one of billions of people inhabiting the planet and that she is no more unique or special than anyone else – in fact, she is essentially just the same as everyone else. She must now fight to differentiate herself, to not conform, perhaps. This is also a 'War' of sorts, and she now knows that she is very much 'in it'.

MOMENTS OF AWARENESS

Like many of Bishop's poems, 'In the Waiting Room' features someone carefully observing their surroundings and subsequently experiencing a moment of insight or awareness. Here, we have the young poet in a dentist's waiting room. Even at the age of six, the young poet loved to observe and make sense of the world around her.

When she enters the waiting room, the young girl has a rather simple and definite idea about who she is: she is six, she is young, she can read. She clearly defines herself against both her aunt and the other people in the waiting room. Her aunt is 'foolish' and 'timid', whereas the young poet is smart, self-composed and self-assured. The other people sitting close by in the waiting room are 'grown-up', whereas she is a child.

The young poet notes that it was winter and got dark early. When she reads the magazine, she carefully studies every photograph and every word. When she has read the magazine, she studies the cover. What the young poet does not realise is that her careful study of the magazine, with all its bizarre and unsettling images, is not just distracting her from the awkwardness of being in the waiting room; it is also slowly causing or building on some inner trauma or anguish that finally erupts in the involuntary emission of a cry.

The young poet is thrown into total consternation when she associates her voice with that of her aunt, and it begins to dawn on her that she and her aunt are not so different; in fact, they are in many ways the same. This leads to a disturbing realisation that she is not entirely unique, and that she shares traits and characteristics not only with her 'foolish, timid' aunt,

In an autobiographical story, 'The Country Mouse', Bishop concluded with a description of the very moment she describes in 'In the Waiting Room': 'A feeling of absolute desolation came over me. I felt ... myself. In a few days it would be my seventh birthday. I felt I, I, I, and looked at the three strangers in panic. I was one of them too, inside my scabby body and wheezing lungs.'

but with the strangers in the waiting room and, indeed, the entire human race.

Essentially, the young poet is reaching an understanding that she is a member of the vast human race that populates the planet – and that there is more that unites her with every other human being (especially the female members of the population) than sets her apart. Whereas at the start of the poem the young poet focused on what she believed made her unique, she now realises that she has more in common with everyone else. It is as if she has undergone a procedure – something far more distressing than a filling or a root canal – that has altered her outlook and the way she thinks about herself. It is as if a door within her mind has been thrown open and can never be shut again.

CHILDHOOD

Bishop doesn't trivialise or romanticise childhood. It is a time of innocence, but it is also the time when we learn some of the hardest lessons in life. It can, therefore, be a traumatic, painful, and difficult time.

Bishop's poems register the fact that children are highly alert and open to the world around them, even if they cannot make full sense of what it is they are experiencing. The young poet in the waiting room is sensitive to her surroundings, taking everything in. She carefully reads the magazine from cover to cover, paying particular attention to the photographs. However, as we noted already, her experience of being in the waiting room and her exposure to the strange and terrifying images in the magazine trigger ideas and realisations that the young girl is not quite capable of processing and rationalising. For a moment, she is overwhelmed by it all and struggles to reorient herself.

Eavan Boland

Themes

Writing in a Time of Violence

Boland is a poet known for her moving responses to all our all-too-violent world. Both 'The War Horse' and 'Child of Our Time' were written in response to the Troubles, the seemingly interminable conflict that gripped Northern Ireland between 1969 and 1994.

In 'The War Horse', the titular animal symbolises this struggle, which raged only a couple of hundred miles away from the poet's Dublin home. Using a powerful simile, the poet compares the stumbling movement of the horse to a 'rumour of war': 'He stumbles on like a rumour of war'. We can see how this 'huge/ Threatening' animal, with its hissing breath and violently stamping hooves, with its muscles and destructive potential might symbolise the struggle in Northern Ireland. We can also understand how this powerful horse might seem like a physical embodiment of such a vicious civil war, of the terrible news that the poet absorbs each evening.

In 'The War Horse', the Troubles migrate in a symbolic way from Northern Ireland to Dublin. In 'Child of Our Time', however, they spill southward in a fashion that is all too real, since the poem laments the death of a victim of the Dublin and Monaghan bombings of 1974.

The poet laments the fact that we live in an age of violence and bloodshed. Although 'Child of Our Time' is set in 1970's Ireland, it's message, surely, still rings true today. For it can seem, as we look around the world, that we're still existing in a time of violence, in an age that, tragically, still robs cradle after cradle.

Ireland: Myth and History

One of the most powerful aspects of Boland's poetry is its engagement with Irish history. This is especially evident in 'Outside History', where the poet experiences a sudden emotional connection with Ireland's past. She is suddenly aware of the 'darkness' of Irish history. It is 'only now', she says, that this darkness is finally 'reaching' her; it is only now that she realises the true extent of the suffering that her countrymen and countrywomen have endured over the centuries.

Boland's engagement with the suffering is also evident in 'The Famine Road', where she confronts arguably the country's most tragic episode, the Great Famine of 1845-47. Boland powerfully conveys the starvation that stalked the land, reminding us that many Irish people were so hungry that they contemplated cannibalism. But the poem reminds us that disease, as much as hunger, was a bane of famine times; Boland powerfully evokes the terrible effects of contagious diseases like typhus.

The poem also highlights the prejudiced, indeed racist, attitudes held by the British elite towards the Irish people in the 1840s. The British elite, represented by Lord Trevelyan and Colonel Jones, regarded the Irish as subhuman, as troublesome, untrustworthy creatures. This view of the Irish as subhuman especially comes across in the poem's portrayal of the road-building scheme. The workers were forced to labour with their bare hands, rather than with tools, and were forced to work even when they were sick with terrible diseases and 'directionless' with starvation.

Lord Trevelyan, the British aristocrat who was in charge of famine relief, regarded the Irish as being genetically pre-disposed to laziness, suggesting that they needed 'toil' in order to improve themselves. This negative view of the Irish was shared by Colonel Harry Jones, Trevelyan's assistant and the Chairman of the Irish Board of Works, the public body that oversaw the implementation of a road-building programme designed to provide work for the starving Irish. Jones believed that these relief works would ultimately have 'cured' the Irish of their 'idleness'.

In Boland's poem, Colonel Jones expresses this attitude when he reports to Trevelyan from his trip around the countryside. He seems unperturbed by the corpses that fester by the roadside until only the bones remain. We sense that people like Jones and Trevelyan are happy to see Irish population reduced in number, just as they might cull a population of deer or badgers that threatened to grow out of control.

'The War Horse' also features a meditation on Ireland's troubled past. The poet, as we've seen, associates the trespassing horse with the Northern Ireland Troubles. As she watches the horse depart her 'short street', she finds herself meditating on the complicated history – between England and Ireland, between Protestant and Catholic – that lies behind this contemporary conflict.

As an Irish Catholic woman, the poet remembers the disasters her ancestors endured over the centuries, thinking, no doubt, of how the 'cause' of Ireland was 'ruined' in defeat after defeat at the hands of the British. She thinks of 'days of burned countryside' when her ancestors were driven from their lands.

She has in mind, no doubt, the great wrongs that were inflicted on the Irish people over centuries of occupation, including the wrongs that inspired 'The Famine Road'.

The poet, then, experiences a moment of 'atavism', which suggests the return of some long-lost impulse or emotion. For a moment, she feels all the rage and humiliation experienced by her ancestors over that endless series of defeats and disasters, of mistreatment at the hands of a conquering enemy. Indeed, the poet says that her 'blood is still / with atavism', which suggests that intense anger has somehow frozen her blood and stopped it from flowing.

The poem, then, highlights how difficult it can be to escape the history and mythology associated with one's country. Of course, it easy to experience such raw emotion when we think about the injustices that our compatriots have endured. And its easy, too, to be led by such impulses towards acts of violence and destruction.

In 'Outside History', the poet suddenly becomes conscious that the Irish landscape is filled or 'clotted' with the remains of the dead, with the countless generations of Irish people who went before. She wishes that there were something she could do for her dead fellow countrymen and women. But she realises that we are 'always too late' to provide such consolation to those who are already dead. All we can do is keep their memories alive, recounting the tales not only of famous generals and politicians, but also of ordinary people who made a contribution to their own communities. By doing so, we can ensure that their memories survive, so that their lives and deaths will not have been in vain.

Suburban Living

The idea of the suburb and suburban living is one that recurs often in Boland's poetry. Suburbs have seldom been regarded as offering much in the way of inspiration to the writer or artist. Suburbia is generally regarded as a place of humdrum family life, lacking both the energy and excitement of the city and the natural beauty of the countryside.

This view of the suburbs is especially evident in 'White Hawthorn in the West of Ireland'. The suburb where the speaker lives is depicted as a place of little significance, compared to the untamed West of Ireland. The suburbs are boring, fake and manmade, whereas the West is natural, authentic and thrillingly beautiful.

'The War Horse', however, takes a different view of suburban life, emphasising that even the average suburban street can be a site of wonder, with the poet stunned by the sudden appearance of this huge creature on an ordinary evening. In 'This Moment', too, Boland demonstrates that even the most banal and comfortable housing estate can be inspirational. Such places can seem dull and boring on the surface. But beautiful,

magical and inspirational things are always happening 'out of sight': moths fluttering through the dark, fruit ripening, a child running into a woman's arms, stars flickering in the evening sky.

Both 'White Hawthorn in the West of Ireland' and 'The Pomegranate' present the suburbs as a safe and comfortable environment, a far cry from the untamed West, with its sense of disorientation and even danger. In 'The Pomegranate', the poet's daughter sleeps untroubled by the terrors of the outside world, her 'teen magazines' and her 'can of Coke' beside her. The poet, however, is all too aware that eventually her daughter must face the trials and difficulties of the outside world, difficulties represented by the wintry rain and the hard flint roads.

'The War Horse' reminds us that the safety of the suburbs is far from complete and can be compromised at any moment by a stray wild animal, by human criminality or even by political conflict. Boland has described how the horse represents an 'intrusion of nature...menacing the decorous reductions of nature that were the gardens'. The image of the powerful horse stumbling through the suburbs reminds us that nature is always out there, waiting to reclaim our cities and our neatly ordered housing estates.

The Subjugation of Women

'The Famine Road' movingly depicts a woman who is told by her doctor that she's incapable of having children. The poem makes a surprising but powerful connection between the sufferings of the Irish during the famine, on one hand, and the sufferings of modern women, on the other.

The doctor displays no sympathy or empathy for his female patient, just as the British elite, in famine times, had little compassion for the Irish people over whom they ruled. The doctor effectively silences his female patient, just as the British elite s effectively silenced the Irish population that was under their control.

The doctor, it's important to note, should not be thought simply as uncaring individual. Rather, he represents an entire society and system, one that views women simply as vessels for reproduction. A woman incapable of reproduction, of ever feeling the 'load' of a child inside herself, is of no value. She is as useless as a road going from nowhere to nowhere: 'what is your body/ now if not a famine road?'

'The Shadow Doll', too, deals with the subjugation of women. This poem presents marriage as an institution that silences women, degrading their humanity and suffocating their personalities. Marriage, Boland suggests, is a system that defines women as little more than servants, slaves or possessions.

These poems, then, present a very negative view of society, suggesting that women are treated by men just as the Irish were treated by the British during famine times and that marriage was just one more tool that society uses to keep women in their place.

Some might feel that these poems, written in the 1970s and 80s, take perhaps too bleak a view of gender relations. After all, isn't society – and the institution of marriage – far more equal today? But these poems remind us that the struggle for women's rights has gone on for a long time and that, even in our more equal world, it is far from complete.

Motherhood

Mothers play a vitally important role in most of our lives, raising us from helpless children so that we become responsible adults. Alas, all too often, the work of mothers goes unappreciated and uncelebrated, their unstinting efforts taking place 'out of sight'.

Both 'The Pomegranate' and 'The Famine Road' deal with hardships relating to motherhood.   But whereas a poem like 'The Pomegranate' deals with the difficulties of rearing children, 'The Famine Road' touches on the agony of a mother who can't have children in the first place.

'The Pomegranate' powerfully conveys the fears and uncertainties that all mothers feel at various times. Such anxiety is especially evident in the poet's description of that long-ago 'summer twilight' when her daughter failed to come home on time. We can imagine the poet growing more anxious, perhaps even panicking, as she walks around the housing estate where she lives, desperately searching for her missing daughter.

'The Pomegranate' also touches on the strains of motherhood when the poet looks in on her sleeping child. The poet is overcome by the desire to shelter her daughter from knowledge and experience of the adult world, with all the 'grief' that such knowledge brings. But the poet ultimately realises that such experience is not only a 'grief' but also a 'gift'. She realises that her daughter needs to make her own way in the world, overcoming life's hardships along the way. If the poet defers or delays 'the grief' associated with such experience, she will 'diminish the gift' of living.

Small wonder, then, that 'This Moment' presents a world where nature itself celebrates motherhood, the work that mothers do and the sufferings that they undergo. The poem focuses on three different aspects of the natural world: the stars, apples and moths. Each is preparing to do something: 'But not yet'.

It seems as if it's only when the mother picks up the child that these beings begin to do what they do naturally.. Only then do the stars rise, moths flutter and apples sweeten. It's as if they celebrate her daily work of nurture by waiting until 'this moment', until this everyday instant of motherly care and affection. The poem, then, presents a world where even the stars pay tribute to the role of this particular mother, and by extension, to mothers everywhere.

Love and Marriage

'The Black Lace Fan' powerfully captures the tension and uncertainty that can exist at the beginning of a relationship. New love, of course, is characterised by great excitement. But it can also bring feelings of dread and exposure. How do I really feel about this person? How do they feel about me? Am I letting myself in for heartbreak?

Such tension, no doubt, is represented by the 'stifling' and 'killing' heat that grips the city, by the 'airless' and humid atmosphere, by the turbulent weather that marks the tail-end of the heat-wave. It is especially evident on the night when the mother received the black lace fan. The air practically crackles with electricity, so that one can almost smell the coming storm.

'Love', is another poem in which Boland depicts a relationship at its most intense. When the speaker and her husband lived in Iowa, the love between them was so passionate and vibrant that it seemed almost like a physical presence in their home: 'love … had come to live with us'. The love they shared was so strong and 'formidable' that even to contemplate it filled them with ecstasy: 'it offered us ascension'.

In both 'Love' and 'The Black Lace Fan', Boland focuses on the progress of a long-term relationship. In 'The Black Lace Fan', she uses the fan as a symbol of her parents' marriage, seeing this heirloom as a record of the ups and downs they enjoyed and endured, of the good and bad times they went through together.

'Love' is similarly balanced. The poet laments the sad fact that in any marriage or long-term relationship it is difficult to maintain the same level of passion year after year: 'Will we ever live so intensely again?' Yet she also celebrates the ability of marriages to endure and survive over long periods. The passion in her marriage may have become somewhat less intense, and the couple's lives may be more 'day-to-day and ordinary'. Nevertheless, they 'love each other still' and continue to communicate effectively: 'We hear each other clearly'. The poem, then, celebrates how, even after years of togetherness, a husband and wife continue to offer one another support, un derstanding and companionship.

A far less favourable view of marriage is presented in 'The Shadow Doll'. Using the doll as a symbol or metaphor, the poem suggests that marriage turns women into pretty possessions for their husbands. Like dolls and children, brides are to be seen rather than heard. They are to be admired for their beauty, for the 'oyster gleam' of their pretty dresses, rather than for their experiences and their ability to express themselves. Perhaps it's fitting, then, to conclude with another, much more positive, symbol of marriage: the blackbird that the poet describes at the end of 'The Black Lace Fan'.

The poem's closing lines sound a triumphant note, celebrating the survival and endurance of Boland's parents' love – its lavish and beautiful 'span' of years. What really matters, then, is not the detailed story of their marriage, with its ups and downs and weathered storms, but the fact that their relationship survived and flourished for so long.

Family: Myth and History

Both 'Love' and 'The Black Lace Fan' engage with the area of personal and family history. 'The Black Lace Fan' movingly depicts the impossibility of fully understanding our family's past, of reconstructing events that occurred before we were born. We may have some evidence of such past events – photos, videos, stories, heirlooms – but we can never truly reconstruct what happened in all its detail. So much of the past must remain forever lost to us.

At the same time, however, the poem celebrates the artist's ability to recreate the past, to improvise or imagine what might have happened. The speaker, therefore, chooses to represent her parents' love by means of the triumphant symbol of the blackbird, with its extended wing. It is not clear, however, how much this glorious symbol reflects the actual facts of the parents' life together and how much it reflects the speaker's artistic imaginings.

'Love', also, deals with a family's past, with the poet revisiting Iowa city, a place where she and her husband lived many years ago, when their relationship was at its most intense. The poem shows how memory can sometimes play tricks on us, how something or someone long gone can suddenly appear before us in a way that seems vividly real. Perhaps this 'vision' has been caused by a combination of the falling darkness and the memories that the poet's return visit has brought flooding back.

Perhaps, then, the dominant emotion in 'Love' is that of nostalgia. We sense that the poet is filled with longing for that golden period in her life. She would love to somehow recover this lost era, to live those days all over again and experience her husband as he was during that unique and special time: 'I want to return to you … as you were'. However, there can be no going back. It's simply impossible to relive earlier periods of our lives, no matter how much we might like to.

Language

Form

Boland is a poet who displays a diverse mastery of form. 'The War Horse', for instance, is written in rhyming couplets or two-line stanzas. Some couplets have full rhymes, like those between 'fear' and 'care' and between 'head' and 'dead'. Others have half rhymes, like that between 'limb' and 'climb' and between 'street' and 'wait'.

'Child of Our Time', meanwhile, is written in three six-line stanzas with an irregular rhyme scheme. (The first stanza rhymes ABACBC, the second ABCABC and the third ABCACB). There are a number of half-rhymes: 'order' and 'murder', 'instruct' and 'protect', 'child and 'rebuild'.

'The Famine Road' is a further display of diversity, consisting of two interwoven poetic texts. The primary text, which deals with the evils of the famine, consists of six- and seven-line stanzas. The shorter italicised text, which deals with the plight of the woman unable to conceive, consists of three-line stanzas. Both texts have with an irregular rhyme scheme. Boland deftly alternates between these two texts, highlighting the parallels between the treatment of the female patient and that of the Irish in famine times.

'The War Horse' features several inventive line-breaks. Lines 6 to 9, for instance consist of single sentence that winds over no

fewer than five lines, mimicking the horse's meandering path through the housing estate. It's a sentence full of stops and starts, caused in no small part by the way in which the words 'Pass' and 'Down' are isolated at the beginning of lines 8 and 9. In this regard, the movement of the verse cleverly enacts the horse's nightly journey, which is full of stops and starts, as he pauses, again and again, to snuffle against the ground.

'Child of Our Time' is similarly inventive. It consists of three long sentences, each spread over a number of lines of verse. Each sentence contains a number of clauses, which can make it quite hard to follow on a first or even second reading. For instance the subject of the second sentence, 'We', occurs in line7, but the verb that goes with it – the 'must' in 'must learn' – does not appear until line 12.

Tone and Atmosphere

Boland's mastery of atmosphere is evident in 'The War Horse', which powerfully captures the sense of unease, or perhaps even dread, experienced by the poet and her neighbours each time the horse comes down their street. The presence of this huge unruly creature has them cowering behind their curtains, watching nervously as it passes by. This atmosphere of tension is reinforced by the poet's sigh of relief when the horse finally disappears.

Most readers of 'The Black Lace Fan' detect a sense of tension in the poem's first twelve lines. Lurking beneath the few straightforward details we are given about that long-ago Parisian summer night. The verse here has an edgy, restless quality, reflecting the almost palpable tension that clogs the air during the hours before the storm.

To a large extent, this sense of tension is due to Boland's extensive use of short, clipped sentences that shift focus rapidly from one subject to the next. This rapid-fire burst of short sentences conveys the agitation of the young man as he hurries to keep his appointment and the nervous tension of the young woman who is anxiously waiting for her lover to appear: 'She ordered more coffee. She stood up'.

'The Pomegranate', too, is rich in atmosphere and imagery. The poet captures not only the swirling fogs of 1950s London, but also 'summer twilight' on a Dublin housing estate, with its flourishing white flowers, buzzing wasps and 'buddleias' with their distinctive honey-like scent. Especially memorable is Boland's depiction of the underworld. The underworld is depicted as a dark and cavernous 'place of death'. According to the poet, it is a place of 'crackling dusk', which leads us to envisage a vast underground cave system, only faintly illuminated, where the very air crackles with some dark magical energy.

Figures of Speech

'The War Horse' is distinguished by a number of inventive metaphors and similes. The horse is compared to a 'rumour of war', while the metaphor of minting a coin is used to capture the power of its legs: 'he stamps death/ Like a mint on the innocent coinage of earth'.

The three plants that the horse damages, meanwhile, are compared to victims of the Troubles, all three being described as 'corpses' that have been 'crushed' or 'mutilated'. The damaged laurel hedge, in a wonderful simile, is compared to someone maimed in such a terrorist attack: 'Only a leaf of our laurel hedge is torn … like a maimed limb.' The uprooted rose, in another simile, is compared to a 'volunteer', which was the name used for ordinary, 'expendable' members of the IRA, the paramilitary organisation that was central to the conflict.

There's an element of synecdoche in lines 5 to 6 where the poet refers to the horse as an 'ambling feather/ Of hock and fetlock'. Synecdoche occurs when we use part of an object to symbolically represent the object as a whole. . In this instance, the poet refers to the feathery clumps of hair at the horse's joints, using them to indicate the horse as a whole. Obviously, it is the horse that is ambling down the road, not just his hock and fetlocks.

In 'The Famine Road', Boland uses a fine simile to convey the cannibalistic impulses experienced by the starving Irish workers. She compares the famine victims to housewives that behave in a 'cunning' fashion while shopping at the local butchers: 'cunning as housewives, each eyed –/ as if at a corner butcher – the other's buttock'.

We imagine such housewives eyeing the butcher's choicest cuts of meat. But they do so stealthily, not wanting to let on that they're looking at anything in particular. Perhaps they intend to haggle with the butcher and don't want to signal their interest in any particular cut. For if they do so, the butcher is less likely to negotiate about the price. As Boland imagines it, the starving workers behaved in a similar fashion. They were so hungry that they couldn't help eyeing each other's bodies and thinking of them as food. But they did so stealthily or surreptitiously, like the 'cunning' housewife at the butcher's shop.   After all, no one, not even a famine victim, wants to signal that they're contemplating cannibalism.

Equally memorable is the simile used to describe the typhoid victim dying alone on the bare mountainside, shunned by friends and family members. One piece of snow doesn't 'attend' to another piece of snow as it melts and disappears. Similarly, a starving worker will not pray beside or attend to a companion who is dying: 'No more than snow/ attends its own flakes where they settle/ and melt, will they pray by his death rattle'. The sheer need to survive means that these workers can no longer act on normal human instinct, but must in their behaviour resemble unthinking, inhuman forces like the wind and snow.

'Child of Our Time', meanwhile, features several paradoxes or seemingly contradictory statements. The fact that the dead child 'cannot listen' is precisely what motivates the poet to address that child. It might seem strange to write a poem addressed to someone who is deceased, to someone who will never read or hear your words. Boland's hope is that her poem will focus the minds of her readers on this dead child, thereby highlighting for us the cost of our current way of thinking and opening us up to the possibility of change.

The poet aims to find 'reason' in the utterly 'unreasoned' act of the dead child's murder. The dead child, according to the poet, was the victim of an act that seems utterly senseless, devoid of any sanity or logic. She is determined, however, to find some sense in this apparently meaningless atrocity.

The poet is determined to make something beautiful from the ugliness of the dead child's passing. She will focus on the horrific sounds associated with his murder: the horror of his 'final cry'; the 'discord' of the bombings with all their roaring explosions; the cries of the wounded; the sirens of the emergency vehicles. But she will use these terrible sounds as inspiration for a tuneful, rhythmical piece of writing: 'This song, which takes from your final cry/ Its tune … Its rhythm from the discord of your murder'.

The War Horse

LINE BY LINE

This poem is set in the Dublin suburb of Dundrum, where Boland lived for over twenty years. The poet's house was on an ordinary suburban street. We imagine a row of comfortable semi-detached houses, of greenery, of neat and carefully tended lawns.

Not far from her home, on the nearby Enniskerry Road, a group of travellers have set up a temporary halting site, which the poet refers to as 'tinker camp'. This phrase might strike us problematic nowadays. When Boland wrote the poem, however, it would not have been considered offensive.

The travellers keep a large horse tied-up in their halting site. Each evening, the horse is 'loosed from its daily tether', freed from the ties that constrain it all day long. The horse takes this opportunity to get some exercise. It wanders off alone, taking a stroll around the neighbourhood. Each evening, its route takes it directly past the poet's house.

Boland, in an essay, described the origin of the poem: 'One evening, at the time of the news, I came into the front room with a cup of coffee in my hand. I heard something at the front door...A large dappled head —a surreal dismemberment in the dusk- swayed low on the doorstep, then attached itself back to a clumsy horse and clattered away'.

The poem is set on one particular 'dry' summer's evening. The horse, as usual, has been released from its constraints. And its wanderings, as usual, take it down the poet's neat suburban street. The sound of the horse's hooves is clearly quite loud, their 'clip, clop' sound audible inside the poet's house. The poet hears the horse approaching and goes to the window to look out.

The horse, we're told, comes 'ambling' along, moving in a slow and meandering fashion. The poet describes its iron shoes as 'casual', reinforcing our sense of the horse's relaxed gait: 'the clip, clop, casual/ Iron of his shoes'. It walks with its head 'Down', its nose 'snuffling' against the ground.

And yet the poet clearly finds this 'huge' creature a 'threatening' or intimidating presence on her street. The horse's breath, we're told, makes a 'hissing' sound every time it exhales. The poem's title suggests that the horse resembled one of the tank-like chargers that were ridden into a battle by medieval knights. It's a massive and muscular beast, then, one utterly out of place on this ordinary suburban road.

The poet uses the metaphor of a coin mint to capture the ferocity of the horse's stamping:
- The horse's shoes are compared to the mint's stamps.
- The earth on which the horse walks is compared to 'planchets' or blank coins.
- The horse's legs are compared to the powerful pistons that drive the stamp into the unmarked coins.

The horse, then, is presented as a relentless, powerful machine that 'stamps death/ Like a mint on the innocent coinage of earth'. It brings death and destruction to the harmless plants and flowers om which it treads. The horse, it seems, wanders not only on the road and footpath but also into the gardens of the poet and her neighbours. The poet describes how the horse 'stumbles' down the street, suggesting that there's something clumsy, perhaps even uncoordinated, about its movement: 'He stumbles on … He stumbles down our short street'.

The poet notes the damage that the horse causes to her property. The horse tears a leaf from her 'laurel hedge'. A crocus plant is 'blown' from its place of 'growth' by the horse's huge limbs. A climbing rose plant, which was meant to scale the stone façade of the poet's new home, is uprooted: 'a rose which now will never climb/ The stone of our house'.

Using a wonderful phrase, the poet tells us how her neighbours use 'the subterfuge// Of curtains' as they watch the horse. We can imagine them peeping out from behind their blinds, eager to observe the horse, but also keen not to attract the attention of this huge and stumbling beast. Perhaps they're worried that the horse will approach their houses, butting against their doors and windows, or that it might even attempt to forcibly enter their homes.

'Thankfully', however, the horse passes through the street without hurting anyone or causing too much damage to property: 'He is gone. No great harm is done'. Only a few plants, as we've seen, have been smashed and uprooted by its passage.

The poet is still at her window, watching as the horse disappears from view. She waits, however, as if she wants to make sure the horse is really gone before expressing her relief at its departure. Finally, she leans against the window sill and sighs with relief: 'I pause, wait,/ Then to breathe relief lean on the sill'.

WRITING IN A TIME OF VIOLENCE

This poem was written at a time when the poet was greatly exercised by the Troubles, the seemingly interminable conflict that gripped Northern Ireland between 1969 and 1994. As the poem's title suggests, the horse symbolises this struggle, which raged only a couple of hundred miles away from Dublin. As Boland put it in one of her essays: 'It was the early seventies, a time of violence in Northern Ireland. Our front room was a rectangle with white walls, hardly any furniture and a small television chanting deaths and statistics at teatime'.

Using a powerful simile, the poet compares the horse to a 'rumour of war': 'He stumbles on like a rumour of war'. We can see how this 'huge/ Threatening' animal, with its hissing breath and violently stamping hooves, with its muscles and destructive potential might symbolise the struggle in Northern Ireland. We can see how it might seem like a physical embodiment of such a vicious civil war, of the terrible news that the poet absorbs each evening.

The horse, as we noted, moves in an 'ambling' rather than a focused fashion, stumbling clumsily as it meanders along the road. The damage that it causes is accidental rather than deliberate. This powerfully suggests the chaotic and random nature of war, where many victims are completely innocent and simply happen to be in the wrong place when the bullets fly or a bomb goes off.

The poet and her neighbours react to the horse just as they react to the Troubles in Northern Ireland:

- They watch the horse's progress from their living rooms, peeping out from behind the curtains. Similarly, they watch the Troubles from the comfort of their living rooms, seeing each day's tragedy unfold on television.
- The poet and her neighbours are unconcerned about the plants the horse 'uproots'. They are similarly unconcerned about the victims of the Northern Ireland Troubles, with their 'crushed' and 'mutilated' limbs: 'why should we care/ If a rose, a hedge, a crocus are uprooted/ Like corpses, remote, crushed, mutilated?'
- The poet and her neighbours worry that the horse might attack someone or attempt to enter their homes. Similarly, they worry that the Troubles in Northern Ireland might spread southwards, bringing death and destruction to Dublin and other cities.
- The poet seems relieved that the horse uproots the climbing rose rather than attempting to enter the house itself. She views the rose, then, as a useful distraction, as 'a mere line of defence' against the horse's depredations. Perhaps she views the Northern Irish victims of the Troubles, too, as a 'line of defence'. As long as the people of the North are targeting each other, the conflict is less likely to spread south.
- They are relieved each night when the horse passes by without attacking anyone or attempting to enter anyone's home. Similarly, they are relieved every day that the violence in the north has not spread southward: 'But we are safe. We are safe'.

The poet, then, brilliantly captures the attitude of those living in the Republic of Ireland toward the Northern Ireland Troubles, especially during the violent, chaotic days of the early 1970s. The Troubles, as we've already noted, unfolded a mere car ride away from the poet's Dublin suburb. For her, though, these terrible events seemed so utterly 'remote', that they might have been happening in another world.

It seems then that the endless succession of bombings and shootings was only of 'distant interest' to the poet and to the people of the Republic. The Troubles is a series of events they are vaguely concerned about and half-listen to on the news each evening. Ultimately, however, they care no more about the 'maimed limb[s]' of their Northern Ireland cousins than they do about damaged plants in their front gardens.

And a similar situation, of course, prevails today. We sit in our comfortable homes, in a relatively peaceful and prosperous part of Europe, hearing about and listening to various terrible conflicts, from Yemen to Syria to Niger. We care a little about the horrors we witness, or at least we pretend to care. But are such terrible events, ultimately, only of 'distant interest' to us, so much so that it's easy for us to switch our screens off, to turn our attention to more pleasant matters?

IRELAND: MYTH AND HISTORY

The Northern Ireland Troubles had their roots long-standing tensions between England and Ireland and between Protestant and Catholic that can be traced back at least to 1641, and maybe even to as far back as 1169. As she watches the horse depart, the poet is keenly aware of this complicated history. As an Irish Catholic woman, she remembers the disasters her ancestors endured over the centuries.

- She thinks, no doubt, of how the 'cause' of Ireland was 'ruined' in defeat after defeat at the hands of the British.
- She thinks of how victory for her ancestors, say in 1601 or 1798, might have led to a very different 'world', to an Ireland unrecognisable from the one we know today. But alas this world was 'betrayed' and never came into being.
- Perhaps the poet is referring to actual traitors who sold out their cause during the various rebellions against British rule. Or maybe she's using the term 'betrayed' more generally, to describe how this imagined world was thwarted and prevented by the consequences of war.
- She thinks of 'days of burned countryside' when her ancestors were driven from their lands. She has in mind, no doubt, the great wrongs inflicted on the Irish people over centuries of occupation, such as those touched on in 'The Famine Road' .

These historical disasters, the poet feels, are symbolised by the rose that the horse 'smashed' on its passage through her garden. The rose lies in ribbons 'across [her] hedge'. As she looks at it, the poet can't help thinking about this litany of defeats, about how Ireland's hopes, again and again, were smashed and left in ribbons.

The poet, then, experiences a moment of 'atavism', which suggests the return of some long-lost impulse or emotion. For a moment, she feels all the rage and humiliation experienced by her ancestors over that endless series of defeats. Indeed, the poet describes how her 'blood is still / with atavism', which suggests that anger has frozen her blood and stopped it from flowing.

For a moment, perhaps, she feels like acting on this impulse and intervening, somehow, on the Catholic or Republican side in the Northern Irish Troubles. The poet imagine that she and her neighbours might experience this urge, a sense of 'fierce commitment' to the Irish cause that might cause them to take such action. And they have a vague or 'unformed' fear of such emotions, dreading where they might lead. But this moment of atavism, she emphasises, lasts for 'a second only'. The poet, we sense, is unlikely to actually contribute to the Troubles in any way.

The poem, then, highlights how difficult it can be to escape the history and mythology associated with one's country. It is easy to experience such raw emotion when we think about the injustices our countrymen have endured. And it's easy, too, to be led by such impulses towards acts of violence and destruction.

SUBURBAN LIVING

The suburbs are usually thought of as dull and uninspiring. But this poem shows us that even the average suburban street can be a site of wonder, with the poet stunned by the sudden appearance of this 'huge' creature on an ordinary evening. The suburbs are also generally considered to be safe and comfortable environments. But the poem reminds us that such safety is far from complete and can be compromised at any moment by a stray wild animal, by human criminality or even by political conflict.

The poem also emphasises our fragile and tenuous grip on nature. As our cities expand, we tame the natural world, transforming hills and fields into suburbs with their neat square gardens. Boland describes how, when she wrote the poem, this very process was underway in the suburb to which she had recently moved: 'It was our first winter in the suburb. The weather was cold; the road was half finished ... At night, the streetlamps were too few. And the road itself ran out in a gloom of icy mud and builders' huts'.

Boland has described the horse's arrival in her suburb as an 'intrusion of nature ... menacing the decorous reductions of nature that were the gardens'. The poem, then, reminds that nature, as symbolised by the horse, is always out there waiting to return. Grass is waiting to grow over our cities and animals are waiting to reclaim our neatly ordered suburbs, when human kind, with all its wars and pollution, finally leaves the stage.

The Famine Road

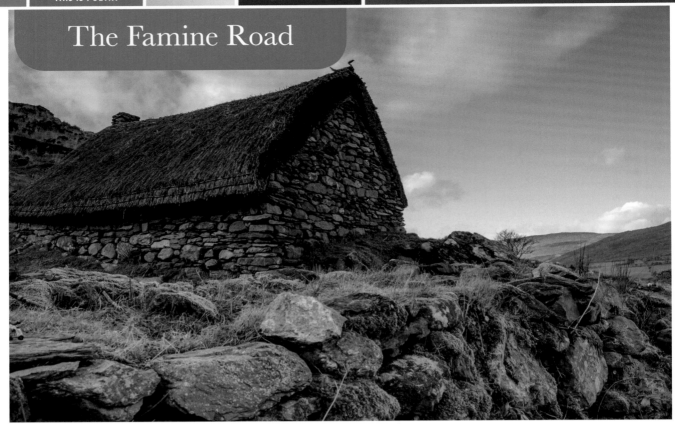

LINE BY LINE

This poem is set in the 1840s when Ireland was in the grip of the greatest famine the country has ever seen.

- Ireland, for centuries, had been under British Rule. For decade after decade, the native Irish had been oppressed by the 'penal laws' and by other measures, that left them poverty-stricken, downtrodden and uneducated.

- Most of the country's land was owned by English landlords. The native Irish rented small farms, in many cases little more than half-acre plots, from these foreign aristocrats.

- In the years leading up to the famine, the native Irish had come to rely on the potato as their main food source. This is because potatoes are a high-yield product; even tiny farms, such as those worked by the native Irish, could produce enough potatoes to feed a family.

- In the years leading up to the famine, the population of the country had reached over eight million, placing further strain on resources.

Boland recalls how she visited Achill when she was in her late teens, staying alone in a 'cottage that was in sight of the Atlantic'. She recalls how the cottage 'had no water and every evening the caretaker, an old woman who shared a cottage with her brother at the end of the field, would carry water up to me. I can see her still'. It was while conversing with this old woman that the poet first properly engaged with the history of the famine: 'She was the first person to talk to me about the famine. The first person, in fact, to speak to me with any force about the terrible parish of survival and death which the event had been in those regions'. In subsequent years the famine would haunt Boland's imagination, leading to this and several other poems.

Finally, in 1845, disaster struck. An infestation popularly known as 'the blight' spread throughout the country, causing the potato crop to rot in the ground. Millions of people faced starvation. To make matters worse, such diseases as typhoid, dysentery and smallpox began to spread throughout the malnourished population. The potato crop failed again in 1846 and 1847, leading to unprecedented misery. This poem deals with the British Government's response to the disaster.

1)

It is 1846. Sir Charles Trevelyan, a leading aristocrat and civil servant in the British government, has been placed in overall charge of Irish famine relief. But he remains in London throughout the crisis, using letters to communicate with the Relief Committee in Dublin.

The Relief Committee has gathered in Dublin Castle. Colonel Harry Jones, one of Trevelyan's deputies, presides over the meeting. We imagine the committee members sitting around a 'deal table' in a plush drawing room, at a far remove from the misery that stalks the land.

Colonel Jones has received a letter from Trevelyan. The letter, as was the custom in those days, has been closed with a wax seal. Jones breaks the seal, and little pieces of red wax fall on the table. These clumps and crumbs of wax, according to the poet, resemble drops of blood tumbling on to the table's surface: 'Trevelyan's/ seal blooded the deal table'.

Colonel Jones reads Trevelyan's letter to the assembled committee members. Trevelyan is opposed to simply giving the famine victims money, an emergency hand-out that could be spent on bread and other kinds of food. He insists that under no circumstances are the starving native Irish to be given such financial aid: 'give them no coins at all'.

Trevelyan has what can only be described as a racist view of the Irish people. The Irish, he claims, are naturally inclined toward slaziness: 'Idle as trout in light Colonel Jones/ these Irish'. Some hard physical labour, according to Trevelyan, would do the Irish good. Such work, he declares, would toughen them up physically. But it would also help their 'characters' or person-alities. They'd get used to hard work and would be less inclined to laziness in future: 'their bones/ need toil, their characters no less'.

Colonel Jones, we imagine, finishes reading and puts down Trevelyan's letter. He leads the committee members in debate or deliberation, as they ponder the best way to proceed: 'The Relief Committee deliberated'. The Committee's job is to draw up and implement a response to the ever-worsening situation in the countryside. But they must also carry out Trevelyan's wishes: the Irish need hard physical labour, and they are to be given no money.

Finally, one committee member makes a suggestion. What if the Irish are given pointless building projects to work on? For example, they might be instructed to build roads 'from nowhere, going nowhere', roads that serve no practical purpose, that lead from one empty field to another?

The Irish, under such a scheme, would have two choices. They could choose to starve to death. Or they could choose to work on these meaningless projects, in return for which they would receive a meagre ration of food each day. And this grim suggestion, as we shall see, is the one the committee chooses to implement.

2)

The poem now takes us forward in time. It is a few months after the Relief Committee's meeting, and their plan has been put into effect. All over the country, starving famine victims are busy building roads 'from nowhere, going nowhere'. We focus on one such group:

- They are 'Sick', not only from hunger but also from the various diseases that raged throughout the countryside.
- They are so exhausted that they move in a 'directionless' fashion. They hardly know what they're doing anymore as they shuffle like zombies around the building site.
- They have been given no tools, no 'fork' or 'stick'. Instead,

they must build the road with their bare hands, lifting and laying stones until their knuckles are all bloody.

- The workers labour in Iron Age conditions. Their situation is so backward that the conditions of the Iron Age, with its primitive tools, seemed almost futuristic: 'Fork, stick/ were iron years away;
- It is the worst of April weather, with snow and hailstones and freezing rain. But still the work must go on.
- Each day's labour earns the workers a meagre ration of food. But the workers remain tormented by hunger and thirst. They suck on hailstones in an effort to ease their thirst and to momentarily fill their bellies: 'suck/ April hailstones for water and for food'.

The workers are so hungry that they contemplate cannibalism. They find themselves eying the buttocks of their fellow workers, imaging what it would be like to eat their flesh.

3)

One of the workers is terribly sick with typhus, a deadly bacterial infection. His fellow workers realize that the sick man is unlikely to make it through the night: 'they will work tomorrow without him. / They know it'. They also realise that he's highly contagious and are careful to 'walk clear' of him, avoiding him so that they themselves don't contract the disease.

The sick man, then, has become a 'pariah' or outcast: 'He has become/ a typhoid pariah'. He is related, we're told, to some of his fellow workers: 'he shares [his blood] with some there'. But even his relatives, in an effort to protect themselves, avoid all contact. The poet, in a powerful turn of phrase, says that this sick man's blood has been 'tainted', suggesting that his fellow workers view him not merely as ill, but also as toxic and unclean.

4)

Colonel Jones writes to Trevelyan, updating him on the road-building scheme. Jones is delighted with progress so far. The scheme, he suggests, has eliminated two problems, that of idleness and that of sedition: 'It has gone better than we expected, Lord/ Trevelyan, sedition, idleness, cured/ in one.'

Trevelyan demanded that the Irish be put to work as a remedy for their natural laziness. This wish has been carried out, with thousands of starving Irish people working on pointless building projects up and down the country: 'From parish to parish, field to field;/ the wretches work'. Furthermore, any threat of 'sedition' or rebellion against the British government has also been eliminated. The Irish have been worked so hard that they no longer have the energy to resist.

In his letter, Jones notes that how the British government has continued to export 'corn' from Ireland. We imagine columns of British solders marching alongside wagons of grain, escorting this precious cargo to the various ports of Ireland, from where it will be shipped overseas. And the starving Irish people, worked almost to death, are incapable of intervening in this process, by attacking the wagons and seizing the grain. Jones seems delighted, therefore, that such exports can continue unimpeded: 'We march the corn/ to the ships in peace'.

It seems that Jones has been travelling around the countryside by carriage in order to personally witness the effects of the road-building scheme. He has seen Irish people work on these famine roads until they are 'quite worn', until they're exhausted to the point of death. He has also seen them collapse and die, their bodies rotting or festering beside the very roads that they've been building: they 'fester by their work'. Fear of contagious disease, no doubt, prevented these 'wretches' from getting a proper burial, making their fellow workers afraid to move or even touch their bodies.

Some of these misfortunate people have lain there so long that their bodies have decomposed, leaving only their bones behind. Jones signs off his letter to Trevelyan by describing how only 'This Tuesday' he saw such bones while travelling by carriage through the countryside.

A Woman's Plight
After each stanza of this famine narrative, we find fragments of another, very different text. This text is set in the present day and describes a woman who has been having difficulty conceiving. She has been for tests in order to discover the cause of the problem. She visits her doctor and receives the bad news that she will never be able to conceive.

The doctor, it must be said, displays no sensitivity or empathy towards her plight. He bluntly confirms that the woman will never be able to have children: 'You never will, never you know'. He offers his patient no words of consolation, simply urging her to 'take it well, woman', to absorbs his crushing news with a minimum of fuss. He comes across as downright rude, dismissing her with a blunt 'good-bye'.

The doctor speaks in a cold, detached manner. He quotes statistics, stating that 'One out of every ten' couples are affected by infertility and that in a third of such cases the

issue lies with the woman's body: 'and then/ another third of those again/ women'. He idly wonders what might have led to the woman's infertility, declaring that 'in a case like yours/ anything may have caused it'. It might have been caused by 'spores', for instance, or by 'a childhood accident'.

To the doctor, then, the woman is more a specimen or a case file than a human being. To him, she is just another patient, just one of the hundreds who walk through his door each year: 'one sees/ day after day these mysteries'

WHY DIDN'T TREVELYAN DO MORE TO HELP THE IRISH?
Trevelyan and the British government were committed to the economic doctrine known as 'laissez-faire'. This doctrine held that the state shouldn't intervene in matters relating to business and the economy. Trevelyan and the British elite held to this view even during the extraordinary catastrophe that was the Irish famine.

Giving the famine victims money, they believed, would mean interfering improperly in the financial market. Giving out free food would mean an improper intervention in the market for grain. Even having the famine victims work on useful projects (such as building bridges, schools or barracks) would mean interfering in the market for construction.

In the years leading up to famine, British landlords and business-owners had exported vast quantities of food from Ireland, everything from beef and butter to barley, wheat and maize. With his laissez-faire beliefs, Trevelyan was determined that, even during the famine's worst years, this food would continue to be exported and would not be diverted to feed the starving Irish.

It's also worth noting that Trevelyan had a rather racist view of the Irish people and felt that the famine was 'The judgment of God sent to teach the Irish a lesson. The real evil with which we have to contend is not the physical evil of the Famine, but the moral evil of the selfish, perverse and turbulent character of the people'.

THEMES

IRELAND: MYTH AND HISTORY

The sufferings of the famine
Boland is a poet known for her engagement with Irish history and in this poem she confronts arguably the country's most tragic episode, the Great Famine of 1845-47. Boland powerfully evokes the great hunger that stalked the land, reminding us that many Irish people were so hungry that they contemplated cannibalism. But the poem stresses that disease, as much as hunger, was a bane of famine times. The poet powerfully captures the scourge

of contagious diseases, such as typhus. There is something heart-breaking about how the famine's victims were declared outcasts or 'pariahs', how they were regarded as corrupt or 'tainted' and were shunned by friends and even family.

The Racism of the British
The poem highlights the British elite's prejudiced, and arguably racist, attitudes toward the Irish people in the 1840s. Trevelyan, as we've seen, regards the Irish as genetically predisposed to laziness, suggesting that they need 'toil' in order to improve

THEMES

themselves. Colonel Jones, it seems, agrees with this view, declares himself pleased that the relief works have 'cured' the Irish of their 'idleness'.

The British elite, the poem suggests, regarded the Irish as subhuman, as troublesome untrustworthy creatures. This attitude is evident when Trevelyan insists that the Irish be given 'No coin', suggesting that, in his opinion, they can't be trusted with money. (Even the phrase 'these Irish', as used by Trevelyan in his letter, suggests such disdain and disregard). We see this attitude, too, when one of the committee members asks if it might be 'safe' to permit the Irish to engage in road-building.

Colonel Jones, too, expresses this attitude when he reports to Trevelyan from his trip around the countryside. Jones expresses no sympathy for the Irish people he has seen starving or diseased or working till 'they are worn'. He seems unperturbed by the corpses that fester by the roadside until only the bones remain. He says that the scheme has 'gone better than expected', as if he were reporting from a particularly successful hunting trip. We sense that people like Jones and Trevelyan are happy to see Irish population reduced in number, just as a population of deer or badgers that threatened to grow out of control might be subjected to a cull.

Roads Going Nowhere

The road-building scheme, as portrayed in this poem, can only be described as a great evil. As we've seen, the workers were forced to labour with their bare hands rather than with tools. They were compelled to work in all kinds of weather, even when they were sick with terrible diseases and 'directionless' with starvation. And the rations they received as payment were so meagre that they sucked on hailstones to stave off hunger.

There is something degrading, too, about being forced to work on a project that serves no practical purpose. It is dehumanising to be forced to build a road 'From nowhere, going nowhere'. It could be considered a cruel form of mockery: being forced to waste the last of one's strength building a road that's never intended to be used

THE SUBJUGATION OF WOMEN

The poem draws a surprising but powerful connection between the sufferings of the Irish during the famine, on one hand, and the sufferings of modern women, on the other.

- The doctor effectively silences his female patient, giving her no opportunity to speak or express herself. Instead, he lectures her about 'spores' before curtly sending her on her way. The British elite, similarly, silenced the Irish population over which they ruled. The native Irish, of course, are unrepresented at the committee meeting and are never consulted about possible solutions to the calamity that faces them.
- The doctor, as we've seen, displays no sympathy or empathy towards his female patient. The British elite, similarly, displayed little compassion towards the Irish people over whom they ruled.
- The doctor, as we've seen, treats his female patient in a cold and clinical manner. This echoes the cold and clinical manner in which members of the British elite, like Jones and Trevelyan, discuss the lives and deaths of the Irish people over whom they rule.
- The doctor, as we've seen, treats his female patient as less than fully human, regarding her as little more than an object of medical study. The British elite, in their own way, regarded the Irish people as less than human, treating them as little more than an animal population in dire need of culling.

The doctor, it's important to note, should not be thought of as a single uncaring individual. Rather he represents an entire society and system, one that silences women and treats them as second-class citizens. This society views women simply as vessels for reproduction. A woman incapable of reproduction, of ever feeling the 'load' of a child inside herself, is of no value. She is as useless as a road going from nowhere to nowhere: 'what is your body/ now if not a famine road?' According to this view, women who can't bear children should occupy themselves with domestic tasks like gardening and housekeeping: 'grow/ your garden, keep house'. There's no sense that women might have any other contribution to make to society.

The poem, then, presents a very negative view of society, suggesting that women are treated by men just as the Irish were treated by the British during famine times. Some might feel that the poem, written in the 1970s, takes a perhaps too bleak view of gender relations. But it reminds us that the struggle for women's rights has gone on for a long time and that, even in our more equal world, it is far from complete.

MOTHERHOOD

'The Famine Road', like many of Boland's poems, engages with the trials and tribulations of motherhood. But whereas a poem like 'The Pomegranate' deals with the difficulties of rearing children, this poem touches on the agony of a mother who can't have children in the first place. Her suffering is exacerbated, no doubt, by having to deal with a chauvinistic and male-dominated medical profession, one that treats her with cold indifference, rather than with empathy and care.

Child of Our Time

LINE BY LINE

1

On 17 May 1974, there was a series of co-ordinated car bombings in Dublin and Monaghan. Three bombs were detonated in Dublin during rush hour, and a fourth exploded in Monaghan almost ninety minutes later. Altogether, thirty-three innocent people were killed, and a further 300 injured.

In the days following this terrible event, the poet, like so many other Irish people, has been wandering around in a state of shock and horror. She has been overcome by the urge to write a poem that might somehow respond to this tragedy, that might make sense of this most senseless act of violence.

The poem that she wants to write would function as a kind of 'lullaby'. Just as a lullaby soothes a crying baby, so her poem might somehow soothe those affected by the bombings: the survivors, the relatives of victims, the ordinary Irish people who have been left mentally anguished by this unspeakable event.

For several days, then, the poet has sought a way to 'order' this poem or 'song'. She has tried to come up with a poetic structure that might somehow make sense of her country's troubled history: Ireland and England, North and South, Protestant and Catholic. Right up until 'Yesterday' she found herself unable to do so. The composition of such a poetic response, of such a song or lullaby, seemed utterly beyond her: 'Yesterday I knew no lullaby'.

Overnight, however, inspiration has struck. Instead of focusing on these big themes of Irish history, she will focus on a single individual. Instead of focusing on abstract notions like nationhood or religion, she'll focus on one of the children who perished in the bombings. Focusing on this one lost individual, this one dead child, enables her to structure or 'order' her poetic response: 'But you have taught me overnight to order/ This song'.

2

The poet claims that 'We', the adults in a society, must 'instruct' the children in our midst. The poet mentions several different ways in which such instruction takes place:

- When children are very young, for instance, we hum them rhythmic, almost wordless songs as we rock them to sleep. Then, when they're awake, we amuse them with nursery rhymes: 'rhymes for your waking, rhythms for your sleep'.
- We should teach children the words for the various objects that surround them. We might teach them, for instance, the 'Names for the animals you took to bed', saying that this stuffed toy is a giraffe, this one a bear and so on.
- Then, when the children are a little older, we should tell them stories. For even silly 'Tales', as the poet points out, can 'distract' an upset child, soothing them and causing them to forget all about their agitation.
- We should also teach children various 'legends'. Such legends, the poet suggests, can protect them from making mistakes as they journey through life. Remembering the legend of King Midas, for instance, might warn them against being excessively greedy. The legend of Icarus, meanwhile, might protect them from their own over-confidence.
- 'Later', as children move into adolescence, we should teach them how to use language in a more sophisticated fashion. Each child, according to the poet, should be encouraged to acquire their own 'idiom', their own personal manner of speaking and writing. This 'idiom' will remain with the child as he or she journeys through life, growing deeper and richer as they grow and learn: 'Later an idiom for you to keep/ And living, learn'.

Such 'instruction', then, involves not only teaching but also nurturing children. It must be carried out not only by parents but also by society as a whole. It's a process that involves carers and teachers, friends and neighbours, brothers and sisters.

Irish society, then, 'should have known' how to instruct not only the children killed in the bombings but also all the other children that surround us. It is as if 'We', as a society, have forgotten how to instruct the children in our midst. Instead of focusing on the language of nurture and instruction, we've become distracted by a different type of language, one associated with hatred, division and conflict.

3

The poet, writing in 1974, reflects on how the people of Ireland, both North and South, have been captivated by a language of hatred, conflict and division.

- They have argued about the rights and wrongs of the various actions that have taken place since unrest broke out in 1969.
- They have argued about the problematic aspects of Northern Ireland since its foundation in 1923, especially the mistreatment of its Catholic population.
- They have even argued about the complicated relationship between Ireland and Britain dating back to medieval times.

In 1923, most of Ireland gained independence from Great Britain. Northern Ireland, however, remained under British rule. Its society was deeply divided. On the one hand, there were Catholic Nationalists, who wanted a united Ireland. On the other, were Protestant Unionists, who wanted Northern Ireland to remain part of Great Britain.

For decades, tensions simmered between these two groups. Finally, in 1969, these tensions came to the surface and there was an explosion of protests, riots and general civil unrest. By 1974, when 'Child of Our Time' was written, this unrest seemed on the verge of transforming into a full-scale civil war.

To the poet, such discussion seemed like 'idle talk', a series of harmless, if heated, historical debates.

Too late, however, she realizes that such 'talk' has consequences. For these endless, bitter debates have amplified the divisions between Northern Ireland's two communities. They have fuelled the atmosphere of conflict, creating a climate in which riots and unrest have escalated into bombings and other atrocities.

Indeed such talk, indirectly, has led to the death of the young victim of the bombing 'whose life our idle/ talk has cost'. Irish society, then, has failed the dead child in a most unspeakable manner. We should have used the language of nurture and instruction to protect him. Instead, however, our addiction to the language of conflict has contributed to his death.

4

The dead child, as we've seen, should have been learning from Irish society, as he grew from a boy into a man. But now, in a bitter irony, these roles have been reversed. And it's Irish society that must learn from the dead child and his tragic passing: 'We ... must learn from you, dead'.

- According to the poet, the 'images' of Irish society have been 'broken'. Society's priorities and moral values have become messed up. We no longer have a clear idea of who we are or how we should behave.

- We must meditate on the 'broken image' of the dead child, on his 'limbs', which were shattered by the explosion.
- Doing so will encourage us to 'make our broken images rebuild/ themselves'. It will encourage us to work to restore our old moral values, to prioritise kindness, understanding and forgiveness rather than bitterness and hatred.

All that's left for the dead child now is the eternal 'final sleep' of death. But the poet hopes that his loss won't have been for nothing. She hopes that his passing will 'wake' a whole new world, will encourage Irish society as a whole to change in a radical fashion: 'Sleep in a world your final sleep has woken'.

If we meditate on the dead child's passing, and on the deaths of other victims of the Troubles, we might leave behind the language of hatred, conflict and division, this seemingly 'idle talk' that leads to tragedy and bloodshed.

We might instead adopt a 'new language', a new and more inclusive way of speaking about nationhood and nationality. We might change our conception of Ireland to one that accommodates Northerner and Southerner, Protestant and Catholic. We might realise, above all, that our ideas of nationhood aren't worth the life of a single innocent child. We must do so, the poet says, for the 'sake' of the dead child. Otherwise his death will have been in vain.

THEMES

WRITING IN A TIME OF VIOLENCE

The poet laments the fact that we live in an age of violence and bloodshed. For the dead child, tragically, is a 'Child/ of our time', born into the bloody world that we, as a society, have created for him. And these bloody times have 'robbed [his] cradle', stealing him away from his parents and his loved ones.

The poem, as we have seen, was set in 1970s Ireland. But its message, surely, still rings true today. For it can seem, as we look around the world, that we're still existing in a time of violence, in an age that, tragically, still loses many of its children to violence and war.

MOTHERHOOD

In poems like 'This Moment' and 'The Pomegranate' Boland engages with the theme of motherhood, focusing especially on the essential, unsung work that mothers do. But this poem, as we've seen, looks beyond the role of mothers – and even that of fathers – by suggesting that society as a whole must work to 'instruct' and nurture the children in its midst: 'We who should have known how to instruct [you]'.

The Black Lace Fan My Mother Gave Me

LINE BY LINE

Back in the 1930s the poet's father gave her mother a black lace fan as a gift. This was at the beginning of their relationship; it was 'the first gift he ever gave her'. The poet's mother kept the fan for many years before passing it on to the poet herself. The poet contemplates this family heirloom and recalls the beginning of her parents' relationship.

1

Her mother and father met when they were both living in Paris. This was during the 1930s, which is also known as the 'pre-war' period. Their relationship, it seems, blossomed in the spring-time, that most romantic of settings. They both decided to remain there for the summer months: 'They stayed in the city for the summer'.

The speaker has heard how her parents, during that long-ago summer, would meet on dates in various cafés around town: 'They met in cafés'. Her mother would always arrive on time for these encounters. Her father, however, would always be late: 'She was always early./ He was late'.

The speaker has heard how, during that long-ago summer, Paris was in the grip of a heat-wave. The air was unpleasantly humid or 'stifling', making it difficult to breathe. Weeks with little or no rainfall had lead to a 'drought' in the city.

As the heat-wave wore on, the nights started to become 'stormy'. We imagine night after night of thundery, unsettled weather. We imagine a blanket of dense clouds concealing the sky, so that the nights seemed 'starless'. But still the heat continued; still there was no rain.

2

The poet, it seems, has been told by her parents about the evening on which her father gave her mother the fan. The poet recounts everything she knows about this occasion. Her parents were, as usual, due to meet at a café. However, on this occasion her father was even later than usual: 'That evening he was later'.

The poet's mother, understandably, grew impatient as she waited on the terrace outside the café. Although she had finished her first drink, there was still no sign of her new boyfriend. She stared down the street, hoping, no doubt, that he would appear at any moment: 'She looked down the Boulevard des Capucines'.

She ordered 'more coffee', which suggests that she intended to wait a bit longer. But she also 'stood up', which suggests that she intended to leave. The speaker's mother, then, felt agitated and uncertain as she waited. Was her boyfriend's persistent lateness a sign of disrespect, one that she should respond to by walking away right there and then? Or had she been stood up; was her boyfriend ever going to appear on this particular evening? Should she stay, or should she go?

On this evening, the heat was even more oppressive than usual: 'The heat was killing'. It seems, however, that the heat-wave was finally about to end causing a great storm to wash over the city. The streets started to empty because the city's inhabitants wanted to be indoors when the storm arrived. As the poet's mother waited on the cafe terrace, she could almost smell the approaching rain, could almost sense the electricity that we associate with lightning crackling in the air: 'She thought the distance smelled of rain and lightning'.

At that very moment, the poet's father was in a nearby department store known as the 'Galeries', where he was buying a gift for his impatiently waiting girlfriend. He picked out the black lace fan and had it wrapped by the shop assistant. He glanced at his watch, aware, no doubt, that he was even later than usual for his date: 'They wrapped the fan. He looked at his watch.'

3

The poem's focus shifts from pre-war Paris to the present day. The poet contemplates the fan, which, as we've seen, has been passed on to her by her mother. She focuses on each of the fan's components in turn.

First, she focuses on the fan's lace. Even when the fan is opened out, this material remains opaque. The poet uses a wonderful metaphor to describe this effect, referring to the lace as 'overcast', because the black lace, like cloud cover, is difficult to see through.

She pushes this metaphor even further, referring to the long-ago evening in Paris when the fan was first 'opened' to relieve or 'offset' the heat. According to the poet, it's as if the evening's storm clouds had somehow entered the fan's very fabric: 'The lace is overcast as if the weather/ it opened for and offset had entered it'.

The poet next focuses on the roses that decorate the lace. Appliqué is a technique whereby smaller pieces of fabric are sewn onto a larger piece. In this instance, red pieces of fabric have been stitched onto the fan's lace to form the shape of 'wild roses': 'These are wild roses, appliqued on silk by hand'.

The unpleasantness of the continuing heat wave is reflected in the father's choice of gift; the fan will be used to relieve the discomfort caused by the evening's heat and humidity. The gift, then, seems a thoughtful one. Though it also, of course, might be seen as a sort of apology for the father's persistent lateness!

The roses, no doubt, are a beautiful design feature, having been skilfully stitched 'by hand' on to the lace. But there's something about them that makes the poet feel uneasy:

- According to the poet, the roses have been 'darkly picked', which suggests that they're a brooding crimson in colour rather than a cheery pink.
- The poet studies the roses' stitching, concluding that they were sewn onto the fan in a fierce, almost aggressive manner: 'darkly picked, stitched boldly, quickly'
- The instinctive, unconstrained quality of the stitching is further emphasised, perhaps, by the fact that the roses being depicted are 'wild'.

Finally, the poet focuses on the fan's 'rest' or frame. The frame is manufactured from tortoiseshell and the poet praises the attractive clarity of this substance or 'element': 'The rest is tortoiseshell and has the reticent/ clear patience of its element'.

The fan's frame, then, is presented as something beautiful and precious. The poet associates its tortoiseshell material with 'patience'. Perhaps she has in mind the many years it took to grow and develop as a carapace on some long-dead tortoise's back. She also compares tortoiseshell to 'Underwater bullion', to gold bars discovered on a wrecked vessel at the ocean's bottom. This is because tortoiseshell, like gold, is an extremely valuable material. And tortoiseshell, like such sunken bullion, must be recovered from the ocean's depths.

But the frame also has certain negative associations. It has become 'worn out' over years of use. And it brings with it a suggestion (or 'inference') of the poor tortoise that was killed so it could be manufactured: 'it keeps,/ even now, an inference of its violation'. The poet describes the harvesting of this creature's shell as a form of 'violation'. To her, it is a violent, intrusive act, like theft or rape.

All in all, then, the speaker has mixed feelings about the fan. On the one hand, she praises its beauty, but on the other she associates it with storms and darkness, with violence and violation.

4

We return to Paris long ago where we left the poet's mother sitting on the café's terrace, waiting impatiently for the poet's father to arrive. The storm, it seems, is even closer to breaking over the city. The poet uses a wonderful turn of phrase to describe the calm that precedes this great tempest, referring to the 'airless dusk before thunder'. Humidity has reduced the oxygen-level in the atmosphere, making the late evening so humid that it now seems 'airless' and almost impossible to breathe.

Everyone, by now, has found their way indoors to escape the coming downpour. Only the poet's mother is still outside, on an otherwise empty café's terrace, still waiting for her date to arrive: 'The past is an empty café terrace'. The poet's father, meanwhile, runs through the emptying streets, clutching the fan he's just bought as a gift.

What will happen next? Will the father get there before the mother gets tired of waiting and storms off? How exactly did events pan out on that long-ago evening? And what will happen to the lovers over the course of their relationship?

The poet, as we noted, has been told certain facts about her parents' courtship. Of course, she doesn't know everything. She doesn't know all the details of what happened on that Parisian evening and over the years that followed.

The poet's parents, alas, are no longer around to fill in the blanks for her. And even if they were, their account could only be partial, with so many details forgotten or left out. The only way for her to truly know what happened would be to somehow travel back in time! There is an air of sorrow, then, when the poet declares that such things can never really be discovered: 'And no way now to know what happened then/ none at all'.

All the speaker can do, therefore, is 'improvise'. She must use her creativity to fill in these blanks in the story by imagining all the details of how her parents' relationship worked out. Perhaps she's considering an essay or a series of poems that would tell her parents' story, one that combines the known facts with her improvised imaginings.

5

The poem's conclusion brings us back to the present day once more. The poet's attention, as we've seen, has been gripped by the black lace fan. But suddenly she finds herself distracted by a female blackbird that is flitting around her garden, searching 'buds, worms, fruit'.

It is the first humid or 'sultry' morning of the summertime. The blackbird 'feels the heat', and responds by stretching out its wing: 'Suddenly she puts out her wing'. The blackbird, then, uses its wing just as the poet's mother would have used the black lace fan. The bird's wing, like a fan, acts a shield from the sun's aggressive heat. Perhaps the bird even flaps its wing gently back and forth, as one would a fan, in order to create a cooling breeze.

Let's dwell, for a moment, on the fact that the poet's father was never on time for these dates with his future wife. Perhaps the father is simply a poor time-keeper, an unpunctual person by nature. Or perhaps his persistent lateness indicates a lack of enthusiasm about the relationship.

But it might also suggest that this new couple are 'out of synch', that they have yet to properly connect on an emotional and psychological level. Even the father's choice of gift suggests that they aren't quite on the same wavelength: he buys the mother a fan just as the hot weather breaks, rendering his gift useless at least for the time being. We're presented, then, with a couple who are a little out-of-step, who are still finding their way in this new relationship.

THEMES

MARRIAGE

This poem powerfully captures the tension and uncertainty that can exist at the beginning of a relationship. New love, of course, is characterised by great excitement. But it can also bring great feelings of dread and exposure. How do I really feel about this person? How do they feel about me? Am I letting myself in for heartbreak?

- Such tension, no doubt, is represented by the 'stifling' and 'killing' heat that grips the city, by the 'airless' and humid atmosphere, by the turbulent weather that marks the tail-end of the heat-wave.

- The mention of the cloudy or 'starless' sky, too, might represent this tension, reflecting the mother's lack of clarity about her relationship's status.

- Such tension is especially evident on the night when the mother receives the black lace fan. The air practically crackles with electricity, so that one can almost smell the coming storm.

- We can sense the tension in the mother's agitated behaviour as she waits for her date to arrive: she stands, sits down, orders more coffee, looks anxiously down the street.

- The father, too, exhibits such agitation, nervously checking his watch while his gift is wrapped in the Galeries, before running through the empty city streets.

It has also been suggested that the coming storm serves a symbolic function. Does it represent the difficulties and tribulations that the couple will later experience? Or does the storm symbolise something more positive? The storm, after all, will break the heat-wave and relieve the oppressive heat and humidity that has gripped the city. Perhaps, then, the storm represents an easing of the tension that seems to have characterised the early days of the couple's relationship.

OUT OF SYNCH

An interesting feature of this poem is how Boland uses the fan as a symbol of her parents' marriage. In this heirloom, she sees an account of the ups and downs that they enjoyed and endured, of the good and bad times they went through together. The good times are represented by the beauty of the hand-stitched roses and by the exquisite clarity of its tortoise-shell frame, which as we've seen, is associated with gold bullion, suggesting the precious nature of their love. Also, the tortoise shell from which the frame is made took a very long time to grow. This parallels the patient development of the couple's loving relationship over many years.

But the fan also symbolises the negative aspects of the marriage: The lace's opacity, as we've seen, recalls cloudy, unsettled weather, symbolising, perhaps the turbulent times in the couple's relationship. The appliqued roses might also allude to such unhappy times, having been stitched fiercely, almost violently, onto the silk. The fan's frame, we remind ourselves, is described as 'worn-out', which suggests the feelings of boredom and exhaustion that creep into any long-term relationship from time to time.

The tortoise-shell frame, too, has violent associations, being linked with the killing and 'violation' of an innocent creature. Perhaps we sense here Boland's negative feelings toward marriage as a whole, which, in poems like 'The Shadow Doll', she seems to regard as violation of women's independence and individuality.

It is fitting, then, that Boland concludes the poem with another, very different, symbol of her parents' relationship, the blackbird that she sees flitting round her garden. In a sense, the bird's wing echoes the black lace fan: they have a similar physical appearance, and both are unfurled or extended to 'offset' heat. Whereas the fan is a 'worn-out' antique, however, the blackbird is full of life and energy. The fan is made from the shells of dead tortoises, whereas the bird is a living, breathing part of nature. It is associated with rebirth and fertility, with the 'first sultry morning, / in summer', with 'buds, worms, fruit'.

The long duration of the parents' relationship is represented by the wing's broad 'span'. The wing is described as 'whole' and 'full', which suggests the fulfilment and satisfaction that Boland's parents found in their long partnership. The wing is also described as 'flirtatious', which suggests the physical and erotic side of her parents' marriage over the years.

The poem's final lines, then, sound a triumphant note, celebrating the survival and endurance of her parents' love – its lavish and beautiful 'span' of years. What matters, then, is not the detailed story of their marriage, with its ups and downs and weathered storms, but the fact that the relationship survived and flourished for so long.

FAMILY: MYTH AND HISTORY

'The Black Lace Fan', like many of Boland's poems, engages with the area of family history. It movingly depicts the impossibility of fully understanding our family's past, of reconstructing events that occurred before we were born. We may have some evidence of such past events – photos, videos, stories, heirlooms – but we can never truly reconstruct what happened in all its detail. So much of the past must remain forever lost to us.

This is what the poet means when she refers to the tortoise shell's 'reticence', its reluctance to speak. She feels that in the fan she can see aspects of her parents' marriage. But it can can only reveal so much. She is unable, then, to tell the full story of her parents' love, of its beginnings in Paris and its continuation through their many years together. She simply does not have the information to do so.

At the same time, however, the poem celebrates the artist's ability to recreate the past, to improvise or imagine what might have happened. The speaker, therefore, chooses to represent her parents' love by means of the triumphant symbol of the blackbird with its extended wing. It is not clear, however, how much this glorious symbol reflects the actual facts of the parents' life together and how much it reflects the speaker's artistic imaginings.

There's sense, too, in which the story of that long-ago Paris evening is as much a family myth as it is a piece of family history. We sense that this story, like most myths, has been retold and passed down. Like many myths, the story of the fan concerns the foundation of a group or tribe, in this case the little 'tribe' of Boland's immediate family. And, perhaps, like many myths, the story of the fan combines fact and fiction. For who knows what details of that Parisian evening have been exaggerated or misremembered over the years?

The Shadow Doll

LINE BY LINE

THE DOLL

The speaker is visiting a museum. In a glass case, she sees a porcelain doll wearing a tiny wedding dress. Dolls like this were used in the 19th century to help brides choose an appropriate gown. Miniature gowns would be made and placed on the dolls, allowing brides to evaluate them without the expense of having a full-size dress created. Using these tiny 'models' as a guide, the bride and her family could accept or reject the design on offer, and could suggest alterations.

The speaker examines the doll and describes its tiny dress. The veil is made from tulle, a soft, silky material. The dress itself has been sewn from crinoline, a stiff, linen-like fabric. The dress seems to be incredibly detailed:

- It has been 'neatly sewn'.
- It has been fitted with a miniature version of the hoops that were a feature of many 19th-century gowns.
- It has been decorated with a spray or pattern of tiny 'seed pearls', which have a pale 'shell-tone' colour.
- The veil's tulle material 'gleams' with a kind of spotless whiteness that puts the speaker in mind of ivory and oysters.
- The hem or edge of the veil has been stitched with a pattern that resembles little flowers.
- The doll's makers have even placed tiny fake flowers in her porcelain hands: petals from roses and from the white flowers of the stephanotis plant.

The doll's little dress, then, is clearly a thing of beauty, given the lavish material involved in its production, its rich detail and its blazing whiteness.

THE DOLL AS PRISONER

Yet the speaker feels nothing but pity for the well-dressed doll. She thinks of the doll as a prisoner, one that is kept 'Under glass, under wraps' in its transparent display case. The doll is a glamorous and stylish creation, but its glamour is an 'airless' glamour, since it remains trapped in the unventilated atmosphere beneath a glassy dome.

Another tragic aspect of the doll's predicament is that it has outlived its usefulness. It has survived long past the 'occasion' when it served a purpose. Now, it is just a toy, a trinket in a museum to be admired by visitors.

Boland uses a poetic technique called personification, whereby an inanimate object is presented as if it had human qualities. In this instance, the doll is depicted as being capable of human experiences, such as 'fevers' and 'lusts'. The doll is also presented as having the power of speech, of being able to express these experiences if it hadn't been silenced in its prison of glass. Boland, of course, doesn't literally mean that the doll possesses these qualities. Rather, she is using the technique of personification in order to make a point about the institution of marriage.

The speaker is particularly conscious of the fact that the doll is doomed to silence. It has been placed 'under wraps'. As a prisoner behind glass, it can never talk about or express the things it has experienced.

It is forced to remain especially 'discreet' about its body and its sexuality: 'it stays/ even now, after all, discreet about/ visits, fevers, quickenings and lusts'. 'Quickenings' and 'fevers' suggest the heat and excitement of sexual arousal, the accelerated heartbeat and the quickening of the pulse. Because it is associated with 'fevers, quickenings and lusts', the word 'visits' itself suggests sexual encounters and pleasure.

THE YOUNG BRIDE-TO-BE

The speaker thinks of the young, 19th-century woman who used the doll to choose her wedding dress. She imagines of how this young bride-to-be must have 'looked at' the doll in its miniature gown, examining its many exquisite features: 'when she looked at/ the shell-tone spray of seed pearls,/ the bisque features'.

The speaker imagines that this young woman had a nightmarish experience. According to the speaker, the young woman could feel herself being transformed into a ceramic doll just like the one she was looking at. The young woman felt herself turning from a creature of flesh and blood into a 'porcelain bride'. She felt that she would never again experience bodily processes like breathing. The young woman felt herself taking the doll's place in its glass display dome, trapped forever in its transparent case, clutching its fake flowers: 'she could see herself// inside it'.

It is significant that the young woman seems to imagine this transformation occurring just as she utters her wedding vows before the altar: 'never feeling/ satin rise and fall with the vows'. It's as if the vows will change her from an organic human being into some weird ceramic statue. Even as she utters the vows, she'll feel her bodily processes, including breathing, cease. She'll no longer feel the satin of her dress rising and falling as she inhales and exhales.

THE NIGHT BEFORE THE SPEAKER'S WEDDING

The speaker then thinks about her own wedding. She remembers the night before the ceremony. She was in a room full of gifts that she and her fiancé had received to mark the occasion: 'the cards and wedding gifts –/ the coffee pots and the clocks'. She remembers packing up her wedding dress, folding this garment of cotton and lace into a 'battered tan case'. The case also contained tissue paper to prevent the dress creasing and wrinkling. We might imagine here that the speaker was preparing the dress for transport from her home to the wedding venue.

The speaker seemed to regard her upcoming marriage with fear and trepidation. She describes herself as being 'astray among the cards and wedding gifts', indicating that she felt lost, confused, and perhaps even desperate at the looming prospect of her marriage. We sense her nervous tension in how she repeated her wedding vows over and over: 'the vows/ I kept repeating on the night before'.

We sense too that she was testing the vows' meaning, wondering about the restrictions they would place on her life. Is she prepared to embrace these vows and surrender herself to the institution of marriage? Is she ready to obey her husband, to embrace his name and be guided by him in all things?

There is a real sense of claustrophobia in these lines. The speaker seems trapped and overwhelmed by the clutter of wedding gifts that surrounds her. Indeed, this claustrophobic atmosphere is reinforced when the speaker depicts herself 'pressing down, then/ pressing down again' on the case's lid.

The poem's final sentence or sentence fragment can be read in two ways: 'And then locks'. On the one hand, the item that 'locks' here is simply the bulging tan suitcase, which has finally been closed by the pressure that the speaker has exerted. On another level, however, the 'locks' refer to the vows of marriage, which are reinforced and policed by tradition and society. These 'locks' will soon click into place and confine the speaker in marriage's 'airless glamour'.

MARRIAGE

This poem, it must be said, presents an extremely negative view of marriage.

Marriage turns women into pretty possessions of their husbands.	The doll in its case symbolises how marriage is little more than a glamorous prison.
	This is reinforced when the 19th-century bride-to-be imagines herself as the doll in its dome of glass. She will survive only as a possession of her husband – a kind of 'living doll' to be displayed by him and admired by society.
Marriage robs women of their freedom and independence.	Wedding vows are associated with 'locks' that trap women, keeping them 'under wraps'.
	Women, the poem suggests, are as confined by the vows and institutions of marriage as the doll is within its glass case.
	The 19th-century bride-to-be imagines herself trapped beneath the doll's glass display case.
	Marriage is presented as an 'airless glamour', as a suffocating and claustrophobic institution.
	The speaker describes herself as being hemmed in and overwhelmed by the clutter of gifts on the night before her wedding.
	This air of claustrophobia is reinforced by the image in the poem's final lines of the speaker 'pressing down' on the suitcase.
Marriage places women 'Under wraps', robbing them of their ability to speak.	Brides, like dolls and children, are to be seen rather than heard. They are to be admired for their beauty, for the 'oyster gleam' of their pretty dresses, rather than for their experiences and their ability to express themselves.
Marriage robs women of their ability to speak about their bodies.	Married women are forced to remain 'discreet' about their bodies and the sexual side of their being, about 'visits, fevers, quickenings and lusts'.
Marriage robs women of their usefulness.	The poem suggests that married women have 'survived their occasion'. Like the doll in the display case, they have outlived their purpose and their usefulness as productive members of society, and continue to exist only as the possessions of their husbands.

It is hardly surprising; therefore, that marriage is regarded with dread. The 19th-century bride-to-be is filled with fear at the prospect of her upcoming marriage. She has a horrific vision of herself transforming into the doll beneath its glass display case. The speaker, too, regarded her upcoming marriage with fear and trepidation. On the night before her marriage she felt 'astray', agitated and claustrophobic, nervously repeating her wedding vows over and over.

THE SUBJUGATION OF WOMEN

Surely the view of marriage in this poem is outdated or too harsh? Today, we think of marriage as a loving partnership in which both partners share life's burdens and protect one another. Why then does Boland present marriage as something that suffocates women's personalities, that degrades their humanity and silences them?

Boland is partly referring to the history of marriage here. In the 19th century, when the doll was manufactured, married woman were often regarded as little more than possessions of their husbands. Disobedience and independence were unthinkable. Yet even in the 20th century, women were regarded as subservient to their husbands and were restricted in various ways by marriage. In Ireland, for example, it was only in the mid-1970s that it became acceptable for a married woman to work outside the home.

Boland writes about a system or society that marginalises and oppresses women, that maintains them as little more than servants, slaves or possessions. And to many women of her generation, marriage was just one more tool society used to keep women in their place. It is in this context, therefore, that we should consider the poem's devastating critique of marriage and its institutions.

White Hawthorn in the West of Ireland

LINE BY LINE

A JOURNEY FROM EAST TO WEST

For centuries writers and artists – from this country and from abroad – have been fascinated by the West of Ireland. They have responded to the wild and rugged nature of its landscape, to its people, to its uniquely shifting light and perhaps above all to the sense that something survives there of an ancient Celtic heritage. The poet, too, experiences such an attraction and in this poem journeys by car from her home in the Dublin suburbs to the West of Ireland: 'I drove West … I left behind suburban gardens'.

The poet presents suburbia as a safe and comfortable environment – but also perhaps as a boring one. She associates it with 'suburban gardens', 'Lawnmowers' and 'Small talk'. We might imagine here a housing estate where neighbours gossip over the fences that divide their well-kept properties. There's a sense in which these people's lives are neat, orderly, confined and predictable – just like their carefully manicured lawns. The poet seems relieved, then, to leave this dull suburban world behind.

She reaches the untamed beauty of Ireland's Atlantic coast and in a few short lines wonderfully captures the region's unique atmosphere:

- This is no place of regular fields and gardens. It is rather a wild and random landscape, marked here and there by 'splashes' of yellow coltsfoot flowers.
- The light is complex; it is hard and glaring but somehow also soft and fuzzy: 'The hard shyness of Atlantic light'.
- The phrase 'low skies', meanwhile, wonderfully captures how, near the ocean, the sky and sea often seem to blend together.

However, there can also be something oppressive, melancholy or even menacing about these looming western horizons. The west of Ireland, then, is a beautiful place. But its beauty can be strange, haunting and even unnerving.

THE HAWTHORN BUSHES

The poet is fascinated by a hill covered with hawthorn bushes whose flowers seem to pour down the hillside in a 'rush' of flickering whiteness. She is suddenly filled with the desire to pick some of the hawthorn's prickly blooms. She wants to climb the hawthorn-covered hill and wander among the bushes, so that someone watching from a distance might see her blend into their whiteness: 'to seem, from a distance, to be part of that ivory, downhill rush'. She wants to pluck armfuls of the hawthorn's distinctive 'sharp flowers'.

She knows, however, that to do so would go against the traditions of the region. In Ireland the hawthorn tree has long been associated with other worlds and with dangerous magic. Indeed, as the poet points out, such superstitions continue to this day; even in modern Ireland people are reluctant to touch this particular plant: 'I had always known/ the custom was/ not to touch hawthorn'.

People are equally reluctant to bring the plant into their homes. To do so is to lose or 'forfeit' luck, to invite misfortune into the household. To 'constrain' this wild plant by bringing it indoors is to risk a terrible punishment. As the speaker puts it, 'a child might die' or farm animals might suddenly become sick: 'an unexpected fever [might] speckle heifers'. (Here, the speaker imagines heifers 'speckled' with sores and rashes as a result of illness.) In keeping with 'custom', therefore, the speaker decides not to pick the flowers of the hawthorn tree: 'So I left it'.

The poet describes how, in the complex western light, the bushes are surrounded by an 'aura' or glowing halo of light. To her, this aura seems to represent the superstitions associated with the plant. It puts her in mind of the supernatural forces with which hawthorn has been traditionally linked: 'superstitious aura of hawthorn'.

THE HAWTHORN ON THE HILL

The poet describes how the hawthorn flowers ripple as the breeze blows through them. The mass of hawthorn, flowers, she declares, resembles a body of water, or some other liquid substance, rushing down the hillside. The plants even seem capable of reshaping the hills on which they're located, just like a stream or river erodes and alters the landscape through which it flows: 'like water, able/ To re-define land'.

The speaker says that she travels West in 'the season between seasons'. In one sense this refers to the changeable Irish weather; how certain days seem to combine features of summer, autumn, winter and spring – while certain weeks seem like 'mini-seasons' all of their own.
Yet the phrase is also reminiscent of something we might find in a legend or a folk tale. This 'season between seasons' seems to be a brief, enchanted moment – neither winter, spring, summer nor autumn – during which everything in the West seems shifting and uncertain.

The poet imagines that the hawthorn, as a liquid substance, is utterly 'free'. She imagines that it isn't confined – as a solid, rooted plant would be – to any one position. Instead, she imagines, the hawthorn can pour itself through the landscape with great ease or fluency, rippling through hills and valleys 'with a fluency/ only water has'.

The poet imagines 'anglers' or 'travellers' that have gone 'astray' in this remote, western landscape. We imagine anglers, walkers and cyclists travelling through the region at the start of summer, relishing its mountains, hills and waterways. When such tourists lose their way, however, the West can often seem an eerie and isolated landscape especially as the 'May dusk' begins to fall.

To visitors in this unnerving situation, the West can seem like an uninhabited wilderness, a place devoid of people, buildings and human language. Indeed the poet suggests that to such lost travellers the hawthorn will seem like the 'only language' spoken in the area.

We can imagine how, to such a lost walker or fisherman, the hawthorn might, for a moment, seem to be communicating. He might see the sunlight glinting on its flowers as a strange form of code, or hear, as the wind pours through its blossoms, an almost human whispering.

THEMES

SUBURBAN LIFE

This is a poem that contrasts two very different worlds: the suburbs of Dublin, on the one hand, and the West of Ireland, on the other. 'White Hawthorn in the West of Ireland' presents suburbia in a distinctly negative light. The suburb where the speaker lives is depicted as a place of little significance, compared to the untamed West:

The suburbs are boring.	The West is thrillingly beautiful.
The suburbs are a fake, manmade environment.	The West is natural and authentic.
The suburbs are a shallow place of trivial 'small talk'.	The West provides experiences that are deep and meaningful.
The suburbs are associated with modernity and technology (lawnmowers for instance).	The West is associated with ancient beliefs and superstitions.
In the suburbs nature has been trapped and tamed into neat suburban gardens.	In the West nature is free; it consists of irregular fields and hawthorn that can never be 'constrained'.
The suburbs are rigidly ordered, places of houses and gardens, where the borders between different properties are always clearly laid down.	The West is fluid and shifting, a place where any given thing seems constantly on the verge of blending into something else: • Fields blend into other fields. • The 'low skies' blend into sea and land. • The light is complex and ever-changing. • The hawthorn seems to flow. • Even the earth is capable of being 'redefined'.
The suburbs are safe and secure.	The West can be threatening, with its 'low skies' and ancient superstitions. It can be a place of eerie isolation, where all human occupation seems to have been stripped away.

IRELAND: MYTH AND HISTORY

The poet's pilgrimage into the West can be seen as an attempt to 'return to her roots'. She longs to recover her heritage as an Irish woman, to reconnect with what remains of ancient Ireland with all its beliefs, traditions and superstitions.

Her desire to return to her roots is represented by her longing to touch the hawthorn: 'All I wanted then was to fill my arms with/ Sharp flowers'. We see it too in her desire to wander among the hawthorn bushes, where she imagines herself blending into the Irish landscape: 'All I wanted then was to seem, from a distance, to be part of/ that ivory downhill rush'.

Yet she knows she must never touch the hawthorn bushes. To do so is to go against superstition and to turn her back on the very traditions she longs to rediscover. This 'paradox' or dilemma represents the poet's status as an outsider in the world of the countryside. As a city dweller and a suburbanite, she will never truly be part of this world. She will never really connect with this landscape. She will never, metaphorically speaking, touch the hawthorn.

As we've seen, the poem's final lines depict anglers and travellers completely out of their element, lost in the eerie isolation of the western dusk. Perhaps the poet realises deep down that she is no different from such holidaymakers. She will only ever experience this environment at a remove, in a shallow and touristic manner.

Outside History

INTRODUCTION

In this poem, Boland grapples with the notions of myth and history. History, as Boland uses the term, can be defined as the written record of events. Irish history, therefore, began with our earliest surviving documents, which were written by Saint Patrick in the 5th Century. Irish history, since then, has been recorded in a wide variety of narrative accounts, from the chronicles of ancient monks to the Wikipedia articles of the 21st Century.

Myths, on the other hand, are fictional stories handed down from one generation to the next. They are often fantastical in nature, featuring gods, monsters and heroes with superhuman attributes. Myths often have an explanatory function. Some myths attempt to explain why the world is the way that it is. Others attempt to explain the origins of a particular tribe or nation.

The poet feels that women have been excluded from Irish history. There are several ways in which this might be the case:

- The Irish historical record has been composed almost entirely by men. For women, until relatively recently, were excluded from the profession of historian.
- Male historians all too often neglected women of real achievement, preferring to focus instead on prominent men.
- Women who did make it into the historical record were often included because of the men in their lives, rather than because of their own contributions to Irish life.
- It might also be suggested that the male writers of Irish history were extremely narrow in their outlook, focusing too much on stereotypically 'masculine' concepts like battles, warriors and kings.

It could even be argued that, in the Irish context, female figures from mythology have received more attention and respect than the real women of history. .

THE STARS AS OUTSIDERS

It is a January night in Ireland. The poet is in the countryside, surrounded by fields and rivers. She is looking up at the stars in the night sky. She finds herself contemplating the extraordinary distance between the Earth and these glittering celestial bodies.

Even the nearest stars, like Alpha Centuari and Wolf 359, are unimaginably distant. Wolf 359, for instance, is about 50 trillion kilometres from Earth. To write it out fully that's 50,000,000,000,000 kilometres. And the vast majority of visible

stars are much, much further away than these our nearest galactic neighbours.

Because the stars are so distant, it can take an extraordinarily long time for their light to reach us. Take, for instance, the star HD 10180, which, at a distance of about 1,990 light years, is still relatively close to Earth:

- A pulse of its light might have 'happened' in the year 0 CE, generated by violent nuclear reactions within its core. At that moment, billions of kilometres away on planet Earth, Jesus Christ had just been born and Augustus still ruled the Roman Empire.
- Such a pulse of light would then spend 1,990 years travelling across the emptiness of space.
- Finally, in 1990, the year Boland wrote the poem, that pulse would have reached our little planet, striking the poet's retina as she stands in a field in Ireland, looking up at the night sky overhead.

The poet describes how the remoteness of the stars places them 'outside history': 'they are, they always have been/ outside history'. They are simply too far away to be involved in the story of Ireland, or of humanity in general. Nothing that happens here can affect them, can dim them or make them shine brighter. Nor can anything that happens on or around the stars affect events here in our long-suffering country.

Even their light is 'outside history'. 'History', as Boland uses the term, can be defined as the written record of events. Irish history, therefore, began with our earliest surviving documents, which were written by Saint Patrick in the 5th Century. But most of the star-light we see was generated hundreds, or even thousands, of years before Patrick penned the first words of Ireland's painful story: 'whose light happened/ thousands of years before/ our pain did'.

The stars, in a wonderful piece of personification, are described as outsiders: 'These are outsiders, always'. They are compared to hermits or recluses, to people who choose to 'keep their distance' from society at large. For the stars, in their own way, 'keep their distance,' hovering light-years above us in the heavens. Such outsiders might be visible, but they remain aloof and remote. We might see them coming and going from time to time, but they avoid all human interaction. The stars, similarly, are visible to us, but are utterly aloof to our affairs.

It is significant that the poem is set in January, the month of new beginnings and resolutions. As we shall see, the poet resolves to make a new start, to engage with history, especially

women's history, in a new and more productive manner.

The stars, in a beautiful turn of phrase, are described as 'iron inklings'. The word 'iron' wonderfully captures the stars' metallic glow, suggesting that they resemble a handful of iron filings scattered on a night-black background.

The light from each star was emitted hundreds or even thousands of years ago. When we look up, therefore, we see each star not as it is now, but as it was hundreds or even thousand of years in the past. We get therefore only an 'inkling' of each star's current appearance, only a hint of what it actually looks like today.

A CONTRAST BETWEEN EARTH AND STARS

The poet, as she stands looking up at the night sky, draws a contrast between the stars, on the one hand, and the Irish landscape on the other.

- The stars, being 'outside history', are associated with myth. The Irish landscape, in contrast, iwhere actual history has taken place. It's the site where the 'ordeal' of history has been experienced. Its 'fields', 'rivers' and 'roads' have been shaped by everything from Viking raids in the 8th Century to the Northern Irish Troubles of the 20th.
- Just as the night sky or 'firmament' is 'clotted' with an innumerable mass of stars, the Irish landscape is 'clotted' with the innumerable bodies of the dead. Boland's comparison underlines the fact that the landscape contains everyone who ever died and was buried on Irish soil, some only recently laid to rest, others long ago absorbed into the earth.
- The stars in the night sky, as we've seen, emit light. The Irish landscape, meanwhile is depicted as emitting 'darkness'. This is hardly surprising, given that the written history of Ireland, beginning with the earliest surviving 5th-Century documents, is in many respects a succession of disasters and defeats, of violence and bloodshed.
- The stars, as we've seen, are utterly remote from human life. The landscape 'Under them', however, is where all human life occurs. This is where each one of us lives and learns, where we discover what is to be a human being, with all the faults and glories that entails.
- The stars above us are constant and utterly unchanging. (Or at least they seem that way to us when we look at them from planet earth.) The landscape, on the other hand, is a place of constant change. It's where each one of us is born, lives and dies. It's where, all too quickly, we realise that we and everything around us are 'mortal' and doomed to pass away: 'a landscape in which you know you are mortal'.

THEMES

THE SUBJUGATION OF WOMEN

As a woman, the poet feels that she must choose between myth, which is represented by the stars, and history, which is represented by the landscape. It is time, she says, 'to choose between them'.

- She can accept the status quo, in which women are largely excluded from the historical record, are feature only as characters of mythology.
- Alternatively, she can attempt to change things.

The poet's choice in this matter is clear: 'I have chosen'. She is no longer willing to accept the exclusion of women from the historical record. She is no longer content for history to be composed by men who are writing about men for the eyes of other men.

Instead, she will herself become a historian of sorts, in her poems essays and other texts. She will be a 'part of [the] ordeal' of Irish history with all its 'darkness', engaging with that troubled past in a new and more focused manner. She will write her own version of history, one that focuses on women and women's experience. She will tell the stories of at least some of the women previously excluded from the historical record.

The poet uses a wonderful phrase to describe this decision, saying that she is moving from myth into history: 'Out of myth into history I move'. The poet, we sense, feels that she's moving between two worlds, between two different phases of being, as she embarks on this new phase of her writing life.

IRELAND: MYTH AND HISTORY

Due to this new engagement with history, the poet experiences a sudden emotional connection with Ireland's past. She is suddenly aware of the 'darkness' of Irish history. It is 'only now', she says that this darkness is finally 'reaching' her, it is only now that she realises the true extent of the suffering that her countrymen and countrywomen endured over the centuries.

She becomes conscious, as we noted above, that the Irish landscape is filled or 'clotted' with the remains of the dead, with the countless generations of Irish people who went before. She wishes there was something she could do for her dead fellow countrymen and women.

This desire is represented by an extremely powerful image. The poet imagines herself kneeling beside these departed Irish people, comforting them as they pass away: 'How slowly they die/ as we kneel beside them'. She imagines whispering to them, easing their passage as they take their last breaths: 'we … whisper in their ear'.

But all this, alas, is completely impossible. No one possesses a device that will allow us to go back and comfort those who are already dead. We are 'always too late' to provide such consolation.

What we can do, however, is keep their memories alive. Of course, we can't do this for every deceased Irish person. But we can tell and retell the stories of some of those people. We can recount the tales not only of famous generals and politicians but also of ordinary people who made a contribution to their own communities. By doing so, we can ensure that their memories survive, that their lives and deaths won't have been in vain.

This Moment

LINE BY LINE

The poem describes an ordinary street or neighbourhood. Night is falling: 'A neighbourhood. At dusk'. A light is on in one of the houses, making the window seem 'yellow as butter'. There is a tree that looks 'black' in the falling darkness: 'One tree is black'. This seems like a quiet and uneventful scene. It strikes us as peaceful but also maybe a little dull. There seems to be little that is dramatic or engaging taking place.

- The poet, however, assures us that 'Things are getting ready/ to happen/ out of sight'.
- Moths lurk in the street's hidden places, preparing for flight. When it gets dark enough, they will emerge and flutter through the neighbourhood.

- The stars, too, are 'out of sight' for the moment. But when it gets dark enough, they will suddenly become visible in the sky above the neighbourhood.
- The poet also mentions apples that hang hidden in the tree's branches. She beautifully describes how the apples' skins curve or slant around the sweet inner flesh: 'rinds slanting around fruit'.
- Stars are preparing to shine, apples are ripening and moths are getting ready to fly. But it is as if nothing will really happen until the poet has found her missing daughter: 'But not yet'. Line 8, then, brings a sense of suspense and tension to the poem. It represents a pause or moment of calm before the action commences.

Then somewhere in the neighbourhood a child runs into a woman's arms. (It is generally presumed that the woman is the child's mother.) As if triggered by this event, the moths, stars and flowers finally act. We're told that the stars 'rise', suggesting they suddenly become visible in the darkening sky. The moths leave their hiding places and begin to 'flutter' through the neighbourhood. The apples hanging from the trees' branches 'sweeten', suggesting that they advance a stage toward ripeness and maturity.

THEMES

SUBURBAN LIFE

The idea of the suburbs and suburban living is one that recurs often in Boland's poetry.

Suburbs have seldom been regarded as offering much in the way of inspiration to the writer or artist. Suburbia is generally regarded as a place of humdrum family life, lacking both the energy and excitement of the city and the natural beauty of the countryside.

In this poem, however, Boland attempts to rediscover the suburbs as a site of artistic inspiration. She shows that beauty, magic and inspiration can be found in even the most humdrum neighbourhood or housing estate: moths fluttering through the dark, fruit ripening, a child running into a woman's arms, the stars flickering in the evening sky. The poem suggests that even a window that is filled with light from the room behind it is a beautiful sight: 'One window is yellow as butter'.

The poem demonstrates that even the most banal and comfortable housing estate can provide the impetus for art and

writing, Such places can seem dull and boring on the surface, but there are always things happening 'out of sight'. 'This Moment' shows that this ordinary place, with its humble, everyday events could be a source of wonder and delight, if only we took the time to appreciate it.

MOTHERHOOD

Mothers play a vitally important role in most of our lives, raising us from helpless children to responsible adults. Alas, all too often the work of mothers goes unappreciated and uncelebrated, their unstinting efforts taking place 'out of sight'.

This poem, however, presents a world in which nature itself celebrates motherhood and the work that mothers do. The poem focuses on three different aspects of the natural world: stars, apples and moths. Each is preparing to do something. However, they hold off on taking action as if they are waiting for some signal or command: 'But not yet'. Only when the mother picks up the child do they swing into action. It almost seems as if the mother's love inspires the rising of the stars , the fluttering of the moths and the sweetening of the apples.

Their actions seem almost a tribute to the mother in the poem. It's as if they celebrate her daily work of nurture by waiting until 'this moment', until this everyday instant of motherly care and affection. The poem, then, presents a world where even the stars themselves pay tribute to the role of this particular mother and by extension to mothers everywhere. Even the apples choose this moment to advance another stage toward ripeness. All in all, then, by showing us how motherhood is connected with other 'ordinary' marvels, including the stars and the changing world of nature, this poem reminds us of how often mothers and their work are taken for granted in our everyday lives.

The Pomegranate

1

This poem takes inspiration from the Greek legend of Ceres, who was the goddess of fertility, and her daughter, Persephone. Hades, ruler of the dead, fell in love with Persephone. One day, while she was out picking flowers, he kidnapped her and carried her off to his underworld realm, which Boland refers to as 'hell'. Persephone, then, became 'a daughter lost in hell'.

Ceres was shocked to discover that Persephone had gone missing. Distraught, she wandered the earth, searching everywhere for her missing daughter. In her distress, she neglected her duties as goddess of fertility, so that nothing grew and the entire world fell into a never-ending winter of barrenness and famine.

Finally, Ceres tracked Persephone down to Hades' underground kingdom. Hades was persuaded by Jupiter, king of the gods, to let Persephone go. But there was a catch. The laws of the gods stated that if you ate anything while in the underworld you had to remain there forever. And it emerged that Persephone, during her captivity, had eaten six pomegranate seeds.

Eventually, a compromise was reached. Persephone would spend six months of each year above ground with her mother, and six months in the underworld with Hades, a month for each seed that she consumed.

According to the legend, these events explain the origins of the seasons. For six months of the year, while Persephone is in her company, Ceres is overjoyed. She causes plants to flourish and crops to grow. But for the other six months, while Persephone is in the underworld, Ceres is distraught. And in her distress, she cancels all growth and flourishing, letting the world's plant-life wither.

2

The poet has always felt a deep connection to this myth. In fact she says that it's the 'only legend' she has ever 'loved', the only one that ever affected her on a personal and emotional level.

The poet first read the story when she was a child. At that time, she was living in London, having been taken there with her family when her father was appointed Irish ambassador to the United Kingdom. The young poet missed Ireland terribly during her time in London. She felt that she was a 'child in exile', that she'd been cut off from her homeland and was forbidden, at least for the time being, to return.

In one of her essays, Boland recalls the sense of disorientation that came with this move: 'I had no choice…One morning I was woken before dawn, dressed in a pink cardigan and skirt, put in a car, taken to an airport. I was five … hardly anything else that happened to me as a child was as important as this: that I left one country and came to another. That an ordinary displacement made an extraordinary distance between the word *place* and the word *mine*.'

To the young poet, London seemed like a hostile, alien environment. She describes it as a 'city of fogs', suggesting its murky and polluted air. As she puts it in her essay: 'But the vista was almost always, that first winter anyway, of a yellow fog … If you went into the street, you entered a muddled and frightening mime … The lights of buses loomed up suddenly. All I knew of the country was this city; all I knew of this city was its fog'. London's people, too, seemed very foreign, their accents filled with 'strange' consonants that she found harsh and unnerving.

It was during this time in London that the poet first read the story of Ceres and Persephone. She immediately felt an intense identification with the character of Persephone: 'I read it first and at first I was/ an exiled child in the crackling dusk of/the underworld'. There are several reason for this feeling of affinity:

- The young poet felt that she, like Persephone, was an 'exiled child'. Persephone, in the story, was exiled to the underworld. Similarly, the young poet, as we've seen, felt that she'd been exiled to the city of London.
- The young poet felt that both she and Persephone were trapped in gloomy, dreary environments. Persephone was forced to reside in the gloom of the underworld with its permanent 'crackling dusk'. The young poet, meanwhile, was forced to reside in the gloom of London with all its smogs and fogs.
- Trapped in the underworld, Persephone was unable to see the stars. Trapped in London, the young poet was also unable to see the stars. (This, no doubt, was due to a combination of smog and light pollution).

The comparison of London to the underworld is both inventive and unexpected. It brilliantly captures the dimness and pollution of London in the post-war period when the the smog sometimes grew so intense that the entire city was shut down. The comparison also suggests how a young girl from Ireland might have been unnerved and overwhelmed by this sprawling metropolis, having been transplanted there, suddenly and unwillingly, from the relative quiet of her native Dublin.

3

The story of Ceres and Persephone continued to resonate with the poet as the years went by. She recalls one particular moment when the legend seemed especially relevant. The poet, by this time, had a young daughter of her own and was living in the Dublin suburbs.

She recalls one particular summer's evening when her daughter was playing in the housing estate where they lived. The daughter's bedtime arrived, but she didn't return home. The poet grew concerned and went out to look for her: 'I walked out in a summer twilight/ searching for my daughter at bed-time'. Eventually, she managed to locate her daughter, who came running into her arms as she approached. The poet's relief is indicated by the fcat that she 'carried her' back home.

Years earlier, in London, the poet had identified with the character Persephone. On this occasion, however, she identified with the character Ceres: 'I was Ceres then'. After all, the poet's daughter had gone missing, just like the daughter of Ceres in the legend. And, like Ceres, she had wandered out in search of her lost child.

Winter, for Ceres, meant the loss of her daughter for another six months. The poet realised she too would eventually face her own winter, that, sooner or later, her own daughter would slip away as she began to live a life of her own. The poet, then, realised that 'winter was in store' not only for the plants that filled the housing estate but also for her.

4

The poem's focus shifts to the present day. The poet's daughter, now a teenager, is asleep in her bedroom. The poet goes upstairs and looks in at her: 'I climb the stairs and stand where I can see/ my child asleep'. Next to the daughter's bed are some 'teen magazines,/ her can of Coke' and a 'plate of uncut fruit'.

The fruit reminds the poet of the pomegranate that played such an important role in the story of Ceres and Persephone. She imagines how miserable and frightened Persephone must have been, having been whisked away, against her will, to Hades' underground domain. She imagines the underworld as a vast cavern, referring to it as 'the place of death', because it was filled with the spirits of those who had passed on. She imagines this terrified young girl, overcome with hunger, reaching out for one of the pomegranates that grew in that bleak place: 'she reached/ out a hand and plucked a pomegranate'.

And this, of course, was the crucial moment. For if Persephone hadn't eaten the seeds the story would have had a very different ending. She could have returned home forever and wouldn't have had to spend six months of each year confined to the underworld: 'She could have come home and been safe/ and ended the story'.

5

In the poem, when the poet looks in on her daughter, the daughter is still a teenager. Until now, she has lived under her mother's roof and has been sheltered from the harsher realities of life. But all too soon, in at most a few short years, she will be a young adult.

- The poet considers the fruit at the daughter's bedside table. This symbolises the painful knowledge and experience that she will acquire as she matures into adulthood.
- Eventually, the daughter will wake up and eat the fruit at her bedside. This symbolises the fact that the daughter must eventually leave the comfort of her parents' house and make her own way in the world. By doing so, she will acquire knowledge and experience, along with all the 'grief' that they bring.
- The poet feels that she could prevent her daughter from eating the fruit: 'I could warn her. There is still a chance'. This symbolises the poet's desire to keep her daughter to at home forever, thereby avoiding such painful knowledge and experience of the outside world.
- Or maybe the poet simply wants to 'defer' her daughter's departure. Maybe she wants to keep her daughter at home – safe and sound – for another while, so that her innocence, at least for a few more years, will remain intact.

Eating the pomegranate in the underworld brought disaster to Persephone. Eating the fruit – or acquiring the knowledge and experience it symbolizes – will bring disaster to the poet's sleeping daughter. Such experience, inevitably, will bring with it heartbreak and loss. She will, inevitably, realise how painful the world beyond her mother's house can be.

The poet knows that once you leave your parents' house, it can never truly be your home again. You have to forge your own path, find your own accommodation. She realises, then, that once her daughter makes her own way in the world, she can never truly come back.

And this, of course, echoes the story of Persephone who, even after she was 'found and rescued' in the underworld, was allowed only a partial return to her mother's house.

The poet, as we've seen, dwells on the hunger that Persephone must have experienced in the underworld, noting that 'even in the place of death … a child can be hungry'. This, no doubt, reflects her worries about her own daughter, the fear that her daughter might experience poverty or want or hunger once she leaves the shelter of the family home.

The poet paints a fascinating picture of the world beyond the shelter of her home. This, she says, 'is another world'. It is not, of course, the hellish underworld where Persephone was exiled. But nor is it the world in which the poet herself grew up. Instead, it is a modern world of constant and bewildering change. Innovations like the 'cars and cable television' that are part of life in their suburb are, of course, extremely useful. But technology also has dangerous, unnerving aspects. And the poet, alas, will not be able to protect her daughter from these forces.

The dangers of this modern world, in which the daughter must make her own way, are symbolised by the unpleasant conditions outside their home:

- The poet emphasises the fact that it is winter and that a 'cold' rain is falling.
- The stars are 'hidden' or 'veiled' by cloud, which suggests that the night is very dark.
- Even the hard, 'flint-coloured' road of the housing estate suggests the harsh lessons that the daughter will have to learn.

MOTHERHOOD

'The Pomegranate' powerfully conveys the fears and uncertainties that come with motherhood. Such anxiety is evident in the poet's description of that long-ago 'summer twilight' when her daughter failed to come on time. We can imagine the poet growing more anxious, perhaps even panicking, as she walks around the housing estate where they lived, desperately searching for her missing daughter.

The poem also highlights the willingness of mothers to do absolutely anything in their power to protect their children, to avoid losing them. In the legend that inspired the poem, Ceres made a terrible bargain with Hades, coming to an agreement that her daughter would spend six months of each year with her and six months in the underworld. The sense of desperation that Ceres would have felt then must also have been experienced by the poet on the evening her daughter went missing. By the time she located her daughter, she was ready to do literally anything, – to 'make any bargain' – in order to avoid losing her again.

The strains of motherhood are also evident in the poem's present-day setting, when the poet looks in upon her sleeping child. The poet, as we've seen, wants to shelter her daughter from knowledge and experience of the adult world, with all the 'grief' it brings.

But the poet ultimately realises that such experience is not only a 'grief' but also a 'gift'. She realises that her daughter needs to make her own way in the world, overcoming life's hardships along the way. If the poet defers or delays 'the grief' associated with such experience, she will 'diminish the gift' of living.

This is symbolised when she decides to let her daughter eat the fruit on her bedside. She will issue no warning: 'I will say nothing'. Instead, she will let her daughter reach out, touch the fruit's 'papery skin' and place it 'to her lips'.

'The Pomegranate', then, is in part a poem about how motherhood involves letting go. The poet decides that she will not prevent her daughter from setting out into the real world, with all its painful knowledge and experience, with all its challenges and triumphs.

Using a wonderful metaphor, the poet tells us that she can at any time 'enter' the legend of Ceres and Persephone. This of course emphasises her strong sense of identification with the story. When she thinks about the story the poet feels as if she is somehow participating in its events.

The metaphor also suggests how the story has provided the poet with succour and consolation throughout her life, ever since she was a five-year-old girl in London. She knows the legend so well that she can recite it to herself 'anywhere' and relate it to her own experiences and emotions.

Now she will pass the tale on to her daughter: 'The legend will be hers as well as mine'. She hopes that her daughter, too, will view this ancient tale as a source of consolation and wisdom, especially when she finds herself confronted by life's inevitable heartbreaks and disappointments.

THE SUBJUGATION OF WOMEN

It's worth noting that Hades, Persephone's abductor, is never mentioned in the poem. (In fact, no male characters are mentioned). But it was his violent act that set the whole story in motion, that led to Persephone becoming 'lost in hell', trapped in that stony 'place of death'. And it was his 'blackmail' that ensured she would have to spend half of each year in that dismal realm.

We should also be aware that in some versions of the story Hades not only abducts but also rapes Persephone. And in others he tricks her into eating the pomegranate seeds, ensuring that she will never be truly free of his clutches.

Hades' predatory behavior, then, haunts the entire poem. The poet is fully aware that such behaviours exist in the real world and that women are all too often subject to such violence and harassment. No doubt, such awareness informs the fear that the poet experiences when she thinks about her daughter leaving behind the family home and making her own way in the world.

Love

LINE BY LINE

GOLDEN MEMORIES OF IOWA

Some time ago, the poet worked for a while in Iowa City, which is in the American Midwest. She lived there with her husband and their infant children. Many years have passed. The speaker has returned to visit Iowa and goes for a walk at twilight, as 'Dark falls on this mid-western town'. She comes upon a bridge that is difficult to make out in the fading light: 'Dusk has hidden the bridge in the river'. She realises that she's in an area of town near where she and her husband used to live: 'Not far from here is our old apartment'.

The period in Iowa seems to have been a golden one in the poet's marriage. She has fond and very vivid memories of their stay, which come flooding back as she crosses the bridge. She remembers many little details of the apartment in which they lived at that time: the view from its windows, its kitchen and its Amish table. (The Amish are a reclusive religious community in North America, known among other things for manufacturing beautiful objects.)

During that special time, the love between the poet and her husband was so intense that it resembled a physical presence in their home. Love, she says, 'had come to live with us'. She depicts love as an angel or a cupid, as a muscular male figure with feathered wings: 'And we discovered there/ love had the feather and muscle of wings'. She later describes it as 'formidable', suggesting its great strength.

This poem refers to the great hero Aeneas, who according to legend fought in the Trojan War and founded what would become the city of Rome. In one of his many adventures, Aeneas travelled down into the land of the dead, here referred to as 'hell'. To access the underworld, he crossed the mythical River Styx, becoming one of the few living people to do so.
As he travelled through the land of the dead, Aeneas encountered the souls of his fallen comrades. They attempted to speak with him, to hear news of what was happening above in the land of the living. However, these dead souls were forbidden from communicating with their still-living former comrade. When they opened their mouths to speak with him, no words came out. As the poet puts it: 'and when the hero/ was hailed by his comrades in hell/ their mouths opened and their voices failed'.

This strange creature spent a period of time 'at rest' in their home and wenever they looked at it they experienced 'ascension', a type of happiness, joy or ecstasy: 'it offered us ascension/ even to look at him'. The poet, of course, isn't suggesting that this actually happened. She isn't saying that this weird winged being actually turned up in their apartment. Rather, she is using personification to convey the depth and strength of the emotions that she and her husband felt at that time.

The couple's time in Iowa wasn't all sweetness and light, however. While they lived there, one of their two young children became seriously ill. Indeed, the poet tells us that the unfortunate child 'was touched by death in this town'. Thankfully, however, the infant survived the illness and was 'spared'.

A CHANGED RELATIONSHIP

It is a long time now since that period in Iowa. However, the poet's marriage has endured. She and her husband still love each other: 'I am your wife … We love each other still'. They still communicate well with one another: 'we speak plainly. We hear each other clearly'. Of course there are occasionally 'distances' between them. But these are merely the 'day-to-day and ordinary distances' that affect any long-term relationship. Overall, their marriage is still strong.

Yet the poet is forced to acknowledge that their relationship has lost some of the intensity it had when they lived in Iowa. Their current 'day-to-day and ordinary' relationship is fine, but it cannot compare to the magic that flourished all those years ago. She wonders if she and her husband will ever again experience love and life in such an intense and vivid manner: 'Will we ever live so intensely again?/ Will love ever come to us again?' She longs to somehow return to those glory days and experience her husband as he was all those years ago: 'And yet I want to return to you … as you were'.

A VISION ON THE BRIDGE

As the speaker crosses the bridge she has a strange experience. She is struck by an exceptionally vivid memory of her husband as he used to be. She remembers him when he was young, crossing this very bridge with 'snow on the shoulders' of his coat. This memory seems so incredibly vivid that the speaker can almost see her young husband before her on the dusk-shrouded bridge.

- She imagines this vision of her young husband as the great hero Aeneas: 'I see you as a hero in a text'.
- She thinks here of the ancient manuscripts in which Aeneas's story was first written down, of scrolls with 'blazing' illustrations and 'gilded', or golden, edges.
- She imagines this ordinary Iowa waterway transforming into the River Styx, becoming 'the water/ the hero crossed on his way to hell'. The river's waters start to 'slide,' which suggests it that it became slick and dangerous. It 'deepens', suggesting it acquired treacherous reaches that one might associate with the mythical Styx.
- She imagines her present-day self as one of Aeneas's companions in the underworld.

- She longs to reach out, to communicate with this strange vision of her young husband.
- But she can no more talk to this memory than the souls of the dead could talk to Aeneas when he visited the underworld. Her 'words are shadows', which he cannot understand or even hear: 'you cannot hear me'.
- She wants to walk with this vision of her young husband through the town's darkening streets. But she can no more follow this memory than the souls of the dead could follow Aeneas out of the underworld: 'You walk away and I cannot follow'.

THEMES

LOVE AND MARRIAGE

'Love' provides a powerful depiction of a relationship at its most intense. When the speaker and her husband lived in Iowa, the love between them was so passionate and vibrant that it seemed almost like a physical presence in their home: 'love … had come to live with us'. The love they shared was so strong and 'formidable' that even to contemplate it filled them with ecstasy: 'it offered us ascension'.

The poem could also be regarded as the story of how even the most intense emotions fade over time, as the couple's relationship no longer reaches the heights of epic intensity that it did in Iowa all those years ago. The speaker wonders:,'Will we ever live so intensely again?'

The poem, then, reflects the sad fact that in any marriage or long-term relationship it is difficult to maintain the same level of passion year after year.

An interesting feature of this poem is that the past is associated with the living, whereas the present is associated with the dead. Usually, it is the other way around. The poet depicts her long-gone youthful husband as a living hero and her present-day self as a ghostly dead companion, whose words are inaudible 'shadows'. The past, then, is depicted as more intense, real and vivid than the present. She wonders if her life and her marriage will ever regain this intensity : 'Will we ever live so intensely again?'. Indeed, this is the great 'epic' or central question that haunts her in the poem.

Yet the poem also celebrates how marriages endure and survive over long periods. The couple's passion may have faded in intensity, and their lives may be more 'day-to-day and ordinary'. But the poet and her husband 'love each other still'. They still communicate well: 'we speak plainly. We hear each other clearly'. The poem, then, celebrates how even after years of togetherness, a husband and wife continue to offer one another support, understanding and companionship.

FAMILY: MYTH AND HISTORY

This poem deals with the power of memory. It shows how, when we revisit a place where we used to live, the memories come flooding back. We remember even trivial or seemingly insignificant details: a kitchen with an Amish table, for example.

The poem also shows how memory can sometimes play tricks on us, how something or someone long gone can suddenly appear before us in a way that seems vividly real. The poet, for instance, thinks she sees her young husband crossing the bridge. Maybe she has spotted a stranger in a coat similar to that worn by her husband all those years ago. Or perhaps this 'vision' is caused by a combination of the falling darkness and the memories that her return has brought flooding back.

Perhaps, then, the dominant emotion in 'Love' is that of nostalgia. We sense that the poet longs to follow this vision of her young husband through the darkening Iowa streets. She is filled with longing for that golden period in her life, for the time when her relationship with her husband was at its most intense. She would love to somehow recover this lost era, to live those days all over again and experience her husband as he was during that unique and special time: 'I want to return to you … as you were'.

However, there can be no going back. It's simply impossible to relive earlier periods of our lives, no matter how much we might like to. And we can never experience the ones we love as they were in past times or previous incarnations.. The poet's use of Aeneas's story wonderfully illustrates this tragic point. The poet cannot interact with this memory of her young husband, just as Aeneas's companions couldn't interact with him as he journeyed through the underworld.

Paul Durcan

Themes

Romantic Love

Both 'Nessa' and 'The Girl with the Keys to Pearse's Cottage' depict the poet falling in love with imposing and beautiful young women. This latter poem wonderfully captures the intensity and passion of teenage love. The poet is clearly smitten by the striking young Cáit and lovingly describes her sallow complexion, her dark hair and her bright smile. We almost get the impression that he'd hang around Patrick Pearse's former cottage waiting for her to appear so he could bask in her dark beauty. Though years have passed, he still fondly looks back to this youthful crush, and even today bitterly regrets that she was forced to emigrate.

'Nessa' is different in that a relationship actually develops between the poet and the object of his affection. The poem highlights the heady excitement that so often marks the beginning of a new relationship. The poet and his lover spontaneously leave behind the wedding party, go swimming in the sea and lie together in a field on the way back. We sense the energy and passion of this first meeting, the exhilaration and elation that must fill them as they begin to fall in love.

Yet the poem also deals with what might be described as love's darker side. The poet might feel excitement on this first meeting, but he feels like his life's spinning dangerously out of control. He compares this sensation to that of falling down a well or being sucked in by a whirlpool. It's as if the poet is keenly aware of how falling in love leaves us exposed and vulnerable, how it costs us a great deal of control over our own lives.

Marriage

Durcan's poetry typically avoids an idealistic or fairytale view of marriage. Instead, his poems tend to be honest about the difficulty and conflict that lie at the heart of many marriages. 'Father's Day, 21 June 1992' is especially moving in this regard, highlighting the difficulties that often arise when a couple have been married for a long time: how sexual passion fades, how traits and habits become annoying over time, how the very presence of one's spouse can become suffocating.

Other poems pick up this theme. 'The MacBride Dynasty' documents how the marriage between Maud Gonne and Major John MacBride ended in recrimination and betrayal, leaving bitterness that still lingers within the extended family decades

later. In 'Windfall', relations between the poet and his wife break down and he is forced to leave the beloved house in Cork where they had forged so many treasured memories. Yet surely the relationship presented in 'Wife Who Smashed Television Gets Jail' is the most dysfunctional of all. The husband, it seems, is absorbed in his TV shows to such an extent that relations between him and his wife have completely broken down, so much so that his wife reacts by smashing in the screen.

Yet Durcan is never black and white, and his work also frequently highlights the positive side of marriage. 'The Difficulty that is Marriage', despite its title, depicts how, for the poet, marriage is the one thing that makes life bearable. Despite their many differences, the poet loves his wife deeply. He cannot believe his luck that this woman came into his life and fell in love with him: 'How was it I was so lucky to have ever met you?' ''Windfall', 8 Parnell Hill, Cork' shows how for many years the poet and his wife enjoyed a contented relationship. Durcan describes moments of bliss as he relaxes by the window and his wife reclines on the couch smoking and 'Knitting a bright-coloured scarf'. Married life seems to have afforded the poet an opportunity to be at peace with himself and the world.

'The Arnolfini Marriage' offers another positive – though enigmatic – portrayal of marriage. The poet imagines the 'plurality' of marriage as being of great significance to the couple depicted in the painting. They are particularly proud of their ability to say 'we' now that they are married, and seem to hold the poet in contempt for being single: 'Imagine being able to say 'we'.' There is a suggestion here that it is the proper condition of man and woman to be married, and that having achieved this the couple now feel more content: 'The most relaxing word in our vocabulary is 'we'.'

Family

A family, Durcan suggests again and again, is a network of connections that stretches across the generations, one that provides individuals with a sense of support, meaning and belonging. Both 'Rosie Joyce' and 'The MacBride Dynasty' offer just such a positive view of family and belonging. 'Rosie Joyce' highlights how the arrival of a new baby can fill an entire family with joy. Rosie's birth has a profound effect on the poet himself, relieving the terrible depression that has dominated his life for the past three years. 'The MacBride Dynasty', too, highlights the great pleasure extended families take in new additions to the fold. The poet's mother is filled with 'motherly pride' over her 'walking, talking little boy',

and is eager to 'show off' this 'latest addition to the extended family'. His great-aunt Maud, too, takes great pleasure in seeing 'the children of the family'.

"Windfall', 8 Parnell Hill, Cork' is a celebration that focuses more on the immediate, or nuclear, family. The poet leafs through photograph albums and is 'exhilarated' as he remembers the many shared moments and adventures that he, his wife and his children have enjoyed together over the years. The poem also suggests that each family is a complex unit that can only ever be properly understood by its own members.

'Wife Who Smashed Television Gets Jail' highlights the negative impact technology can have on these intimate family bonds. Increasingly, family members relate to screens rather than to each other. These screens have insinuated themselves into our lives and living rooms to such an extent that they function almost as extra members of the family.

Durcan's poetry also highlights the terrible loneliness that can arise when family bonds break down or become less intense and relevant over time. The title of the poem 'Father's Day, 21 June 1992' is significant as, in an important sense, the poet is no longer required to function in a father's role. He still has daughters, of course, but they are 'grown up and gone away'. "Windfall', 8 Parnell Hill, Cork' also touches on such loneliness. It depicts how the poet had to leave the family home in Cork and return alone to Dublin, which now felt to him like an 'alien, foreign city'.

'Sport' too focuses on how the bonds of family can break down, highlighting a bitter personality clash between father and son. The young poet was a sensitive, talented and artistic individual. But to his father these traits meant nothing. The father regarded his son's only success as playing on a 'winning team' for Grangegorman Mental Hospital: 'In your eyes I had achieved something at last'. 'Madman' touches on a similar theme, highlighting how difficult it must have been to live with his father's increasingly volatile personality.

Ireland and Irish History

Durcan is a poet well known for his criticisms of Ireland and Irish society. This is especially evident in 'The Girl With the Keys to Pearse's Cottage'. The poem shows how Ireland in 1960 was a country that had failed, that was wracked with economic stagnation, and that had to watch thousands of its young people emigrate. The poet describes himself as being 'here in the dark', suggesting that he viewed the Ireland of the day as a dark, tormented place that had 'no future'. There is a real tone of sorrow, despair and rage in the poem's final stanza, where the poet vocally addresses young Cáit Killann, lamenting her forced departure from her homeland.

Pearse dreamed of an Ireland that would 'cherish all the children of the nation equally'. In 'Windfall', however, Durcan witnesses and criticises a society that is shockingly unequal, where some of the great citizens are 'homeless', while some of the 'worst' are allowed to build and live in 'ugly' and monstrous houses: 'the worst/ Erect block-house palaces – self-regardingly ugly'. In modern Ireland, Pearse's dream of a fair and equal society seems little more than a cruel joke, for this is a land where 'all the children/ Are not cherished equally'. Those close to the centre of power grow wealthy while the rest go wanting.

Inequality also features in 'Rosie Joyce'. This poem takes the form of a journey from east to west, and it highlights the economic differences between Ireland's eastern and western halves. As the poet crosses the Shannon, the traditional 'Great Divide' between the two regions, the poet remembers his father lamenting the west of Ireland's impoverished status and how its people were forced to move east (to Dublin or to England) in search of work: 'We are the people of the West,/ Our fate to go East'.

While many of Durcan's poems focus on the evils of poverty, 'Ireland 2002' deals with the dangers of sudden wealth. We can read the poem as criticising the vulgar and conspicuous consumption that was evident in the country during Ireland's economic boom of the 2000s. 'Rosie Joyce', however, takes a longer view of Ireland and Irish history, one that presents such shifts in social and economic status as ultimately irrelevant. Durcan looks back into geological time, into the millions of years it took for the landscape itself to form. The poem describes this great cycle of nature as a 'higher power than politics'. Kings, politicians and dictators, conflicts, wars and peace treaties – all of these have come and gone and will come and go again.

Yet the Irish landscape with its flora, fauna and people remains and will remain after all such power-grabs have long ago been forgotten. Durcan ultimately celebrates the fact that Ireland is plural rather than uniform, that it consists of wildly varied people and places, and hopes it'll stay like this forever: 'No such thing, Rosie, as a Uniform Ireland/ And please God there never will be'.

Mental Suffering

Again and again, Durcan's poems deal with individuals in various states of mental torment:

- In 'Rosie Joyce' the poet confesses that for three years he has suffered terribly from depression. He describes how he's been 'subsisting' or surviving rather than really living; the phrase 'slums of despair' brilliantly captures the misery he's suffered.
- 'Sport', too, deals with individuals in extreme mental distress, providing a bleakly humorous insight into the psychological ailments afflicting the Mullingar mental-hospital football team.
- In 'Father's Day, 21 June 1992', the poet is wracked with guilt, as he blames himself for the dimming of his wife's affections: 'It's a killer, this guilt'.
- The final stanza of 'Nessa', meanwhile, contains several powerful images that remind us of the doubts and insecurities that all too often arise in even the most loving of relationships.
- 'Windfall' describes the terrible homesickness that arises when the home you long to return to is no longer there.
- 'En Famille, 1979' highlights the traumatic early experiences encountered in the 'dark school' of childhood.

Religion

Durcan is somewhat unusual among modern poets in that he remains what can only be described as a spiritual or even religious writer. His work is sometimes critical of organised religion, deploying dark humour to underscore what he perceives to be the unhealthy and repressive aspects of the Church's teaching. Yet he retains something of the Christian faith many of his fellow poets have long abandoned.

'Rosie Joyce', too, features such an emphasis on religion and spirituality. It can be read as one long prayer of thanksgiving and celebration in which the poet thanks God for the safe arrival of his granddaughter. We see this at the poem's conclusion when the poet declares, 'Thank You, O Lord, for the Descent of Rosie onto Earth'.

'The Difficulty that is Marriage' has an unusual take on religion and the afterlife. The poet is no atheist or 'brave pagan' and clings to the belief that heaven's 'changeless kingdom' awaits us after death. However, he would much rather live for eternity on this troubled earth with his wife than in such a place of endless bliss.

'Six Nuns Die in Convent Inferno' highlights both the ridiculous and the sublime aspects of religious belief:

- The poem focuses on the enormous self-sacrifice of religious vocation. The speaker describes the 'exotic loneliness' of being an nun, mentioning how she had to relinquish the things that many young girls dream about – the prospect of falling in love and getting married, of having a family and a home of her own.
- The poem suggests that religious faith is something that is all but impossible to explain and rationalise. The speaker's decision to become a nun is described as 'the weirdest thing a woman can do' and she finds it hard to explain the sacrifices she has made: 'All for why and for what?'
- Those who have strong religious faith are likened to a group that exists on the fringes of society, much like the punks that the speaker passes on Grafton Street. The nun considers herself to be the 'ultimate drop-out', a true 'delinquent' and 'subversive'.
- The poem also touches on how religious faith provides great comfort. The nun greets the moment of her death with great calmness.
- This is another poem where Durcan seems to cling to a belief in the afterlife. However, the poem seems to highlight how absurd such a notion is in the modern world. In the second part of the poem Durcan describes a somewhat farcical and bizarre scene, with the six nuns hiding under a bandstand in the park.

Nessa

LINE BY LINE

STANZAS 1 TO 3

The poet remembers how he first met Nessa O'Neill, the woman who would become his wife. The couple were introduced at the wedding of Patrick Kavanagh, a great Irish poet. This event took place on 1 August 1968 at the Shangri-La Hotel, which was located in Dalkey, County Dublin: 'I met her on the first of August/ In the Shangri-La Hotel'. We can imagine their eyes meeting across the hustle and bustle of the wedding celebration.

Because the couple are by the sea in summertime, they decide to leave the wedding reception and go for a swim: 'I hopped into the Irish Sea'. On their way back to the hotel, they lie down together in a field: 'On the way back I fell in the field/ And she fell down beside me'. Perhaps they kissed and embraced, or merely lay together in the summer sunshine. He describes how he could have happily lain beside her in the field for the rest of his life: 'I'd have lain in the grass with her all my life/ With Nessa'.

The poet, then, is clearly immediately smitten with Nessa; he feels intoxicated, out of control, overcome by emotion. He uses a wonderful metaphor to capture these sensations, describing how Nessa 'took me by the index finger/ And dropped me in her well'. These lines powerfully suggest his sense of being out of control, of falling helplessly toward something new and unknown. This is reinforced by the refrain that occurs in some form at the end of each stanza: 'And that was a whirlpool, that was a whirlpool,/ And I very nearly drowned.' The refrain shows how the intensity of the poet's feelings is almost too much for him to bear; he feels as if he's losing himself or drowning in emotion.

Nessa is portrayed as an energetic, carefree and spontaneous young woman. She seems confident and self-assured as she takes the lead in her budding relationship with the poet: 'She took me by the index finger'. It's she who suggests they leave the party and go for a swim together: 'Take off your pants, she said to me … Would you care to swim? she said to me'. When the poet tumbles in the field, she's quick to advance their courtship by lying down beside him.

STANZA 4

That was then and this is now. The poem was published in book form in 1975, seven years after the couple first met. Its final stanza clearly takes place sometime after that memorable first meeting, shifting from the past to present tense. The poet and Nessa are still together. However, at this time the poet's feelings about their relationship are fraught with uncertainty, dread and desperation. Perhaps their relationship has taken a turn for the worse, entering a rocky period. Or perhaps the poet feels for some reason that Nessa might be about to leave him. Or perhaps he simply feels insecure – aware of how vulnerable love makes us, of the devastation he'll feel if Nessa chooses to leave him.

The poet uses images from their first meeting to describe his current dark state of mind. He describes himself languishing on the rocks of Dalkey, from which he and Nessa went swimming on the day they first met. This hard and desolate shoreline serves as a powerful metaphor for his bleak mental state. He pictures himself swimming in the Irish Sea, just as he and Nessa did at their first meeting. He imagines himself in trouble in the water, the waves that threaten to drown him serving as another powerful metaphor for his distressed mental state.

He pleads with Nessa to relieve the feelings of dread and uncertainty that grip him regarding their relationship. He asks her to 'stay with [him] on the rocks', to promise herself to him and to relieve his fear and insecurity. He asks her to 'come for [him] into the Irish Sea' as if he longs for her to rescue him from the waves of doubt and dread that threaten to overwhelm his mind.

THEMES

ROMANTIC LOVE

In some respects 'Nessa' highlights the heady excitement that so often marks the beginning of a new relationship. The poet and his lover spontaneously leave behind the wedding party, go swimming in the sea and lie together in a field on the way back. We sense the energy and passion of this first meeting, the exhilaration and elation that must fill them as they begin to fall in love.

Yet the poem also deals with what might be described as love's darker side. The poet might feel excitement on this first meeting, but he feels like his life's spinning dangerously out of control. He compares this sensation to that of falling down a well or being sucked into a whirlpool. It's as if the poet is keenly aware of how falling in love leaves us exposed and vulnerable, how it costs us a great deal of control over our own lives.

This is especially evident in the poem's final stanza, where the poet seems gripped with fear and uncertainty about the status of his relationship with Nessa. We get the distinct sense that he fears for the relationship's future, and worries whether Nessa

still loves him with the same intensity. The images of the poet languishing on the rocks, drowning in the Irish Sea and riding in the dust-wrapped taxi all convey his misery as he grapples with the feelings of doubt and insecurity that threaten to overwhelm him completely.

THE STRENGTH AND POWER OF WOMEN

Durcan's poetry contains many portraits of strong women. His former wife Nessa, as portrayed in this poem, certainly falls into this category. As we've seen, she takes the lead in their budding relationship, taking the young poet 'by the index finger' and leading him on an intense romantic journey. Again and again on that first day we see her taking the initiative, suggesting to the poet that they go for a swim and lying beside him when he falls in the field on the way back to the hotel.

All in all, then, she comes across as by far the more self-assured, confident and assertive of the two. This vivacious, spontaneous young woman is portrayed almost as a force of nature – a whirlpool whose powerful energy threatens to overwhelm the poet.

FOCUS ON STYLE

FORM

Durcan's poetry is known for its 'looseness', for its use of long lines and irregular stanzas. 'Nessa' is perhaps more formal than much of Durcan's later work, being divided into three stanzas of six lines each with a concluding stanza of eight lines.

Repetition is another recurring feature of Durcan's work. As we've seen, this poem features a refrain that occurs in some form at the end of each stanza, lending the piece an almost song-like quality and reinforcing our sense of the young poet's vulnerability.

A SENSE OF VOICE

In this poem we get a real sense of the young poet's character and personality as he portrays his younger self in a typically unflattering and self-deprecating manner. He seems far less self-assured than Nessa when they first meet and is led by her throughout this first meeting. He's reluctant to enter the water, suggesting he's far less carefree and spontaneous than his new love. In the end, however, he was unable to resist both her charms and her dare to go swimming in the Irish Sea.

STRANGE AND SURREAL IMAGERY

The image of the couple riding 'in a taxi-cab wrapped up in dust' is unexpected and unsettling. This image, too, recalls the day of the couple's first meeting; how after the wedding in Dalkey they must have caught a cab back into the city centre. Now, however, the poet envisages a taxi

surrounded by a dust cloud, as if this cloak of dust represents the doubts and uncertainties that blur the poet's mind.

Alternatively, perhaps the poet imagines a taxi caked with a layer of dust from having waited for him for years while he languished on the rocks at Dalkey. In any event it is a memorable and peculiar image, one whose disturbing qualities are amplified by a final desperate repetition of the poem's refrain, one that conveys the poet's despairing state of mind as he sinks beneath waves of doubt and uncertainty: 'Oh you are a whirlpool, you are a whirlpool,/ And I am very nearly drowned'.

METAPHOR AND FIGURES OF SPEECH

The poet uses several fine metaphors in this poem. He compares the sensation of falling in love to that of falling down a well into a pool of dangerous, swirling water: 'And dropped me in her well/ And that was a whirlpool, that was a whirlpool,/ And I very nearly drowned'. This powerfully captures the dizzying, headlong feeling of excitement that often accompanies a new relationship.

A similar effect is created when he compares Nessa herself to a whirlpool in the third and fourth stanzas. In the third stanza this powerfully captures the force of her personality and the dizzying effect she has on the poet. In the final stanza, however, the metaphor takes on a somewhat darker quality, suggesting that the poet is on the verge of being overcome with feelings of doubt and insecurity regarding their relationship.

The Girl with the Keys to Pearse's Cottage

BACKGROUND

The Irish revolutionary leader Patrick Pearse had a small cottage in Rosmuc, Co. Galway, which he used as a kind of country retreat. Pearse was a leader of the 1916 Easter Rising against British rule in Ireland, and was executed in the Rising's aftermath. However, he was also a poet and writer, and it was in his Rosmuc cottage that he composed many of his best-known pieces. Because Rosmuc lies in the heart of the Connemara Gaeltacht, spending time there also allowed Pearse to increase his fluency in the Irish language. Pearse's cottage still exists, and is today maintained as a heritage site.

LINE BY LINE

THE GIRL

The poet remembers a summer he spent in Rosmuc during his mid-teens. While there, he fell in love with a girl named Cáit Killann. He describes Cáit as a 'dark girl', suggesting she possessed the sultry complexion common to many people in Connemara. Her hair was dark, her legs were brown, and her eyes, we're told, resembled those of the Spanish ladies painted by El Greco, suggesting their hazel or almond colour. Her bright and sunny smile made a wonderful contrast with her sallow and sultry features: 'Her dark hair was darker because her smile was so bright'.

For some reason this young woman possessed a set of keys to Pearse's cottage. Perhaps her family had been formally appointed caretakers of this local monument. Perhaps care of the cottage had been entrusted to her father because he was a postman and therefore a government employee. Or perhaps a set of keys had simply come into her possession by accident.

THE COTTAGE

That summer the poet spent a great deal of time hanging around Pearse's former home. He seems to have been attracted to the girl with the keys but also to the cottage itself. The cottage was built into the side of a hill and is described as having only 'two windows', suggesting its small size. Its interior was sparse and simple, with its 'bare brown rooms' and its 'white washed walls'. On its walls hung photographs showing Pearse to be 'passionate and pale'. We get a sense of Pearse not only as an intense and devoted revolutionary but also perhaps as a bookish and indoorsy type.

To the poet the cottage seemed a place of 'cosmic peace'. The peace he experienced there was so mystical and profound that he felt at one with the cosmos or universe. The cottage, however, had fallen into disrepair: its thatched roof was damp and the paint on its door frames was flaking away. He remarks that the cottage always looked better from a distance: 'all was best seen from below in the field'. From up close one could see how the cottage was afflicted by rot and disrepair. From down in the field, however, it looked like a picture-perfect country dwelling.

THE POET'S FEELINGS FOR CÁIT

The poet was clearly smitten with Cáit. He describes how Cáit would sit inside the cottage. She would perch on a windowsill and gaze out at the world: 'Often she used linger on the sill of a window'. He remembers her wearing a dress as red as the sunset and blazer as black as the dark side of the moon: 'In sun-red skirt and moon-black blazer'.

Meanwhile, he'd sit in the rushes below the cottage composing poems about her in a ledger book, which was a type of copybook used by shops and businesses to record transactions. The poems he wrote for Cáit were filled with passion, suggesting the intense feelings he had toward this young woman.

Cáit was due to emigrate at the end of the summer: 'She was America-bound at summer's end./ She had no choice but to leave her home'. The poem is set in 1960, a time when Ireland, especially the west of Ireland, was gripped by poverty. Cáit Killann was one of thousands forced to leave the country in search of a better life.

We get a sense that Cáit had already mentally moved on from Ireland. Though she wasn't leaving until the end of summer, it already felt like a foreign country: 'Looking toward our strange world wide-eyed'. Ireland couldn't offer her a living or a future. She was unneeded in her own country, a stranger in her own native place: 'Our world was strange because it had no future'.

The poet movingly laments how Cáit was forced to leave the country in which she was born: 'O Cáit Killann, O Cáit Killann,/ You have gone with your keys from your own native place'. Yet though she is long gone from her native place, the poet remembers her face and her dark El Greco eyes.

THEMES

IRELAND AND IRISH HISTORY

Pearse and his fellow revolutionaries were idealists, dreaming of the perfect Ireland that would be created once the country had gained independence from Britain. Their hopes, however, were not fulfilled. The poem shows how Ireland in 1960 was a country that had failed, that was wracked with economic stagnation and had to watch thousands of its young people emigrate. The poet describes himself as being 'here in the dark', suggesting how he viewed the Ireland of the day as a dark, tormented place that had 'no future'.

There is a sense, therefore, in which the poem suggests we've failed Pearse and the country's other founding fathers. The grim reality of poverty and emigration is a far cry from their vision of a prosperous land in which every Irish person would have a place. It is bitterly ironic that the girl who holds the keys to Pearse's country retreat – who walks the very floors he walked – is herself forced to leave the nation he gave up his life to forge.

There is a real tone of sorrow, despair and rage in the poem's final stanza. The poet vocally addresses Cáit, lamenting her forced departure: 'O Cáit Killann, O Cáit Killann,/ You have gone with your keys from your own native place'. There is a powerful song-like quality to these lines, as if they could be the chorus to a bitterly sorrowful emigration ballad.

It is tempting to view the cottage as a metaphor for Ireland in 1960, a time when the country was undeveloped not only economically but also socially, culturally and technologically.

The cottage's spare, almost primitive, decor reflects the backward, almost primitive state of Ireland at the time. It is a spiritual place, a place of cosmic silence, just as the Ireland of the day was an intensely spiritual and religious country. But its lapse into decay reflects the rotten state of Ireland's economy and society.

The poet, then, seems to suggest that the perfect image of 1950s Ireland is a crumbling cottage containing nothing but photographs of Patrick Pearse. Perhaps the poet is suggesting that Ireland was too obsessed with Pearse, with the heroics and sacrifices of the past, to develop a social and economic future. There's a sense in which Ireland is portrayed as too inward and backward-looking to become a truly modern state.

ROMANTIC LOVE

This poem wonderfully captures the intensity and passion of teenage love. The poet is clearly smitten by the striking young Cáit. He remembers not only her physical beauty but also her particular posture and the outfits that she wore: 'Hands by her side and brown legs akimbo;/ In sun-red skirt and moon-black blazer'. The poem features an exquisite image of longing: the poet sitting in the rushy field while the object of his affection sits on the window sill staring out distractedly at the world. We almost get the impression that he'd hang around the cottage waiting for her to appear so he could bask in her dark beauty.

FORM

Durcan's poetry is known for its 'looseness', for its use of long lines and irregular stanzas. 'Nessa' is perhaps more formal than much of Durcan's later work, being divided into six stanzas of four lines each. Repetition is another recurring feature of Durcan's work. In this instance the repetition of Cáit's name in lines 8, 12 and twice in line 21 suggest the intensity of the poet's feelings for this young woman and the sorrow he must have experienced at her departure.

A SENSE OF VOICE

In this poem we get a real sense of the young poet's character and personality. There is something ridiculous and self-deprecating about his portrayal of his younger self. The sixteen-year-old poet is shown playing the role of the romantic, of the doomed but glamorous rebel artist, as he writes poems in his ledger and worships his distant would-be lover. We might think here of musicians like Kurt Cobain and Jim Morrison, of poets like Keats and Shelley, and perhaps even of Pearse himself.

METAPHOR AND SYMBOL

There are a number of striking metaphors in this poem. As we've seen, Pearse's cottage can be taken as a metaphor for Ireland in the 1940s, 1950s and early 1960s. There is an element of metaphor, too, when the red of Cáit's skirt is compared to a sunset and the blackness of her blazer to the moon's dark side.

Cáit herself could be said to symbolise the plight of young people with regard to emigration. She has been given the keys to Pearse's cottage, just as the young people of Ireland in the 1940s and 1950s finally inherited their own state after centuries of occupation. Yet Cáit must leave the cottage behind, just as thousands of young people were forced to depart forever the country that had been gained for them through so many years of struggle.

The Difficulty that is Marriage

LINE BY LINE

The poet lies in bed beside his wife. She's 'curled up' fast asleep but he lies awake beside her. The poet describes how she seems 'faraway', capturing the sense of distance we sometimes feel when we lie beside a sleeping loved one. As he lies there, the poet thinks about his marriage and his life.

It seems that he and his wife have more than their fair share of arguments. They 'differ' or disagree a lot. They are split or divided on a great many issues: 'We divide, we differ'. Sometimes the parties to an argument 'agree to disagree'. They accept that neither side can be convinced of the other's point of view so they agree to stop arguing and put the issue to one side. However, the poet and his wife cannot even manage this. They 'disagree to disagree'. They argue even about the possibility of taking a break from arguing.

Despite their many differences, the poet loves his wife deeply. He cannot believe his luck that this woman came into his life and fell in love with him: 'How was it I was so lucky to have ever met you?' The closeness they share is evident when he describes her as 'my sleeping friend'. He knows that his wife must have flaws and denies idolising or worshipping her: 'I do not put you on a pedestal or throne'. Yet he simply cannot see any faults that she might possess: 'You must have your faults but I do not see them'. To him she seems almost perfect.

The poet is not 'a brave pagan', one of those atheists convinced that only eternal nonexistence waits for us beyond the grave. Such people are almost 'proud of [their] mortality'. They accept or even celebrate the fact that this life is all we have and concentrate on living it to the full. But the poet cannot join them in this. Instead he clings to the belief that there is something more.

The poet believes in life after death, in some afterlife or heaven that awaits us when we die. The contrast bet-ween heaven and earth is clear. Heaven is a 'changeless kingdom', an eternal and constant state of being where nothing ever alters. This world, on the other hand, is a 'changeling earth', a site of flux and motion where nothing ever stays the same. In heaven our existence would be free of cares and worries. During our earthly existence, however, we will always be faced with troubles: 'I have my troubles and I shall always have them'.

The poet, however, would gladly sacrifice heaven if he could live here on earth forever with his wife: 'Yet gladly on this changeling earth I should live for ever/ If it were for you my sleeping friend'. He would swap an eternity of unchanging bliss for an eternity in this troubled and changing world, provided he could spend it with his wife: 'But I should rather live with you for ever/ Than exchange my troubles for a changeless kingdom'.

THEMES

MARRIAGE

This poem provides an honest and deeply moving portrait of a marriage. The complexity of married life is suggested not only by the poem's title but also by the fact that the poet lies awake at night pondering the questions that arise from his relationship. The poet's marriage – like any other – has both positive and negative aspects.

As we've seen, the poet's relationship with his wife is fairly intense and tempestuous. They argue a lot, disagreeing and differing about many things. In fact there are times when they cannot even agree to disagree, yet their relationship is ultimately a positive one. The poet cannot believe his luck that this woman is in his life. If he could he would sacrifice heaven to spend eternity on earth with her. The poem, then, is realistic and unflinching; it highlights the ups and downs of any long-term relationship.

Indeed, there's almost a sense that the poet loves his wife too much. He would rather live on earth with his wife than enter heaven. His love for his wife makes heaven seem downright unappealing. Perhaps this, then, is the 'difficulty' referred to in the poem's title. This world is a place of change and trouble. But love makes the thought of leaving it unbearable, even if we believe that heaven's changeless kingdom is waiting.

RELIGION

Durcan's poetry can sometimes be critical of organised religion, deploying dark humour to underscore what he perceives to be the unhealthy and repressive aspects of the Church's teaching. Yet as this poem makes clear the poet never fully abandoned his faith and clung to the idea that heaven – in some form or other – actually exists. He never quite joined the ranks of those atheists or 'brave pagans' who almost celebrate their unbelief. In 'The Difficulty that is Marriage' heaven is imagined as a 'changeless kingdom', a place of unfaltering bliss where all our earthly troubles are left behind.

FORM

This is one of the few poems by Durcan on the course that features a formal structure. The poem is a form of sonnet, although it does not use any formal rhyming scheme. Like many sonnets, however, it does feature something of a turn or change in focus in the ninth line when the poet begins to describe his 'troubles'.

SOUND EFFECTS

The opening line features repeated 'd' sounds, creating a somewhat jarring effect that seems to correspond with the fractious nature of the relationship: 'We disagree to disagree, we divide, we differ'. The third line also features alliteration, with the poet using repeated 'm' sounds. Here, the effect is softer: 'I array the moonlit ceiling with a mosaic of question marks'.

METAPHOR AND SIMILE

The poet describes the thoughts that crowd his mind when he lies awake at night as a 'mosaic' of question marks upon the ceiling.

HUMOUR

The poet is quick to use self-deprecating humour when describing his own life, especially when it concerns some problem or difficulty that he is facing. In 'The Difficulty that is Marriage' he tells us that he is 'no brave pagan' to convey the fact that he would not find it easy to live with the thought that there is no afterlife when we die.

Wife Who Smashed Television Gets Jail

Telly Savalas as Kojak

LINE BY LINE

This poem is unusual in that it takes the form of a newspaper report. The report concerns a woman who is put on trial for smashing her family's television set. The poem reports how the woman's husband testified against her, telling the judge how 'She came home, my Lord, and smashed in the television'. He was at home with his children watching a detective series called *Kojak*: 'Me and the kids were peaceably watching *Kojak*'.

Midway through the episode, his wife returned from the local pub and 'marched' angrily into the living room. She seems enraged by the fact that families spend all their time watching television rather than engaging in conversation. She threatens to smash the television if he doesn't turn it off: she 'declared/ That if I didn't turn off the television immediately/ She'd put her boot through the screen'.

He refuses to do so and she makes good on her threat, using her boots as a hammer to smash the appliance: 'I didn't turn it off, so instead she turned it off … And then she took off her boots and smashed in the television.' The husband responded by taking his children to his mother's house so they could watch the remainder of the *Kojak* episode: 'I had to bring the kids round to my mother's place;/ We got there just before the finish of *Kojak*'. He came home afterwards to find his wife had dumped the remnants of the TV set: 'When I returned home my wife had deposited/ What was left of the television into the dustbin'.

She despises how television has taken over modern life. Television sets, she suggests, have infiltrated family life and now play the role of parents and spouses: 'I didn't get married to a television'. Where family members once interacted with one another, now they 'interact' with their television sets, sitting there dumbly and passively as they absorb show after show and advertisement after advertisement. In her opinion, the family would be better off spending time in the pub together rather than watching television. This is not necessarily for the purpose of drinking alcohol but because pubs are places of human interaction, where people chat and play games like bar billiards: 'We'd be much better off all down in the pub talking/ Or playing bar-billiards'. According to the husband, after this little speech she returned to the pub, 'Whereupon she disappeared off back down again to the pub.'

The report switches from relating the husband's testimony to describing the reaction of the presiding judge, Justice O'Brádaigh. The judge is unimpressed with the wife's behaviour. He suggests that television sets should be considered members of the families that own them: 'As indeed the television itself could be said to be a basic unit of the family'.

The judge deems that any wife who shows a preference for bringing her family to the pub rather than watching television is a 'threat to the family'. And because the family is the basic unit of society, she might also be said to threaten society as a whole. He decrees that any wife who displays this preference for the pub in such a violent manner must serve time in prison. He sentences her to an unspecified period in jail, with no chance of appeal.

FAMILY

This poem highlights the negative impact technology can have on family life. The wife laments how increasingly families sit stupefied in front of the television rather than interacting with one another. Each family member spends their evenings lost in their own private relationship with the screen. The old traditions of eating together, of talking together, of sharing news and opinions are all long gone.

TV addiction has permeated society to an extraordinary extent. The husband's reaction to his wife's astonishing attack on the TV set is simply to rush off elsewhere so he and his kids can catch the remainder of the *Kojak* episode. The older generation, too, seems vulnerable to this insidious addiction. We see this when the husband declares: 'My mother has a fondness for *Kojak*, my Lord'. Small wonder, then, that the wife feels compelled to take such extreme and aggressive action against the offending apparatus. Both the wife and the judge take the view that television sets have become almost members of the families that own them. They have insinuated themselves into our lives and our living rooms. As the judge puts it, 'indeed the television itself could be said to be a basic unit of the family'. Without us really noticing it, they have come to provide the companionship once provided by parents, siblings and spouses: 'I didn't get married to a television/ And I don't see why my kids or anybody else's kids/ Should have a television for a father or mother'.

The poem, then, presents a conflict between human interaction on one hand and machine interaction on the other. We see this especially when the wife declares she'd rather have her children in the pub that have them sitting in front of the television set. Pubs may be slightly disreputable places that are often considered inappropriate for children, but at least there people engage with each other, whether it be through conversation or through playing games like bar billiards. They are not sitting stupidly getting lost in a little screen.

MARRIAGE

Durcan's poetry often presents a gritty and realistic view of marriage, yet surely the relationship presented in 'Wife Who Smashed Television Gets Jail' is the most dysfunctional of all. The wife comes to feel so ignored and marginalised that she's provoked into the action described in the poem. This surely is marital

breakdown at its most extreme. Yet to make matters worse, the husband presumably reports the wife's action to the police, testifies against her in court and effectively gets her locked up.

THE STRENGTH AND POWER OF WOMEN

Durcan's poetry is full of strong and impressive women. Indeed, much of his work can be read as an ode to the power of femininity. Yet among these heroines, surely the wife who smashed the television stands out. This is a woman not afraid to rebel. She has been ignored in favour of the television for long enough. She has watched television destroy family life across the country for long enough. She responds with her own small but unforgettable act of rebellion. It's unsurprising, then, that she's associated with Queen Maeve, who in Irish legend was the fierce and powerful ruler of Connacht, and the equal of any king.

IRELAND AND IRISH HISTORY

This poem presents Ireland as an oppressive place – especially toward women. The role of women is to maintain the stability of the family unit, and thereby the stability of society itself. Women must function as loyal and obedient wives who look after the household and tend to their husband's needs. Any women who rebel against this role will be regarded as a social menace and dealt with severely by the authorities.

Tellingly, there is no mention in the report of the wife's testimony. Perhaps the judge felt her husband was the only one worth listening to and was happy to convict based on his evidence alone. Or perhaps she was invited to speak in her own defence but the reporter felt her words were not worth relating. Either way her 'silencing' reflects the marginalised status of women in Ireland at that time.

The poem was written at a time when televisions were the only form of electronic entertainment. Yet its message is even more pertinent today in our world of smart phones, laptops and consoles. We now have so many different screens to get lost in, so many different ways to ignore each other.

The bias against women is perhaps also suggested when the husband describes how the detective Kojak shoots a woman who just happens to share his wife's name: 'I remember the moment exactly because Kojak/ After shooting a dame with the same name as my wife/ Snarled at the corpse – Goodnight, Queen Maeve'. We're left with the impression that this is a world where women are controlled and oppressed, and where necessary in a violent manner.

FORM

The poem's most notable feature is its presentation as a newspaper report. The title, for instance, is written in the style of a newspaper headline, while the body mixes quotes and reportage just as an actual court report would. The husband's testimony is quoted verbatim, while in the last six lines Durcan skilfully captures the clipped, neutral style of the court reporter.

A SENSE OF VOICE

Durcan brilliantly captures the tone of the husband's speech as he gives his testimony. There is something very realistic about the way he moves from a casual style of phrasing ('me and the kids', 'my mother's place', 'my mother has a fondness', *Kojak* references, and so on) to a more ceremonial or formal one ('peaceably', 'my Lord', 'deposited', 'whereupon', and so on). We are left with a vivid impression of a man used to speaking in a colloquial and casual manner who throws in a few big words to impress the judge and win his favour.

It's also important to look at the types of words used by the husband to describe his wife's behaviour. He frames her outburst in emotionally charged language, designed to make her actions seem violent and unreasonable and uses words like 'marched', 'smashed', 'declared', 'disappeared'.

HUMOUR

This poem is rich in the surreal humour that flavours much of Durcan's poetry. We see this in the wife's assault upon the television set and in the husband's equally bizarre response as he rushes around to his mother's house to catch the end of *Kojak*. We see it in the strangely accurate notion of television sets as family members and in the judge's overreaction as he imprisons the wife for breaking what is after all her own appliance. There are also several quirky little details like the husband's mother also being a *Kojak* fan and in the wife's fondness for the now obscure game of bar billiards.

Durcan uses this bizarre scenario to make a serious point, attacking both the destructive influence of television and the oppression of women in the Ireland of the day. The poem may be zany but it is also a powerful piece of satire or social criticism.

Parents

LINE BY LINE

Durcan compares sleep to an ocean. When we fall asleep we slip beneath this ocean's surface and 'drown' in its depths. He depicts parents looking down on their child who is lost in these swirling reaches of unconsciousness: 'A child's face is a drowned face:/ Her parents stare down at her asleep'.

The ocean of sleep separates or 'estranges' those who slumber from those who are awake. Sleepers remain on one side of the ocean's surface, waking people on the other. The surface of this ocean, then, is like a barrier separating the parents from their child: they are 'Estranged from her by a sea;/ She is under the sea/ And they are above the sea'. Indeed Durcan reinforces this point by repeating it almost exactly in lines 16 to 17.

The parents long to connect with their child but the impassable barrier of sleep prevents them from doing so. They are 'stranded' on one side of this divide and cannot cross over. Durcan uses a wonderful simile to describe this, suggesting that the parents resemble people who have been 'locked out of their own home'.

Sleep is like a pane of glass separating the parents from their child: 'Their big ears are fins behind glass'. But it is a twisted or distorting pane that makes the parents' ears resemble huge fish-like fins. It seems to suggest that even if the sleeping child could somehow sense what was happening around her it would seem bizarre, distorted and incomprehensible. This is a strange but powerful image that reinforces our sense of the great divide between the waking and the sleeping worlds.

We sense, however, that this is no ordinary sleep, that this particular child may well be very ill. After all, the parents seem to be highly anxious and concerned about their child. They stay up all night watching over her: 'And through the night, stranded, they stare'. As they watch they are open-mouthed in fear and suspense. Their foreheads are 'furrowed' with lines of worry. According to Durcan their clenched and puckered foreheads are like the mouths of fish: 'Pursed-up orifices of fearful fish'.

We sense, too, that the child is experiencing some kind of fever that brings vivid, unpleasant and chaotic dreams.

Even though she's unconscious she realises something is wrong. And in her dreams she longs to connect with her parents: 'And in her sleep she is calling out to them/Father, Father/ Mother, Mother'. But of course her parents can't hear what she shouts out in her dreams. If she woke she would see her parents standing there watching over her: 'If she looked up she would see them'. But she is lost in her fevered sleep and cannot do so. The repetition of the word 'drowned' in the poem's last line reinforces our impression that the child is sick and perhaps even dangerously so: 'At the drowned, drowned face of their child'.

THEMES

FAMILY

The poem highlights how far away our loved ones and family members seem while they're sleeping. Sleep is likened to a barrier or pane of glass that leaves us 'locked out' or 'stranded'. When our loved ones sleep beside us we experience a strange kind of loneliness. For they are lost in another world, adrift deep within the ocean of their slumber where we cannot reach them. 'The Difficulty that is Marriage' is another poem that touches on this topic, depicting how the poet lies beside his sleeping wife and contemplates the ups and downs of their relationship.

Durcan is a poet who presents an honest and rounded view of family life, celebrating the joys of family life but also its difficulties. This poem seems to deal with the agony of having a sick and feverish child, highlighting the stress and worry experienced by parents in that terrible situation. We sense the tension as they stay up all night watching over their child, their foreheads 'furrowed' with worry.

FORM

Although many of Durcan's poems are composed in a 'loose' style, featuring long lines and irregular stanzas, 'Parents' is more regular and restrained. However, it does not feature any particular formal structure or rhyming scheme.

METAPHOR AND SIMILE

This poem turns on a 'conceit' or extended metaphor that compares sleep to an ocean. Sleepers slide into this ocean and 'drown' within its depths while waking people remain 'stranded' above its surface: 'She is inside the sea/ And they are outside the sea'. The ocean's surface, as we've seen, is presented as some unreachable barrier between sleep and waking.

Other metaphors are used to describe the parents' faces as they watch their sleeping child. Their ears are compared to fins. And in an especially bizarre comparison their clenched brows are likened to the mouths of fish. A fine simile, meanwhile, is used to describe the distance between the waking parents and the sleeping child, with the parents compared to people who have been locked out of their own home.

En Famille, 1979

This poem was written in 1979 when Durcan was thirty-five years old and had two daughters of his own. The term 'en famille' means together as a family, suggesting that the piece was inspired by the poet spending time with his children. The poem presents a complex double-sided view of childhood. In one sense, childhood is depicted as a 'dark school'. It is a 'school', where we learn and develop. But it is also a 'dark' school, a place where the lessons learned can often be harsh, uncomfortable and scary. The repetition of the phrase 'dark school' powerfully reinforces this, evoking a sense of tension, foreboding and loneliness.

No doubt Durcan has his own difficult childhood in mind here, which was darkened, especially after the age of ten or so, by the difficult relationship he had with his father. Poems like 'Sport' and 'Madman' touch on these fraught and painful memories.

Yet the poet longs to return to some kind of childhood, to revisit that dark period with all its harsh lessons: 'Take me back to the dark school'. Why does he long for such a return? Perhaps he longs for the simplicity of childhood, for a time when everything was either black or white, good or evil, 'tiny' or 'massive'. Perhaps he longs to return to a more innocent state of mind, one lacking the complexity and uncertainty of the adult world, where things are all too often neither black nor white but one of infinitely varied shades of grey.

It is also possible that the poet is being ironic or sarcastic here, that he has no desire whatsoever to return to childhood's 'dark school'. On this reading, the words 'tiny' and 'massive' refer not to comforting certainties but to victimisation. They evoke how in childhood the small are often bullied, abused and prosecuted by those larger and more powerful, whether by adults or by other more 'massive' children.

Madman

LINE BY LINE

The poem begins with the statement: 'Every child has a madman on their street'. This can be understood to mean that there is in fact a madman living on every residential street. But it is more likely that the poet is saying that children will always identify someone as mad on their street, regardless of whether or not there is an actual 'madman' present. There is always someone labelled 'mad' by children (just think of the area in which you grew up). Unfortunately for the poet, the person marked as the 'madman' in his neighbourhood was his own father: 'The only trouble about our madman is that he's our father'.

FAMILY

This brief poem touches on the very difficult relationship Durcan had with his father. It gives us a sense of how hard it must have been growing up in the house of a 'madman'. The term 'madman' suggests a volatile and violent temperament. Living with such a person must have been extremely difficult. The poem also suggests that everyone on the street was aware of the poet's father's behaviour and that the other children identified him also as a 'madman'. This must have been very awkward and unpleasant for the young poet.

FORM

This poem again demonstrates Durcan's mastery of the short poem as he encapsulates a sentiment or experience using only two lines.

HUMOUR

The impact of this poem seems to very much depend on the tone in which it is read. Read in one way, it can seem like the kind of thing we might hear a comedian say on stage – the first line setting up the joke and the second delivering the punch-line. However, the poem can also be read in a very sombre and sad voice, rendering it much more tragic and painful. Try reading it using different tones to see how the effect of the lines changes.

'Windfall', 8 Parnell Hill, Cork

LINE BY LINE

LINES 1 TO 117

The poet describes a time in his life when he lived at 8 Parnell Hill in Cork city. He lived there with his wife and children. They decided to name the house 'Windfall' because they felt so fortunate to have a home of their own: 'What a windfall! A home of our own!' A windfall is an unexpected boon or benefit. It is also used to refer to something blown down by the wind, such as fruit or leaves from a tree.

The poet used to relish his time at home. He was content to 'stay at home' for 'weeks' at a time. He would sit in 'a winged chair by the window' and daydream. Here, it seems, the poet was free of worry and could spend time pondering such strange and paradoxical thoughts as 'life is a dream that is real'. When he was at home, the poet experienced a form of calm and peace that he thought was only known to Buddhist monks. He could close his eyes contentedly and breathe in and out: 'I closed my eyes and breathed in and out'. The deep feeling of serenity he experienced at home is likened to a leaf floating upon the waters of a tranquil stream: 'In the gut of my head coursed the leaf of tranquillity'.

Being able to say that he was 'going home' at the end of the day filled the poet with pride, and made him feel very special. It was as if life had singled him out, and he felt very fortunate: 'I felt elected'. Having a home also meant that the poet felt more comfortable about life: 'It is ecstasy to breathe if you are at home in the world'. It made him feel safe and secure, offering protection to him and his family, shielding them from the dangers lurking in the outside world: 'Having a home of your own can give to a family/ A chance in lifetime to transcend death'.

Due to its location on a hill above the city, the poet's house afforded him a fine view. From the 'high window' he could see ships and trawlers arriving into Cork port 'from all over the world'. He would watch them being 'borne up and down' the River Lee by the pilot tugs. Beyond the river he could see the 'control tower of the airport on the hill', which he likens to a 'lighthouse' far in the distance, 'flashing green to white to green'.

LIFE INSIDE THE HOME

Durcan describes the family home as a place where you can be uninhibited and free. It is a space that affords freedom of expression, a place where extreme moods are common and natural: 'climbing the walls is as natural/ As making love on the stairs'. The poet compares the home to having a 'sea of your own'. It gives you the space to be who you are and to act without restriction and inhibition. The poet says that at home you are free to 'hang upside down from the ceiling' and that you could do this without stress or worry: 'With equanimity'.

The home was his children's 'private sea' in which they 'swam about'. The home also provided the poet's children with a healthy environment in which they were free to be themselves: it was like a 'private sea' in which they 'swam about'. The children, in turn, made the home a special place. In this regard, they were dependent upon each other – the home was home because of the children and the children were able to be themselves because they were at home. The poet describes the relationship as mutually beneficial, or 'symbiotic'.

The poet paints a very pleasant picture of life in the family home. While he would be contemplating his own thoughts, his children would be sitting on his knees 'watching TV'. The poet's wife would recline on the couch 'Knitting a bright coloured scarf, drinking a cup of black coffee,/ Smoking a cigarette'. The family cat would snooze 'in the corner of a chair'. The walls of the house were decorated with paintings, 'Pastels and etchings on the four walls, and over the mantelpiece'. There were also many books and photograph albums: 'A room wallpapered in books and family photograph albums'. These albums contained a photographic record of the family's many adventures and the changes that had occurred over the years: 'Chronicling the adventures and metamorphoses of family life'. The description of these photographs gives a sense of how the home functions as a repository for the family's mementoes and shared memories.

The poet describes how he would pore over these albums every year, 'accumulating' the family's history, his child 'looking over [his] shoulder' as excited as he is to see the various pictures. It is as if viewing the pictures allows him to relive these cherished moments. He describes the enormous pleasure that this activity afforded him, speaking of being 'exhilarated'.

LINES 118 TO 141

The last two sections of the poem describe how, 'with good reason', the poet was forced to leave his home: 'But then with good reason

Although the view from his window was essentially industrial, the poet considered it to be beautiful. He says that the 'industrial vista' was his Mont Sainte-Victoire. The Mont Sainte-Victoire is a mountain in southern France that inspired a number of famous paintings by the artist Cézanne. The poet seems to be able to draw similar inspiration from his view of the city.

/ I was put out of my home'. When this happened his life crumbled. It was as if a violent wind had suddenly cut him down: 'By a keen wind felled'. The description of his experience plays on the name of the family home 'Windfall'. The poet feels as if he is something blown down by the wind.

Durcan tells us that when he left the family home he moved to Dublin and tried to find a way to live and survive there 'without a home'. This, of course, was anything but easy. Dublin is an 'alien, foreign city' to the poet, and he suffers from a terrible form of homesickness: homesickness for a place that he can never return to. It is one thing to be homesick when you know that you 'will be going home next week'. It is quite a different thing to feel homesick 'knowing that there is no home to go home to'. The poet says that it is an 'eerie' feeling that is all but impossible to describe.

The poet now spends his days moving from place to place. He spends his nights in bed and breakfasts, 'Hostels, centres, one-night hotels'. In the evening, he often wanders the streets 'Peering in the windows of other people's homes,/ Wondering what it must feel like/ To be sitting around a fire'. It is a great pleasure, whether you are an Indian living in a tepee or a middle-class Westerner living in a house, to sit around a fire and see the 'firelit faces of your family'.

THEMES

MARRIAGE

The poem presents us with a very positive view of marriage. For many years, it seems, the poet and his wife enjoyed a contented relationship. Durcan describes moments of bliss as he relaxes by the window and his wife reclines on the couch smoking and 'Knitting a bright-coloured scarf'. Married life seems to have afforded the poet an opportunity to be at peace with himself and the world.

We also get a sense of the intimacy of marriage. Durcan describes a particular moment when the telephone rings and he and his wife become 'smiling accomplices' as they both decline to answer it: 'when the telephone rings/ Husband and wife are metamorphosed into smiling accomplices,/ Both declining to answer it'. The poem also celebrates the erotic love that married life can foster: 'climbing the walls is as natural/

As making love on the stairs'. Rather than kill the attraction between husband and wife, marriage seems to strengthen it. The poet describes how the telephone interrupting the couple's lovemaking leads to an increase in their desire for one another: 'Initiating, instead, a yet more subversive kiss –/ A kiss they have perhaps never attempted before'.

FAMILY

The poem is a great celebration of family. It focuses on the many shared moments and adventures that the poet and his family enjoyed over the years. These events and experiences seem to have greatly enriched the poet's life and afforded him enormous pleasure and satisfaction. As the poet leafs through the numerous albums of photographs in the house, he is 'exhilarated' by the sight of so many special moments, from the birth of his children to the many family holidays taken.

THEMES

The poem suggests that the family is a unit that can only ever be properly understood by the individual members of that family. Durcan talks about decoding or detecting hidden or deeper significances in conversations between family members that would never be obvious or apparent to someone outside the family: 'Sifting the sands underneath the surfaces of conversations'. The family share a collective 'psyche' that is complicated and fascinating. Durcan considers the family to be 'subversive'. He describes the family home as a space in which a group of people are free to behave as they wish. Such freedom of expression is considered by the poet to be a threat to society: 'The most subversive unit in society is the human family'.

The poem ultimately documents just how painful it is to lose one's family. Durcan describes the terrible homesickness that he experiences, living away from his family and the city he knows so intimately. What is especially difficult is the notion that there is no home to return to: 'It is an eerie feeling beyond all ornithological analysis/ To be homesick knowing that there is no home to go home to'.

IRELAND AND IRISH HISTORY

The poem describes the city of Cork and its environs. We get a picture of a small, 'intimate' and vibrant city, full of hustle and bustle. The poet describes the activity on the river, the arrival of ships from all over the world: 'shipping from all over the world/ Being borne up and down the busy, yet contemplative, river'. It is a city of industry, of 'factory chimneys' and 'car assembly works'. But it is also an 'intimate' and peaceful place. Though the river might host traffic from all over the world, it is considered a 'contemplative' river.

However, the poet touches on the dangers that lurk within its streets. He likens the city to Marseilles, the second-largest city in France that has a reputation for violent crime and corruption: 'as homicidal as a Little Marseilles'. Durcan also passes critical comment on the country, saying that Ireland is an unequal society, a place where 'all the children/ Are not cherished equally'. It is a place where some of the great citizens are 'homeless', while some of the 'worst' are allowed to build and live in 'ugly', monstrous houses: 'the worst/ Erect block-house palaces – self-regardingly ugly'.

FORM

Durcan's poetry is known for its 'looseness', for its use of long lines and irregular stanzas. This is very evident in the structure of "Windfall" which features stanzas of varying lengths and sentences that run on over many lines.

STRANGE AND SURREAL IMAGERY

The poem features a number of strange and surreal images, which are so typically and uniquely Durcan. There is, for example, the image of him hanging 'upside down from the ceiling ... while postcards from Thailand on the mantelpiece/ Are raising their eyebrow markings benignly'. Durcan also describes the surreal thoughts that would sometimes occupy him when he was at home. He imagines 'Goya sketching Goya among the smoky mirrors', a truly bizarre and surreal image.

METAPHOR AND SIMILE

The poet uses a metaphor to describe the affection he felt for the factories and power stations that he could see when he looked out the window. He says that 'industrial vista was my Mont Sainte-Victoire'. The suggestion here is that the poet feels a similar affection for the factories and power stations that Cézanne felt for the mountain range.

He compares Cork to Marseilles, saying that it is as 'intimate and homicidal' as this French city renowned for its intricate streets and violence.

The poet uses the sea as a metaphor for the family home. He says that the home is a 'private sea' in which the children and parents can swim freely.

The home is also likened to some 'symbiotic fluid', a substance upon which the family members are dependent and which keeps them together.

The poet compares his experience of having to leave the family home to being knocked down by a violent wind: 'By a keen wind felled'.

HUMOUR

The ability to find humour in almost any circumstance or situation is a strong feature of Durcan's poetry. Here again we are presented with moments of light-hearted mirth, such as the time when the telephone was ringing and the husband and wife used the opportunity to initiate a kiss 'they have perhaps never attempted before' while the children watched 'solemnly' their 'parents at play'.

A SENSE OF VOICE

When we read "Windfall" we get a strong sense of the poet's personality and character. The lines are at times painfully honest and they feature many very personal thoughts, memories and feelings. As mentioned above, Durcan's quirkiness and humour are very much evident in the poem, as is his ability to reflect.

Six Nuns Die in Convent Inferno

BACKGROUND

This poem is based on an actual event that occurred in the Loreto convent on St Stephen's Green in Dublin in 1986. A fire spread through the building, killing six nuns – Sisters Rosario Flavin, Margaret Keane, Gonzaga Kehoe, Edith Kennedy, Seraphia Kennedy and Eucharia Scully. The nuns were aged between sixty and eighty-three years. According to an Associated Press report, three of the six dead nuns were found 'huddled together in a corridor', while the remaining three were 'elsewhere in the dormitory'. The cause of the fire was never discovered.

LINE BY LINE

PART I

The nuns were based in the Loreto convent on St Stephen's Green. The speaker recalls the hustle and bustle of nearby Grafton Street. She describes it as a *paseo*, a Spanish term meaning promenade or passage. This is the hub of Dublin city, and everybody passed along this street. We get a sense of how familiar this part of the city was to the speaker. She describes attending Mass at the Carmelite church in Clarendon Street but never using the conventional entrance. She would slip in 'by way of Johnson's Court,/ Opposite the side entrance to Bewley's Oriental Café'.

At the Grafton Street entrance to St Stephen's Green is a memorial to the Fenian leader Jeremiah O'Donovan Rossa.

Here groups of punks would gather 'round the base of the great patriotic pebble of O'Donovan Rossa,/ Knelt tableaus of punk girls and punk boys'. The nun recalls the striking appearance of the punks, with their shaved heads, Mohawks, bright or garish hair dye, and dark clothing embellished with safety pins or razors: 'half-shaven heads and the martial garb/ And the dyed hair-dos and the nappy pins'. Rather than being shocked and outraged at their appearance, the nun thought the punks 'looked so conventional'. She found them bemusing and felt pity for them, seeing them as vulnerable teenagers desperately trying to belong to a group: 'Clinging to warpaint and to uniforms and to one another'.

THE NUN'S VIEW OF HER VOCATION

The speaker describes the emotions she experienced when she made the decision to become a nun. She seems to have been joyful, saying that she was 'smiling'. But her desire to become a nun also filled her with a certain horror: 'I was also afraid'. The decision to become a nun involved a lot of courage and faith. The speaker says that she was surprised and shocked at the extent of her own courage and the intensity of her belief: 'Appalled by my own nerve, my own fervour'.

The speaker associates her vocation with a rejection of the world and all the world has to offer. She says that deciding to become a nun meant opting 'out of the world'. She turned her back on the things that most young girls dream of, what the speaker refers to as the 'marvellous passions of girlhood'. Unlike the punks who gather in St Stephen's Green, the nun has turned her back permanently on what most people would consider a normal life. She has opted out of the conventional life, denying herself the possibility of marital love, of becoming a mother and of having a home of her own. Hers was not a casual commitment, something done for 'a night or a weekend or even a Lent or a season'. It is a decision that will shape and determine her whole life.

The speaker places little or no stock on her corporeal existence. When she dies in the fire, she thinks how 'lucky' she is to 'lose' her life, as though it were something of a burden that she is happy to shrug off. Her body holds no value for her. The fact that it is consumed in the fire does not bother her, and all she can think is that some 'poor fire-brigade men' will have to shovel up her remains 'into black plastic refuse sacks'. Death is something that she welcomes, and she seems to even long for the end of the world to arrive. She even mentions her 'apocalyptic enthusiasm', a longing for the world to be destroyed, as foretold in the Bible.

Her attitude to life seems to both excite and shock her. She thinks that there is something almost criminal or subversive about her way of seeing things, and she describes herself as a 'delinquent' and a 'recidivist'. She is a 'wild woman', someone who lives outside the norms. When she became a nun, the speaker was essentially abandoning life on earth in favour of a life to come after death: 'Such terrestrial abandonment'. This choice filled her with excitement but also trepidation. Preferring another world to life on earth seemed arrogant, as though she was presuming to know better than others what mattered: 'my other-worldly hubris'.

And yet for all the 'fervour' of her faith and her wildness, the life of the nun is ultimately lonely and dull. The nun describes the entirely predictable life that awaited her when she chose to become a nun, a 'lifetime of bicycle lamps and bicycle pumps/ A lifetime of galoshes stowed under the stairs'.

LIFE WITH THE OTHER NUNS

The speaker is conscious of the fact that her life must strike many as strange: 'I knew what a weird bird I was'. She describes herself as a 'beadswoman', someone whose duty it is to pray for others. But she is not ashamed or embarrassed by her vocation, and she does not consider herself in any way foolish: 'I was no daw'. The speaker is also aware of how odd her shared life in the convent might have appeared. She imagines how if the roofs were ever ripped off the buildings in the city at night, theirs would have offered one of the stranger sights. You would have caught a glimpse of a group of elderly women 'Scuttling' about their dorm, 'wheezing, shrieking' and 'croaking', dressed in 'yellowy corsets, wonky suspenders' and 'strung-out garters'.

Though the nuns are described somewhat comically – they are forever moving hurriedly like small animals or birds, 'scuttling', 'scurrying', 'Fluttering' and 'scampering' – we get a sense of how hard a life they lived. The speaker likens them to sailors on a ramshackle boat, cobbling together a frugal living and keeping the ship afloat with nothing but their own guts and gumption. Sleeping at the top of the convent is akin to being at the masthead of an old ship: 'Sleeping up there was like sleeping at the top of the mast/ Of a nineteenth-century schooner'. The nuns are like hardworking sailors, doing what they can to keep the old ship afloat: 'in the daytime/ We old nuns were the ones crawled out on the yardarms/ To stitch and sew the rigging and the canvas'.

We also get a sense that these were fun-loving and lively women. The speaker tells us that they were 'frisky girls', and compares herself and her fellow nuns to 'kittens in the sun', a comparison that suggest playfulness. She describes a 'seaside holiday' that they took together in 1956. The picture that the speaker paints of this occasion is humorous, but it illustrates the playful nature of the nuns, 'fluttering up and down the beach' and 'Scampering hither and thither' in their 'starched bathing-costumes'.

THE FIRE

The nun describes how the fire happened on a Sunday night. They had finished their evening prayers and, because she was eager to get back to a book she was reading, the speaker 'skipped bathroom' so that she could 'hop straight into bed/ And get in a bit of a read'. However, she was so tired that she fell asleep 'with the book open'. She was woken by the violent sounds of the fire: 'the racket of bellowing flame and snarling glass'.

The thoughts that went through the speaker's mind during the fire were not what you might expect at such a terrible moment. She tells us that the 'first thing' she thought was that she would never be able to return the book she was reading to its owner. She also thought about the grim job of the firemen who would have to 'shovel up our ashes and shovel/ What is left of us into black plastic refuse sacks'.

Ultimately, the speaker is philosophical about dying suddenly. She considers it a blessing to die at an unexpected time: 'Isn't it a marvellous thing how your hour comes/ When you least expect it?' She also perceives her death as a form of liberation: 'in so many ways, losing things is such a refreshing experience/ Giving you a sense of freedom you've not often experienced?' There is a sense in which her mortal existence is somehow burdensome. Perhaps it is the freeing of her immortal soul that the nun has in mind here when she speaks of 'freedom'.

The speaker remembers a particular holiday that the nuns took in 1956. They stayed by a 'secluded beach' belonging to 'an affluent buddy of the bishop's'. The speaker remembers this as one of the most pleasant times of her life. She recalls with particular fondness the day they went swimming. She paints a rather humorous picture of the group of nuns 'fluttering up and down the beach' in their 'starched bathing-costumes'. What calls this particular occasion to mind is the way in which the flames of the fire remind the speaker of the waves of the sea: 'Tonight, expiring in the fire, was quite much like that,/ Only instead of scampering into the waves of the sea,/ Now we were scampering into the flames of the fire.'

HOW THE NUN UNDERSTOOD/IMAGINED THE EVENT

The speaker considers the fire to be a manifestation of Christ. She imagines that he has come to them in the form of fire to consume their bodies and deliver their souls to heaven. The speaker considers her death to be a 'strange Eucharist'. The Eucharist is the sacrament that involves bread and wine. When the priest performs the Eucharist, the bread and wine become the body and blood of Christ. The bread, in the form of communion, is then consumed by those attending the Mass. The speaker sees her own death as a form of Eucharist. However, in this case it is Christ consuming her body: 'To be eaten alive by fire and smoke'.

The nuns' death is imagined, paradoxically, as a form of birth. It is as if they are 'giving birth to their deaths'. She likens the flames and smoke to a host of maternity staff who help the nuns with this birth: 'Doctors and midwives weaved in and out/ In gowns of smoke and gloves of fire'. Christ is now imagined as an elder, an authoritative father figure, wearing a 'dressing gown' and tearing 'up and down the corridor, splashing water' on the nuns' 'souls'. These very bizarre images are perhaps the result of the nun inhaling smoke and losing the ability to think rationally. It is as if the fire is causing her to hallucinate.

The nun also imagines the angel Gabriel to be present in the room. In the Bible, Gabriel is an archangel who typically serves as a messenger sent from God to certain people. In the Gospel of Luke, Gabriel appears to Zacharias and to the Virgin Mary, foretelling the births of John the Baptist and Jesus, respectively. In keeping with traditional depictions of Gabriel, the speaker describes the angel's lips as 'boyish'. However, rather than using wings to fly, he is seen frantically 'pedalling' a 'skybike', some form of pedal-operated plane. The speaker imagines Gabriel to be 'darting in and out of the flames of the dormitory'. He has 'an extraordinary message' on 'his lips'. The angel has come to tell the nuns that they are to die. He whispers this message in the speaker's ear: 'He whispers into my ear what I must do/ And I do it — and die'.

PART II

Just when we thought things couldn't get much stranger or more surreal, the second part of the poem introduces a number of strange and bizarre twists.

- We are told that the first part of the poem is actually spoken by some 'female punk' standing at the 'top of Grafton Street'. This punk has been speaking as if she is one of the nuns who died in the inferno.
- In another bizarre development, we are told that Jesus is present on Grafton Street and has been listening to this punk speak. He is being followed by 'a gang of teenagers' and eccentric street performers or 'dicemen'.
- In a final bizarre twist or development we are told that the six nuns who died in the fire have been reincarnated and now spend their days 'hiding under' the 'bandstand' in St Stephen's Green.

The punk is described as being small and very thin or 'emaciated'. The fact that she is 'agéd' might not necessarily mean she is old, but just appears old because she has not taken care of herself. This punk is dressed entirely in black, like someone in mourning: 'Clad all in mourning clothes'. She also appears to be very distressed and sorrowful. She is described as wailing or 'grieving like an alley cat'.

Jesus is 'astonished' by what he has just heard: 'annulled with astonishment'. The word 'annulled' means to be obliterated or wiped out and suggests that Jesus has been blown away by these words. When the punk has finished speaking Jesus turns to those following him and declares that 'not even in New York City' has he 'found faith like this'. (This declaration is an allusion to a story in the Bible in which a Roman soldier asks Jesus to heal a favoured servant. Jesus is moved by the soldier's faith in his power and says 'I tell you, I have not found such great faith even in Israel.')

At night when the gates have been locked and all the 'courting couples' have left (Durcan suggests that these couples go to the local cinemas to make love or 'die' in), the six nuns creep out from their hiding place and 'kneel together by the Fountain of the Three Fates', a statue in the park of mythical Scandinavian female beings who rule the destiny of gods and men. They kneel by this statue and recite the 'Agnus Dei', the invocation to the Christ sung or recited during the breaking of the consecrated bread during the Eucharistic rite.

The nuns recite this prayer as if it were a sentimental song of yearning or frustrated hope for help or support: 'as if it were the torch song/ Of all aid'. The poet mentions a number of contemporary events or phenomena associated with the word aid: 'Live Aid, Self Aid, Aids, and All Aid'.

The final lines of the poem are a short prayer recited during Mass before the Agnus Dei, the Prayer of Humble Access.

These words are again derived from the same story in the Bible mentioned above, in which Jesus helps a Roman soldier by going to his house and healing his servant.

This part of the poem is wonderfully strange and surreal. The reader ends up flabbergasted at the audacity of Durcan's poetic imaginings. There is an almost hallucinatory or intoxicated element to the scene he presents, a form of madness in keeping perhaps with the drug culture of the streets where the poem takes place.

THEMES

RELIGION

The poem highlights the enormous self-sacrifice religious vocation demands, and gives us a sense of how tough and lonely such a life can be:

• The speaker tells us how when she became a nun she had to relinquish the things that many young girls dream about – the prospect of falling in love and getting married, of having a family and a home of her own: 'Surrendered the marvellous passions of girlhood,/ The innocent dreams of childhood'.

• She describes the 'exotic loneliness' of her life and hints at the monotony of her existence when she talks about a 'lifetime of galoshes stowed under the stairs,/ A lifetime of umbrellas drying out in the corner'.

• The nuns are compared to a crew upon a rickety old ship, struggling each day to keep the vessel afloat: 'We old nuns were the ones who crawled out on the yardarms/ To stitch and sew the rigging and the canvas'.

The poem presents the nun's vocation as an act of rebellion. She is the 'ultimate drop-out', someone who has permanently turned their back on what society has to offer. She humorously refers to herself as a 'Christnik', part of some subculture that refuses to conform to social expectations.

The poem suggests that the Catholic religion is ultimately life-denying and preoccupied with death. The speaker seems to be infatuated with death and the end of the world – what she terms her 'apocalyptic enthusiasm'.

The poem also suggests that nuns play a rather servile role in the Catholic Church. This is highlighted in the nun's mentioning of Cardinal Mindszenty, a Hungarian priest persecuted for opposing the communist government of his country. The speaker describes him as a 'great hero' of the nuns, and says that any of them would have 'given [their] right arm/ To have been his nun – darning his socks, cooking his meals'.

Religious faith is ultimately something that is hard to rationalise. The speaker's decision to become a nun is described as 'the weirdest thing a woman can do', and even she finds it hard to explain the sacrifices she has made: 'All for why and for what?/ To follow a young man – would you believe it –/ Who lived two thousand years ago in Palestine'. She is conscious of how peculiar and ridiculous her life seems – 'To be sure we were weird birds, oddballs' – but she is quick to say that she is no fool: 'I was an old nun … But I was no daw'. The poet seems to find the idea of such fervent faith bizarre and ridiculous. His imagining of the fire and the nuns' response to it is farcical and surreal. At one point, he introduces the angel Gabriel and has him 'pedalling a skybike' through the flames.

The second part of the poem presents religious faith in an especially bizarre light. Durcan presents with a strange scene on Grafton Street in which Jesus is said to be listening to a 'female punk' tell the nun's story as if she were actually the nun. Jesus is said to be followed by 'gangs of teenagers and dicemen'. We are also presented with an image of the six deceased nuns crawling out from under a bandstand in St Stephen's Green to pray.

There is a suggestion here that, in the modern world, strong or fervent religious belief is no longer commonplace and has become the preserve of eccentric individuals such as the 'female punk'. It is only 'gangs of teenagers' and street performers that follow Jesus. Everyone else seems to be oblivious to His presence or do not believe that He is who He says He is. The fact that Jesus says that 'not even in New York City' has he found faith like this, suggests that it is amongst the crazies and the freaks that one now finds believers.

THE STRENGTH AND POWER OF WOMEN

The speaker of the poem demonstrates enormous strength and resilience. She has chosen a hard way of life, rejecting many of life's comforts and joys in order to devote herself to her faith. Her life is one of few creature comforts, and the building that she lives in is old and in poor shape: 'No fire-escapes outside, no fire-extinguishers inside'. Though she and her fellow nuns are old and frail, they must fend for themselves. They are likened to the 'bony crew' of a ship, each day having to deal with the essential chores in order to keep the vessel afloat: 'We old nuns were the ones who crawled out on the yardarms/ To stitch and sew the rigging and the canvas'.

METAPHOR AND SIMILE

The speaker uses a number of comparisons when describing herself and her fellow nuns. She likens them to exotic birds and compares the convent to an aviary: 'I knew what a weird bird I was, I knew that when we/ Went to bed we were as eerie an aviary as you'd find'. She also compares the nuns to sailors – 'A bony crew' – and says that the convent was like a rickety old ship. She likens sleeping at the top of the building to sleeping at 'the top of the mast/ Of a nineteenth-century schooner'. She also compares their daily chores to the essential maintenance work on a ship, saying that each day they would have to crawl out to the tips of the mast arms to 'stitch and sew the rigging and canvas'.

The speaker uses different metaphors to describe the powerful presence of Christ in her life. She says that he is the 'ocean/ Forever rising and falling on the world's shore'. Christ is also imagined as the fire that consumes the building. She imagines the flames to be his arms embracing her: 'Burning to death in the arms of Christ'.

The fire is also compared to a 'dragon', which the speaker clasps and strokes: 'I clasped the dragon to my breast/ And stroked its red-hot ears'. It is like a beast that has come to consume her: 'To be eaten alive by fire and smoke'.

A SENSE OF VOICE

Durcan is renowned for his ability to infuse a poem with a strong sense of voice. The speaker of the first part of 'Six Nuns Die in Convent Inferno' is given a unique character all her own. Durcan uses expressions such as 'I skipped bathroom so that I could hop straight into bed/ And get in a bit of a read' and 'Fire-brigade men are salt of the earth' to bring the speaker to life.

HUMOUR

This poem displays again the fun and humour that is a feature of many of Durcan's poems. Although the story that inspired the poem is a tragic one, Durcan presents it in his own inimitable way. His description of the nuns at home in the convent and on the beach in Tramore is very humorous. The nun's expression of surprise at the cost of the book she was reading is also funny, especially considering the moment in which this occurs. This lightening of mood in the midst of tragedy and suffering is typical of Durcan. It is evident also in poems such as 'Sport' and 'Windfall'.

FORM

The poem is written in the rather loose style that is a feature of many of Durcan's later poems. There is no formal structure or rhyming scheme and the lines are often long and free-wheeling.

STRANGE AND SURREAL IMAGERY

Like many of Durcan's poems, this poem is marked by its many strange and surreal images. There is the bizarre image of the nuns in their undergarments running around their sleeping quarters 'wheezing, shrieking, croaking'. Durcan also presents us with an image of the nuns 'Scampering hither and thither in [their] starched bathing-costumes' when on holiday in Tramore.

The images of the nuns burning to death in the fire are especially strange and surreal. The angel Gabriel is imagined to be 'pedalling his skybike' and the nuns are compared to women 'frantically in labour' and doctors and midwives are described weaving 'in and out/ In gowns of smoke and fire'. There is also an image of Christ 'in his dressing gown' tearing 'up and down the dormitory, splashing water' on the nuns' souls. We might imagine that the smoke that the nun is inhaling and the heat of the fire are causing her to see and experience very strange things.

The second part of the poem features perhaps the strangest images of all. We are presented with an image of Jesus on Grafton Street listening to a 'female punk' speak the nun's tale. We are also presented with an image of the dead nuns crawling out from under a bandstand in St Stephen's Green and praying by a statue.

Sport

BACKGROUND

In this poem the poet addresses his father, with whom he had a difficult relationship. As Durcan himself describes it: 'When I was ten, he began to be somewhat problematic. When I think about it there were gratuitous beatings and he was incredibly severe about things like examinations. If I hadn't got second or third place it was bad news, and sometimes he would take the strap off his trousers and beat me. A man has to be so very complicated if he takes a school report for a ten-year-old that seriously'.

Durcan's father was a high-ranking judge, and in the poet's account emerges almost as a stereotype of that profession – as a stern, severe and uncompromising man to whom discipline was everything. He could make no sense of his son's sensitive personality and artistic inclinations. To him these seemed like signs of insanity or mental disorder.

Over the poet's teenage years the relationship between father and son became increasingly tense and then broke down completely. Finally, when the poet was nineteen, his father, along with other family members, had him committed to a psychiatric hospital. He spent the next several years in and out of various mental institutions.

LINE BY LINE

'Sport' recalls a memory from that difficult period. As he turned twenty-one, the poet was being held in Grangegorman Mental Hospital: 'I was a patient/ In B Wing'. He was selected to play in goal for the hospital's Gaelic-football team in a match against Mullingar Mental Hospital. Both teams, it appears, consisted solely of inmates rather than of staff members.

The poet provides a vivid portrait of the opposing team. He emphasises the great size and bizarre appearance of the Mullingar players, describing them as 'big country men' who had 'gapped teeth, red faces,/ Oily, frizzy hair, bushy eyebrows'.

As goalkeeper, the poet was unsurprisingly focused on the Mullingar forward division, who would be bearing down on the goal he was tasked with protecting. He stresses the enormity of their full-forward line, which was 'over six foot tall/ Fifteen stone in weight'. The three full-forwards were all schizophrenics, while the centre half-forward was rumoured to be an alcoholic solicitor locked up for castrating his best friend.

Yet the poet held his nerve and bravely defended his goal against the intimidatingly crazy Mullingar attack: 'To my surprise/ I did not flinch in the goals'. He played far better than he had expected to, executing several 'spectacular saves'. He found himself 'leaping high' to tip what would have been a 'certain goal' over the bar, and 'diving full stretch' to deny the Mullingar team.

The poet credits his impressive display to the fact that his father was present at the game. So keen was he to witness his son's performance that he drove all the way from Dublin to Mullingar: 'You drove all the way down,/ Fifty miles,/ To Mullingar to stand/ On the sidelines and observe me'.

The poet was determined not to disappoint his watching father: 'I was fearful I would let down/ Not only my team but you'. Indeed, he wanted to captivate, or 'mesmerise', him with the quality of his performance. His father's presence gave him the 'will to die', the motivation to ignore pain, risk and potential injury that he deems 'essential' to all sportsmen: 'It was my knowing/ That you were standing on the sideline/ That gave me the necessary motivation'. Because his father was watching, he was willing to throw himself at the ball even in the teeth of the burly and demented Mullingar attack.

The poem suggests that both artists and sportsmen share a particular, almost dysfunctional, mentality. According to the poet, both require a 'will to die', a willingness to do whatever it takes to attain their goals. We can see how this might be true of athletes, how they are required to train long after they have passed through the pain barrier, to throw themselves heedlessly into tackles, to keep fighting long after their bodies ache. But how is it true of artists? Perhaps Durcan has in mind here the artist's need to take risks with his or her own mental health. The artist, he seems to suggest, must expose him or herself to mental suffering and perhaps even to the risk of suicide. He or she must probe the darkest recesses of the mind, must explore all kinds of painful memory and emotion in the creation of art.

FORM

'Sport', like much of Durcan's poetry, is notable for its 'looseness', for its use of long lines and irregular stanzas.

A SENSE OF VOICE

In this poem we get a real sense of the young poet's state of mind and personality. We sense his vulnerability as he stands between the goalposts but also his hope and determination to impress his watching father.

STRANGE AND SURREAL IMAGERY

Like much of Durcan's poetry 'Sport' features imagery that is memorably strange, in particular the depiction of

the Mullingar players with their 'gapped teeth' and 'bushy eyebrows', of their centre half-forward who was rumoured to be an alcoholic solicitor locked up for castrating his best friend.

HUMOUR

This poem bristles with the zany humour for which Durcan's poetry is so often celebrated: the bizarre set-up of the match between two mental hospitals, the almost cartoonish depiction of the Mullingar team, the farcical final scoreline: 'Having defeated Mullingar Mental Hospital/ By 14 goals and 38 points to 3 goals and 10 points'. There is also the fact that one of the Mullingar players allegedly castrated his best friend but 'meant well' by doing so.

THEMES

FAMILY

This may seem like a funny and light-hearted poem but it provides a moving portrait of a complicated relationship between father and son. The father comes across not as loving and supportive but as severe, critical and judgmental. He seems to have a low opinion of his son and is dismissive of his talents and abilities: 'There were not many fields/ In which you had hopes for me'. Even the use of the word 'observe' in the first stanza indicates the father's cold and critical manner.

The poem also highlights the personality clash between father and son. The young poet was a sensitive, talented and artistic individual. But to his father these traits meant nothing. The father regarded his son's only success as playing on a 'winning team' for Grangegorman Mental Hospital: 'In your eyes I had achieved something at last'. The son would go on to become a famous and successful poet, but, again, to the father these achievements would mean little or nothing compared to his success in goal that day: 'Seldom if ever again in your eyes/ Was I to rise to these heights'.

This, then, is a highly dysfunctional relationship. And yet we sense that some affection remains between the two. The father, after all, turns up to support his son, travelling fifty miles to an obscure football match between two mental institutions. At the end of the game he seems to take genuine pride in his son's display: 'Sniffing your approval, you shook hands with me./ 'Well played, son.''

Perhaps he felt that at last his son was doing something he could understand, something manly and robust. Perhaps he felt that on this, his son's twenty-first birthday (the day traditionally thought to be the beginning of adulthood), his son was finally starting to act like a man. The poet's twenty-first birthday should have been a day of family celebration, yet it turns out to be a grim parody of togetherness, the father shaking hands with the son he's had incarcerated after a match between two mental hospitals.

The poet, too, displays a kind of affection toward the father who had him locked up. He is desperate to impress or 'mesmerise' him, and terrified of letting him down. The fact that his father is watching from the sidelines drives him on to play with the fearlessness and abandon of the true sportsman.

We are left, then, with an agonising sense of what might have been, that this father-and-son pair could, under different circumstances, have had a healthy and happy relationship. We sense the poet's anger at being incarcerated, at being misunderstood, dismissed and disregarded by his father. We perhaps also sense anger at his younger self for trying so hard to impress the man who had essentially had him locked up. And yet there is also a real sense of sorrow here, as if the poet acknowledges the residual love that continued to exist between them even after he had been committed. We sense him lamenting his father's own mental and emotional issues, and the terrible impact they had on their relationship.

Father's Day, 21 June 1992

LINE BY LINE

THE POET DEPARTS FOR CORK

The poet is preparing to leave his home in Dublin for two weeks. He will travel by train to Cork. A taxi has arrived to take him to the train station. The taxi driver waits outside the poet's house: 'The taxi was ticking over outside in the street'. The cab attracts the attention of the poet's neighbours: 'All the neighbours noticing it'. We can imagine how neighbours relaxing on this summer Sunday might find themselves idly gawking at this waiting vehicle.

The poet, meanwhile, is running late and feels he's in danger of missing his train. He seems flustered and disorganised, telling us twice how he's 'dashing' around the house. He runs up and down the stairs searching his pockets as if he's convinced he's forgetting something.

The poet's wife asks him a favour, requesting that he bring an axe to her sister in Cork: 'She told me that her sister in Cork wanted a loan of an axe'. The sister needs the axe to prune the buddleia tree in her back garden, which, because it is high summer, has 'grown out of control'.

The poet is initially reluctant to oblige, telling his wife that 'A simple saw would do the job, surely to God/ She could borrow a simple saw'. His reluctance is perhaps understandable. The axe is a large and fearsome weapon, 'all four-and-a-half feet of it'. Furthermore, his wife has made no effort to wrap it up in any way: 'She handed the axe to me just as it was,/ As neat as a newborn babe,/ All

in the bare buff '. We can understand how the poet might feel awkward about carrying around such a dangerous implement with nothing to conceal its blade: 'not a blanket, an old newspaper … not even a token hanky/ Tied in a bow round its head'.

However, the poet agrees to bring the axe to Cork. He's in a rush and simply doesn't have time to argue. Furthermore, he seems reluctant to quarrel with his wife just as he's about to leave her for two weeks: 'I decided not to argue the toss. I kissed her goodbye'. He also seems self-conscious about the taxi waiting outside under his neighbours' idle scrutiny.

GUILTY ON THE TRAIN

The poet realises that his wife is happy to see him depart for his two-week stay in Cork: 'I could see that she was glad/ To see me go away for a while'. The poet feels his wife will be glad of a break from him; she'll have the bed to herself, she won't have to put up with his sexual advances or dubious eating habits. Because the couple's daughters 'are all grown up and gone away', she'll have the house to herself, and she seems 'Glad at the prospect of being/ Two weeks on her own'.

The poet's reaction to this is most unusual. We might expect him to respond with anger and resentment, but instead he finds himself beset by terrible feelings of guilt: 'The whole long way down to Cork/ I felt uneasy. Guilt feelings./ It's a killer, this guilt'. The poet always feels guilty leaving his wife behind. But somehow the knowledge she's glad to see him go makes the guilt even more pronounced: 'I always feel bad leaving her/ But this time it was the worst'.

As the train approaches Portarlington station, the poet comes to a strange and sudden conclusion: he feels guilty because his wife has fallen slightly out of love with him. His wife's feelings have dimmed to the extent that she's glad to see the back of him for a fortnight. This makes the poet feel guilty. It's as if he's failed his wife by allowing her to fall out of love with him, by not remaining sexy, youthful or interesting enough over their years of marriage.

THE PASSENGER

The poet finds himself blurting out this sudden realisation to the passenger sitting opposite, asking 'I am feeling guilty because she does not love me/ As much as she used to, can you explain that?' This is obviously a bizarre question to ask a stranger. The poet describes how he 'overheard' himself speak, as if he spoke out loud without intending to. We can imagine how this happens sometimes, how we might find ourselves blurting out the answer when we are deep in thought and have a 'eureka' moment.

The poet's fellow passenger, however, is understandably taken aback by this sudden question from a complete stranger. The sight of the axe disturbs him further: 'The passenger's eyes were on the axe on the seat beside me'. The poet must strike him as a crazy and possibly dangerous individual, as some kind of madman who carries this dangerous weapon around while talking to himself.

The poet attempts to convince the passenger that he's actually normal. He tries to explain why he's carrying such a potentially deadly implement: 'Her sister wants a loan of the axe'. He finds himself babbling, as we often do in such awkward moments, and for no real reason he announces the name of Portarlington in Irish: 'As the train threaded itself into Portarlington/ I nodded to the passenger 'Cúl an tSúdaire!''

The passenger, however, is not convinced by this display. If anything, he's even more freaked out. Eager to escape what seems to him like a crazy person, he moves off to another area of the train: 'The passenger stood up, lifted down a case from the rack,/ Walked out of the coach, but did not get off the train'. The poet is left alone with the axe until the train reaches Cork.

THEMES

MARRIAGE

Durcan's poetry typically avoids an idealistic or fairytale view of marriage. Instead, poems such as 'Wife Who Smashed Television Gets Jail' and 'The MacBride Dynasty' are honest about the difficulty and conflict that lie at the heart of many marriages. 'Father's Day, 21 June 1992' is no exception to that rule. The poem highlights the difficulties that often arise when a couple have been married for a long time: the sexual passion between the couple has seemingly begun to fade. According to the poet, his wife now regards his sexual advances as a crude or vulgar form of pestering.

The poet also highlights how over time one's quirks and habits – such as eating habits – can become extremely annoying: 'Two weeks of not having to look up from her plate/ And behold me eating spaghetti with a knife and fork'.

The poem paints a frank and sorrowful picture of a couple who have fallen a little out of love, something that brings great guilt and distress to the poet: 'I am feeling guilty because she does not love me/ As much as she used to, can you explain that?'

The poem also highlights how suffocating it can become when you've lived with your partner for many years. The poet's wife is glad of the break his trip to Cork brings, is relieved to have the house and the bed to herself for two whole weeks. It has been suggested that the humorous image of the settee snapping shut 'with herself inside it' symbolises this suffocation. She is physically trapped by the settee bed just as she is emotionally stifled by the marriage.

The poem also describes the difficult transition that occurs when children leave home. The poet's daughters 'are all grown up and gone away'. The poet and his wife, then, have in a sense 'served their purpose' as a couple; they have raised their daughters and have successfully seen them off into the wider world. This requires a major readjustment of the couple's routines and daily lives, as well as a refocusing of their energies. Their marriage must change if it is to survive at all.

The symbol of the axe is important in this regard. The poet's wife gives him this dangerous naked blade, a dangerous implement that is to be used in the destruction of a tree. Perhaps the wife's 'gift' of this weapon to the poet symbolises the conflict that will emerge between them. Furthermore, at the end of the poem the poet sees the axe as a representation of his wife herself: 'we sat alone,/ The axe and I … All our daughters grown up and gone away'. Perhaps this suggests that the poet has come to view his wife as a source of conflict and pain; just as the axe poses physical danger, so she now poses emotional danger.

THEMES

However, it is also possible to view this symbolism in a more positive light. The axe, after all, may be dangerous but it is also a useful tool. The poet's wife is insistent that it be delivered to her sister so a particular job can be accomplished. In a sense, then, the axe might be seen as symbolising the wife's positive qualities: her practicality, attentiveness and generosity. The fact that the poet sees the axe as 'standing in' for his wife might mean that she is somehow always with him. It might suggest that, despite their difficulties, even when they are physically apart she is still at the forefront of his mind.

FAMILY

In Durcan's poetry, the notion of family is very much a double-headed axe. It can offer great comfort and consolation but can also be a terrible source of conflict. This poem focuses on the difficulty that arises when children leave home. The poem is entitled 'Father's Day, 21 June 1992', but in an important sense the poet is no longer a father. He still has daughters, of course, but they are 'grown up and gone away'. They no longer require him to play the father's role of carer and protector. Tellingly, the poet twice states that his daughters have left, in lines 42 and 59.

We get the impression that their departure not only contributes to the tension in the poet's marriage but also leaves him feeling abandoned, empty and perhaps even a little useless. His care and attention are now sadly surplus to his daughters' requirements.

MENTAL SUFFERING

Again and again, Durcan's poems deal with individuals in various states of mental torment. In 'Rosie Joyce', for instance, the poet confesses that for three years he has suffered terribly from depression, describing how he has existed 'in the slums of despair/ Unable to tell one day from the next'. In 'Sport', meanwhile, the poet finds himself confined to a mental institution.

The mental suffering in 'Father's Day, 21 June 1992' is much less extreme. Yet we must not dismiss it entirely. The poet comes to the grim and sudden realisation that his wife doesn't love him in the way she used to, that she's actually glad to have him out of the house. This realisation leaves the poet wracked with guilt, as if he blames himself for the dimming of his wife's affections: 'It's a killer, this guilt'. The knowledge that his daughters have left home also contributes to his negative state of mind. Their departure has left the poet feeling sad, useless and abandoned.

THE STRENGTH AND POWER OF WOMEN

Durcan's poetry frequently presents us with strong and powerful female figures. In this poem we get a sense that the poet's wife possesses such a strong personality. We are left with the impression that this is a cool, calm and competent woman who knows her own mind. For instance, she easily overcomes her husband's reluctance to bring the axe with him to Cork city. She is completely unfazed when the fold-up settee snaps around her pregnant body, while her husband panics and loses the plot completely. At the end of the poem, she is symbolically associated with the axe itself, which, as we've seen, might suggest her general competence, attentiveness and usefulness.

FORM

Like many of Durcan's poems 'Father's Day' is written in a loose free verse with lines and stanzas of an irregular length.

HUMOUR

This poem features a hint of Durcan's trademark surreal and zany humour, especially in the image of the flustered poet wandering around with a massive axe and talking to himself on the Dublin-to-Cork train. It is also evident in the image of the sofa-bed snapping shut to swallow his pregnant wife.

METAPHOR AND SYMBOLISM

The poem also features some very effective symbolism. The axe might symbolise the conflict that threatens to emerge in the poet's marriage, or might perhaps represent the wife herself. The bed snapping shut, too, serves a symbolic function, representing how the poet's wife feels stifled or suffocated by their relationship.

The Arnolfini Marriage

BACKGROUND

This poem comes from Durcan's 1994 collection entitled *Give Me Your Hand*, a series of poems loosely inspired by paintings in the National Gallery, London. This particular poem is inspired by Jan Van Eyck's painting *The Arnolfini Marriage*.

The painting's likely subjects, Giovanni Arnolfini and Giovanna Cenami, were wealthy merchant-class Italians. It is considered one of the most original and complex paintings in Western art. The painting is much admired for its unusual perspective, the richness of its imagery, and the use of the mirror to reflect space (the view in the mirror shows two figures just inside the door that the couple are facing). The portrait is also considered unique by some art historians as the record of a marriage contract in the form of a painting.

The couple are shown in an upstairs room containing a chest and bed. The two figures are very richly dressed, with both their outer garments trimmed and fully lined with fur. These outfits would have been enormously expensive, and appreciated as such by a contemporary viewer.

LINE BY LINE

THE SUPERIORITY OF THE ARNOLFINIS

We get a sense of the couple's privileged social status throughout the poem. They speak in an authoritative and superior manner, telling the poet plainly what he may not do: 'Do not think you may invade/ Our privacy because you may not'. They also make mention of their 'magnitude' or greatness, saying that the artist has so masterfully captured them that it is as if the greatness of their minds has been exposed in the painting: 'Our brains spill out upon the floor … The minutiae of our magnitude'.

Observing the couple in the painting seems to leave the poet feeling inadequate in comparison. Their 'magnitude' contrasts sharply with his more humble existence. He describes how he cycles to the gallery each day with his dog tied to the handlebars of his bike. It is as if the couple are judging him as he stands before the painting, and challenging him: 'Are you? Who eat alone? Sleep alone?'

THE COUPLE'S TOGETHERNESS

The couple place great stock on their marriage. They emphasise how they now think of themselves as a 'we' rather than two individuals 'I's. Their unity has brought an element of serenity into their lives: 'The most relaxing word in our vocabulary is 'we'.' The couple seem to feel that their ability to say 'we' also makes them superior to those who are not in a position to do so: 'Most people are in no position to say 'we'.'

The couple also state that their portrait is the 'most erotic portrait ever made'. Although there is little or nothing in the painting that might suggest eroticism to the modern viewer, there are certain details that represent or symbolise lust. For example, the little dog can be seen as an emblem of lust. Also, the curtains of the marriage bed have been opened and their redness is thought by some viewers to allude to the physical act of love between the married couple.

Again, the poet is left feeling inadequate in comparison. He is not in a 'position to say 'we'.' When he leaves the gallery in the evening, he goes home to 'eat alone' and to sleep 'alone'. The magnificent bed and furnishing of the Arnolfinis also likely show up the more humble abode that the poet is occupying while he works at the gallery.

A CELEBRATION OF THE ARTIST

The poem celebrates the great skill of the artist Van Eyck, who has captured the couple and the room in which they stand in extraordinary detail. He has managed to do 'justice' to the subjects of his painting, and the Arnolfinis seem to be very pleased with the results. The couple state that they chose Van Eyck because they had 'faith in the artist' to represent the things that matter most to them.

Once again, we can almost sense the poet's own feeling of inadequacy as he stands before this masterful work. Van Eyck has done such a magnificent job representing the Arnolfinis that there seems to be little or nothing left for the poet to say or write that will reveal anything further. The couple seem

One of the painting's most celebrated features is the mirror that hangs on the wall behind the couple, and in which two figures can be seen. Perhaps it is to this feature that the speaker alludes when he says that the artist has done 'justice' to their 'life as a reflection'. Van Eyck also painted the furniture in the room with incredible skill, and again the couple speak of their faith in his ability to do 'justice to their bed'. Perhaps most importantly, the artist has managed to convey a certain view of marriage that the poet suggests was important to the Arnolfinis. The couple associate marriage with specific ideas or concepts, and again they express their faith in Van Eyck's ability to represent these.

to hint at this when they tell the poet that he should not think that he can 'invade' their 'privacy'.

In the end, the poet seems to have had all he can take of being scrutinised and found wanting by these stern and powerful people. When he says that we 'will pause now for the Angelus', it is as if he is taking a much needed break. His final lines seem to have an air of resignation or acceptance. It is as if he is wearily acknowledging the fact that there are those like the Arnolfinis, with their magnificent lives and perfect marriages, and others like him, who 'eat alone' and sleep alone, and 'at dawn cycle to work'. Ultimately, however, it takes all kinds to make the world go around: 'Here you have it:/ The two halves of the coconut'.

THEMES

MARRIAGE

The painting is thought by many to represent the conventional 15th century views of marriage and gender roles. The poet lists four particular values that the couple wished the painter to convey: plurality, fertility, domesticity and 'barefootedness'. The 'plurality' of marriage, of being numerous rather than single, seems to be of great significance to the Arnolfinis. They are particularly proud of their ability to now say 'we'. There is a suggestion here that it is the proper condition of man and woman to be married, and that having achieved this the couple now feel more content: 'The most relaxing word in our vocabulary is 'we'.' Domesticity, the taking care of household affairs, is considered intrinsic to marriage. The ability of married couples to reproduce is also considered important. The Arnolfinis place particular emphasis on this, telling us that their bed is their 'most necessary furniture'. The fourth value associated with marriage is 'barefootedness'. It is not clear what the poet intends by this, but it might be a reference to the humbling nature of marriage, the relinquishing of individuality. There is a suggestion here that marriage entails an exposing of the self, a sort of nakedness before the other partner.

A CELEBRATION OF ART

'The Arnolfini Marriage' is one of a collection of poems that Durcan was commissioned by the gallery to write. When he was working on the project he spent his days at the gallery studying the paintings. 'The Arnolfini Marriage', spoken by the painting's subjects, clearly celebrates the artist's achievement. The couple say that they are only 'standing to [their] portrait' because of the belief they have in the artist as someone to 'do justice' to both them and their values. Van Eyck has managed to capture the 'minutiae' of this couple's magnificent life.

So faithful and penetrating is his work that it is as if he has revealed the Arnolfinis' inner thoughts. Using a rather bizarre and gruesome image, the speaker says that their 'brains spill out upon the floor', allowing the dog to sniff at the 'minutiae of [their] magnitude'. The suggestion here is that the artist has thoroughly cracked and exposed his subject. The effect of the work is so powerful that the couple seem to challenge and taunt the poet as he stands before the painting.

Ireland 2002

FORM

Durcan's poetry is known for its looseness, its use of long lines and irregular stanzas. 'The Arnolfini Marriage' is perhaps more formal than many of the poems on the course, being divided into eight stanzas of three lines each.

STRANGE AND UNUSUAL IMAGERY

Many of the images in the poem correspond closely with the painting that the poet describes, but there is one image that is very strange and bizarre. Durcan imagines how the couples' 'brains spill out upon the floor' for the 'terrier' at their feet to sniff.

A SENSE OF VOICE

The poem captures the rather stiff and arrogant voice of the Arnolfinis as they pontificate and preach to the poor poet. They needle him with questions and exhaust him with notions that his own life is inadequate compared to theirs.

HUMOUR

Durcan often uses self-deprecating humour in his poems. This is evident towards the end of 'The Arnolfini Marriage' where he mentions how he cycles to work each day with an 'Alsatian shepherd dog' attached to the handlebars of his bike. The image is especially humorous when compared with the grandeur and splendour of the Arnolfinis evident in the portrait he is studying.

LINE BY LINE

This poem is set in 2002, a time when the Irish economy experienced incredible growth. A new sense of confidence was palpable throughout the country. People were better off than ever before, and even those with average incomes could afford to purchase luxury items and go on foreign holidays. The poem captures this newfound sense of wealth and confidence. It is no longer a big deal to take a holiday in America. It is no longer a treat or something special. Indeed, such journeys have become so commonplace, whether they be short shopping trips to New York or extended vacations in Las Vegas, that it no longer feels like going abroad at all.

Yet it might also be argued that the poem highlights a spirit of brashness and boastfulness. Pride, after all, often comes before a fall, and there's only a thin line between confidence and overconfidence. And we can read the poem as criticising the vulgar and conspicuous consumption, the competitive spending and showing off that was evident in the country during the period around 2002, and which contributed to the demise of the economic boom and the country's slide back into recession.

The poem also touches on the relationship between Ireland and America. The person who answers the question doesn't view America as 'abroad'. To him or her, Ireland and America are essentially part of the same country. Perhaps the poem, therefore, can be read as criticising the 'Americanisation' of Ireland, lamenting the enormous influence American culture has on Irish people. We might think here of our favourite American movies, video games, TV shows, fashions and music. It isn't hard to identify the massive impact these have had on how Irish people speak, dress and even think. This process, the poem suggests, has progressed to such an extent that the two countries are now virtually indistinguishable.

Durcan is a master of the very short poem. His short poems often work like punchlines or visual gags. We stare for a second or two before the penny drops and the meaning dawns. In 'Ireland 2002', as in 'Madman' and 'En Famille', he manages to pack a great deal of meaning into a couple of lines. Such poems often work through juxtaposition, by combining two unlikely statements. In this instance, we are confronted with a question and a most unexpected answer.

Rosie Joyce

LINE BY LINE

The poet is staying near Achill in Co. Mayo. His daughter goes into labour in Dublin's Holles Street hospital. The poet drives from Mayo to Dublin, hoping to make it in time for the birth.

ACHILL AT DAWN

The poet rose very early that morning, and he paints a lovely picture of Achill Sound 'before daybreak'. The weather is warm and the first wildflowers of the year have started to bloom. The poet describes a riot of colour, emphasising the great variety of flower species to be found in this beautiful area of Ireland.

He mentions no fewer than eleven different species that have suddenly burst forth. Their bright colours fill the entire landscape, covering Achill Island and the mainland, bogs, cemeteries and the banks of streams. There is a real sense of hope in these lines as the poet captures the fertility, energy and freshness of an early summer morning.

THE POET SETS OUT ON HIS JOURNEY

That afternoon the poet sets out on his journey to Dublin. He will travel 'the waters and the roads of Ireland', on the 'two hundred miles from west to east'. He begins along the Old Turlough Road, passing the farm of his relative Walter Durcan, which a canopy of ash trees shelters like an umbrella. He continues eastward, driving down side roads and main roads, over bridges, up ramps and through roundabouts.

THE POET IS FILLED WITH JOY AND ELATION

This is his grandchild's 'Incarnation Day', the day when her soul or spirit will enter the world, and he seems almost intoxicated with happiness and anticipation. The knowledge that his grandchild is about to be born fills the poet with great joy.

It makes everything seems magical to him, not only the beautiful flowers of Achill Sound but also the cloudy sky that resembled 'blue-and-white china' and the furze bushes that made the fields resemble 'tartan rugs'. Even dull, ordinary things like roundabouts and bypasses seem filled with mystery and wonder: 'To drive such side-roads, such main roads, such ramps, such roundabouts,/ To cross such bridges, to by-pass such villages, such towns'.

THE POET OUTLINES HIS WISHES FOR HIS SOON-TO-BE-BORN GRANDCHILD

The poet outlines his hopes for his soon-to-be-born grandchild. Like a character in a fairy-tale, the poet makes three wishes, hoping for three distinct things for his granddaughter. He wishes that she will have a long life, that like the poet himself she will live to the age of fifty-six and beyond. He wishes that she will go on to have children and grandchildren of her own.

Finally, he wishes that she too will be lucky enough to experience a day like this, a day when even the most ordinary things are filled with mystery and wonder: 'May you some day in May/ Fifty-six years from today be as lucky/ As I was when you were born that Sunday'.

THE POET HEARS ABOUT ROSIE'S BIRTH

The poet does not reach Dublin in time for the birth. He's still in Mayo, on the Swinford bypass, when he receives a call from his son-in-law telling him that his granddaughter has been born: 'I heard Mark your father say:// 'A baby girl was born at 3:33p.m.' Thankfully, both the poet's daughter and newly born granddaughter are safe and well.

The poet refers to the Swinford bypass as 'P. Flynn's highway'. This is a reference to the controversial Mayo-based politician Pádraig Flynn. Flynn served as minister in several Fianna Fáil governments in the 1980s. The poet presumably feels that Flynn used his influence as a minister to secure funds for the building of the bypass and gain favour with his local constituents.

On this day, however, the poet seems unconcerned with such political matters. He doesn't even seem upset that he failed to reach Dublin in time for Rosie's birth. If anything, the news of Rosie's safe arrival into the world leaves him even more elated than he was before: 'That was that Sunday afternoon in May/ When a hot sun pushed through the clouds/ And you were born!'

THE POET CROSSES THE SHANNON

The poet continues driving quickly toward Dublin, eager to see his newly born granddaughter for the first time. He slows down only at Tarmonbarry, where he crosses the River Shannon, the traditional division between Ireland's western and eastern parts.

The poet remembers crossing the Shannon at this exact spot when he was a child, sitting in the back seat of his father's car: 'in my father's Ford Anglia half a century ago'. He remembers how at Tarmonbarry back then there stood a 'Bailey bridge', which was a type of cheap prefabricated bridge used commonly in Ireland and elsewhere in the 1940s and 1950s. He remembers how his father's car 'crashed, rattled, bounced' across this temporary structure.

His father always regarded crossing the Shannon as a special and significant act, one that meant traversing the 'Great Divide' between the West of Ireland and the rest of the country. He would slow down as he drove over the bridge, just as the poet himself slows down on this special day fifty years later. He would solemnly 'enunciate' the name of the great river, almost as if he was saying a prayer. In his own small way he felt like Moses, who in the Bible led his people on an epic voyage across the Red Sea: 'Daddy relishing his role as Moses'.

The poet's father would lament the state of Ireland's West, which for centuries has been the country's poorest region. He would complain how for generations the people of the West were forced to leave their homes, moving to Dublin or to England in search of employment and a better life. As they crossed that old Bailey bridge, the poet's father would solemnly declare that 'We are the people of the West,/ Our fate to go East'.

THE POET REACHES DUBLIN

Eventually the poet reaches Dublin. Usually, he hates returning to the capital from his stays in Mayo. He has several poems describing how he finds the city grubby and depressing after Co. Mayo's great beauty and serenity.

On this occasion, however, he is delighted to make his return, to drive past Kilmainham and the Grand Canal: 'Never before had I felt so fortunate/ To be driving back into Dublin city'.

His granddaughter's birth has filled him with such happiness that even the banal city sights seem beautiful. The canal bridges, for instance, resemble silvery or 'pewter brooches'.

THE POET HOLDS HIS GRANDDAUGHTER FOR THE FIRST TIME

The poet reaches Holles Street hospital and sees Rosie for the first time. He describes how her birth brought joy to the assembled members of the family: 'Popping out of my daughter, your mother –/ Changing the expressions on the faces all around you'.

Not surprisingly, he finds holding her an incredibly moving experience. He finds himself laughing out loud, overcome with emotion: 'How I laughed when I cradled you in my hand'. He describes her as a 'seashell at my ear', suggesting that her cooing and breathing sounds resemble the repetitive and rhythmic noises of the ocean.

He describes how Rosie's birth lifted a great depression that had overwhelmed him. For three years, he says, he had 'subsisted' or survived in the 'slums in despair'. Life, it seems, had taken on a kind of monotonous greyness, and he was 'Unable to distinguish one day from the next'. He describes how Rosie's birth 'saved my life', suggesting perhaps that in his depression, life had become unbearable and that he was contemplating ending it all.

The poet will return to Mayo a happy man. Rosie's birth has relieved the great depression that threatened to overwhelm him. In a single day, three years of suffering have been cancelled out.

THE POET RETURNS TO MAYO

On his way back West, the poet stops in Charlestown, where he meets an acquaintance of his, an organic farmer called John Normanly. Normanly is travelling back from a meeting of the Western Development Commission, an organisation devoted to promoting economic and social development in Ireland's western region.

The meeting between the two men seems a little awkward, as chance encounters between acquaintances can sometimes be. The poet 'wavers' on the street as if he's uncertain whether to move on or continue with the conversation. Meanwhile, Normanly 'crouches' in his car, as if he's uncertain about whether he should step out and engage the poet more deeply in conversation.

The poet and Normanly praise the work of John Moriarty, an Irish philosopher and writer who preached that human beings can and should live in harmony with nature and with one another. He describes how he and Normanly bless themselves or 'wet their foreheads' in the autobiography of this great thinker. Perhaps the poet is being metaphorical here, comparing the activity of praising and honouring a writer's work to the activity of blessing oneself in that writer's name. Or perhaps he and his friend actually do half-jokingly bless themselves in honour of Moriarty's new book. In any case, we get the impression they regard Moriarty as a kind of saintly presence in Irish life.

The poem concludes with a prayer of thanks. The following Sunday, we're told, is the Feast of the Ascension, on which Christians celebrate how Jesus was lifted body and soul into heaven. The poet, however, is more interested in celebrating Rosie's birth, which he views as an example of the opposite process. Rosie's body and soul, he suggests, descended from heaven into this world: 'Thank You, O Lord, for the Descent of Rosie onto Earth.'

THEMES

MENTAL SUFFERING

Like many of Durcan's poems, 'Rosie Joyce' presents us with an individual in a state of extreme emotional distress. The poet describes how for three years he has been suffering through a terrible bout of depression.

He describes how he's been 'subsisting', or surviving, rather than really living, the phrase 'slums of despair' brilliantly capturing the misery he's suffered. Like many depressed people, he's found life grey, monotonous and unchanging; he's been 'Unable to distinguish one day from the next'.

The birth of his granddaughter, however, changes all that. Indeed, he claims that Rosie's birth saved his life. This might suggest that the poet was so depressed he considered taking his own life. Yet it might also suggest how Rosie has given the poet his life back by lifting the cloud of despair that hung over him. Tellingly, the poet mentions how the 'sun pushed through the clouds', and he lovingly describes the colourful wild flowers that have sprung up all over Achill. The light and colour returning to the world in springtime reflects how Rosie's birth has brought joy and hope back to the poet's life, lifting the grey fog of depression that clouded his existence.

RELIGION

Durcan is somewhat unusual among poets in that he remains a religious writer, retaining something of his Christian faith while his fellow poets are overcome with doubt. 'Rosie Joyce' can be read as one long prayer of thanksgiving and celebration in which the poet thanks God for the safe arrival of his granddaughter. We see this at the poem's conclusion when the poet declares: 'Thank You, O Lord, for the Descent of Rosie onto Earth'. This tone of ecstatic and joyous prayer runs through the entire piece. The poet captures how special and miraculous he regards Rosie's birth by referring to two Christian mysteries: the Incarnation and the Ascension.

Importantly, the poem is set during springtime, during the Church's Easter season between the Feast of Easter itself and the Feast of the Ascension. This is a time of rebirth and hope in nature, as emphasised by the poet's description of sunlight and freshly emerging wildflowers. It is also the period when Christians celebrate rebirth and salvation; Christ rises from the tomb and saves mankind from sin and death. This particular year it also proves a time of salvation and rebirth for the poet himself; Rosie's arrival saves him from depression ('You saved my life') and gives him the hope to begin afresh.

IRELAND AND IRISH HISTORY

This poem takes the form of a journey from east to west, and it highlights the economic differences between Ireland's eastern and western halves. As the poet crosses the Shannon, the traditional 'Great Divide' between the two regions, the poet remembers his father lamenting the west's impoverished status and how its people were forced to move east in search of work: 'We are the people of the West,/ Our fate to go East'.

Yet the poem is not all doom and gloom in this regard. The poet is keenly aware that there are people, like the organic farmer John Normanly, who bring to the West sustainable economic activity. He knows that there are organisations like the Western Development Committee that attempt to foster economic and social growth in the region. We are left with the impression that in the poet's eyes the West is not doomed to remain eternally poor, but that with sufficient effort and ideas it can have a bright future.

An important aspect of Durcan's outlook is his emphasis on plurality rather than uniformity. Again and again, he stresses the uniqueness of individuals in all their quirks and strangeness. He resists the idea that people should be forced to conform with some uniform or preconceived idea of what a human being should be. He celebrates the fact that Ireland is plural rather than uniform, that it consists of wildly varied people and places, and hopes it'll stay like this forever: 'No such thing, Rosie, as a Uniform Ireland/ And please God there never will be'.

The poem describes nature as a 'higher power than politics'. Kings, politicians and dictators, conflicts, wars and peace treaties – all of these have come and gone, and will come and go again. Yet the Irish landscape with its flora, fauna and people remains, and will remain after all such power grabs have long ago been forgotten.

FAMILY

It could be argued that the theme of family dominates Durcan's poetry like no other. 'Rosie Joyce' offers a positive view of family and belonging, highlighting how the arrival of a new baby can fill an entire family with joy: 'Popping out of my daughter, your mother –/ Changing the expressions on the faces all around you – /All of them looking like blue hills in a heat haze'.

We've already seen the profound effect her birth has on the poet himself: it makes not only his day but his week and his year, relieving the terrible depression that has dominated his life for the past three years. It transforms his view of the world so that everything – even canal bridges, side roads, ramps and roundabouts – seems magical. To him Rosie's birth seems nothing less than miraculous, a religious or spiritual experience that transforms his consciousness and leaves him feeling hopeful and renewed.

This poem, like 'The MacBride Dynasty', highlights how families stretch across the years, passing on a sense of inheritance from generation to generation and providing its members with a sense of support, meaning and belonging. The poet is highly concerned with the newer generations of his family: he races across the country to be with his daughter and her husband, and celebrates the arrival of his granddaughter. Yet on this joyful occasion, he also takes time to remember his own father. He slows down when crossing the Shannon at Tarmonbarry, just as his father did when the poet was a boy.

An unusual feature of this poem is that it extends the notion of family into the landscape itself. The poet regards the rivers and mountains of Ireland as relatives, as a large extended family of a kind: 'There is only the River Shannon and all her sister rivers/ And all her brother mountains'. The mountains are described as enjoying 'family prospects'. They look down from their lofty heights and take in members of their own family – the hills, woods and valleys that make up the Irish landscape. The country's plants and flowers – and even its people – are all members of this great clan, tribe or family. Everything in nature is in an important sense related.

A SENSE OF VOICE

We get a real sense of the poet's joy, relief and gratitude as we follow him on his journey eastward to greet his newborn granddaughter. This expressive, celebratory tone is nowhere more evident than when the poet holds Rosie for the first time: 'How I laughed when I cradled you in my hand'. The poet's tone throughout might be described as one of praise or prayer, as if he's offering up a hymn of thanksgiving for Rosie's birth: 'Thank You, O Lord, for the Descent of Rosie onto Earth'.

METAPHOR, SIMILE AND FIGURES OF SPEECH

This poem is especially rich in metaphor. In a brilliantly inventive phrase, the poet compares the landscape to a picnic scene, describing how the fields resemble 'tartan rugs', while the sky resembles 'blue-and-white china'. The thin blooms of the Arum lilies are compared to 'yellow forefingers', while the hawthorns are compared to white powder smeared across the landscape: 'The first hawthorns powdering white the mainland'.

The ash trees on Walter Durcan's farm are compared to 'joined handwriting', and we can imagine how their branches might be said to resemble an elaborate cursive script. They are also compared to an 'umbrella' because the canopy they form shelters the farmhouse from the elements.

In another memorable phrase, the poet compares suffering from depression to living in a miserable slum: 'For three years/ I had been subsisting in the slums of despair', while Rosie herself is likened to a seashell at the poet's ear, suggesting how to him her cooing and breathing resembles the noises of the sea. The poem features several instances of personification. The River Shannon, for instance, is depicted as a female presence, almost as a goddess whose presence flows through the entire country. Ireland's mountains and rivers, meanwhile, are depicted as this great waterway's brothers and sisters. The night-time, too is personified almost as a goddess or mythical being that pushes the Arum lilies up through the soil.

Another metaphorical phrase occurs when the poet declares that 'neither words nor I/ Could have known that you had been named already'. The poet seems to be suggesting that Rosie's mother had already picked a name for the child she was expecting but had told no one of her choice. The name 'Rosie' had yet to be spoken in relation to this child. The choice of name was still beyond words and language.

The MacBride Dynasty

LINE BY LINE

A CHILDHOOD VISIT

The poet remembers a childhood visit to his great-aunt, a woman called Maud Gonne. The visit took place in 1949 when the poet was only four years old and had just started to walk and talk: 'Now that I have become a walking, talking little boy'. Maud Gonne lived in Roebuck House, which was near what at the time were the outskirts of Dublin. His mother drove herself and her son in a 'black Ford Anglia'.

The poet's mother seems eager to 'show off' her young son, taking him to see Maud Gonne just as soon as he can walk and talk. She is filled with 'motherly pride' and wants her aunt to see this 'latest addition to the extended family'. Maud Gonne is no ordinary relative. She was a famous patriot, political activist and campaigner for Irish independence from British rule. She was also an actress known in her youth for her great beauty. She had a famously turbulent relationship with the great poet W.B. Yeats.

The poet's mother dislikes Maud because of an event that took place in 1905, forty-three years before this visit. Maud married Major John, the pride of the MacBride family. In 1905, however, the couple's marriage was breaking down and relations between them became very difficult. At that time, Maud accused Major John of abusing Iseult, her daughter from a previous relationship, accusations now almost universally believed to be false.

Maud had entered the MacBride family when she married the poet's great-uncle, Major John MacBride, who became a national hero when he was executed for his part in the 1916 Easter Rising. He was also a hero within the family: 'most … courageous of soldiers,/ The pride of our family'.

The poet brings to mind Maud's storied past, referring to her as 'Cathleen Ní Houlihan', a character she played in her most famous stage performance. He also refers to Maud as 'the servant of the Queen', which was the title of Maud's autobiography. The 'Queen' Maud served was of course not the ruler of England but the spirit of Irish independence itself.

He was celebrated within the family not only for his bravery but also for his humility. He was the 'most ordinary of men', a man without any airs and graces. Furthermore, he was a most 'gay' or 'Humorous' person who brought laughter to all who remembered him: 'Whose memory always brought laughter/ To my grandmother Eileen's lips'.

AN AGED BEAUTY

At the time of the visit, Maud was eighty years old. Age had ruined her once-beautiful face: 'her lizards of eyes darting about/ In the rubble of the ruins of her beautiful face'. Her hands had withered so they resembled 'claws', and her eyes now had a 'lizard' quality. The elderly Maud had 'taken to her bed', seemingly not well enough now to be up and about.

There are indications, however, that despite her old age Maud remains somewhat vain and egotistical. She was keen, we're told, to receive 'admirers', suggesting that despite her ill health she was eager to see those who would compliment her and remind her of former glories.

The great actor and director Micheál Mac Liammóir was one such 'admirer'. He had behaved in a most theatrical and flattering fashion when he visited Maud the previous week, kneeling before her with a rose in one hand and the other clutched to his heart. He theatrically recited the poems of Maud's famous former lover, many of which were dedicated to Maud herself. We can imagine Maud relishing this worship.

We also get the impression that even in her old age Maud remains a regal and dignified presence. She lives in Roebuck House, a mini-mansion on the edge of Dublin with a walled orchard, a 'wrought-iron balcony' and extensive grounds. She 'receives' guests who are 'announced' into her presence as if she were a noble lady. Perhaps the descriptions of her as 'Cathleen Ní Houlihan' and 'a servant of the Queen' reinforce this impression.

THE YOUNG POET GETS A FRIGHT

The young poet and his mother are brought in to see Maud, who we're told loved to be visited 'Especially [by] the children of the family'. She seems to genuinely like children and reaches out to embrace the young boy who has been brought into her presence. The young poet, however, is frightened by Maud's aged and withered appearance, by her hands that resemble 'claws' and her 'lizards of eyes'. He rejects the old woman's embrace and flees in panic: 'Terrified, I recoiled from her embrace/ And, fleeing her bedroom, ran down the stairs/ Out onto the wrought-iron balcony'. His uncle calms him and takes him for a soothing walk in the orchard.

THE MOTHER'S REACTION

The poet's mother was understandably embarrassed and awkward about this incident. Yet she was not overly embarrassed. As the poet puts it: 'Mummy was a little but not totally mortified'. It turns out in fact that the poet's mother was never too fond of Maud in the first place: 'She had never liked Maud Gonne'.

The MacBride family, it seems, are still bitter about these long-ago accusations, which they regard as a terrible betrayal. The poet's mother, for instance, had 'never liked Maud Gonne because of Maud's/ Betrayal of her husband, Mummy's Uncle John'. The MacBrides must put up with Maud because through marriage she is a part of their extended family: 'For dynastic reasons we would tolerate Maud'. They may dislike her for that long-ago betrayal, but she remains John's widow and the mother of Seán, the poet's uncle. Yet while they must tolerate Maud, they would 'always see through her'. They would always be aware of the disloyal and treacherous streak that lay beneath her regal exterior.

THEMES

FAMILY

This poem stresses the difference between family and dynasty. A 'dynasty' is usually considered to be a line of rulers from the same family. The poem's title, 'The MacBride Dynasty', refers not to a succession of rulers exactly but to a succession of successful and prominent people, all members of the extended MacBride clan.

The poet's mother 'never liked' Maud and is only a 'little but not totally mortified' by her son's embarrassing behaviour. Yet they 'tolerate' Maud for 'dynastic reasons': she has contributed to the dynasty, to the extended family's renown, both through her own fame and through her son Seán, who became a prominent public figure in his own right.

The poem's opening lines highlight this distinction between family and dynastic loyalty. The poet's mother experiences 'motherly' pride; pride in her own children and perhaps in her immediate blood relatives. But she also experiences 'dynastic' pride; pride in the standing and achievements of the broader MacBride clan. It could be argued that Maud's betrayal of Major John brings these two types of pride into conflict.

In one sense, 'The MacBride Dynasty' celebrates the importance of family. A family, the poem suggests, is a network of connections that stretches across the generations, one that provides individuals with a sense of support, meaning and belonging. Through the mention of Major John, it stresses how each family remembers its dead, and perhaps how we ourselves might be remembered by our own families when we pass on.

Yet it also shows the delight we take in new additions to our families. The poet's mother is filled with 'motherly pride' over her 'walking, talking little boy'. She is eager to 'show off' this 'latest addition to the extended family'. Maud, too, takes great pleasure in seeing 'the children of the family'.

MARRIAGE

A feature of Durcan's poetry is that it presents marriage in a realistic and unflattering light. We see this in 'The MacBride Dynasty', which highlights how the marriage between Maud

Gonne and Major John MacBride ended in recrimination and betrayal. Indeed, the bitterness of that break-up still lingers within the family decades later. The poem, then, reminds us how often marriage is not a fairy-tale union but a journey full of difficulty and conflict.

The poet's mother takes what might strike us as a very traditional view of marriage. She resents Maud for being a 'disloyal wife': 'loyalty/ In Mummy's eyes was the cardinal virtue'. For the poet's mother, Maud's disloyalty makes her unworthy of affection: 'Maud Gonne was a disloyal wife/ And, therefore, not worthy of Mummy's love'.

IRELAND AND IRISH HISTORY

Many of Durcan's poems deal with the topic of Irish history. What makes 'The MacBride Dynasty' stand out is that it approaches this theme in a very personal way. The poet highlights his own membership of an important dynasty in Irish life; he belongs to a long line of prominent and successful individuals, all linked to the same extended family.

The poet has family ties to historical figures like Maud Gonne, Major John MacBride and Seán MacBride, Furthermore, through them he is connected to famous artists, such as W.B. Yeats and Micheál Mac Laimmóir. All of these individuals, of course, played a significant role in Irish public life.

THE STRENGTH AND POWER OF WOMEN

Durcan entitled one of his books *The Laughter of Mothers*, so it shouldn't surprise us that he holds mothers and motherhood in the greatest of esteem. He describes each young mother as a kind of 'goddess'. Mothers, in his eyes, play arguably the most important role in society. He stresses how mothers take great 'pride' both in their own children and in the greater dynasty to which they belong.

Yet he stresses that motherhood has a 'vengeful' and 'spitting' aspect, reminding us how mothers protect their families just as female animals protect their young. We see this in the way the poet's mother had never forgiven Maud for her treatment of Major John. The mother would never deem Maud worthy of her love, and would always be convinced she could 'see through' her likeable exterior. Who would cross such an unforgiving and spitting 'goddess' of vengeance?

The strength and power of women is also evident in the figure of Maud herself. She, too, possesses familial and dynastic pride, taking great delight in meeting new additions to her extended family. Though age has left her 'great beauty' in ruins, we get the impression that she retains much of her poise and elegance. This, we're reminded, is a strong and powerful woman who achieved prominence and influence, and is happy to be reminded of this earlier success by famous visitors like Mac Liammóir.

Robert Frost

Themes

Nature

Frost was famous as a poet of the American outdoors who celebrated the New England countryside. In 'After Apple-Picking' the poet captures the beauty and atmosphere of the late autumn harvest, describing the frost-covered grass and the wonderful colours of the apples that are being gathered. Even in the otherwise bleak "Out, Out –", Frost takes the time to praise the natural world, celebrating the 'Sweet-scented' freshly cut sawdust, and memorably describing how the Vermont landscape stretches into the distance. 'The Tuft of Flowers', too, celebrates the beauty and power of the natural world. The speaker likens the tuft with its dramatic colours to flames leaping from the ground: 'A leaping tongue of bloom'.

'Spring Pools' provides a vivid portrayal of nature's fragile beauty. There is a peculiar icy charm to the description of the leafless trees, the shivering winter flowers, and the freezing pools that reflect the sky with crystal clarity. Similarly, 'Birches' describes ice melting in the trees in the morning sun. The image of the shards of ice falling and shattering on the ground is wonderful. There is also the beautiful description of the birches when they have been bent to the forest floor, their trunks arched and their leaves trailing on the ground. Frost likens these trees to 'girls on hands and knees that throw their hair/ Before them over their heads to dry in the sun.'

Many of Frost's poems present the natural world as a source of consolation and inspiration. In 'Birches' he describes how the forest can be a source of fun for the boy working on his father's farm. The activity of climbing and 'swinging' birches provides valuable lessons for the boy, teaching him the value of patience and composure. In later years, the poet turns to the natural world as a means of escape from the tribulations of life. He thinks of the birch as a temporary escape from life's troubles, a way to leave earth behind for a while and to return refreshed and rejuvenated.

In 'The Tuft of Flowers', the natural world consoles the speaker, enabling him to overcome the gloomy, introspective mood that he experienced when he first arrived to work in the field. The flowers cause him to notice other aspects of the natural world that surround him, opening his ears to the sounds of 'the wakening birds'. They serve as a 'message from the dawn', a signal to the speaker that others share his appreciation of beauty: 'feel a spirit kindred to my own'. They teach him the lesson that no man works in isolation.

However, for Frost nature isn't all sweetness and light. 'Spring Pools' reminds us how death and life coexist at the heart of nature. With the changing of each season some elements of nature are destroyed and some are born again. The spring pools and winter flowers will be swept away so that the trees can flourish and put out their leaves. The poem considers the way nature moves in cycles of death and rebirth. Each element of nature dies and is reborn as the seasons change.

'Design' reminds us that the natural world can be bloody and unpleasant just as often as it is beautiful and serene. The image of the spider catching the moth reminds us the natural world is full of dangerous predators, and often one creature must die for another to live. In 'Mending Wall' nature is associated with supernatural forces, in this case with the malevolent woodland 'elves'. There is a menacing sense in the poem that nature barely tolerates human civilization. Nature is depicted as resisting man's attempts to impose order with our walls, bridges and boundary lines.

Transcience and Brevity

Frost's work often focuses on situations that pass away; moments that exist for only a fleeting instant before disappearing. 'Spring Pools', for example, concerns the loss of pools that were formed 'only yesterday' when melted snow poured down into the forest. These pools will likely begin disappearing in a few days' time, sucked up by the surrounding trees. 'After Apple-Picking' describes the end of the harvest and the arrival of winter. It seems only a short while ago that the trees were loaded with apples. Now their branches are barren and frost covers the grass. In 'The Tuft of Flowers' the description of the butterfly searching for a flower that it had rested upon the previous day also suggests the transience of life.

Frost's poems also explore the fragility of human life. "Out, Out –" reminds us that in the middle of even the most ordinary day life can be snatched away from us. All it takes is a moment's loss of concentration with a vehicle or power tool to turn an ordinary day to tragedy. The poem urges us not to take life for granted. 'Provide, Provide', makes a similar point, highlighting how transient beauty, youth and fame can be. The Hollywood star described in the opening lines suddenly

finds that she is a 'withered hag' that no one recognises, reduced to cleaning steps for a living.

'The Road Not Taken' also touches on the transience of life. When the poet decides to take one road he hopes that he might return to the same place sometime in the future and try the other road. However, he knows that this is not likely to happen: 'I doubted if I should ever come back.' Life is too short for us to get the chance to try different options. We choose our paths and must stick with them.

Sorrow and Despair

'Acquainted With the Night' is probably Frost's greatest depiction of despair. It provides a moving portrayal of a mind in the grip of insomnia and depression. The speaker's demons will give him no rest. His inner turmoil will not allow him to sleep, relax or even sit still. He must always keep moving, his restlessness mirroring the agitated condition of his mind. The grim urban landscape through which he walks serves as the perfect metaphor for his despair.

'The Tuft of Flowers' begins with a similar feeling of dejection and loneliness, as the speaker arrives to work in a field alone. However, in this case the speaker's spirits are eventually lifted when he finds a tuft of flowers that the mower has preserved.

A number of Frost's poems describe a need to escape the world for a while. In 'After Apple-Picking', the tiredness that the speaker describes seems more than physical exhaustion – there is a weariness with life itself evident in the poem. The very thing that motivated him – the prospect of a bountiful harvest – has lost its gloss. The speaker is mentally worn out and unable to muster any enthusiasm for the work that is now almost done. He longs for a long sleep, similar to the woodchuck's hibernation, to restore his enthusiasm for life.

The poem can be compared to 'Birches' where the speaker talks about being 'weary of considerations' and needing to get away from life for a while.

In 'The Road Not Taken', the poet laments that he is unable to travel both roads and has to choose between them. There is a real sense of sorrow to the acknowledgement that he will never be able to return to this fork and see where the other road led.

Sorrow is also a major theme in "Out, Out –". However, here it is the apparent absence of sorrow at the tragic accident that is most noteworthy. The farm workers permit themselves little or no time to grieve for the dead boy before they turn 'to their affairs'. There is something brutal about the way the people on the farm just get on with their lives after the boy's death. Many readers are inclined to criticise the farm workers for expending so little grief on behalf of the dead boy; however, the poem highlights the uncomfortable truth that life must always go on. This was especially true on a New England farm a century ago, when conditions were extremely tough. A livelihood must be created and the dead boy has no more to contribute to this process: 'No more to build on there.'

A Cold Universe

In 'Design', Frost argues that the world is a meaningless place. He suggests that there is no God or higher intelligence that runs the universe. Instead everything that happens to us, both good and bad, is entirely random. Our lives are just a series of flukes that serves no higher purpose.

'Acquainted With the Night' also depicts a universe where there is no God to hear our prayers and pleas. At the poem's conclusion the speaker gazes up at the moon's 'luminary clock'. He seems to be looking to the heavens for a solution to his troubles. However, there is nothing out there and the speaker gets no answers. The moon will only proclaim, mysteriously, that the time is 'neither wrong nor right'. Perhaps Frost is referring to the concept of morality – of right and wrong – in these lines. In a world where God doesn't exist, how can the concepts of 'right' and 'wrong' make any sense?

'Provide, Provide' also depicts the world as a cold and brutal place. The poem tells us that it is our responsibility to take care of ourselves and that we should not expect anything from society. If we want to survive with dignity, we must be self-reliant and not fool ourselves that the world is anything other than cruel and uncaring. Frost's description of the old woman in the opening lines is pitiless, a reflection of this grim philosophy.

"Out, Out –" is similarly cold and unflinching in how it depicts the farm workers turning 'to their affairs' immediately after the boy's death. They cannot allow grief to interfere with the business of survival. The boy's death is depicted as accidental and futile, with no greater meaning to be drawn from it.

Childhood

In 'Birches' Frost memorably celebrates the freedom and imagination we associate with childhood, depicting the young speaker as a champion swinger of birches. The poet longs to be able to return to this time and escape the troubles of life.

He also captures the mentality of childhood in "Out, Out –". The boy in the poem is a 'big boy' capable of doing 'man's work'. However, even this strong adolescent is really just a 'child at heart'. The boy still feels the delight a child takes in being given a break from the routine of work or study: 'the half hour/ That a boy counts so much when saved from work.'

Isolation and Community

Many of Frost's poems deal with isolated individuals. In 'Birches' the poet describes a solitary boy living in the country, 'too far from town to learn baseball'. Though he is without companionship, the boy finds pleasure in his solitary activities, challenging himself to bend every one of his father's birch trees to the ground. The poem is a celebration of the pleasures of solitude. A similar need for solitude is evident in 'After Apple-Picking', where the speaker has left the company of his fellow workers and now longs to sleep.

In 'The Tuft of Flowers' the speaker must come to terms with the isolation he feels from working alone. The speaker's initial loneliness leads him to a gloomy conclusion about the human condition. He states that 'all must be [alone] … Whether they work together or apart.' However, the discovery of the tuft of flowers changes the speaker's mind. Although the mower likely spared the flowers purely for his own enjoyment, the fact that they were left standing means that the speaker can also experience the same joy. The sight of the flowers gives the speaker a sense of connection and community.

No such sense of community is offered in 'Provide, Provide'. Here Frost describes the isolation of old age. The poem warns us to do everything in our power when we are young to avoid being alone when we are old. It is all too easy to neglect the future when we are young, but Frost tells us that we would be foolish to assume everything will just work itself out as we get older. We should act now to ensure comfort and support for our later years. We should not expect care from the community but should provide for ourselves.

'Acquainted With the Night' is a similarly hard-hitting study of isolation. The speaker spends his nights cut off from his friends and family, walking alone through the city. The streets he walks through are mostly empty, with the speaker himself producing the only 'sound of feet'. Even when he encounters other people his isolation holds. He silently passes the watchman without talking to him or even looking him in the eye. The cry he hears is 'interrupted' and is not meant for him in the first place. The speaker is utterly and terrifyingly alone.

'Mending Wall' reminds us that people must have clear and defined boundaries between them if community is to be maintained. We must respect other people's property – and society's rules and regulations – if we are to live in harmony together. A failure to respect boundaries would lead to chaos. As the poet's neighbour puts it: "Good fences make good neighbors." The spring ritual of mending the wall is a social event that brings the poet and his neighbour together each year. Paradoxically, reinforcing the boundaries between their lands reinforces their sense of community, too.

The Tuft of Flowers

LINE BY LINE

LINES 1 TO 10

The speaker of the poem has come to a field to 'turn the grass'. This grass was cut by another man very early in the morning, 'before the sun' had risen. The mower used a scythe – a long, curved blade – to cut the grass. The grass was wet with dew when it was cut, helping the blade to slice cleanly through the grass: 'The dew … made his blade so keen'. The dew has since gone but the piles of cut grass are still wet, so the speaker has come to turn the grass so it can dry in the sun.

The speaker looks to see if the mower is still around. He checks behind an 'isle' of trees and then listens to see if he can hear the mower sharpening his blade: 'I listened for his whetstone on the breeze.' But the mower has gone, his work done. The speaker resigns himself to the fact that he must get on with his work alone, just as the mower had been alone when working earlier that morning. He feels dejected and thinks to himself that it is man's lot to be alone, even when he works with others: "As all must be [alone]… Whether they work together or apart."

LINES 11 TO 19

Just as he is saying this to himself, a butterfly flies past. The butterfly seems 'bewildered' as it searches for a flower that it rested on the previous day. However, its memory of where this flower is has faded overnight: 'Seeking with memories grown dim o'er night/ Some resting flower of yesterday's delight.'

The speaker watches the butterfly circling a patch of ground where a particular flower lies 'withering on the ground'. The butterfly then flies off into the distance before returning excitedly to the speaker: 'And then on tremulous wing came back to me.' The butterfly's actions intrigue the speaker and he becomes philosophical about life, thinking 'of questions that have no reply'.

LINES 20 TO 30

The speaker would have begun working but the butterfly's flight again attracts his attention, drawing his eye to 'a tall tuft of flowers beside a brook' that the mower's work has exposed. These flowers stand out dramatically, like flames leaping from the ground, in a field that has been otherwise levelled by the mower's scythe. Having cut everything else, the mower 'spared' these flowers. The speaker examines the flowers and discovers that they are 'butterfly weed'.

The mower left these flowers 'to flourish' because he 'loved them'. He didn't consciously spare them for others to enjoy, or expect any credit for leaving them: 'Nor yet to draw one thought of ours to him.' The mower spared the flowers because they brought him joy when he was working by himself that morning: 'from sheer morning gladness at the brim.'

LINES 31 TO 42

The flowers inspire the speaker and he begins to think very differently about his circumstances. Suddenly his ears are open to the sound of the birds that are waking in the trees: 'made me hear the wakening birds around'. He also imagines that he can hear the mower's scythe 'whispering to the ground', as though the mower is there with him in the field.

The fact that the mower spared the tuft of flowers and makes the speaker feel that the mower is someone like him, a kindred spirit. He no longer feels alone. It is as if the mower is helping the speaker with his work and sitting with him in the shade when he pauses to rest: 'glad with him, I worked as with his aid,/ And weary, sought at noon with him the shade'. The speaker now works in a dreamlike state, having made a connection with the mower. He converses with the mower in his mind: 'And dreaming, as it were, held brotherly speech/ With one whose thought I had not hoped to reach.'

The speaker now thinks very differently about man's condition. Whereas earlier he believed that it was man's lot to always work alone, he now thinks that men always work together, even when they are 'apart'.

NATURE

Like many of Frost's poems, 'The Tuft of Flowers' celebrates the beauty and power of the natural world. The speaker is inspired by the beauty of the flowers. He likens their dramatic colours to flames leaping from the ground: 'A leaping tongue of bloom'. The mower also appreciates the beauty of the natural world. He spared the tuft of flowers because the sight of them made him feel good: 'from sheer morning gladness at the brim.'

The natural world consoles the speaker, enabling him to overcome his initial gloomy, introspective mood. Before spotting the flowers, the speaker had been preoccupied with his own thoughts, contemplating 'questions that have no reply'. However, once he sees the flowers he starts to engage with the world around him. He examines the flowers to see what type they are, and opens his ears to the sounds of 'the wakening birds'.

THEMES

THEMES

The natural world also acts as a guide and mentor for the speaker. The butterfly draws the speaker's attention to the flowers and is ultimately responsible for the speaker overcoming his initial sorrowful mood. The tuft of flowers acts as a 'message from the dawn', a signal to the speaker that others share his appreciation of beauty: 'feel a spirit kindred to my own'. The flowers enable the speaker to feel the mower's presence in the field and to overcome his loneliness. They teach him the lesson that no man works in isolation but is always part of a community, even when he is working alone.

ISOLATION AND COMMUNITY

The speaker's initial loneliness leads him to a gloomy conclusion regarding the human condition. He feels that 'all must be [alone] … Whether they work together or apart."' He denies the existence of community, suggesting that we are isolated beings, only concerned with our own lot.

However, the discovery of the tuft of flowers changes the speaker's mind. Although the mower likely spared the flowers purely for his own enjoyment, the fact that they were left standing means that the speaker can also experience the same delight. These flowers give the speaker a sense of community and show him how the actions of others have a bearing on our lives. The mower's decision to spare the flowers has enriched the speaker's day and enabled him to overcome his sense of isolation. He realises that he and the mower share a common love of nature and that the mower is a 'kindred' spirit. In the end, he must acknowledge that we cannot operate completely independent of others and that 'Men work together … Whether they work together or apart.'

SORROW AND DESPAIR

The poem opens with the speaker feeling dejected and alone. He seems weary with life and the condition of man, convinced that we are all ultimately alone. His sorrow is compounded by the sight of the butterfly circling a flower that it enjoyed the previous day, but has since been cut and now lies 'withering on the ground'. However, the speaker is able to overcome his sorrow when he finds the tuft of flowers that the mower spared. The beauty of the natural world, and the sense that someone else was also gladdened by these flowers, gives the speaker a very different outlook on life.

TRANSIENCE AND BREVITY

The image of the butterfly searching for a flower that it had rested on the previous day suggests the brevity of life. What is here to be enjoyed today might be gone tomorrow.

FOCUS ON STYLE

ATMOSPHERE AND TONE

The first half of the poem is melancholic, as the speaker struggles to come to terms with his loneliness and dwells on deep questions 'that have no reply'. The appearance of the butterfly, searching for the flower that has since been cut down, adds to the mournful atmosphere. This changes dramatically when the speaker's eye is drawn to the tuft of flowers. The field suddenly comes to life with the vibrant colours of the flowers and the sounds of the birds singing in the trees. The speaker is renewed and the tone becomes one of hope rather than despair. The final lines have a contented atmosphere as the speaker rests in the shade.

VERBAL MUSIC

Lines 7 and 8 feature long-vowel sounds that convey the speaker's despondency: 'But he had gone his way, the grass all mown,/ And I must be, as he had been – alone'. Shorter vowel sounds feature in the later lines, reflecting the speaker's lighter mood: 'And feel a spirit kindred to my own'.

IMAGERY

Frost dramatically likens the tuft of flowers to flames rising from the ground: 'A leaping tongue of bloom'. He creates a melancholic picture of the butterfly circling the withered flower it had rested on the day before: 'I marked his flight go round and round,/ As where some flower lay withering on the ground.'

FORM

The poem features everyday language and is written in iambic pentameter, which gives it a rhythmic beat.

The Road Not Taken

LINE BY LINE

The poet describes how he once came to a fork in the road when walking through the woods. It was autumn and the leaves on the trees and the ground were yellow: 'Two roads diverged in a yellow wood'. The poet wished that he could have travelled both roads simultaneously: 'sorry I could not travel both/ And be one traveler'. Since this is impossible, he had to choose between the two.

The poet stood for a long time, weighing up his options. He inspected the first road carefully, looking 'as far as [he] could' to a point where it turned and his view was obstructed by trees and bushes.

The poet then 'took the other' road, since it was 'just as fair' or suitable as the first. The poet was drawn to it because it was 'grassy' and hadn't had as many travellers as the first road: 'having perhaps the better claim,/ Because it was grassy and wanted wear'. Almost immediately, however, he acknowledged that actually both roads were equally worn: 'the passing there/ Had worn them really about the same'. The two roads, in fact, were almost identical, both carpeted with leaves that had yet to be trampled underfoot: 'both that morning equally lay/ In leaves no step had trodden black.'

The poet told himself that he would return to the first road sometime in the future: 'I kept the first for another day!' But he knew, even then, that it was unlikely he would ever get back to the same point. Once we set off down one road we soon encounter more forks, more decisions, and before we know it we have travelled too far from the starting point to ever be able to return: 'knowing how way leads on to way,/ I doubted if I should ever come back.'

The poem finishes with the poet imagining how he will recount this moment later in life. He says that he will tell this story 'with a sigh'. But the story that he will tell in the future will not reflect the truth. He will say that he came to a divergence in a wood and that he took the more difficult road: 'I took the one less traveled by'. He will then say that this decision to take the rougher path made 'all the difference' to his life.

Perhaps the poet's sigh is an expression of his sadness that this version of events is not strictly true, that life is not as clear-cut as his story illustrates. Though he might like to believe that his choice made 'all the difference', life is often random and the choices we make are less significant than we might like them to be.

FORM

The poem consists of four stanzas with five lines each. The rhyme scheme is ABAAB.

TONE

Depending on how we interpret the speaker's tone in the final stanza, the poem can mean very different things. The speaker imagines how he will be telling the story of the choice he had to make when he is a much older man: 'Somewhere ages and and ages hence'. He imagines how he will tell this story with a 'sigh'. Will this be a sigh of satisfaction at a life well lived? Or will it be a melancholic sigh, one that expresses sadness or regret?

The poem's final three lines involve a misremembering of the options that lay before the speaker. The speaker tells us that when he is an old man he will say that the road he decided to take was the 'one less travelled by'. Yet, we know that the 'roads' he faced at the time were as 'fair' as each other. Is the speaker suggesting that as time goes by his memory of events will become gradually less clear? Or is he suggesting that he will deliberately distort the truth to make his life sound more heroic? Is there a note of defiance in the last two lines, or is the speaker ruefully aware that he never made such a brave choice in his life?

METAPHOR

The poem uses the extended metaphor of the fork in the road to represent important choices we face in life. It suggests that life is a journey and that there are different paths we can take along the way.

The fact that both paths appear the same suggests that the choices we face are often not as clear-cut as we might like them to be and that chance plays a large part in everything we do. The bend 'in the undergrowth' suggests that we can only see so far into the future.

THEMES

THE NATURE OF CHOICE

The poem is ultimately a reflection on how important choices are made. We might deliberate at length before making our decision, just as the poet stood for a long time before choosing his road: 'long I stood'. But the choice is never easy.

For one thing, we can only see so far into the future, only anticipate so much. Frost describes how he could only see so far down one of the paths before it turned into the undergrowth. Secondly, the right choice is not always obvious. We might have to choose between two ways that are equally appealing. The two roads that the poet faces are 'just as fair' and even though one seems grassier, it turns out that both are 'really about the same'. 'The Road Not Taken' also suggests that the important choices we make in life are often based on impulse and chance. The way the poet closely inspects the first path but 'Then took the other' suggests that the choice was ultimately impulsive, and that he had no way of knowing then that he had made the right choice.

The poem finishes by highlighting how people can be less than truthful when it comes to remembering certain moments in their lives. The first three stanzas make it quite clear that the two paths appeared the same to the poet when he had to choose between them. But Frost says that in the future when he is old and telling the tale of the choice he had to make, he will say that one of the roads was much rougher than the other and that is why he chose it. He will also say that deciding to go the hard way made 'all the difference' to his life.

This version of events will make it seem that he was courageous, that the choices he faced at the time were clear – take the easy road or the tough road. But the fact is that at the time both roads appeared 'just as fair' and the poet could see no difference between them. The poem demonstrates how we often impose narratives on our lives and decisions, even though our choices are often arbitrary.

SORROW AND DESPAIR

The title of the poem suggests that it is what the poet did not get to experience that preoccupies him, more than the memories of what he experienced. He regrets that he will never be able to return to this fork and see where the other road led.

The poem finishes on a sorrowful note as the poet imagines how he will tell the story in the future. He knows already that when he is older he will not be absolutely honest when it comes to recounting his life. He will make out that he was adventurous and brave, that he took the 'less traveled' path and knew when he made his choice what lay ahead. But he will sigh as he tells this tale, because it was not quite like that at all.

TRANSIENCE AND BREVITY

The poet realises that, due to the transient nature of life, it's unlikely he'll be able to return to the same place sometime in the future and try the other road: 'Yet knowing how way leads on to way,/ I doubted if I should ever come back.'

Mending Wall

LINE BY LINE

Where is this poem set?

Like many of Frost's poems, 'Mending Wall' has a rural setting. The speaker is a farmer. Each spring he repairs gaps that have appeared in the wall dividing his property from his neighbour's. This is a dry stone wall: it has no cement and is built by carefully piling stones and boulders on top of one another.

What causes the gaps in the wall?

Freezing conditions cause the ground under the wall to expand: 'the frozen-ground-swell under it'. When the frost melts 'in the sun' the ground contracts again. This process continues throughout the winter and causes the stones that make up the wall to topple: 'spills the upper boulders in the sun'. As a result, large gaps appear in the wall. This process of swelling and contraction 'makes gaps even two can pass abreast'.

How does the speaker feel about these gaps?

Though there is a straightforward scientific explanation for the appearance of the gaps, the speaker presents it as a strange, almost supernatural phenomenon. He claims there is a mysterious force in nature that dislikes walls: 'Something there is that doesn't love a wall,/ That sends the frozen-ground-swell under it'.

> The task of replacing the boulders is presented as difficult but strangely enjoyable. It is physically demanding: 'We wear our fingers rough with handling them.' However, it also has the rewards of a sport or outdoor activity: 'just another kind of outdoor game'. Like tennis or golf, the task of repair requires skill, focus and physical effort.

Are these the only gaps that appear in the wall?

No. Hunters often pursue rabbits across the speaker's fields, causing damage to the walls: 'they have left not one stone on a stone'. The speaker suspects that the hunters tear down the stones from the wall to scare out the rabbits who have taken shelter among the stones: 'But they would have the rabbit out of hiding,/ To please the yelping dogs.' The speaker is used to tidying up after the hunters: 'I have come after them and made repair'. He draws a distinction between the hunters' vandalism from the naturally occurring gaps he wishes to repair on this spring day: 'The work of hunters is another thing'.

How are these naturally occurring gaps repaired?

The speaker informs the neighbour that the wall is in need of repair: 'I let my neighbor know beyond the hill'. The two men arrange to meet up and set about the task of reconstruction: 'And on a day we meet to walk the line/ And set the wall between us once again.' Though the men work as a team, each remains on his own side of the wall: 'We keep the wall between us as we go.' The speaker replaces the boulders that have fallen onto his property, the neighbour those that have fallen onto his: 'To each the boulders that have fallen to each.' They both respect the boundary between their farms.

What does the speaker suggest? How does the neighbour react?

They come to a section of farmland where there are no animals, only trees: apple trees on the speaker's side, pine trees on the neighbour's. The speaker suggests to the neighbour that this portion of the wall is unnecessary: 'There where it is we do not need the wall'. After all, there are no animals that might cross the boundary and cause tension between the two farmers: 'My apple trees will never get across/ And eat the cones under his pines, I tell him.'

The neighbour, however, insists on rebuilding the wall even in this area where it serves no practical purpose. He quotes an old proverb: "Good fences make good neighbors." He believes that the boundary lines between neighbours should always be clearly marked and respected. According to the proverb, this is the only way good relations can be preserved between people who live side by side.

What is the speaker's attitude to this proverb?

The fresh spring air makes the speaker feel mischievous: 'Spring is the mischief in me'. He wants to challenge his neighbour on the wisdom of the old proverb: "Why do they make good neighbors?" He expresses how foolish it seems to build a wall that serves no practical purpose: 'Isn't it/ Where there are cows? But here there are no cows.'

The critic George Montiero wrote that 'Mending Wall' brings to mind an ancient Roman ritual: 'The festival of the Terminalia was celebrated in Rome on 23 February. The neighbours on either side of any boundary gathered around it with their wives, children, and servants, and crowned it, each on his own side, with garlands, and offered cakes and bloodless sacrifices. In later times, however, a lamb or suckling pig was sometimes slain, and the stone sprinkled with the blood. Lastly, the whole neighbourhood joined in a general feast.'

He tells the neighbour his theory that there is a force in nature that 'doesn't love' walls and knocks them down whenever it can. This mysterious force might be offended by the building of unnecessary walls: 'Before I built a wall I'd ask to know/ What I was walling in or walling out'. To an extent, this force reminds the speaker of mischievous elves: 'I could say 'Elves' to him,/ But it's not elves exactly'. The speaker wants the neighbour to acknowledge the existence of this mysterious force: 'I'd rather/ He said it for himself.'

What does the speaker think of the neighbour?

The neighbour has a firm belief in the proverb handed down to him by his father and seems pleased with himself for remembering it. He has no time for the speaker's objections to building a wall where it seems pointless to do so. He has no truck with the notion of this 'Something' in nature that despises walls. He answers the speaker's objections by quoting the old proverb again: 'He says again, 'Good fences make good neighbors.''

According to the speaker, the neighbour 'moves' not only in the physical darkness of the woods where they work but also in a philosophical darkness: 'He moves in darkness as it seems to me,/ Not of woods only and the shade of trees.' This 'darkness' is caused by his failure to question the wisdom of the old proverb, by his refusal to even attempt to think for himself: 'He will not go behind his father's saying'.

FOCUS ON STYLE

TONE

Some readers describe the speaker's tone as mocking and condescending. He seems to have contempt for his neighbour, a simple countryman so mired in tradition that he insists on building a wall even where there's no need for one. The speaker's tone is ironic and playful when it comes to these traditions. Yet his tone is never fully snobbish or mocking. We're left with a sense that he still clings to a certain level of respect for the countryside and its ways.

IMAGERY

Memorable images in this poem include the 'frozen-ground-swell' under the wall, the two farmers using a 'spell' to keep the round rocks balanced, the neighbour moving like 'an old-stone savage armed' with a rock in each hand. Also effective is the humorous image of the speaker's apple trees sneaking onto the neighbour's land to eat the 'cones under his pines'.

FORM

The poem features plain, everyday language written in iambic pentameter, which gives the poem a persistent, rhythmic pulse.

VERBAL MUSIC

The verbal music in 'Mending Wall' is perhaps less rich than that in other poems by Frost. However, the poet makes interesting use of repetition. He repeats two key phrases, 'Something there is that doesn't love a wall' and "Good fences make good neighbors", in order to reinforce the poem's two competing viewpoints.

316

THEMES

THE MEANING OF BOUNDARIES

This poem explores the significance of walls. It reminds us that people must have clear boundaries between them if order is to be maintained. We must respect other people's property – and society's rules and regulations – if we are to live in harmony together.

The poet believes in boundaries. Throughout the winter he has repaired the damage to the wall caused by hunters: 'I have come after them and made repair'. When spring arrives he is the one who contacts his neighbour so they can meet up and fill the gaps caused by the frost.

It is also important to the neighbour that the wall between the farms are maintained. He is convinced that "Good fences make good neighbors" and even insists on building it where there are no cows or other animals to wall in or wall out. Both the speaker and the neighbour show their respect for boundaries by remaining on their own property even as they work together: 'One on a side.'

The rebuilding of the wall is presented as a spring ritual that must be performed if society is to survive for another year. It is associated with old sayings handed down through generations, with 'elves', and with magic in the form of the 'spell' the farmers use to make the round stones balance. We get a sense this ritual has been taking place since the time of the 'old-stone savage'.

However, the speaker also questions these old traditions. The spring air, he says, makes him mischievous, and he can't help pointing out the silliness of building a wall where there are no animals to contain. He questions the need for boundaries in places where they serve no practical purpose. He seems convinced that there is 'Something', some power in nature that despises walls and 'wants them down' though he doesn't specify what this is.

The speaker is quite critical of his neighbour in the poem. He presents the neighbour as a foolish and unthinking character who is set in his ways. He goes so far as to depicting his neighbour as an 'old-stone savage', a kind of caveman. The speaker's irritation stems from the fact that the neighbour refuses to think for himself. His only response to the speaker's questioning of the need for the wall is to quote an old proverb. The neighbour is either unwilling or unable to engage the speaker in a proper debate, relying instead on the wisdom passed down to him from his father: 'He will not go behind his father's saying'.

The speaker feels that the neighbour should learn to think for himself, to question the old sayings that have been passed down to him. To simply accept old sayings as the complete truth is to move 'in darkness'. The poem suggests that we should move out of this darkness by learning how to think for ourselves, by questioning the traditions, attitudes and beliefs that have been handed down to us by our ancestors.

'Mending Wall' provides an insight into Frost's personality. He said of this poem: 'Maybe I was both fellows in the poem ... a wall builder and a wall toppler. He makes boundaries and he breaks boundaries. That's man.'

Some critics think that Frost is alluding to himself in the poem – he is the 'Something' that doesn't love a wall. The gaps, after all, are caused by frost.

NATURE

The speaker also seems in two minds about the cause of the gaps that appear in the wall each spring. In one sense, the speaker offers a perfectly valid explanation for how these gaps are made, suggesting that they are the result of natural processes whereby the ground swells and contracts.

On the other hand, the speaker claims that they are caused by a strange and invisible 'Something', a sinister force that hates walls and causes the frost to swell under them so that they topple: 'That sends the frozen-ground-swell under it'. This mysterious power, the speaker suggests, is offended by the existence of walls: 'And to whom I was like to give offence.' It is determined, he tells the neighbour, to tear the walls apart.

'Mending Wall' personifies nature as the force 'that doesn't love a wall,/ That wants it down." Nature is depicted as resisting man's attempts to tame her, to impose order on her wildness with our walls, bridges and boundary lines. There is a menacing sense in the poem that nature barely tolerates our human civilization. In the poem, frost almost topples a farmyard wall. But who knows, perhaps tomorrow it is an entire city that will be shrugged aside.

ISOLATION AND COMMUNITY

An important feature of 'Mending Wall' is that walls unite as well as divide. The task of rebuilding the wall brings the two men together. It is described as an annual social occasion, a 'kind of outdoor game'. Every spring, the maintenance of the walls brings the neighbours together and gets them working as a team. Their work is a celebration of community and a reaffirming of the boundaries that are needed for that community to function. By carrying it out they are in keeping with a tradition that goes back centuries. In this way, the wall unites the farmers even as it divides and separates their land.

After Apple-Picking

LINE BY LINE

The apple harvest is coming to an end, the winter just beginning. The speaker has been working hard picking apples and is now exhausted: 'I have had too much/ Of apple-picking: I am overtired'. It is night and he has just finished his last day's work. He is somewhere on the farm, possibly already in bed, close to sleep: 'I am drowsing off.'

Outside he can still hear the barrels of apples being emptied into the cellar bin: 'I keep hearing from the cellar bin/ The rumbling sound/ Of load on load of apples coming in.' He left his ladder standing against a tree in the orchard: 'My long two-pointed ladder's sticking through a tree/ Toward heaven still'. Beside the tree is a barrel that he didn't quite fill and there may be a few apples 'upon some bough' that he didn't pick. But the speaker is exhausted and is 'done with apple-picking now'.

The speaker is so exhausted, he still experiences sensations associated with the recent work:
- He still sees the apples. They are 'Magnified' and every detail and spot of colour is visible as the apples 'appear and disappear': 'Stem end and blossom end,/ And every fleck of russet showing clear.'
- He feels as if he is still standing on the ladder. The 'instep arch' of his feet still hurt and he feels as if the ladder is still pressing beneath his feet: 'My instep arch not only keeps the ache,/ It keeps the pressure of a ladder-round.' He also feels as if he is swaying on the ladder as the tree bends in the breeze.
- He describes a strange moment earlier that morning when he took a sheet of ice from 'the drinking trough' and held it up to his eyes. The sheet of ice was like a 'pane of glass' that distorted the world around him. He has not being able to overcome the 'strangeness' he experienced: 'I cannot rub the strangeness from my sight'.

There was a time at the beginning of the season when the speaker was full of enthusiasm for the work that lay ahead. He mentions the 'great harvest' that he then 'desired', when the trees were full of apples: 'There were ten thousand thousand fruit to touch'. Back then he could think of the care that such work involves, how each apple has to be handled lovingly, gently taken down and 'not let fall'. Each apple that is dropped, even if not bruised or dirtied by the fall, has to go to the 'cider-apple heap', as though it were 'of no worth'.

But the speaker has 'had too much/ Of apple-picking' for the moment and just wants to sleep. He has been tired all day and says that he was 'well/ Upon [his] way to sleep' when he started work in the morning. His experience that morning of seeing the world distorted through the sheet of ice skimmed from the drinking trough gave him a sense of the dreams he could later expect. He knows that when he does finally sleep, he will be troubled by thoughts of the apples that were dropped and condemned to the cider-apple heap.

As he begins 'drowsing off' the speaker wonders what kind of sleep he is entering. Is he about to enter a deep hibernating sleep like the woodchuck? Or will he just experience 'some human sleep'? The speaker feels that the woodchuck could tell him what lies ahead were he not already 'gone' to sleep himself.

ATMOSPHERE

The atmosphere of the poem is wonderfully strange and dreamy. The speaker is hovering between the waking world and sleep, and both seem to be merging. The way the poem jumps from the present to the past and back again only adds to this atmosphere, as does the fact that the poet is still experiencing the effects of the work when he is no longer apple-picking: 'I feel the ladder sway as the boughs bend.'

VERBAL MUSIC

Frost uses repeated 't' sounds in the opening lines that seem to reflect the tiredness that he is feeling: 'My long two-pointed ladder's sticking through a tree/ Toward heaven still'. Lines 7 and 8 feature soft 's' sounds that convey a sleepy feeling: 'Essence of winter sleep is on the night,/ The scent of apples: I am drowsing off.'

Assonance and alliteration are used to great effect throughout the poem. Line 12 features both, with the repeated 'h' and 'o' sounds creating a dreamy atmosphere: 'And held against the world of hoary grass.' In lines 25 to 26, the poet uses repeated 'o' sounds to convey the endless loads of apples entering the cellar: 'The rumbling sound/ Of load on load of apples coming in.'

IMAGERY

Much of the poem's imagery is open to interpretation. The image of the poet's ladder standing against the tree pointing 'Toward heaven still' is melancholic and hints at the poet's desire to abandon the world.

The image of the poet staring at the world through a sheet of ice introduces a strange aspect to the poem. It hints at the dream world that the poet is about to enter in sleep, as though he is passing from one world into another.

This strange, dreamy world is again evident in the image of the oversized apples that revolve before the poet's tired eyes: 'Magnified apples appear and disappear,/ Stem end and blossom end'. The repetition in these lines also conveys the poet's tiredness.

FIGURES OF SPEECH

Line 30 features an example of hyperbole. The poet uses an extraordinary number to convey the enormity of the harvest: 'There were ten thousand thousand fruit to touch'.

NATURE

Like many of Frost's poems, 'After Apple-Picking' celebrates the beauty of the natural world. Here Frost focuses on the harvesting of apples in late autumn. He captures the time of year beautifully with his descriptions of the 'hoary grass' and the ice that he skims from trough that he holds up to his eyes, as well as a wonderful description of the apples themselves: 'Stem end and blossom end,/ And every fleck of russet showing clear'.

SORROW AND DESPAIR

The tiredness that the speaker describes in the poem is more than just physical exhaustion: he is weary with life itself. The speaker tells us that he is 'overtired/ Of the great harvest I myself desired.' The very thing that excited and motivated him – the prospect of a bountiful harvest – has lost its gloss. The speaker is worn out and unable to muster any enthusiasm for the work that is now all but done. When he wonders what kind of sleep he will experience, the long hibernating sleep of the woodchuck or just 'some human sleep', we get the impression that it is the woodchuck's that he desires – a proper break that will allow him to regain his lust for life.

The poem can be usefully compared to 'Birches' where the speaker talks about being 'weary of considerations' and needing to get away from life for a while. Both poems describe a loss of appetite for life but stop short of desiring death as a means of escape. In 'Birches' the poet speaks of a desire to climb 'Toward heaven' but to not actually reach heaven. In 'After Apple-Picking' Frost mentions a ladder that is pointing 'Toward heaven still' which he has abandoned, suggesting that he is reluctant to make this journey for the moment.

TRANSIENCE AND BREVITY

The poem is set in late autumn just as winter is about to set in. The grass is covered in frost and the woodchuck has already gone into hibernation. The last apples have been taken from the trees and the 'Essence of winter sleep is on the night'. There is a strong sense of transience, of things coming to their natural end. The speaker, too, experiences this with regard to the work he has just completed. There was a time when he looked forward to this harvest with enthusiasm, but that time has passed and he is left feeling exhausted. The shattering of the sheet of ice that he holds before his eyes symbolises the end of a certain phase in his life.

ISOLATION AND COMMUNITY

'After Apple-Picking' touches on the need to be alone every once in a while. The speaker has left the orchard and is somewhere by himself, no longer a part of the harvest. Perhaps there was a time early in the harvest when the speaker enjoyed the company of those he was working with, but we get the impression that he now wants to be alone.

Birches

LINE BY LINE

The poet describes the birch trees that he sometimes comes across in the woods. The birches are bent in different directions, some even to the extent that the tops of the trees touch the ground.

WHAT MAKES THE TREES BEND LIKE THIS?

'Ice storms' cause the birch trees to bend in this manner. During winter when it rains, the water held in the trees freezes. Frost describes how you would come across the trees on a 'sunny winter morning/ After a rain' and find the trees 'Loaded with ice'. The weight of this frozen water is too much for the trees to bear and so they bend to the ground. Frost describes this process in lines 7 to 18:

- As the wind picks up, the frozen trees begin to shake and the cracking ice makes a clicking sound: 'They click upon themselves/ As the breeze rises'.

- The ice around the bark is like an 'enamel' coating that cracks as the trees begin to move in the breeze. As the ice cracks, the trees turn different colours: 'turn many-colored/ As the stir cracks and crazes their enamel.'

- When the sun begins to shine, the ice starts to melt. Shards of ice like 'crystal shells' fall from the trees, shattering when they hit the 'snow crust' on the ground.

- The weight of the ice in the trees eventually drags the trees to the ground: 'They are dragged to the withered bracken by the load'. The trunks of the trees are quite flexible and 'seem not to break' when this happens.

- However, when the ice brings them to the ground they 'never right themselves'. As a result, one can find birch trees with 'their trunks arching in the woods/ Years afterwards'.

HOW WOULD THE POET LIKE TO IMAGINE THEY HAVE BEEN BENT?

The poet would like to think that the trees have been bent as a result of 'some boy' swinging them. Swinging birches involves climbing carefully to the top and then leaping out from the tree while holding onto the top branches. The weight of your body pulls the tree to the ground. However, the tree will not remain bent but will spring back upright when you release your hold: 'swinging doesn't bend them down to stay'.

Frost imagines a young boy walking through the woods as he goes to 'fetch the cows'. This boy lives 'too far from town to learn baseball' and has to find ways of entertaining himself as he goes about his daily chores: 'Whose only play was what he found himself '. Frost likes to imagine that this boy will climb every birch he can find on his father's land again and again, pulling the trees to the ground until he has worn them down and they never spring back upright: 'he took the stiffness out of them'.

This boy would learn over time the best technique for bringing the trees to the ground. He would learn that you should not jump out 'too soon' as this would mean that the tree would not bend all the way to the ground. Instead, he would keep 'his poise' and climb carefully to the 'top branches' before jumping out and pulling the tree to the ground: 'Then he flung outward,

THEMES

NATURE

Like many of Frost's poems, 'Birches' celebrates the beauty and wonder of the natural world. Particularly memorable is the poet's description of the ice melting in the trees in the morning sun. The image of the shards of ice falling and shattering on the ground is wonderful: 'Soon the sun's warmth makes them shed crystal shells/ Shattering and avalanching on the snow crust'. There is also a beautiful description of the birches when they have been bent to the forest floor, their trunks arched and their leaves trailing before them on the ground. Frost likens these trees to 'girls on hands and knees that throw their hair/ Before them over their heads to dry in the sun.'

'Birches' also presents nature as a source of consolation and inspiration. Frost describes how the forest can be a source of fun for the boy who is working on his father's farm. As he journeys to and from the fields he can pause to play in the woods, climbing each of the birches and bending them to the ground. This activity also contains valuable lessons for the boy, teaching him the value of patience and composure: 'He learned all there was/ To learn about not launching out too soon … He always kept his poise'.

In his later years, the poet turns to nature as a source of consolation and means of escape from the tribulations of life. He thinks of the birch as the perfect means of temporary escape from life's troubles, a way to leave earth behind for a while only to return refreshed and rejuvenated. In this regard, the poem can be compared to 'After Apple-Picking' which also describes a longing to take a break from life.

ISOLATION AND COMMUNITY

'Birches' celebrates the pleasures of solitude. The poet describes a solitary boy living outside of the community, 'too far from town to learn baseball'. This boy must deal with the fact that he is without companionship. However, unlike the isolated speaker in 'The Tuft of Flowers', the boy in 'Birches' finds pleasure in his solitary activities, challenging himself to bend every one of his father's birch trees to the ground.

SORROW AND DESPAIR

Towards the end of the poem, the poet describes how he sometimes becomes weary with life and its concerns. Life can seem like a journey through 'a pathless wood' full of irritations, like cobwebs and twigs that lash you in the eye. Sometimes the poet longs 'to get away from earth awhile'. Like the speaker in 'After Apple-Picking', who longs for a sleep that will last for months, the poet here describes a need to get away from all his troubles so that he can recharge his batteries and regain an appetite for life: 'I'd like to get away from earth awhile/ And then come back to it and begin over.' Swinging the birch tree provides him with a perfect metaphor for this escape and return.

CHILDHOOD

The poem celebrates the joys of childhood and especially the importance of play. Frost describes the thrill the boy experiences when he takes time from his chores to climb the trees in the woods. The poet looks back with great fondness on his own youth, when he had the freedom and the imagination to climb the birch trees and bend them to the ground. He says that he dreams about 'going back to be' a 'swinger of birches'. However, the poem suggests that is not possible to experience the same sense of freedom and fun later in life. As we get older we become too over-burdened with worries to be able to play like children and forget all our cares.

feet first, with a swish,/ Kicking his way down through the air to the ground.'

The poet speaks about getting 'away from earth awhile'

The poet tells us that he used to swing birches when he was younger. Now that he is an older man, he dreams about 'going back' to this activity to escape the frustrations of life. When he is 'weary of considerations' and his life seems to have no direction ('life is too much like a pathless wood'), Frost dreams about getting away from it all by climbing birches:

Where your face burns and tickles with the cobwebs
Broken across it, and one eye is weeping
From a twig's having lashed across it open.
I'd like to get away from earth awhile

The poet would like to escape life 'awhile' but not forever; he eventually wants to come back and 'begin over'. Frost does not want some 'fate' or spiritual power to cruelly misunderstand his desire to escape as a death wish: 'May no fate wilfully misunderstand me … and snatch me away/ Not to return.' Life on earth might be painful and wearisome at times but it is also the place where 'love' occurs and the poet cannot imagine a better place for this to happen: 'Earth's the right place for love:/ I don't know where it's likely to go better.'

The poet would like to get 'away from earth' by climbing a birch tree. He would like to climb 'Toward heaven' as far as he could until the tree could bear his weight no longer. At this moment the tree would bend and lower the poet back down to the ground: 'dipped its top and set me down again.' Climbing the birch would enable the poet to fulfil his wish: to escape from earth awhile but to then return. Being able to do this would make life more bearable: 'That would be good both going and coming back.' Swinging birches becomes a metaphor for a desirable way to live, a way that would enable you to get away from everything but would always ensure that you returned: 'One could do worse than be a swinger of birches.'

- The poem is constructed around a number of contrasts and opposites. Frost contrasts the flexibility of the birches with the rigidity of the 'straighter darker trees'. This flexibility and rigidity is associated with another important contrast in the poem: reason and imagination.

- The poem ultimately celebrates the imagination and its ability to describe and understand the world in different ways. The poet would like to imagine that the trees have been bent by some boy swinging them but has to acknowledge that the correct reason is ice storms. 'Truth' or reason is seen as the enemy of the imagination, something that interferes with its efforts to play with the world that it encounters.

- The poem also contrasts the freedom that the young have to play and escape with the claustrophobic world of adult responsibility. Frost longs for an escape from this world, back to the world of the young boy climbing his father's trees.

FOCUS ON STYLE

METAPHOR AND SIMILE

Frost uses the idea of birch swinging as a metaphor for escape from life. The poet longs to 'get away from earth awhile' but he also wants to come back. The birch is seen as the ideal method for this escape because it reaches towards the heavens but remains firmly rooted in the earth.

The birch is also a metaphor for the flexibility of the imagination. Unlike the 'straighter darker trees', which might correspond with the matter-of-factness that the poet despises, the birches are flexible and can 'bend to left and right'. This flexibility corresponds with the freedom of the imagination to describe and understand the world as it likes.

In a memorable simile, the poet likens the bowed trees to girls drying their hair in the sun. He also compares life to a 'pathless wood' and life's frustrations to cobwebs and twigs that scratch us as we try to forge our way through.

VERBAL MUSIC

Lines 7 to 11 use alliteration to great effect. Frost uses repeated 'c' sounds to convey the sound of the ice cracking: 'They click upon themselves … and turn many-colored/ As the stir cracks and crazes their enamel.' He uses softer 's' sounds when describing the melting ice: 'Soon the sun's warmth makes them shed crystal shells'.

Soft 's' sounds along with repeated 'f' sounds are used when describing how the boy eventually flings himself out from the tree: 'Then he flung outward, feet first, with a swish'. The line wonderfully captures the excitement of the leap.

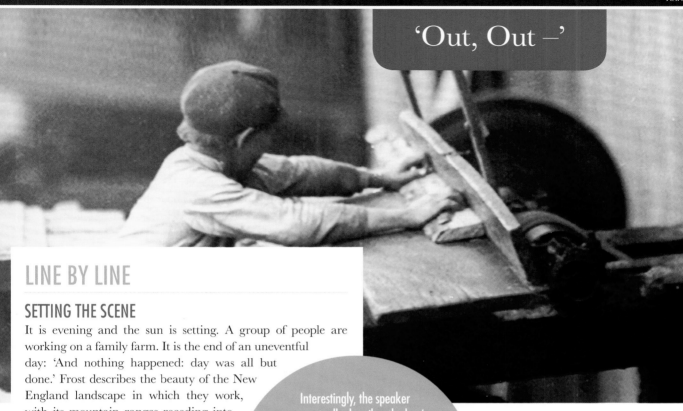

'Out, Out –'

LINE BY LINE

SETTING THE SCENE

It is evening and the sun is setting. A group of people are working on a family farm. It is the end of an uneventful day: 'And nothing happened: day was all but done.' Frost describes the beauty of the New England landscape in which they work, with its mountain ranges receding into the distance: 'And from there those that lifted eyes could count/ Five mountain ranges one behind the other/ Under the sunset far into Vermont.'

Among the workers is a boy using a buzz-saw to cut firewood for the family's stove, creating 'stove-length sticks of wood' as he works. The sawdust and freshly cut firewood give off a rich smell: 'Sweet-scented stuff when the breeze drew across it.' Frost captures the ugly and aggressive sound of the buzz-saw, describing how it 'snarled and rattled'. The saw is presented in a menacing light, snarling like a wild animal. The phrase 'snarled and rattled' is repeated three times, which emphasises its repetitive, relentless din.

THE ACCIDENT

The speaker wishes that the workers had finished up early: 'Call it a day, I wish they might have said'. By doing so they would have given the boy an extra half hour away from his duties, which he would have really valued: 'To please the boy by giving him the half hour/ That a boy counts so much when saved from work.' The farm workers, however, decide to continue working until suppertime. The boy's sister comes to tell them that their evening meal is ready: 'His sister stood beside them in her apron/ To tell them 'Supper.''

At that very moment, tragedy strikes as the boy loses concentration and cuts himself with the buzz-saw. Once again the saw is depicted as a living thing, a dangerous animal. The speaker describes it leaping at the boy as if it wanted to consume him for supper: 'the saw,/ As if to prove saws knew what supper meant,/ Leaped out at the boy's hand'. In lines 16 and 17, however, the speaker says that the saw only 'seemed' to leap out at the boy. In reality the boy must have 'given the hand', accidentally putting his hand in harm's way.

Interestingly, the speaker never actually describes the boy's injuries in detail. His response to the tragedy is conveyed in the simple but moving exclamation: 'But the hand!' It's as if the speaker is unable or unwilling to describe the saw slicing through flesh and bone, instead leaving us to imagine the terrible damage its blade must have done to the youngster's arm.

THE BOY'S REACTION

The boy's initial reaction, bizarrely, is to laugh at the disaster: 'The boy's first outcry was a rueful laugh.' The laugh indicates his disbelief at his injuries. He is clearly in shock as he turns toward his workmates holding his damaged arm: 'As he swung toward them holding up the hand'.

He holds up his hand to limit the amount of blood that gushes from the wound: 'half as if to keep/ The life from spilling.' However, it is also a pleading gesture: 'Half in appeal'. He raises his hand in protest against the injury, like a soccer player appealing to the referee for a penalty.

Despite his shock, the boy quickly realises the gravity of his situation. According to the speaker, he is a 'big boy' doing 'man's work' and has probably seen his fair share of farmyard injuries. He has been around long enough to know that his wounds are extremely serious. His life, he realises, will never be the same again: 'Then the boy saw all … He saw all spoiled.' The poor boy pleads with his sister not to let the doctor amputate his damaged hand: ''Don't let him cut my hand off –/ The doctor, when he comes. Don't let him, sister!''

THE BOY'S DEATH

The doctor arrives too late to save the damaged hand: 'But the hand was gone already.' All he can do is give the boy ether, an anaesthetic drug, to numb the pain: 'The doctor put him in the dark of ether.' We can imagine the boy being sucked down into the dark of unconsciousness as this general anaesthetic takes effect.

The boy's breathing becomes laboured: 'He lay and puffed his lips out with his breath.' Suddenly, the person monitoring the patient realises something is wrong: 'the watcher at his pulse took fright.' The boy's heartbeat gets fainter and fainter: 'They listened at his heart./ Little – less – nothing!' The people on the farm can hardly believe that the boy is dying in front of them: 'No one believed.' But finally his heart stops altogether: 'and that ended it.'

THE AFTERMATH OF THE BOY'S DEATH

The poem's final lines are abrupt and matter of fact. Life, the speaker maintains, has to go on. They people on the farm have work to do and mouths to feed. They can't afford to spend time mourning the boy but must go about their business: 'And they, since they/ were not the one dead, turned to their affairs.'

FOCUS ON STYLE

ATMOSPHERE

The poem's opening is a masterpiece of atmosphere. The scene is peaceful and idyllic, with country people working on a day when 'nothing happened' and the sun setting behind New England's glorious mountains. However, the presence of the buzz-saw constantly snarling and rattling like a ferocious animal adds tension to the scene. This unsettling presence gives us a sense that something bad is about to happen.

TONE

We can imagine the speaker of "Out, Out –" relating the events of the poem in a matter-of-fact tone of voice. The language, while at times superbly descriptive, is informal and conversational. We see this especially when the speaker corrects himself, first saying that the saw leaped out at the boy, then stating that it only 'seemed' to leap, that he must have 'given the hand'.

For the most part, the speaker simply describes the scene without criticism. This is especially true of the poem's conclusion and the workers' seemingly cold reaction to the boy's passing. However, a closer reading reveals instances where the speaker expresses sorrow at the boy's fate – for example, when he wishes that the workers had avoided the accident by finishing early, or in the brief phrase of lament: 'But the hand!'

IMAGERY

Frost uses great economy in "Out, Out –", crafting vivid images with a minimum of words. As always with Frost, images of the natural world feature prominently; he wonderfully depicts the family working at sunset in the shadow of vast American mountain ranges.

Perhaps the most striking images are that of the saw leaping for the boy's hand and the boy subsequently holding up his damaged hand 'Half in appeal, but half as if to keep/ The life from spilling.'

FIGURES OF SPEECH

Frost makes excellent use of personification in describing the buzz-saw. It is presented as a living thing, a vicious snarling animal that is capable of leaping out at the boy and maiming him.

VERBAL MUSIC

Frost uses effective word-music in the lines that describe the pleasant smell of the freshly cut sawdust. Alliteration is present in the repeated 's' sound in 'Sweet-scented stuff'. Assonance features in 'breeze drew across it', with its repeated 'e' sounds. There is also a pleasant euphonious sound to the lines that describe the New England landscape. Here, the repetition of broad vowel sounds creates a slow, easy music: 'mountain ranges one behind the other/ Under the sunset far into Vermont.'

Frost's use of hidden rhymes also contributes to the verbal music of the poem. We see this where 'count' at the end of line 4 rhymes with 'Vermont' at the end of line 6. There is also a half-rhyme effect between 'Under' and 'sunset' in line 6. The pleasant verbal music used to reflect the beauty of nature is in sharp contrast to the harsh cacophonous sound effects used in the description of the buzz-saw. The repeated use of harsh-sounding consonants in the phrase 'snarled and rattled' suggests the din and racket made by the saw. Furthermore, the fact that the phrase 'snarled and rattled' is repeated three times suggests the monotony of this din, which dominates the yard for the entire day's work.

THEMES

SORROW AND DESPAIR

The theme of sorrow is dealt with in a complex way in "Out, Out –". The people on the farm permit themselves little or no time to grieve for the dead boy before they turn 'to their affairs'. There is something brutal about the way the people on the farm just get on with their lives after the boy's death. However, business must always be taken care of. A livelihood must be maintained, and the dead boy has no more to contribute to this process: 'No more to build on there.'

Many readers are inclined to criticise the people on the farm for spending so little time grieving his death. Other readers have branded Frost as callous because in the poem he fails to condemn this behaviour. He simply describes the workers' reaction to the boy's death without comment.

The poem highlights the uncomfortable truth that life must always go on. This was especially true on a New England farm a century ago, when conditions were extremely tough and survival itself was an issue. Such people could afford to spend little time exploring their feelings of bereavement. There was always wood to be chopped, a hard winter to be provided for, animals to be hunted.

Even in our comfortable, modern existences, life must always go on. How often have we heard about the death of a neighbour or relative, and after a moment's pause, simply got on with our day? Even when we lose a close friend or relative our lives must continue after a mourning period. The world doesn't stop to let us grieve forever. Because we are 'not the one dead', we are all expected to eventually turn to our affairs.

NATURE

Frost is well known as a nature poet. Even in this bleak poem, Frost takes time to praise the natural world, celebrating the 'Sweet-scented' freshly cut sawdust and memorably describing how the Vermont landscape stretches into the distance. These pretty images create an atmosphere of calm in the poem before the horrific accident.

TRANSIENCE AND BREVITY

Transience is another of Frost's great themes. "Out, Out –" reminds us that even in the middle of everyday routine, life can be snatched away from us. All it takes is a moment's loss of concentration with a vehicle or power tool to turn an ordinary day into a tragic one. The poem urges us not to take life for granted.

A COLD UNIVERSE

"Out, Out –" powerfully illustrates the idea, also hinted at in 'Design', that the world is a meaningless place. The boy's death is random, accidental and futile. The poem's title, a quote from Shakespeare's Macbeth, reinforces this theme. It is taken from a speech in which Macbeth laments the utter futility of living and dying.

CHILDHOOD

In "Out, Out –" Frost skilfully captures the mentality of childhood. The boy is by no means naive or ignorant. He is a 'big boy' capable of doing 'man's work'. He is 'old enough to know' that he is in a dire situation, that he will lose his hand and possibly faces death: 'He saw all spoiled.' However, the boy is still really a 'child at heart'. Frost captures the giddy excitement that the boy feels at being let go from work half an hour early: 'To please the boy by giving him the half hour/ That a boy counts so much when saved from work.'

One of the poem's most moving lines occurs when the speaker wishes that the workers had finished early: 'Call it a day, I wish they might have said'. By doing so they would not only give the boy the bonus of a half-hour off, but would also unknowingly save his life by avoiding the accident with the buzz-saw.

We can also detect here the speaker's regret that this boy, 'a child at heart', was expected to do 'a man's work' in the first place. His sister also works, preparing a meal for the workers: 'His sister stood beside them in her apron/ To tell them 'Supper.'' These children have no time to be children. Perhaps the poet feels that children should get to enjoy a time of fun and innocence before they are forced to deal with the difficulties of the adult world.

Spring Pools

LINE BY LINE

The poem is set in a forest at the beginning of spring. Ice has melted on the surrounding mountaintops. Melt water has poured down from the mountains and formed pools on the forest floor. These pools are so cold that they 'chill and shiver'.

Because it is very early springtime, there are as yet no leaves on the trees' branches to obscure the sky. The pools reflect an almost perfect mirror image of the sky above them: 'These pools that, though in forests, still reflect/ The total sky almost without defect'.

Some winter flowers have taken root in the moisture around the pool's edges. These pale and fragile blooms also seem to 'chill and shiver' in the cold spring air.

While the trees in the forest are presently leafless, each has thousands of 'pent-up buds' that are bursting with life. Soon leaves will come sprouting from each and every one of these buds. The bare forest will be transformed into lush and leafy 'summer woods'.

In the process of flowering, however, the trees will destroy the spring pools. The water in the pools will be sucked up by the trees' roots rather than draining away through a woodland 'brook or river'. The trees will 'drink up' the pool water and use it to grow their leaves: 'to bring dark foliage on.'

The trees will also destroy the flowers that grow beside the pools. Their new leaves will 'darken nature' and prevent sunlight from reaching the floor of the forest. Without light, the new flowers will wither and die.

The poet regrets that both the pools and the flowers will 'soon be gone'. He urges the trees to 'think twice' before they destroy this lovely scene:

Let them think twice before they use their powers
To blot out and drink up and sweep away
These flowery waters and these watery flowers

Summer is often associated with joy and beauty, and winter with darkness and hardship. However, in 'Spring Pools' Frost performs an unusual reversal of these stereotypes. To most of us, the sight of leaves appearing on the trees in springtime is a cheerful one, an indication that winter is over and summer is on its way. In this poem, however, the sight of the leafing trees is presented in a sinister, destructive light. The trees will 'use their powers' to 'darken nature'. The 'summer woods' are destined to 'blot out' the light on which the 'watery flowers' depend, bringing an end to this scene that the speaker enjoys so much.

THEMES

NATURE

'Spring Pools' is one of Frost's classic nature poems, a moving and vivid portrayal of nature's fragile beauty. We are presented with a scene that has a peculiar icy beauty: leafless trees, the shivering winter flowers, and the freezing pools that reflect the sky with crystal clarity. The water in the pools is described as 'flowery' because it allows flowers to grow around its edges and reflects their beauty on its surface. The description of the flowers as 'watery' reminds us that they grow at the pools' edges, while also suggesting their fragility.

'Spring Pools' also reminds us how death and life coexist at the heart of nature. With the changing of each season some elements of nature are destroyed and some are born again. The spring pools and winter flowers will be swept away so that the trees can flourish.

The poem is keenly aware of just how destructive nature can be. The trees are presented as having sinister 'powers'. They are powerful and strong, with 'pent-up buds' full of energy waiting to be unleashed. They possess the ability to 'darken nature' and to create 'dark foliage'. The trees are portrayed as a destructive force, associated with such negative verbs as 'blot out' and 'sweep away'. In stark contrast, the flowers and the pools are presented as fragile and vulnerable. They are 'watery' and 'flowery', innocent aspects of the woodland that have little capacity for resilience or survival.

The poem also considers the way nature moves in cycles of death and rebirth. Each element of nature dies and is reborn as the seasons change. Though the spring pools will 'soon be gone', they will return next year when the snows melt again. In this they are like the 'summer woods' that disappear each autumn only to re-emerge in spring. Nothing in nature, the poem suggests, is ever permanently destroyed. Things only disappear temporarily to be recreated when the seasons shift again.

TRANSIENCE AND BREVITY

Perhaps the most important theme in this poem is that of transience. 'Spring Pools' concerns the loss of a few puddles, pools that were formed only 'yesterday' and that will probably begin disappearing in only a few days' time.

The poet seems to resent the trees for sucking up the pools and for blotting out the light that keeps the flowers alive, urging them to 'think twice' before they do so. However, he must know deep down that nature has to take its course. The trees cannot hear his pleas. The blooming of the forest means that the pools and the 'watery flowers' beside them must disappear. We get the impression that the pools' transient nature, the very brevity of their existence, only adds to their beauty in the speaker's eyes.

ATMOSPHERE

Frost wonderfully captures the atmosphere of a forest at the end of winter. We sense the wet stillness of the thaw, the peace and quiet of the forest's interior. There is also a melancholy aspect to this wintry, chilly landscape.

IMAGERY

The spring pools possesses a strange, wintry beauty. We are presented with images of leafless trees, frail flowers and icy pools that 'chill and shiver'. It's an uncluttered scene of light and clarity, with the pools reflecting the sky perfectly. There is also a great sense of fragility in the various images: these weak 'watery flowers' and 'flowery waters' will be swept away as the trees' foliage begins to appear.

FIGURES OF SPEECH

Frost refers to the trees in the forest as if they possessed human reasoning, as if they were capable of deciding whether or not to use their 'powers' to 'darken nature'. By doing so, he powerfully conveys his appreciation of the spring pools and his dismay at their destruction.

FORM

As always, Frost marries the everyday language of New England with carefully constructed poetic lines. 'Spring Pools' is written in two stanzas, each rhyming AABCBC. The two stanzas mirror each other almost perfectly, just as the pools reflect the sky above them 'almost without defect'.

VERBAL MUSIC

Though 'Spring Pools' is in many ways a sorrowful poem, it is filled with pleasant verbal music. Assonance, in particular, is used skilfully throughout. We see this in line 3 with its repeated 'i' sound ('chill and shiver'), in line 6 with its repeated 'a' sound ('dark foliage') and in line 8 which also has a repeated 'a' sound ('darken nature').

Repeated broad vowel sounds also feature in the phrases 'summer woods', 'pent-up buds' and in the wonderfully descriptive 'flowery waters' and 'watery flowers'. This preponderance of broad vowel sounds slows the pace of the verse, giving it a lilting but melancholy beauty, appropriate to this poem of transience and loss, and to the scene of icy beauty it describes.

Acquainted With the Night

LINE BY LINE

The speaker says that he is 'acquainted with the night', that he knows the hours of darkness well. He does not, like most people, spend his nights tucked up in bed. Instead, he spends them walking alone through the deserted city streets. The speaker depicts himself walking 'out' and 'back' for long distances, sometimes going so far that he leaves the city behind: 'I have outwalked the furthest city light.'

The city at night is depicted as a melancholy environment. It rains constantly: 'I have walked out in rain – and back in rain.' The streets are almost completely deserted; when the speaker stops walking, when he 'stood still', there is no one else around to make 'the sound of feet'. The lanes are desolate and depressing: 'I have looked down the saddest city lane.'

The city at night is also depicted as a menacing environment. It is difficult to read the lines about the 'interrupted cry' without the suspicion that the person crying out is the victim of some violent act. The sighting of the night watchman further reinforces this sense of menace, suggesting that city streets are dangerous by night and need to be kept in order by a police presence.

The speaker is utterly isolated as he wanders through this depressing urban landscape. However, even when he encounters other human beings he is unable or unwilling to communicate. He makes no attempt to speak to the night watchman. In fact, he is barely able to look him in the eye as he passes him on the street: 'And dropped my eyes, unwilling to explain.' Furthermore, the 'interrupted cry' he hears coming from another street is not meant for him: 'But not to call me back or say good-bye'.

The speaker looks up at the moon. Using a striking metaphor, he describes it as a 'luminary' or glowing clock: 'at an unearthly height/ One luminary clock against the sky'. We can imagine how the full moon resembles a round clock face set at an 'unearthly height' in the sky.

To the speaker, the moon suggests that the time 'was neither wrong nor right'. There are several ways in which this enigmatic line can be interpreted. It may refer to the blank numbness associated with the speaker's experience of depression. Alternatively, it may refer to the whole notion of morality, of right and wrong, which has become more ambiguous in the modern world where fewer people believe in the old certainties of religion.

The structure of 'Acquainted With the Night' echoes that of Dante's Inferno, a great 14th-century poem that describes a journey into hell. Like 'Acquainted With the Night,' Inferno used three-line stanzas and triple rhymes. Just as Dante describes a journey into a literal, physical hell, so Frost describes a journey into a psychological hell – a state of total despair.

Sufferers of depression often describe how difficult they find it to communicate and to connect meaningfully with other people. This aspect of depression is reflected in 'Acquainted With the Night'. The speaker never tells us what misfortune, if any, has plunged him into despair; communication between the poet and his readers is blocked. This theme of communication breakdown is evident in several lines: the speaker silently passing the night watchman, the 'interrupted cry', even the moon's lack of answers.

THEMES

SORROW AND DESPAIR

'Acquainted With the Night' provides a moving portrayal of a mind in the grip of depression. The speaker's inner turmoil will not allow him to sleep, relax or even sit still. He must always keep moving, his physical restlessness mirroring his agitated state of mind.

The dark, desolate city streets through which he walks reflect the speaker's depression. Consider the empty and menacing streets, the sad and sordid lanes, the darkness at the edge of town where the streetlights are no longer visible. This grim urban landscape serves as the perfect metaphor for the speaker's troubled mind.

Sufferers of depression often describe it as a static state. It can seem that nothing can ever change; that the world is locked in a constant cycle of despair. 'Acquainted With the Night' illustrates this powerfully. Night after night, the speaker is compelled to make his journey through the streets. Nothing changes. The speaker appears trapped in a loop, wandering the city in circles. The fact that the speaker wants someone 'to call [him] back or say good-bye' suggests that he may have lost someone close to him. However, this is never made clear in the poem.

Those with clinical depression often describe themselves as feeling nothing at all, just a numb blankness. Perhaps the speaker is referring to this emptiness when he describes the luminary clock in lines 12 to 13. For the speaker, the time is neither 'wrong nor right'. He has moved beyond a point where times are good or bad in a conventional sense, and exists in a numb state of apathy and indifference.

ISOLATION AND COMMUNITY

'Acquainted With the Night' is a powerful study of isolation. The speaker spends his nights cut off from his friends and family, walking alone through the city. The streets he walks through are almost completely empty, with the speaker himself making the only 'sound of feet'. Even when he encounters other people his isolation remains. He silently passes the watchman without talking to him or even looking him in the eye. The cry he hears is 'interrupted' and is not meant for him in the first place. The speaker is utterly and terrifyingly alone.

A COLD UNIVERSE

It is possible to read 'Acquainted With the Night' as depicting a universe where there is no God to hear our prayers. At the poem's conclusion, the speaker gazes up at the moon's 'luminary clock', as if looking to the heavens for a solution to his troubles. However, there is nothing out there apart from endless, empty space, and the speaker gets no answers. The moon will only proclaim, mysteriously, that the time is 'neither wrong nor right'.

Perhaps Frost is referring to the concept of morality – of right and wrong – in these lines. In this modern 'time' where fewer people subscribe to religious morality, do the concepts of 'right' and 'wrong' make any sense? In a godless universe, is any action – no matter how horrible – justified? .

ATMOSPHERE

Frost vividly conjures up the sinister and melancholy atmosphere of the city at night, a lonely world of darkness, street lights and interrupted silences.

IMAGERY

In a few short lines, Frost sketches a moody landscape of deserted and rain-drenched streets, rundown lanes, and darkness illuminated only by feeble streetlights that fade to nothing at the city's edge. The 'luminary clock' is a brilliant metaphor for the moon poised against the dark night sky.

FORM

'Acquainted With the Night' is a sonnet. Like all sonnets it has fourteen lines. Sonnets are usually divided into an eight-line octet and a six-line sestet. Unusually for a sonnet, 'Acquainted With the Night' it is divided into four three-line stanzas and a final two-line couplet. Frost makes skilful use of triple rhyme throughout. 'Rain' at the end of line 2 rhymes with 'lane' and 'explain', while 'beat' at the end of line 5 rhymes with 'feet' and 'street'.

The poem's form is in keeping with its theme. Its first and last lines are the same, reflecting the fact that the speaker is going round in circles. The poem consists of six sentences spread over its fourteen lines. Tellingly, each sentence begins with the word 'I', suggesting that the speaker is trapped in his own mind and cannot see beyond his tortured mental state.

VERBAL MUSIC

There are a great deal of long vowel sounds throughout the poem which contribute to the haunting, despairing mood. They slow the pace of the verse and create a sad, aching music. We see this in line 4 with its repeated 'o' and 'a' sounds: 'I have looked down the saddest city lane.'

In line 7, the repeated 'st' sounds suggest footsteps: 'I have stood still and stopped the sound of feet'. The slow, steady iambic rhythm of the lines also suggests the sound of footsteps echoing on a midnight street.

Design

He has witnessed a weird and unsettling coincidence. The mutant white heal-all flower has been joined by a rare white moth and an even rarer white spider. All three are 'kindred' or related in the sense that they share the same unusual colouring.

Most of all, however, the sight gets under the speaker's skin because it triggers a dark train of thought about the universe in his mind.

What does this scene remind the speaker of?
The speaker associates the moth, the flower and the spider with death and disease. As he memorably puts it, they are 'Assorted characters of death and blight'. This association is reinforced by the description of the moth as a 'white piece of rigid satin cloth'. This reminds the reader of a shroud, a cloth that bodies were traditionally wrapped in for burial.

The scene also makes the speaker think of witchcraft. The scene's three components – a white heal-all, a spider and a moth – are reminiscent of the stomach-churning ingredients used in dark magic: 'Mixed ready to begin the morning right,/ Like the ingredients of a witches' broth'.

The three creatures are 'ready to begin the morning right' – up early and ready to go about their business. There is also a pun here on the word 'rite', as if Frost is suggesting they are ready to start the day with a dark ritual.

The poet Randal Jarrell has compared the images of the three creatures to a witches' black mass or satanic ceremony. The flower, he suggests, serves as the altar on which the moth is sacrificed, just as an animal (or even a human) might be killed in some dark ritual.

What does the speaker ask himself?
The speaker wonders what brought this grim scene into existence and mixed its three 'ingredients' together. Something, he implies, must have brought the unnaturally white heal-all into existence. Something must have caused the spider to rest on top of the flower: 'What brought the kindred spider to that height'. Something must have 'steered' the moth into danger: 'What … steered the white moth thither in the night?'

What does the speaker conclude?
Only an evil power, the speaker suggests, could have created this unnerving scene: 'What but design of darkness to appall?' The speaker suggests that there are dark forces in the universe that are capable of influencing life on earth. This 'design of darkness' has conspired to turn the heal-all white and bring the spider and the moth to rest on it. There is an evil cosmic 'design' behind the appalling little scene.

LINE BY LINE

What does the speaker see?
The speaker is out walking when he sees a heal-all flower. A 'fat' spider is resting on the heal-all. The spider has snared a moth and holds it in its legs, preparing to devour it.

Heal-all flowers have healing properties and usually grow on a 'wayside' or roadside. They are famous for their bright blue appearance. Here, however, the speaker has stumbled on a white one. The spider is also white, pale as a 'snow-drop'. The moth is white as well. Frost vividly captures its appearance, comparing it to 'a paper kite' and 'a white piece of rigid satin cloth'.

How does the speaker react, and why?
- This little scene – the white flower, the white spider and the white moth – unnerves the speaker. It is fair to say that he's a little freaked out by what he's seen.
- He might be disgusted by the sight. Many people have an aversion to spiders and moths, and the sight of a spider on the verge of devouring a moth is not exactly a pretty picture.
- He might be unsettled by the flower's genetic mutation. Finding a white heal-all is like meeting a five-legged dog or an elephant with two trunks. What the speaker has encountered is a bizarre freak of nature, a flower that should not exist.

THEMES

A COLD UNIVERSE

Throughout history, mankind has been preoccupied with the question of whether or not God exists. One of the most well-known arguments to justify the existence of God was the 'argument from design'. Philosophers would point to a beautiful flower like a rose, or a complex natural mechanism like the human eye, and claim that its perfection proved that God must exist. How could things as perfect and complex as a rose or the human eye have just randomly sprung into existence? There must have been a designer, some intelligent and all-powerful being who created them.

In 'Design', Frost offers a chilling variation on this argument from design. Nothing in the world happens randomly. Even the tiniest and most insignificant occurrences happen for a reason. Therefore 'something' must have brought the little scene in lines 1 to 8 into existence. Something must have caused the heal-all to be white instead of blue. Something must have brought the spider to rest on it and 'steered' the moth into its clutches. The scene is so horrible that only some dark power could have caused it. Frost concludes that evil forces not only exist, but are capable of interfering in our world and manipulating the behaviour of plants, animals and perhaps even people. It is 'design of darkness', he claims, that has made our terrible world the way it is.

The poem's final line suggests that perhaps there is no design at all behind the arrangement of the spider, the moth and the heal-all flower: 'If design govern in a thing so small.' Maybe it is just a random event. However, if there is no design behind this small thing, then maybe there is no design behind more significant events either. Perhaps the entire universe the entire universe is nothing but a random arrangement of molecules. And that, perhaps, is the most terrifying vision of all.

NATURE

In 'Design', Frost presents us with nature's darker side. The poem reminds us that the natural world can be violent and unpleasant just as often as it is beautiful and serene. The image of the spider catching the moth reminds us the natural world is full of dangerous predators and that all too often, one creature must die for another to live.

ATMOSPHERE AND TONE

Frost presents us with a world where things we usually associate with good are instead linked with evil. The colour white, for example, is usually associated with innocence and purity. Here, however, it is linked with death and disease. The heal-all flower was famous for its medicinal properties. In this poem, however, the heal-all is associated with a sinister 'witches' broth' rather than with healing.

This vivid imagery conjures up an atmosphere of menace. The mood is reinforced by the use of a cluster of sinister words such as 'death', 'blight', 'dead', 'witches' and 'darkness'. (To this list might also be added 'kindred', meaning similar or related, which also has supernatural associations.)

The speaker's tone in the octet is simple and straightforward as he describes unflinchingly what he's seen. In the sestet, however, his tone seems more emotional and despairing. When he considers the mutant white heal-all, he seems disturbed or perhaps even offended. Heal-alls, he reminds us, are blue flowers. They should have nothing to do with whiteness: 'What had that flower to do with being white,/ The wayside blue and innocent heal-all?'

METAPHOR AND SIMILE

'Design' is rich in powerful similes. In line 3 the moth is compared to a 'piece of rigid satin cloth' while in line 8 it is compared to a 'paper kite'. In another wonderful simile, the heal-all is compared to a 'froth', suggesting its foamy white appearance. Perhaps the most interesting simile of all, however, suggests that the three little organisms have been combined 'Like the ingredients of a witches' broth'. In line 7, meanwhile, a metaphor compares the spider to a 'snow-drop' flower.

FORM

'Design' is a Petrarchan sonnet. It is divided into an eight-line octet and a six-line sestet. The poem rhymes ABBA ABBA ACAACC. In many Petrarchan sonnets the octet presents a situation while the sestet considers what meaning can be drawn from the situation. In 'Design', the octet describes the flower, the spider and the moth, while the sestet meditates on the significance of this little scene.

VERBAL MUSIC

There are several instances in this poem where Frost deploys a harsh and grating verbal music. We see this in phrases like 'dimpled spider, fat and white', 'Assorted characters of death and blight', and 'dead wings carried like a paper kite'. In each instance, the clash of hard consonants creates a cacophonous musical effect, appropriate to the poem's unsettling imagery.

Provide, Provide

LINE BY LINE

The first four lines describe a woman who has lost her looks, status and wealth in society. When she was young she was beautiful and famous: 'The picture pride of Hollywood.' The poet compares her to Abishag, a character from the Bible renowned for her beauty. However, her beauty has vanished with age. Frost refers to her as a 'witch' and a 'withered hag'. She has also lost any wealth and status that she would have enjoyed when she was a Hollywood star. This unfortunate woman now washes steps in order to survive.

Frost uses the woman's fall from grace as a cautionary tale. Be careful, he warns us, for 'Too many fall from great and good' for us to think that we can avoid a similar fate. Frost tells us to act now to ensure that we never end up like the woman described in the opening lines. There are a number of options that he suggests:

- Don't get old: 'Die early and avoid the fate.'
- If you are destined to live a long life, make sure you die in a high-ranking position: 'Make up your mind to die in state.'
- Become very rich: 'Make the whole stock exchange your own!'
- Become as powerful as a king so that nobody will have the courage to insult you: 'If need be occupy a throne,/ Where nobody can call you crone.'

For some, the knowledge and skills acquired in early years provide them with the means to take care of themselves when older: 'Some have relied on what they knew'. Others have avoided the fate of 'the beauty Abishag' by being realistic about life and not living in a fantasy world: 'simply being true.' According to the speaker, both approaches are worth considering: 'What worked for them might work for you.'

Some who achieve fame in their youth think that they will always be wealthy, beautiful and loved. These people consequently 'disregard' what is to come. But memories of fame and fortune will not compensate for a failure to plan for later years: 'No memory of having starred/ Atones for later disregard'. If we disregard the future, we will pay the price when we are old and sick.

Frost's advice is summed up in a single word which he repeats at the end of the poem: 'Provide, provide!' He tells us to do whatever is required to make sure we are not alone and without support in our final years. If this means that we have to pay people to take care of us, then so be it. It is better to live in comfort, surrounded by false friends, than it is to live helplessly alone: 'Better to go down dignified/ With boughten friendship at your side/ Than none at all.'

FORM
The poem consists of seven three-line stanzas and follows an AAA, BBB, CCC rhyme scheme.

TONE
Frost adopts a blunt and unsentimental tone in 'Provide, Provide'. The opening line is particularly harsh in its description of the former Hollywood beauty. The poet remains matter-of-fact throughout, dishing out his advice without sentiment and never softening his tone. The rhyme scheme adds to the cold tone, lending the poem a certain flippancy.

THEMES

ISOLATION AND COMMUNITY
Frost deals with isolation in a number of his poems. In 'After Apple-Picking' and 'Birches', solitude is portrayed in a positive light. However, the isolation that Frost presents us with in 'Provide, Provide' is terrible and bleak. When we are young and healthy we are able to find ways to enjoy time by ourselves. When we are old, sick and helpless it is a very different matter. The poem warns us to do everything in our power when we are young to avoid being alone when we are old. It is all too easy to neglect the future when we are young, or to imagine that everything will just work itself out as we get older. But Frost tells us that we would be foolish to act or think this way. We should act now to ensure that we enjoy as much comfort and support as possible in our later years.

A COLD UNIVERSE
The poem tells us that it is our responsibility to take care of ourselves and that we should not expect anything from society. It portrays the world as an uncaring place where we must fend for ourselves. Frost's description of the old woman in the opening lines is pitiless and unsentimental, a reflection of the brutality of life.

The poem offers no sense of community or of people caring for one another. (In this regard, the poem can be compared with "Out, Out —" which also describes the world as a cold and brutal place.) If we wish to survive with dignity, we must depend on ourselves and not pretend that the world is any different than it is. The poem suggests that money and power are necessary to avoid indignity in old age.

TRANSIENCE AND BREVITY
The poem highlights how transient beauty and fame can be. The Hollywood star described in the opening lines suddenly finds that she is a 'withered hag' that no one recognises, reduced to cleaning steps for a living. In an age of celebrity, when so many people get fifteen minutes of fame, the poem offers sound advice. Looks fade and fame is often short-lived. If we don't acknowledge this fact then we will pay a heavy price: 'No memory of having starred/ Atones for later disregard'.

Seamus Heaney

Themes

Art, Craft and Creativity

Celebration of Craft

'The Forge' is one of Heaney's most passionate and vivid celebrations of craft. The poet admires the effort and exhaustion that goes into the labour, evident in the way the blacksmith 'expends himself'. The poet is also attracted by the physicality of the work – by the beating of metal; the sudden, almost dangerous 'fantails of sparks'; and the settling of roasting hot metal in water: 'hiss when a new shoe toughens in water'.

But the blacksmith's work is not only practical and everyday but also artistic and creative. Working in 'shape and music', the blacksmith seems to combine the sound and rhythm of a musician with the transformative, sculpting ability of a fine artist.

Heaney compares the anvil to an 'altar', bolstering the idea of the forge as a special, almost sacred place. All the poet knows of it is 'a door into the dark'. We get the sense that the forge is reserved for blacksmiths only, that laypeople have no business crossing the threshold of this sacred space.

'The 'Harvest Bow' is a similar celebration of craft and manual labour. The poet praises the skill with which his father wove the bows, tightening the strands of straw 'twist by twist' until the 'love-knot' came together. He describes the 'fine intent' or intense concentration his father brought to this task and how eventually his fingers seemed to move automatically, as though he no longer needed to think about what he was doing: 'Until your fingers moved somnambulant'.

The father's inherent craftsmanship also features in 'A Call'. The father exhibits great care and precision, combing carefully through the leeks and ensuring that he's careful ,too, to remove each weed at the root, ensuring that they won't grow back. But he also possesses the gentleness and sensitivity necessary to nurture a garden, removing the weeds 'gently', so as not to upset the soil bed.

'Sunlight' and 'The Pitchfork' also celebrate different aspects of craft. 'Sunlight' celebrates the everyday precision of the aunt as she goes about her baking, following her through the process of preparing and baking the scones as she wrestles dough into shape, places it in the oven, cleans off the bakeboard and waits for the scone to rise. 'The Pitchfork' meanwhile celebrates how the titular instrument has been carefully shaped and sculpted until it has become smooth and balanced. The farmer appreciates just how well-suited it is to the task at hand, admiring the 'springiness, the clip and dark of it'.

The Nature of Art

'The Forge' is a potent allegory for the poetic process.

- The poet, like the blacksmith, must expend himself in his efforts. He must work really hard to produce 'shape' (form, stanzas etc) and 'music' (sound effects and verbal music).
- Poetry must be at centre of the poet's life, just as the anvil is 'somewhere in the centre' of the forge.
- Poetry must be an immovable priority in the poet's life, just as the anvil is 'Set there immovable' in the forge.
- Poetry, like the anvil, has a 'square' part (representing form, hard work, drafting) and a part that is 'Horned as a unicorn' (representing fantasy, imagination, wonder and invention).

Poetry and art originate from a mysterious and unknowable place in the psyche. Like the forge, this part of the mind remains hidden and mysterious. We can experience only glimpses into its workings, just as the poet knows only the door of the forge and the darkness of its interior.

'Bogland' too focuses on the poetic process. Heaney was keenly aware that memory was important to him as a poet: 'memory was the faculty that supplied me with the first quickening of my own poetry'. It is memory, perhaps above all, that sustains Heaney as a poet, nourishing his talent and arousing his inspiration. There is a sense in which he feels that a poet must excavate the layers of his remembrance, much as the turf-cutters and archaeologists dig into the layers of bog, in an attempt to extract the material for poetry from his personal store recollection.

In 'The Harvest Bow', the poet comes to see the bow not merely as a humble piece of craftsmanship but as a genuine piece of art. He thinks of it as a 'device', as a tool or implement that allows his father to communicate things that otherwise would have remained unsaid. But the term 'device' in its older usage also means an emblem, and the bow works as a powerful symbol for the poet, representing not only the father's personality but also the harvest and the traditions associated with it in the parish where he grew up.

'The Skunk' and 'The Pitchfork' also focus on aspects of poetic creativity. 'The Skunk' celebrates the fascination of words themselves, especially ancient, fundamental words like 'wife'. For such words, especially when we haven't used them for a while, possess the power to intrigue and captivate us. In the right circumstances, the poet suggests, language can be more potent and intoxicating than a freshly broached cask of wine. 'The Pitchfork', meanwhile, acknowledges that no poem can achieve perfection that the poet imagined at the beginning of its composition. Each work, at best, can only come 'near' such perfection.

The Anxiety of the Artist

In 'The Forge' we sense that the poet cannot help but compare the hands-on usefulness of the blacksmith's craft with the more abstract utility of poetry. There is a thread of this concern through Heaney's work: an anxiety about the legitimacy of writing poetry, about whether it is a 'proper' job for a man. This is more understandable if we consider Heaney's traditional rural upbringing, where men did practical physical labour and poetry was possibly considered pretentious or grandiose.

Though the poet admires the blacksmith, there is a sense in which he also feels inadequate by comparison, working with a pen and paper rather than 'the bellows'. The blacksmith does real work involving 'real iron'. The material that Heaney works with, on the other hand, is only imagined in his readers' heads.

This anxiety about the uselessness of poetry is also present in 'The Skunk'. We see this in lines 13 to 14: 'The beautiful, useless/ Tang of eucalyptus'. The smell of the eucalyptus tree may be beautiful but it serves no practical value. Similarly the lines themselves may be beautiful but also serve no practical value. Like all poetry they are 'useless' in any practical sense.

Such anxiety also features in 'The Harvest Bow', heightened no doubt by the fact that Heaney's father was a no-nonsense, pragmatic man. However, on this occasion the poet detects a similarity between them. For harvest bows, like poems, are beautiful but serve little practical value. Making the harvest bow, then, shows the father's hidden artistic side, with the poet remarking on how his father's hands 'Harked to their gift and worked with fine intent'. The father weaves the bow with the same skill and intensity with which the poet puts together a poem.

Perhaps the father's weaving grants the poet a sense of permission – if it's okay for his father to produce the beautiful but useless bows, it is okay for him to compose his poems. The similarity between the poet and his father only goes so far, however. Heaney responds to the harvest bow with the intense spirituality of a poet, feeling that he is able to glean 'the unsaid' from its loops. To his father, however, it is more 'throwaway': part of a tradition and nothing more.

Imagined Spaces and Landscapes

Again and again, Heaney provides intensely vivid descriptions of places he has only imagined, places he has never been.

- In 'The Forge', for instance, we have to remind ourselves that the poet has never actually been inside the door of the forge, that he knows it only through sounds and occasional glimpses.
- In 'Tollund Man', Heaney vividly imagines his journey to Jutland, to the 'flat country' where Tollund Man's body was discovered.
- In 'A Constable Calls', the young speaker imagines 'the black hole in the barracks', envisaging an almost dungeon-like cell into which he and his father will be cast for deceiving the constable.
- In 'The Pitchfork', the farmer, a man given to playful imagination, imagines the space probe drifting on and on, far past its intended destination, eventually reaching 'an other side'.
- In 'A Call', the poet imagines his parents' hallway and his father working the garden, picturing the hallway's 'sunstruck pendulums' and his father kneeling beside the leek rig.
- Heaney's descriptions of such places are so realised that as readers of the poem we experience them ourselves.

'Sunlight' describes an actual place, the poet's childhood farm in Mossbawn. However, the poem presents us with an idealised version of the place. Similarly in 'Postscript', the poet presents us with an idealised version of the Flaggy Shore: the wild, glittering ocean; the 'slate-grey lake'; the swans that look like balls of 'earthed lightning'. Perhaps the poet has actually experienced the Flaggy Shore under such conditions. But it is more likely that the image he paints for us fuses elements of different trips he has taken there over the years. Perhaps he's seen the Flaggy Shore on an exquisitly blustery afternoon, but surely he has never actually witnessed the splendour he advises us to seek out.

Crediting the Marvellous

'Lightenings VIII' powerfully makes the point that the marvellous is very much a matter of perspective. What is ordinary and mundane to one person is extraordinary to another. To the monks, the flying ship is an extraordinary sight – it is like nothing they have ever seen before or will ever see again and they will remember it for the rest of their lives. To the crewman, however, the flying ship is just his place of work. But the opposite is also true. To the monks the oratory is just a place where they eat, work and pray. But to the crewman it is truly extraordinary. It is as wonderfully alien to him as the bed of a deep-sea trench would be to us. The poem suggests then that the ordinary world around us can be a source of awe, mystery and inspiration, if we look at it in the right way. If we are open to experience and view our lives with fresh eyes, as the crewman views the oratory, the world might suddenly appear as the truly marvellous place it actually is.

'The Forge' and 'the Pitchfork' show the poet finding the marvellous in the most unlikely workday scenarios. In 'The Forge', he sees the humble workshop as a space of truly marvellous creation. 'The Pitchfork', meanwhile, presents the simple, everyday instrument, comprising of 'Riveted steel' and 'turned timber' as being almost perfect.

'Bogland' features a similar sense of mystery and wonder. The poet seems awestruck as he contemplates the different objects that have been preserved by the bog: the butter dug out after a hundred years, the preserved trees, the 'astounding' Great Irish Elk. He also seems awestruck at the thought of how endlessly deep the bog is, how layer after layer can be stripped away to reveal yet more bogland underneath.

'The Skunk' is yet another poem where Heaney finds the marvellous in the everyday. The skunk is a familiar sight in California – as common as a fox or a squirrel would be in Ireland. However, he knows that to native Californians, the skunk is a nuisance, barely a step above vermin. Yet the poet finds great mystery in this everyday creature. To him it is the 'Ordinary, mysterious skunk'. He realises that it's a common rodent, but he also, as we've noted, sees it as something special, as a creature of poise and elegance.

'Postscript' too is a poem that stresses the the importance of being present in the moment, and of keeping oneself open to life and its sensations. The opening line emphasises the importance of making the time for such experiences 'And some time make the time to drive out west'. Doing so, the poem suggests, is by no means a frivolous activity; it's necessary for a sense of perspective, for our mental and emotional wellbeing.

The Process of Memory

In 'Bogland', the bog is like a museum preserving the history of the Irish race. It holds the evidence of the past, the flora and fauna that once existed on the island and the remains of past civilizations, all the layers that have been 'camped on before' by Ireland's previous occupants.

Yet the bog also serves as a metaphor for the mind or consciousness of the Irish race. As Heaney puts it: 'I had a tentative unrealised need to make a congruence between memory and bogland and, for the want of a better word, our

national consciousness'. Within our national consciousness we remember all that has happened to us as a race, handing it down to the next generation in history, song and story.

'Sunlight' and 'A Constable Calls' are in their very different ways wonderful poems of childhood memory. In 'A Constable Calls', the poet vividly reconstruct and imaginatively re-enter an incident from his childhood, wonderfully capturing a child's perspective on events. We see this in the way he describes the speaker's boyish fascination with the officer's gun. He is captivated by the details of the constable's weapon: 'its buttoned flap, the braid cord/ looped into the revolver butt'.

'Sunlight' illustrates how we often remember distant times and places in a positive light, how our minds filter out the negative details and enable us to imagine that things were better than they actually were. When the poet thinks back on the summers he spent at Mossbawn, it seems that the rain never fell and there were no disturbances or interferences from the outside world. His memory seems to combine the best elements of these summers and to fuse them into a single perfect afternoon.

'The Skunk', 'The Harvest Bow' and 'Tate's Avenue' all provide fascinating insight into the strange and surprising ways that memory functions. The poet's memory, the skunk and his wife are inextricably linked in 'The Skunk'. When the poet was lonely in California, the skunk's appearance triggered memories of his wife. In turn, when he is back in Dublin with his wife, Heaney can't help but be reminded of the skunk: 'It all came back to me last night'. Heaney, then, describes the powerful, irresistible manner in which smells, tastes, sights, sounds and even words trigger memory.

In 'The Harvest Bow', as the poet examines the 'golden loops' of the bow pinned up on his dresser he finds himself vividly remembering an occasion from his childhood. With astonishing clarity, the poet recalls an evening walk with his father to a local fishing spot. Heaney uses a typically brilliant metaphor for this process of memory, for how the bow stimulates such intense recollection. The loops of the bow, he suggests, are a kind of screen on which footage of long-ago events is replayed for him to savour and relive.

'Tate's Avenue', meanwhile, describes the process of memory as an almost inner Instagram. We find the poet flicking through different mental images, as if he were swiping through an internal photo stream. The poem, we might imagine, is set during a moment of ease or relaxation, one in which the poet finds his mind idling or drifting through memories of the past. Maybe he is on a train or a plane, in a space where it is possible to tune out from what is going on around you and become lost in your own thoughts.

Love and Relationships

'The Skunk' and 'Tate's Aveneue' are both powerful celebrations of married love, showing how the love between two people can grow and remain intense even after years of marriage. When the poet was in California he had been with his wife for 'eleven years'. Yet his feelings towards her were still passionate, and he missed her deeply during this spell abroad. He wrote her love letters and was reminded of her by the sensual delights of California: by the sweet smell of eucalyptus trees or by a sip of Californian wine.

'Tate's Avenue' similarly celebrates the resilience and longevity of a long-term relationship, not the just the excitement and passion of the young love in its earliest stages. The poet fondly recalls how he and his wife explored the world together as the years went by and their relationship continued to flourish and deepen. He relishes how their horizons expanded over time, from the the claustrophobic walled yard, to the Northern Irish seashore, to the exotic Guadalquivir river in Spain, and then, no doubt, even further afield.

'The Underground' presents an arguably more complicated picture of marriage. The poem's first nine lines capture the joy and excitement of early married life. We can imagine the feelings of freedom and exhilaration they experience as they begin their honeymoon in London, the wife still proudly wearing the 'going-away coat' from her wedding. The second half of the poem is dark and unrealistic, perhaps even a little bizarre, as the poet presents himself in a similar situation to Orpheus: forced to lead his wife on a journey through the darkness but doomed to lose her if he looks behind. The nightmarish scenario suggests the poet's feelings of anguish and confusion as he takes up his role as husband. He has been thrust into a new set of responsibilities that will eventually require him to function as father, breadwinner and protector.

'A Constable Calls' provides a subtle but effective portrait of the poet's father. It's fair to say that in this poem the father comes across as the strong silent type:

- He's a farmer, a man well used to the physical demands of making a living off the land, as he sows and harvests various crops.
- He's a man of few words; as we noted above, the only thing he says to the constable is 'No'
- He's not afraid to defy the authorities by growing illicit turnips.
- He's not afraid to face down the constable, another powerful masculine presence.
- He calmly lies about the hidden crops, giving no evidence of being frightened or intimidated by the constable and his revolver. The father's composure contrasts starkly with the fear the young speaker experiences.

'The Harvest Bow' is poem that explores the complicated relationship between the poet and this rough, tough no-nonsense man. Specifically it focuses on the difficulties they experienced in communicating. Like many men of his background and generation, the poet's father wouldn't have been given to self-expression or to talking about his feelings.

The poet, however, suggests that his father could express his inner self, the mellowed silence that existed within him, through making the harvest bows: 'As you plaited the harvest bow/ You implicated the mellowed silence in you'. To 'implicate' means to convey or communicate. Making harvest bows, then, allowed the father to convey or communicate something of his personality. He expresses himself through making these little bows, just an artist might express himself by creating a sculpture or a painting.

According to the poet, the bow is a 'knowable corona', because it allows him to know his father. As we noted, the bow functions almost like a Braille text, for when the poet touches it, he feels he can learn unsaid things about his father's life and personality.

'A Call' also focuses on such difficulties in communication. The poet is a highly articulate man who loves to express his thoughts and feelings in words. Why then does he struggle to express his feelings for his father when they speak on the phone?

Perhaps it has to do with the difficulty that many men seem to have when it comes to expressing their feelings – it is not something that comes naturally to them. Perhaps it is a generational thing – the poet would have grown up in a time when fathers and sons would rarely articulate their feelings for one another. Perhaps the poet knows that if he speaks these words he will make his father uncomfortable, and he does not want to do this. The result will just be silence at the other end of the phone.

The Forge

LINE BY LINE

The poet is fascinated by the forge, and by the blacksmith who works there. It seems he's drawn to this little workshop and likes to hang around outside. We sense that he's spent hours staring at the pieces of scrap metal in the forge's yard. He's studied 'old axles' the blacksmith would have removed from carts before replacing them with new ones. He sees wheels that the blacksmith decided were beyond repair and that now sit 'rusting' outside the forge.

When the poet lingers outside the forge, he can hear the noises of the blacksmith's trade. For instance, he hears the sound of the blacksmith's hammer colliding with his anvil. Each tap of the hammer produces a 'short-pitched ring', a chime that seems to be both high-pitched and short in its duration. The blacksmith, then, produces a kind of tinkling sound, as he shapes and thins out a piece of metal with continuous well-aimed tapping.

Sometimes the poet hears a sharp hissing sound emanating from the forge. He imagines that the blacksmith is thrusting a freshly beaten, red-hot horseshoe into a bucket of water to cool. This cooling process solidifies and toughens the iron, fixing it in shape: 'hiss when a new shoe toughens in water'.

The poet, however, has never actually been inside the forge itself. The blacksmith, it seems, has never offered to show him around the building's interior. And he's probably too intimidated by the blacksmith to request such an invitation. This particular tradesman, as we shall see, comes across as a rather gruff and unapproachable individual.

From time to time, the poet has looked through the building's open door, peering into the gloom of its interior. It's too dark inside, however, for him to see much. All the poet 'knows' of the forge, therefore, is its doorway and the darkness to which it leads: 'All I know is a door into the dark.'

On occasion, however, as he peers in through the door, the poet has witnessed little eruptions of sparks, the result of heat and friction as metal grinds against metal within the forge. Such bursts occur suddenly, and at 'unpredictable' intervals, as the blacksmith goes about his work. The poet describes how these surges issue outward from the anvil, expanding in a 'fantail' shape.

The poet imagines what the interior of the forge might be like, focusing especially on the blacksmith's anvil.

338

He imagines that this particular anvil follows the classic design, having one square end, known as the heel, and one horned end, known - unsurprisingly - as the horn: 'Horned as a unicorn, on one end square'. (The 'horn' of an anvil is used for hammering metal into curved shapes.)

- He imagines the anvil as a solid rectangular block, resembling 'an altar' in a church.
- He imagines that it must be extremely heavy, an 'immoveable' object.
- He imagines that the anvil 'must be somewhere in the centre' of the forge.

This of course makes sense from a practical point of view, permitting the blacksmith to move around the anvil as he works, striking the metal on its surface from a variety of different angles. But it also seems appropriate that the anvil, the blacksmith's largest and most important piece of equipment, should be his workroom's focal point.

The poet imagines the blacksmith at work within the forge. His labours are exhausting; as he drains or 'expends himself' in his efforts at the anvil. The blacksmith's work, of course, is practical in nature as he produces marketable products for everyday use, things like horseshoes, wheels and axles.

The blacksmith's negative attitude toward the traffic stems partly from the fact that he resents being left redundant and superfluous by technology's ever-onward march. One of the blacksmith's main jobs, after all, is making horseshoes. As cars and other new technologies become more common, his skills become less relevant and less sought-after.

But the poet also presents the blacksmith as a kind of artist, as someone working in 'shape and music'. He's a kind of musician whose 'hammered anvil', as we've seen, produces music of a kind, a tinkling pitch and rhythm. But he's also a sculptor of sorts, shaping raw metal into useful and even beautiful objects.

The poet often sees the blacksmith standing at the door of the forge, taking a break from his work. He leans against the door's side jamb, smoking a cigarette and watching the world go by: 'Sometimes, leather-aproned, hairs in his nose,/ He leans out on the jamb'.

Heaney provides us with a memorable portrait of the blacksmith. Given his hairy nose and the 'iron hoops rusting' outside his business, we get the impression that he isn't too bothered with superficial things like grooming and branding. He is a tough, country workman of the old school: a no-nonsense, slightly gruff character.

As he smokes, the blacksmith watches cars passing by his forge. He can remember a time when most people travelled by horse and cart rather than by car, when roads were filled with the 'clatter/ Of hoofs' rather than with the zoom of car engines.

The poet describes how the 'traffic is flashing in rows' as it passes the forge, a phrase that conveys several meanings at

once. The word 'flashing' suggests the greatly increased pace of modern life. Once people travelled on horseback or on foot and had time to take in their surroundings. Nowadays we tend to whizz around in our cars, utterly unmindful of the environments we pass through. (And even when we do find ourselves walking, we're in such a hurry, so preoccupied with the stresses and strains of modern living, that we pay little attention to what's going on around us).

'Flashing', no doubt, also suggests the blacksmith's opinion of the automobiles he watches from his doorway. These might be fancy or "flash", as the expression goes, and they might have glossy 'flashing' paint jobs. But they're also flimsy, mass-produced, and ultimately disposable, especially compared to the carts the blacksmith would have worked on, each of which was unique and designed to last a lifetime.

The fact that the cars go flashing by in 'rows' suggests the conformity of modern living.

We travel to and from school and work, in an orderly and regulated fashion, each of us sealed in our almost identical, mass-produced pods. We allow ourselves to be herded 'in rows' like obedient cattle

The blacksmith grunts at the sight of the passing traffic, almost as if he can't find the words to express his contempt for this flashily conformist procession and the new world it represents. He flicks his cigarette in its direction, a classically aggressive gesture of contempt. Then he retreats back into the forge, slamming the door behind his as he does so: 'Then grunts and goes in, with a slam and a flick'.

These gestures reveal not only the blacksmith's scorn for the traffic and the modernity it represents but also his anger and frustration that his skills are no longer as valued as they once were. But surely there is also an element of defiance; we sense the blacksmith's determination to persevere with his craft even in the face of the world's indifference.

The poet imagines that, once the blacksmith's back in the forge, he gets down to business: 'To beat real iron out, to work the bellows.' The mass-produced vehicles passing outside are manufactured from cheap artificial alloys and various plasticky materials. The blacksmith, however, still works with genuine metal . It's only the blacksmith, and those few others that practise his dying art, who continue to use 'real iron'.

THEMES

CELEBRATION OF CRAFT

'The Forge', perhaps more than anything else, is a celebration of the blacksmith's craft. The poet admires the effort and exhaustion that goes into the labour, evident in the way the blacksmith 'expends himself'. The poet is also attracted by the physicality of the work – by the beating of metal; the sudden, almost dangerous 'fantails of sparks'; and the settling of roasting hot metal in water: 'hiss when a new shoe toughens in water'.

But the blacksmith's work, as we noted above, is not only practical and everyday but also artistic and creative. Working in 'shape and music', the blacksmith seems to combine the sound and rhythm of a musician with the transformative, sculpting ability of a fine artist.

He also compares the anvil to an 'altar', bolstering the idea of the forge as a special, almost sacred place. All the poet knows of it is 'a door into the dark'. We get the sense that the forge is reserved for blacksmiths only, that laypeople have no business crossing the threshold of this sacred space.

The blacksmith, as we have seen, has a dismissive and defiant attitude to modernisation. We sense that the poet celebrates the blacksmith's individuality and authenticity: this is someone who does his own thing and follows his own calling, irrespective of the changes in the world at large. Perhaps the poet even shares a little of the blacksmith's hostile attitude towards our conformist, mass-produced society.

The poet associates the anvil with a unicorn, a mythical horse that has a single horn protruding from its forehead. The unicorn is a fantastic beast, a purely imaginary creature. This suggests that the blacksmith's work involves a degree of fantasy and imagination, as well as hard physical labour. Scottish mythology celebrated the unicorn as a beast that would die rather than be captured, suggesting the blacksmith's dogged refusal to change his ways in the face of modernity.

The unicorn also suggests the boundless imagination that poets and artists strive for. In spiritualism, for example, the unicorn is a symbol of change and transformation, while modern day investors use the term for new companies and ideas that can literally change the world: Skype or Google, for example.

THE NATURE OF ART

'The Forge' can be read as an allegory for writing poetry. Different aspects of the poem function as metaphors for creativity:

- Poetry and art originate from a mysterious and unknowable place in the psyche. Like the forge, this part of the mind remains hidden and mysterious. We can experience only glimpses into its workings, just as the poet knows only the door of the forge and the darkness of its interior.
- Poetic inspiration is 'unpredictable', just as the appearance of the blacksmith's 'sparks' is random. When it occurs, however, it is wonderful.
- The poet, like the blacksmith, must expend himself in his efforts. He must work really hard to produce 'shape'

(form, stanzas etc) and 'music' (sound effects and verbal music).

- Poetry must be at the centre of the poet's life, just as the anvil is 'somewhere in the centre' of the forge.
- Poetry must be an immovable priority in the poet's life, just as the anvil is 'Set there immovable' in the forge.
- Poetry, like the anvil, has a 'square' part (representing form, hard work, drafting) and a part that is 'Horned as a unicorn' (representing fantasy, imagination, wonder and invention).
- Like smithing, poetry has somewhat fallen out of fashion. It is undervalued in the modern mass-produced world.

THE ANXIETY OF THE ARTIST

We sense that the poet cannot help but compare the hands-on usefulness of the blacksmith's craft with the more abstract utility of poetry. There is a thread of this concern through Heaney's work: an anxiety about the legitimacy of writing poetry, of whether it is a 'proper' job for a man. This is more understandable if we consider Heaney's traditional rural upbringing, where men did practical physical labour and poetry was possibly considered pretentious or grandiose.

Though the poet admires the blacksmith, there is a sense in which he also feels inadequate by comparison, working with a pen and paper rather than 'the bellows'. The blacksmith does real work involving 'real iron'. The material that Heaney works with, on the other hand, is only imagined in his readers' heads.

In the title, Heaney is possibly playing on the dual meaning of the word 'forge'. Besides being the name for the blacksmith's workplace, 'to forge' means to fake or to imitate. Perhaps this pun expresses Heaney's anxiety that the work he does has no real-world application – at least, not in the way that the blacksmith's work does.

IMAGINED SPACES

This is yet another poem where Heaney provides an intensely vivid description of a place he has only imagined, a place he has never been. We have to remind ourselves that the poet has never actually been inside the door of the forge, that he knows it only through sounds and occasional glimpses. But his depiction of this workshop is so realised that as readers of the poem we almost feel like we have been inside the forge ourselves.

CREDITING THE MARVELLOUS

On the face of it, the forge is an unpromising location for a poem. It's not aesthetically pleasing, with the rusty 'old axles and iron hoops' piled up outside, and the unpolished grumpy blacksmith with 'hairs in his nose'.

However, the poet sees this humble workshop as a place of truly marvellous creation. The 'unpredictable fantail of sparks' that explodes as the blacksmith strikes the metal is beautiful and unexpected. The blacksmith creates 'music' as he works, causing the anvil to 'ring' with his hammer. The anvil itself is marvellous, described as being 'Horned as a unicorn' and standing like an 'altar', 'immovable' in the centre of the forge.

FORM

'The Forge' is written in the form of a sonnet. It has fourteen lines. The octet is concerned with the forge itself whilst the sextet focuses on the blacksmith. It has an ABBACDDC EFGFEF rhyming scheme.

VERBAL MUSIC

The poem is full of sounds. Heaney describes the 'short-pitched ring' of the anvil, the 'hiss' of the red-hot horseshoe as it is plunged in water, the 'clatter/ Of hoofs', and the 'grunts' of the blacksmith. These various sounds underscore the poet's assertion that there is a kind of 'music' in the work of the blacksmith.

METAPHOR, SIMILE AND FIGURES OF SPEECH

The anvil is central to the poem and Heaney uses effective figures of speech to describe it. Using a simile, he describes it as being 'Horned as a unicorn'. This gives us a striking visual of the anvil's horn and also suggests that there is something mystical and magical about the anvil.

Using a metaphor, Heaney also describes the anvil as 'an altar'. This emphasises how central the anvil is to the blacksmith's work, and how there is something mysterious and sacred about it.

IMAGERY

'The Forge' is filled with vivid imagery, from the rusty 'axles and iron hoops' outside the forge, to the beautiful plumes of sparks that randomly fly off the anvil: 'The unpredictable fantail of sparks'.

Perhaps the most memorable image in the poem, however, is that of the blacksmith himself. He is a little scruffy in his work gear: 'leather-aproned, hairs in his nose'. He is a traditionalist with little patience for the modern world, who 'grunts' at the rows of traffic outside the forge. He is brusque in his manner, returning inside 'with a grunt and flick'. In just a few lines, Heaney portrays the blacksmith's appearance, his personality and the way he carries himself.

Bogland

LINE BY LINE

A COMPARISON BETWEEN IRELAND AND AMERICA

'Bogland' opens by comparing the landscape of Ireland to the prairies of North America:

Prairies of North America	Irish Landscape
Prairies are vast grasslands reaching for hundreds of kilometres.	The Irish landscape is relatively tiny; you can travel for only a few hours by car before reaching the sea. One might say it's cramped and claustrophobic in comparison to the prairies' endless plains.
The prairies exhibit an endless flatness.	The Irish landscape on the other hand is known for being rugged, mountainous and uneven.
The prairies are almost featureless, stretching out monotonously in every direction.	The Irish landscape, on the other hand, is filled with geographical features; with mountains, lakes and hills.
In the prairies you can see for tens or even hundreds of kilometres.	In the Irish landscape, however, you can only see as far as the next hill, lake or mountain. Then the eye must 'concede' or give way: 'Everywhere the eye concedes'. The rugged horizon seems to 'Encroach' or push up against the viewer.
In the prairies, because there are no distractions, one's gaze tends to drift all the way toward the horizon.	In Ireland, however, some feature of the landscape will inevitably attract or distract the eye. Heaney, for instance, mentions how the eye is 'wooed' or seduced by the sight of a mountain lake: 'the eye … is wooed into the cyclops' eye of a tarn'.

This 'big sun' can be usefully compared to the description of a 'tarn', or mountain lake, in the Irish landscape. In a wonderful metaphor, Heaney likens this tarn to a 'cyclops' eye'. (The cyclops was a mythical one-eyed giant.) He emphasises how the eye is 'wooed' or seduced by the tarn, which gently draws the gaze into its depths.

Heaney, using a wonderful phrase, refers to the prairies as 'unfenced country'. This describes how the prairie ranges were kept open, without walls or barriers, so cattle could wander freely, grazing on their abundant grass lands. But it also suggests how, as we've noted, the prairies possess few natural impediments, such as hills and mountains. The prairies, therefore, permit one to travel for hundreds of miles without encountering the slightest obstacle.

While the Irish landscape, of course, has no such wide-open spaces, it has its own 'unfenced country' in the form of its bogs: 'Our unfenced country/ Is bog'. Just as the prairies allow one to wander vast distances along the surface of the earth, so the bogs allow one to burrow vast distances into the earth, striking deeper and deeper into its depths.

A JOURNEY INTO THE BOG'S DEPTHS

In the 19th century, the voyagers who traversed the great plains of America were known as pioneers. These men and women were fearless and intrepid explorers, setting out to encounter environments and landscapes no European had ever before witnessed.

The closest Irish equivalent to these pioneers are the turf cutters who dig into the bog, revealing its secrets. As Heaney puts it: 'Our pioneers keep striking/ Inwards and downwards'. The American pioneers witnessed extraordinary sights as they journeyed westwards across the American plains. But our turf-cutting pioneers have made some incredible discoveries of their own:

- They found the perfectly preserved skeleton of a 'Great Irish Elk', which has been extinct for approximately 11,000 years. Heaney uses a wonderful metaphor to depict the elk's skeleton set up in a museum, describing it as 'an astounding crate full of air'. (We can imagine the skeleton's bare bones resembling a kind of crate or box).
- They found butter that had been buried in the bog over 'a hundred years' ago. It was 'salty' after its decades amid the peat and had been leached of its original yellow colour but was nevertheless still perfectly edible.
- They have found the trunks of ancient trees, of 'great

firs'. These trunks had been softened by the bog's swampy wetness until they were 'waterlogged' and reduced to a spongy or pulpy consistency. But their oiginal shape was still preserved.

Each layer of bogland the turf cutters remove reveals evidence of earlier civilisations: 'Every layer they strip/ Seems camped on before'. Each level of the bog contains remnants of the people who were alive when that level formed the bog's surface. In this way, those who probe the bogs of Ireland are on an archaeological journey into the country's past.

Heaney's description of how each layer of bog seems 'camped on' wonderfully captures the brevity of human life. Each generation of Irish people is only 'camping' on the island. We're here only temporarily before we must give way to the younger generations coming up behind us.

The word 'camped' also underlines the impermanence of each civilisation – Celtic, Viking, Norman – that invaded and occupied the island over the preceding centuries and millennia. Each was only 'camped' here. Though they didn't realise it at the time, each civilisation was only passing though, was occupying the island for only a relatively brief period before being replaced by the next civilisation to come along.

The word 'camp', of course, can also refer to a military force, especially one in medieval times, reminding us how each civilisation had to forcibly remove the one that came before in order to settle here.

A DESCRIPTION OF BOGLAND

The poem emphasises the strange splendour of Ireland's boglands, which Heaney once described as 'a very beautiful, benign place.' Heaney praises the oddly pleasant texture of the peat that comprises this boggy landscape, comparing it to 'black butter'. This memorably conjures the peat's pleasant softness and its yielding, almost creamy qualities.

Heaney seems especially fascinated by the bog's shifting, malleable nature:
- The buttery material of which the bog consists constantly changes shape. Merely to step on it is to alter its contours, for it is contantly 'melting and opening underfoot'.
- The bog's surface, too, is constantly altering. Its exterior cools and solidifies each night, 'between sights of the sun', generating a crusty upper layer. However this crust melts again each morning when the sun rises, bringing with it the relative heat of the day.
- Bogland exhibits no definition. There is nothing lasting,

The phrase 'big sun' refers to an optical illusion whereby the sun seems bigger when it's close to the horizon. This effect is especially pronounced in locations, like the American prairies, where the horizon is often far off in the distance. As the sun sinks down over the edge these of these great plains 'at evening', it seems like it's being 'sliced' or cut in half by the horizon line.

Using another fine metaphor, Heaney compares a tarn or mountain lake to a 'cyclops' eye'. (The cyclops was a one-eyed giant in greek mythology). Such tarns, he suggests, seduce the eyes of all who see them, gently drawing our gazes into their depths: 'the eye … is wooed into the cyclops' eye of a tarn'.

crisp or distinct about its shape. The shifting, melting substance of the bog is 'Missing its last definition/ By millions of years'. It's millions of years since the bog was last 'defined', was last cast in an enduring definite shape, and millions of years until it will be again.

- It seems as if nothing solid could ever exist in such an environment: 'They'll never dig coal here'.

Heaney presents the bogland as a 'kind' landscape, an adjective that encompasses its haunting physically beautiful character, the softness of peat that makes it up and the almost miraculous preservative qualities it exhibits.

THE BOTTOMLESS BOG

Heaney imagines that the bog reaches ever downward in stratum after stratum, that each layer stripped away will only reveal another. He imagines that that turf cutters could keep delving through the bog until they encounter the island's very foundations. He suggests that the turf cutters might even encounter the Atlantic Ocean, which he imagines is constantly percolating through or under the bedrock of the island.

He fancies that the 'bogholes' we witness on the bog's surface are filled with ocean water that has filtered up through the bog's countless layers, all the way from the Atlantic as it ripples through the foundations of the country: 'The bogholes might be Atlantic seepage'.

The edges of the bog, where it blends into ordinary farmland, are relatively dry. But the centre is incredibly moist. Heaney concludes by imagining that this central portion of the bog might in fact be 'bottomless'.

If the turf cutters were to dig here, at the bog's 'wet centre', their 'downward and inward' voyage of discovery would never end. They would be able to strip away new layers of bogland for hundreds or even thousands of years, with each one revealing new historical treasures and evidence of ever earlier civilisations.

FORM

'Bogland' features short lines arranged in four-line stanzas. Perhaps the poem's long progress down the page suggests digging or excavation. We might think of its stanzas as a pictorial representation of great shafts dug into the bog's depths as its pioneers keep striking downward.

METAPHOR, SIMILE AND FIGURES OF SPEECH

There are several memorable metaphors in this poem:

- Heaney uses an excellent metaphor to describe the impressive American sunset, claiming that the prairies 'slice a big sun at evening'. We can imagine how the sun's disc might seem to be sliced or cut in half by the horizon as it sinks slowly downward.
- A tarn is described as the eye of a cyclops, a mythical one-eyed giant.
- A similarly fine metaphor is used to depict the elk's skeleton set up in a museum. It is described as 'an astounding crate full of air'. (We can imagine the skeleton's bare bones resembling a kind of crate or box).
- Heaney memorably compares the bog's melting, shifting soil to 'black butter'.
- He compares those who dig into the bog to the 'pioneers' of the American west.

The poem concludes with an instance of hyperbole, or deliberate poetic exaggeration: 'The wet centre is bottomless'. Of course Heaney doesn't believe that the bog is actually bottomless. He exaggerates for effect, to emphasise how incredibly deep the bogs actually are.

IMAGERY

'Bogland' is replete with imagery of softness and wetness, as Heaney masterfully conjures up the yielding nature of the bog. He describing its buttery soil 'Melting and opening underfoot'. He emphasises the moistness of the this landscape, featuring a centre so wet you could sink down into it forever and holes that are filled with 'seepage' from the Atlantic itself. He describes a substance than can never be defined or cast into any kind of definite shape, where nothing hard like coal could ever be discovered. Only items that are waterlogged and pulpy can be salvaged from its depths.

As we have noted, the bog is depicted in terms of wholesome food, of 'butter' and 'crusting' bread, emphasising what Heaney regards as its nurturing, nourishing qualities. This is further reinforced when he personifies the bog's soil, describing it as 'kind', an adjective usually associated with human beings.

THEMES

THE PROCESS OF MEMORY

Heaney had this to say about 'Bogland' and memory: 'I began to get an idea of bog as the memory of the landscape, or as a landscape that remembered everything that happened in and to it. In fact, if you go round the National Museum in Dublin, you will realise that a great proportion of the most cherished material heritage of Ireland was 'found in a bog''.

In a sense, then, the bog is like a museum preserving the history of the Irish race. It holds the evidence of past, the flora and fauna that once existed on the island and the remains of past civilizations, all the layers that have been 'camped on before' by Ireland's previous occupants.

Yet the bog also serves as a metaphor for the mind or consciousness of the Irish race. As Heaney puts it: 'I had a tentative unrealised need to make a congruence between memory and bogland and, for the want of a better word, our national consciousness'. Within our national consciousness, we remember all that has happened to us as a race, handing it down to the next generation in history, song and story. Similarly the bog records an impression of 'everything that happened in and to it', serving as a potent metaphor for our national consciousness:

- Like the 'bottomless' bog, our national consciousness goes back thousands of years.
- Like the bog, it contains different layers of memory, each one closer to the present.
- Like the bog, our national consciousness is shapeless and fluid, rather than solidly defined. The story of Irish civilisation changes depending on who is recounting it, with different individuals regarding historical events in radically different lights.
- The other sense of 'definition', that of meaning or significance, is also relevant here. Our national consciousnesses cannot be pinned down to any one such meaning , to any one coherent or definite narrative. Like the bog it is 'missing its last definition/ By millions of years'. It's a story that shifts and alters like the peat itself.

It is also possible that Heaney is suggesting the Irish race is overly introspective and excessively inward looking. Our pioneers, he says, keep striking 'inward and downward'. On one level this refers to those digging into the bog. Yet on a metaphorical level it refers to the Irish people generally. We constantly 'strike inwards', obsessing about our own present, and downwards, obsessing about our own past, in particular the injustices the country has suffered.

ART, CRAFT AND CREATIVITY

The poem can also be taken as a symbol for the poet's memory. Heaney was keenly aware that memory was important to him as a poet: 'memory was the faculty that supplied me with the first quickening of my own poetry'. It is memory, perhaps above all, that sustains Heaney as a poet, nourishing his talent and arousing his inspiration. There is a sense in which he feels that a poet must excavate the layers of his remembrance, much as the turf-cutters and archaeologists dig into the layers of bog, in an attempt to extract the material for poetry from his personal store recollection.

CREDITING THE MARVELLOUS

Like many of Heaney's poems, 'Bogland' features a sense of mystery and wonder. The poet seems awestruck as he contemplates the different objects that have been preserved by the bog: the butter dug out after a hundred years, the preserved trees, the 'astounding' Great Irish Elk. He also seems awestruck at the thought of how endlessly deep the bog is, how layer after layer can be stripped away to reveal yet more bogland underneath.

Each layer of bog that is stripped away reveals evidence of an earlier civilization: 'Every layer they strip/ Seems camped on before'. The choice of the word 'camped' is masterful; suggesting the temporary nature of each occupation. In archaeological terms even centuries are only a brief period. The word 'camped' suggests that in the great sweep of history each civilization only briefly occupied the land before the world changed yet again.

Heaney's affection for the bog is evident in how he describes it as a gentle and nourishing location. Its soft soil is described as 'melting' and 'kind'. It is depicted in terms of wholesome food, of 'butter' and 'crusting' bread. Its gentleness preserves and maintains all that is placed within it: the Great Irish Elk, the salty white butter and the trunks of fire trees.

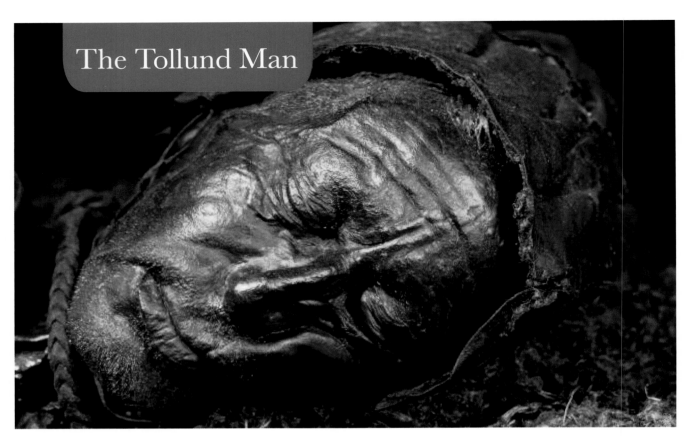

The Tollund Man

LINE BY LINE

Tollund Man is a naturally mummified corpse of a man who lived during the fourth century BC, in what is now Denmark. He was discovered in 1950 by two brothers cutting turf on a bog near Tollund, on the Jutland peninsula. Heaney first learned of Tollund Man in archaeologist PV Glob's book *The Bog People*, and became fascinated by the subject: 'The unforgettable photographs of these victims blended in my mind with photographs of atrocities, past and present, in the long rites of Irish political and religious struggles.'

In lines 17 to 18, Heaney briefly details the discovery of Tollund Man. He imagines how the turfcutters' digging riddled the bog with holes, comparing the effect to a honeycomb pattern: 'Honeycombed workings.' As they dug, they came across an unexpected 'Trove' or treasure: Tollund Man's corpse. The bog had preserved the body so well that the brothers were convinced they'd discovered the body of a recent murder victim. Today, Tollund Man's remains reside in a museum near the town of Aarhus: 'Now his stained face/ Reposes at Aarhus.'

PART I: THE POET'S WISH

The poet resolves to 'Some day' go to Aarhus in Denmark, on a pilgrimage of sorts, to see the preserved body of Tollund Man. He describes Tollund Man's features in exquisite detail, revealing the extent to which he has scrutinised this perfectly preserved face in photographs:

- He mentions Tollund Man's 'peat-brown head', which has

been 'stained' over time by the bog which preserved him.
- He mentions the 'mild pods of his eye-lids', brilliantly describing the rather mild-mannered, sleepy expression of Tollund Man. The poet likens the shape of the eye-lids to seed 'pods' – waxy vessels for a plant's seeds, which typically split when ripe. (The poem will pick up on this seed metaphor again in Part II.)
- He describes the perfectly preserved cap that Tollund Man wears. It has the same brown, leathery appearance as Tollund Man, so that it looks almost indistinguishable from the skin: 'His pointed skin cap.'

He describes how Tollund Man is 'Naked' apart from this cap, the 'noose' around his neck, and a 'girdle' or belt around his waist. The poet also describes how the bog even preserved Tollund Man's stomach contents, his last meal consisting of a sort of porridge made from seeds: 'His last gruel of winter seeds/ Caked in his stomach'.

The poet imagines standing still for a long time on the 'flat country' or bog land where Tollund Man was buried and recovered: 'I will stand a long time.' Here, the poet will contemplate Tollund Man's fate.

What happened to Tollund Man?

Tollund Man was hanged: the 'noose' that killed him was still around his neck when his body was recovered. Though the custom in Scandinavia during this era was for bodies to be cremated, Tollund Man's corpse was buried in the bog. This is because Tollund Man's death was a ritualistic killing. He was placed in the earth as a sacrifice to the earth goddess to ensure continued good harvests.

Heaney presents this ritual sacrifice as a bizarre kind of marriage. The earth goddess is the bride and Tollund Man her groom: 'Bridegroom to the goddess'. Instead of wedding ring, Tollund Man gets a 'torc' or necklace – the noose that is used to hang him: 'She tightened her torc on him'.

The goddess, personified as the 'fen' – the bog itself – accepts Tollund Man as a worthy sacrifice. Like a bride, she embraces the body of her groom on their wedding night: 'She … opened her fen'. We can imagine the soft bogland giving way, making it easier for Tollund Man's body to be interred and preserved in the earth.

Bogs are capable of preserving bodies because of their high acidity levels; they conserve bodies in a way that resembles the use of vinegar to pickle fruit. The poet refers to this process as the bog's 'dark juices working' on Tollund Man's body. These juices keep him perfectly preserved – a sort of relic – just as in Catholicism, saints' bodies are said to remain intact after death: 'working/ Him to a saint's kept body.'

This allusion to sainthood and martyrdom strongly suggests that Tollund Man was a willing sacrifice. Perhaps it was an honour to be chosen from his community to be the goddess's mate and make the crops flourish. It is possible he died willingly for the greater good of his society.

PART II: VIOLENCE IN IRISH HISTORY

The poet begins to think about the victims of Ireland's troubled history. Firstly he recalls a photograph he once saw in Tom Barry's book *Guerilla Days in Ireland*. The photograph depicted the corpses of a farming family laid out in their own farmyard. There bodies were 'stockinged' or dressed in nightclothes, suggesting they had been surprised or ambushed in their sleep, dragged from their beds and shot. They seem to have been machine-gunned, absolutely mangled by bullets, so that pieces of their flesh lay all around the farmyard.

He also recalls a story, 'part of the folklore where [he] grew up', about four Catholic brothers who were murdered and had their corpses tied to a train. The poet vividly describes the damage that this did to their remains as they were dragged 'For miles along the lines'. We can imagine the friction grinding away at their faces, at their noses, their lips and their teeth, so that afterwards flecks of their skin and teeth could be seen on the railway sleepers. He describes these horrible flecks as 'Tell-tale', as if they intimate or tell a story, that someone does not want told, that even the perpetrators are ashamed of in the morning

Embracing the Ancient Religion

Heaney considers embracing the pagan religion that Tollund Man believed in. This would be an act of blasphemy, turning against the Christianity he was raised in: 'I could risk

blasphemy'. He would 'Consecrate' the bogs back at home to the earth goddess. The bogs of Ireland would become 'holy ground', dedicated to this ancient religion, just as the bogs of Denmark were sacred in Tollund Man's day.

He would pray to the earth goddess through Tollund Man, her martyr and saint, just as Catholics pray to God through Saint Anthony or Saint Teresa. He would pray for the earth goddess to make whole or 'germinate' the remains of murder victims he mentioned above: 'pray/ Him to make germinate// The scattered, ambushed/ Flesh'.

Heaney thinks of the murder victims described above. He imagines that he could somehow gather the particles of their remains, pieces of flesh the machine guns had scattered around the farmyard, particles of skin and teeth that had 'flecked' the sleepers. He imagines placing these particles within the Irish bog. If his prayers to the goddess are answered, the preservative powers of the bog will go into overdrive, not only preserving but restoring these particles of flesh, which would then 'germinate', sprouting into life like seeds do in the springtime.

Perhaps the poet imagines that the bog could bring these long-ago victims back to life. Or perhaps he imagines it could restore their mutilated bodies, thereby allowing them the possibility of a proper, dignified burial.

Of course, we must remind ourselves that this is merely a bizarre but powerful flight of fancy. Heaney is not seriously entertaining the idea of embracing an ancient, pagan religion. He is not considering tracking down the remains of these victims and reinterring them in the bog. He doesn't really believe that an ancient earth-goddess might help restore their bodies or bring them back to life.

What we have here is a powerful metaphor for the poet's longing that something positive might come from the agonies of Irish history. He hopes that murder victims like those described above won't have died for nothing, that their deaths might somehow bring about a new era of peace. He hopes that just as the death of Tollund Man allowed the crops to flourish each summer, the deaths of these poor murder victims might somehow allow a period of peace and reconciliation to flourish in his troubled country.

PART III: JOURNEYING TO AARHUS

The poet returns once more to imagining his trip to Aarhus to see Tollund Man's body. He imagines driving through the Danish countryside. We can imagine him sounding out the names of the towns as he drives – 'Tollund, Grauballe, Nebelgard' – savouring their sounds and their strangeness, maybe even noting how they're both similar and different to the names of places back home.

He imagines asking the locals for directions. This might be an awkward exchange, since he doesn't speak any Danish: 'Not knowing their tongue.' He will have to be guided by their 'pointing hands' as they gesture toward where he needs to go.

As he drives, he will imagine Tollund Man's last journey in a tumbril or wagon: 'As he rode the tumbril'. This tumbril would have brought him to the place where he was hanged, then to the bog for burial. The poet imagines Tollund Man's 'sad freedom' as he goes to his death, the tumbril allowing him one last look at the countryside, one last breath of fresh air. The phrase 'sad freedom' also emphasises Tollund Man's stoic acceptance – even embrace – of his fate.

The poet views the bog as a 'cauldron' where he might brew up some sort of redemption or meaning for the murder victims of Irish political violence. Like a cauldron, the bog is a deep, dark receptacle containing 'dark juices' and possessing strange powers – in the bog's case, the ability to preserve bodies. The poet portrays the bog as a magical, potent, even dangerous force, but one that might also be used for good.

The poet will feel a similar 'sad freedom' as he muddles his way around the Danish landscape. On the one hand, he is on holiday and free to do what he likes; on the other hand, he doesn't know the language and keeps getting lost. Nevertheless, he feels certain he will feel 'at home' in Jutland: 'In the old man-killing parishes'. Heaney, too, hails from a place of ancient tribal violence, where people are put to death in the name of religion. Though he is a stranger in Denmark, it will feel all too familiar: 'I will feel lost,/ Unhappy and at home.' For Heaney, 'home' is not a comforting notion, but a reminder of violence – something he can never fully escape.

FOCUS ON STYLE

FORM

The poem consists of eleven four-line stanzas and does not feature any formal rhyme scheme.

TONE AND ATMOSPHERE

A general tone of melancholy and sadness seems to pervade the poem. Although Tollund Man's death is not described as harrowing or violent, there is something touching and sad about the description of his final meal, that 'last gruel of winter seeds' and the manner in which he was dressed for the occasion.

The tone and atmosphere of the third part of the poem is particularly melancholic, as the poet imagines not only the 'sad' journey of Tollund Man to the place where he was to be sacrificed but also the rather bleak trip that the poet imagines he will one day take through 'the man-killing parishes' of Jutland. He imagines how he will feel 'lost,/ Unhappy and at home' in this unfamiliar country.

The tone and atmosphere of the second part of the poem is perhaps somewhat different to the other parts of the poem. Here the sadness is laced with something of the anger and desperation that the poet feels when it comes to the seemingly intractable violence of his home country.

METAPHOR, SIMILE AND FIGURES OF SPEECH

The poet compares Tollund Man's eye-lids to seed vessels or 'pods' that split open when the seed is ripe. The image perfectly captures the appearance of this feature of the preserved head, conveying how the texture and colour of the skin has hardened and darkened over the centuries that the body lay in the bog. The comparison also draws to mind the notion of germination that the poet describes in the second part of the poem.

Heaney uses a wonderful metaphor to describe how the bog appears after the turfcutters have completed their work, likening it to a honeycomb. The image beautifully conveys the lines and cube-shaped hollows that result across the bog after the turf has been cut out: 'Honeycombed workings'.

VERBAL MUSIC

Heaney uses soft sounds and long, sonorous vowels when describing Tollund Man's appearance. He describes how the 'stained face/ Reposes at Aarhus'. The repeated 's' sounds and the long 'a' sounds seem to capture something of the peace, serenity and acceptance that Tollund man experienced at the moment of death.

The poet uses harsh, cacophonous language when describing the brutal murders of the men in Ireland. Line 27, for example, features repeated 'c' sounds, 'Stockinged corpses', while lines 29 to 30 feature harsh 't' and 'c' sounds: 'Tell-tale skin and teeth/ Flecking the sleepers'. The sounds explicitly contrast with the softer sounds of the first part of the poem and capture some of the violence and discord surrounding these terrible killings.

IMAGERY

The poet imagines the bog as a goddess, a bride to whom Tollund Man's corpse is wedded. The noose around his neck is compared to a 'torc' or ornamental band and the manner in which the bog opens to receive the body is very sexual, suggesting that the wedding between the sacrificial victim and the bog to whom he has been offered has been consummated.

CONFLICT AND VIOLENCE

The poet considers the conflict and violence that has been a significant feature of Irish history in the 20th century. He calls to mind just how brutal and savage this conflict has been, recounting the horrific murders of certain farm labourers and 'four young brothers'.

What is especially tragic about the the killings described in the second part of the poem is that they were often perpetrated by people belonging to the very towns and parishes to which the victims belonged. During such conflicts as the recent Troubles in the North and the War of Independence in the early part of the 20th century, parishes were often bitterly divided over political and religious beliefs.

Heaney identifies certain parallels between the the parishes of 20th Century Ireland and ancient Jutland. In Jutland, just as in Ireland, men were killed by members of their own communities. Thousands of years ago, these Jutland villages sacrificed men like Tollund Man to the earth goddess. And just as with many of the killings in Ireland, these Jutland sacrifices were carried out in the name of religion.

Those who conducted the killings in Ireland and in Jutland shared a belief that they were acting for the greater good of the communities to which they belonged. In Jutland, the community believed that it was necessary to sacrifice one of their members in order to ensure that the harvest would flourish and there would be food enough for everyone. Those who killed in the Troubles in Ireland also believed they were acting for the greater good. They wished to renew, save or restore the land in a more abstract political sense.

However, there are a number of important ways in which the killings in Ireland and Jutland differ. Tollund Man was, as the poet imagines it, a willing victim and martyr. He would have believed, just as the rest of his parish did, that his death was a good and necessary thing for the community at large. Most victims of the Troubles, such as those mentioned in part II, were not willing victims. In the case of the labourers described in the second part of the poem, these men were dragged from their beds in the middle of the night and executed.

Tollund Man was killed in a manner that involved as little violence as possible. He was likely hung from a tree and his body was intact after his death. When he died his remains were also treated with the greatest of respect, his body gently placed in the bog. The victims of political violence in Ireland, in contrast, often died and suffered in the most appalling manner, their bodies mangled and desecrated.

On the one hand, then, the poem shows how the impulses of religious murder go very deep. These instincts have always been and, perhaps, will always be with us. However, Heaney leaves the door open for a sense of hope. Perhaps something can be salvaged from all this religious violence; perhaps some form of renewal can occur: 'make germinate// The scattered, ambushed/ Flesh'.

But the poet seems to have his doubts about the possibility of anything good coming from all the violence in his home country. At the end of the poem, Heaney describes how he will imagine feeling 'lost' and 'Unhappy' as he travels through the unfamiliar Danish peninsula of Jutland. In a time before GPS and Google Maps, we can imagine how unsure he would be of where he was going. But we can imagine how the poet might feel 'lost' and 'Unhappy' at home in Ireland for different reasons. Having experienced decades of violence and conflict in the North, the poet understandably feels depressed and bewildered by the seemingly intractable violence of the Troubles.

MASCULINITY AND FEMININITY

One of the most interesting aspects of this poem is its depiction of the bog as female: 'Bridegroom to the goddess'. This earth goddess was central to the iron-age society depicted in the poem, a hugely important deity who had control over the harvest. She is personified by the bog: 'She tightened her torc on him/ And opened her fen'.

Heaney portrays the bog as a site of feminine energy. It is powerful and undoubtedly sexual: 'She … opened her fen,/ Those dark juices working/ Him'. The bog is also imbued with nurturing, maternal traits. It is protective, having preserved Tollund Man perfectly for thousands of years: 'a saint's kept body'. It is also restorative and fertile, providing the people with another year of good harvests and plenty. Interestingly, however, this feminised bog also demands violence, in the form of a sacrifice.

IMAGINED SPACES AND LANDSCAPES

In 'Tollund Man', Heaney explores a landscape that he has never actually visited. In the first and last part of the poem, he vividly imagines his journey to Jutland. He imagines the 'flat country' where Tollund Man's body was discovered. The poet imagines the manner in which the locals of the towns through which he travels will greet and interact with him, 'pointing' their hands when he asks for directions in an unfamiliar tongue. Heaney even imagines what he will be saying to himself as he drives along the Jutland roads. Perhaps tracing the place names on a map, he imagines repeating them to himself when he drives there, some time in the future: 'Saying the names// Tollund, Grauballe, Nebelgard'. We must wonder whether the poet, having made such a vivid journey in his mind, now feels the need to actually visit the country in order to experience the very feelings and emotions he describes at the end of the poem.

Sunlight

LINE BY LINE

I

'Sunlight' is a love poem of sorts, a love poem dedicated to a place. The poem celebrates the Heaney family farmhouse called Mossbawn, where the poet was born and where he lived until he was fourteen. In the poem, Heaney remembers with great affection the summers of his childhood at Mossbawn.

The poem recalls a summer's afternoon from this period of his life. The afternoon that he describes is not that of any particular day, but represents all of the summer afternoons of his childhood at Mossbawn. The poet remembers long summer days of sunshine: 'each long afternoon'. Many people have such memories, recalling their childhood summers, perhaps, as warmer than they really were.

The poet uses a wonderful simile to describe the sun on those hazy afternoons. The sun is compared to a griddle, a circular iron plate used for cooking. The sky is compared to a wall against which the griddle has being placed to cool. This captures how the sun's heat would diminish as the afternoon wore on: 'the sun stood/ like a griddle cooling/ against the wall/ of each long afternoon'.

The poet recalls the iron pump that stood in the yard outside the farmhouse. The pump was typical of its era, having a bulbous top, which the poet compares to a helmet: 'The helmeted pump in the yard'. He recalls how these long days of sunshine would heat the pump's iron, making it warm to the touch. The poet also remembers how a bucket full of water would often be 'slung' over the pump's handle. The water in the bucket would reflect the sunlight, which lent it a golden or honey colour: 'water honeyed/ in the slung bucket'.

The poet remembers how on such afternoons his aunt would bake scones in the kitchen of the farmhouse:
- He recalls how her hands 'scuffled' as they massaged the dough into scone shapes on the bake board. We can imagine her fingers colliding, weaving and scrambling, moving in an emphatic manner as she moulds the dough into shape: 'her hands scuffled/ over the bakeboard'.
- He recalls how she would stand before the worktop by the kitchen window dressed in a 'floury apron'.
- As she stood there, she would feel the heat of the stove against her legs. The poet recalls how the oven would redden as it heated, sending a 'plaque of heat/ against her where she stood'. We can imagine the heat emanating in a cube of heat, one that corresponds to the square or plaque shape of the oven door.
- When the scones were finally in the oven, the aunt would clean up after herself, dusting the bakeboard with 'a goose's wing'.

With the process complete, she would sit and wait for the scones to rise, her nails 'whitened' from working with the flour. The aunt's shins would have reddened from the heat coming from the stove. The poet compares the patchy or spotted red marks on the aunt's shins to measles: 'measling shins'.

II

Heaney associates these childhood summers at Mossbawn with security, calmness and love. He begins the poem by saying there was an 'absence' of something during these sunlit days.
- Perhaps the poet is describing how these long summer days were devoid of stress and hurry. There was a lazy, relaxed atmosphere about the farm and the poet was free to what he wished with his time
- Perhaps the poet is alluding to the innocence of childhood, to the absence of the fears and anxieties that we often experience as we get older.
- Perhaps the poet is referring to the absence of the violence and conflict that had engulfed the North when he was writing the poem. The Mossbawn of his childhood is presented as a refuge from such conflict.

The poet describes the absence as 'sunlit', suggesting that the sun perhaps facilitated this absence. Its bright rays allowed no room for anything unpleasant to lurk and hide. On these long summer afternoons, there was an 'absence' of darkness.

The absence of stress and anxiety is also suggested when the poet later says, 'here is a space/ again'. It is as if these long afternoons afforded everyone a breathing space, an opportunity to relax and to take timeout from the hustle and bustle of the day-to-day life. When the aunt has put the scones in the oven, she sits down and relaxes, waiting for them to bake.

But the 'space' that the poet describes might also be an imagined space. Whenever he thinks about this place and this time in his life, he is reminded of the security and peace that he experienced back then. Now that the poet is older, he can revisit this place in his mind and experience some of its calm.

Heaney also refers to 'love' in the poem's closing lines, suggesting that above all else, it was this that he experienced most on those long summer afternoons. Perhaps it is the thought of his aunt going about her business in the kitchen that epitomises such love. The aunt is depicted as a nurturing and wholesome presence with her 'broad lap' and whitened nails. We can imagine how her presence in the warm kitchen must have made the young poet feel safe and secure. But it is also likely that it is Mossbawn itself that epitomises this love, that within its grounds and its walls the poet felt perfectly happy and secure.

The poet compares the love that he experienced in Mossbawn to a scoop that has been sunk deep into a bin of flour: 'here is love/ like a tinsmith's scoop/ sunk past its gleam/ in the meal-bin'. A scoop is a utensil with a short hand and deep bowl used, for example, to take flour from a bag or a bin. In this case, the scoop has been crafted from tin by a tinsmith. The shiny metal surface of the scoop would reflect or 'gleam' in the sunlight. However, in this instance, the scoop is sunk deep into the flour in the bin, to the point where its surface is no longer exposed to the light: 'sunk past its gleam/ in the meal-bin'.

The image suggests perhaps the abundance of the love that the poet felt during these summer days in Mossbawn. The image suggests a sense of almost womb-like security. Like the tinsmith's scoop, which is sunk deep in the flour, the poet felt that the love he felt here was all-embracing, that it surrounded him and cushioned him from harm.

THEMES

IMAGINED SPACES AND LANDSCAPES

Although the place that the poem describes, the poet's childhood home, Mossbawn, is an actual place where the poet spent his childhood, there is a sense in which the description is very much imagined. Just as we all tend to recall the summers of our childhood as perhaps being graced with more sunshine than was actually the case, so the poet seems to imagine a rather idealised version of the place where he grew up. The place that he describes is soaked in sun and seems blissfully peaceful. The poet vividly remembers his aunt baking in the kitchen.

THE PROCESS OF MEMORY

Just as he does in such poems as 'A Constable Calls' and 'The Forge', Heaney convincingly conveys to us a child's mentality. The poem captures the innocence of the child's mind. We get the sense that the poet at this time was barely conscious of the larger world beyond his family home, that he was utterly unaware of any happenings beyond this place.

The poem also illustrates how we often remember distant times and places in a positive light, how our minds filter out the negative details and enable us to imagine that things were better than they actually were. When the poet thinks back on the summers he spent at Mossbawn, it seems that the rain never fell and there were no disturbances or interferences from the outside world. His memory seems to combine the best elements of these summers and to fuse them into a single perfect afternoon.

MASCULINITY AND FEMININITY

There has been much discussion about the poem's final comparison of love to a scoop sunk into a meal bin: 'like a tinsmith's scoop/ sunk past its gleam/ in the meal-bin'. Many critics interpret this image symbolically, as suggesting the perhaps old fashioned view that men cause most of the conflict and violence in the world while women are associated with care and nurture.

The metal scoop made by a tinsmith is associated with masculinity, with forges and tools. The meal bin is associated with femininity, with cooking and domesticity. Perhaps the poem suggests that love and the absence of conflict become possible only when feminine values predominate over masculine ones, when the scoop is sunk into the meal bin's flour. Mossbawn, associated with the poet's 'broad-lapped' aunt is one place where such feminine values predominate and love is allowed to exist.

ART, CRAFT AND CREATIVITY

Heaney often uses traditional skills as a metaphor for his own poetic craft. This is especially evident in 'The Harvest Bow', which draws many analogies between the craft of weaving the bows and that of writing poetry. We also see this in 'The Forge' and in 'The Pitchfork'. This tendency is arguably also present in 'Sunlight'. This poem stresses the care and patience involved in baking bread, characteristics that are also important in the creation of poetry.

This is one of many poems where Heaney praises craft and manual labour. He celebrates his aunt's baking ability, following her through the process of preparing and baking the scones as she wrestles dough into shape, places it in the oven, cleans off the bakeboard and waits for the scone to rise.

CONFLICT AND VIOLENCE

Heaney wrote this poem around the same time he wrote 'A Constable Calls' and 'The Tollund Man', poems that deal with the bitter conflict in Northern Ireland. Yet in this poem, there is the sense of Mossbawn as a place of refuge from conflict. The poet's childhood home is presented as place of complete security and comfort:

- It is a place associated with nourishment and wholesomeness; with water in the bucket and bread in the oven. Depictions of the sun as a griddle and of the water as honey reinforce this association.
- The aunt is depicted as a nurturing and wholesome presence, with her 'broad lap' and whitened nails.
- It is a place of warmth, both from the sun and from the oven. There is almost a sense in which the poet thinks of Mossbawn as a place of permanent good weather: the sun fills 'each long afternoon'.
- Heaney stresses that this is a place of love and kindness: 'and here is love'
- The 'helmeted pump' seems to stand guard, so no trouble can enter.

This is a place from which violence and conflict are completely absent. The sun pours down upon this welcome absence. The poem depicts a breathing space, a refuge where conflict cannot enter: 'here is a space/ again'.

TONE AND ATMOSPHERE

This is a poem that is all about atmosphere. The various images that the poet presents us with conjure up the atmosphere of his childhood home on these long summer days. There is a perfect stillness and calmness to the place. There is an almost-entire absence of movement in the poem. In fact, the only movement described is that of the aunt's hands scuffling or scurrying over the bakeboard as she prepares the scones for the ovens. There is also almost an entire absence of sound. The only sound the poet describes features in the poem's second last stanza, where he mentions the ticking of the 'two clocks' in the kitchen.

This atmosphere of stillness and silence seems to correspond with the process of memory that is happening here. The poet is recalling an idealised version of these childhood days, rather than a specific, actual event. As we observed above, such recollections of treasured times often preserve the positives and eliminate the negatives, until we are left with a memory that is ideal.

SOUND EFFECTS

There are several examples of alliteration in this poem. We see this with the repeated 'h' sound in 'helmeted pump in the yard/ heated its iron,/ water honeyed' and with the repeated 's' sound in 'measling shins:/ here is a space/ again, the scone rising'.

Assonance occurs throughout the poem, through the constant repetition of 'u' and 'o' sounds. We see this in lines 4 and 5 for example: 'water honeyed// in the slung bucket'. Assonance also occurs with the repeated 'ea' sound in 'meal' and 'gleam'.

Assonance and alliteration produce a pleasant and euphonious musical effect, appropriate to the poem's atmosphere of peace and comfort. The repeated broad-vowel sounds slow the pace of the verse, lending it a relaxed easy quality appropriate to the peaceful and sunny afternoon it describes.

METAPHOR AND SIMILE

There are several metaphors and similes in this poem:
- Using a metaphor, Heaney compares the top part of the pump to a helmet.
- Using a metaphor, he compares the oven's door to a plaque.
- As we have seen in a fine simile, he compares the sun to a griddle and the sky to a wall the griddle cools against.
- In a final simile, love is described as a scoop half sunk into a meal bin.

NEOLOGISM

An interesting feature of this poem is that Heaney uses two neologisms or words he makes up himself. These are 'honeyed' as in to become like honey and 'measling' as in to develop measles or a measle-like appearance

A Constable Calls

LINE BY LINE

INTRODUCTION

Seamus Heaney grew up on a farm in Co. Derry, Northern Ireland, during the 1940s. The Northern Ireland of the poet's youth was a divided place. On one hand, there was the Protestant majority who dominated the state; controlling the parliament, the civil service and the police. On the other, was the Catholic minority, to which Heaney and his family belonged. This Catholic minority suffered discrimination and inequality at the hands of the Protestant-dominated state institutions.

This poem is based on a memory from the poet's childhood. A constable, or police officer, arrives on a routine visit to the farmhouse. He's come to note the 'tillage returns', to record the different varieties of crop growing on the farm and the area of land devoted to each one. This would enable the authorities to determine how much tax the poet's father had to pay and to bill him accordingly.

THE CONSTABLE ARRIVES

The constable arrives on a bicycle, which he leaves leaning 'at the window-sill' of the house. Heaney provides a typically vivid and detailed description of the bike's various features.

- He describes its 'mud-splasher', which was a piece of rubber fabric draped over the front wheel. Like the mud-guard, it protected the constable's uniform from getting dirty as he cycled around the countryside performing his duties.
- He describes the 'fat black' grips on its handlebars.
- He describes the bike's dynamo, a little electrical device that charged as the constable pedalled and powered the bike's front light. The dynamo, because of its stubby shape, reminds the childhood speaker of a 'spud' or potato.

We might think of bicycles as a simple and old-fashioned means of transport, but in the 1940s, when cars were still extremely rare in Ireland, a bike was an important piece of equipment. Without his bicycle, the constable would not have been able to travel around the district and carry out his duties.

The speaker presents the bike almost as a kind of weapon. Its dynamo is depicted as 'gleaming and cocked back', like a gun ready to fire. Similarly, its 'flat black handlegrips' resemble the handle of a gun. There's even something menacing about the speaker's depiction of the 'mud-splasher', which is presented as 'cowl' or hood that might be draped over a prisoner's head. Tellingly the constable keeps it 'gleaming', just as he keeps the holster of his revolver 'polished'. For the speaker, then, the constable's bicycle is a machine of menace and violence, one that facilitates an agent of a hostile regime.

ARITHMETIC AND FEAR

The constable enters the farmhouse and takes a seat. He removes his cap and places it beside his chair: 'The cap was upside down/ On the floor, next his chair'. His hair is described as 'slightly sweating', suggesting the exertions of his cycle to the farmhouse.
The constable begins recording the tillage returns, taking down this information in his ledger or record book: 'He had unstrapped/ The heavy ledger'.
The father lists the different crops growing on his farm, describing the amount of land devoted to each in terms of 'acres, roods and perches', which are measurements of area.

The poet describes this moment as one of 'Arithmetic and fear'. The 'arithmetic' relates to the calculations the constable makes in his ledger, adding up the volumes of the various crops that grow on the farm and working out the taxes due on each one.

The 'fear', meanwhile, is experienced by the young speaker. Any small child might be frightened by the presence of an armed police officer in their kitchen. But in this instance the unease is even greater. For the constable is a member of the RUC, the Protestant controlled police force; to the young speaker he represents oppressive state power.

The young speaker's fear is evident in how he finds himself 'staring' at the constable's gun, taking in its every detail: 'the polished holster/ With its buttoned flap, the braid cord/ Looped into the revolver butt.' We sense that he is simultaneously horrified and fascinated by this weapon; though it terrifies him, he can't take his eyes off it.

Throughout the poem, the constable is associated with an oppressive weight. His boots are associated with heaviness and his pedals are described as being 'relieved' when he steps off them. Tellingly, the speaker associates these boots with the 'law', suggesting that like many Northern Irish Catholics he regards 'the law' as an oppressive force.

His policeman's cap is also associated with heaviness and pressure, leaving a wedge-shaped indentation in his sweat-damp hair: 'The line of its pressure ran like a bevel'. Its weight is also hinted at when he uses both hands to replace it on his head: 'fitted his cap back with both hands'. The ledger in which he makes his returns, too, is described as 'heavy'.

There is an interesting reference to the 'domesday book' in line 30. The Domesday Book was a record of all the lands of England made in 1086 by King William I, twenty years after he had violently conquered the country. Heaney describes the constable's ledger as a kind of mini-Domesday Book. Instead of recording the wealth of an entire country, it records what's growing on the farms of a single district.

A SMALL DECEPTION

The speaker's father has 'a line/ Of turnips' growing on his land that he doesn't want the authorities to know about. (Presumably the father wants to avoid paying tax on the sale of these vegetables). The turnips have been planted far from prying eyes. They grow at the very end of the potato field, where the father ran out of potato seed when he was sowing the season before.

The constable has nearly completed the tillage returns. But he wants to be sure he's recorded absolutely everything, asking the father: 'Any other root crops?/ Mangolds? Marrowstems? Anything like that?' The father, of course, says no, failing to mention the secret turnips. The young speaker, already uneasy in the constable's presence, is terrified by this little piece of fraud. He imagines that his father might be taken to the 'barracks' for lying to the constable. Perhaps the speaker himself might be jailed also, for not speaking out against his father's deception.

The verb 'assume' in line 25 has two meanings. In one sense it means to understand or realise. The speaker, then, realises that his father isn't being totally honest with the constable, is practising a small deceit on the state. But it also means to take on responsibility. The speaker then 'assumes small guilts' in the sense that he feels implicated in and responsible for the deception that is taking place.

Thankfully, the constable leaves without inspecting the fields and discovering the illicit turnips. He replaces his cap, adjusts his baton and closes his ledger. Then he gives the speaker a look as he takes his leave: 'And looked at me as he said goodbye'. We can imagine that the young speaker was terrified by the constable's gaze. Maybe he felt the constable was inspecting him for signs of guilt. Maybe he felt the constable somehow suspected the existence of the illicit crops.

The constable is briefly visible outside the window, securing the ledger to his bicycle's carrier: 'A shadow bobbed in the window./ He was snapping the carrier spring/ Over the ledger'. Then the only sign of him is the ticking sound his bike makes as he cycles down the lane away from the speaker's house: 'the bicycle ticked, ticked, ticked'.

CONFLICT AND VIOLENCE

In many respects, the poem describes a minor incident, a routine visit by a police officer to a farm. Yet the poem skilfully highlights the tensions that existed between Catholics and Protestants in the Northern Ireland of the poet's youth.

The constable represents the institutions that oppress the speaker's family and other Catholics all across Northern Ireland. Nevertheless, the speaker's father has no alternative but to invite him in, to answer his questions, to account for himself to this representative of an alien authority. The constable's presence in the speaker's home, then, represents a kind of violation, perhaps even a humiliation.

It's unsurprising, therefore, that throughout the poem the constable is presented as a menacing or even terrifying figure, one who brings with him not only 'arithmetic' but also 'fear':

- As we've seen, he is associated with an oppressive heaviness, suggesting the repression to which Northern Ireland's Catholics were subjected.
- His bicycle, as we noted, is depicted not only as an innocent mode of transport, but also as a kind of weapon, as a machine associated with menace and violence.
- He is associated with weaponry, with his baton in its case, with his revolver in its 'polished holster'.
- He is also associated with enforcement and imprisonment, with 'the black hole in the barracks'.
- As we have seen his ledger is described as a 'domesday book', associating it too with conquest and violence.
- Even the depiction of him, in the poem's closing stanza, as a 'shadow' adds to this sense of menace and unease.

Tellingly, the speaker records only one word his father uttered to the constable: 'No'. But this single syllable captures the father's anger and resentment at having to account for himself to this oppressive government, which refuses to recognise his rights.

Perhaps this is part of his motivation for not being completely honest with his tillage returns. On one hand, of course, he simply wants to avoid paying tax on the sale of 'a row of turnips'. But there's also a sense in which he wants to 'get one over' on what he regards as a hostile and oppressive state.

It's important to note, however, that the constable, as far as we can tell, doesn't behave badly during this brief visit. The speaker's father doesn't shout at him, abuse him or defy him in any way. All these tensions remain bubbling beneath the surface.

Eventually, however, the tensions described in the poem would flare up into the terrible conflict known as the Troubles, which began several decades after the events described in this poem. The constable's bike, as we've noted, produced a ticking sound as he cycled.

Perhaps it's not too fanciful to hear in that ticking a timer counting down to the beginning of the Troubles, which at that time were still years in the future. It's a noise that also brings to mind the many bombs that exploded with such terrible loss of life in that devastating conflict.

THE PROCESS OF MEMORY

'A Constable Calls' is a wonderful poem of childhood memory, one in which we witness the poet vividly reconstructing and

THEMES

imaginatively re-entering an incident from his childhood. Heaney wonderfully captures a child's perspective on events. We see this in the way he describes the speaker's boyish fascination with the officer's gun. He is captivated by the details of the constable's weapon: 'its buttoned flap, the braid cord/ looped into the revolver butt'.

Heaney also wonderfully evokes the 'small guilts' of childhood, the silly and naïve worries that can seem so great to us when we are children. The young speaker, as we've seen, 'assumes' or takes on the guilt of his father's little deception, worrying that by not alerting the constable to this fraud he's become implicated in a terrible crime.

The fact that he mentions how the constable looked at him as he departed further reinforces our sense of the fear that gripped him. The young speaker, we imagine, worries that the constable is scanning his face for signs of deception. He even worries that he and his father might be hauled off to the barracks for not being completely honest with the tillage returns. Here we see Heaney wonderfully capturing the fears that strike us as ridiculous when we're adults but seem very real and vivid when we're children.

MASCULINITY AND FEMININITY

'A Constable Calls' provides a subtle but effective portrait of the poet's father. It's fair to say that in this poem the father comes across as the strong silent type:

* He's a farmer, a man well used to the physical demands of

making a living off the land, as he sows and harvests various crops.
* He's a man of few words; as we noted above, the only thing he says to the constable is 'No'
* He's not afraid to defy the authorities by growing turnips without reporting doing so.
* He's not afraid to face down the constable, another powerful masculine presence.
* He calmly lies about the hidden crops, giving no evidence of being frightened or intimidated by the constable's and his revolver, his composure contrasting starkly with the fear the young speaker experiences.

The father, then, comes across as a rough, tough no-nonsense farmer. However, poems like 'The Harvest Bow' and 'A Call', present a different and arguably softer side of the father's personality.

IMAGINED SPACES AND LANDSCAPES

Heaney's poetry is littered with imagined landscapes and locations. We see this in 'A Constable Calls', where the young speaker sits there nervously during the constable's visit, 'Imagining the black hole in the barracks'. He seems to envisage an almost dungeon-like cell into which he and his father will be cast for carrying out this deception. Perhaps the young speaker has visited the barracks on business with his father and has had occasion to glimpse this cell. Or maybe he's simply imagining it, based on what he's read in books and comics.

IMAGERY

Heaney is nothing if not a poet of description. We see this in his comprehensively detailed descriptions of the bicycle with its handle-bars, dynamo and mud-splasher. It's also evident in his description of the constable's holstered weapon with its flap and cord.

The constable's movements are also precisely described: how he unstraps, closes and secures his ledger, how he adjusts his 'baton-case', how he carefully replaces his cap. It is important to note, however, that the speaker never describes the constable's demeanour or facial expressions. He is presented only in relation to his uniform and equipment. It's as if for the young speaker the constable is completely identified with his job, with the role he plays as representative of an unloved and oppressive regime.

VERBAL MUSIC

Cacophony occurs in lines 19–20, where the repeated hard 'b', 'd', 'p' and 't' sounds create a harsh verbal effect suited to the tough and rigid material of the constable's gun.

The phrase 'black hole in the barracks' is also satisfyingly cacophonous, the harsh verbal music appropriate to the imagined horror of the barracks' jail cells.

METAPHOR, SIMILE AND FIGURE OF SPEECH

The metaphors in 'A Constable Calls' capture the aggressive , invasive nature of the constable's visit, at least as it would have been perceived by the young poet and his family. The bike's mud-splasher, as we've seen, is compared to sinister rubber hood, one that might perhaps be used in the abduction of a prisoner. There's a sense, too, in which the bike's 'cocked' dynamo is compared not only to a potato but also to a gun. Even the constable's hair is associated with pressure, as the line left by his cap is compared to a bevel drilled into concrete surface.

There is an interesting use of metonymy in line 8. Metonymy occurs when a person or thing is called not by its own name but by the name of something closely associated with it. In this instance the constable is referred to as 'the law'. For this reason, the boot of this individual constable is referred to as 'the boot of the law'.

The Skunk

LINE BY LINE

THE POET MISSES HIS WIFE

The poet remembers a period he spent working in California during the 1970's. He was obliged to spend a few months away from his wife and children, who remained behind in Ireland. The poet, naturally enough, felt very lonely for his family during this time of separation. In fact he missed his wife so much that many aspects of California's landscape and lifestyle reminded him of her. He thought of her, for instance, when he caught the scent of the eucalyptus trees that are ubiquitous in that part of the world: 'The beautiful, useless/ Tang of eucalyptus spelt your absence.'

Perhaps the poet longed to share this beautiful aroma with his wife. Or maybe it reminded him of her perfume. In any event, this wonderful phrase suggests that the trees were communicating with the poet, speaking to him through the medium of scent in order to emphasise just how far away his wife was. Californian wine, too reminded the poet of the wife he'd left behind, particularly the 'aftermath' of every sip. This aftertaste or lingering finish reminded him of his wife's scent, He was reminded especially of how, when they lived together back in Dublin, he'd inhale her aroma from her cold pillow after she'd left the bedroom in the morning.

THE WRITING DESK

While in California, the poet would spend his evenings writing. His desk, it seems, was situated at a large French window, or glass door, that gave on to the yard of the property where he was staying. Beyond this window was a 'verandah', or covered porch.

The light from his desk lamp would illuminate this verandah. But its glow would 'soften', or diminish in intensity, as it reached the verandah's edge and blended with the darkness of the yard beyond: 'My desk light softened beyond the verandah'.

The poet recalls how on these evenings the house would be extremely quiet, its silence broken only by the humming of the refrigerator: 'The refrigerator whinnied into silence'. He also recalls the orange tree that grew in the yard, specifically how its fruit seemed larger in the evening time: 'Small oranges loomed in the orange tree'. This effect was created, no doubt, because the fruit's bright rind seemed even brighter as the darkness gathered.

No doubt, the poet composed poetry during these evenings at his writing desk. But he also found himself writing love letters to his wife. This was something he hadn't done for a long time, not since the early days of their relationship eleven years ago: 'After eleven years I was composing/ Love letters again'. Remember that this poem is set during the 1970's, a pre-internet era when there was no Skype, social media or even email to keep in touch. Furthermore transatlantic phone calls were extremely expensive, making letters by far the most efficient and cost-effective means to communicate.

THE SKUNK'S NIGHTLY VISITS

Each evening, as the poet sat at his writing desk, a skunk would appear in the garden of the property. The poet was fascinated by this creature and was especially taken by its lustrous, glossy tail:

- He describes the tail as 'damasked', suggesting not only its luxuriance but also its distinctive black and white patterning.
- He compares the tail to a black and white chasuble, the vestment worn by a Catholic priest as he celebrates a funeral: 'damasked like the chasuble/ At a funeral Mass'.
- The tail was so extravagant that it seemed to parade the skunk around the place: 'the skunk's tail/ Paraded the skunk.' It seemed to the poet that the tail was leading the animal, rather than the other way around.
- He describes how the tail was 'Up', as if the skunk, peacock-like, was keen to show off its most extravagant feature. The word 'Paraded', too, conveys the skunk's confident, self-assured demeanour, how it strutted around the yard like it owned the place.

The skunk would sniff the verandah on the other side of the

A voyeur is someone who gains pleasure from watching others. The poet, then, is a voyeur in the sense that gets a thrill from watching the skunk about its business each evening.

Voyeurs topically enjoy watching others when they are naked or engaged in sexual activity. The poet's observing of the skunk, of course, isn't sexual in this strict sense. But it does have a slightly erotic component. For the poet, as we've seen, reagrds the skunk as an elegant, sensual creature and associates it with his wife's confident, expressive

Voyeurs are typically tense and nervous because their activities involve an invasion of privacy. The poet, as we watches the skunk, experiences something of this tension: 'I began to be tense as a voyeur.' Perhaps the poet feels that watching the skunk is an intrusive act. Perhaps he feels that that at night the verandah and the yard belonged to the skunk more than to him, and that the creature should be left to do its thing unobserved Or maybe this tension stems from his fear that the skunk won't make an appearance in this particular evening and that hell be denied the thrill of watching it wander and snuffle about the yard.

French door, just 'five feet' from where the poet sat at his writing desk: 'Snuffing the boards five feet beyond me'.

The word 'Snuffing' brilliantly conveys the skunk's action of rubbing its nose against the verandah, suggesting the sniffling, snorting sounds it produced as it checked the wooden boards for scents.

THE POET WATCHES THE SKUNK

The poet found himself waiting each evening for the skunk to appear: 'night after night/ I expected her like a visitor.' We can picture him at his writing desk, anticipating the skunk's arrival and wondering when it will show up. We can imagine his heart skipping a beat each time it finally appeared in the garden: 'And there she was'. We sense that he was surprised, perhaps even a little shocked, at how important its nightly visits became to him.

- It seems that the skunk, just like the taste of wine and the smell of eucalyptus, began to remind the poet of the wife he missed so much:
- The skunk, like the poet's wife, is female and exhibits a peculiarly feminine beauty.
- It's a 'glamorous' creature, showing off its glossy, patterned tail as if it were sporting the latest and most fashionable gown from Paris or Milan.
- As we've seen, the skunk swaggers around the yard with great self-confidence, with poise and assurance worthy of a runway model.
- Unlike a model, however, the skunk doesn't care who's looking.

The link between the skunk and the poet's wife, while it seems bizarre at first, actually makes a certain kind of sense. For in the skunk, he sees a little of his wife, of her beauty, her demeanour and her attitude. In his loneliness, then, the poet nearly began to depend on the skunk's visits. It's as if, when the skunk was nearby, he no longer missed his wife quite so much.

THE POET REMEMBERS THE SKUNK

The poem's first five stanzas, as we've seen, are set some years ago, during the poet's stint in California. The final stanza, however, is set in the present day when the poet is back in Dublin with his wife and family.

He describes how 'last night' he was 'stirred', or sexually aroused, by the sound of his wife undressing: 'stirred/ By the sootfall of your things at bedtime'. His wife, having disrobed, reached into a bottom drawer for her nightdress: 'Your head-down, tail-up hunt in a bottom drawer/ For the black, plunge-line nightdress'.

Suddenly the poet finds himself reminded of the skunk. The position and motion of his wife searching for the nightdress remind him of the skunk 'snuffing' the boards of the verandah. The black nightdress on her white skin, no doubt, reminds him of the skunk's damask coat. Suddenly he is transported back to his time in California all those years ago, when he would spend each night waiting for the skunk to make its appearance: 'It all came back to me last night'.

LOVE AND RELATIONSHIPS

'The Skunk' is a powerful celebration of married love. It shows how the love between two people can grow and remain intense even after years of marriage. When the poet was in California, he had been with his wife for 'eleven years'. Yet his feelings towards her were still passionate, and he missed her deeply during this spell abroad. He wrote her love letters and was reminded of her by the sensual delights of California: by the sweet smell of eucalyptus trees or by a sip of Californian wine.

The poem also celebrates erotic and sexual love, showing how the desire between the poet and his wife is undiminished by a over a decade of marriage. In the poet's mind, the skunk becomes associated with his wife. The poet looks forward to the nightly visits of the skunk, because its glamour, mystery and confidence remind him of his wife's sexuality.. The eroticism of married life is also celebrated in the poem's concluding stanza, where the poet is 'stirred' or aroused by the sound of his wife undressing and by the sight of her 'tail-up hunt' for her nightdress.

It could also be argued that the poem illustrates how 'absence makes the heart grow fonder'. The time spent in California is the poet's first extended period of separation from his wife since the beginning of their marriage. This separation seems to have intensified his feelings toward her. The whole idea of marriage, of her being his 'wife', began to seem fresh and new once more. He found himself 'writing love letters again', as he did when he was a love-struck young man at the beginning of their relationship.

THE PROCESS OF MEMORY

This poem provides fascinating insight into the strange and surprising ways in which memory functions. In the poet's memory, the skunk and his wife are inextricably linked. When the poet was lonely in California, the skunk's appearance triggered memories of his wife. In turn, when he is back in Dublin with his wife, he can't help but be reminded of the skunk: 'It all came back to me last night'.

The poem also explores the sensory aspects of memory. Heaney describes the powerful, irresistible manner in which smells, tastes, sights, sounds and even words trigger memory:

- The skunk's tail reminds the poet of a priest's robe at a funeral: 'damasked like the chasuble/ At a funeral Mass'.
- The smell of the eucalyptus tree reminds him of his wife: 'The beautiful, useless/ Tang of eucalyptus spelt your absence.'
- The aftertaste of wine reminds him of his wife's scent: 'The aftermath of a mouthful of wine/ Was like inhaling you off a cold pillow.'

An interesting feature is how the poet remembers remembering. In present day Dublin, his wife's hunt for the nightdress reminds him of how in California, all those years ago, wine and eucalyptus reminded him of his wife! The processes of memory, then, are complex and irregular, operating through all kinds of unpredictable layers and circuits.

CREDITING THE MARVELLOUS

'The Skunk' is another poem where Heaney finds the marvellous in the everyday. The skunk is a familiar sight in California – as common as a fox or a squirrel would be in Ireland. However, the poet knows that to native Californians, the skunk is a nuisance, barely a step above vermin.

Yet the poet finds great mystery in this everyday creature. To him it is the 'Ordinary, mysterious skunk'. Hhe realises that it's a common rodent but also, as we've noted, sees it as something special, as a creature of poise and elegance.

The poet, then, simultaneously holds two contradictory views of the skunk. On one hand he's 'mythologized' the animal, building it up into a symbol of his wife's sexuality: confident, mysterious and even glamorous. On the other hand, he constantly 'demythologizes' the creature, reminding himself, even as he waits each night for its appearance in his garden, that it's only a skunk.

ART, CRAFT AND CREATIVITY

This poem celebrates the fascination of words themselves, especially ancient, fundamental words like 'wife'. Such words, especially when he haven't used them for a while, possess the power to intrigue and captivate us. In the right circumstances, the poet suggests, language can be more potent and intoxicating than a freshly broached cask of wine.

THE ANXIETY OF THE ARTIST

Several critics feel that this poem also contains a commentary on the business of writing poetry itself. We see this in lines 13 to 14: 'The beautiful, useless/ Tang of eucalyptus'. The smell of the eucalyptus tree may be beautiful, but it serves no practical value. Similarly, the lines themselves may be beautiful but serve no practical value. Like all poetry they are 'useless' in any practical sense.

This anxiety about the uselessness of poetry is one that runs through Heaney's work. It is hinted at in several poems that compare the writing of poetry to other, more practical crafts. This occurs in 'The Harvest Bow', in 'The Pitchfork' and perhaps even in 'Sunlight'. The comparison is suggested very strongly in 'The Forge'.

VERBAL MUSIC

There are several instances of assonance in this poem. We see this in line 5 for instance with its repeated 'i' sound. Lines 6 and 7 feature a profusion of broad-vowel sounds that create a pleasant musical effect. A similar pleasant verbal music is created by the broad-vowel sounds throughout the fourth stanza. An example of euphony occurs in the phrase 'beautiful, useless/ Tang of eucalyptus', where the pleasant musical effect is appropriate to the tree's sweet smell.

MOOD & ATMOSPHERE

In 'The Skunk' Heaney masterfully evokes the atmosphere of a Californian evening: the smell of eucalyptus, the humming refrigerator, the soft light spilling onto the verandah and the orange trees in the yard at the edges of its glow. Even the word 'refrigerator' is masterfully chosen. This American usage suggests how the poet finds himself in a location that is for him exotic and mysterious.

There's a wonderful build up of tension in stanzas 3 and 4, which depict the poet, 'tense as a voyeur', waiting for the skunk to appear, an anxiety that finds release at the beginning of stanza 5, when it finally shows up: 'And there she was'.

IMAGERY

'The Skunk' features some intensely sensual imagery. There are several memorable visual images. The oranges 'looming' in their tree and the skunk being 'paraded' by its own tail. Particularly vivid is the description of how the light from the desk lamp 'softened'. We can imagine its glow being hard or intense around the desk, then softening as it illuminates less and less the further away from the lamp one goes.

METAPHOR, SIMILE AND FIGURES OF SPEECH

There are several memorable similes in this poem. The poet compares the skunk's tail to a priest's 'chasuble', emphasising how mysterious and sacred the creature has become to him. Because the poet and his wife live together, he has not written her love letters for a long time. He is not used to writing the word 'wife' and the word seems strange and mysterious to him. He evokes this strangeness and mystery by comparing the word to an old and precious cask of wine. The cask has long been in storage, but now the poet is about to open it once more.

Heaney is well known for his ability to vividly capture different sounds. There are several instances of this in 'The Skunk'. In line 5 he compares the soft hum of the refrigerator to a horse whinnying. In line 22 he memorably compares the swishing sound of his wife removing her underwear to the soft noise of soot falling down a chimney.

Taste and smell are evoked in stanza 4, which memorably describes the smell of the eucalyptus tree and the after taste of wine. The senses of smell and taste are intermingled in line 16. The wine's aftertaste reminds the poet of the aroma his wife's hair would leave on the pillow when they were back home in Ireland together.

LOVE LETTERS

We can imagine him writing phrases like 'I miss you dear wife' or 'Let me tell you what happened today dear wife'. The poet realises that he hasn't addressed his spouse in writing for a long time, that he hasn't written the word 'wife' in over a decade. Suddenly, this short everyday word strikes him as being very mysterious and beautiful, almost as if it were a word from some strange and unknown language.

The word 'wife', in an unexpected but effective metaphor, is compared to a cask of wine.
Because the poet hadn't written this word for a long time, it's compared to a cask that's had been stored in a cellar, put aside until needed.
We 'broach' a cask by inserting a syringe, known as a 'barrel thief' and drawing up a portion of the liquid, allowing us to taste and sample the vinatge within.
By writing the word 'wife' again, after many years, the poet felt as if he were sampling a rare and valuable vintage.

As he wrote the word 'wife', the slender 'i' vowel seemed to release from the word into the night air, just as the opening of a cask would release the scent of wine: 'as if its slender vowel/ Had mutated into the night earth and air/ Of California.'

The description of the vowel as 'mutated' suggests how the poet's relationship with his wife has changed and matured over the course of their relationship. The word 'wife' meant something different to the poet eleven years into their marriage than it had done at the beginning. This is similar to how the taste of wine will mature and deepen with time.

The Harvest Bow

LINE BY LINE

The poet remembers his father's skill as he wove the bow

Where Heaney grew up, there was a tradition of weaving small bows from straw each autumn at harvest time. The poet now has one of these bows in his house, 'pinned up on [his] deal dresser'. He contemplates this bow, recalling how it was woven by his father several years before:

- It was made from several stalks of harvested wheat, which his father 'plaited' or intertwined.
- It was created 'twist by twist', the father wrapping one strand of wheat around another again and again. The strands would gradually be tightened into a very rigid plait or braid: it 'tightens twist by twist'.
- This length of braided straw would be knotted into an elaborate bow shape, which Heaney describes as a 'love-knot'.

Using a wonderful metaphor, Heaney compares the wheat in the bow to some kind of metal capturing its golden, metallic sheen. But this is a 'metal' that does not rust or decay, because the process of plaiting the harvest bow dries out the straw, preventing it from rotting.

We sense that the poet's father made a number of these bows each year, and quickly got back into the knack of weaving them each harvest time. The poet suggests that his father had a talent for this kind of work, a 'gift' to which his fingers 'Harked' or

responded. He recalls how his father worked a 'fine intent', with intense concentration as he interlaced the straw.

Eventually the father's fingers seemed to move automatically, as though he no longer needed to think about what he was doing. Heaney, in a typically inventive turn of phrase, describes how his father's fingers were sleepwalking, how they 'moved somnambulant'. This suggests the unconscious ease with which the father wove the bows, his fingers seeming to operate independently of his conscious mind. He no longer needed to concentrate or even look at his fingers as they interlaced the straw.

WHAT TYPE OF PERSON WAS THE FATHER?

The poet's father worked as a farmer and cattle dealer. The poet recalls how he carried a stick, an 'ash plant' or a 'cane stick', with him everywhere he went. Such implements would be used not only as a walking sticks but also, no doubt, for driving livestock along the country roads.

Heaney remembers his father working with roosters or 'game cocks' on their farm, recalling how he 'lapped the spurs' of these unruly birds, trimming back the sharp growths of bone that protruded from their claws. The poet recalls how his father had devoted his whole lifetime to practical tasks such as this on and around the family farm.

We sense that the poet is surprised – and perhaps even a little charmed – that his father took so readily to making the harvest bows. This is a man who was a stick-wielding cattle-dealer, a farmer used to working out in the elements, a man devoted to difficult, practical tasks around the farm. There is something incongruous about seeing such an individual engrossed in the intricate, almost dainty, craft of making the harvest bows.

THE FATHER EXPRESSES HIS PERSONALITY THROUGH THE BOW

All through his life, the poet's father remained a man of few words. In his younger days, his silences seemed tense and sullen, maybe even a little cranky. In his later days, however, his silences seemed tranquil and almost welcoming. This is because the father mellowed as he aged, becoming calmer and more at peace with himself. The poet artfully describes the transformation of his father's personality. The 'silence' contained within his psyche changed over time, just as wine in a barrel ages to become smoother and more soothing.

> The poet uses a wonderful turn of phrase to describe how, as the years passed, the father's hands 'aged around' these various sticks. This is wonderfully cinematic image – we visualise the hand ageing in time-lapse cinematography, as if we are fast-forwarding through a video.

The poet, however, feels that his father can communicate with him through the harvest bow. The surface of the bow, in an unusual but effective comparison, is likened to a piece of braille text. When the poet touches the bow he can 'read' this text, just as a visually impaired person might read a passage of braille: 'I tell and finger it like braille'.

The poet, then, describes a form of communication that takes place through the medium of touch. Such messaging occurs through items that, like the harvest bow on the poet's dresser, are 'palpable', that can be felt and handled. Touching the bow allows to poet to 'glean' or understand aspects of his father's life and personality, aspects that the father had always left 'unsaid': 'Gleaning the unsaid off the palpable'.

The poet, it seems was given the harvest bow by his father and has treasured it ever since, having it pinned on the dresser before him as he writes. He describes it, therefore, as a 'love-knot', as if it were a token of affection from father to son. However, he's aware that this bow was a 'throwaway' love token, a most casual gift. Maybe the poet just happened to be visiting his father as he finished one of the many bows he would make during that particular harvest time. We can imagine the father casually tossing the completed bow to his son and thinking no more about it. And even if it was a more meaningful gift, we can imagine the poet's father playing it down and not wanting to make a big deal out of it.

> The bow is 'throwaway' in another sense, of course. It is fragile and disposable, a 'frail device' made out of straw. These objects were not intended to last a long time. They were usually worn for a brief time during the harvest, and then cast aside.

CHILDHOOD MEMORIES

The poet remembers walking with his father through the countryside near their home. He recalls how he carried his fishing rod, indicating that his father was taking him to a nearby river or lake to do a spot of fishing: 'Me with the fishing rod'. He remembers how his father, as always, was carrying his walking stick, which he used to whack 'the tips off weeds and bushes'. We can imagine him doing this almost absent-mindedly as they walked along, simply for the enjoyable sensation of whipping the heads off the plants.

The way his father whacked the hedgerows reminds the poet of shooters beating bushes to scare up birds that might be hiding in them. The father, however, manages to flush nothing from the undergrowth as they walk along. This is, no doubt, because he was striking the bushes idly or absent-mindedly.

But it's hard not to detect here a note of sorrow about the father's life, a suggestion that he never flushed out or revealed the opportunities that life had for him, that he never fulfilled his potential. The poet's father, as we have seen, was in his own way a contemplative, creative man. However, he was never afforded the opportunity to explore this creative potential. Instead he spent a 'lifetime' herding cattle and tending to game cocks. Perhaps if he had being born in a different place or a different time, he could have been a diplomat or an investment banker, or even a writer like his son.

The poet describes how his father's stick 'Beats out of time', a phrase that suggests several different meanings. Perhaps the poet's suggesting that his father had little or no sense of rhythm, that the beating of his stick doesn't keep time with their steps as they walk along.

Or perhaps the poet is suggesting that his father was 'out of time' in the sense that he was born at the wrong time, coming of age in an Ulster that had changed little since the 1700's, where the only profession and lifestyle open to him was that of a farmer or cattle dealer. Had he come of age, as his son did, in the rapidly modernising Ireland of the 1950's, he would have had far more opportunities in training and self-development.

The poet thinks of the 'townland' or parish in which he was raised as a 'tongue-tied' place. To be tongue-tied, of course, is to be lost for words, to be unable to explain or articulate oneself clearly. The poet suggests, therefore, that the people surrounding him as he grew up were a tongue-tied lot, that they never learned the vocabulary with which to express themselves in a deep and complex fashion. There is a sense, too, in which these people were suspicious of such fluency. Their natural language was silence.

THEMES

PROCESS OF MEMORY

As the poet examines the 'golden loops' of the bow pinned up on his dresser, he finds himself vividly remembering an occasion from his childhood. It all comes back to him with astonishing clarity. As we noted, he recalls an evening walk with his father to a local fishing spot:

- He remembers how they followed the route of a railway line, walking in between the banks that sloped upward from either side of the tracks: 'I see us walk between the railway slopes'. (The nearest town to where Heaney grew up, Castledawson, had a train station, and the railway line ran behind the back of the family home).

- He remembers how it was harvest season, late August or September, and how his father was wearing one of the bows he made every year at this time: 'You with a harvest bowl in your lapel'.

- He remembers the grass was high, having flourished over the summertime, but the midges that signal autumn in many parts of Ireland were already making their presence felt.

- He remembers how the weather was cool enough for fires to be lighting in many of the surrounding farmhouses. But the smoke from their chimneys rose 'straight up' because the hard winds of winter were still someway off: 'Into an evening of long grass and midges,/ Blue smoke straight up'.

- He remembers how, as they walked, they passed the various landmarks of an 'ordinary' townland or country parish. They saw discarded pieces of furniture and farm equipment that lay rusting in the hedgerows: 'old beds and ploughs in hedges'.

- They passed an outhouse onto which an advert for an upcoming auction had been pasted.

- Heaney remembers how such evenings had a 'big lift', suggesting the optical effect by which the sky can seem higher and further away on those evenings when summer transitions into autumn.

Heaney uses a typically brilliant metaphor for this process of memory, for how the bow stimulates such intense recollection. The loops of the bow, he suggests, are a kind of screen on which footage of long-ago events is replayed for him to savour and relive.

As he looks at the bow on his dresser, the poet recalls his tongue-tied townland with heartbreaking clarity. It's as if this long-ago parish has been woven into the bow's fabric. He recalls how, even as he walked along beside his father,

he was 'already homesick' for those harvest evenings. This is a phrase that wonderfully captures the nostalgia we sometimes feel for a golden moment, even while that moment is still going on! Our enjoyment of such special times can sometimes be tinged with a sorrow born from our knowledge that these moments can't last, that everything must change.

LOVE AND RELATIONSHIPS

This is another poem that explores the complicated relationship between the poet and his father. Specifically, it focuses on the difficulties they experienced in communicating. Like many men of his background and generation, the poet's father wouldn't have been given to self-expression or to talking about his feelings.

The poet, however, suggests that he father could express his inner self, the mellowed silence that existed within him, through making the harvest bows: 'As you plaited the harvest bow/ You implicated the mellowed silence in you'.

The 'motto' that the poet associates with the bow is something of a paradox, having contradictory meanings. On one hand, it suggests that the objective of art is to create peace. On the other, it suggests that peace will be the conclusion of art; that art can only be made out of conflict and turmoil. We sense here an anxiety experienced by many writers and artists — they long for a life of serenity and tranquillity but worry about what would fuel their art were serenity to ever be achieved.

To 'implicate' means to convey or communicate. Making harvest bows, then, allows the father to convey or communicate something of his personality. He expresses himself through making these little bows, just an artist might express himself by creating a sculpture or a painting.

But the verb to 'implicate' can also mean to interweave or entwine, suggesting that the poet's father wove his inner self into the very harvest bows he created. It's as if the 'mellowed silence' that existed in him was infused into the bows themselves, as if his father's personality is somehow encoded in the straw: 'You implicated the mellowed silence in you/ In wheat'.

In making the bow, the poet's father tied the plaited straw into a complicated crown-like knot, which the poet describes as a corona. According to the poet, it is a 'knowable corona', because it allows him to know his father. As we noted, the bow functions almost like a Braille text, for when the poet touches it, he feels he can learn unsaid things about his father's life and personality.

But this communication brings sorrow as well as happiness. The poet realises that his father never had the chance to realise his full potential. He realises that his father had hidden depths, gifts that were destined to remain unexplored. He realises that father never managed to 'flush out' all the opportunities life might have had in store for him. But he realises too that his father was born 'out of time'. As we noted already, he grew up at a time before educational opportunities were widely available. He grew up in place, a 'tongue-tied townland', where

there was little scope for self-expression and self-development and where such concepts, if anything, were frowned upon.

Despite all this complication, however, the poem conveys the strong connection that existed between father and son. This is beautifully suggested in the portrait of them walking together through a late summer's evening, strolling through the railway slopes together in companiable silence. It's a moment that, even while it was happening, the poet realised he would always remember and return to again in his mind.

CELEBRATION OF CRAFT

This is one of many poems where Heaney celebrates craft and manual labour. He praises the skill with which his father wove the bows, tightening the strands of straw 'twist by twist' until the 'love-knot' came together. He describes the 'fine intent' or intense concentration his father brought to this task and how eventually his fingers seemed to move automatically, as though he no longer needed to think about what he was doing: 'Until your fingers moved somnambulant'.

THE NATURE OF ART

The poet comes to see the bow not merely as a humble piece of craftsmanship but as a genuine piece of art. He thinks of it as a 'device', as a tool or implement that allows his father to communicate things that otherwise would have remained unsaid. But the term 'device' in its older usage also means an emblem, and the bow, as we have seen, works as a powerful symbol for the poet, representing not only the father's personality, but also the harvest and the traditions associated with it in the parish where he grew up.

The poet associates the bow with a saying by Coventry Patmore: 'The end of art is peace'. In what sense might the 'end' or objective of this artwork be described as 'peace'?

- Creating the bow, as we have seen, allowed the father to express the peace or 'mellowed silence' that existed within him.
- Creating the bow allowed the father to express creativity, that otherwise would have lain dormant within him forever, granting him a measure of peace or release.
- The bow generates an element of peace or reconciliation between the poet and his father, allowing him to understand his father in a new way.

THE ANXIETY OF THE ARTIST

Heaney, like many artists, experienced a sense of anxiety about his work as a poet. Although his poems necessitated a great amount of commitment, time and effort to produce, they had no practical value. His anxiety was heightened by the fact that his father was, in contrast, a no-nonsense, pragmatic man, someone whose whole lifetime was devoted to practical tasks.

However, on this occasion the poet detects a similarity between himself and his father. Harvest bows, like poems, are beautiful, but serve little practical value. Making the harvest bow, then, shows the father's hidden artistic side, with the poet remarking on how his father's hands 'Harked to their gift and worked with fine intent'. The father weaves the bow with the same skill and intensity with which the poet puts together a poem. Perhaps the father's weaving grants the poet a sense of permission – if it's okay for his father to produce the beautiful but useless bows, it is okay for him to compose his poems.

It's worth nothing, however, that the similarity between the poet and his father only goes so far. Heaney responds to the harvest bow with the intense spirituality of a poet, feeling that he is able to glean 'the unsaid' from its loops. To his father, however, it is more 'throwaway': part of a tradition and nothing more.

In pagan times, people wore harvest bows to honour the spirit of fertility, a magical god-like presence that brought a bountiful harvest each autumn. People believed this 'spirit of the corn' somehow inhabited these bows at harvest time. Pinning such a bow to your lapel would gain the spirit's favour, coaxing it to keep you safe through harvest season and beyond.

The bow's looped design reminds the poet of a snare, which, in ancient times, would have been used to catch 'the spirit of the corn' rather than a wolf or deer. He thinks of a 'snare' that's been stepped in, that's been triggered or 'drawn' tight.

The bow, therefore, managed to snag 'the spirit of the corn', which, for a moment at least, would have inhabited its loops. It also, as we've seen, managed to capture the father's personality.

It's a snare, however, that's been 'slipped', whose target has somehow managed to escape from its drawn or tightened loops. For the 'spirit of the corn', it was believed, would inhabit such bows for a short time, around the harvest, before moving on. It's also been 'slipped' by the father's personality, for his character was best expressed during the process of the construction as he delicately wove it 'twist by twist'.

He thinks of a snare whose strands have been polished or 'burnished' by an animal's efforts to free itself, that is still warm from having closed around an animal's ankle. This wonderfully suggests how the spirit of the corn would leave a trace itself behind in the bow's loops, even when harvest time was over and it had departed this golden corona.

Similarly, a trace of the father's personality, of the mellowed silence that existed within him, is expressed by the bow even now, sitting mutely as it does on the poet's deal dresser.

FOCUS ON STYLE

METAPHOR, SIMILE AND FIGURES OF SPEECH

There is an interesting simile in line 11 where the poet compares the feel of the harvest bow to a braille manuscript, as if he can read it by touch: 'I tell and finger it like braille'. Another simile occurs at the poem's conclusion when the bow's loops are compared to a snare or small trap: 'Like a drawn snare'.

A metaphor occurs in line 5 where the bow is compared to a 'corona' or crown. There is also a metaphorical expression in line 20, where the late summer evenings are described as having a 'big lift', suggesting the open and expansive evening sky. Heaney also uses a wonderful metaphor to describe the vividness of his childhood recollection, saying that when he looks into the bow's loops he can actually see the past. The bow is described almost as a magical object: 'And if I spy into its golden loops/ I see us walk between the railway slopes'.

There is an interesting pun in line 26 where the word 'device' can have two meanings. In one sense it means a tool or gadget. In another, however, it means symbol or emblem.

VERBAL MUSIC

The poem has a pleasant verbal music throughout, partly due to its AABBCC rhyme scheme. The poem features many half-rhymes, such as the rhyme between 'peace' and 'device' and that between 'midges' and 'hedges'.

The Underground

LINE BY LINE

AN EVENING IN LONDON

This poem describes evening in London. The poet and his wife had just been married and had arrived in that great city for their honeymoon. The poet's wife was still wearing her 'going-away coat'. These were fancy white coats worn by brides when they left their weddings and set off on their honeymoon.

The couple, according to the poet, had been 'mooning around' London. They'd been wandering around the city in a relaxed and casual fashion, and taking in the sights, maybe stopping into a favourite pub for a drink or two.

On this evening they were due to attend one of 'the Proms', a series of concerts that takes place each year in London's famous Albert Hall venue. They travelled there by underground rail: London's famous Tube service. They got off the train in a 'vaulted tunnel', in one of the many older Tube stations with an ornate and arching roof.

However, all their 'mooning around' had left them late for the concert: 'mooning around, late for the Proms'. They exited the train and ran through the Underground station, rushing to reach the Albert Hall before the performance began: 'There we were in the vaulted tunnel running'. The poet recalls how his wife, was 'speeding ahead' as they ran through the station.

The poet's wife was still in front as they left the station and continued rushing through the streets toward the Albert Hall. The poet remembers how, as she ran, her going-away coat 'flapped wild' in the breeze. The coat was blown vigorously this way and that, causing its buttons to fall off. The poet describes how the fallen buttons lay in the street, leaving a kind of trail between the tube station and the Albert Hall.

OUR ECHOES DIE

Line 10 presents us with a sudden jump forward in time. Whereas lines 1 to 9 are set before the concert in the Albert Hall, lines 11 to 16 are set later that evening, as the poet struggles to make his way from the Albert Hall back to the Underground station. (It's notable that in the poem's first nine lines the poet uses the past tense, whereas in the last six he uses the present tense).

The poet uses the image of echoes dying to symbolise the passage of time between these events: 'Our echoes die in that corridor'. This refers to the corridor that led from the station itself to the street above. We can imagine the couple laughing and exclaiming as they dashed down this corridor in an effort to get to the Proms in time. We can imagine how the echoes produced by their laughter bounce around the corridor's walls, diminishing in intensity until they 'die' or completely fade away.

In one of the Greek myths the goat-god Pan chased a nymph called Syrinx through the fields in an effort to have sex with her. As she ran, she called out to the other gods for help. The gods responded by transforming her into a reed, thereby rescuing her from Pan's attentions. Presumably, in the gods' opinion, life as a plant was preferable to the ravishes of Pan.

The poet thinks of his wife running through the London streets as Syrinx. He thinks of himself as Pan running behind her: 'me then like a fleet god gaining/ Upon you before you turned to a reed'.

We must remember that the poem describes a newly married couple at a time when sex before marriage was extremely uncommon. The poet's comparison of himself to Pan captures the sexual anticipation and excitement he feels on his honeymoon. The comparison between his wife and Syrinx, meanwhile, suggests the unease and apprehension she might have felt regarding sex, especially in this era when information about sexuality was scarce and such issues were rarely openly discussed.

THE POET AS ORPHEUS

The poem refers to the Greek myth of Orpheus and his wife Eurydice, who died after being bitten by a snake. Orpheus journeyed into the underworld, the land of the dead, determined to recover his wife and return with her to the land of the living. A gifted musician, he used his musical abilities to charm the Lord of the underworld and was permitted to take Eurydice back with him.

However, there was a catch: he had to walk ahead of his wife and not look back until they had safely returned to earth. If he turned around before they'd made it out of the underworld, Eurydice would remain forever with the dead. Orpheus had nearly led Eurydice to the surface when he was startled by a noise behind him and tragically looked back, causing him to lose his wife forever.

As the poet makes the return journey from the Albert Hall, he compares himself to Orpheus:
- Just as Orpheus led Eurydice through the underworld, so the poet must lead his wife from the Albert Hall back to the Underground Station: 'retracing the path back'.
- His wife walks behind him on this journey, just as Eurydice was forced to walk behind Orpheus.
- Like Orpheus in the underworld, the poet leads his wife through an unnerving alien landscape. He passes through dark disorientating streets, the phrase 'moonlit stones'

suggests that only the moon illuminates the cobblestones he walks upon. He passes through an eerily empty station, one that is dark, cold and draughty 'after the trains have gone', their service finished for the night.
- He listens intently for his wife's footsteps following behind, just as Orpheus must have listened for the footsteps of Eurydice as he guided her from the land of the dead: 'all attention/ For your step following'.
- The poet finds himself in an agitated state of mind, just as Orpheus must have been as he led Eurydice on their ill-fated journey from the underworld. He feels 'tensed', suggesting the worry and nervousness that fills him. He describes himself as 'bared', suggesting he feels exposed and vulnerable as he makes his way through the city and the station.
- Orpheus lost Eurydice by looking back. Similarly, if the poet looks back his wife will be 'damned' or lost forever: 'and damned if I look back'. The poet seems terrified that if he looks behind his wife will simply disappear for good.

The poem's last line can also be read as a statement of determination, one that suggests the poet's stubborn refusal to look behind. The colloquial expression 'damned if I do something' conveys a great reluctance or refusal to do the thing in question. In this instance it conveys the poet's refusal to look back until he has lead his wife to safety.

The poet, as we noted, feels lost and disorientated as he walks the city streets. But he is guided by the buttons that fell from his wife's coat earlier that evening. As he comes across each fallen button he picks it up: 'lifting the buttons'. Finding each one reassures him that he is on the right track, that he is indeed retracing his steps from the Albert Hall to the station.

The poet, therefore, compares himself to Hansel in the fairy story. Hansel led Gretel through the forest, using white pebbles as a guide. Similarly, the poet leads his wife through the streets of the city, using the fallen going away coat's buttons to trace his route.

FOCUS ON STYLE

METAPHOR, SIMILE AND FIGURES OF SPEECH

'The Underground' is particularly rich in allusions. As we've seen, the references to Hansel and Gretel and Orpheus and Eurydice in the last two stanzas highlight the fears the poet feels as he begins married life.

The reference to the lustful god Pan chasing the nymph Syrinx, meanwhile, captures the poet's sexual excitement on his honeymoon. It also captures the trepidation he imagines his wife to be experiencing, one common to many newly-wed brides in earlier times.

The poet imagines his wife being transformed not only into a 'reed', as Syrinx did in the legend, but also into 'some new white flower'. Here we imagine this woman in her white going-away coat being transformed into some never-before-seen blossom.

The fact that this flower would be 'japped' or stained with 'crimson' has two different meanings. It refers to how, while they were in a pub on the night in question, the poet's wife accidentally stained her coat with beetroot. But this image also evokes sexual relations between the couple and suggests the loss of virginity.

VERBAL MUSIC

The poem has an irregular rhyme scheme. Each line rhymes with another in the same stanza, but in an irregular pattern. Furthermore, many of these are half or even quarter rhymes. In the first stanza, for instance, 'running' rhymes with 'gaining' while 'ahead' rhymes with 'reed'. In the second stanza, meanwhile, 'crimson' rhymes with 'button' while 'trail' rhymes with 'hall'.

TONE AND ATMOSPHERE

This is a poem with two very different atmospheres. The opening section is realistic, joyous and full of life. The poet describes the excitement that he and his wife felt as they raced to the Albert Hall. In stark contrast, the atmosphere of the second section is unrealistic, eerie and haunting, with its stark streets and empty tube station.

LOVE AND RELATIONSHIPS

The poem's first 9 lines capture the joy and excitement of early married life. We can imagine the feelings of freedom and exhilaration they experience as they begin their honeymoon in London, the wife still proudly wearing the 'going-away coat' from her wedding. They spend their time 'mooning around, enjoying what the city has to offer in a relaxed and casual fashion. We sense their excitement at going to a show in the famous Albert Hall, the two of them racing in order to get to the performance. in time

The second half of the poem is dark and unrealistic; perhaps even a little bizarre, as the poet presents himself in a similar situation to Orpheus: forced to lead his wife on a journey through the darkness but doomed to lose her if he looks behind.

These closing lines brilliantly convey an atmosphere of dread and loneliness. They summon up not a bustling, brightly-lit city but an eerie unnerving landscape of empty streets and deserted stations, one lit only by the moon and the flickering lamps of the underground. The poet's feelings of anxiety and vulnerability, of being 'bared and tensed' also contribute to this sinister atmosphere. As does his sense of being lost and disorientated, of having to navigate his way back to the station by means of the buttons that fell from his wife's coat earlier.

A reference to Hansel and Gretel further reinforces this menacing, lonesome atmosphere. We might think of "Hansel and Gretel" as a harmless fairy story. But it's also, in its own way, a dark and frightening tale, one that depicts two children abandoned in the depths of an unfamiliar and terrifying forest.

This is a poem, then, that describes two very different sides to a new marriage or relationship. The opening 9 lines, as we've seen, capture the energy and exhilaration of beginning something new, of really getting to know this new person, of setting out on the journey that every marriage or relationship represents.

However, the poem also registers the poet's fears and anxieties as he sets out on married life. The nightmarish scenario depicted in lines 11 to 16 suggests the poet's feelings of anguish and confusion as he takes up his role as husband. He has been thrust into a new set of responsibilities that will eventually require him to function as father, breadwinner and protector.

The tensions experienced by the poet also stem from a larger unease, typical of the 1960x, about the nature of sexuality. The poet's fears find their greatest expression when he depicts himself as an Orpheus-like figure, terrified to look behind. Here we sense his fear that this new marriage, only just begun, might not last, that his new bride might eventually be lost to him.

The Pitchfork

INTRODUCTION

At the heart of this poem is the notion of perfection and the possibility of its existence in the world. When we say that something is perfect, we can mean a number of things:

- It is highly suitable for something or exactly right.
- It is precisely accurate or exact.
- It is as good as it is possible to be.
- It is flawless.

But nothing that actually exists is completely perfect or flawless. True perfection is something that we can only imagine. It is something that exists in the abstract, but not in reality.

Take circles, for example. Mathematically speaking, a circle is the set of points in a plane that are equidistant from a given point. For a circle to be perfect, you'd need all those points in the circle's circumference to match up exactly. And for all those points to match up exactly, you'd need this precision to remain constant no matter how closely you looked. But the closer you look at any drawn circle or any object that is circular, you will begin to see inconsistencies. Only in the abstract world of pure mathematics can we find our perfect circle – a world of points and infinitely-thin lines.

The same goes for any other object or thing that exists in the world. We might have an idea or an understanding about what constitutes a perfect chair or a perfect apple, but no actual chair

or apple will be absolutely perfect. Each individual object that exists has its own flaws and quirks, no matter how small or insignificant, that render it less than perfect. Some objects will come closer than others to reaching a state of perfection, but each will ultimately fall short.

LINE BY LINE

The poem describes a farmer who has given some thought to this notion of perfection. The farmer reflects that perfection can only be imagined, although some objects come closer to it than others do.

The farmer considers the different implements he uses in his work and thinks about which one comes closest to being perfect. We can imagine him looking at the various tools in his shed, at the shovels and forks and other implements. Having given the matter some thought, he decides that it is his pitchfork that comes 'near to an imagined perfection'.

The pitchfork is a simple object, comprising of a steel head that is riveted or fixed to a timber handle. The timber of the handle has been 'turned' or machine-carved to a rounded state. Yet the farmer considers it to be almost perfect.

The pitchfork's perfectness can be assessed according to the criteria we gave above:

It is highly suitable for something or exactly right

The pitchfork is well 'balanced' and the ideal 'length'. The weight of the head in proportion to the weight of the handle allows it to be handled with ease. In fact, the farmer sometimes holds it aloft like a javelin, noting how 'accurate and light' it feels.

The pitchfork has been 'sharpened', perhaps though use or with a sharpening tool. It has the right amount of "give" or flexibility: 'The springiness'. It has been 'tested' and proven to work. When it comes to threshing wheat at harvest time, there is no better implement or tool. It can be used with speed, allowing the farmer to swiftly work through the wheat: 'the clip and dart of it'.

It is precisely accurate or exact

The pitchfork achieves an almost mathematical state of perfect. The farmer considers the abstract qualities 'Smoothness', 'straightness' and 'roundness', and how the these are present in the pitchfork.

It is as good as it is possible to be

To the farmer, the pitchfork is not just a useful tool that is easy to handle and work with. He considers it to be an almost perfect object, independent of the use for which it is intended. To him, it is an object of great beauty. The details on the grain on the ash handle strike him as beautiful: 'He loved its grain of tapering, dark-flecked ash'. The polished handle is beautifully shiny or lustrous: 'sheen'.

The farmer thinks about how the pitchfork feels almost perfect. The timber handle has been 'Sweat-cured', polished through repeated use, lending the tool a wonderfully tactile feel. He seems to love to handle this implement, even when he is not working. In playful moments he imagines himself being a 'warrior' or an 'athlete', and that the pitchfork is his spear or javelin.

It is flawless

The farmer considers the pitchfork to be an all-but-perfect implement. It is ideal for the work for which it is used. The pitchfork feels great to work with and is aesthetically pleasing. But of course, the pitchfork is not absolutely flawless. As we have already said, the farmer does not believe that this implement is perfect, only that it comes 'near to an imagined perfection'. Yet the farmer would probably be hard-pressed to say where the flaws lie in this tool.

THE PITCHFORK AS SPACE PROBE

The farmer has an interest in space travel and exploration. He has learned about 'probes', robotic spacecraft that explore the outer reaches of space. His curiosity is sparked by them. He imagines how, when their mission is complete, they drift beyond their destination, ending up in the farthest reaches of the solar system: 'when he thought of probes that reached the farthest'. They no longer have engines propelling them along; they are merely drifting: 'Evenly, imperturbably through space'. There is something quite serene about this image of a space probe 'sailing' quietly through space, 'absolutely soundless'.

When the farmer thinks about this space probe, he imagines it as a long, cylindrical vessel with sharp metal 'prongs' at one end. In short, he sees it as being shaped like a pitchfork: 'He would see the shaft of a pitchfork sailing past'.

This pitchfork-probe was launched with a certain destination in mind – given a 'simple lead' – and propelled in that direction. Once it reached its destination, however, it was switched off and left to drift. It continues to move with intent through space, rather than aimlessly drifting. It is as if, somewhere along the way, the probe has learned 'at last to follow that simple lead'. It surpasses its original trajectory, goes 'Past its own aim' and carries on through to the 'other side'.

DIFFERENT VISIONS OF PERFECTION

The farmer imagines the probe travelling far beyond the known parts of space, eventually reaching 'an other side' or dimension. Here too those who live in this dimension also have an idea or understanding of perfection. Like the farmer, they believe that perfection can only be imagined, that nothing perfect actually exists. Certain objects or things can approach or come near to this imagined perfection, but nothing that actually exists can be considered perfect.

However, here in this place far removed from our planet, they have a different understanding of what perfection entails. On earth, we imagine that achieving perfection is all about careful planning and plotting. Something can be considered perfect if it achieves its goal or hits its target. In the other dimension that the probe reaches, they do not place the same value on such control. Perfection is something that happens when things are out of our hands. This understanding of perfection entails spontaneity and surprise; it arises in the unexpected rather than the expected.

The poet uses the image of a javelin being held and aimed to represent how we think about perfection on earth: 'perfection... is imagined... in the aiming'. He uses the image of the 'opening hand', the moment that the javelin is thrown and released to represent the different vision or understanding of perfection that exists in this other dimension: 'perfection... is imagined' in the 'opening hand'.

THEMES

CREDITING THE MARVELOUS

The poem reminds us how fascinating and marvellous the everyday world can be, if we are capable of looking at it in a certain way. Even the most mundane, everyday items can be a source of wonder and admiration. The farmer is fascinated by the pitchfork he works with. This simple, everyday instrument, comprising of 'Riveted steel' and 'turned timber' strikes him as being almost perfect. It is smooth and pleasant to handle. It is beautifully balanced and enables allows him to work with speed and ease: 'the clip and dart of it'. It is a thing of great beauty: 'He loved its grain of tapering, dark-flecked ash'.

The farmer is someone with an almost childlike sense of wonder and imagination. We see this in the description of him playing with the pitchfork, imagining it to be a 'javelin' or a 'spear': 'he played the warrior or the athlete'. He is fascinated by space travel, thinking about how the probes that travel through space are capable or journeying far beyond their intended destination. We also get the sense of how playful his imagination is when he associates the shape of such probes with the pitchfork: 'He would see the shaft of a pitchfork sailing past'.

ART, CRAFT AND CREATIVITY

The idea of perfection presented in the poem is something that might apply to the poet and his work. We can imagine how each time the poet writes a poem he is aiming for perfection. But no single poem can ever be perfect; so each work can only come 'near to an imagined perfection'.

The different understandings or visions of perfection described in the poem's closing lines might also be relevant to the poet and the manner in which he approaches his work. On the one hand, we can think of the perfect of the

FORM

The poem consists of five four-lined stanzas and features an AABB rhyme scheme. It is interesting to note that all of the rhymes are either half rhymes or imperfect rhymes. For example, Heaney rhymes 'one' with 'perfection' and grain' with 'sheen'. It is as if the poet is acknowledging or illustrating the poem's preoccupation with perfection and how it can only be imagined.

VERBAL MUSIC

The poet uses rich verbal music to suggest the rich beauty of the pitchfork's handle. The poet uses repeated 'a' sounds in line 8 to convey the pleasing tone and colour of the timber that has been polished through use: 'its grain of tapering, dark-flecked ash'. Heaney also uses some wonderfully sonorous, lush language in lines 9 to 10, words such as 'burnish' and sheen' to convey the lustrous quality of the handle that has been achieved through repeated handling and rubbing.

Assonance is also used when the poet describes the probe journeying through space: 'Its prongs starlit and absolutely soundless'. The long 'o' sounds seem to convey or correspond with the vast, silent space through which the probe travels.

The poet uses short, one-syllable words, that trip off the end of the tongue to convey how the pitchfork can be deftly handled: 'the clip and dart of it'.

METAPHOR, SIMILE AND FIGURES OF SPEECH

The poem describes how the farmer thinks of the pitchfork as a 'javelin'. Both are 'light' to handle and the pronged and sharpened head of the pitchfork allows for 'accurate' work, just as a javelin's pointed head allows for precise aim.

IMAGERY

The poet's description of the probe, shaped like a pitchfork and drifting silently through space, is wonderful. Heaney captures the manner in which the probe moves in a perfectly straight line, without any external interference: 'Evenly, imperturbably'. The probes 'prongs' reflect the light of the surrounding stars: 'Its prongs starlit'. The probe also emits no sound as it travels. It is in a constant state of motion and has no need for engines or thrusts: 'absolutely soundless'. It is a beautifully serene and peaceful image.

To convey a certain understanding of perfection, Heaney also uses the image of the hand of a javelin thrower opening to release the javelin. As we discussed above, the image suggests that perfection can be understood very differently to the way we normally think about it. Rather than being achieved through careful planning and calculation, perfection arises in a more spontaneous fashion, when things are released from our control and allowed to behave as they need or want to behave.

perfect poem as one that conforms to established criteria of form and rhyme etc. The poet careful plans and structures his writing in order to come as close as possible to this notion of perfection. Perhaps, however, the perfect poem is not the one that achieves technical excellence and conforms to such traditional understandings of form and meter. Perhaps the perfect poem can be imagined in a different way, arising out of a more free-flowing, spontaneous effort, surprising the poet when it happens rather than being the product of careful planning.

Like a number of Heaney poems, 'The Pitchfork' is a great celebration of craftsmanship. The pitchfork has been carefully shaped and sculpted until it has become smooth and balanced. The farmer appreciates just how well-suited it is to the task at hand, admiring the 'springiness, the clip and dark of it'. We also get a sense of craftsmanship from the description of the probe that has been carefully designed to travel to the remotest parts of space. To the farmer, this vessel has very similar qualities to the pitchfork he works with – both have been shaped and streamlined to a state approaching perfection.

IMAGINED SPACES AND LANDSCAPES

The ability of the mind to conjure up places, whether real or imagined, is a recurring theme in Heaney's poems. Here the farmer, a man given to playful imagination, imagines the space probe drifting far past its intended destination, eventually reaching 'an other side'. Here the farmer imagines the possibility that those who live here have a very different understanding of what constitutes perfection. In this imagined place, perfection does not result from careful planning and control but from spontaneous action.

Lightenings VIII

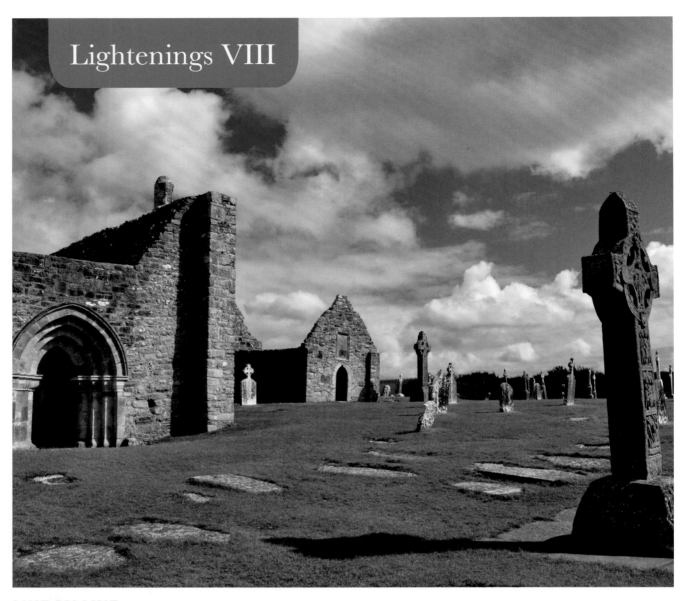

LINE BY LINE

The poem describes an incident from the 'annals' or historical records of Clonmacnoise, a monastery in County Offaly founded in 544 AD by Saint Ciarán. The opening lines describe an ordinary part of the monastery's routine'. There is a peaceful atmosphere as the monks gather to pray in their 'oratory' or chapel: 'when the monks of Clonmacnoise/ Were all at prayers inside the oratory'. The oratory was and still is open-roofed, so that as the monk prayed they were exposed to God's creation.

These lines suggest the silence, order and repetition of life at the monastery, where everything is regulated and scheduled. The monastery's large community is highly organised. Each monk has a role – some are blacksmiths, carpenters or farmers. Some are artists, who spend their days

> Though they lead lives of strict routine, peace and quiet, the monks at Clonmacnoise also occasionally endure Viking raids. They associate strange ships with danger. This time, however, the ship is not coming up the Shannon but is directly over their heads – a truly awesome sight.

creating precious metal objects or illuminated manuscripts. The monks lead simple lives of prayer and routine, with up to eight prayer services a day. They are in the midst of one of these services at the beginning of the poem.

Suddenly, however, in this orderly and predictable setting, something utterly unexpected happens. Through the open-air roof of the oratory, the monks see a ship floating in the sky: 'A ship appeared above them in the air.' This must have been an extraordinary sight for the monks, as shocking and unexpected as the sighting of an alien spacecraft might be to us today.

These people live in the earth's upper atmosphere just as we live on its surface. The earth's surface is to them what the seabed or ocean floor is to us. They travel through the clouds, their natural environment, dropping their anchor whenever they want to stop. We can imagine how the anchor might nestle or lodge in the crook of a tree, bringing the ship to a halt in the clouds above.

But now the anchor seems to have fallen off by accident – it trails along behind, connected by the anchor line. The anchor drags along the ground, while the ship proceeds through the sky, maybe a couple of hundred meters above it. Suddenly, however, the anchor gets stuck in the rails of the open-air oratory, causing the ship to shake violently in the air as its progress is halted: 'the big hull rocked to a standstill'.

Then the monks see a figure leave the deck of the airborne ship above. This 'crewman' begins to lower himself down the rope. His legs or shins are crossed over the rope in an effort to secure himself. He grapples his way down the rope, hand after hand laboriously: 'shinned and grappled'.

When he reaches the bottom of the rope, he attempts to pull the anchor free with one hand, while clinging to the rope with the other. However, he struggles 'in vain' to release the huge, heavy anchor.

It soon becomes apparent that the crewman cannot breathe the air on the surface of the earth, in the same way that humans can't breathe under water, neither can this crewman breathe earthly air. For, as we noted, he and his kind have their natural environment in the higher reaches of the earth's atmosphere. To him, the oratory floor might as well be the bottom of the ocean.

For a moment, the monks are frozen in shock, staring at the crewman as he struggles for breathe and attempts to free the anchor from the altar rail. For them, this must have been a moment of true shock and awe - not just to have witnessed this unidentified flying object in the sky, but to have it physically intrude into their world.

The abbot calls on his fellow monks to wake up and take action. He realises that this other-worldly crewman can't breathe on the earth's surface and that he's in danger of drowning: 'This man can't bear our life here and will drown … unless we help him.' At this, the other monks spring into action and help the crewman to free the anchor: 'So/ They did, the freed ship sailed'.

The crewman then scuttles back up the long anchor rope to the safety of his ship. We can picture him gasping as he breathes his own atmosphere again. We can imagine how he is stunned by his experience of the earth's surface, an environment like nothing he has ever seen before 'the man climbed back/ Out of the marvellous as he had known it.'

THEMES

CREDITING THE MARVELLOUS

The poem powerfully makes the point that the marvellous is very much a matter of perspective. What is ordinary and mundane to one person is extraordinary to another. To the monks, the flying ship is an extraordinary sight – it is like nothing they have ever seen before or will ever see again and they will remember it for the rest of their lives. To the crewman, however, the flying ship is just his place of work.

But the opposite is also true. To the monks the oratory is just a place where they eat, work and pray. But to the crewman it is truly extraordinary. It is as wonderfully alien to him as the bed of a deep-sea trench would be to us.

The poem suggests then that the ordinary world around us can be a source of awe, mystery and inspiration, if we look at it in the right way. If we are open to experience and view our lives with fresh eyes, the way the crewman views the oratory, the world might suddenly appear as the truly marvellous place it actually is.

FORM

The poem is one of a series of twelve-line poems that Heaney wrote at this period. The poem's structure is simple and straightforward, consisting of twelve lines broken up into four three-line stanzas.

IMAGERY

The poem centres on an extraordinary image, the sudden appearance of a ship above the open-aired oratory at Clonmacnoise. It is an incredible sight: 'A ship appeared above them in the air.' However, the language used to depict this fantastical occurrence is understated. Heaney focuses on the small, practical details, such as the 'big hull' coming 'to a standstill', and the efforts of the crewman to climb down and free the anchor: 'shinned and grappled'. By not sensationalising the wild, incredulous sights described, Heaney's language lends the events of the poem a quiet authority.

TONE AND ATMOSPHERE

The poet doesn't spend any time speculating about the origins of the airborne ship – whether it is ghostly, angelic, or just a mass hallucination on the part of the monks. He merely describes what happens in a matter-of-fact way. This down-to-earth, almost deadpan reporting of the events provides a striking and effective contrast to the poem's fantastical imagery.

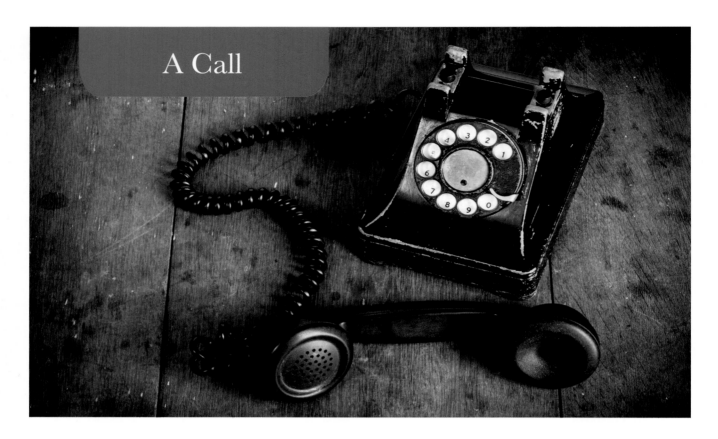

A Call

LINE BY LINE

The poet makes a phone call to his father. He calls the landline in his parent's house, which is located on a table in the hallway. His mother answers the phone and says that his father is busy in the garden: 'The weather here's so good he took the chance/ To do a bit of weeding'. She asks him to hold the line while she fetches his father from the garden: "Hold on', she says, 'I'll just go out and get him'".

While he waits, the poet pictures his father gardening. The poet imagines his father kneeling beside a 'rig' or bed of leeks: So I saw him/ Down on his hands and knees beside the leek rig'. We sense that the father approaches this work with real care and finesse. The poet pictures him closely examining the leek plants as he searches for weeds growing between them: 'Touching, inspecting, separating one/ Stalk from the other'. He imagines that is father is careful to pluck each weed by the root so that it won't grow back. We sense that the father is not one for half measures and feels satisfaction in a job well done: 'Pleased to feel each little weed-root break'.

We sense that the father has a great love for the leeks that he takes such pains to grow, that he really appreciates these graceful, fragile plants. Strangely enough, it also seems that the father has a certain affection for the weeds that he plucks. He seems 'rueful' or regretful that he must end their lives in order that his leeks might thrive.

The poet continues to wait for his father to come to the phone. He can hear a loud ticking as he waits, reminding him that there are several clocks in his parent's hallway, their noise amplified by the emptiness of the hallway: 'The amplified grave ticking of hall clocks'.

He imagines how his parent's hallway must look in the sunlight. He pictures the phone lying 'unattended' on the hall table. He thinks of sunlight reflecting on the pendulums of the clocks. He finds the hallway to be a very calm and pleasant environment.

The medieval story of Death and Everyman comes to the poet's mind. The poet imagines that if this story took place in modern times, Death would probably summon Everyman over the phone. The poem was written in the early nineties. If it were today, we might imagine Death summoning Everyman by Twitter or Instagram!

The poet is just thinking about his father's death when the man himself comes to the phone. We can imagine that having just contemplated his death, the poet is relieved to hear the old man's voice. He wants to tell his father how much he loves him and cares for him, but he doesn't do it. The words are almost spoken, but the poet checks himself and holds them back: 'I nearly said I loved him'.

THEMES

LOVE AND RELATIONSHIPS

In 'The Harvest Bow', Heaney describes his father as a strong silent farmer with 'almost a contempt for speech'. In 'A Call' we get the impression that the father is perhaps most comfortable when he is out working in the garden. It is hard to imagine that he is very talkative on the phone. We can imagine him taking the call but saying relatively little, happy to get back to his work when the conversation ends.

The poet, however, is someone who is given to expression. He is a highly articulate poet who loves to express his thoughts and feelings in words. Why then does he struggle to express his feelings for his father when the old man comes to the phone?

Perhaps it has to do with the difficulty that many men seem to have when it comes to expressing their feelings; it is not something that comes naturally to them, and they may have been taught to think of it as 'unmanly'. Perhaps it is a generational thing – the poet would have grown up in a time when fathers and sons would rarely articulate their feelings for one another. Perhaps the poet knows that if he speaks these words he will make his father uncomfortable and he does not want to do this. The result will just be silence at the other end of the phone.

Although the poet's father is not given to expressing his feelings in words, we get the impression that he is a gentle and sensitive man. The poet imagines his father ruefully removing the weeds from his leek bed, seeming to regret the need to kill these invading plants. We also get the impression that the poet's father is a man who takes pride in his work, deriving great pleasure from doing things properly.

ART, CRAFT AND CREATIVITY

We sense that the father is someone who takes great pride in his work. He exhibits great care and precision, combing carefully through the leeks and removing each weed at the root to ensure that they won't grow back. But he also possesses the gentleness and sensitivity necessary to nurture a garden, removing the weeds 'gently', so as not to upset the soil bed. 'A Call', then, is a poem that celebrates the craft of gardening, just as 'The Forge' celebrates the craft of the blacksmith.

IMAGINES SPACES AND LANDSCAPES

Many of Heaney's poems feature a speaker who imagines a location or environment. In this instance the speaker imagines his parents' hallway and his father working in the garden. We have to remind ourselves that the speaker never actually sees the hallway's 'sunstruck pendulums' or his father kneeling beside the leek rig. He's on the other end of the phone the whole time. However his description of this imagined space is so vivid that we feel we've witnessed it ourselves.

FOCUS ON STYLE

FORM

The poem is almost a sonnet. The poem has fifteen lines, one more than the traditional sonnet. The sonnet portion of the poem, the first fourteen lines, concludes with the father's imagined death. The fifteenth line, where the poet describes the father speaking, is set apart and stands on its own. It's very much an after-thought. The poet's imagining of his father's death has been so deep that he is so surprised to hear his father's voice. The father was quite old when the poet wrote this poem and we sense that the poet is preparing himself mentally for his eventual passing.

> The medieval tale of Death and Everyman emphasises the inevitability of death. In the medieval story, Death appeared at the door of a character called Everyman in order to summon him to the next world.

to, imagining the stalks as 'tapered, frail and leafless'. The various objects described in the poem serve as effective metaphors for or symbols of the father's frailty and pending death. Like the leeks, the father is 'frail' and can be seized by death at any moment.

Particularly striking is the image if the father being summoned by Death, just as Everyman was in the medieval play. We imagine the father walking in from the garden to the beautifully sunlit hallway, with its 'sunstruck pendulums' to answer the phone. No sooner does he pick up the receiver though, than he disappears, vanishing into the afterlife, leaving the phone unattended on the hall table.

VERBAL MUSIC

The assonance in line 7 with its broad vowels creates a pleasant, euphonious sound. Assonance also features in the phrase 'sunstruck pendulums' with its repeated 'u' sounds. Onomatopoeia occurs in line 12: 'The amplified grave ticking of the hall clocks'.

IMAGERY

The poem is rich with vivid, memorable imagery. The poet describes the leek rig that his father is attending

The father's imagined passing is oddly peaceful and beautiful. It is the departure of a man who lived a gentle, fulfilled life. But there is also an element of sorrow here, in the emptiness of the hallway he leaves behind, a hollowness that amplifies the 'grave ticking' of the hall clocks. Of course, 'grave' here has two separate meanings, suggesting both the sombre sound of the pendulums and the grave where the poet's father will eventually be buried.

Postscript

LINE BY LINE

In *Stepping Stones*, a book of interviews, Heaney describes the joy he derives from driving: 'Often when I'm on my own in the car, driving in spring or early summer … I get this sudden joy from the sheer fact of the mountains to my right and the sea to my left, the flow of the farmland, the sweep of the road, the lift of the sky.' 'Postscript' captures something of this 'sudden joy', being a great hymn to the energy and locomotion of driving, to the pleasures of being behind the wheel.

The poet advises a visit to the Flaggy Shore, a stretch of coastline in County Clare, famous for its limestone rock formations and fossils. 'September or October', he suggests, is the perfect time to visit this rugged location. At this time of year the wind and light go 'working off each other', combining to create spectacular effects across this mile-long stretch of coast road.

The title captures the manner in which the poem was composed, quickly, fluently and with relatively little effort. Heaney commented on the writing of this piece: 'Now and again a poem comes like that, like a ball kicked in from nowhere.' The poem, then, was written outside or after the poet's usual writing process, which involves painstaking thought, effort and revision.

Postscripts are often more casual and relaxed in tone than the main body of the work. And the poem has something of this carefree zest.

The word 'postscript' comes from the Latin postscriptum, which means 'after writing'. A postscript can be a remark added to a letter after the letter has been signed. It can be a section added to a book, usually just before the book goes to print.

There's a wonderful element of personification in this line. The wind and light caress the landscape like two sculptors shaping a single piece of clay. Sometimes they work in tandem, collaborating to generate particular visual effects, the breeze rippling a mountain lake so that it perfectly reflects the pale autumn sun. But sometimes, we sense, they compete or tussle with one another, each altering and revising the other's handiwork.

Imagine looking out 'one side' of the car, toward the ocean, as we zip along the coast road. We'd see the interplay of these two elemental forces, the wind and the light, producing a magnificent effect: 'So that the ocean on the one side is wild/ With foam and glitter'. We can imagine the wind making the ocean tempestuous or 'wild', stoking its surface into mountainous, foaming waves. We can picture the autumn sunlight glittering as it reflects on this turbulent surface

Now imagine looking out the other side of the car, so that your gaze turns 'inland'.

- You'd see a place of 'stones'. The landscape surrounding the Flaggy Shore is extremely stony and rugged, full of boulders, erratics and moraines.
- You'd see the lake known as Lough Muree, with 'a flock of swans' adrift on its waters. The swans, with their 'headstrong-looking heads', would come across as proud and assertive creatures.
- Some swans would have their heads '[t]ucked' in tight to their bodies. Others would have their heads 'cresting' on the lake's surface. Still others would have their heads plunged below the waterline, keeping 'busy underwater' as they search industriously for food.

Wind and light would once again contribute to the beauty of the scene. Their interplay would lend Lough Muree a 'slate-grey' appearance, so it almost blends it with the stony surrounding landscape. The swans' feathers would be 'roughed and ruffling', tousled, disarrayed and rearranged by the wind's gusts.

The feathers of particular swans might stand on end, revealing different layers and shades of white. The underside of some feathers would be spotlessly white, others a dusky grey: 'Their feathers roughed and ruffling, white on white'.

A lightning rod attracts a bolt of lightning and leads it down into the earth where its energy dissipates. Heaney imagines a bolt of lightning that remains on the earth's surface, a crackling and fizzing ball of electricity. This is the comparison used to describe the swans, wonderfully capturing their intense white plumage. Each swan, he says, is a bolt of earthed lightning, a creature of pure white light that illuminates the lake on which they glide.

Remember, we're driving. We have to keep at least one eye on the road, meaning we can manage only a few fleeting glances at the beauty that surrounds us. The poet, however, advises that there's no point in parking and getting out of the car. For doing so won't allow us to get more out of this experience: 'Useless to think you'll park and capture it/ More thoroughly'.

We can 'capture' this landscape 'thoroughly', then, in a few brief glimpses, snatched and savoured from our station behind the wheel. Indeed there's a sense that stopping would diminish the experience of this particular vista. The energy and propulsion of driving, its endless forward momentum, contributes to the exhilaration we experience as we glance at the lake on one side of us, at the ocean's 'foam and glitter' on the other.

The poet wonderfully captures how driving makes one feel both present and absent, how it promotes a sense of being both in the landscapes through which we drive and also somehow at a remove from them: 'You are neither here nor there'. On one level, of course, as we motor along the coast we're a part of the Flaggy Shore's landscape. But on another we're sealed away from the world around us, ensconced within the bubble of the car.

The poet, in another unexpected turn of phrase, describes how we'd be a 'hurry' as we drive. We wouldn't be merely 'in a hurry'; we would actually be a hurry. This phrase wonderfully captures the exhilarating sense of speed we'd feel as we power along the coastline. We'd feel that our bodies, minds and very souls were filled with energy and propulsion.

The poem also shows how experienced drivers often enter a strangely meditative state while driving. While their attention, of course, remains focused on the road, another part of their mind drifts freely, experiencing unexpected images and associations as one thought leads on to another. As we traversed the coast road, the poet suggests, we'd enter just such a reflective state of mind, with 'known and strange things' passing through our minds. We'd find our minds drifting not only to known or familiar topics, but also to strange or unexpected ones.

The poem's final lines emphasise the importance of mindfulness, of being open to the world around us. The beauty of the Flaggy Shore will render our hearts off-guard, making us susceptible to such a state. Then finally, as we drive along between the ocean and the lake, we will find our hearts opening as we experiences a sense of oneness with the world around us.

Heaney uses a wonderful metaphor to describe this sense of mindfulness: As we drive along, winds from the sea would buffet or forcibly nudge the car in which we drive, impacting the side of the vehicle: 'big soft buffetings come at the car sideways'.

The poet imagines these gusts of wind, affecting not the car's position on the road but our very hearts, blowing them open so we for once are truly present in the landscape that surrounds us.

THEMES

TONE

The tone of the poem is conversational and informal. The fact that it begins with the word 'And' gives the sense that we are being dropped into the poem in mid-conversation. It has a free-flowing and unconstrained feel, containing no full stops in its first ten lines.

VERBAL MUSIC

Also contributing to the poem's lively rhythm are its many examples of alliteration. Lines such as 'inland among stones/ The surface of slate-grey lake is lit', with its repeated 's' and 'l' sounds, contribute to the poem's rapid flow of imagery. Similarly, the description of the swans with 'Their feathers roughed and ruffling, white on white', with its repeated 'r' and 'w' sounds, lends the poem an urgent rhythm.

The poet imagines a car being struck reasonably forcibly by the wind as it drives along the coast. However, this impact is presented as benign, as an oddly soothing disturbance, rather than a violent and dangerous one. He describes how these gusts are not only big and imposing, but also soft and gentle. The word 'buffeting' itself contributes to this paradoxical effect. It describes a reasonably violent, forceful action but the word has a soft almost soothing verbal music.

METAPHOR, SIMILE AND FIGURES OF SPEECH

Perhaps the most striking metaphor in the poem is that of the swans as 'earthed lightning'. The long-necked, elegant swans are like forks of lightning tethered to the earth. With their 'white on white' colouring, they seem to light up the 'slate-grey lake'. Their 'ruffling' feathers, meanwhile, give them the flickering appearance of flames.

IMAGERY

'Postscript' is full of energetic, kinetic imagery. Everything seems to be busy and on the move, from the poet in his car to the wind and light 'working off each other'. Every surface seems to be dancing in the breeze, such as the surface of the ocean 'wild/ With foam and glitter' and the swans' feathers 'roughed and ruffling'.

IMAGINED SPACES AND LANDSCAPES

The poet advises us to go the Flaggy shore at a particular time when conditions are just so, when the wind and light are interacting perfectly, when the weather conditions are in a particularly atmospheric state. In a sense, then, the poet presents us with an imagined space, an idealised version of this coastline: the wild, glittering ocean; the 'slate-grey lake'; the swans that look like balls of 'earthed lightning'.

Perhaps the poet has actually experienced the Flaggy Shore under such conditions. But it is more likely that the picture he paints for us fuses elements of different trips he has taken there over the years. Perhaps he's seen the Flaggy Shore on an exquisitively blustery afternoon, but surely he has never actually witnessed the splendour he advises us to seek out.

CREDITING THE MARVELLOUS

This is a poem that has the idea of mindfulness very much to the fore. For it stresses the importance of being present in the moment, and of keeping oneself open to life and its sensations. The opening line emphasises the importance of making the time for such experiences 'And some time make the time to drive out west'.

On the one hand, the poet is reminding himself to take time out of his busy life 'to drive out west' to one of his favourite places. This opening line, however, it can also be read as a general address to all of us to 'make the time', to make room in our busy lives for the places and experiences that really move us and replenish us. Doing so, the poem suggests, is by no means a frivolous activity - it's necessary for a sense of perspective, for our mental and emotional wellbeing.

We are often advised, when we see something spectacular on our journey, to stop, to pull over and take it all in. We can only be mindful, we are told, by slowing down. The poet, however, gives us the opposite advice. Our trip to the Flaggy Shore should suffer no such interruptions – we must keep driving. There is a certain species of mindfulness, the poem suggests, that comes from movement, pace and rhythm. The heart can be open to experience, even when we are in the driver's seat.

Tate's Avenue

LINE BY LINE

THE CAR RUG (CIRCA 1963)

The poet finds himself thinking about various rugs that he has shared with his wife over the many years they have been together. The first rug he remembers is a 'car rug' from the early sixties. This was the 'first' rug he and his future wife owned as a couple. It likely came with the poet's first car, which he purchased in 1963, a time when many cars came with a rug intended for picnics or day trips.

He remembers how, when they drove in his new car to the seaside, this car rug was 'Spread on sand by the sea'. We can imagine the couple relaxing on the rug as they watch the waves come crashing in. This is a beautiful image, one that captures not only the sense of adventure involved in embarking on a new relationship, but also the sense of freedom that comes from owning your first car.

The rug itself, it should be pointed out, doesn't strike us as being especially attractive, Around its edges were old-fashioned woollen tassels or tails: 'Edged with a fringe of sepia-coloured wool tails'. Its colour scheme was a mixture of various browns: brown and 'fawn', or greyish brown, for the main body of the rug, with sepia or reddish brown for the tassels.

In a wonderful phrase, the poet describes how the rug was 'Breathing land breaths' capturing its stale and musty odour from being stowed in the car. Its staleness, we imagine, must have been especially pronounced when compared to the freshness of the sea breeze.

But this rug, despite its unattractiveness, was their 'comfort zone'. In one sense of course, this simply means, that it was a comfortable place to sit, that it spared them the discomfort of the seaside's sand and rocks. But the term 'comfort zone' as we shall see also serves as a powerful metaphor for their relationship.

THE SPANISH RUG (CIRCA 1969)

The poet finds himself thinking about a different rug, one they shared on their first trip to Spain in 1969. The poet has now achieved some success and is already a minor literary celebrity, having just published his second book of poems *Door into the Dark*. It is quite possible, therefore, that the poet and his wife have been invited to Spain to attend a literary gathering there. Perhaps their trip has been paid for and they are enjoying some V.I.P. treatment.

The description of the rug certainly suggests that the poet and his wife had a great time. We get the impression that they ventured off by themselves, out into the Spanish heartlands, with a basket of local wine and food. The poet remembers sitting on a rug by the banks of the Guadalquivir river, which flows through Cordoba and Seville in Southern Spain, and enjoying their feast.

The rug that the poet remembers from this particular occasion was eventually strewn with scraps from the meal they enjoyed. Scattered all over its surface are 'crusts' from the baguettes, shells from the cooked eggs, bits of the local cheese, olive stones and 'rinds' from the salami scattered all over the rug. Heaney

The poet in an interesting turn of phrase describes the car rug as 'vestal', meaning related to virginity. Perhaps this suggests that rug is new and unsullied. They unfold it carefully, almost gingerly, spreading it out for the first time by the sea. It's a phrase that also tells us something about their relationship in its earliest stages, suggesting perhaps that it had yet to develop fully physically. We must remember that during the early 1960's, when this stanza is set, sex before marriage was still relatively uncommon.

The parks in Belfast were locked-up on Sundays because the civic authorities were heavily influenced by the Presbyterian community, who believed that Sundays should be preserved for worship and reflection. Work and even recreation were to be avoided as much as possible. For this reason, until 1965, Sunday saw Belfast parks under lock and key.

describes the rug as 'scraggy', with food scraps entangled in its fibres. These scraps made the rug uncomfortable to lie on.

The description of the rug gives us a sense of how relaxed and carefree the couple were on this occasion, 'drunk' from the local Spanish wine. We can imagine that this is one of their first trips abroad, and likely their first trip to Spain, and they are just lapping and soaking up the culture. We also get a sense of how at ease they are with each other, having been together for a number of years.

THE BELFAST RUG (CIRCA 1961)

Now the poet finds himself remembering another rug, one that he and his wife lay on briefly back in 1961. At this time, the poet and his future wife were both living in Belfast. But at this stage they were only acquaintances rather than lovers. It is likely, in fact, that they were both attached to other people at the time.

One Sunday, they found themselves in the same back yard on Tate's Avenue in central Belfast. We imagine that this is some kind of social gathering, that they have both been invited around for lunch by a mutual friend, for example.

The yard, in which they found themselves, seemed claustrophobic, with its 'walls' and 'high and silent' dustbins. We can imagine that these dustbins might have been smelly on such a warm afternoon. The back yard that the poet remembers consisted of lumpy earth, suggesting that it was barren and uncared for rather than a well-attended garden. The overall portrait of the backyard suggests rented accommodation for students or graduates rather than a family home.

The poet remembers how his future wife was lying on a rug in the yard reading. He recalls how she twirled her hair distractedly, lost in her book: 'a finger twirls warm hair'. The poet was deeply attracted to this woman and felt that she was deeply attracted to him as well. He took the brave step of lying down beside her on the rug.

The poet's future wife didn't respond positively to this advance, but she didn't push him away either. She just ignored him and went on reading. The poet uses the colloquial expression 'nothing gives' to describe this lack of response, meaning 'nothing doing' or 'nothing happening'. But the expression 'nothing gives' also refers to the ground on which they both lay, suggesting the unyielding nature of the surface.

The poet lay 'at [his] length', his body stretched out alongside his future wife. The lumpy earth made him deeply uncomfortable but he was determined not to move from the rug. He wanted to remain pressed against her for every second possible: 'But never shifted'.

The poet describes how he was 'Keen-sensed' during these minutes he spent next to his future wife. His senses were heightened by his attraction to her, and he was keenly aware of her smell and her touch. But the poet also remained conscious of the discomfort of lying on this hard, lumpy earth.

Finally they moved. Maybe they were called in for dinner by the mutual friend who has been hosting them. Maybe they were disturbed by one of the flies that populate the 'high and silent' dustbins! But now they know they have something. Though nothing has been said, they know they like each other. It is the first move in what will become a life-long attachment.

THEMES

TTHE PROCESS OF MEMORY

This poem describes the process of memory as an almost inner Instagram. We find the poet flicking through different mental images as if he were swiping through an internal photo stream. The poem, we might imagine, is set during a moment of ease or relaxation, one in which the poet finds his mind idling or drifting through memories of the past. Maybe he is on a train or a plane, in a space where it is possible to tune out of what is going on around you and become lost in your own thoughts. Somehow the poet finds himself thinking about the rug that came with his first car. But this memory triggers a remembrance of another rug and then another, wonderfully illustrating the associative manner in which the memory works, how one thought leads on to another and then another, in an endless chain of associations.

The poet, as have seen, finds himself remembering the rug he and his wife would use when they visited the beach in the early stages of their relationship. He remembers a rug they sat on during an exquisitely sensual trip to Spain. These are two fine memories, but they are not the ones that he recalls most fondly. They are not the ones that he finds himself returning to again and again.

Instead he finds himself dwelling 'again' and again on a rug associated with an ordinary morning in an ugly back yard in Belfast in the early 60's: 'Instead, again, it's locked-park Sunday Belfast'. Maybe it's easy to see why this is the rug that he always returns to, for this was the beginning of the beginning of his relationship with his wife, the earliest moments of their flirtation when everything seemed fresh and new and full of possibility.

LOVE AND RELATIONSHIPS

But 'Tate's Avenue' celebrates the resilience and longevity of a long-term relationship, not the just the excitement and passion of the young love in its earliest stages. The poet celebrates how he and his wife explored the world together as the years went by and their relationship continued to flourish and deepen. He relishes how their horizons expanded over time, from the the claustrophobic walled yard, to the Northern Irish seashore, to the exotic Guadalquivir river in Spain, and then, no doubt, even further afield.

The rugs described in the poem serve as a symbol of their relationship over the years. Placing a rug on the ground creates a space apart from the surface in which it has been laid. Similarly, the bond the couple share can be thought of as a place apart, as being somehow separate from the surrounding network of human commitments and relationships. We think of it as a comfortable space – usually it is more comfortable to sit on a rug rather than on sand or earth. Similarly, the poet views his relationship with his wife as a comfort zone, for it provides them both with calmness and reassurance, nourishing them as they journey through life.

FOCUS ON STYLE

IMAGERY

This is a poem where Heaney's imagery is at its deftest and most economical. He manages to place us in space and time with just a single phrase or image, such as the musty rug breathing land-breaths, the 'scraggy' rug by the Spanish river covered in scraps of food, the 'locked-park Sunday Belfast' and the wife twirling her hair as she reads, condensing a whole love-story into a mere sixteen lines.

Gerard Manley Hopkins

Themes

The Beauty of Nature

Perhaps the first thing to strike readers of Hopkins' poetry is his intense love of the natural world. His inspired and ecstatic response to nature can be summed up by his declaration in 'Spring' that the thrush's song strikes him 'like lightning'. Hopkins is 'electrified' by the beauty of the natural world. He regards spring as a time when nature can offer us a cleansing sense of personal rebirth and renewal.

A similarly ecstatic response to the natural world can be found in 'The Windhover', where Hopkins lovingly describes the flight of a falcon, its 'riding of the rolling-level-underneath-him steady-air'. To Hopkins the falcon is something majestic, a prince or 'dauphin' of the 'kingdom of daylight'. His heart 'stirs' as he watches the bird, suggesting the great exhilaration that the poet experiences at the sight.

A perhaps more restrained appreciation of nature is evident in 'Inversnaid' and 'Pied Beauty'. 'Inversnaid' delights in the sights and sounds of a 'burn' or brook crashing down a slope in the Scottish Highlands. 'Pied Beauty', meanwhile, celebrates the beauty of 'dappled things', sights that have a complex visual pattern, such as a trout's speckled skin, finches' wings and a landscape divided into many different fields and 'plots'.

Environmentalism

There are also instances where Hopkins displays what might almost be described as an environmentalist attitude toward nature. In 'Inversnaid', for instance, he is worried that the wild places of natural beauty like Inversnaid might be consumed by urbanisation and industrialisation: 'What would the world be, once bereft/ Of wet and of wildness?' He concludes the poem by calling for such beauty spots to be left alone: 'Long live the weeds and the wilderness yet'.

A similar attitude is evident in 'God's Grandeur'. The poem describes how we have stripped the soil, 'seared' or burnt the landscape and left the sky itself 'bleared' or darkened with pollution. To Hopkins it seems that the filth arising from our industrial activities has 'smeared' the entire world so that it 'wears man's smudge and shares man's smell'. Hopkins, writing in the 19th century, laments how man has lost contact with the earth, has forgotten his role as a guardian of God's creation. This is symbolised by the fact that our feet are 'shod' and no longer touch the soil: 'nor can foot feel, being shod'. And in today's world, surely, it is even more obvious that we have lost our way when it comes to stewardship of the environment.

God's Presence in Nature

In Hopkins' poetry, thoughts of nature often lead to thoughts of God:

- In 'Spring', for instance, the earth in springtime reminds Hopkins of the Garden of Eden, which in turn leads him to think about sin. Specifically he thinks about children, who are sinless and innocent as Adam was before he ate the apple.
- In 'The Windhover' the sight of the soaring falcon causes Hopkins to think about Christ's role as our redeemer.
- In 'As Kingfishers Catch Fire' considering nature's variety leads him to think about the 'just man', who 'justices' or lives in a just way and keeps himself in a state of grace with God.
- In 'Pied Beauty' a celebration of 'dappled things' leads Hopkins to praise God.

Hopkins was keenly aware of God as the creator of every living thing we see around us. This is evident in 'Pied Beauty', where he describes God as the force that gives birth to the wonders of the natural world, to everything that is 'original', 'spare' and 'strange'. God, he said, 'fathers forth' every thing we see around us in nature.

A similar point is made in 'God's Grandeur', where Hopkins describes God's energy flowing through all living things. It is like an electric 'charge' or current that pulses through everything in creation: 'The world is charged with the grandeur of God'. God's energy is an eternal source of freshness that exists deep down in the natural world, ensuring that it will always restore itself: 'nature is never spent;/ There lives the dearest freshness deep down things'. The Holy Spirit protects and shelters the world like a bird 'brooding' over the eggs in its nest.

'As Kingfishers Catch Fire' also focuses on God's presence in the natural world. God, the poem suggests, has given everything in the world a unique spiritual essence. This essence 'dwells' inside each creature and object: 'that being indoors each one dwells'. We can think of it as a spiritual spark or soul that resides within. Each creature and object reveals its unique essence to the world through its actions and appearances: the way it looks, the sounds it makes, the things it does. Everything acts in such a way that it spells out or expresses the essence God has placed within it: 'Selves – goes itself; *myself* it speaks and spells'.

Sin and Redemption

Hopkins was keenly aware that mankind was sinful. In 'God's Grandeur', for instance, he laments that humankind goes against God's will, smearing and despoiling the beautiful world he has given us. Hopkins despairingly asks why man fails to 'reck' or obey God's will: 'Why do men then now not reck his rod?'

'Spring', too, is highly conscious of sin. Hopkins celebrates the innocence of the young, claiming that an 'innocent mind' exists in every child. Yet Hopkins is all too aware that as children grow older their innocent minds will be corrupted by sin: 'before it cloy … Before it cloud … and sour with sinning'. The speaker calls on Jesus to preserve the innocence of these children, requesting Christ to 'Have' and 'get' each boy and girl, to take them to him before their innocence is destroyed: 'Have, get … Christ, lord … Innocent mind and Mayday in girl and boy'.

There are several other poems where Christ is depicted as overcoming sin. In 'Felix Randal', for instance, Hopkins claims that Christ, through communion, is our 'reprieve and ransom', the thing that saves us from sin and death. When Hopkins gives Felix communion his heart becomes 'heavenlier': his soul becomes cleansed of sin and more fit to enter heaven. In 'The Windhover' Christ is depicted as a knight or 'chevalier' who does battle on our behalf against the forces of sin. Christ opposes sin like a knight riding into battle against an enemy army or the falcon battling against the 'big wind'.

'As Kingfishers Catch Fire' also focuses on the notion of sin and redemption. The poem calls on us to 'justice', to behave as 'just men', to turn away from sin and live in a good or graceful fashion: 'the just man justices;/ Kéeps gráce: thát keeps all his goings graces'. When we behave in such a fashion we resemble Christ.

Mental Suffering

Hopkins' earliest mention of despair comes in 'Inversnaid'. He describes a little whirlpool in the highland brook as a black hole of despair. It has a black and 'fell' or evil look about it. This little black whirlpool of despair suggests Hopkins' unhappiness at the time. When he wrote 'Inversnaid' he was ministering in the slums of the great Northern English industrialised cities. Hopkins, who never enjoyed good health, found this work mentally and physically exhausting. This whirlpool image ominously suggests the despair into which the poet would later sink. 'Felix Randal' also seems to prefigure the poet's own suffering. The sick blacksmith's mind begins to 'ramble' as his sanity slips away, suggesting the madness-inducing torment that would soon grip the poet himself.

The 'terrible sonnets' describe this descent into mental torment. They were written over the last few years of the poet's life when he was working in University College Dublin. During this period Hopkins was in poor mental and physical health. He found his duties exhausting and unrewarding. Furthermore, he was lonely and miserable in Ireland, a country where he found it difficult to fit in and had few friends. As he put it in a letter these 'terrible sonnets' were the product of a 'continually jaded and harassed mind'.

'No worst, there is none' could be described as a howl of mental torment. The poet has been 'pitched past pitch of grief'. He is experiencing a mental state that is far beyond ordinary grief or sorrow. Hopkins' mental torment is more or less unrelenting, with only the briefest of pauses between one bout of suffering and the next. His torment also keeps getting worse. To Hopkins it seems that his sufferings will keep increasing in intensity forever, that there is 'no worst', no rock-bottom for him to hit.

'I wake and feel the fell of dark' powerfully captures 'black hours' of misery, comparing the poet's mental anguish to a terrible unending journey of dark 'ways' and awful 'sights'. Furthermore, we get a sense that the poet has been living with such despair for all his life: 'But where I say/ Hours I mean years, mean life'. The poem is also wonderful on the misery of insomnia, capturing how for an insomniac the night seems to stretch on and on as the light seems to take forever to arrive.

'Thou art indeed just, Lord' is perhaps less intense than the other three. Here Hopkins presents his suffering in a more rational, restrained and subtle fashion. However, his despair and mental torment still resonate throughout the poem. It powerfully conveys Hopkins' desperate and 'straining' attempts to make something of his life and his sense of failure and disappointment when these attempts come to nothing. Hopkins feels completely barren, that he is incapable of 'building' or producing anything worthwhile. The only element of hope in the poem is Hopkins' desperate plea for God to do something to relieve his situation.

Doubting God's Goodness

We first encounter the theme of religious doubt in 'Felix Randal', where the powerfully built blacksmith curses God for allowing him to become ill: 'Impatient he cursed at first'. However, Felix 'mended' his ways when Hopkins 'anointed' him and gave him the sacraments. Felix, it seems, became reconciled with God and somehow learned to accept his illness as part of God's plan.

'I wake and feel the fell of dark' and 'No worst, there is none' explore intense states of religious doubt. Hopkins is in a terrible state and calls out to God for help. God, however, fails to answer, leaving Hopkins feeling abandoned in his time of greatest need. As he puts it in 'No worst, there is none'': 'Comforter, where, where is your comforting?/ Mary, mother of us, where is your relief?' In 'I wake and feel the fell of dark,' God is presented as someone distant and uncaring who 'lives alas! away' and fails to respond to the poet's 'cries' for help. The speaker, therefore, describes his prayers as 'dead letters', mail that has been posted to an abandoned or false address.

There's even a sense in which the poet thinks that God wants him to suffer. It's as if God willed or 'decreed' that the poet should experience this intense mental and physical suffering. Furthermore, he seems to resent that God decided to trap his soul in the scourge of a 'sick' and 'sweating' physical body. In a very real sense, the poet is angry with God for causing him to be born.

Hopkins's most powerful statement of religious doubt comes in 'Thou art indeed just, Lord'. In it Hopkins asks an age-old question: if God is good why does he let wicked men triumph and sinners get ahead in life? Furthermore, why does he let his faithful servants suffer? Hopkins has sacrificed so much for God yet nothing in his life succeeds. Meanwhile sinners who have sacrificed nothing, who are the slaves or 'thralls' of lust, get ahead in life. There is a strong sense of frustration in this poem. Hopkins suspects that God has turned against him and is actually his enemy rather than his friend.

Hopkins' Poetic Style

Inscape and Instress

Hopkins was convinced that everything in nature was unique. His term for the individuality of each thing, for the qualities it and it alone possessed, was 'inscape'. Everything, he believed, from the tiniest pebble to a soaring falcon to the mind, had its own 'inscape', or set of unique qualities. This view is evident in 'As Kingfishers Catch Fire, Dragonflies Draw Flame' which suggests that each object and living thing has its own unique inner essence and expresses this essence through its behaviour in the world.

Hopkins' poetry is driven by the desire to grasp the inscapes of the natural world, to capture in words the unique individuality of each bird and flower he described. Again and again, he sets out to capture the inscape of various natural objects by stretching language to its very limits. Very often Hopkins uses sound effects in an attempt to capture the uniqueness and character of a natural phenomenon. He was master, in particular, of assonance and alliteration. 'Spring' provides a good example of alliteration, the repeated soft 'l' sounds capturing the season's lushness and abundance: 'shoot long and lovely and lush;/ Thrush's eggs look little low heavens'.

'Instress' is another important term in Hopkins' work. According to Hopkins instress was God's divine energy, a force that flowed through everything like electricity and preserved the natural world in all its variety and beauty. 'God's Grandeur', in particular, explores the theme of instress. In this poem 'instress' is represented as an electrical charge that emanates from God and crackles through the universe, maintaining the beauty and individuality of each living thing.

Sprung Rhythm

Hopkins's greatest contribution to English poetry was his concept of 'sprung rhythm'. The theory of sprung rhythm can be difficult to grasp, and has been the subject of many scholarly articles (including Hopkins' own almost incomprehensible 'Preface'). The best way to understand 'sprung rhythm', however, is to compare it to standard English verse. In traditional English poetry each line had a set amount of 'stressed' and 'unstressed' syllables. This creates a predictable rhythmic effect, something you could tap your foot to. A good example is the rhythm of the following lines from Wordsworth's 'The Solitary Reaper':

Will no one tell me what she sings?-
Perhaps the plaintive numbers flow
For old, unhappy, far-off things
And battles long ago:

Hopkins, however, changes the rules by focusing only on 'stressed' syllables. Each line has a set amount of 'stressed' syllables, but can have any amount of 'unstressed' syllables. The effect created by sprung rhythm will be obvious if the following passage from Hopkins is compared to the one above from Wordsworth:

As a skate's heel sweeps smooth on a bow-bend:the hurl and gliding
Rebuffed the big wind. My heart in hiding
Stirred for a bird — the achieve of the mastery of the thing!

The only way to really understand sprung rhythm, however, is to read Hopkins' poems aloud. The technique generates a powerful, unpredictable music, which, while it may lack the regular pulse of traditional poems like the 'The Solitary Reaper', can bring the movement of natural phenomena, a falcon or a roaring stream, vividly to life in the mind of the reader. To Hopkins sprung rhythm was 'the least forced, the most rhetorical and emphatic of all possible rhythms, combining opposite and, one would have thought, incompatible excellences'. ⌧

God's Grandeur

LINE BY LINE

LINES 1 TO 3

According to the poet God is present in all things. His presence or energy flows through every aspect of creation like an unstoppable electrical current. Hopkins describes how the world is 'charged' with his greatness like a battery charged with electricity: 'The world is charged with the grandeur of God'.

Take a piece of aluminium foil. Shake it and watch how it glitters and shines. Rays of light or 'shining' emanate from such silvery material when it's agitated. Similarly, energy emanates from God and flows through all things. Hopkins describes how energy bursts or 'flames' from God and pours through nature: 'It will flame out, like shining from shook foil'.

God is present in countless individual aspects of creation – in the various plants, animals and insects that inhabit the earth for example. But his presence 'gathers to a greatness'. Every single aspect of nature combines to make an extraordinary global system, to produce an incredible illustration of God's magnificence.

Hopkins often uses words that have more than one meaning. In this instance the word 'charged', as we've seen, is used in the sense of electricity. However, we also detect here a shade of the word's other meanings. To be 'charged' is to be accused of a crime, in this instance bringing to mind mankind's crime of failing to respect God's creation. To be 'charged' is also to be given a task, in this instance bringing to mind how humanity is charged with the great duty of protecting God's creation.

Hopkins uses the simile of oozing oil to explain this. This image can be hard to visualise precisely but he seems to have in mind the idea of an old-fashioned olive press. Thousands of olives are crushed, resulting in little streams of olive oil that ooze down the press's surface before gathering in a vat of precious glistening liquid.

LINES 4 TO 8

Hopkins imagines God wielding a great staff or 'rod' that symbolises his authority – and indeed his ability to punish us. However, we no longer 'reck', heed or even notice this rod, this great and terrible symbol of office. According to Hopkins, then, mankind no longer respects God's authority. Nor do we fear His punishment. Hopkins seems amazed at the disrespect humanity shows God, especially when He has given us the gift of this magnificent world: 'Why do men then now not reck his rod?'

This disrespect is evident in the ecological disaster we've created, in the mess we've made of God's creation. Hopkins, we remember, was writing at the time when the consequences of the Industrial Revolution were becoming clear. Vast polluted

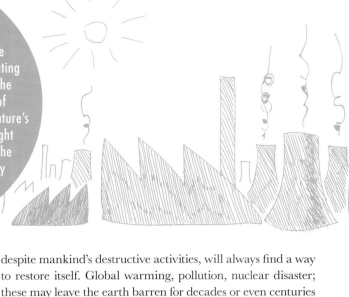

cities had sprung up in England and around the world. Huge factories endlessly belched out gouts of acrid smoke. Pollution was rife and nature seemed everywhere in retreat.

For generations, Hopkins declares, people have inhabited the world without any regard for its magnificence. The word 'trod', repeated three times, suggests mindless, ignorant activity that tramples down nature's beauty.

It seems to Hopkins that industry has left everything 'seared' or burned. We might think here of furnaces and factories, of natural resources burned away, of forests scorched to make room for more production.

Commercial activity has left everything 'bleared' or blurred. We might imagine here clouds of dank smoke pouring from the factory towers of the industrial revolution and darkening the sky itself.

Our toil, our industrial activities, have left the world 'smeared' with pollution. The dirt and stench we produce has seeped into nature, leaving it indelibly stained: 'And wears man's smudge and shares man's smell'.

The soil is 'bare' now and no longer sprouts crops. Much soil, no doubt, has been left barren by pollution. Elsewhere soil has been built over by towns and industrial facilities.

Hopkins laments that human beings are 'shod', that we wear shoes and as a result no longer feel the soil against our feet: 'nor can foot feel, being shod'. Hopkins, of course, doesn't want everyone to start going around in bare feet. Rather he uses the notion of footwear to symbolise how we are no longer at one with the natural world that surrounds us. We have lost all sympathy with and understanding of nature just as our feet have lost contact with the earth.

LINES 9 TO 14

And yet there is hope. Despite the damage inflicted by man, 'nature' can never be fully 'spent', exhausted or destroyed: 'And for all this, nature is never spent'. The natural world,

despite mankind's destructive activities, will always find a way to restore itself. Global warming, pollution, nuclear disaster; these may leave the earth barren for decades or even centuries but eventually growth will return.

Hopkins uses the sunrise to illustrate nature's infinite capacity for renewal. At night the sun sets in the blackness of the western sky, the 'last lights' of the day slowly going out: 'And though the last lights off the black West went'. In the morning, however, the sun 'springs' back to life in the eastern sky. It rises up from the 'brink' or edge of the sky as it emits the dull brown light of early dawn: 'Oh, morning, at the brown brink eastwards, springs'.

This endless renewal is possible because God's presence flows through the entire world. His energy may not be immediately evident but it resides 'deep down' in the things of this earth. Hopkins refers to it as a 'dearest freshness' because it is a precious force that ensures nature will always be refreshed or reborn: 'There lives the dearest freshness deep down things'.

Hopkins uses an inventive metaphor to describe how God presides over the world. The planet Earth is compared to an egg. The Holy Spirit is compared to a bird with a 'warm breast' and bright wings. The Holy Spirit 'broods over' the world, nourishing and protecting it, just as a bird 'broods over' an unhatched egg.

THE BEAUTY OF NATURE

'God's Grandeur' is more abstract than other poems by Hopkins and contains less direct descriptions of nature than, say, 'Spring' or 'Pied Beauty'. However, he does provide a memorable portrait of the sun rising in the east each morning, springing triumphantly up from the 'brink' of the world.

The word 'Crushed' completes the statement begun in line 3 but stands alone by itself at the beginning of line 4, its isolation highlighting its significance. It signals a change in the poem's focus, introducing the theme of environmental damage, the crushing of nature's beauty by man. The word 'Crushed' might also suggests the disappointment that the poet feels when he looks at the beauty of nature and the damage that man does.

Hopkins refers to the world as 'bent', which can be understood to mean different things. Perhaps it is a reference to the curved nature of the globe. However, the world 'bent' can also mean corrupt or morally crooked and so might be describing the activities of man.

GOD'S PRESENCE IN NATURE

The poem describes how God's presence throbs and pulses through the world. Hopkins compares it to a current of electricity that 'charges' the universe and to pulses of energy that 'flame out' like beams of light. God's presence exists 'deep down' in things so it can sometimes be overlooked. But He is there in every single aspect of creation. And everything on the planet 'gather[s] to a greatness', combining to offer an extraordinary testament to His grandeur or magnificence.

Because God is present in nature it can never be 'spent', destroyed or exhausted. Mankind in his greed and stupidity may pollute and ruin the natural world, but God's presence nourishes and sustains it. Hopkins wonderfully captures this idea with the metaphor of the 'Holy Ghost' tending to the world just as a bird tends to an unhatched egg. Despite man's destructive efforts, therefore, nature will always restore itself. The beautiful image of the sunrise captures nature's endless capacity for self-renewal.

ENVIRONMENTALISM

This is one of several poems where Hopkins exhibits what might be described as environmentalist tendencies, where he shows a keen awareness of how the Industrial Revolution had ravaged the English landscape. For generations we have carelessly trampled God's creation, guided only by selfishness and greed.

We have stripped the soil, 'seared' or burnt the landscape and left the sky itself 'bleared' or darkened with pollution. For Hopkins it seems that the filth arising from our industrial activities has 'smeared' the entire world so that it 'wears man's smudge and shares man's smell'. Hopkins, writing in the 19th century, laments how man has lost contact with the earth, has forgotten his role as a guardian of God's creation. And in today's world, surely, it is even more obvious that we have lost our way when it comes to stewardship of the environment.

SIN AND REDEMPTION

Hopkins is a poet greatly concerned with the idea of sin. In this poem he laments how mankind no longer pays any attention to God, no longer heeding his glory and authority: 'Why do men then now not reck his rod'. Hopkins suggests that we sin against God not only by murdering, lying and cheating but also by failing to respect his creation. We sin through our greed and our industry. We sin when our 'toil' stains the magnificent world he has gifted us and in which he is everywhere present.

FORM

Like many of Hopkins' poems, this is a perfectly formed Petrarchan sonnet. It has the typical Petrarchan rhyme scheme: ABBAABBA CDCDCD. It is divided into an octet (eight lines) and a sestet (six lines). It could also be argued that there is a shift in focus between the octet and the sestet. These defining features of the Petrarchan sonnet are also evident in 'Spring', 'As Kingfishers Catch Fire, Dragonflies Draw Flame' and 'I wake and feel the fell of dark'.

SYNTAX

Hopkins' compression of language is evident in the line 'There lives the dearest freshness deep down things'. Ordinarily of course we would say something like 'the dearest freshness lives deep down in things'. His unique approach to sentence structure or syntax is also evident in the phrase 'the ooze of oil/ Crushed', which as we've seen has the effect of energising the verse and leaving the key word 'Crushed' highlighted in a prominent position.

VERBAL MUSIC

The poem derives its intense energy from Hopkins' extensive and highly original use of assonance and alliteration. In the phrase 'ooze of oil' for example, with its onomatopoeic quality, we can almost hear the oil slicking and flowing. The sestet, however, is dominated by a gentler, more soothing – though still energetic – word music. The assonance of the phrase 'dearest freshness', with its repeated 'e' sounds, for example, lends it a pleasant musical feel. A similar euphonious effect is created by the alliteration in 'last lights' with its repeated 'l' sound. The poem's concluding lines, which describe the redemptive qualities of the Holy Spirit, are particularly rich with alliteration, generated by the repeated 'b' sound in 'bent', 'brood', 'breast' and 'bright', and the 'w' sound in 'world', 'warm' and 'wings'.

IMAGERY

The poem uses images of light to describe the powerful presence of God in the world. His magnificence is said to erupt brilliantly in many individual rays of light, 'like shining from shook foil'. The 'Holy Ghost' that broods lovingly over the world protects it with 'bright wings'. The poem also features a wonderful description of the rising sun, used to illustrate the potential the world has for renewal. Hopkins suggests that man is doing everything he can to dull and smudge God's sheen and brilliance.

As Kingfishers Catch Fire, Dragonflies Draw Flame

LINE BY LINE

LINES 5 TO 8

This is the thinking behind the poem:

- God has given everything in the world a unique spiritual essence.
- This essence 'dwells' inside each creature and object: 'that being indoors each one dwells'. We can think of it as a 'spiritual spark' or soul that resides within.
- Each creature and object reveals its unique essence to the world through its actions and appearances: the way it looks, the sounds it makes, the things it does.

Therefore the actions and appearances of each creature and object are like a cry declaring its unique spiritual essence: 'Crying *What I do is me: for that I came*'. Every single thing 'came' into the world to express the unique essence God has placed within it: 'Each mortal thing does one thing and the same'. Everything acts in such a way that it spells out or expresses its essence: 'Selves-goes itself; myself it speaks and spells'.

LINES 1 TO 4

Hopkins gives us several examples of creatures and objects expressing their unique inner essence. Firstly, he describes kingfishers and dragonflies. These creatures express their essence through their beautiful appearance, especially through the way they look when sunlight strikes their bodies. So bright are kingfishers and dragonflies that when the sunlight hits them they blaze with colour, appearing to go up in flames: 'As Kingfishers Catch Fire, Dragonflies Draw Flame'.

Even humble, ordinary stones have a unique essence that dwells within them. They express this essence through the sounds they make when they are thrown ('tumbled') into wells: 'As tumbled over rim in roundy wells/ Stones ring'. (Many readers find this phrase difficult because Hopkins plays around with the usual order of the words. We would ordinarily put it like this: 'Stones make a ringing sound when they are thrown over the rims or edges of roundy wells'.)

Finally, Hopkins describes a string on a musical instrument and a church bell. A string 'tells', or expresses its essence, through the note it produces when plucked: 'each tucked string tells'. ('Tucked' is an old word for plucked.) Similarly, a church bell expresses its essence through the sound it makes when somebody rings it. The 'hung bell' dangles from the church tower, and when it is 'swung' its chime ring out.

LINES 9 TO 14

In the poem's final six lines, Hopkins focuses on 'the just man', a man who lives in a just and right-eous manner: 'I say more: the just man justices'. He is someone who 'keeps gráce', who lives in accordance with God's law and stays free of sin. All the just man's activities (referred to here as his 'goings') are

> The eyes of the just man are not Christ's eyes. They are 'not his'. However Christ can be seen in them each time the just man does good. When God looks down from heaven, therefore, He sees Jesus in the appearance and actions of just men. And to Him that is a 'lovely' sight.

carried out in a decent and sinless way: he is someone 'that keeps all his goings graces'.

Christ is present in each of us when we live according to God's law, when we act like the 'just man'. Christ, therefore, is present all over the world wherever someone is doing the right thing: 'Christ plays in ten thousand places'. He is present in the limbs, eyes and faces of each just man:

Lovely in limbs, and lovely in eyes not his
To the Father through the features of men's faces.

THEMES

THE BEAUTY OF NATURE

Like much of Hopkins' work, this poem emphasises the beauty of the natural world. It conjures up the fiery colourful beauty of kingfishers and dragonflies. The poem suggests that even something as humble and ordinary as the noise of stones dropping down a well deserves to be celebrated. Hopkins also celebrates the beautiful sounds made by certain manufactured objects: strings on musical instruments and church bells. While these man-made objects are not technically part of the natural world, they blend with it in the poem's celebration of life's rich tapestry.

A similar celebration of nature can be found in 'Pied Beauty', 'Inversnaid', 'Spring' and 'The Windhover'. In each of these poems, Hopkins focuses on the uniqueness, or 'inscape', of each creature and object, devising complex and original poetic lines to capture that uniqueness. 'Kingfishers' is arguably Hopkins' greatest expression of this individuality. Everything, the poem suggests, acts in a way that expresses or spells out the unique essence that exists within it.

GOD'S PRESENCE IN NATURE

'Kingfishers' also refers to another of Hopkins' central themes: the presence of God in nature. God has placed a unique essence inside each creature. Each creature expresses this essence through its actions and appearances. Therefore, God is present in every creature and object that makes up the natural world. A similar theme is evident in 'God's Grandeur', where Hopkins claims that the whole world is 'charged', or electrified, with God's presence.

In this poem, Hopkins draws a moral or religious lesson from his contemplation of the natural world. A similar move is made in 'Spring', 'God's Grandeur' and 'The Windhover'. In each of these poems, Hopkins moves from meditating on

nature's beauty to thinking about the sinfulness of man and the possibility of being saved from sin through God's grace. An interesting exception to this might be 'Thou Art Indeed Just, Lord', where the sight of the riverbanks becoming 'thick' with leaves makes Hopkins question God's fairness and justice.

SIN AND REDEMPTION

This poem emphasises the distinction between humanity and the rest of God's creations. Non-human creatures and objects come into this world with a simple purpose: to express through their actions and appearances the essence God has placed within them. Human beings have a higher purpose: to make Christ present in the world by behaving as a 'just man'.

Non-human creatures fulfil God's plan for them automatically, simply by existing. They have no choice in the matter. Human beings, on the other hand, have been given free will. We can choose to go against the purpose God has in mind for us by living in a sinful rather than a just manner.

The poem, therefore, calls on us to turn away from sin and live in a 'just' and 'graceful' fashion. We will fulfil God's plan for us. We will make Christ present in the world through our good deeds. We will seem 'lovely' in the eyes of God as we remind Him of his son.

This preoccupation with sin and redemption can be found throughout Hopkins' poetry. It is also evident in 'Spring', where Hopkins calls on God to preserve the innocence of children against the ravages of sin. We see it in 'The Windhover', where Hopkins celebrates the possibility of salvation through Christ. We also see it in 'God's Grandeur', where Hopkins calls on men to 'reck' God's laws and treat the world He has created for us with respect.

FORM

'As Kingfishers Catch Fire' is a perfectly formed Petrarchan sonnet. It has the typical Petrarchan rhyme scheme: ABBAABBA CDCDCD. It is divided into an octet (eight lines) and a sestet (six lines). There is a shift in focus between the octet and the sestet. In the octet, Hopkins discusses how every creature and object expresses its inner essence through its actions and appearances. The sestet, on the other hand, deals with issues of morality. These defining features of the Petrarchan sonnet are also evident in 'Spring' and 'God's Grandeur'.

VOCABULARY

Another signature feature of Hopkins' poetry is the usage of nouns as verbs. In line 7, the noun 'self' is transformed into the verb 'to self', meaning to be oneself or express one's inner qualities. In line 9, the noun 'justice' is transformed into the verb 'to justice', meaning to live in a just and righteous fashion according to God's law.

SYNTAX

Unusual sentence structure and compression are also signature features of Hopkins' poetry. For example, the line 'As tumbled over rim in roundy wells/ Stones ring' is structured in a peculiar manner and it seems be missing words that we might use in ordinary speech. If we were to convert this line into 'normal' speech' it might go something like this: 'Stones make a ringing sound when they are thrown over the rims of roundy wells'.

VERBAL MUSIC

'As Kingfishers Catch Fire' highlights Hopkins utterly unique poetic style. He believed that one of the main purposes of poetry was to describe an object's 'inscape', or unique qualities. In this poem, and in many others, he uses a series of complex sound effects in an attempt to capture the qualities of the objects he describes:

- In line 1, Hopkins uses assonance and alliteration to create a pleasant verbal music, reflecting the colourful splendour of kingfishers and dragonflies. Assonance is present through the repeated broad 'a' sound in 'dragonflies draw flame'. Alliteration, meanwhile, features through the repeated 'f' sound in 'fire', 'flies' and 'flame'.

- It could be argued that there is an 'onomatopoeic' quality to lines 2 and 3. The large number of broad-vowel sounds and the alliteration of 'rim into roundy', with its repeated 'r', create a hollow, echoing music that mimics the sound of a stone falling down a well.

- Onomatopoeia also occurs in lines 3–4. The repeated 'b' sound in 'bell' and 'bow', and the rhyme between 'swung' and 'tongue' gives these lines a loud, booming quality, suggestive of the ringing bell they describe.

METAPHOR

Hopkins uses a metaphor to describe the effect of sunlight striking the dragonflies' and kingfishers' bodies. It appears, he says, that these beautiful creatures have caught fire. Hopkins also uses a wonderful metaphor to describe the sound of the bell ringing, declaring that the bell is shouting out its name. The bell, he suggests, 'flings' its name throughout the surrounding countryside: 'each hung bell's/ Bow swung finds tongue to fling out broad its name'.

Spring

LINE BY LINE

LINES 1 TO 8

The poem's first eight lines focus on the delights of springtime, celebrating various features of the season. The poem begins by celebrating 'weeds'. It is probable that Hopkins has wildflowers such as daisies or dandelions in mind here. To Hopkins, these 'weeds' are not a pestilence or an irritation but have a beauty of their own that deserves to be praised. They are 'long and lovely and lush'.

Spring, Hopkins claims, is a 'strain' of the earth's early days. This word 'strain' can be read in a number of ways: in this instance, however, it can be best interpreted as a remembered snatch of melody, or a piece of song. Springtime, then, is a kind of 'faint echo' of the way the world was in its early Eden-like state. It reminds the speaker of a time before Adam defied God's will and ate the apple, before sin and wickedness entered the world.

The poem also celebrates the beauty of a thrush's eggs: 'Thrush's eggs look little low heavens'. Hopkins celebrates the delicate blue of the thrush's eggs. Their colour resembles that of the 'heavens' or sky above. But they are 'low' or close to the ground. The eggs, he declares, are 'little low heavens'. They are like little patches of sky that have somehow fallen to the ground.

The poem also celebrates the thrush's song, which floats through the forest, echoing from the trees' wooden boughs. It moves, as Hopkins puts it, 'through the echoing timber'. To Hopkins, then, the thrush's music is a thrilling feature of the springtime. He uses an unusual simile to describe this, comparing the notes of the thrush's song to lightning bolts: 'it strikes like lightnings to hear him sing'.

Hopkins next focuses on a pear tree, which is starting to put out leaves and blossoms: 'The glassy peartree leaves and blooms'. (The tree is described as 'glassy' because its fruit and leaves are shiny and glistening with morning dew.)

The trees' branches seem to 'brush' against the blue sky: 'they brush the descending blue'. To Hopkins, the sky's blue has a deep, rich texture: 'that blue is all in a rush with richness'.

Finally, Hopkins describes the newborn lambs that are racing about the place: 'The racing lambs too have fair their fling'. The lambs, it seems, are having a 'fling', a wild and happy time.

Spring, then is a beautiful time of year: 'Nothing is so beautiful as spring'. It is a time of lovely wildflowers, glistening fruit trees, of bird song and blue skies.

These lines emphasise the 'fertility' of springtime. Spring is depicted as a time of birth: newborn lambs gambol in the meadow and the thrush's nest is full of eggs from which chicks will soon emerge. It is a time of growth: wildflowers 'shoot', or burst, from the soil and blossoms grow on the pear tree. It is a time when the natural world seems full of 'richness', 'lushness' and abundance.

For Hopkins, spring is a time of renewal and regrowth. This is evident in his description of the thrush's music. The thrush's song, he says, cleanses the ears of those who hear it, just as one might clean a garment or a towel. Firstly, it 'rinses' our ears, washing away the noise and babble we have to put up with on a daily basis. Then it 'wrings' them, squeezing out any unpleasantness that might remain.

LINES 9 TO 14

Hopkins considers the meaning of spring, this time of abundance and beauty, of juice and joy: 'What is all this juice and all this joy?' Because spring is a time of freshness and newness, it makes Hopkins think of the earth's early days, bringing to mind the time when God had just made the world and man was still living in the garden of Eden: 'a strain of the earth's sweet being in the beginning/ In Eden garden'.

These thoughts of Eden lead Hopkins to consider children who are sinless and innocent, as Adam was before he ate the apple. Hopkins claims that 'innocent mind' and 'Mayday' exist in every child: 'Innocent mind and Mayday in girl and boy'. (To Hopkins, 'Mayday' is associated with purity and innocence, perhaps due to the fact that May is traditionally regarded as the month of the Virgin Mary.)

The speaker calls on Jesus to preserve the innocence of these children. He requests Christ to 'Have' and 'get' each boy and girl, to take them to Him before their innocence is destroyed: 'Have, get … Christ, lord … Innocent mind and Mayday in girl and boy'. Jesus, he says, must move to claim these children 'before' their innocent minds are corrupted by sin: 'before it cloy … Before it cloud … and sour with sinning'.

According to the speaker, the majority of these children are 'worthy the winning'. They are worth the effort it would take for Christ to 'win' them, to take them to Him and preserve their sinless nature: 'Most, O maid's child, thy choice and worthy the winning'. (Jesus is referred to as a 'maid's child' because he was given birth to by a maid, or virgin.)

THE BEAUTY OF NATURE

Hopkins was extremely sensitive and responsive to the natural world, and like many of his poems, 'Spring' celebrates the delights of nature. It celebrates deep-blue skies, the cleansing music of a thrush's song, glistening eggs and pear trees. A similarly ecstatic response to nature's beauties can be found in 'As Kingfishers Catch Fire', 'The Windhover', 'Pied Beauty' and 'Inversnaid'.

Perhaps above all else, spring is depicted as a time of fertility: of birth, growth and abundance. It is a time when nature can offer us a cleansing sense of personal rebirth and renewal. (This is evident when Hopkins describes his ears being 'rinsed' and 'wrung' dry by the thrush's song.) For Hopkins spring is such a magical time of year that it brings to mind the Garden of Eden. In springtime, the world is no less than a kind of paradise.

SIN AND REDEMPTION

Hopkins' poetry is greatly concerned with sin and redemption. In this poem he calls on Christ to preserve the innocence of each girl and boy, to take these children to Him before sin can corrupt their perfect natures. The notion of Christ as our redeemer, the one who saves us from sin and damnation, is also present in 'Felix Randal' and in 'The Windhover'. In 'Felix Randal', Hopkins refers to Christ as that which 'reprieves' or 'ransoms' us from sin. In 'The Windhover', Christ is depicted as a knight, or 'chevalier', who does battle on our behalf against the forces of sin.

The conclusion of 'Spring', however, is a little vague. It is unclear exactly how Hopkins wants Christ to preserve the innocence of each child. Does the speaker want Jesus to keep the children young forever, to preserve them from the guilts and complications of adulthood? Yet surely Hopkins realises that everyone must grow up eventually, that we cannot spend our lives in the blissful innocence and naiveté of childhood. It is more likely that Hopkins wishes the children might grow up to be adults but remain 'childlike' in that they will be somehow free of sin. It is this remarkable and miraculous task that Hopkins calls on God to undertake.

FORM

Like many of Hopkins' poems, this is a Petrarchan sonnet. It has the typical Petrarchan rhyme scheme: ABBAABBA CDCDCD. It is divided into an octet (eight lines) and a sestet (six lines). There is a shift in focus between the octet and the sestet. In the octet, Hopkins discusses the beauty and joy of springtime. The sestet, on the other hand, deals with issues of innocence and sin. These defining features of the Petrarchan sonnet are also evident in 'God's Grandeur'.

SYNTAX

The syntax that the poet uses in lines 11 to 14 is very unusual — the words are ordered in a very different way from how such a sentence would be structured in everyday speech. The speaker asks Christ to preserve the innocence of the children before it is destroyed: 'Have, get, before it cloy,/ Before it cloud, Christ, lord, and sour with sinning,/ Innocent mind and Mayday in girl and boy'. Were we to express this in normal speech, we might say something along the lines of 'Take hold of the innocent minds of all girls and boys before they are clouded, cloyed and soured with sinning'.

VERBAL MUSIC

In this sonnet, Hopkins sets out to write lines that are as breezy and energetic as the springtime itself. Assonance and alliteration contribute greatly to the poem's pleasant or 'euphonious' musical effect. We see alliteration in lines 2 and 3, for example, with their repeated 'l' sounds (long, lovely, lush, little and low). Assonance, meanwhile, features in 'racing lambs', with its repeated 'a' sound. There are many more examples scattered throughout the poem, combining to make a rich verbal music that suggests the lushness and abundance of springtime.

Hopkins uses a number of musical effects to capture the power and energy of the thrush's song. The phrase 'echoing timber', for instance, has a strangely onomatopoeic quality, in which we can almost hear the thrush's singing echoing from the tree trunks. The use of powerful monosyllabic verbs such as 'rinse', 'wring' and 'strike' capture some of the energy Hopkins hears in the thrush's singing. It has also been suggested that the phrase 'sour with sinning' is onomatopoeic, the repeated 's' sounds bringing to mind the hissing of the snake in the Garden of Eden.

IMAGERY

Hopkins uses an interesting metaphor to describe the weeds in line 2, referring to them as 'wheels'. It is possible to imagine the central portion of the wildflower as the wheel's 'hub' and its petals as the 'spokes'. A powerful simile, meanwhile, is used to describe the thrush's song, with Hopkins declaring that it strikes the ear like lightning. Perhaps the most beautiful image in the poem is the description of how the thrush's eggs resemble the sky above them. Hopkins memorably refers to them as 'little low heavens', comparing them to tiny patches of sky that have somehow settled on the ground.

'Spring' is full of images of movement in which Hopkins uses verbs that capture the freshness and energy of springtime. The weeds, we're told, 'shoot' out of the earth. The thrush's song 'strikes', 'rinses' and 'wrings'. Lambs 'race' through the meadows. Even the blue sky is depicted as being full of movement. It is 'descending … in a rush' as if it were pouring down from heaven. ⊠

Pied Beauty

LINE BY LINE

In this poem, Hopkins marvels at the variety of the natural world. In particular, the poem praises God for the existence of things that are 'dappled'. If something is dappled, it means that it has spots or patches of colour. The poet lists some dappled things that impress him:

- Skies that contain a variety of colours ('couple-colour'). These skies are compared to a 'brinded cow'. Brinded means having a grey or brownish streak or a patchy colouring. Hopkins is likely thinking of skies with streaks of clouds of different shades.
- The rose-coloured 'moles' or spots that feature on the skin of the trout. These rose-coloured moles are dotted all over the trout ('in stipple').
- Chestnuts that fall and crack open to reveal their inner colours. These are compared to coals freshly taken from the fire, black and glowing red.
- The variety of colours that feature on 'finches' wings'.
- The different forms of land that make up the landscape.

Hopkins thinks of the way the countryside is divided up into plots of farmland, with different plots being used for different things. He thinks of the 'fold' or enclosure for animals. (A 'fold' could also be a hill.) He also mentions 'fallow' land, land that has been ploughed and left unseeded.

Finally, the poet speaks of all the 'trades' that people have and the variety of equipment and clothing they use: 'And all trades, their gear and tackle and trim'.

In the last five lines of the poem, Hopkins marvels at the incredible variety of God's creation. He wonders how it is possible for God to do what He has done: 'who knows how?' God has created such a variety of things and yet each thing is perfectly beautiful and unique.

God creates or 'fathers-forth' things that contrast ('counter'), are unique, rare ('spare') and 'strange'. He brings into existence all that is capable of sudden change ('fickle') and everything that is 'freckled'. There are fast things, slow things, things that are 'sweet' and things that are 'sour'. There are things that glow and sparkle ('adazzle'), and there are things that are dull and 'dim'. Every individual thing is perfectly beautiful and requires no alteration: 'whose beauty is past change'. For all this God should be praised.

THEMES

THE BEAUTY OF NATURE

The poem praises the great diversity and beauty of the natural world. Hopkins celebrates the wonderful colours and textures that are to be found in nature. Everything from the sky to the fields, from the smallest detail on the wing of a finch to the varied plots of farmland are included. In contrast to 'God's Grandeur', the poet even celebrates the various work that man does: 'And all trades, their gear and tackle and trim'. 'Pied Beauty' does not set man apart from nature and criticise him for his lack of care. Instead, Hopkins celebrates all that exists on the planet and marvels at the wonderful variety.

GOD'S PRESENCE IN NATURE

Once again, Hopkins perceives the work of God in the natural world and celebrates His greatness. He marvels at God's creation and glories in the fact that there is such variety in the world. The wonderful variety of colours, shades, tastes and textures is testament to God's genius and goodness.

What is particularly praiseworthy is the fact that God could create such diverse things: 'things counter, original, spare, strange'. The poem suggests that, though there is great variety and contrast evident in the world, everything ultimately comes together to form a perfect whole. This is the genius of God. Hopkins coins a special verb to describe God's creative powers: 'He fathers-forth' all these amazing things and combines them. It also fascinates the poet how the world can be in a constant state of flux, yet God never changes: 'He fathers-forth whose beauty is past change'. How God does this incredible work is a mystery ('who knows how?') but warrants our praise: 'Praise Him'.

FORM

'Pied Beauty' is an example of what Hopkins termed the 'curtal sonnet'. The curtal sonnet is a form invented by Hopkins and used in three of his poems. It is an eleven-line (or, more accurately, ten-and-a-half-line) sonnet. The first six lines replace the traditional octet, and the last four-and-a-half lines replace the sestet. It is essentially a reduced Petrarchan sonnet.

VOCABULARY

The poem features a number of neologisms or newly coined words or phrases. Hopkins coins a special verb to describe God's creative powers: 'He fathers-forth' all these amazing things and combines them. He also uses the word 'adazzle' to describe the brightness or gleam of certain objects.

VERBAL MUSIC

There is a joyous word music to 'Pied Beauty', reflecting the poem's light-hearted atmosphere of celebration. Typically, Hopkins makes extensive use of assonance and alliteration, lending the poem a pleasant euphonious effect. Line 9 provides a wonderful example of alliteration, with its repeated 's' sounds – 'swift, slow, sweet, sour' – generating a pleasant sound. A similar musical effect is created by 'Fresh-firecoal' and 'fathers-forth', with their repeated 'f' sounds.

Assonance features in lines 3 and 4 in phrases such as 'rose-moles', with its repeated 'o' sound, and 'finches-wings', with its repeated 'i' sound. The phrase 'couple-colour' in line 2 employs both assonance and alliteration, with its repeated 'c' sound and its repeated broad vowels. A similar effect is created by the playful combination of 'fickle' and 'freckled' in line 8, with their repeated 'f' and 'ck' sounds.

This feast of assonance and alliteration reflects the joy with which Hopkins responds to nature's variety. The poem's music, however, is also intended to help us imagine the beauty of 'dappled things'. In conjunction with the vividness of Hopkins' descriptions, it is intended to bring their vividness and uniqueness to the mind of the reader.

The Windhover

LINE BY LINE

THE BIRD

When the poet was on his morning walk he 'caught' or caught sight of a falcon soaring through the sky. He was clearly impressed by this fierce and powerful creature.

- The falcon, he says, is 'morning's minion'. In this instance the word 'minion' suggests the darling or favourite of a powerful noble.
- The falcon, he says, is the crown prince or 'dauphin' of the kingdom of daylight: 'king-/dom of daylight's dauphin'.
- The falcon, he says, has been 'drawn' by the dawn. This might suggest that the early morning light has attracted or 'drawn' the falcon into the sky to hunt. It also suggests how the dawn-light makes the falcon visible, almost as if the dawn were sketching or drawing the bird as it hovers in the sky.
- 'Dapple', one of Hopkins' favourite words, means being spotted or patterned with colour. In this instance it may describe the bird's feathers, the colours of the dawn, or both.

> The phrase 'rolling level underneath him steady' is like an adjective describing the thermals of air on which the falcon glides. These air-currents are sometimes rolling and sometimes level as the falcon passes over them. Yet they remain firm and steady underneath him as they support him on his journey through the sky.

The falcon, then, is associated with light; with morning, dawn and daylight. It is also presented as a noble or regal being, as a courtly 'minion' or a princely 'dauphin'. This is reinforced by the word 'kingdom' being split so that the word 'king-' is left hanging at the end of the first line.

THE BIRD'S MOVEMENT

The falcon is compared to a horseman or a jockey. For it rides through the sky on currents of air: 'in his riding/ Of the ... air'. In its movement the bird exhibits great poise and control, the verb 'stride' suggesting its power and confidence: 'striding/ High there'.

The bird 'rung' or spiralled around the sky, using one of its wings to control this circling pattern of flight. Just as a rider uses reins to control his mount, so the bird uses this 'wimpling' or folded wing to coax and manipulate the air through which it flies: 'rung upon the rein of a wimpling wing'. To the poet it seems that the bird moves in 'ecstasy', as if it were overcome with pleasure at its own strength and power.

The falcon then flies off on a sudden swinging arc over the landscape: 'then off, off forth on a swing'. It cruises away in a smooth and even fashion, reminding the poet of a skater effortlessly gliding over ice and expertly taking a curved 'bow bend': 'As a skate's heel seeps smooth on a bow bend'.

Its flight path takes it directly into a 'big wind'. It scorns or rebuffs the danger posed by this challenging gale. And its strength and skill (its 'hurl and gliding') allow it to make progress against the breeze's force.

POET'S REACTION TO THE BIRD

The poet suggests that he has been suffering from some sort of depression or mental anguish. His heart, he tells us, has been in 'hiding'. We get the impression that the poet's heart or psyche has been covered by a cloud of despair. Or maybe he's felt a terrible inner numbness, an inability to experience any emotion at all. Or maybe he's felt intimated and repressed by life, feeling that he must hide his heart away and avoid expressing his true feelings and personality.

In any event, witnessing the falcon's glorious flight has lifted his spirits. His heart is 'stirred' by this exhilarating sight, filling him with energy, hope and excitement.

The poet associates the falcon with achievement and mastery: 'the achieve of the mastery of the thing'. This may refer to the falcon's own achievement and mastery, to the strength and skill it displays as it powers through the sky. However, it might also refer to God, who displayed great achievement and mastery by creating the falcon in the first place.

THE FALCON AND CHRIST

The poet lists various aspects of the bird's sweeping arc into the big wind. He mentions the bird's physical beauty and the 'plume' of its feathers. He mentions the 'air' on which it glides and the stunning 'act' or action it undertakes. He mentions the 'valour' it displays in tackling the big wind and the 'pride' it seems to exhibit in its own power and control. For the poet all these things 'Buckle' or combine to create one extraordinary moment of flight.

The bird's struggle with the big wind reminds the poet of Christ, specifically of how Christ struggled with and overcame sin at the

> The poet may have been inspired to make this comparison by the many medieval paintings that depict Christ as just such a knight battling the dragons of sin and death. The falcon, like the knights of old, is depicted as being regal and noble. It rides air-thermals the way a knight rides a horse. Even its 'plume' of feathers recalls the decorations knights would often wear on their helmets.

> The word buckle is unusual because it has two very different meanings. It can mean to join together (as in how the various aspects of the falcon's flight combine in one glorious image) or it can mean to fall apart (as in how Christ buckled on the cross) or in how the falcon might ultimately buckle in its assault on the big wind. 'Buckle' might also suggest the suit of armour a knight dons before going into battle, reinforcing the image of Christ as a chevalier battling against sin.

moment of the crucifixion. Both events involved great courage and great beauty:

• Just as the bird exhibits courage in challenging the gale, so Christ exhibited courage in allowing himself to be sacrificed for humanity's wrongdoings.

• The crucifixion, like the bird's flight, was a beautiful thing. For Hopkins, this was the moment that saved the human race from sin and allowed us to become right with God once more.

The crucifixion, however, was of far greater significance than the flight of any bird. It involved suffering that was a 'billion/ times' more dangerous and beauty that was a 'billion/ times' lovelier.

The poet calls out to Christ as: 'O my chevalier!' Chevalier is another word for knight, suggesting that the poet views Christ as a mounted warrior riding into battle on his behalf and indeed on behalf of all mankind. The poet describes how during the crucifixion, fire seemed to burst forth from Christ's broken body: 'And the fire that breaks from thee then'. The poet doesn't mean this literally. Rather the fire symbolises the extraordinary magnificence of this moment, one that would change forever the nature of man's relationship with God.

BEAUTY THROUGH SUFFERING

It's 'No wonder', the poet declares, that Christ exhibited his greatest beauty, courage and magnificence when he was broken on the cross. For many things are at their most magnificent when worn or broken.

A ploughman's utterly monotonous and plodding labour (his 'sheer plod') turns a field into 'sillion', into furrows of cut earth. Though the earth has been broken it has also been refreshed and its newly exposed minerals 'shine' in the sun. This line might also refer to the plough itself, which shines as it is worn and polished by endless use.

The poet also thinks of dead emb[ers] a stove or fireplace. The embers [fall] from the fireplace and hit the gr[ound] impact they 'gall themselves' or break [apart and] shatter to reveal tiny sparks of deepest red an[d] gall themselves, and gash gold-vermillion'. Th[ese embers] exhibit their greatest beauty just as they brea[k]

THEMES

THE BEAUTY OF NATURE

Like many of Hopkins' poems, 'The Windhover' reveals the poet's love of the natural world.

The poet relishes the sight of the falcon, which is depicted as a fierce and dangerous hunter. The falcon, then, possesses a 'Brute beauty', beauty of a brutal and ferocious kind. This contrasts with the gentler aspects of nature celebrated in 'Spring' and 'Pied Beauty'.

The falcon is presented as a regal being, reminiscent of a knight or prince. It exhibits poise, confidence and control as it goes 'striding' through the sky, manipulating the air-thermals on which it cruises. It is also an elegant creature, gliding smoothly and crisply through the air. To the poet the falcon seems caught up in an 'ecstasy' as if it relished its own strength, power and control. Perhaps most notable of all is the bird's 'valour' or bravery, which we see in its willingness to test itself against the 'big wind'.

Hopkins was unusually sensitive to natural beauty. In this poem, the mere sight of a falcon 'stirs' his heart, leaving exhilarated. It lifts the terrible gloom that had The poet is simply blown away by the the falcon's soaring flight, by the in which it operates.

kins to ponder
strength, bravery
rifice Christ made
aved mankind from

ers in
umble
ound. At
part. They
d gold: 'Fall,
embers, then,
and fall apart.

SIN AND REDEMPTION

Like many of Hopkins' poems, 'The Windhover' deals with the theme of sin and redemption.

In this instance Hopkins focuses especially on the crucifixion. For Hopkins, as for many Christians, this was the greatest moment in human history. For through his sacrifice on the cross Christ made up for the great sin that had stained humanity since the beginning of time. His agonising death afforded human beings the possibility of being right with God once more.

For Hopkins, the falcon's charge into the big wind recalls the bravery and beauty of Christ's sacrifice, though of course the crucifixion was a 'billion/ times' more significant that the bird's journey through the sky. We can imagine the bravery and danger involved in Christ's terrible death. It might seem strange, however, to describe this bloody event as lovely.

Yet for Hopkins this was a magnificently beautiful spectacle. For it meant that mankind was redeemed from sin and that the very fabric of our relationship with God had been altered. He even imagines flames bursting from Christ's ailing body as it hangs there on the cross, as if to mark the grave significance of this occasion. He points out that Christ's body, like many other aspects of the physical world, was at its most beautiful when at its most broken.

The poem, as we've seen, utilises the medieval depiction of Christ as a knight or 'Chevalier', riding into battle against the forces of sin and death. Tellingly, Hopkins addresses him as 'my chevalier' since he goes into battle on our behalf, as our representative, just as a medieval knight would fight for the honour of his Lord or Lady.

FORM

The poem is written in the form of a Petrarchan sonnet. It has the typical Petrarchan rhyme scheme: ABBAABBA CDCDCD. It is divided into an octet (eight lines) and a sestet (six lines). There is a shift in focus between the octet and the sestet. In the octet, the poet is concerned with the falcon. In the sestet, however, the focus shifts to Christ.

VOCABULARY

One of the distinguishing features of Hopkins' poetry is his use of long adjectival phrases. A number of these occur in 'The Windhover'. For example, in the opening line he uses the compound adjective 'dapple-dawn-drawn' to describe the falcon. In the third line he uses a particularly long phrase to describe the currents of the air, describing these as 'rolling level underneath him steady'.

The poem also features some old, obscure vocabulary. For example, the poet refers to the falcon as the 'dauphin' of the morning and later on to Christ as his 'chevalier', both archaic terms for certain royal figures.

Hopkins also coins a word to capture the rich texture of the soil, referring to it as 'sillion'.

SYNTAX

Hopkins often compresses sentences in his poems, omitting words that we would ordinarily use in everyday speech. Line 12, for example, 'sheer plod makes plough down sillion/ Shine' converted into 'normal' speech might go something like this: 'The sheer plod of the farmer pushing his plough down the field makes the soil or sillion shine'.

SPRUNG RHYTHM

Hopkins' poetry features a unique form of meter that he called 'sprung rhythm', which requires an equal number of stressed syllables per line, but the number of unstressed syllables can vary (and therefore so can the line length). The opening line of the poem, with its regular stressed and unstressed syllables, is very close to the standard iambic pentameter meter but the second line is a perfect example of Hopkins' use of sprung rhythm: 'dom of daylight's dauphin, dapple-dawn-drawn Falcon, in his riding'. It features the same number of stressed syllables as the first line, but a greater number of unstressed syllables.

VERBAL MUSIC

Hopkins uses incredible word play to relay his joy and excitement, and also to express the action of the bird. Taking even the first three lines, the music of the poem is evident. It opens with the soft alliteration of 'm's and 'n's and with the assonance of the 'o's. This is followed by a succession of 'i's – 'this morning morning's minion'. This fluid movement, broken by a comma, is succeeded by the alliteration of 'd's in a similar fashion: 'king-/ dom of daylight's dauphin, dapple-dawn-drawn Falcon'.

The alliteration and controlled use of commas in the first five lines work to give a sense of excitement. They also enrich the image of the bird as a noble horseman, which develops throughout the poem, and you can feel the clip-clop of a horse in the staccato rhythm. This eases as the flight of the bird takes hold. Smooth 's's and rolling 'r's begin to dominate, set against 't's. The lines reveal both the falcon's majestic mastery of the air and the poet's breathless admiration.

In the last two lines of the poem, Hopkins again uses alliteration to great effect. The soft 's' sounds of 'sillion/ Shine' works perfectly when describing the smooth beauty of the earth. And the slightly harsher 'g' sounds of the final line enhances the description of the embers as they fall and break.

IMAGERY

The poem uses a number of powerful images to illustrate the falcon's flight. There is the metaphor of the 'rein' illustrating the controlled flight of the bird as it spirals in the air. The poem also features the wonderful simile of a 'skate's heel' sweeping smoothly across the ice. Again, the image is one of masterful control and elegance.

The bird itself ultimately becomes a powerful metaphor for Christ and His noble actions. Hopkins fuses the falcon and Christ in the sestet of the poem. He then uses some wonderful imagery to reveal the magnificent beauty of Christ. Both the image of the earth rubbed smooth by the plough's blades and the embers exploding in dramatic colour are so wonderfully and vividly portrayed.

Inversnaid

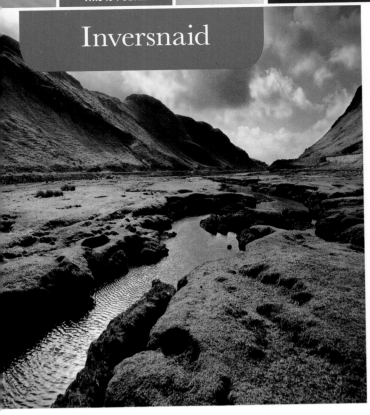

metaphor to describe this foam, comparing it to a fleece of white wool.

We're told that the foaming water 'Flutes' as it nears the lake that is its 'home' or final destination: 'Flutes and low to the lake falls home'. The word 'flute' may refer to the musical instrument, suggesting that the water 'Flutes' or makes a pleasant musical sound as it meets the lake. Or it may refer to flutes as in champagne glasses, suggesting that the foam breaks into fizzy flute-shaped rivulets as it finally falls toward the lake.

Hopkins captures the stream's strength and power by comparing it to a galloping horse. The stream's surface bucks, rocks and tosses like the muscled back of a race horse galloping at full pelt. The brown colour of its surface, as we've seen, is compared to that of the hair on a horse's back. Its fleecy foam meanwhile can be visualised as the horse's tossing mane.

STANZA 2

Hopkins' attention now focuses on a kind of mini-whirlpool that has formed midway down the stream's path. The water in this pool is so dark that Hopkins describes it as 'pitchblack'. It seems unpleasantly thick and soupy, as if it were a broth or stew: 'the broth/ Of a pool so pitchblack'.

On the surface of this pool he sees a froth that is brownish 'fawn' in colour. He compares this surface foam to pool's cap or 'bonnet'. It is puffed out and tossed around the place by the breeze across the pool's surface: 'A windpuff-bonnet of fáwn-fróth'. The foam moves on the surface of the whirlpool in a kind of spiral pattern before being sucked down into its depths: it 'Turns and twindles'. ('Twindles' is a verb that Hopkins made up himself, meaning to 'twist' and 'dwindle' at the same time.)

This black little whirlpool is described as 'féll-frówning'. The fact that it is 'frówning' suggests its depressing, gloomy appearance. In Hopkins the word 'fell' usually means malevolent suggesting its gloomy pitch-black waters are sinister, evil and threatening.

To Hopkins, then, this little whirlpool that goes 'round and round' is a bleak and terrible sight. Contemplating it causes him to be overcome by sorrow. His mind is left 'drowning' in 'Despair' just as a little woodland creature might become trapped in the whirlpool before drowning in its black waters.

STANZA 3

At times the stream's banks are so close together that they almost

LINE BY LINE

STANZA 1

This poem was inspired by a trip Hopkins made to the Scottish Highlands. He was very taken with the wild beauty of this landscape and in this poem celebrates the movement of a stream, or 'burn', as it flows down the hillside to the lake below. Its surface is a dark or 'darksome' shade of brown, one that Hopkins compares to the colour of the hair on a horse's back.

The stream, we're told in line 2, goes 'roaring down' the slope, suggesting the power and force with which it thunders to the lake below. Its course is described as a 'highroad', suggesting the great height from which it rushes. Its travels this path in a 'rollrock' fashion: it twists and turns, rocks and rolls; changing directions constantly as it is deflected by the obstacles in its path.

The stream passes through 'coops', a word Hopkins coined to describe enclosed hollows, and 'combs', which he defined as uneven and rippling stretches of water. Foam forms on the water's surface as it navigates these features: 'In coop and in comb the fleece of his foam'. Hopkins uses a highly visual

The water 'Flutes' before it enters the lake that is its final destination. The word 'flute', in this instance, is open to two different interpretations:
• We can interpret 'flute' in terms of the musical instrument. On this reading, Hopkins is suggesting that the sound of the roaring water is more pleasant and enjoyable than the music of a flute or any other instrument.
• 'Flute' can also be taken as describing the shape of the stream's course. It is like an upside-down champagne glass, thinner at its source way up on the hillside, broader at its bottom where it enters the lake.

form a 'groin' or little dam. The stream 'threads' or weaves its way through these obstructions and continues down the hillside: 'the groins of the braes that the brook treads through'. The banks by these narrows are sprinkled, or 'degged', with dew. When light shines on the dew-covered grass it creates a multicoloured or 'dappled' effect: 'Degged with dew, dappled with dew/ Are the groins of the braes.

Lines 11 and 12 focus on some of the plant life that blooms beside the stream, and that its waters nourish and sustain. Hopkins mentions packs or clusters of wiry heather ('heathpacks') and 'flitches' or thin strands of fern: 'Wiry heathpacks, flitches of fern'.

An ash tree 'sits over' the brook. The tree, we're told, is beautiful or 'beadbonny'. It's beautiful or 'bonny' because beads of water hang on its branches, having been splashed up from the gushing stream below: 'And the beadbonny ash that sits over the burn'. In this stanza Hopkisn uses a number of words from the Scottish dialect, including 'braes', 'degged', 'bonny' and 'burn', which reinforce our sense of the poem's Highland setting.

STANZA 4

The poet is well aware that places like Inversnaid are under threat in our industrial age. 'What would the world be, once bereft/ Of wet and wildness?', he asks, wondering what this earth will resemble once it's 'bereft' or deprived of such beautiful wilderness locations. The answer, of course, is that the world would be a terrible place without 'wet and wildness', without unspoilt countryside and unpolluted rivers.

'Let them be left,/ O let them be left', he says, pleading for such areas of unspoiled countryside to be left alone by industry and development. The poem's last line, therefore, is a defiant cry for the wilderness to survive long into the future: 'Long live the weeds and the wilderness yet'.

Each stanza of 'Inversnaid' deals with a different theme. The poem twists and turns from subject to subject like the meandering river it describes. The opening stanza describes the power and energy of the brook as it rushes down the hill. The second stanza, meanwhile, focuses on a dark whirlpool that interrupts the river's flow. The last line of this stanza, with the repetition of 'rounds' and repeated 'o' sounds, mimics the swirl of the water. The third stanza marks another change of direction, celebrating the fertility the brook brings to the wilderness around it. The sprightly rhythm used in these lines reflects this life and energy. With the final stanza, the poem's focus shifts yet again as it becomes a desperate environmentalist plea for the wilderness to be left alone. The poet's use of a rhetorical question and repetition reveal his concern and desperation.

THEMES

THE BEAUTY OF NATURE

Once again, Hopkins reveals the beauty and splendour of the natural world. He captures the colours and the textures of the burn as it courses over the rocks. The water is 'horseback brown' and the foam a 'windpuff-bonnet'. We get a sense of the power and energy of nature as the water roars and falls. As in 'The Windhover', the poet uses images of a horse to capture the brute strength of nature.

However, unlike poems such as 'The Windhover' and 'Pied Beauty', which also describe the beauty and magnificence of the natural world, 'Inversnaid' contains a darkness that is lacking in both. The 'pool' is 'so pitchblack' and it 'rounds and rounds Despair to drowning'. Though the poet can admire the landscape that he observes and make a heartfelt plea for its preservation, there is a darkness at the centre of the poem, something disturbing in the description of the water that was absent in earlier poems such as 'Pied Beauty'. The poet has discovered a darkness lurking within the natural world that seems to chime with his own inner despair.

ENVIRONMENTALISM

Though Hopkins wrote a long time ago he often exhibits an environmentalism fitting to our own age. We see this in the poem's final stanza where he points out what an unimaginably terrible place the world would be without such places of wild and unspoilt beauty. He concludes with a desperate plea that locations like 'Inversnaid' be spared by industry, building and development: 'Let them be left, let them be left'. As we know today, however, such pleas all too often go ignored in the name of progress.

MENTAL SUFFERING

The poem looks forward to Hopkins' 'terrible sonnets' such as 'No worst, there is none' and 'I wake and feel the fell of dark' in which he explores personal feelings of incredible despair and devastation. Though stanzas 1 and 3 praise nature's splendour, it is a celebration that is tinged with sadness.

The burn is fertile and productive, its waters nourishing the plant life that grows around it. (Hopkins presents the

THEMES

brook's role of 'fertilising' the soil around it in explicitly sexual terms, saying it treads through the 'groins' of its banks.) Hopkins, on the other hand, considered his life barren and infertile. This infertility takes three forms:

- Firstly, he was sexually infertile, forbidden by his priestly vows from having children or a loving sexual relationship. (Hopkins' feelings on this subject are evident in 'Thou Art Indeed Just, Lord', where he refers to himself as 'Time's eunuch'.)

- Secondly, he was artistically infertile. The heavy workload of his clerical duties left him little time or energy to write his poetry, and cut him off from nature – his chief source of inspiration.

- Finally, he felt that this life as a whole was barren and empty, as the parish and teaching work that consumed so much of his resources left him frustrated and unfulfilled. There is something almost mocking about the beauty and fertility of the Inversnaid landscape, then, as it seems to taunt Hopkins with the very things he longs for so much but are denied him.

'Inversnaid' was written at a time when Hopkins was on the verge of the depression and despair that would characterise the last period of his life. He had sacrificed an incredible amount for God and had served His Church faithfully only to be rewarded with mental anguish and physical illness. (The doubts and inner turmoil this inspired are movingly documented in 'Thou art indeed just, Lord' and the other 'terrible sonnets'.)

Perhaps the poem's central image, then, is 'the pool so pitchblack' – the little whirlpool in the brook's path that fills Hopkins with such horrified fascination. It's as if staring into its murky 'fell-frowning' depths gives him some premonition of the personal abyss into which he soon will fall, the despair in which he will soon find himself drowning.

FORM

The poem consists of four four-line stanzas each featuring an AABB rhyme scheme

VOCABULARY

Hopkins is famous for playing with language. He often invented or coined new words to convey his desired meaning. In the second stanza he uses the word 'twindles' to capture the water's unique movement.

The poet is also renowned for the way he combines existing words to create new compound words. For example, he uses the word 'rollrock' in line 2 to convey the rolling of the water over the rocks and the word 'pitchblack' to describe the darkness of the pool. In line 5 he combines the words 'fáwn' and 'fróth' to capture the colour of the foam that the churning water creates.

VERBAL MUSIC

As with so many of Hopkins' poems, 'Inversnaid' is rich with musical effects. The poem's first stanza pulses with a powerful rhythm, capturing the freshness and energy of the brook as it rushes down the slope. Alliteration predominates in this stanza. We see this with the repeated 'r' sounds in line 2: 'rollrock highroad roaring down'. Line 3, also, is rich in alliteration with the repeated 'c' sound in 'coop and in comb', and the 'f' sound in 'fleece of his foam'.

This preponderance of alliteration contributes to the vibrancy of the stanza's music, as does the internal rhyme in line 3 between 'comb' and 'foam'. A similar vibrancy is evident in stanza 3. Once again, alliteration is used extensively. We see it in the repeated 'd' sound in 'Degged with dew, dappled with dew', the 'br' sound in 'braes of the brook', and the 'f' sound in 'flitches of fern'.

Felix Randal

This poem was written in the early 1880s when Hopkins was working as a priest in various parishes between Liverpool and Manchester. Hopkins was horrified by the circumstances of the poor in those industrial cities, which were polluted, dirty and ridden with disease. This poem was inspired by the death of one of his parishioners, a thirty-one-year-old blacksmith. (The real-life blacksmith was called Felix Spencer. It is unclear why Hopkins felt compelled to use a different name in his poem.)

LINE BY LINE

LINES 1 TO 4

As part of Hopkins' priestly duties, he tended to the sick. One man he tended to was Felix Randal, a 'farrier' or blacksmith. Hopkins had heard the news of Felix's death: 'Felix Randal the farrier, O he is dead then?' Hopkins' duty of care to Felix is now at an end: 'My duty all ended'.

Hopkins recalls Felix growing ill. The blacksmith was a big, strong and handsome man: ' big-boned and hardy-handsome'. Yet as his illness progressed, he began 'pining', or wasting away. Hopkins describes Felix's body as his 'mould of man', suggesting that it was crafted by God in the same mould as that of all other men, according to His likeness.

By the end, Felix was desperately sick in both mind and body. His powers of reasoning failed and his mind began to ramble: 'reason rambled'. Four different diseases, each of them 'fatal', had infected his body: 'some fatal four disorders, fleshed there'. Hopkins describes how the different diseases 'contended' or competed with one another to finish Felix off. The strong and big-boned blacksmith was destroyed by illness: 'Sickness broke him'.

LINES 5 TO 8

At the beginning of his illness, Felix cursed God for making him sick: 'Impatient, he cursed at first'. However, when Hopkins anointed him as part of the Last Rites, he mended his ways and made his peace with God: 'but mended/ Being anointed and all'. Hopkins would come to Felix's house and give him communion: 'since I had our sweet reprieve and ransom/ Tendered to him'. Because of this, in the months before his death the blacksmith's heart became 'heavenlier' or holier. He began to focus in his heart and mind upon God and the next life: 'a heavenlier heart began some/ Months earlier'.

LINES 9 TO 11

Hopkins thinks about the relationship between priests and the sick people they visit. The sick person becomes close ('endeared') to the priest, but the priest also becomes close to the sick person: 'This seeing the sick endears them to us, us too it endears'. Hopkins had a positive effect on Felix, comforting him as he lay weeping in agony. But Felix also had an effect on Hopkins. The sight of the blacksmith crying touched the poet in a deep and meaningful way: 'thy tears that touched my heart'.

LINES 12 TO 14

Hopkins thinks of Felix in his prime, in the years before he became ill. In these years, Felix was more 'boisterous'. He was loud, rough and noisy. He was as physically powerful as any of his 'peers' – as any other blacksmith in the area. Hopkins thinks of him working at his forge, 'fettling' or shaping a horseshoe for a workhorse:

When thou at the random grim forge, powerful amidst peers
Did fettle for the great grey drayhorse his bright and battering sandal!

Felix's forge is described as 'random' because like a dry-stone wall, it is made from uncut, irregular stones. In those years of strength and health Felix never predicted or 'forethought' that he would end up broken by sickness, that he would spend his last days weeping in agony as he wasted away. All such thoughts of sickness and death were 'far' from the mind of this powerfully strong and handsome blacksmith.

FORM

Like many of Hopkins' poems, this is a Petrarchan sonnet. It has the typical Petrarchan rhyme scheme: ABBAABBA CCDCCD. It is divided into an octet (eight lines) and a sestet (six lines). There is a shift in focus between the octet and the sestet. In the octet, Hopkins describes the course of Felix's illness. It could be argued that in the sestet he meditates on the significance of these events.

VOCABULARY

Hopkins was a great lover of language and delighted in using unusual words in his poetry. In line 8 the poet asks God to grant Felix his rest in the next life, whatever offences he might have committed in this one. Hopkins uses the phrase 'all road ever', which was a Lancashire term meaning 'whatever'. It has also been suggested that 'sandal' was a Lancashire slang term for horseshoe.

Hopkins also uses some terms that had all but disappeared from English is his own day: 'farrier' for blacksmith, 'fettle' for shape and 'random', which means built from uneven blocks. It could also be argued that he uses the word 'boisterous' in its medieval sense – meaning huge or massive – in reference to the youthful Felix's big-boned physique. 'Heavenlier', on the other hand, is a neologism, a word Hopkins has made up himself.

VERBAL MUSIC

Like most Hopkins poems, 'Felix Randal' is littered with assonance and alliteration. We see alliteration in 'mould of man', with its repeated 'm' sound, in 'big-boned and hardy-handsome', with its repeated 'b' and 'h' sounds, in 'fatal four', with its repeated 'f' sound, in 'reprieve and ransom', with its repeated 'r' sound, and in 'bright and battering', with its repeated 'b' sound.

Examples of assonance include 'four disorders', with its repeated 'o' sound, 'fleshed there, all contended', with its repeated 'e' sound, 'heavenlier heart', with its repeated 'ea' sound, and 'great grey drayhorse'. It could be argued that onomatopoeia occurs in the poem's final two lines, where the powerful movement of the verse and the clashing consonants bring to mind the sound of the blacksmith's hammer clashing against an anvil.

THEMES

PHYSICAL AND MENTAL SUFFERING

This poem provides a moving portrayal of mental and physical suffering. There is something horrific about the description of four terrible diseases taking root in Felix's flesh and 'contending' with each other for the right to finally kill him. Felix suffers mentally, too. As his illness progresses his mind slips into insanity and his 'reason rambles'. 'I wake and feel the fell of dark' and 'No worst, there is none' also depict suffering, though in those poems the suffering is perhaps more mental than physical. Felix's tears are reminiscent of Hopkins' 'cries' in these two terrible sonnets. Like Hopkins in the later poems, it could be said that Felix goes through 'black hours' of unimaginable suffering.

The poem movingly depicts how serious illness can make the strongest of us weaker than a little child. Felix, once a 'powerful', 'big-boned' and 'hardy-handsome' worker, is reduced to weeping like a baby: 'child, Felix, poor Felix Randal'. He is comforted by the priest's words and touch the way a child might be comforted by its mother: 'My tongue had taught thee comfort, touch had quenched thy tears'. The poem also makes the point that when we are young and strong we seldom think about illness. We give no 'forethought' to the difficulties that may await us. Perhaps the message here is that we shouldn't take health for granted and should make the most of it while we have it.

SIN AND REDEMPTION

An important theme in Hopkins' poetry is that of sin and redemption In poem after poem, Hopkins stresses that it is only through Christ that we can be cleansed of sin and enter heaven. In this poem, Felix, like all men, is a sinner. Yet when Hopkins gives him communion his heart becomes 'heavenlier'. His soul becomes cleansed of sin and fit to enter heaven. Christ, through communion, is our 'reprieve and ransom', the thing that saves us from sin and death.

DOUBTING GOD'S GOODNESS

Another recurring theme in Hopkins is that of doubt regarding God's fundamental goodness. If God is so good, Hopkins wonders, then why does he allow his faithful servants to suffer? In this poem, Felix begins to doubt God's goodness, cursing Him for making him ill. Felix's doubts are overcome when Hopkins administers the sacraments and he 'mends' his relationship with God. In the later sonnets, however, there is no such easy answer to the poet's doubts. ⊠

No worst, there is none

The poem was probably written in 1885 toward the end of the poet's life when he was working in University College Dublin. At the time, Hopkins was in poor mental and physical health. He found his duties exhausting and unrewarding. Furthermore, he was lonely and miserable in Ireland, a country where he found it difficult to fit in and had few friends. As he put it in a letter, these and the other 'terrible sonnets' were the product of a 'continually jaded and harassed mind'.

LINE BY LINE

A CRY OF DESPAIR

The poem's first eight lines are a cry of total mental torment: Hopkins declares that he has been 'Pitched past pitch of grief'. His torment occupies a place on the scale of suffering that is beyond ordinary 'grief'. He is close to complete despair and possibly even to madness.

Furthermore, his mental torment keeps getting worse. Each new pain he experiences has learned from earlier pains how best to make him suffer. He describes each new 'pang', therefore, as having been 'schooled' by the pangs that went before ('forepangs'). Each new pain 'wrings' his mind in a way that is 'wilder' and more violent than the last.

Hopkins, therefore, feels that there is no limit to his torment. There is no such thing as rock bottom, no 'worst' possible situation for him to be in. No matter how badly he's suffering, new and more vicious pains will come along.

The poet says his mind is being 'wrung' like a damp dishcloth. This image conveys the extreme nature of his suffering. His psyche is being choked and mangled by the mental torment that afflicts him.

The poet says his mind is being beaten on an anvil, the 'age-old anvil' of mental torment. This image also powerfully conveys the extreme nature of his suffering. Mental torment makes the poet 'wince' in pain and 'sing' out in agony.

The poet cries out in torment and distress. His 'cries heave': we can imagine his chest heaving as he moans and groans in despair. His cries are 'long' and drawn-out and there are a great number ('herds') of them.

Hopkins enjoyed using words that have multiple meanings. This is evident in his use of the word 'pitched' in the opening line: 'Pitched past pitch of grief'. This phrase can be interpreted in at least three different ways:
• To 'pitch' is to throw or hit an object. Hopkins' mind has been thrown beyond grief into some new and even more terrible emotional state.

- To 'pitch' something can also mean to blacken it, to roll it round in wet tar. Hopkins' mind has been blackened by suffering. It is now more 'pitch' black than the blackness we associate with grief and mourning. It has entered a new kind of darkness.
- The word 'pitch' also suggests the notes on a musical scale. On this reading, Hopkins is suggesting that there is a 'scale' of suffering just as there is a scale of musical notes. As you go up the musical scale the pitch of the notes becomes higher and higher, each note having a more intense effect upon the ear than the last. Similarly, as you go up the scale of mental suffering, each new torment has a higher 'pitch': each degree of suffering has a more intense effect on the soul than the one that came before it.

> There is some disagreement about what is beaten on the 'age-old anvil' in line 6. Grammatically, it is the speaker's 'cries' that 'wince and sing' on the anvil: 'My cries heave … huddle … wince and sing'. But this seems to make little sense. How, after all, can 'cries' be beaten on an anvil? As the critic Norman White suggests, it makes more sense to read this as the poet's soul or mind being hammered on an 'age-old anvil', suffering mental torment as thousands have before throughout the ages. (It has also been suggested that the poet's soul 'sings' God's praises even as he suffers.)

Hopkins probably intended the word 'pitched' to be understood simultaneously in these three ways. Yet the phrase has a clear meaning. Hopkins has moved beyond mere grief into a darker emotional state.

RELIGIOUS ISSUES

In the face of such torment, Hopkins calls out for help to Jesus, his 'comforter', and to the Virgin Mary: 'Comforter, where, where is your comforting?/ Mary, mother of us, where is your relief?' On this occasion, however, no relief appears to be forthcoming. The poet seems to have been abandoned by the God he has served so faithfully.

The poet's torment is caused not only by his own miserable circumstances but also by some universal problem, some great sorrow that affects the entire world: 'a chief woe, world-sorrow'. Hopkins doesn't describe the precise nature of this 'world-sorrow'. Some critics feel that Hopkins is referring to the tragedy of sin, that the great 'sorrow' he has in mind is mankind's failure to obey God's law. However, Hopkins could also be referring to the apparent distance between God and man. On this reading, the 'world-sorrow' is God's apparent unwillingness to answer our prayers and his apparent willingness to let evil men triumph.

NO REAL RELIEF FROM SUFFERING

There seems to be a brief interval or 'lull' in the poet's torment when his sufferings pause ('leave off'): 'Then lull, then leave off'. However, this reprieve is only momentary. No sooner has one bout of suffering ended than the next one begins. There will be no real let-up in the poet's mental agony.

The poet personifies his mental torment as one of the Furies – the terrifying demons from Greek mythology whose purpose was to drive their victims mad. The Furies were 'fell', or malevolent, beings who constantly tormented their victims, never allowing them a moment's rest. These beasts had no interest in pausing or 'lingering'. They wanted to be 'brief', to be quick, to drive their victims into insanity in as short a time as possible. The poet thinks of his mental torment as a Fury because it is constant and relentless. He feels that there will be no real let-up until he has finally been driven insane.

DESPAIR'S ABYSS

Hopkins comes up with yet another powerful image to describe his mental torment, comparing himself to a man hanging off the edge of a mountain: 'O the mind, mind has mountains'. He says he's dangling from the edge of a steep and jagged ('sheer') cliff above a terrifying drop: 'cliffs of fall/ Frightful, sheer'. Beneath him lurks an abyss so deep that no one has ever managed to 'fathom' it, to explore or comprehend it fully. The poet seems aware that most people simply won't understand the kind of suffering that he is forced to put up with. Only those who have 'hung there' above despair's abyss can fully understand what he's going through: 'Hold them cheap/ May who ne'er hung there'. The rest of us who have never (ne'er) dangled above this chasm will 'hold [his words] cheap'. We will not understand his complaints or take them seriously.

A CRUMB OF COMFORT

The poet maintains that human beings are simply not cut out for the kind of mental torment he's going through. The human mind, he claims, is a weak and fragile thing with limited powers of endurance ('small durance'). It cannot deal with the 'steep' cliffs and 'deep' abyss that form the landscape of despair: 'Nor does long our small/ Durance deal with that steep or deep'. We cannot cope with this kind of extreme suffering for very long without simply falling apart.

Yet there is some comfort for the beleaguered poet, some shelter from the storm that has engulfed his mind: 'Here! Creep,/ Wretch under a comfort serves in a whirlwind'. Though his existence is miserable, he can take comfort from the fact that his life will one day be over: 'all life death does end'. Death will bring a final halt to his trials and sufferings. Furthermore, there is the comfort of sleep. When the poet is sleeping, it seems, his sufferings disappear or are at least diminished. The poem's conclusion, then, is a shocking indication of the extent of the poet's misery: his only relief comes from death or unconsciousness.

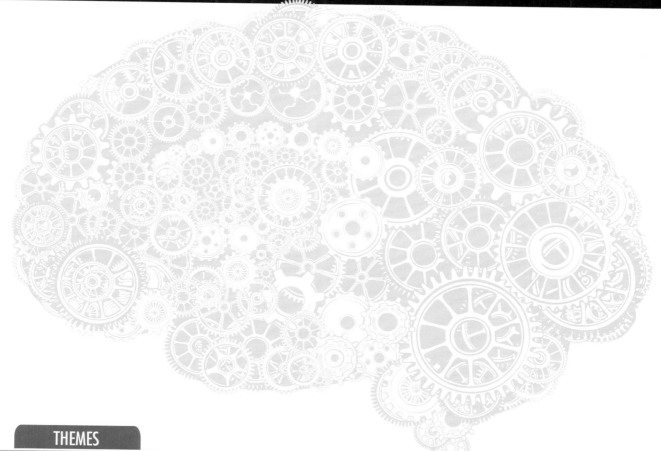

THEMES

MENTAL SUFFERING

This poem could be described as a howl of mental torment. The poet has been 'pitched past pitch of grief'. He is experiencing a mental state that is far beyond ordinary grief or sorrow. Hopkins uses a number of very powerful images to describe the extraordinary torment he suffers:

- His mind is being violently 'wrung' like a piece of cloth.
- His mind is being beaten on an anvil.
- He personifies his suffering as a Fury, a malevolent demon from Greek mythology.
- He thinks of himself as dangling from a mountain above a seemingly bottomless pit of despair.
- He compares his mental torment to a violent 'whirlwind'.

Hopkins' mental torment is more or less unrelenting, with only the briefest of pauses between one bout of suffering and the next. His torment also keeps getting worse. To Hopkins, it seems that his sufferings will keep increasing in intensity forever, that there is 'no worst', no rock-bottom for him to hit. It is hardly surprising, therefore, that the poet thinks of himself as a pitiful 'wretch', crying out in agony over and over again. His only 'comfort' is the oblivion offered by sleep or death.

A similarly bleak portrayal of mental torment is evident in 'I wake and feel the fell of dark', which powerfully describes 'black hours' of mental distress. We also see it in 'Thou art indeed just, Lord', where the poet bitterly laments the barrenness, frustration and disappointment that have consumed his life. Mental torment is also portrayed in 'Felix Randal', when the sick blacksmith's reason or sanity begins to slip away.

DOUBTING GOD'S GOODNESS

This poem powerfully deals with what is arguably Hopkins' darkest theme: his sense of abandonment by God. In the throes of mental torment, Hopkins calls out to God and the Virgin Mary for comfort and relief. God, however, is unable or unwilling to help him. Hopkins, who was a loyal and devoted priest, feels abandoned by the God he has served so faithfully.

A similar sense of abandonment is evident in 'I wake and feel the fell of dark', where Hopkins describes his prayers to God as 'dead letters' that will never reach their destination. We also see it in 'Thou art indeed just, Lord', where Hopkins accuses God of 'thwarting' him and treating him like an enemy while allowing sinners to get ahead in life. This theme is arguably also present in 'Felix Randal', where the dying Felix curses God for making him ill.

FORM

Like many of Hopkins' poems, this is a perfectly formed Petrarchan sonnet. It has the typical Petrarchan rhyme scheme: ABBAABBA CDCDCD. It is divided into an octet (eight lines) and a sestet (six lines). It could also be argued that there is a shift in focus between the octet and the sestet. These defining features of the Petrarchan sonnet are also evident in 'Spring', 'God's Grandeur', 'As Kingfishers Catch Fire, Dragonflies Draw Flame' and 'I wake and feel the fell of dark'.

SYNTAX

There are several examples in this poem of what we might describe as Hopkins' 'shorthand' style. We see this in the following phrase: 'Hold them cheap/ May who ne'er hung there'. A more conventional writer might express a similar sentiment like this: 'Those who have never hung from those terrible cliffs may well hold my words cheap and not take them seriously'. Entire words are left out as Hopkins compresses this sentence into a short, powerful poetic phrase.

A similar effect is created by the phrase 'herds-long'. This combines two distinct pieces of information about the poet's cries. The cries are 'long' and drawn-out and there are a great many ('herds') of them. We also find this technique in line 8, where 'Force' is a shortened version of the old word 'perforce', meaning 'it is necessary'.

VERBAL MUSIC

This sonnet is dominated by an unpleasant verbal music, reflecting the intense despair it describes. The opening lines, in particular, are marked by a jarring cacophony. This cacophonous effect is largely down to Hopkins' use of repetition. The repetition of the word 'pitch' in line 1, and the close proximity of 'pangs' and 'forepangs' in line 2, lend the opening a jerky, grating quality.

This is reinforced by the alliteration in the first line, where the repeated 'p' sound in 'Pitched past pitch' creates a harsh musical effect. The assonance and alliteration in 'wilder wring' with its repeated 'w' and 'i' sounds is also far from easy on the ear. A similarly unpleasant effect is created by the repeated 'h' sound in line 5: 'My cries heave, herds long huddle in a main'. This repetition is almost onomatopoeic, suggesting the speaker's gasps and cries as he laments his suffering.

IMAGERY

In this poem, Hopkins uses several powerful images to describe his mental torment. He compares it to an anvil on which he is beaten and to a whirlwind that blasts him with its force. Perhaps most memorably he compares himself to a man dangling from a 'sheer' cliff above a vast and seemingly bottomless chasm.

The image of 'herds of cries' in line 5 is surreal and peculiar. The poet's cries are presented almost as living things, as poor bewildered beasts that 'huddle' together like cattle on a freezing winter evening. The comparison of the cries to living animals may seem weird and outlandish, but it successfully conveys the poet's distress, suggesting that he finds himself in a debased and animalistic state. His self-respect and dignity have been stripped away.

In line 7 we see an example of personification, The poet uses the image of the Fury to represent the mental torment that threatens to overwhelm him. There is something compelling about this depiction of the poet's inner suffering as a Fury, or malevolent being, from Greek mythology. This technique, whereby an idea or emotion is represented by a person or a mythological character, is known as 'personification'.

I wake and feel the fell of dark

LINE BY LINE

BACKGROUND

The poet is in a state of extreme mental anguish; gripped by doubt, confusion and despair. He is also physically ill. (At this time Hopkins suffered from a staggering list of different ailments). Furthermore, he suffers from severe insomnia. He wakes in the middle of the night and lies there awake for hours suffering in the darkness.

BLACK HOURS

In the poet's distressed state the darkness seems almost solid or tangible. When he wakes on such a night he can almost 'feel' it brushing or pushing against him. He compares it to the 'fell' or hide of an animal: 'I wake and feel the fell of dark'.

Hopkins was fond of using words that have more than one meaning. Fell can also mean evil or wickedness, suggesting that Hopkins experiences the darkness as something sinister or menacing. Fell is also an old word for bitterness, which makes sense given Hopkins' mentions of 'gall' and 'heartburn' later in the poem. Finally, 'fell' is a dialect word for vale or valley, suggesting how Hopkins' mind has been in a bad place, has wandered through some valley of darkness.

Hopkins wonderfully captures how when we experience insomnia, time seems to stretch on and on, each hour of wakefulness seeming like an eternity. He feels like he's been lying there in misery for an incredibly long time; that the morning has 'delayed' itself in arriving for hour after hour. (Indeed this is reinforced by the repetition of the word 'hours' in line 2). But daytime is still far off. He must suffer 'more' as the light delays 'yet longer' in arriving: 'and more must in yet longer light's delay'.

The poet, then, spends 'black hours' lying awake through the night. The word 'black', of course, suggests not only the literal blackness of the night-time but also the poet's despairing state of mind. Hopkins uses the metaphor of the journey to emphasise his mental suffering. He declares that he's travelled down roads or 'ways' so terrible he can hardly bear to mention them. He's witnessed sights so terrible they defy description: 'What sights

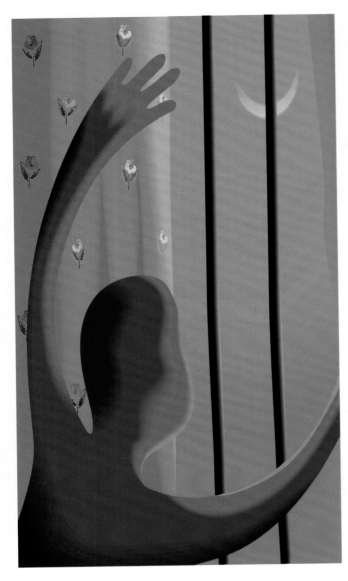

wonderful metaphor Hopkins compares his prayers to 'dead letters', which are letters that cannot be delivered because their intended recipient has moved away.

The poet describes how he experiences the tastes of 'gall', a bitter fluid secreted by the liver, and of 'heartburn', which is caused by stomach acids. In a grim but effective phrase he suggests that what he's tasting is himself: 'My taste was me'. It's as if his entire system is composed of these awful substances: 'I am gall, I am heartburn'.

We can take this literally. Like many sick people the poet probably does experience these bitter tastes rising in his mouth. However 'gall' and 'heartburn' also serve as metaphors for his situation in general, powerfully symbolising how painful and bitter his life has become. The poet feels that God must intend him to suffer in this way. It must be God's will, His solemn or 'deep' decree that the poet experience such misery: 'God's most deep decree/ Bitter would have me taste'.

THE BODY AS BURDEN

The poet's physical body seems a burden to him. He views it as a 'curse' or instrument of torture. He imagines the different stages of his body's construction, almost as if he visualises his accursed body forming in the womb. Firstly its foundations were assembled out of bone: 'Bones built [the curse] in me'. This basic structure was filled out with flesh: 'flesh filled [the curse]'. Finally, blood was introduced to this construct, filling it to the brim: 'Blood brimmed the curse'.

It is as if his body was assembled around his soul, trapping it and confining it in a torturous structure of bone and flesh. The poet's 'spirit' or soul is naturally inclined to rise towards heaven. He compares it to yeast, the cooking agent that causes bread to rise: 'Selfyeast of spirit'. But his physical body prevents his soul from rising toward heaven, trapping it in this earthly realm. He compares his body to an especially 'dull' or heavy dough that envelops the yeast, spoils or sours it, and prevents it from rising: 'a dull dough sours'.

The poet compares himself to the 'lost' souls, those unbelievers who live outside the church's teachings: 'The lost are like this'. They, too, are 'scourged' or tortured by having a body. Like the poet they must be their 'sweating selves', their souls trapped within flesh and blood constructs that sweat and suffer as they age and sicken. However the lost are in a 'worse' situation than the poet, for they lack the consolation of religious belief. Furthermore, they will presumably not get to heaven when their cursed bodies finally give up.

you, heart, saw, ways you went'. This metaphor of a journey through some bleak and frightening landscape powerfully captures the poet's tortured mental state.

The poet is keen to point out that he speaks with 'witness', from deep and intense personal experience: 'With witness I speak this'. This kind of anguish isn't just something he's imagining or has heard about second hand. He's been suffering and surviving bouts of anguish throughout his entire life: 'But where I say/ Hours I mean years, mean life'.

WHERE IS GOD'S COMFORT?

As he lies there through the night, the poet prays to God, asking Him for comfort and relief. He thinks of his prayers as 'cries' for help. The poet has prayed in this desperate fashion 'countless' times. But his appeals have all gone unheeded. Unfortunately Jesus, who he thinks of as his dearest friend, seems very distant at such moments: 'dearest him that lives alas! away'. Using a

THEMES

PHYSICAL AND MENTAL SUFFERING

The poem describes the terrible mental anguish that Hopkins endured, especially toward the end of his life. He powerfully captures the 'black hours' of misery, comparing his mental anguish to a terrible unending journey of dark 'ways' and awful 'sights'. Furthermore, we get a sense that the poet has been living with such despair to some extent for all his life: 'But where I say/ Hours I mean years, mean life'. The poem is also wonderful on the misery of insomnia, capturing how for an insomniac the night seems to stretch on and on as the light delays in arriving.

The poem also describes intense physical discomfort, reflecting the various illnesses Hopkins suffered from at this time. The poet's mouth is filled with bitter tastes – indeed it seems to him that his entire physical system is composed of 'gall' and 'heartburn'. He thinks of his body as little more than a 'scourge' or instrument of torture. He thinks of his flesh, bones and blood as part of a

terrible 'curse'. Ultimately, he regards his body as little more than an impediment to his soul reaching heaven.

DOUBTING GOD'S GOODNESS

Once again, Hopkins speaks of the difficult relationship he has with God. The poet feels isolated from God, abandoned and alone. His 'countless' prayers to God for help are like cries that go unheeded, or like 'dead letters' destined to never reach their intended recipients. Jesus, who he considers his dearest friend, seems very far away indeed.

There's even a sense in which the poet thinks that God wants him to suffer. It's as if God willed or 'decreed' that the poet should experience this intensely bitter mental and physical suffering. Furthermore, he resents that God decided to trap his soul in the scourge of a 'sick' and 'sweating' physical body. In a very real sense the poet seems angry with God for causing him to be born.

FORM

The poem is composed in the form of a Petrarchan sonnet. It has the typical Petrarchan rhyme scheme: ABBAABBA CDCDCD. It is divided into an octet (eight lines) and a sestet (six lines). There is a shift in focus between the octet and the sestet.

SYNTAX

A signature feature of many of Hopkins' poems is the unusual syntax that he deploys. For example, in the second line he says 'what sights you, heart, saw' where we might normally say 'What sights you saw, heart'. The following line features what we might call Hopkins' shorthand technique, where he omits certain words that we would use if we were expressing the same sentiment in everyday speech: 'And more must, in yet longer light's delay'. If we fill in the gaps we end up with a line such as 'And you must endure more sights such as this as the light's arrival is set to be delayed even longer'. Unusual syntax is also a feature of line 12 where the poet says 'Selfyeast of spirit a dull dough sours'. Converted into 'normal' language the line might go something like this: 'A dull dough sours the selfyeast of the spirit'.

VOCABULARY

Hopkins is renowned for his invention of new words. Sometimes he would coin or create a new word by combing two existing words. We see this in line 12 when he combines the words 'self' and 'yeast' to create the word 'Selfyeast'. The word conveys the way in which the spirit naturally rises without any agent acting upon it.

VERBAL MUSIC

The poem features plenty of assonance, frequently using long-vowel sounds to express despair. This despair is evident in the first line, which features long 'a' and 'e' sounds. The drawn-out sounds of the second line continue this, the 'o' sounds in particular expressing the poet's suffering. It is also evident in the long 'a' sounds of 'alas! away'. Alliteration, too, features to express the poet's discomfort. In line 11, the repeated 'b' and 'f' sounds express the bitterness that the poet is experiencing: 'Bones built in me, flesh filled, blood brimmed the curse'.

METAPHORS AND SIMILES

The poem also contains some interesting metaphors and similes. The poet likens his severe discomfort to indigestion, saying that he is 'gall' and 'heartburn'. He compares the negative impact his body has on his spirit with 'dull dough' that prevents yeats from rising. His unanswered cries to God are compared to letters that cannot be delivered.

REPETITION

The poem uses repetition to express despair and anguish. In the second line, Hopkins conveys the terrible nature of the time he has spent awake when he says: 'What hours, O what black hours'. He also emphasises the extent of his suffering in the seventh line through the repetition of the word 'cries'.

Thou art indeed just, Lord …

In this poem, Hopkins expresses his doubts about the goodness and justice of God. It was written toward the end of Hopkins' life when his personal circumstances were dire. He was both depressed and suffering from intense bouts of physical illness. Years of difficult work as a priest had left him exhausted. Hopkins found the teaching duties that occupied the last few years of his life particularly exhausting. To make matters worse he was stationed at the time in Ireland, a country where he felt lonely, out of place and had few real friends.

LINE BY LINE

HOPKINS COMPLAINS TO GOD

As a priest, Hopkins must believe that God acts in a just way. After all, religion teaches us that God is a being of complete goodness. Yet he cannot avoid having certain doubts. He cannot avoid feeling that some of God's actions are actually unjust. He 'contends' – or argues – with God, expressing these doubts:

• Why does God let evil men succeed in life?

• Hopkins is a loyal and dutiful priest, one of God's faithful servants. Why, then, does everything he attempts to do end in disappointment? Why does God persistently 'defeat' and 'thwart' him?

• Hopkins is God's friend but God treats him very badly. (Hopkins can't imagine getting worse treatment even if he was God's enemy.)

• Why do sinful men, who are enslaved by drink and sex, 'thrive' much more than Hopkins, who spends his life loyally serving God's 'cause'?

God may well be the most 'just' being in existence. But Hopkins feels that there is also justice to his own 'pleas' or complaints about God's actions and inactions: 'but, sir, so what I plead is just'.

THE BARRENNESS OF HOPKINS' LIFE

Hopkins describes the richness and fertility of the natural world. He depicts river banks and woods ('brakes') becoming 'thick' with leaves, as life returns to them after the winter. Each spring the banks and hedges become 'laced' again with delicate and complexly interwoven parsley plants ('fretty chervil'). Yet while the natural world is fertile, Hopkins himself is completely barren:

• He is barren since as a priest he can have no children. (He compares himself to a 'eunuch', a man who has been castrated.)

• Hopkins also feels creatively barren. He 'strains' and struggles but can create no 'works that wake', no good poems that have any life in them.

MENTAL SUFFERING

This poem is one of Hopkins' 'terrible' sonnets – poems in which Hopkins describes mental anguish. Other poems in this group include 'No worst, there is none' and 'I wake and feel the fell of Dark'. 'Thou art indeed just, Lord' is perhaps the least intense of the three. Here, Hopkins presents his suffering in a more rational, restrained and subtle fashion.

However, the poet's despair and mental torment still resonate throughout the poem. It powerfully conveys Hopkins' desperate and 'straining' attempts to make something of his life, and his sense of failure and disappointment when these attempts come to nothing. Hopkins feels completely barren, that he is incapable of 'building' or producing anything worthwhile. The only element of hope in the poem is Hopkins' desperate plea for God to do something to relieve his situation.

DOUBTING GOD'S GOODNESS

This is a powerful poem of religious doubt. In it, Hopkins asks an age-old question: if God is good why does He let wicked men triumph and sinners get ahead in life? Furthermore, why does He let His faithful servants suffer? Hopkins has sacrificed so much for God yet nothing in his life succeeds. Meanwhile, sinners who have sacrificed nothing – who are the slaves or 'thralls' of lust – get ahead in life. Hopkins, like many other people throughout history, wonders why God allows this to happen.

• Hopkins also feels professionally barren. His priestly duties were exhausting and repetitive, and involved no worthwhile projects of lasting value.

Birds are busy building nests in the trees but Hopkins is incapable of 'building' anything worthwhile. He can produce no children, no poems and nothing of lasting value in his professional life. Hopkins asks God to give him relief from this barrenness: 'O thou lord of life, send my roots rain'. He presumably wants God to send him poetic inspiration or improve the circumstances of his working life.

There is a strong sense of frustration, perhaps even anger, in this poem. Everything Hopkins tries to do ends in disappointment and failure. He cannot understand why God allows this to happen, especially when Hopkins has served Him so faithfully. Hopkins almost suspects that God has turned against him and is actually his enemy rather than his friend.

A similar sense of abandonment is evident in 'I wake and feel the fell of dark', where Hopkins describes his prayers to God as 'dead letters' that will never reach their destination. We also see it in 'No worst, there is none', where Hopkins calls out in vain for God's comfort. This theme is arguably also present in 'Felix Randal', where the dying Felix curses God for making him ill.

It has also been suggested that in this poem Hopkins expresses doubts about his religious vocation, especially his vow of celibacy. Hopkins sacrificed the sexual side of his nature for God. He also gave up his ability to 'breed', to father children. But in this poem he suggests that God has given him little or nothing in return. There's a sense in which he regrets these huge sacrifices, referring to himself in a demeaning fashion as 'Time's eunuch'. Is it possible that Hopkins envies those sinners who are 'thralls of lust', who are slaves to sexual passion? In

THE LANGUAGE OF THE COURTROOM

An interesting feature of this poem is the way Hopkins uses legal phrases and terminology that we might associate with a courtroom setting. Hopkins has certain issues with the way God has treated him. He 'pleads' his case rationally like a lawyer in a courtroom. He addresses God in a respectful manner, the way a lawyer would a judge, calling Him 'Sir' and being careful to declare at the beginning of his 'plea' that God is just and right.

In many of his poems Hopkins draws a moral message from the natural world. The beauty of nature leads him to contemplate God's goodness. In 'The Windhover', the sight of a soaring falcon causes Hopkins to think about Christ's role as our redeemer. In 'As Kingfishers', the unique beauty of each natural thing causes Hopkins to think that Christ's presence is in each just man.

In this poem, however, the beauty of nature seems to tie in with Hopkins' angry questioning of God's justice. Each spring the riverbanks grow thick with leaves while God lets Hopkins' life remain barren and empty. Hopkins' only hope is that God will make his life fertile and fulfilling, just as He sends rain to water the plants on the riverbank. Hopkins, therefore, calls out desperately for God to 'send my roots rain'.

FORM

Like so many of Hopkins' poems, 'Thou art indeed just' is a Petrarchan sonnet. It has a typical Petrarchan rhyme scheme: ABBAABBA CDCDCD. It is divided into an octet (eight lines) where Hopkins outlines his complaints against God and a sestet (six lines) where he compares himself to nature and hopes for a solution to his troubles.

SYNTAX

The poem's opening is relatively simple in terms of syntax. We are presented with more or less straightforward sentences in which it is reasonably easy to work out what's going on. As the poem goes on, however, the syntax becomes more cluttered, difficult and convoluted. This is evident in lines 5 to 9, where most readers require several readings of the text in order to properly follow the poet's meaning.

This contorted word order reflects his confused and angry state of mind. At the beginning of the poem he speaks rationally and his intense emotions are kept in check. As the poem goes on, however, his confusion, bitterness and frustration come bubbling to the surface and are reflected in the increasingly difficult and tortured syntax.

VERBAL MUSIC

This poem is not as rich in sound effects as some other poems by Hopkins. However, assonance and alliteration do occur in lines 9 to 11. We see assonance in the repeated 'b' sounds ('banks' and 'brakes', 'birds' and 'build'), in the repeated 'l' sound ('leaves' and 'lace') and in the repeated 'fr' sound ('fretty' and 'fresh'). Assonance also occurs in these lines due to their repeated broad-vowel sounds. The phase 'fretty chervil', in particular, creates a pleasing euphonious effect. These lines are typical of Hopkins in that he uses intense and musical language in order to describe the natural world in an effort to capture the uniqueness, or 'inscape', of each natural thing he depicts. ⊠

TAKE CARE OF EACH OTHER!

Well-Being in Post-Primary Schools

Guidelines for Mental Health Promotion and Suicide Prevention

The Well-Being Guidelines are available to download at: **www.education.ie**

Everyone needs someone they trust who accepts and believes in them for who they are. We all should look after ourselves and each other.

Ask your teachers about the **Well-Being Guidelines for Post-Primary Schools.** They give lots of advice for your school on how to work together to make things better for everyone.

SOME USEFUL WEBSITES:

Spunout.ie

Reachout.ie

Letsomeoneknow.ie

An Roinn Sláinte
DEPARTMENT OF HEALTH

AN ROINN
OIDEACHAIS
AGUS SCILEANNA | DEPARTMENT OF
EDUCATION
AND SKILLS

Feidhmeannacht na Seirbhíse Sláinte
Health Service Executive

This Well-Being campaign is supported by the Department of Education and Skills with the co-operation of the Irish Educational Publishers Association.

John Keats

Themes

Nature

When you read Keats' poetry you cannot help but feel that he saw or experienced nature differently from the rest of us. Where the rest of us merely see a 'night sky' he observes a 'starr'd face': where the rest of us see bits of cloud he sees 'symbols of a high romance'. To Keats the sound of a swarm of 'gnats' or midges on a summer's evening is like a 'mournful choir'. The poet's unusual sensitivity to the natural world is perhaps nowhere more evident than in his reaction to the nightingale's singing in 'Ode to a Nightingale'. The nightingale's song fills the poet with an overwhelming mix of emotions; he is happy, melancholy and numb all at the same time.

Keats was enthralled by the rich and varied details of the natural world. In 'To Autumn', for example, he focuses on the many sensual delights of this time of year, from the sights of harvested fields and all the ripening fruit to the wonderful sounds of the birds, animals and insects. But he was also moved and inspired by the vast expanses of the sky, seas and mountains. In 'Bright Star' the poet considers how the earth's oceans, mountains and moors must look from the star's vantage high in the night sky. There is something incredibly seductive and soothing about the 'moving waters' and the 'soft-fallen mask/ Of snow upon the mountains and the moors'. 'To one who has been long in city pent' celebrates the beauty of a clear blue sky, which Keats describes as the smiling and 'open face of heaven'. In 'When I have fears that I may cease to be' the poet celebrates the beauty of the starry night sky and describes his burning ambition to capture such beauty in his poetic works.

Keats's seems to consider the natural world to be most lovely when there is no human presence. In 'To Autumn' the poet describes the various processes of the harvest, from the winnowing of the grain to the pressing of the apples, but the only reference to human existence is the mention of the 'thatch-eves' of the country dwellings. This notion that the natural world is at its most beautiful when there is no one around is also evident in 'To one who has been long in city pent', where the poet seems to relish the fact that he is alone to enjoy the beauty and tranquillity of the countryside. In 'When I have fears that I may cease to be' the poet again takes time 'alone' away from the hustle and bustle of everyday life to stand at the ocean's edge as he contemplates eternity.

Celebrating Artworks

Keats's poetry celebrates the pleasure and serenity people derive from artworks of all types. In 'Ode on a Grecian Urn', for example, the poet is filled with joy and wonder at the sight of an ancient piece of sculpture. The scenes depicted on the urn's surface utterly absorb him and transport him briefly to another place and time. Keats imagines how the urn will help future generations to deal with their troubles or 'woe', describing it as a 'friend to man'. In 'Ode to a Nightingale', the bird's song is considered a piece of artistic ingenuity worthy of praise and celebration. The bird's complex 'full-throated' airs – at once blissful and melancholy, summery and sorrowful – emerge as a moving and bewitching work of art. As such, it seems to take its place alongside Homer's epic poems, Chapman's translations and the Grecian Urn.

'Chapman's Homer' is one of several poems where Keats celebrates the joy and pleasure of reading. Reading poetry, the poem suggests, can be a thrilling voyage of discovery. Exploring a new poet's work is like exploring a new country or island brimming with riches and fantastic sights. For Keats discovering Homer through Chapman's translation is as thrilling as discovering a new planet or a new ocean. 'To one who has been long in city pent' also celebrates the pleasure of reading. Keats cannot imagine anything more pleasant than finding a quiet spot in the countryside to relax with a good book. The reading of the 'gentle tale of love and languishment' allows for a momentary break from the stresses and strains of life.

Artistic Creativity

Keats, like the other Romantic poets of his generation, venerated artistic creativity as one of the greatest human traits, regarding it as something sacred and mysterious. 'When I have fears' presents poetic inspiration as the 'magic hand of Chance', as an almost magical or mystical force. However, the poem also stresses that artistic creation requires hard work. The poet's ideas and inspirations have to be painstakingly worked on and transformed into poems, just as the harvest must be gathered with back-breaking toil. In 'Ode on a Grecian Urn' the poet makes a reference to the care and time that went into the urn's creation, describing it as the product of 'silence and slow-time'.

'On First Looking into Chapman's Homer' is more than anything else a tribute to the creative genius of Homer. Keats indicates Homer's pre-eminent status among poets by referring to his work as a 'vast expanse', which dwarfs the smaller territories represented by the works of other great poets. In 'Ode on a Grecian Urn' Keats praises the artist who created the intricate scenes on the body of the urn. According to the poet, the urn is better able to tell an elaborate or 'flowery tale' than poetry ever can.

Yet Keats' poetry is testament to the power and fertility of his own imagination. In 'Ode to a Nightingale' we find Keats using his poetic powers to envisage in incredible detail the nightingale's woodland environment. His poetic imagination will allow him to join the nightingale in its woodland abode. As he puts it, he will fly there on poetry's invisible wings. A similar escape is evident in 'Ode on a Grecian Urn' where the poet seems to momentarily lose himself in the world depicted on the urn's surface. His imagination enables him to breathe life into the still and silent figures in the various scenes.

Love

Keats, like the other Romantic poets of his generation, celebrates love as a force that is spontaneous, irrational and ungoverned by logic and reason. Love, he suggests, is 'unreflective', being rooted in passion and emotion rather than in analysis and reflection. It is presented as a 'faery power', as a kind of spell or enchantment that takes over our minds and bewitches us. In 'Ode on a Grecian Urn' the poet describes a scene of 'wild ecstasy', where a group of men and women seem to be intoxicated with passion and desire.

But there can also be a dark side to this bewitchment, to the loss of conscious and rational control that love implies. We can find ourselves falling for the wrong person and making dangerous choices and decisions. In 'La Belle Dame Sans Merci', for instance, such 'faery power' is presented as something dark and dangerous: the 'faery child' bewitches the knight and lures him to his doom. The poem can be read as a warning to men about the dangers of falling in love with a beautiful woman. For when a man is betrayed by such a woman, or indeed if she fails to return his affections, he will find himself in a state of total despair. A similar depiction of love as pain and torment is evident in 'Ode on a Grecian Urn' where the poet describes how love often 'leaves a heart high sorrowful and cloy'd'.

'When I have fears that I may cease to be' stresses how people take great 'relish' or delight in the pleasures of romance. The poet himself is clearly captivated by his beloved's beauty and worries that death might take him away from this 'fair creature'. He is terrified that he might die before experiencing true love to the fullest. A similar sentiment is evident in 'Bright Star' where Keats longs to be able to rest his head forever upon his 'fair love's ripening breast'. In 'Ode on a Grecian Urn' the poet envies the young lovers depicted on the urn because their love will never grow old or fade.

Death

Death very much forms the 'background music' of Keats' work. In poem after poem we find him lamenting the reality of death and its consequences for human existence. 'When I have fears that I may cease to be' centres on a terrifying race against time. Keats is haunted by the possibility that death will claim him before he can make the most of his talent and truly relish the pleasures of romantic love. He responds to these fears by standing at the ocean's edge and meditating as he watches the waves come in.

'Ode to a Nightingale' is very much a poem that laments the reality of death and its consequences for human existence. Each of us, even the strongest and most vibrant, is condemned to grow 'pale' and 'spectre-thin', to be faced with the indignities of old age and finally to die. Worst of all, perhaps, the physical beauty we possess in youth inevitably fades away as we grow older.

However, the poet also seems attracted to or fascinated by the notion of death and dying in 'Ode to a Nightingale': 'For many a time I have been half in love with easeful death'. Death, he feels, would be 'easeful', a sweet release from this cruel world. A similar attitude to death seems to be evident in the final stanza of 'To Autumn', describing both the autumn and the day reaching their end. The poet mentions the 'soft-dying day' and describes how the 'light wind lives or dies'. Rather than rage against the season's end, Keats seems to accept it and embrace it. There is a certain beauty to behold in the dying moments of both the day and the season. Keats describes the beautiful effect that the setting sun has on both the clouds and the harvested fields: 'barred clouds bloom the soft-dying day,/ And touch the stubble plains with rosy hue'.

Change and Changelessness

Like many of Keats' poems 'When I have fears' emphasises the transitory nature of the world around us. Everything is changing and passing away: the grain is stripped from the fields, clouds constantly shift formation as they drift across the sky, wave after wave washes and breaks upon the shore. Even love and life itself are fleeting. This is also evident in 'To Autumn' where the poet describes the progression of the season, from the final ripening of the fruits and blossoming of the flowers, to the harvesting of the crops and finally the late stages when the fields are 'stubble plains'.

Yet 'Ode to a Nightingale' also stresses that certain aspects of the universe are utterly unchanging. While crops come and go the process of harvesting itself continue for thousands of years to come. Individual waves last only a few seconds but the ocean itself will continue forever. The stars, too, will continue to shine long after each of our fleeting human lives has passed. In 'Bright Star' the poet considers the star 'unchangeable' and envies its ability to remain the same. It never sleeps or alters its position. The poet wishes that he too could stay awake forever so that he could watch his beloved sleep. Like the star he will never change and never sleep. Frozen in a state of 'sweet unrest', he will happily feel the rise and fall of his beloved's breast and listen to her soft breath.

In 'Ode on a Grecian Urn' the poet celebrates the fact that the urn has not changed over the thousands of years that it has existed. It seems 'unravish'd' or unmarked by the passage of time. In the final stanza the poet states that the urn will continue to exist long after he and his generation have passed away. It will 'remain, in midst of other woe' and offer pleasure to those who view it. The urn is, therefore, a symbol of the timelessness of great art.

'Ode to a Nightingale' is a poem that contrasts change and changelessness. Change is represented by human beings, each of whom finds their youthful beauty stripped away as they age, become 'spectre-thin' and eventually die. Everything we build and create will be destroyed by the passage of time, will be devoured by the 'hungry' years and centuries as they pass. Changelessness, on the other hand, is represented by the nightingale. For this 'immortal bird' has existed for centuries, since 'ancient days', and because it was not 'born for death' will continue to do so long into the future. The nightingale, we're told, will never be 'trodden down' by time's passage. Keats, of course, knows that the particular nightingale he's listening to this summer evening is not really immortal. This particular bird will die like any other. Yet the song it sings is the same song that nightingales have been singing for thousands of years and will continue to sing far into the future.

To one has been long in city pent

LINE BY LINE

LINES 1 TO 8

The poem describes how pleasant it can be to spend a day in the country if you have been stuck in the city for a long time. For anyone who has been 'long in city pent' it is 'very sweet' to be out in the open expanses of the countryside, where you can gaze at the sky and not have your view obscured by tall buildings: ''Tis very sweet to look into the fair/ And open face of heaven'. It is also a great pleasure to lie down in a bed of tall grass and read a good book.

The country is presented as a place of beauty and tranquility. The unclouded 'blue' sky is 'fair' or beautiful. The tall grass that sways gently in the breeze offers the visitor a 'pleasant' secluded place to relax: 'pleasant lair/ Of wavy grass'. This is an 'open' space, a place where someone can 'breathe'. The words 'heaven' and 'firmament' suggest great open expanses. Keats presents the countryside as a loving, benevolent place that warmly welcomes and embraces those who come to visit. The bright blue sky is compared to a smiling 'face'.

The person who spends a day in the country will experience great joy. Keats cannot imagine a greater pleasure: 'Who is more happy'. The experience will inspire a religious or spiritual response. For someone who has spent too long in the city, the sight of the open sky will inspire a 'prayer' of gratitude or awe. There is a sense in which God is smiling back at the person Keats imagines taking this trip to the country. The poet describes the 'open face of heaven' that smiles back at one who says a 'prayer'.

The country offers those who have spent too long in the city respite, an opportunity to rest and relax. Keats describes how 'Fatigued' someone might feel when they arrive and how wonderful it is to just sink into a bed of tall grass. It is here that someone discovers their 'heart's content'.

LINES 9 TO 14

The journey back to the city in the evening will bring mixed emotions. Keats imagines how the person making their way back will hear the song of the nightingale: 'Catching the notes of Philomel'. Keats describes a single cloud drifting quickly across the sky: 'the sailing cloudlet's bright career'.

Such sights and sounds are very pleasant, but someone returning to the city would feel sad that their day had so quickly come to an end: 'He mourns that day so soon has glided by'. Keats compares the swift and silent passage of time to the tear of an angel falling from the heavens: 'passage of an angel's tear/ that falls through the clear ether silently'. It is a melancholic image and seems to suggest that the heavens are sympathetic to the feelings of the person returning to the confines of the city. The idea of the tear falling from the heavens can also be contrasted with the image of the smiling blue sky in the opening lines.

THEMES

FOCUS ON STYLE

FORM

This poem is a sonnet and uses an ABBA ABBA CDCDCD rhyming scheme. The first quatrain describes the pleasure found in gazing up at the open sky. The second quatrain considers the joys of retiring to 'some pleasant lair' with a good book. The sestet then involves a turn. The poet moves from considering the joys of a day spent out of the city to the sadness that will accompany the journey home.

NATURE IMAGERY

Like so many of Keats' poems, 'To one who has been long in city pent' contains a number of memorable images of the natural world. Here Keats concentrates on the sky. He captures the wonderful expanse of the sky when he describes it as an 'open face' and speaks of the 'smile of the blue firmament'. In the poem's closing lines Keats describes a cloud drifting across the sky like a boat sailing upon the ocean: 'the sailing cloudlet's bright career'.

REFERENCES TO OLDER TIMES

Like many Romantic poets, Keats' poetry makes frequent references to characters from Greek myths and legends. Here the poet refers to the song of the nightingale as the 'notes of Philomel'. According to Greek mythology, Philomel was the daughter of an Athenian king, who was turned into a nightingale in order to protect her from a cruel and vengeful man.

METAPHOR AND SIMILES

Keats personifies the sky, likening it to a smiling face. The face is said to be 'fair' and 'open'.

The final two lines of the poem involve a simile. Keats compares the passage of time to the 'passage of an angel's tear'.

NATURE

Keats was typical of the Romantic poets in his worship of the natural world. And his almost overwhelming love of nature is evident throughout his poetry. Here he describes the awe-inspiring beauty of the sky, a sight which inspires one to 'breathe a prayer'. The natural world is presented as a loving, caring environment. The poet presents the sky as the smiling and 'open face of heaven'. He also describes the great pleasure of sinking into long grass and hiding away from the troubles of the world for a while.

As such, the country is presented as an idyllic escape from the hustle and bustle of city life. It is a place that offers the weary city-dweller much needed rest and respite.

CELEBRATING ARTWORKS

The poem celebrates the joys and pleasures of reading. Keats cannot imagine anything more pleasant than finding a quiet spot in the countryside to relax with a good book. The reading of the 'gentle tale of love and languishment' allows for a momentary break from the stresses and strains of life.

On First Looking into Chapman's Homer

BACKGROUND

In this sonnet Keats records his pleasure and excitement at discovering George Chapman's translations of the great Greek poet Homer. Homer was famous for his two epic poems *The Iliad* and *The Odyssey*. Keats could not read ancient Greek so it was only through Chapman's translations that he could explore these epics, which are often considered to be the greatest works of Western poetry.

LINE BY LINE

LINES 1 TO 4: READING AS TRAVELLING

The poem's opening lines present reading poetry as a form of travel and exploration:

- A great poet's collected works is like a country (a 'realm', 'state' or 'kingdom') he or she has painstakingly constructed over years of imaginative effort.
- Each poet's country is a 'realm of gold', a place of great wealth. This suggests the incredible imaginative richness present in each great poet's output.
- The country built by each great poet is described as large or 'goodly', suggesting the breadth of each great poet's vision.
- Reading a poet's work is like visiting and exploring his or her country.
- Keats is very 'well travelled' in this regard because he has read the work of many great poets: 'Much have I travelled in the realms of gold/ And many goodly states and kingdoms seen'.

Keats mentions bards, who were the poets of Britain and Ireland in Celtic times. The bards 'hold' or govern a series of islands in the west. We imagine them ruling these territories like wise old stewards, using their poetic wisdom to govern justly. The bards' overlord is Apollo, who was the Greek god of poetry and song. The bards have sworn 'fealty' or loyalty to Apollo, just as a baron takes an oath of allegiance to his king. We sense, therefore, that the bards preside over their islands in Apollo's name, governing on his behalf.

Each island probably represents the collected works of a given poet that Keats has read over the years. Some readers think Keats is referring to the poets of Britain and Ireland here, which is why he refers to them as 'bards', as this locates their realms in the West.

LINES 5 TO 8: VISITING HOMER'S REALM

Homer's work, too, is described as a realm or 'demesne'. The country he created is particularly vast and expansive: 'One wide expanse … Homer ruled as his demesne'. On the 'map' of poetry, Homer's realm dwarfs even the large or 'goodly' countries constructed by the other great poets of the European tradition. The air or 'serene' in his realm is extremely crisp and pure, suggesting how even after thousands of years his poems retain their energy and freshness.

Keats has often heard about Homer's amazing epics: 'Oft of one wide expanse had I been told'. Yet he has never been able to read them due to his lack of ancient Greek. He has never been able to visit and explore Homer's great realm: 'Yet never did I breathe its pure serene'.

Now, however, Keats has discovered Chapman's translations of Homer's masterpieces: 'I heard Chapman speak out loud and bold'. Chapman's skill as a translator has allowed him to experience Homer's work for the first time. Finally Keats has managed to enter the 'wide expanse' of Homer's realm and breathe its pure clean air.

The phrase 'deep-brow'd' refers to a famous bust of Homer, which depicts Homer's brow or forehead as being marked by deep wrinkles. Presumably the sculptor intended to convey that Homer was always furrowing his brow in deep concentration as he worked on his extraordinary epics.

LINES 9 TO 14: A GREAT DISCOVERY

Keats describes an astronomer or 'watcher of the skies' who discovers a new planet: 'Then I felt as some watcher of the skies/ When a new planet swims into his ken'. The planet, we're told, 'swims' into the astronomer's 'ken' or knowledge. The use of the word 'swims' is interesting. Perhaps it describes the planet moving across the night sky until it slides into view of the astronomer's telescope. Or perhaps it describes new knowledge entering the astronomer's consciousness as he pores over his charts and calculations. (It's often been suggested that these lines were inspired by the astronomer Herschel's discovery of the planet Uranus in 1781.)

Keats also describes the Spanish explorer Cortez, who discovered the Pacific Ocean while travelling through Darien or Panama. We can imagine Cortez's shock when he reached the top of a hill and saw something he'd never expected: a vast and undiscovered ocean shimmering as far as the eye could see.

Keats paints a wonderful picture of Cortez as he makes his astonishing discovery. Cortez is 'stout' or strong and has the 'eagle eyes' of an experienced soldier and explorer. He stands 'silent' on the mountain peak and 'stares' at this new ocean, suggesting that even this hard and seasoned commander is stunned and moved by the magnificent sight of the sparkling Pacific.

His soldiers, too, are stunned by the discovery. They glance at one another with a 'wild' or shocked look in their eyes. Then slowly 'surmise' or understanding dawns: they realise that they are the first Europeans ever to gaze upon this seemingly endless body of water.

Keats is clearly thrilled by Chapman's translations. They permit him for the first time to really discover Homer's poetry. And this excites him as much as if he's discovered a new planet. He feels the kind of exhilaration Cortez must have experienced when he stood on that Panama hill before a freshly-discovered ocean.

In this poem Keats makes a fairly large factual blunder. He mixes up Hernán Cortez with another explorer called Vasco Balboa. It was actually Balboa who discovered the Pacific while Cortez was active around the Aztec regions of Mexico. Most readers feel Keats' error has little impact on the quality of his poem. Do you agree?

THEMES

CELEBRATING ARTWORKS

'Chapman's Homer' is one of several poems where Keats celebrates the joy and pleasure of reading. Reading poetry, the poem suggests, can be a thrilling voyage of discovery. Exploring a new poet's work is like exploring a new country or island brimming with riches and fantastic sights.

The poem also celebrates the incredible excitement of discovering a great new author. For Keat's discovering Homer through Chapman's translation is as thrilling as discovering a new planet or a new ocean. The poem, then, emphasises the emotional intensity with which Keats responded to works of art. Most of us don't share this incredible sensitivity. But maybe we can understand where Keats is coming from when we respond with excitement to a new book, movie or song.

ARTISTIC CREATIVITY

More than anything else the poem is a tribute to the creative genius of Homer. Keats indicates Homer's pre-eminent status among poets by referring to his work as a 'vast expanse', which dwarfs the smaller territories represented by the works of other great poets. He suggests the originality and freshness of Homer's work by referring to his realm's 'pure serene' or fresh clean air. The poem stresses Homer's unparalleled artistic creativity by reminding us that even after thousands of years his work retains all its freshness, originality and power.

The poem also suggests that to fulfil their creativity poets must remain true to their artistic vision. They must maintain 'fealty to Apollo', staying loyal and devoted to their craft. They must follow their artistic intuitions and not be swayed by censorship, by the promise of money or by fear of others' negative reactions to their work.

FORM

This poem takes the form of a Petrarchan sonnet, which means that it is divided into an octet (the first eight lines) and a sestet (the final six lines). The octet rhymes ABBA ABBA while the sestet rhymes CDCDCD. As is often the case with Petrarchan sonnets there is a shift in subject matter between the octet and the sestet. The octet centres on the notion of exploration, while the sestet deals with the notion of discovery.

NATURE IMAGERY

Keats was a typical Romantic poet in how he littered his work with images of the natural world. As a a tribute to Homer, who wrote a great deal about sea voyages, the poem features a great deal of water imagery: we see 'western islands', the swimming planet, the great sailor Cortez and the Pacific Ocean itself.

This poem centres on epic images of discovery in nature. Cortez explores new lands and discovers a whole new ocean. Astronomers, meanwhile, explore the heavens with their telescopes, coming upon new planets. As we've seen the poem also suggests that the act of reading poetry itself can be a form of exploration.

On another note, the poem also contains short but skilful physical descriptions. The fact that Homer is described as 'deep-brow'd' indicates his enormous intelligence and wisdom. The fact that Cortez is 'stout' and possesses 'eagle eyes' suggests his fierceness and determination. In each case Keats manages to reveal much about the man using only a simple phrase.

REFERENCES TO OLDER TIMES

Like the other Romantic poets of his generation Keats was greatly interested in the classical world of ancient Greece. We see this in his reference to the Greek god Apollo and indeed in how he pays tribute to Homer, the very greatest of the Greek poets. The mention of bards, meanwhile, reflects the Romantic interest in the Celtic civilisation.

METAPHOR

The poem's first eight lines are dominated by a 'conceit' or extended metaphor that compares the activity of reading to the activity of travel. A memorable feature of the poem is how it depicts European poetry as a kind of 'map'. The work of each major poet forms a territory on this map: the greater the poet's work, the larger the territory. The vast size of Homer's realm – his 'wide expanse' – indicates his singular greatness in the history of Western verse.

Another metaphor is used to describe the vividness and intensity of Chapman's translation. Chapman's book is compared to someone speaking out 'loud and bold', suggesting the confidence and certainty he brought to his task.

SOUND EFFECTS

Throughout the poem Keats makes extensive use of assonance to create a pleasant verbal music. We see this in line 4 with its repeated 'o' sound: 'Apollo hold'. A similar repetition of the 'o' sound is evident in line 11: 'stout Cortez'. Line 11 also features a repeated 'e' sound in 'eagle eyes'. Assonance also predominates in lines 6 to 7. Here we see a repeated 'o' sound in 'deep-brow'd Homer' and a repeated 'e' sound in 'never breathe its pure serene'.

When I have fears that I may cease to be

LINE BY LINE

LINES 1 TO 4

Keats compares his poetic imagination to a field that's alive with growth and fertility, that's 'teeming' with grain at harvest time:

- Keats claims that his imagination is similarly fertile; it is 'teeming' or overflowing with ideas for poetry.
- These ideas have developed in his imagination so that they are now ready to be turned into poems. In this regard they resemble fully-matured ears of corn at harvest time.
- He will use his pen to 'glean' or gather these ideas, just as farmers use scythes to gather the autumn harvest.
- His ideas will be stored as finished poems in a pile of books filled with 'charactery' or writing, just as harvested grain is stowed in 'garners' or storehouses.

However, Keats worries that he will 'cease to be' before he has the chance to accomplish this great task: 'When I have fears that I may cease to be/ Before my pen has glean'd my teeming brain'. His mind might be brimming with ideas, but he's terrified he'll die before he's had the chance to turn these ideas into poems. He fears that he'll never get to 'harvest' the ideas that teem in his fertile imagination.

LINES 5 TO 8

Keats describes 'Huge' banks of clouds drifting across the starry sky at night: 'When I behold upon the night's starr'd face/ Huge cloudy symbols'. Keats longs to 'trace the shadows' of these cloud formations, to capture in great detail the patterns of light and shade that mark their puffy, irregular surfaces as they drift through the starlight.

Yet Keats is also humble about his poetic ability, describing how poems are written with help from the 'magic hand of Chance'. He presents poetic inspiration as something almost magical or mystical, as something beyond the poet's own control. It strikes by 'Chance' in a random and unpredictable fashion. The poet cannot force the issue. He must remain humble and attentive, waiting for the moment when he is guided by inspiration's 'magic hand'.

These lines, then, remind us how Keats was filled with a burning desire to express the beauty and mystery of nature in his verses. Yet he worries that he will 'never live' to achieve this, that he will die before writing poems that adequately capture the nighttime clouds, and indeed other such instances of nature's majesty: 'That I may never live to trace/ Their shadows'.

LINES 9 TO 14

There is a woman for whom Keats feels great affection and desire. He is never happier, it seems, than when he's gazing upon the beauty of this 'fair creature'. However, he is terrified that death will steal him away from her. He fears that he will die soon and will no longer be able to study this woman's beautiful face: 'And when I feel, fair creature of an hour,/ That I shall never look upon thee more'. He worries that he will die before he can properly 'relish' or enjoy love to the full.

To Keats the clouds symbolise or represent a 'high romance'. What exactly does he mean by this? Maybe for Keats the beauty and majesty of these lofty cloud formations suggest the power and mystery of love and togetherness. Or maybe they bring to mind the perfect existence of the Romantic poet, a life filled with creativity and connected with the natural world.

As we've seen, then, Keats experiences fears relating both to 'Fame' and 'Love'. He worries that he'll die before he can maximise his artistic potential and win lasting fame as a poet. He also worries that he'll die before he can properly experience love.

He responds to these fears by venturing to the 'Shore of the wide world'. We imagine him travelling to England's south coast and looking out over the vast wildness of the Atlantic. We imagine him walking along a beach or cliff as he meditates upon the fears that fill his mind: 'I stand alone and think'. Standing on the seashore allows him to focus on the 'bigger picture'. He contemplates the wide world that surrounds him and the vast ocean, which seems to go on forever and will still be washing against the shoreline millennia from now.

It is unclear if Keats is in a relationship with this woman or if she's merely a member of his social circle that he's fallen in love with and gazes at longingly across the room every time they meet up. Some readers regard this 'fair creature' as Fanny Brawne, the great love of Keats' life. Others feel it makes more sense to think of her as a different woman with whom Keats was briefly infatuated.

When Keats considers this vastness of time and space his own concerns seem petty and unimportant. After all, what significance does any individual person have from the viewpoint of eternity? His fears regarding romantic love and literary success become 'nothing' in his mind: 'Till Love and Fame to Nothingness do sink'.

THEMES

ARTISTIC CREATIVITY

Keats, like the other Romantic poets of his generation, venerated artistic creativity as one of the greatest human traits, regarding it as something sacred and mysterious. This poem, as we've seen, presents poetic inspiration as the 'magic hand of Chance', as an almost magical or mystical force. It is beyond the poet's own control, striking by 'Chance' in a random and unpredictable fashion.

The poem emphasises the pride and delight Keats takes in his own poetic gifts:

• He stresses the great fertility of his imagination. His mind, he says, is 'teeming' with ideas for various poems, just as the field is alive with grain at harvest time.
• He seems confident that if he lives long enough he'll be able to create a high pile of books filled with his poetic words.
• He seems confident, too, that inspiration's 'magic hand' will enter his life, allowing him to capture nature's beauty in his verses.
• He seems convinced, then, that he will prove capable of 'tracing' phenomena like clouds floating across the starry sky.

However, the poem also stresses that artistic creation requires hard work. The poet's ideas and inspirations have to be painstakingly worked on and transformed into poems, just as the harvest must be gathered with back-breaking toil.

NATURE

Keats was typical of the Romantic poets in his worship of the natural world. And his almost overwhelming love of nature is evident throughout his poetry. In this poem he celebrates the beauty of the starry night sky and describes his burning ambition to capture such beauty in his poetic works. The poem also celebrates the bounty of nature at harvest time and the constancy of the waves washing against the shore.

The poem also suggests that Keats somehow 'sees' nature differently than the rest of us. Where the rest of us merely see a 'night sky' he observes a 'starr'd face', where the rest of us see bits of cloud he sees 'symbols of a high romance'. It seems that Keats' poetic imagination is capable of detecting symbols and meanings in nature that simply elude ordinary people.

It's worth noting that Keats's response to nature often seems at its most intense when there's nobody else around. In this instance he stands 'alone' at the ocean's edge as he contemplates eternity. This is a poet who seems to value unpeopled landscapes more than any other.

LOVE

This poem stresses how people take great 'relish' or delight in the pleasures of romance. He himself is clearly captivated by his beloved's beauty and worries that death might take him away from this 'fair creature'. He is terrified that he might die before experiencing true love to the fullest.

Yet there's also a sense in which Keats acknowledges that romantic love is a short-lived, transitory emotion. He may feel great affection for the 'fair creature' mentioned in line 9, but he acknowledges that she is merely the fair creature 'of an hour'. In an hour's time, or tomorrow, or next week, his affections could be directed toward someone entirely different. Keats, it seems, is fully aware of how fickle and changeable love can be.

Like the other Romantic poets of his generation, celebrates love as a force that is spontaneous, irrational, ungoverned by logic and reason. Love, he suggests, is 'unreflective', being rooted in passion and emotion rather than in analysis and reflection. It is presented as a 'faery power', as a kind of spell or enchantment that takes over our minds and bewitches us.

STRUCTURE

'When I have fears' is a Shakespearean sonnet consisting of three quatrains and a concluding rhyming couplet. The poem has the following rhyme scheme: ABAB CDCD EFEF GG. As in most Shakespearean sonnets each quatrain deals with a different topic, while the concluding couplet outlines the poet's final response to the issues that have been raised.

METAPHORS AND SIMILES

The poem's opening lines centre on a conceit or extended metaphor, which compares the act of poetic creativity to that of gathering the harvest. Many critics have praised this conceit for how skillfully it conveys the abundance of Keats' imagination, likening it to a fertile field teeming with 'full ripen'd grain'.

Keats also uses a metaphor to describe the night sky, comparing it to a 'face' which is occasionally hidden from view by the cloud formations that blow across it: 'the night's starr'd face'.

NATURE IMAGERY

This poem is rich with Keats' usual nature imagery. The opening quatrain presents us with several images of ripeness and plenty: the fields alive with full-ripened grain, the 'rich' garners full to bursting with the harvested crops. These images skilfully suggest the 'teeming' fertility of Keats' imagination, which is rich with ideas that are ripe or ready to be transformed into poems.

Another powerful nature image occurs in lines 5 to 6, where Keats depicts the star-filled night sky. Yet perhaps the poem's most melancholic and memorable image is that of the poet standing alone on 'the Shore/ Of the wide world' as he meditates on the notions of love, death and poetic fame.

SOUND EFFECTS

Like most of Keats' poems, 'When I have fears' is rich in assonance and alliteration. Alliteration is particularly evident in line 4 with its repeated 'g' and 'r' sounds: 'rich garners the full ripen'd grain'. Assonance, meanwhile, occurs throughout the poem. We see it in line 3, for instance, with its repeated 'e' sound: 'pen has gleaned my teeming brain'. Lines 5 to 8 also feature a pleasant verbal music, generated by the repeated 'a' sounds. We see this in the phrase 'starr'd face' and in the phrase 'shadows with the magic hand of chance'.

But there can also be a dark side to this bewitchment, to the loss of conscious and rational control that love implies. We can find ourselves falling for the wrong person and making dangerous choices and decisions. In 'La Belle Dame Sans Merci', for instance, such 'faery power' is presented as something dark and dangerous: the 'faery child' bewitches the knight and lures him to his doom.

DEATH

Death very much forms the 'background music' of Keats' work. In poem after poem we find him lamenting the reality of death and its consequences for human existence. This poem centres on a terrifying race against time. As we've seen, Keats is haunted by the possibility that death will claim him before he can make the most of his talent and truly relish the pleasures of romantic love. Sadly, in his case these intuitions regarding an early death turned out to be all too accurate.

Keats responds to these fears by standing at the ocean's edge and meditating as he watches the waves come in. The ocean has been washing against the shore for millions of years before we were born and will still be doing so millions of years after our deaths. From the 'wide world's' point of view we exist for little more than the blink of an eye. So what does it matter if we die tomorrow or in sixty years' time? Eventually the poet's fears come to seem like nothing at all. His hopes and dreams – his very existence – seems to 'sink to nothingness' as he contemplates the greater scheme of things.

This response has been described as extremely bleak. Yet it can also be read as a form of mindfulness or meditation. As he contemplates the ocean the poet finds a form of acceptance, coming to terms with his place in the universe, and learns to look beyond his own ambitions, fears and frustrations.

Perhaps the most important 'message' put forward by 'When I have fears' is that time is of the essence. Each human being has dreams and hopes, goals and ambitions he or she would like to achieve. It is important, however, that we 'seize the day' and begin to realise our potential as soon as possible, for we never know when we might suddenly 'cease to be'.

CHANGE AND CHANGELESSNESS

Like many of Keats's poems, 'When I have fears' emphasises the transitory nature of the world around us. Everything is changing and passing away: the grain is stripped from the fields, clouds constantly shift formation as they drift across the sky, wave after wave washes and breaks upon the shore. There's a sense in which even love and life itself are fleeting.

Yet the poem also stresses that certain aspects of the universe are utterly unchanging. While crops come and go the process of harvesting itself will continue for thousands of years to come. Individual waves last only a few seconds but the ocean itself will continue forever. The stars, too, will continue to shine long after each of our fleeting human lives has passed.

La Belle Dame Sans Merci

The poem's title, from a 1424 French poem by Alain Chartier, means 'the beautiful woman without mercy'.

LINE BY LINE

SETTING THE SCENE

The speaker is travelling through a barren landscape. The harvest is 'done' or completed, indicating that autumn is over and winter is well on its way. The coming cold has already caused the sedge or grass to wither on the nearby lakeside. Squirrels have gathered their supply of nuts for the bitter months to come while the birds have flown away for warmer climes: 'And no birds sing!'

The speaker meets a knight, who seems to be 'loitering' aimlessly on the side of a hill. The knight looks 'woebegone' or extremely mournful and miserable. He appears 'pale', worn and 'haggard'.

The knight also seems to be physically ill. His forehead is pale as a lily: 'I see a lily on the brow'. It is also moist with the sweat or 'dew' of anguish and fever. His cheeks, meanwhile, are marked with the glow of illness; they're the sickly red of a fading, withering rose: 'And on thy cheeks a fading rose/ Fast withereth too'.

The speaker wonders why the knight is loitering in such a bleak and depressing place. He asks the knight what 'ails' or troubles him: 'O what can ail thee knight at arms/ Alone and palely loitering?'

MEETING THE FAERY

The knight begins to tell the story of how he ended up in such a pitiful state. He was riding through the 'Meads' or meadows when he encountered a mysterious lady. She was 'Full beautiful' with long flowing hair. The knight describes how 'her foot was light', suggesting that she had an attractive and shapely body. Yet this was no ordinary woman, but a 'faery's child', a strange magical creature. Her 'wild' eyes seem to suggest the unruly and unpredictable 'faery' magic that dwells within her.

In these stanzas the knight recounts how he spent the day with the faery woman. He made her little pieces of jewellery from the flowers that grow in the meadow, weaving her bracelets, a 'garland', and a belt or 'Zone'. She seemed to be falling for him. She gazed at him as if she were in love with him: 'She looked at me as [if] she did love [me]'. She even moaned or sighed with contentment: 'And made sweet moan'.

He carried her through the meadows on his 'pacing steed' while she entertained him by singing him a 'faery song'. The knight seems to have been so entranced by the Lady's beauty that he couldn't look away from her: 'And nothing else saw all day long'.

She found him nourishment, providing him with wild honey and with roots that were so sweet the knight relished eating them: 'She found me roots of relish sweet,/ And honey wild'. She gave him a strange kind of dew to drink that the knight compares to 'manna'. In the Bible this was the miraculous substance that fell from heaven each morning to nourish the Jewish people as they wandered through the desert.

The Lady said something in a strange language the knight can't understand. He assumed, however, that the Lady was telling him she loved him: 'And sure in language strange she said/ 'I love thee true'.

THE GROTTO

That evening the Lady takes the knight home with her. She lives in an 'elfin grot' or elven grotto. We imagine here some kind of enchanted cave-like dwelling place, perhaps not unlike the elvish environments depicted in Lord of the Rings and in similar fantasy films.

In the grotto the Lady starts weeping and sighing as if she was overcome by a sudden fit of uncontrollable sorrow: 'And there she wept and sigh'd full sore'. The knight attempts to comfort her by kissing her. He kisses her four times and she closes her 'wild eyes' as if soothed or comforted by this gesture: 'And there I shut her wild wild eyes/ With kisses four'.

Finally, the Lady 'lulls' the knight to sleep. Perhaps she sings to him once again, easing him into slumber with some kind of lullaby. Or perhaps she merely holds him in her arms until sleep takes hold.

THE NIGHTMARE

While sleeping in the grotto the knight has a nightmare so terrible that even thinking about it fills him with woe: 'And there I dream'd – Ah! Woe betide!'. His dream takes place in the 'gloam' or twilight. Through the dusk comes a procession of ghostly knights, of kings, princes and warriors. The spectral figures are described as being 'death pale', suggesting they are white as corpses. They also seem to be extremely thin, as indicated by their 'starv'd lips'.

Their mouths open or 'gape' in order to give the knight a terrible warning: 'I saw their starv'd lips in the gloam/ with horrid warning gaped wide'. They warn the knight that he has been enslaved by a beautiful lady without mercy: 'They cried 'La belle dame sans merci/ Thee hath enthrall'. ('On thrall' is another expression for 'enslaved ').

Then the knight's dream ends. He wakes up to find himself not in the faery's dwelling but on the hill where the speaker found him in the opening stanza. He has been magically transported from the grotto to the 'cold hill's side': 'And I awoke and found me her'.

The Lady, it seems, has placed the knight under some kind of terrible spell or enchantment. He has lingered on the hillside ever since and can never leave. He is condemned to loiter there – sickly and despairing – until he dies: 'And this is why I sojourn here/ Alone and palely loitering'.

The Lady, it has been suggested, is a kind of malevolent creature who preys on men like a spider preys on flies. She waits in the meadow for men to pass by and uses her beautiful appearance to attract them. Then she deploys her magical powers to place them under a terrible enchantment: they spend the night in her grotto but wake on a 'cold hill's side' that they can never leave.

The 'Pale warriors' in the knight's dream are the Lady's previous victims. Like the knight, each of these 'Pale warriors' was entrapped and bewitched by the Lady. Each of them was condemned to remain on the hillside until they were claimed by death. While the knight sleeps their ghosts attempt to warn the knight of the danger he is in. Their warning, however, comes too late. For the knight is already 'in thrall' to the Belle Dame Sans Merci.

It also seems that the Lady's enchantment prevents the knight from sleeping. The terrible nightmare in the grotto, he says, was the 'latest' or most recent dream he has experienced. This makes his fate all the grimmer: he must linger pointlessly on the hillside without even the refuge of sleep to break up the monotony.

Several critics have suggested that the Lady uses the 'faery song' she sings while on horseback to enchant the knight. The roots, honey and 'manna dew' that the Lady gives the knight might function as a kind of 'magic potion' that leaves him in her power. The knight assumes that the Lady is telling him she loves him when she speaks to the knight in 'language strange'. But it's also possible that she's speaking the words of a spell that will destroy him.

LOVE

'La Belle Dame Sans Merci' is often regarded as a parable or allegory of love. It's taken as a warning to men about the dangers of falling in love with a beautiful woman. For when a man is betrayed by such a woman, or indeed if she fails to return his affections, he will find himself in a state of total despair.

We see this in the poem's title, which is borrowed from a poem written by Alain Chartier in 1424. It depicted the poet's desperate love for a beautiful woman who was unwilling to return his affections. In Chartier's poem the beautiful woman is 'without mercy' because she refuses to give in to the poet's advances.

The knight finds himself 'in thrall' to the Lady. Similarly, when a man falls in love with a beautiful woman he risks falling under her spell and becoming 'enslaved' by her beauty. If the relationship doesn't go well he can find himself in a state similar to that of the knight languishing on the hill. Like the knight he will find himself feverish and sickly. Like the knight he will be filled with 'anguish', woe and emotional torment. Like the knight he will be unable to sleep. He will find himself trapped in a cycle of negative thoughts and emotions just as the knight is trapped on the hillside.

Female readers, needless to say, often take issue with this view. After all, it in not only men who can find themselves hurt in the context of love and

relationships. Women can and do suffer just as frequently. Why then should women always be portrayed as icy and merciless lovers who delight in torturing their poor male suitors?

A number of feminist critics have also objected to the depiction of the Lady as a kind of supernatural 'femme fatale'. They point out how she resembles the succubus, the siren and other mythical creatures who specialise in luring men to their doom. The poem, they maintain, stems from a sexist tradition of storytelling whereby women always play the part of devious seducers, villains who use their feminine wiles to lead innocent men astray. According to these critics this tradition dates all the way back to the Bible and the story of Adam and Eve.

Some readers also suggest that the knight actually assaults the Lady while they are in the grotto. The Lady, they maintain, 'wept and sigh'd full sore' because she was being violated by the knight. His 'kisses four' were not an attempt to comfort her but represent an unwanted sexual advance. The knight is punished for his misdeeds by being condemned to remain forever on the 'cold hill side'.

Initially, the knight seems to be in control. He places the Lady on his powerful 'pacing steed' and sets off with her across the meadow. Soon, however, the Lady begins to take charge of the situation. It is the Lady, not the knight, who finds food for the couple. Then she takes him to her grotto. Finally, she 'lulls' him into a deep sleep. As the poem progresses, therefore, the knight falls further under the Lady's spell and it is the Lady, not the knight, who is in control.

On this reading, then, the knight is an 'unreliable narrator' and we can't take his account of events at face value. After all, the poem takes the form of a conversation between the knight and an unnamed speaker. And how do we know that the knight is telling the truth? Perhaps he's concealing or omitting certain aspects of his story.

FORM

'La Belle Dame Sans Merci' is a wonderful example of a the poetic form known as a ballad. It has many of the features often associated with the ballad form:

- It is a relatively short poem that tells a story.
- It uses four-line stanzas that have an ABCB rhyme scheme.
- In each stanza the second and fourth lines are shorter than the first and third.
- Like many ballads it deals with events of a supernatural nature.
- Like many ballads it features a great deal of repetition. Both of the poem's first two stanzas, for instance, begin with the same line: 'O what can ail thee knight-at-arms'.

Furthermore, the last three lines of the first stanza are also almost identical to the last three lines of the final stanza. (According to several critics this gives the poem a 'circular structure'. The poem ends precisely where it began, suggesting that nothing can ever change for the knight. He is trapped on the 'cold hill's side' forever).

NATURE IMAGERY

Keats' work is typically rich in nature imagery and this poem proves no exception. The poem's haunting atmosphere is established at the very beginning with its depiction of a barren wintry landscape where the pale and sick-looking knight 'loiters' aimlessly.

REFERENCES TO OLDER TIMES

Keats, like the other Romantic poets of his generation, was greatly taken with the medieval period and images related to the medieval world litter his work. In this instance we have a knight -at-arms with his 'pacing steed' and kings, princes and warriors.

The poem also highlights the Romantic interest in fairy tales and fantasy. We are presented with a beautiful woman who isn't quite human and lives in mysterious 'elfin grot', with a knight struck down by a terrible enchantment, with other-worldly 'death pale' kings and princes. Many readers detect a Celtic reference in this tale of a 'faery's child' and her terrible bewitchments.

Ode to a Nightingale

LINE BY LINE

THE SETTING

It is a summer's evening. The poet is relaxing in a garden when he hears a nightingale singing. The bird is flitting around a little 'plot' of woodland nearby. The woodland is a place of 'beechen green', suggesting that it contains many leafy beech trees. The poet pictures how as night descends their branches must cast countless of shadows ('shadows numberless') on the woodland floor.

THE NIGHTINGALE'S SONG

The nightingale sings in a 'full-throated' manner. It performs with such volume, energy and passion that it fills the little woods with melody, making it a 'melodious plot' of ground. According to the poet, the bird sings with 'ease' and its song seems to welcome or celebrate the summertime: 'Singest of summer in full-throated ease'. We should remember, however, that the nightingale is famed for the melancholy nature of its singing. We might imagine here a sad but also laidback and jazzy melody floating through the neighbourhood on this balmy summer's evening.

THE POET'S REACTION TO THE NIGHTINGALE'S SONG

Keats' reaction to the nightingale's singing is a complex one:

- Listening to its beautiful song certainly gives him happiness and pleasure.
- At the same time its singing fills him with feelings of sorrow and melancholy: his heart 'aches' and his 'sense' or mind is 'pained'.
- It also fills him a sense of drowsiness and numbness that

threatens to lull him into unconsciousness. He feels as if he's consumed the deadly poison hemlock and it was shutting down his bodily systems one by one: 'as though of hemlock I had drunk'.

- He feels as if he's drained a glass of liquid opiate (opiates are a family of narcotic drugs that includes heroin and morphine) and was sinking into a sedated mental blankness: 'Or emptied some dull opiate to the drains'. (The opiate is described as 'dull' because of how it sedates and clouds the conscious mind).

What causes these feelings of sadness and numbness? Keats stresses that it isn't because he's envious of the nightingale's 'happy lot' among the trees. He claims instead that its singing makes him 'too happy'. It's as if the nightingale's joyous performance threatens to overwhelm him with emotion: 'being too happy in thine happiness'. It's as if his mind is so flooded or overcharged with happiness that it suffers some kind of meltdown and tips over into a state of numbness and sorrow.

Keats' reaction to the nightingale's song may seem bizarrely over the top. But we can perhaps understand where he's coming from. Listening to a playlist of sad but beautiful songs on your headphones while lying alone in a quiet place can produce a similar mix of emotions: pleasure or happiness in the music's beauty, melancholy induced by its sorrowful sounds and a sense of numbness or mental relaxation that tends toward sleep and unconsciousness.

The bird's singing makes Keats feel as if he's sinking into forgetfulness and mental blankness. He describes this sensation wonderfully: he feels as if he's dying and his soul is sinking down the river Lethe: 'and Lethe-wards had sunk'. In Greek mythology the Lethe was a river in the afterlife whose waters brought complete forgetfulness. The souls of the newly dead would drink from it in order to forget their lives on earth.

THE POET ENVIES THE NIGHTINGALE

The poet, then, is conscious of the nightingale's 'happy lot', of the joyous, carefree existence it enjoys 'among the trees' of the woodland. According to the poet, the nightingale has 'never known' the troubles and torments we human beings must endure as we make our way through life. Instead it sings with 'ease', relishing the serenity and peacefulness of the woodland it inhabits.

The fact that Keats describes the nightingale as 'light-winged' further reinforces our impression of its carefree existence: 'Thou light-winged Dryad of the trees'. This phrase suggests not only the bird's slightness and agility but also its freedom from the cares and worries that weigh down human beings.

Our lives are dominated by tiredness ('weariness'), sickness ('fever') and worry ('fret'). So it's hardly surprising that the world is full of moaning and groaning: 'Here, where

men sit and hear each other groan'. Indeed, our lives are so terrible that even to consider the reality of human existence is to be filled with sorrow: 'Where but to think is to be full of sorrow'. We find ourselves filled with despair that causes our heads to drop as if our eyes were made of lead that weighed us down: 'And leaden-eyed despairs'.

Keats is especially distressed by the fact that youth cannot last. The young, as we know, often possess great beauty and have shining or 'lustrous' eyes. And of course good looking young people attract many admirers who 'pine' or long for them. Yet such youthful beauty seems to vanish all too quickly. Indeed it sometimes seems that our youthful years rush by in little more than a few days, that our good looks will be gone by the day after tomorrow: 'Where beauty cannot keep her lustrous eyes,/ Or new love pine at them beyond tomorrow'.

Each of us, then, must face the frailty and indignities of old age. And as we age we become weak, pale and thin. Our hair will grow thinner and turn grey. Our bodies will shake with the fever of 'palsy' or sickness: 'palsy shakes a few, sad, last grey hairs'. Until eventually death will claim each one of us: 'youth grows pale and spectre thin and dies'.

THE POET LONGS TO JOIN THE NIGHTINGALE

To sum up: human life is depicted as being full of pain and woe while the nightingale's days are carefree and happy. It is hardly surprising, therefore, that Keats wishes to leave this cruel world behind. He wants to slip quietly away from his present existence, to 'leave the world unseen' and join the nightingale in its dark and peaceful plot of woodland.

He wants his mind or consciousness to somehow leave his body. His spirit would then fade, melt or dissolve into the woodland: 'And with thee fade away into the forest dim// Fade far way, dissolve'. There he would share the nightingale's life of serenity and ease. There he would be able to 'quite forget' this troubled world and the difficulties that fill our day-to-day lives. The poet, then, wants to have some kind of 'vision' of the woodland. While he cannot physically join the nightingale in its woodland home he can do so in his imagination.

THE POET LONGS FOR MAGICAL WINE

Keats longs to drink a glass of wine that has come from the Hippocrene, which was a magical well or fountain in Greek mythology. According to legend anyone who drank from it would be filled with poetic inspiration. He believes that drinking some of the Hippocrene's wine will boost or empower his imagination, allowing him to experience the vision he so desires of the nightingale's woodland home.

Keats provides an intensely vivid description of this magical liquid, describing how it matures for centuries in cool caverns that erosion has cut or 'delved' deep into the earth. It has champagne-like bubbles: 'With beaded bubbles winking at the brim'. It's such a 'blushful' purple in colour that it stains the mouth of anyone who drinks it.

Keats imagines that the Hippocrene's wine would have an extraordinary taste. It would have organic and earthy qualities. To capture this he says it would taste like the countryside, with all its greenness and its flowers: 'Tasting of Flora and the country green'. Its flavour would also be zesty, fresh and exhilarating. To capture this he says it would taste like carefree French peasants having a party, singing and frolicking after a day working in the fields: 'Dance, and Provençal song, and sunburnt mirth!' Keats, then, longs for a 'draught' of this enchanted liquid, for a glass or 'beaker full' of this strange wine from the 'warm south': 'O for a draught of that vintage!'

The Hippocrene, as we've noted, is located in Greece. But Keats imagines that tasting its magically inspirational wine would remind him of the Provence region in the south of France. This is because Provence has long been associated with poetry and music. It gave the world the 'troubadours', medieval poet-minstrels that greatly inspired Keats and the other Romantic writers of his generation.

THE IMAGINATIVE VISION BEGINS

Keats, however, has no such magical beverage to bolster his powers of imagination. Instead he must rely on his mind's natural resources if the vision is to take place. He worries whether his 'dull brain' is up to the task. He seems concerned that the everyday, rational part of his mind will 'perplex' and hold back or 'retard' his imagination, preventing it from envisaging the forest.

But the poet is determined that the vision will occur. He is sure that he will imaginatively join the nightingale: 'Away! away! for I will fly to thee'. And in line 35 he declares that the vision he's longed for has commenced; that in his imagination he is 'Already with' the nightingale in its woodland abode.

The poet uses a wonderful metaphor to describe this process. He claims that poetry has carried him into the woodland with its invisible or 'viewless' wings. 'I will fly to thee … on the viewless wings of Poesy'. It's Keats' poetic creativity that has allowed him to induce this vision, and has to imagine the little plot of forest with such intensity and detail.

THE VISION CONTINUES: THE WOODLAND PLOT

Lines 36 to 50 are devoted to this incredibly detailed 'vision' of the woodland. It features twisting paths that are overgrown with moss: 'winding mossy ways'. It's a place of green or 'verdurous' gloominess, for the trees' branches obscure much of the starlight and moonlight. In his vision, therefore, the poet can see little of what grows upon the forest floor: 'I cannot see what flowers are at my feet'.

His sense of smell, however, is fully engaged by the woodland's gorgeous odours. The pleasant or 'seasonable' month of May lends a different 'sweet' smell to each plant and flower: 'each sweet/ Wherewith the seasonable month endows'. Their perfumes float upwards and combine to form a natural incense that lingers among the trees: 'soft incense hangs upon the boughs'. They 'embalm' the woodland air, filling it with mild and balmy fragrances.

This woodland plot may be small but contains a wide variety of plant life. In lines 43 to 7 the poet lists some of the things that grow there: 'The grass, the thicket, and the fruit-tree wild;/ White hawthorn and the pastoral eglantine;/ Fast fading violets'. (An 'eglantine' is a type of wild rose often referred to as a 'sweet briar'.)

Bacchus was the Roman god of wine and drinking; according to legend he travelled on a chariot pulled by leopards. Keats stresses that he will not be carried into the woodland on this chariot: 'Not charioted by Bacchus and his pards'. This is a metaphor, stressing that Keats' vision of the woodland will be a product of pure poetic imagination. He will not require alcohol or other drugs to induce it.

Keats uses a poetic device called 'synaesthesia' to convey this liquid's extraordinary taste. Synaesthesia occurs when an experience associated with one sense is described in terms of another sense. In this instance the flavour of the wine (associated with the sense of taste) is described in terms of a whole range of different sensory experiences: dance, song, sunburn, greenness, 'mirth' or merriment.

Keats uses a metaphor to describe how the woodland is only faintly illuminated, saying that the summer breeze carries the moonlight and starlight down from heaven and disperses it among the forest's pathways: 'But there is no light,/ Save what from heaven is with the breezes blown'. This is an exquisite piece of writing that captures the softness of this starlight: we can almost imagine it floating slowly downwards on currents of air.

Keats makes a special mention of the 'musk rose' that's just 'coming' into full ripeness. This climbing flower – often found near trees – is known for the sweet moisture of its petals. This musky liquid attracts flies that 'haunt' the roses and fill the air around them with the murmur of their buzzing: 'murmurous haunt of flies on summer eves'.

THE VISION CONTINUES: A DEATH WISH

In his vision Keats continues wandering through the woods, still listening to the nightingale's song: 'Darkling, I listen'. (To be 'darkling' is to be in darkness). For a long time, he says, he has been attracted to the notion of dying. Death, he feels, will be 'easeful', a sweet release from the trials and difficulties of life.

Keats uses personification to describe the moon and stars that are visible in the sky above the woodland. The moon is compared to a fairy Queen seated regally on her throne: 'haply the Queen Moon is on her throne'. The stars are compared to 'Fays' or fairies that surround the Queen, ready to do her bidding: 'Cluster'd around by all her starry fays'.

This night in particular strikes him as a good time to die: 'Now more than ever seems it rich to die'. It would be perfect, he feels, for his life to 'cease' at midnight: 'To cease upon the midnight with no pain'. Then he could savour the nightingale's music for a few more hours before passing quietly and painlessly away. He wants the bird's passionate, ecstatic song to be the last thing he hears on earth: 'While thou art pouring forth thy soul abroad in such an ecstasy'.

Keats uses a typically inventive metaphor to describe this 'death wish', comparing it a courtship or romance. He has, he says, been 'half in love' with death. He has 'courted' death with poems ('rhymes') the way other poets might court a beautiful woman: 'Call'd him soft names in many a mused rhyme'. He has flattered death by calling him 'soft names'. He has implored death to terminate his existence, to gently but firmly put a stop to his breathing: 'To take into the air my quiet breath'.

He imagines that the nightingale would continue singing after his death: 'Still wouldst thou sing'. He imagines that its song would become his 'requiem' or funeral music, echoing through the air over his corpse. Keats, of course, would be unable to hear this 'high requiem' himself. For his dead ears would be 'vain' or useless. His corpse would be a useless and unfeeling thing, little more than a 'sod', an inanimate clump of clay or soil.

THE VISION CONTINUES: THE BIRD'S IMMORTAL SONG

This nightingale, he claims, is an 'immortal Bird'. It has existed for thousands of years, maybe even since the beginning of time. And it will never die: 'Thou wast not born for death'. 'Generations' have come and gone, wearing out and destroying every living thing. Only the nightingale is immune to time's passage. Only this bird escapes being damaged or 'trodden down' by the passing years and centuries: 'No hungry generations tread thee down'.

Keats imagines some of the places this nightingale might have visited over its centuries of existence. He imagines that thousands of years ago the nightingale was present in the empires of the ancient world, maybe in Egypt, Greece or Rome. Its song, he claims, delighted both emperors and their court jesters in those long ago times: 'The voice I heard this passing night was heard / In ancient days by emperor and clown.

A 'generation' in this sense refers to a span of time that can be anything between fifteen and seventy years. These generations are described as 'hungry', suggesting how the passage of time devours youth, beauty, strength and health.

He imagines that the nightingale's song might also have been heard by Ruth, a character from the Bible who lived thousands of years ago: 'Perhaps the self-same song that found a path through the sad heart of Ruth'. The Bible describes how Ruth was forced to leave her native land and work as a farm girl in a foreign country. Keats, therefore. mentions her 'sad heart' and describes her weeping with homesickness as she works in fields that to her seem strange or 'alien': 'sick for home/ She stood in tears amid the alien corn'.

Keats claims that nightingale has even travelled to 'faery lands', to mysterious and supernatural countries humans can never visit. Its charming music has been heard in the 'casements' or windows of magical fairy palaces. But these fairy kingdoms aren't all sweetness and light. They are described as 'forlorn', suggesting a lonesome and desolate landscape that lies beside turbulent or 'perilous seas'.

THE END OF THE VISION

Then Keats' vision comes to an abrupt end. It's as if the word 'forlorn' – meaning sorrowful or despairing – reminds him of the real world with all its woes and difficulties and snaps him out of his happy woodland fantasy. The word 'forlorn', he says, is like a sorrowfully tolling bell, like an alarm clock that cruelly rouses him from his vision: 'Forlorn! The very word is like a bell/ To toll me back from thee to my sole self'. His mind had been filled with an incredibly rich and detailed fantasy of the woodland. But suddenly he is aware only of his 'sole self', of his body and its actual surroundings in the garden where he sits.

Keats refers to the 'fancy' or imagination. He suggests how it's 'fam'd' or famous for 'cheating' us, for leading us to believe in things that are not real. In this regard it resembles some kind of 'deceiving elf' from a fairy tale. Yet Keats feels that the imagination's reputation for deluding us is exaggerated: 'the fancy cannot cheat as she is fam'd to do'. After all, despite his best efforts he cannot maintain his imaginative vision of the forest but must return reluctantly to the real world.

The nightingale begins to move away from the piece of woodland near Keats' garden. He listens to its melancholy singing (its 'plaintive anthem') become fainter as it moves deeper into the countryside: 'Past the near meadows, over the still stream,/ Up the hill-side'. Finally Keats can no longer hear its singing at all: 'Fled is that music'. The nightingale is out of earshot, lost to him in the 'glades' or greenness of the next valley over.

The poem concludes with Keats wondering about the strange mental journey he has just taken through the woodland. Was it simply a daydream (a 'waking dream') or should it be thought of as a 'vision' because of its peculiar imaginative intensity? Keats, it seems, isn't even sure if he's awake: 'Do I wake or sleep?' Perhaps he simply fell asleep and dreamt the whole experience. We are left with little doubt, however, that it was more a 'vision' than either a dream or daydream.

THEMES

NATURE

Keats was typical of the Romantic poets in his worship of the natural world. 'Ode to a Nightingale' highlights the poet's unusual sensitivity to nature, how his responses to nature's beauty seem far more intense and heightened than those of his fellow human beings. This is especially evident in his intensely atmospheric vision of the woodland:

- We sense the relish Keats takes in the woodland's aromas as they linger like incense among its 'boughs' and leave its darkness 'embalmed' with fragrance.
- He delights in nature's variety, in listing the range of plants and flowers that thrive among the woodland's 'mossy ways'.
- Even insects thrill him, as witnessed by his rapturous description of the buzzing flies that haunt the musk rose.
- The beauty of the night sky, too, is celebrated in the memorable personification whereby Keats depicts the moon as the 'Queen' of the night and the stars as her fairy servants.

Yet Keats' unusual sensitivity to the natural world is nowhere more evident than in his reaction to the nightingale's singing. The nightingale's song fills the poet with seemingly contradictory emotions: he is happy, melancholy and numb all at the same time. He describes how the bird's singing makes him 'too happy', as if his system is overwhelmed with emotion at this bird's sweet song 'of summer'.

'Ode to a Nightingale' also demonstrates how the poet regards nature's beauty as a consolation for the strains and difficulties of human existence. This world may be a place of suffering but the poem suggests that there is ease and pleasure to be found in the beauty of nature.

CELEBRATING ARTWORKS

Again and again in his poetry Keats celebrates the pleasure people derive from artworks of all types. And it's perhaps not going too far to suggest that the nightingale's song takes its place alongside Homer's epic poems, Chapman's translations and the Grecian Urn as a piece of artistic ingenuity worthy of praise and celebration. Its melodies, as Keats describes them, seem comparable to those produced by any human musician. The bird's complex 'full-throated' airs – at once blissful and melancholy, summery and sorrowful – emerge as a moving and bewitching work of art.

THEMES

ARTISTIC CREATIVITY

Keats, like the other romantic poets of his generation, venerated artistic creativity as one of the greatest human traits, regarding it as something sacred and mysterious. In this poem we find Keats using his poetic powers to envisage in incredible detail the nightingale's woodland environment. His poetic imagination will allow him to join the nightingale in its woodland abode. As he puts it he will fly there on poetry's invisible wings.

'Ode to a Nightingale' is perhaps above all a celebration of the power of the imagination. Keats, it must be remembered, never actually physically enters the forest. Instead, he simply imagines what the nightingale's leafy abode must be like. Lines 35 to 50 show Keats constructing a little 'imaginary world', creating an intensely detailed and vivid depiction of an environment that exists only in his mind.

The poem, then, shows how Keats retreats from the pain and suffering of the real world into an imaginary haven. 'Fancy', or the power of the imagination, allows him to 'leave the world unseen' and 'quite forget' the trials and tragedies of human existence. Keats' 'fancy' constructs a refuge to which he can flee in his vision or 'waking dream', leaving this troubled world behind.

The imagination or 'fancy' is famous for its ability to 'deceive' or 'cheat' us into believing in things that are not real. Yet there are limitations to its power. The imagination, it seems, will always be 'retarded' or limited by the duller more rational parts of the brain. The poet's powers of imagination can maintain his fantasy of the woodland for only a short time. He cannot remain for long in his imaginary paradise before he must return to his 'sole self' and to reality.

DEATH

Death is a constant presence in Keats' work. 'Ode to a Nightingale' is very much a poem that laments the reality of death and its consequences for human existence. Each of us, even the strongest and most vibrant, is condemned to grow 'pale' and 'spectre-thin', to be faced with the indignities of old age and finally to die. Worst of all, perhaps, the physical beauty we possess in youth inevitably fades away as we grow older. It can be enjoyed by its possessors and admirers for only the briefest time before disappearing completely.

'Ode to a Nightingale', then, presents a fairly negative view of life. The world is depicted as a place full of moaning and groaning: 'here where men sit and hear each other groan'.

Our lives, according to Keats, are dominated by worry, sickness and tiredness. He suggests that to even think about the human condition is to be filled with 'sorrow/ And leaden-eyed despairs'.

However, the poet is also fascinated by the notion of death and dying: 'For many a time I have been half in love with easeful death'. Death, he feels, would be 'easeful', a sweet release from this cruel world. He longs to stop breathing, for death to 'snatch' his breath away. He seems especially pleased by the notion of slipping peacefully into death on this particular night, with the song of the nightingale ringing in his ears.

'Ode to a Nightingale', then, reveals what might be described as a Romantic attitude to death. Death is memorably personified as a kind of lover that the poet 'courts' or woos. The poet flatters death with beautiful words in the hope that death will snatch his breath away and end his troubled existence. Like many romantic poems, 'Ode to a Nightingale' presents the notion of dying, especially of dying young, as something glamorous and attractive.

Keats uses a number of memorable images to reinforce this notion of the world as a bleak and lonely place. Stanza 7, for instance, depicts Ruth working in the fields as she weeps with homesickness. Even the 'faery lands' are described as being 'forlorn' or sorrowful, with their castles that look out over dangerous, lonely oceans.

CHANGE AND CHANGELESSNESS

This is a poem that contrasts change and changelessness. Change is represented by human beings, each of whom finds their youthful beauty stripped away as they age, become 'spectre-thin' and eventually die. Everything we build and create will be destroyed by the passage of time, will be devoured by the 'hungry' years and centuries as they pass.

Changelessness, on the other hand, is represented by the nightingale. For this 'immortal bird' has existed for centuries, since 'ancient days', and because it was not 'born for death' will continue to do so long into the future. The nightingale, we're told, will never be 'trodden down' by time's passage.

Keats, of course, knows that the particular nightingale he's listening to this summer evening is not really immortal. This particular bird will die like any other. Yet the song it sings is the same song that nightingales have been singing for thousands of years and will continue to sing far into the future.

Though countless individual nightingales have died the song has been passed on from generation to generation. Like Homer's poetry or the Grecian Urn, the song of the nightingale is eternal and everlasting while all around 'hungry generations' come and go. The nightingale's song, therefore, serves as a powerful symbol for the kind of everlasting art that Keats admires and that he longs desperately to create.

FORM

'Ode to a Nightingale', like all odes, is addressed to something that has captured the poet's imagination and fired up his poetic faculties. It is written in eight ten-line stanzas, each of which rhymes ABAB CDEC DE. This is a most complex and intricate rhyme scheme, but one that Keats pulls off with aplomb.

REFERENCES TO OLDER TIMES

Like the other Romantic poets of his generation Keats was greatly interested in the classical world of ancient Greece and Rome. And 'Ode to a Nightingale' contains several references to Greek and Roman mythology.

- Alcohol, for instance, is associated with Bacchus, who was the Roman god of wine.
- Flowers are associated with Flora, who was the Greek goddess of flowers, plants and gardens.
- Keats also refers to the nightingale as a 'Dryad'. (The dryads, as we have seen, were magical tree spirits in Greek mythology).
- The depiction of the moon as a 'Queen' might also owes something to the Roman goddess Diana.
- Keats also refers to mythical places such as Lethe and Hippocrene.

Celtic mythology was also of great interest to the Romantics and this is perhaps evident in the several references to fairies throughout the poem. Stanza 4, for instance, depicts the stars as 'Fays' or fairies. Stanza 7, meanwhile, describes the nightingale singing in a bleak and haunting 'faery' landscape.

Stanza 7, meanwhile, contains a reference to the Book of Ruth from the Old Testament, describing Ruth's sorrow and homesickness when she was exiled from her homeland.

METAPHORS AND FIGURES OF SPEECH

Entire chapters can and have been written about Keats' use of metaphors in 'Ode to a Nightingale'. In stanza 1, for instance Keats uses a wonderful metaphor to describe the nightingale, comparing it a Dryad. Another two memorable metaphors are to be found in stanza 4. Keats wittily compares being drunk to being carried off by Bacchus on his magical chariot which was pulled by leopards. Poetic inspiration, meanwhile, is compared to a set of 'viewless' or invisible wings that take the poet on wonderful imaginary journeys: 'the viewless wings of Poesy'.

Keats also uses metaphors to describe nature. In line 49 the moisture in the petals of the musk-rose is compared

to 'dewy wine'. Another memorable metaphor is used to describe the emotion and soulfulness of the nightingale's singing. Keats captures the joy and beauty of the nightingale's singing by declaring that the bird's soul is emanating from its mouth: 'thou art pouring forth thy soul abroad/ In such an ecstasy'.

In this poem Keats makes extensive use of the literary device known as 'personification'. Personification is a figure of speech that depicts objects and abstract concepts as if they had human traits and qualities. In stanza 3, for instance, the concepts of love and beauty are presented almost as human beings. 'Beauty', it has been suggested, is presented as a woman with bright 'lustrous' eyes, while 'Love' is presented as a man who 'pines' or longs for her affection.

The moon, for instance, is described as the 'Queen' of the night sky, sitting on her throne amid the heavens as she gazes down on humanity. The stars, meanwhile, are described as her fairy servants that 'cluster' around their radiant mistress: 'Haply the Queen-Moon is on her throne/ Cluster'd around by all her starry Fays'.

In stanza 8, the concept of 'fancy' or imagination is personified as a kind of semi-human 'elf'. Keats suggests that the 'fancy' has the all-too-human quality of deceitfulness. Yet perhaps the most memorable 'personification' of an abstract concept is that of death in stanza 6. Death is depicted as a person with whom the poet has fallen in love: 'for many a time/ I have been half in love with easeful Death'. Keats portrays Death as his lover, as someone he has flattered and courted by writing beautiful poems about him.

Ode on a Grecian Urn

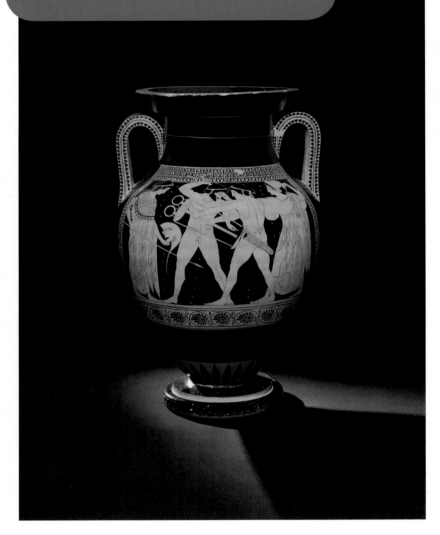

LINE BY LINE

STANZA 1

The poet stands before an urn or pot that was made in Ancient Greece. We might imagine that he is standing in a quiet room in a museum. He is fascinated by the urn, particularly with the decorations upon its surface.

The poet speaks to or addresses the urn. He considers it to be the 'bride of quietness', suggesting that the urn and 'quietness' are somehow connected or wedded:

- Perhaps the urn is associated with 'quietness' because it is a silent and static piece of sculpture.
- The association may also refer to the quiet spaces in which the urn has resided,

The poet also associates the urn with 'silence and slow time'. This is likely a reference to the urn's creation. It is the product or 'foster-child' of some sculptor's painstakingly slow and silent labour. The term 'slow time' may be another reference to how the urn seems unaffected by the passage of time. It is almost as if time acts differently upon this object, passing by more slowly than normal.

such as the museum in which it now on display.

The urn is still in remarkably good condition. Keats describes it as a 'still unravish'd bride'. The word 'ravish' normally means to make love in a violent and passionate manner. So the poet is saying that the urn is in some way virginal or has yet to be violated – it has not been 'ravish'd' by the passage of time.

The urn is elaborately decorated, with a number of scenes depicted on its surface. Each scene is set in the countryside or the woods. Keats, therefore, describes the urn as a 'Slyvan historian' (the word 'sylvan' means 'of the woods'). So the urn is like someone who tells stories (a 'historian') of the woods or countryside.

The stories that the urn tells are 'flowery' or full of fine detail (the word 'flowery' also plays upon the fact that the scenes are set in the country). Keats thinks that the images on the surface of the urn 'express' a richer or more vivid tale than his words can achieve: 'express/ A flowery tale more sweetly than our rhyme'.

A variety of characters, both male and female, appear in the scenes depicted on the surface of the urn. The poet cannot say whether the characters are gods or human: 'deities or mortals, or of both'. Nor can he say whether the setting is some mythical location of the gods or an actual place in ancient Greece: 'In Tempe or the dales of Arcady'.

The images upon the surface reveal a 'mad pursuit'. It seems that a group of men or gods are chasing a group of women or 'maidens'. The women are struggling to free themselves from the men's clutches: 'What mad pursuit? What struggle to escape?' There are also instruments depicted, 'pipes and timbrels'. The overall scene seems to be one of great excitement or 'wild ecstasy'. But the poet cannot say exactly what is happening.

STANZA 2

Keats describes a handsome or 'Fair' young man sitting 'beneath the trees'.

He is a musician and he plays the 'pipes' or some form of flute. Of course, no sound can be heard – this is, after all, only a scene depicted on the surface of an urn. Keats describes the music as 'unheard' and 'ditties of no tone'. But the image of the musician inspires him to imagine the music that the young man plays. These imagined 'melodies' are thought to be even 'sweeter' than music that can actually be heard: 'those unheard/ Are sweeter'. Whereas actual music is heard and appreciated by the ear, imagined music appeals to the 'spirit'. As such, it is considered to be more valuable or 'endear'd'.

Because he is a character depicted on the surface of an urn, the young musician will never move or change. As long as the urn survives, he will remain seated beneath the tree playing the 'pipes': 'Fair youth, beneath the trees, thou canst not leave/ Thy song'. For the same reason the tree beneath which the young man sits will never shed its leaves: 'nor ever can those trees be bare'.

Keats now focuses on another character depicted on the urn. It is a man who is attempting to kiss a beautiful young woman. The poet describes him as a daring or 'Bold' lover. But like the young musician he will never move or change. The lover will, therefore, never achieve his 'goal' and kiss the woman: 'never canst thou kiss'. However, the poet urges this character not to be saddened by this. The fact that the scene will never change means that the woman will never vanish or lose her beauty: 'She cannot fade'. The lover might not experience the 'bliss' of the kiss, but he will always be in love with this woman: 'though thou hast not thy bliss,/ For ever wilt thou love'.

STANZA 3

Keats considers the fact that the musician, the tree and the lover can never change to be a 'happy' state of affairs:

- The tree's branches are 'happy, happy boughs' because they can never shed their leaves. For them it will be as if it is eternally spring: 'cannot shed/ Your leaves, nor ever bid the Spring adieu'.
- The musician or 'melodist' is considered 'happy' because he will never tire or grow weary of playing the flute. He can also be 'happy' because the music that he plays will always remain fresh or 'new'.
- Keats considers the 'Bold Lover' to be in a 'happy' position because the love or passion he feels will never cool: 'happy love!/ For ever warm'. He will always desire this woman and his love for her will never grow old and tired: 'For ever panting, and for ever young'.

The poet contrasts this eternal love and longing with 'human passion', the love that living, 'breathing' people experience. He considers it to be 'far above' this love.

Human love always results in heartache and disappointment: 'leaves a heart high-sorrowful'. The love that people feel for each other often sours and becomes tedious and tiresome: 'cloy'd'. Keats likens human passion to a form of fever: 'A burning forehead, and a parching tongue'.

STANZA 4

In the fourth stanza the poet focuses on another scene entirely. A group of people are on their way to witness 'the sacrifice' of a cow. The cow is being lead by a 'priest'. It is decorated or dressed in garlands of flowers: 'all her silken flanks with garlands drest'. The poet is fascinated by the scene depicted and he wonders who these people are and where exactly they are headed: 'Who are these coming to the sacrifice?/ To what green altar, O mysterious priest'.

The poet also wonders about the town that these people come from. It is not depicted on the urn but Keats imagines how this town must now be empty, as all its citizens are on their way to the sacrifice. He wonders whether the town is situated 'by river or sea shore'. Perhaps it is a fortified town in the mountains: 'Or mountain-built with peaceful citadel'.

This imagined town will forever remain deserted now that all its inhabitants are frozen in time on their way to the sacrifice. Keats thinks about the silent, empty streets: 'thy streets for evermore/ Will silent be'. The town will never know the reason why it is abandoned, as no one can ever return to say what is happening: 'and not a soul to tell/ Why thou art desolate, can e'er return'.

STANZA 5

In the poem's final stanza the poet seems to take a step back and consider the urn as a whole. He speaks directly to the urn, describing its form and features:

- The urn's shape is typical of ancient Greek pottery: 'O Attic shape'.
- Keats considers it to be a particularly beautiful or 'fair' shape or 'attitude'.
- The urn is elaborately decorated with different characters in woodland settings: 'with brede/ Of marble men and maidens overwrought'.

The poet also focuses on the effects that this piece of sculpture is capable of having on those who view it:

- It perplexes or teases our minds with complicated notions. Keats likens the experience to thinking about such concepts as 'eternity'. The suggestion here is that the human mind is just not capable of processing or understanding such ideas.
- It offers us consolation and comfort. Keats describes the urn as 'a friend to man' and suggests that it is capable of helping us with the inevitable troubles or 'woe' that each and every generation must face.

What is remarkable is that the urn is capable of doing these things whilst being a 'silent' piece of sculpture. Despite being a 'silent form', the urn can tell us stories and challenge us with complicated thoughts and ideas: 'Thou, silent form, dost tease us out of thought'.

Keats considers how he and those of his generation will eventually age and die: 'old age shall this generation waste'. The urn, however, shall continue to exist, seemingly unaffected by the passage of time. The troubles of the poet's generation will pass, but new troubles or woes will arise for future generations. The urn will exist in the midst of these: 'Thou shalt remain, in midst of other woe/ Than ours'.

'BEAUTY IS TRUTH, TRUTH BEAUTY'

Keats believes that the urn has something to say to us about the nature of beauty and truth. Both, it suggests, are linked. In fact, they are one and the same thing: 'Beauty is truth, truth beauty'. What does Keats mean by this?

'COLD PASTORAL'

The scenes depicted on the urn are described as pastoral, meaning that they depict idyllic scenes of rural life. But Keats says that this is a 'Cold' pastoral. Why does he describe it in this manner? Perhaps the word 'Cold' is a reference to the fact that the urn is made out of cold materials such as clay and marble. Some readers feel that Keats is being critical of the urn here. For all its scenes of human life and love, the urn is an inorganic object, incapable of feelings or emotions. Perhaps the word 'Cold' is also a reference to the fact that the scenes presented on the urn are static, depicting characters frozen in time.

First of all, we might consider what the poet might mean by 'beauty'. It is likely that Keats is thinking of anything that offers us sensory pleasure and inspires feelings of wonder and awe: a sky at sunset, a great piece of art etc. Our response to such things is often natural and instinctual and does not require any rationalisation or explanation. Keats seems to be suggesting that such feelings or responses are in some sense absolutely true or real – they are the one thing we can completely trust. Everything else that we 'know' is open to debate or question, even things that we might consider scientific fact. As such, this is 'all [we] know on earth'. In fact, this, the final line states, is all we 'need to know'.

The urn, as a wonderful piece of art that inspires awe in those who observe it, embodies or expresses this view.

FORM

'Ode on a Grecian Urn' is a form of ode, a lyrical poem that addresses and praises some person or object. It consists of five stanzas with ten lines in each stanza. The first seven lines in each stanza follow an ABABCDE rhyme scheme. However, the last three lines of the stanzas are not the same. For example, in the first stanza, the rhyme scheme of the last three lines is DCE, and the rhyme scheme of the last three lines in the third stanza is CDE.

METAPHORS AND SIMILES

The poet compares the urn to a virginal 'bride', suggesting that it has been untouched or untarnished by the passage of time: 'Thou still unravish'd bride'. The urn is like a 'historian' that relates legends or tales from a time long ago: 'Sylvan historian'.

The poem is loaded with paradoxes:
• The urn is 'silent', yet it tells 'tales'.
• The musician is motionless yet he is 'for ever piping songs for ever new'.
• The poet describes the music that the musicians depicted on the urn play as 'unheard' melodies.
• The urn is a static piece of art, yet it manages to convey 'wild ecstasy' and depict love that is 'For ever warm' and 'For ever panting'.

• The urn is considered a 'silent form' yet it still manages to utter the only 'truth' that we 'need to know'.

The poem also features a lot of repetition. In the third stanza, the poet repeats the word 'happy' six times, conveying his almost giddy excitement at the scenes before him.

REFERENCES TO OLDER TIMES

The urn that the poem describes is a piece of sculpture from Ancient Greece. Like many Romantic poets, Keats was fascinated by such ancient civilisations. The scenes depicted on the urn reveal an idyllic way of life. The people depicted on the urn live close to nature. The description of the 'mad pursuit' and the 'pipes and timbrels' suggest that these people knew how to enjoy themselves and that music and art played an integral role in their lives. The fourth stanza also presents us with an image of community, of an entire townsfolk taking in a ceremonial event. We get the impression that the poet longs to live in society like this.

SOUND EFFECTS

There are soft, sibilant 's' sounds in the second line: 'silence and slow'. The poet also makes use of long vowel sounds here to correspond with the slowness of time being expressed: 'Thou foster-child of silence and slow time'.

LOVE

The scenes depicted on the urn's surface present the poet with idyllic scenes of love. In the opening stanza Keats describes a scene of lust and desire. A group of men are chasing or in 'pursuit' of some women. The poet says that the women 'struggle to escape' from the clutches of the men. Although such a 'struggle' would seem to suggest an unwillingness on the women's part, Keats describes the scene as one of 'wild ecstasy', a riotous display of physical love.

In the second stanza Keats describes a man boldly attempting to kiss a beautiful young woman. As this is a static piece of art, the depicted lover will forever be frozen in his attempt to achieve this kiss. As such, his desire and longing will never be fulfilled or satisfied. Keats considers this to be a 'happy' state of affairs. If the man never actually kisses the woman, his longing for her will never die. In contrast, actual human love and desire, the poet says, ultimately leads to disappointment and heartache: 'leaves a heart high-sorrowful and cloy'd'.

CELEBRATING ARTWORKS

Keats' fascination and admiration for this piece of sculpture is evident throughout the poem. There are times when the poet seems almost breathless and giddy with excitement.

The poem suggests a number of things about the power or significance of great artworks:

- They spark the imagination. Looking at a static piece of sculpture inspires the poet to imagine the world that the characters inhabit and even the sounds of the music that they play.
- They 'tease us' or challenge us to think about important or complex things. The urn, for example, inspires the poet to think about beauty, truth and the eternal. In fact, the poet believes that great works of art offer us the most important truths.
- They afford people great pleasure and serenity. Keats imagines how the urn will help future generations to deal with their troubles or 'woe'. He describes the urn as a 'friend to man'.
- They allow us an insight into the past. The urn presents the poet with a 'flowery tale' from Ancient Greece. Keats wonders who these people are and what it is that they are doing.
- Their appeal is timeless. The urn fascinates the poet, just as we might imagine it fascinated those who would have seen it when it was first made. Keats imagines how future generations will continue to enjoy the urn long after his generation has passed.

ARTISTIC CREATIVITY

Keats, like the other Romantic poets of his generation, venerated artistic creativity as one of the greatest human traits, regarding it as something sacred and mysterious. In the poem's opening stanza the poet seems to make a reference to the care and time that went into the urn's creation, describing it as the product of 'silence and slow time'. Keats also praises the sculptor's ability to tell an elaborate or 'flowery' story using marble, saying that the urn is better able to 'express/ A flowery tale' than his own poetry.

But the poem is perhaps even more a testament to Keats' creativity and the fertility of his imagination. Taking what he describes at one point as a 'Cold' or lifeless piece of sculpture, the poet brings the urn to life. It is as if he enters the world depicted on the urn's surface and interacts with the different characters who inhabit this world.

CHANGE AND CHANGELESSNESS

The poet begins by celebrating the fact that the urn has not changed over the thousands of years that it has existed. It seems 'unravish'd' or unmarked by the passage of time. In the final stanza the poet states that the urn will continue to exist long after he and his generation have passed away. It will 'remain, in midst of other woe' and offer pleasure to those who view it. The urn is, therefore, a symbol of the timelessness of great art.

In stanzas 2 to 4 the poet seems to lose himself in the scenes that are depicted on the urn's surface. He engages with the characters as if they were real, actual people. Keats considers how these characters are frozen in time and envies the fact that they and their circumstances will never change or alter. The musician will forever be playing music and the lover forever reaching to kiss the beautiful woman. This, the poet believes, is a very happy state of affairs.

The musician will never tire of playing his music and the lover will never have to deal with the disappointments and pains that Keats associates with real human love.

To Autumn

LINE BY LINE

STANZA 1

The poet begins by describing typical characteristics of the autumn season. He thinks of the 'mists' that often occur at this time of year. He also calls to mind the 'fruitfulness' of autumn, a time of year when many fruits ripen and late flowers bloom. The season's fruitfulness is, however, considered 'mellow', perhaps when compared with the rapid growth and bloom of spring and summer. The word 'mellow' also suggests the slightly cooler weather of the season and perhaps the fact that colours of the various blossoms are less vivid than in spring or summer.

The poet personifies the season and imagines that it is a very close friend of the sun: 'Close bosom-friend of the maturing sun'. The word 'maturing' suggests the weakening light of the sun as we move from summer to winter. It is as if the intensity of the sun's light is dimming with age.

Together the sun and the season cause fruit to ripen and late flowers to bloom. Keats uses the word 'conspiring' to describe their alliance, suggesting a certain mischievousness and playfulness:

- They will 'load and bless' the ivies or vines that grow up around the edge of the thatched roofs of houses with plenty of fruit.
- They will fill the branches of the mossy apple trees with fruit until they are bending under the weight: 'To bend with apples the moss'd cottage trees'.

- Other fruits will also be ripened through: 'fill all fruit with ripeness to the core'.
- They will cause the skins or 'gourds' of certain fruits to 'swell' as they ripen.
- The shells of the nuts will also expand as the kernels within are plumped up: 'plump the hazel shells/ With a sweet kernel'.
- They will cause the flowers to bud again and again, producing flowers from which the bees can continue to gather nectar.

There is a wonderful sense of abundance here. The trees are being weighed down by their fruit, the gourds and the nuts are set to burst and the hives, already 'o'er-brimm'd' with the nectar gathered during the summer months, will have to somehow cope with even more honey.

STANZA 2

In this stanza the poet focuses on the harvest that occurs in autumn. The growth that the poet described in the opening stanza has ended and the crops must now be gathered. Again the poet personifies the season, and suggests that she can be found in many different settings throughout the countryside, should we wish to go looking.

Keats first imagines Autumn 'sitting' on a granary floor. The granary is where the threshed grain is stored. Here the chaff is separated from the grain by a process called 'winnowing', which involves blowing a current of air through the grain in order to remove the chaff.

The 'winnowing wind' lifts and separates the hair of Autumn: 'Thy hair soft-lifted by the winnowing wind'.

The poet then pictures Autumn 'sound asleep' on a furrow that has been 'half-reap'd'. A furrow is a long narrow trench made in the ground by a plough. Only half of the crops in this furrow have been gathered or 'reap'd', but Autumn has fallen asleep. Keats says that she has been made sleepy by the 'fumes of poppies'. Poppies are flowers renowned for their opiate properties and are classically associated with sleep. Autumn's scythe or 'hook' lies idle next to her as she sleeps, thus sparing the next tuft of crop and intertwining flowers: 'thy hook/ Spares the next swath and all its twined flowers'.

Autumn is then described crossing a 'brook' or stream. Her head hangs down like that of a 'gleaner', someone who gathers the grain left behind by the reapers. Such workers would have their heads bent as they crouch to gather the cut grain. Autumn's head seems to be hanging heavy as though it were 'laden' down by some weight: 'like a gleaner thou dost keep/ Steady thy laden head across a brook'.

Finally the season is depicted standing by 'a cider-press' watching patiently as 'the last oozings' of juice are pressed from the apples.

There is a great sleepiness and languid quality to this stanza, as though nature has exhausted itself with all that it has produced. The personified season sits 'careless on a granary floor' or sleeps in the field by its sickle. The harvesting has been done and now it is time for nature to take a breather before the whole process starts again with the coming spring.

STANZA 3

In the final stanza the season is nearing its end. Not only that, but the day is also ending. It is evening time. There is a scattering of long, thin clouds in the sky that resemble bars through which patches of sky can be seen. These 'barred clouds' catch the colours of the setting sun and Keats compares them to flowers in bloom: 'While barred clouds bloom the soft-dying day'. The day is softly drawing to a close and the evening sun casts a gentle reddish light over the bare, harvested fields: 'And touch the stubble plains with rosy hue'.

Keats focuses on the sounds of autumn and contrasts them with those of spring. He argues that autumn's music is as lovely, if not lovelier, than that of spring, a season renowned for its pleasant sounds. The poet does not wish Autumn to be intimidated by the spring's reputation for such sweet music, telling it to 'Think not of' the 'songs of Spring'. The spring has long ended and its songs can be heard no more: 'Where are the songs of Spring? Ay, where are they?'

The music of autumn can now be heard throughout the countryside.
- The buzzing of the 'small gnats' sounds mournful and the poet compares them to a 'wailful choir'. Keats describes this 'choir' of insects rising and sinking along the riverbanks as the 'light wind' gusts and 'dies'.
- 'Full-grown lambs loud bleat' by a stream ('bourn') in the hills.
- The 'Hedge-crickets sing'.
- The 'red-breast' joins the chorus 'with treble soft' from a nearby garden.
- The 'gathering' swallows 'twitter in the skies'.

THEMES

NATURE

Keats was typical of the Romantic poets in his worship of the natural world and his almost overwhelming love of nature is evident throughout his poetry. In 'To Autumn' he focuses on the many sensual delights of this time of year, from the sights of harvested fields and all the ripening fruit to the wonderful sounds of the birds, animals and insects.

The poem also gives us a sense of the harmony and tranquillity of the natural world. Keats describes how the sun works to bring the various plants to fruit and flower. This notion of perfect harmony is perhaps most evident in the poem's third stanza, where Keats brings all the elements of the evening together. The 'small gnats' rise and fall with the soft breeze ('borne aloft/ Or sinking as the light wind lives or dies') and their mournful buzzing

blends with the bleating of the lambs and the singing of the birds.

The poet seems to consider the natural world to be most lovely when there is no human presence. Although Keats celebrates the harvest that occurs in autumn, the farmers and workers are entirely absent from the picture. The poet describes the various processes, from the winnowing of the grain to the pressing of the apples, but the only person that he mentions is the personified season. The only reference to human existence in the first stanza is the mentioning of the 'thatch-eves' of the country dwellings. This notion that the natural world is at its most beautiful when there is no one around is also evident in 'Bright Star' and 'To one who has been long in city pent'.

DEATH

In poem after poem we find Keats lamenting the reality of death and its consequences for human existence. However, there are also moments when the poet seems attracted or fascinated by the notion of death and dying.

The third stanza of 'To Autumn' describes both the autumn and the day reaching their end. The poet mentions the 'soft-dying day' and describes how the 'light wind lives or dies'. The gnats are described as a 'wailful choir' and the image of the 'stubble plains' reminds us of the fact that the harvest has come to an end.

But rather than rage against the season's end, Keats seems to accept it and embrace it. There is a certain beauty to behold in the dying moments of both the day and the season. Keats describes the beautiful effect that the setting sun has on both the clouds and the harvested fields: 'barred clouds bloom the soft-dying day,/ And touch the stubble plains with rosy hue'.

CHANGE AND CHANGELESSNESS

In contrast with poems such 'Ode on a Grecian Urn' and 'Bright Star' which celebrate the unchanging natures of the urn and star, 'To Autumn' seems to relish the fact that the natural world is in a constant state of flux. Keats charts the progression of the season, from the final ripening of the fruits and blossoming of the flowers, to the harvesting of the crops and finally the late stages when the fields are 'stubble plains'.

FORM

'To Autumn' is a lyric poem, comprising three eleven-line stanzas. Like 'Ode on a Grecian Urn' and 'Ode to a Nightingale', it is a form of ode, a poem that addresses a person or object that cannot respond. The rhyme scheme of each stanza is ABAB CDEDCCE.

The poem's three stanzas each focus on different stages of autumn: the first stanza describes the early stage of the season when flowers are still blooming and fruits and vegetables ripening, the second stanza describes the harvesting of the crops, while the third stanza concentrates on the final days of autumn, when the fields are bare.

The poem also moves through the three phases of the day: morning, afternoon, and evening. The first stanza describes the morning when the sun is 'maturing' in the sky. The second stanza centres round the afternoon when the labourers are resting after their morning's work. The last stanza is set in the evening. Keats speaks of the 'soft-dying day' as the setting sun casts a warm glow over the harvested fields.

SOUND EFFECTS

The poem features many fine examples of assonance and alliteration. The opening line, for example, has alliteration in the repeated 'm' sounds of 'mists and mellow'. There is also alliteration in the repeated 'b' and 'd' sounds in the third line of the final stanza: 'barred clouds bloom'. Assonance and alliteration feature in line 15, with the repeated 'w' and 'i' sounds in 'winnowing wind'. Repeated 'i' sounds also occur in line 29: 'sinking as the light wind lives or dies'.

There is a certain onomatopoeic quality in line 15, the words 'winnowing wind' giving us a sense of the sound of the wind itself. Onomatopoeia is also used in line 22 where the poet speaks of the 'last oozings' of the apple juice.

NATURE IMAGERY

The poet focuses on the many sensual delights of the natural world, describing the sights and sounds he associates with this time of year. We are presented with images of superabundant growth, as fruits ripen to the point of bursting and flowers blossom. In a particularly wonderful image the poet describes the evening sky and the effect that the setting sun has on the harvested field: 'barred clouds bloom the soft-dying day,/ And touch the stubble plains with rosy hue'. The final stanza is also rich with the different sounds of the evening, from the 'wailful choir' of the gnats to the 'loud bleat' of the lambs and the 'treble soft' sounds of the red-breast.

The poem also celebrates the produce of the natural world. Keats describes how the beehives are 'o'er-brimm'd' with honey. He mentions apples and the 'plump' hazelnuts with their 'sweet kernel'. He describes apples being squeezed to make cider.

Bright Star

LINE BY LINE

The poet addresses a star in the night sky, possibly the North Star. He says that he would like to be as 'steadfast' as the star is: 'would I were steadfast as thou art'. To be 'stedfast' means to be firmly fixed in position. The poet envies the star's ability to remain in the same place, never moving and never changing.

However, although the poet admires the star's steadfastness, there is much about the star's existence that he does not envy. The star might look splendid, shining in the night sky, but it is alone and isolated, far removed from the world that it watches: 'in lone splendor … And watching'. Keats likens the star to a religious recluse or hermit: 'Eremite'.

The poet imagines that the star has eyes that never blink and that it watches, for all eternity, the movements of the earth far below: 'watching, with eternal lids apart'. From its lofty height the star can see the movements of the oceans. Keats considers the rise and fall of the tides each day to be some sort of ritual cleansing ('ablution') of the shores: 'their priestlike task/ Of pure ablution round earth's human shores'. The star can also see the snow-covered mountains and moors. The recently 'soft-fallen' snow covers both like a mask: 'the new soft-fallen mask/ Of snow'.

The poet does not wish to be as remote as the star – even though it has a perfect view of these beautiful sights – but he would still like to be steadfast: 'No – yet still stedfast, still unchangeable'. He would like to remain as he is for all eternity, never changing position and never sleeping.

The reason that the poet wishes to be 'stedfast' is given in lines 10 to 13. His head is resting upon his beloved's breast that gently rises and falls as she breathes. The poet would like to remain as he is and experience this for all eternity: 'To feel for ever its soft fall and swell,/ Awake for ever in a sweet unrest'. Like the star he will remain forever motionless so that he can better hear his beloved's 'tender-taken breath'. In such a position he could happily 'live ever'.

However, if he can't live forever in the way he has just described, the poet would rather 'swoon to death'.

FORM AND STRUCTURE

The poem is a sonnet with a ABAB CDCD EFEF GG rhyming scheme.

In the first quatrain Keats describes the star's lonely position in the sky and its remoteness from the world. In the second quatrain he focuses on what the star can see. As is often the case in a sonnet a 'turn' occurs in the first line of the sestet, signaled here by the word 'No'. The sestet then goes on to describe how the poet would prefer to spend a life of eternal sleeplessness.

NATURE IMAGERY

The central image in the sonnet is that of the star. Keats depicts it as something beautiful yet somewhat tragic. It is isolated from the very beauty that it is destined to observe forever.

The poem, like many of Keats', incorporates images of the sky and the sea in order to convey a sense of majesty and mystery. In this sonnet the poet gazes up at the star in the sky and imagines how it must view the sea below. Keats likens the sea to a cleansing body of water, purifying the world. The image of the snow upon the mountains is also one of purity, its pristine whiteness masking the mountains and the moors.

SOUND EFFECTS

The poem contains many wonderful examples of assonance and alliteration. The eighth line contains both: 'Of snow upon the mountains and the moors'. The assonance of the 'o's coupled with the alliteration of the 'm's combine to create a very pleasant line. Again in line 11 the poet uses both to fine effect: 'To feel for ever its soft fall and swell'. The soft 's' sounds mix beautifully with the 'f's of 'feel' and 'fall' to give the line a very sweet and dreamy atmosphere.

THEMES

CHANGE AND CHANGELESSNESS

The poet considers the star 'unchangeable' and envies its ability to remain the same. It never sleeps or alters its position. The poet wishes that he too could stay awake forever so that he could watch his beloved sleep. Like the star he will never change and never sleep. Frozen in a state of 'sweet unrest' he will happily feel the rise and fall of his beloved's breast and listen to her soft breath.

Though the poet longs to be 'stedfast' and unchanging, the poem can also be read as a celebration of the human world of change and flux, from which the star remains eternally remote. It is the earth that the poem ultimately celebrates, with its constantly moving waters and 'new soft-fallen mask/ Of snow upon the mountains and the moors'. The star can only gaze upon this, whereas those who live on earth are part of this beautiful landscape.

NATURE

Keats was typical of the romantic poets in his worship of the natural world. His almost overwhelming love of nature is evident throughout his poetry.

The poem considers the natural world to be something truly awe-inspiring. The oceans, mountains and moors that the star gazes upon suggest that the earth is a place of great beauty. There is something incredibly seductive and soothing about the 'moving waters' and the 'soft-fallen mask/ Of snow upon the mountains and the moors'.

However, Keats suggests that the natural world is at its most beautiful when it is untouched by mankind. The movements of the oceans are described in terms of a cleansing of the 'human shores', as though man is a blight upon the world that needs to be cleansed.

DEATH

In poem after poem we find Keats lamenting the reality of death and its consequences for human existence. However, there are also moments when the poet seems attracted or fascinated by the notion of death and dying. In the final line of the poem he states that if he cannot exist forever with his head resting upon his beloved's breast he would prefer to die: 'And so live ever – or else swoon to death'. The word 'swoon' can mean to be overwhelmed by ecstatic joy. Perhaps the poet cannot imagine a better place to die than where he is, lying in bed with his beloved, his head resting upon her breast.

Sylvia Plath

Themes

Mental Anguish

Many of Plath's poems express feelings of inner turmoil, describing a speaker who is haunted by raging storms of emotion:

- In 'Finisterre', the sea's violent fury is often taken to represent Plath's tumultuous mental state.
- 'The Arrival of the Bee Box' also depicts mental turmoil. The sight and sound of the locked box fills the speaker with dread: 'The box is locked, it is dangerous'.
- 'Mirror' is another poem that illustrates mental turmoil. The woman in the poem is gripped by a fit of loneliness or despair, examining herself in the looking glass as she cries and wrings her hands: 'She rewards me with tears and an agitation of hand'.

'Elm' is perhaps one of Plath's greatest poems of mental turmoil, one in which the poet powerfully reveals her own anguished mental state. The female speaker in the poem is in an intensely agitated and tumultuous state of mind. She suffers from 'bad dreams', she seems to have experienced bouts of madness, and she fears hitting rock 'bottom' – complete and total mental desolation. Perhaps the most disturbing aspect of 'Elm' is the way it suggests that there is no limit or extreme to human suffering. The elm claims to have known the 'bottom'. It has experienced the most intense possible degree of mental anguish. However, we are left with the impression that more knowledge must be borne, that more suffering must yet be undergone.

There is a slight note of hope in 'Finisterre' that this mental turmoil will come to an end and the speaker can enter a new and tranquil mental space. The peasants mention a peaceful place 'tropical and blue', far from the furious waters of the bay where they live. Yet as the poem concludes, we are left with the impression that such inner peace is a distant prospect, as distant as the faraway waters the peasants have 'never been'. 'The Arrival of the Bee Box' also features a note of hope. The speaker can overcome her fear of the bees by releasing them, rather like someone who is afraid of flying stepping onto a plane. If the speaker can overcome this seemingly irrational fear of the bee box, perhaps she can also overcome the deeper mental turmoil that affects her.

Some of Plath's poems explore the feelings of inadequacy and uncertainty:

- The feeling of being an inadequate mother is present in 'Child', where Plath describes the anguish that she feels at being unable to offer her child the kind of joyful experiences it needs.
- Feelings of inadequacy are also explored in 'Mirror'. The speaker looks at her reflection with 'tears and an agitation of hands'. She turns away to the soft glow of candles and the moon, as if she does not like what she sees in the mirror.
- Feelings of self-doubt are powerfully dramatised in 'Elm'. Plath is inhabited by her own self-doubts just as the elm is inhabited by a 'dark' clawed creature with a murderous face.
- Such feelings are also arguably present in 'Morning Star', where the poet struggles to come to terms with her new role as a mother.

There are several instances in Plath's poetry where the speaker expresses what might be described as self-destructive thoughts or desires. Many readers feel that these desires surface in 'The Arrival of the Bee Box'. When the speaker imagines herself wearing the protective garments of a bee-keeper, she describes the face-covering as a 'funeral veil'. There is a sense here that she is anticipating her own demise or, on some level, even desiring it.

A similar desire to be free of human consciousness is also present in 'Poppies in July'. In this poem, the speaker sees only two ways out of her numbing depression: experiencing intense physical pain or slipping into a blissful drug-induced trance: 'If I could bleed, or sleep!' The poem closes with the poet imagining herself within a 'glass capsule' into which she longs for opiates to 'seep'. These 'liquors' will dull and still her until total oblivion is reached and the world fades away.

Such desires are arguably expressed in 'Finisterre', when the speaker describes herself walking into the sea-mist. She describes how this mist 'erases' the rocks and yet she enters it. It's as if on some level she desires to be erased from existence herself. She imagines the mist being composed of dead souls, and yet she enters it, as if on some level she desires to join them in death. Many readers feel that the description of the souls almost choking the speaker also reflects her self-destructive desires: 'They stuff my mouth with cotton'.

Nature

To Plath, nature was often a source of inspiration. We see this in 'Black Rook in Rainy Weather', where the bird's shining feathers aid the speaker in her attempts at poetic composition. The sight of the bird allows her to patch together 'a content of sorts', to engage in some form of artistic creation. It helps stave off the fear of 'total neutrality', the fear that she will never again be sufficiently inspired to write a poem. 'Pheasant' is also a celebration of nature. Once again, the speaker is inspired by the sight of a bird, of this 'fine' thing that visits her garden. The poem praises the 'kingliness' of the pheasant, of this bright bird that fills the speaker with 'wonder'.

'The Arrival of the Bee Box' and 'Pheasant' are both concerned with the power that humans sometimes wield over the natural world. In 'Pheasant', the poet's husband has threatened to kill the bird and it is now up to her to convince him that the pheasant's life is worth preserving. In 'The Arrival of the Bee Box', it is the poet herself who entertains the possibility of killing the bees that are in her possession: 'They can die, I need feed them nothing, I am the owner'. But she cannot be so cruel. In the end, she decides to be 'sweet God' and 'set them free'.

Psychic Landscapes

There are many poems where Plath creates what she described as 'psychic landscapes'. She uses a scene from nature or an element of the natural world in order to convey an inner state of mind. For example, in 'Black Rook in Rainy Weather', the speaker's dull and uninspired state of mind is reflected in the 'dull ruinous landscape' she trudges through and in the rainy, grey and 'desultory' atmosphere that dominates the scene.

This tendency is particularly evident in both 'Elm' and 'The Arrival of the Bee Box'. The bee box serves as a metaphor for Plath's turmoil-filled mind. The box seethes with furious black bees 'angrily clambering' over one another in a chaotic fashion. Similarly, her mind seethes with dark, angry and negative emotions. The elm undergoes various tortures, which serve as metaphors for Plath's turmoil-filled mental state. It is inhabited by a dark creature that serves as a metaphor for Plath's feelings of inadequacy and what might be described as the dark side of her personality. 'Poppies in July' does something similar: the description of the field of poppies corresponds with and illustrates the neutrality and numbness that the poet is experiencing.

'Finisterre' paints a particularly rich and suggestive psychic landscape. The sea's violent fury is often taken to represent Plath's tumultuous mental state. The ocean is presented as a terrifyingly vast 'exploding' force that 'cannons' into the coastline, making an endless and oppressive roaring sound – a 'doom-noise'.

Poetic Inspiration

'Black Rook in Rainy Weather' presents an almost spiritual view of poetic inspiration. It is described as a rare and miraculous event and associated with the descent of angels. Inspiration is presented as inducing almost a religious ecstasy in those lucky enough to experience it. When we are inspired, the things we look at seem to 'shine'. An 'incandescent' light world seems to shine from them. Yet 'Black Rook in Rainy Weather' also stresses that inspiration is something that happens in a random, haphazard and unpredictable way. It is described as an 'accident' and as 'spasmodic'. It is not something we can actively seek out. Instead, we can only wait for it to strike us if we are lucky enough to be in the right place at the right time.

Plath felt that in order to be a true poet, one had to explore one's unconscious mind, delving into the darkest depths of the psyche:

- The bee box in 'The Arrival of the Bee Box' can be taken to represent hidden aspects of the mind, the dark and mysterious parts the true poet must explore. Like the bee box, our unconscious mind is almost completely sealed: we cannot know what it contains until we begin to explore it.
- In 'Elm', the tree's reaching into the soil with its 'great tap root' can be taken as a metaphor for the work of the poet's task of probing the depths of his or her own psyche.
- In 'Mirror', the woman looking into the mirror's depths can be taken as a metaphor for this kind of self-exploration.
- In 'Finisterre', the ocean is often taken as a metaphor for the unconscious mind. Just as the peasants venture into the ocean and extract little shells from it, so the true poet must venture into the depths of his or her own psyche. Just as the peasants produce little toys from the fruit of their explorations, so the poet might create a 'pretty trinket' from her own mental explorations.

Plath was keenly aware that such an inner journey was a dangerous business and involved encountering all kinds of inner demons, dark thoughts, traumas and negative emotions that are usually kept hidden in the mind's deepest recesses. Some critics see the 'terrible fish' at the conclusion of 'Mirror' as not only representing old age but also these inner demons. Similarly, 'Finisterre' depicts the ocean – representing the unconscious mind – as a place of great danger, as being furious and treacherous, with 'no bottom, or anything on the other side of it'.

This notion is powerfully explored in 'The Arrival of the Bee Box'. Just as the speaker is terrified and disgusted by the bee box, so Plath was nervous about exploring her unconscious mind and horrified by the demons that might lurk there. By opening up her unconscious, she will unleash her inner demons, just as the speaker will release the bees. Yet just as the speaker can't stay away from the bee box, so Plath was drawn back again and again to probe around the edges of her unconscious, for she felt that only by exploring this hidden aspect of herself could she create great poetry.

We must remember that for Plath, writing was everything. She was someone who simply couldn't function unless she had the time and space to work on her poetry, and many of her diary entries and letters give the impression that literature mattered as much to her as friendship or family life. There is a sense in which 'Black Rook in Rainy Weather' touches on this artistic insecurity. The speaker is completely uninspired and is 'skeptical' about the possibilities of such inspiration occurring. She dreads 'total neutrality', losing her poetic talent. For her, such creative neutrality meant not only artistic frustration but also a grey, blank and passionless existence. She would be plunged into a limbo-like state of being.

Many readers feel that 'Mirror' also touches on this anxiety, that it depicts a situation where the front, or facade, of the perfect housewife is in danger of choking the artist within. They suggest that the poem's speaker is in danger of forgetting about the artist she really is, and gazes into the mirror's depths in a desperate attempt to reconnect with her own creativity. A similar note is struck by 'The Times Are Tidy'. The poem describes a society that has 'beaten the hazard', that has seen off all threats and enemies. Technological advances make life easy, producing an abundance of wonderful material goods. Such a safe and technologically advanced society might be a comfortable place to live but it will also be a dull and uninspiring place to live, especially if you are a poet.

Order and Chaos

'Black Rook in Rainy Weather' presents the world as a random and chaotic place. It suggests that there is no pattern or meaning to the way that things happen. Everything happens randomly. The leaves fall haphazardly, not according to some 'ceremony' or hidden pattern. Studying events reveals no 'portent', no sign of deeper meaning. Inspiration, too, is random and chaotic. It is 'spasmodic', occurring in a way that is entirely haphazard and unpredictable.

In 'Finisterre' the sea is associated with chaos. Perhaps its key feature is its 'formlessness'. It is presented as a vast, shapeless void churning chaotically. Order, on the other hand, is represented by the solidity and stability of the coastline. Similarly, in 'The Arrival of the Bee Box' the bees are a chaotic force, swarming hectically and frenziedly within their box. They are like a wild and disorderly mob. Only the box imposes order on them, containing their fury.

A similar attitude to order and chaos is evident in 'The Times Are Tidy'. This poem was written during the 1950s, not long after the Second World War had ended. It was a decade of conformity and conservatism in America. There was a sense that the forces of evil had been destroyed and that the future was safe. However, to many artists of the time such a society appeared dull and materialistic. Plath characterises it as the 'province of the stuck record.' The poem suggests that society needs 'hazards' and a healthy degree of fear and unpredictability in order to avoid becoming boring and complacent. These could be the hazards of legend and superstition that terrified people in medieval times or they could be the all-too-real hazards that America had fought against in the world wars.

Femininity and Motherhood

Many of Plath's poems deal with the difficulties of motherhood and touch upon the idea of mothers failing their children. 'Morning Song' describes the poet's initial feelings of uncertainty and doubt following the birth of her child. She does not seem to feel a bond or connection with her child and is left feeling somewhat numb and detached. She feels less secure now that the child has come into her life, saying that the child's 'nakedness/ Shadows' her own safety. In 'Child' the poet's depression makes her feel that she is not capable of offering her child the happiness and joyful experiences that it deserves.

The idea of mothers failing their children is also present in 'Finisterre' through the depiction of Our Lady of the Shipwrecked. Our Lady is often thought of as the 'mother' of the human race. Yet in this poem she is certainly depicted as having failed her children. Despite her serene and beautiful smile, 'her lips sweet with divinity', she is cold, distant and uncaring. She no longer hears the pleas of those who pray to her, either of the despairing sailor or of the peasant woman. She is unmoved by the plight of the lost souls that drift around the place like mists (unlike the speaker, who emerges from their fog 'beaded in tears').

It is also possible to read 'Mirror' as a comment on the pressure women feel to meet certain standards of beauty, pressure that comes from films, magazines and advertising. (Nowadays, it could be argued that men are also subject to such pressure – unlike when Plath wrote the poem.) We see this in the depiction of the mirror as a kind of god that exacts tribute, or payment. Women, the poem suggests, will pay a high price in order that the mirror will be kind to them. The psychological dangers associated with this pressure are suggested by the description of the mirror having treacherous depths and swallowing all it sees. ⌧

The Times Are Tidy

LINE BY LINE

This poem can read as a strange fairytale, one that paints a vivid portrait of an imaginary little town and its community. The town is presented as a rich and comfortable place, its great wealth indicated by its cows producing milk that's incredibly thick with cream: 'The cow milks cream an inch thick'. Cream and fat, we note, are often used as symbols for richness, plenty and prosperity.

It's a place where technological innovation has made life easier. For instance, the town's mayor has a fancy new automated rotisserie that 'turns / Round of its own accord'. (A rotisserie is a spit or skewer that rotates over a fire to ensure that meat is evenly cooked). In these lines we can almost visualise the mayor throwing a gala banquet for the townsfolk to show off this new toy.

The town is also a very safe place. Once it would have been threatened occasionally by fearsome dragons. But that was long ago and these terrible beasts have 'withered' and shrunk over the centuries, evolving from huge and fiery serpents into tiny 'leaf-size' lizards.

Witches once posed a different type of threat to the community. We are presented with the traditional fairy-tale witch, an old woman or 'crone' accompanied by a demonic familiar in the form of a 'talking cat'. According to the speaker, witches wreaked havoc upon the townsfolk. They used their magic to ruin crops, for instance, or used herbs to make love potions that controlled people's minds.

Thankfully, however, such witchcraft is a thing of the past, its last practitioner having been burnt alive over eighty years ago along with her cat and the 'love-hot herb' she used in her

concoctions. The poem's speaker shows little remorse about the witch's deaths. The town's children, we're told, are safer now that witchcraft has been eliminated. Black magic no longer interferes with agriculture, allowing cows to produce their extraordinary milk. For the speaker, then, the witches were simply a threat that had to be eliminated.

The town, then, is a place of great prosperity and safety. But according to Plath such comfort comes at the price of terrible boredom. She describes a place where nothing ever changes, wittily referring to it as the 'province of the stuck record'. A stuck record, of course, endlessly repeats the same few seconds of music. Similarly, it seems that in this town the exact same day occurs over and over again. It's a place where life is unexciting, predictable and dull.

There is no room for heroism in this safe but monotonous place. Once upon a time heroes were called on to don their suits of armour and ride off to defeat the dragons that menaced the town's welfare. But as we've seen the passage of time has eliminated such hazards and threats: 'History's beaten the hazard'.

Now there's 'no career' for a hero in this town and nothing for him to fight against: 'There's no career in the venture/ Of riding against the lizard'. Heroes born here are 'unlucky' because they'll find no opportunity to express their heroism. They're simply born too late to show off their strength, selflessness and courage.

And heroes aren't the only ones surplus to requirement. Skilled craftspeople, too, are increasingly no longer needed, as machines now handle tasks once done by hand. The town's best cooks would once have found employment at the mayor's banquet. But now they remain 'jobless' as the new automated rotisserie turns around on its own.

THEMES

A BITING CRITIQUE OF 1950s AMERICA

This poem was written during the 1950s, which was a time of great success and confidence in American life. This was a moment when the United States loomed over the world as its one true superpower. Nazi Germany and its allies had been defeated in the Second World War while the Soviet Union had yet to emerge as a serious rival to American might. It seemed certain that even outer space itself would soon fall to American conquest.

It was also a time of great economic prosperity in America; where it seemed everyone could find respectable and well-paying employment. Advances in medicine made diseases that had tormented earlier generations a thing of the past. Consumer goods like cars, central heating, fridges and televisions became freely and cheaply available, bringing a level of everyday comfort that would have been unimaginable a decade previously.

The little fairy-tale town Plath sketches so memorably serves as a powerful allegory for the U.S. during this 1950s period of confidence and dominance. The post-war wealth is symbolised by the inch-thick cream issuing from the cows, technological advancement by the mayor's new spinning gadget. America's enemies like Germany and Japan have gone the way of the witches and dragons that once menaced the town. They've been burned up or have been shrunk down to insignificance.

But Plath, like many writers and artists, had mixed feelings about this shiny new America, regarding it as a place of great dullness, conformity and conservatism. Like the town in her little story, 1950s America is a 'province of the stuck record', a place of boredom where nothing ever really changes. She sees little scope for heroism in this monotonous country. Furthermore, she was keenly aware that technology had downsides as well as benefits. For, as the 'jobless' cooks symbolise, in a world increasingly run by machines, many old skills and talents would fall by the wayside.

HEROISM AND THE YOUNG

'But the children are better for it' might be regarded as the poem's most important line. Plath was twenty-five when she wrote this poem and she seems deeply concerned with what this new America meant for young people. In previous generations , young Americans had been ravaged by diseases like polio, had slaved in farms and factories, had bled to death on the battle fields of France. Now they only worried about who to invite to the prom as they drove brand new cars to drive-in movie theatres. A new word – 'teenager' – was coined in order to sell products to these affluent youngsters.

But does Plath really believe that children are better off in this brave new world? She hardly wants a return to poverty and disease. Nor does she want to send young Americans marching off to war. However there's a sense in which she feels her younger countrymen are too pampered and over-indulged. They lack the opportunity for heroism in these 'latter-days' to which they've been born, in this repetitive and monotonous country where 'History' has already run its course. The potential heroes among them are simply 'unlucky', having been born at a time when all the great battles have been fought and all challenges overcome.

ORDER AND CHAOS

In 'The Times Are Tidy', Plath powerfully describes a perfectly ordered environment. She depicts a place where the same things happen over and over again in a perfectly regular and predictable fashion. Anything that might disrupt this regularity has been carefully eliminated. The prevalence of machines – like the mayor's automated rotisserie – reinforce our sense of a mechanised and totally rational world. But it's one where there's little room for heroism, creativity or craft. There's no scope for individualism in this 'province of the stuck record'. In these tidy times no disruptive influences will be tolerated; each human being must conform and funcntion as one of society's obedient cogs.

POETIC INSPIRATION

We sense too that Plath views this ordered, tidy world as somehow deeply uncreative. This mechanical realm is no place for individualists and dreamers, for artists and craftsmen who follow their own course of self-expression. Indeed many artists, writers and musicians found the conformist America of the 1950s a deeply uninspiring place, one in which they struggled to find acceptance.

> This poem comes from a time when America was the only world power. However, later poems like 'Elm' and 'Finisterre' come from a time when America and Russia faced off in what became known as the cold war. While this poem laments the America's unchallenged dominance, those later poems dread the possibility of a nuclear conflict and the horrors it would unleash.

A POET OF STRIKING DESCRIPTIVE POWERS

'The Times Are Tidy' is a playful and witty piece of social critique and its imagery lacks the hallucinatory intensity we see in Plath's later work. Yet it features a number of oddly memorable images that possess a haunting, fairy-tale like quality: the dragon shrunk to 'leaf-sized', the crone burnt with her talking cat, the mayor's rotisserie and the 'jobless' cooks, the milk with its inch-thick cream.

FOCUS ON STYLE

Black Rook in Rainy Weather

LINE BY LINE

SETTING THE SCENE

It is late autumn or early winter, what Plath memorably describes as the 'season of fatigue', a time when nature itself seems worn-out and exhausted. The speaker is trekking through a grim and depressing stretch of countryside: 'a dull ruinous landscape'. It is raining and the falling leaves are 'spotted' with moisture.

As she trudges stubbornly through this wintry scene, she observes a rook perched on a branch: 'On the stiff twig up there/ Hunches a wet black rook'. The rook sits 'hunched' upon its perch, almost as if it's trying to protect itself from the miserable weather.

WHAT IS INSPIRATION?

The speaker thinks of artistic inspiration as a kind of spiritual or religious experience. In line 12, for instance, she wittily describes it as 'backtalk' from the sky, as if being inspired meant being spoken to directly by God. She also describes it as an angel, as a creature of fire and light descending from heaven and exploding into the artist's life: 'whatever angel may choose to flare/ Suddenly at my elbow'. Her view of inspiration as something sacred and spiritual is reinforced in line 4 when she refers to it as a 'miracle'.

When we're inspired we see the world in an intense and heightened way, as if everything around us was filled with light: it will 'set the sight on fire/ In [your] eye'. To be inspired, then, is to experience 'tricks of radiance', strange optical illusions or tricks of the light.

But maybe the speaker is overdoing this talk of spirituality? Maybe it's too much to describe artistic inspiration in such grandiose and over-the-top terms? Lines 36 to 37 suggest that the speaker herself feels she might have gone too far in presenting inspiration as such a holy and miraculous occurrence. She concedes that while she herself is inclined to view inspiration in such a way not everyone will do so: 'Miracles occur,/ If you care to call these spasmodic/ Tricks of radiance miracles'.

Yet it's important to note that inspiration is 'random' as well as rare. In line 5, for instance, we're told that it's an 'accident' while in line 37 it's described as being 'spasmodic', which means fitful or irregular. Inspiration, then, is something that happens in a haphazard and unpredictable way. It's not something we can actively seek out. Instead, we can only wait for it to strike us. We can only hope we're lucky enough to be in the right place at the right time.

THE SPEAKER'S DESIRE FOR INSPIRATION

As she trudges through this wintry landscape, the speaker does not expect the miraculous accident of inspiration to occur: 'I do not expect a miracle/ Or an accident'. She longs to be inspired, to experience some of the 'backtalk' from the heavens mentioned above.

We must remember that Plath, even more than most poets, was terrified of writer's block. She was someone who simply couldn't function unless she was writing; many of her diary entries and letters give the impression that literature mattered as much to her as friendship or family life. For her, then, prolonged lack of inspiration meant a grey, blank and passionless existence. She would be plunged into 'total neutrality', a limbo-like state drained of colour and emotion. Thankfully the inspiration provided by the rook offers 'respite' or relief from this fear. But such respite is only 'brief'. We sense that this fear of total neutrality will be a constant feature of the speaker's life.

THE 'MINOR LIGHT'

The speaker also describes a second and lesser type of inspiration. Proper inspiration is associated with angels, blazing lights and 'backtalk' from the heavens, while this lesser inspiration is associated with only a 'minor light'. Proper inspiration is associated with nature, while this lesser inspiration seems to be associated with domestic scenes. When this lesser inspiration strikes, common household objects seem consumed by heavenly or 'celestial' fire. A blazing, or 'incandescent', light pours out of them: 'light may still/ Lean incandescent// Out of a kitchen table or chair'. This lesser inspiration can 'hallow' or make sacred a moment that would otherwise be completely unimportant: 'hallowing an interval/ Otherwise inconsequent'. It is presented, then, as a holy and benevolent force, associated with honour, love and largesse (generosity). The speaker desires proper inspiration and all that goes with it. Yet she feels she 'honestly can't complain' as long as she has this lesser inspiration and its 'minor light'. While she will always long for proper inspiration, as long as this lesser inspiration is part of her life she will be able to get by.

Unfortunately for her the sky is 'mute' or unspeaking. As she puts it in line 24, she is quite 'skeptical' or doubtful about the possibility of inspiration striking.

Yet the speaker has not completely given up hope. Inspiration, as we've seen, is random and unpredictable. Ultimately the speaker is 'ignorant' as to when she will be inspired and as to what form her inspiration might take. So there's still the possibility that inspiration might strike today, even in a landscape as depressing as this one: 'for it could happen/ Even in this dull ruinous landscape'. She will therefore tread warily and be 'politic', or careful, determined not to miss the moment if it does occur.

INSPIRATION STRIKES

And without warning it does, in the form of the black rook that's hunched on its branch, 'ordering' or tidying its feathers as the rain comes down. Suddenly, the rook begins to 'shine', as the burning light of inspiration emanates from its body. For a few moments it 'seizes' the speaker's senses; there is nothing else she can look at or think about. She describes how the sight of the rook 'hauls' her eyelids open, suggesting that she finds herself unable to close her eyes or look away.

But inspiration is only half the battle, for the poet is determined to turn this moment of inspiration into an actual poem. The poem, she declares, will have to be 'patched together', suggesting a process that requires false starts as well as trial and error. Accomplishing this will require hard work and stubbornness. It will also require an element of luck.

The speaker is bent on creating a poem of some description, a 'content of sorts'. But of course she doesn't know if the thing she manages to patch together will be any good. The poem, then, concludes on a note of grim determination. The speaker will stick relentlessly to this task while she endures the 'long wait' until the next time inspiration descends blazing into her life: 'The wait's begun again,/ The long wait for the angel'.

THEMES

POETIC INSPIRATION

'Black Rook in Rainy Weather' presents an almost spiritual view of inspiration.

- Poetic inspiration, the poem suggests, is a holy or sacred phenomenon. It is associated with the descent of angels and with 'backtalk' from the heavens above.
- Inspiration is also associated with light and fire. It 'sets the sight on fire in [our] eyes' and everything seems to shine or glow.
- Its appearances are also rare and highly unpredictable. The writer or artist must be 'wary' and 'politic', waiting patiently and attentively for it to strike.
- The artist must then work stubbornly and doggedly, using that inspiration to create 'content'.

This poem powerfully depicts artistic insecurity. The speaker is haunted by the fear of long-term writer's block, of what she describes as 'total neutrality'. She associates lack of inspiration with a limbo-like state of greyness, emptiness and inertia.

ORDER AND CHAOS

'Black Rook in Rainy Weather' presents the world as a random and chaotic place. The leaves fall haphazardly, not according to some 'ceremony' or hidden pattern. The weather is described as 'desultory', which means without plan or purpose. Even inspiration is 'spasmodic', occurring in a way that is entirely

THEMES

haphazard and unpredictable. The speaker, therefore, believes that things happen chaotically rather than according to some divine plan or higher purpose. Studying the leaves reveals no 'portent' – no sign of deeper meaning. There's no use looking for any purpose or 'design' in the weather or the natural world.

PSYCHIC LANDSCAPES

There are many poems where Plath creates what she described as 'psychic landscapes'. She uses a scene from nature or an element of the natural world in order to convey

> The poem, it is important to note, has a 'hidden' rhyme scheme in which the first lines of each stanza rhyme or almost rhyme (there … fire … desire … chair) as do the second lines (rook … seek … backtalk … took … walk) and so on. It has been claimed that the poem's unusual structure contradicts its argument that the world is a random and chaotic place. It is possible, after all, that a hidden order lies behind the apparently chaotic and random events we see around us, just as there is a hidden pattern behind the seemingly random arrangement of the poem's lines.

an inner state of mind. In this poem, the speaker's dull and uninspired state of mind is reflected in the 'dull ruinous landscape' she trudges through, and in the rainy, grey and 'desultory' atmosphere that dominates the scene. This, she declares, is the 'season of fatigue'. This phrase describes the time of year – late autumn or winter – when nature itself is exhausted and winding down. Yet it also describes the poet's state of mind, how she is worn out from a period devoid of inspiration and creativity.

PERSONIFICATION

Another important feature of this poem is its use of personification. Inspiration, an abstract quality or concept, is depicted as a kind of person, a supernatural angel that can descend from heaven at any moment, and appear like a burst of flame beside the speaker: 'whatever angel may choose to flare/Suddenly at my elbow'.

A POET OF STRIKING DESCRIPTIVE POWERS

The imagery in this poem isn't as violently memorable as that elsewhere in Plath's work. Yet she still skilfully conjures a depressing, dreary and wintry atmosphere. She depicts a 'dull ruinous landscape' of rain and falling leaves appropriate to the 'season of fatigue' that is late autumn or early winter, a time when nature itself seems tired and worn.

VERBAL MUSIC

This poem features a great deal of assonance, in particular patterns of repeated broad-vowel sounds. These slow our reading of the lines in a way that is appropriate to the rather depressing landscape the poem describes. 'Arranging and rearranging its feathers in the rain … Thus hallowing an interval/Otherwise inconsequent'. The movement of the verse brings to mind the speaker trudging stubbornly through this desolate winter scene. ▨

Morning Song

LINE BY LINE

LINES 1 TO 9

The poem describes the poet's response to the birth of her child. The parents' lovemaking set the child's life in motion. The poet likens the creation of life to the winding of a watch: 'Love set you going like a fat gold watch'.

When the child is born, the midwife slaps its 'footsoles' and it begins to cry. The parents express their enthusiasm at the birth. They 'magnify' the 'arrival' of the child, and 'echo' each other's sentiments.

WHAT SORT OF WORLD IS THE CHILD BORN INTO?

The world into which the child has been born seems cold and unsympathetic. It is unceremoniously greeted with a slap on the footsoles. The room in which it is born is unhomely and lacking in warmth: 'a drafty museum'. There is a sense in which the world is coldly indifferent to the child's existence. The child must take its place 'among the elements'. The word 'elements' might be a reference to the harsh weather that the child will have to endure or it might refer to the basic substances of earth, wind, fire and water. Either way, the world seems unwelcoming.

HOW IS THE CHILD DESCRIBED?

The child is described as a 'New statue', perhaps because it is something to be observed and commented upon. It is also likened to a 'fat gold watch' in the opening line. Both descriptions are lacking in tenderness and warmth.

The child is also described as vulnerable. The poet refers to its 'nakedness' and its 'bald cry', and says that it must now take its place among the 'elements'.

HOW DO THE PARENTS RESPOND TO THE BIRTH OF THEIR CHILD?

The child's birth unsettles the parents. They seem unsure about how to act: 'We stand round blankly as walls'. The child's vulnerability and need for protection makes them feel insecure: 'your nakedness/ Shadows our safety'.

HOW DOES THE POET FEEL ABOUT BECOMING A MOTHER?

The poet seems to feel unsure about her relationship with the child. Now that the child has been born, she does not feel bonded to it. She says that she can no more be considered the mother of the child than a cloud can be considered the mother of the rain that forms a mirror-like pool upon the ground: 'I am no more your mother/ Than the cloud that distills a mirror'. And just as the cloud's destruction, or 'effacement', by the wind will be reflected in the pool it has created, so, too, will the poet's destruction with age be reflected in the child's eyes. The poet seems to be implying that she has created something that will strengthen and grow while she begins to wither and fade with age.

LINES 10 TO 18

In the second half of the poem, the poet is at home with the child. It is night-time. The child is asleep in a room decorated with 'pink roses'. It breathes softly and rhythmically. Its gentle breath is likened to that of a moth. Its breathing sounds like the sea heard from a great distance: 'A far sea'.

The poet wakes 'to listen' to the child. The moment that the child begins to cry, she gets up to feed it. She is wearing a 'floral' nightgown. Her tiredness is evident when she says that she 'stumbles from bed'. Her breasts are heavy with milk, and she likens herself to a cow that needs to be milked: 'cow-heavy'. When she picks up the child, its 'mouth opens clean as a cat's' ready to feed.

As she feeds the child, the day breaks. Slowly, the windows brighten and the stars disappear from the sky: 'The window square// Whitens and swallows its dull stars'. When the child has finished feeding, it makes some happy vowel-like sounds: 'And now you try/ Your handful of notes;/ The clear vowels'.

THEMES

FEMININITY AND MOTHERHOOD

The poem shows how becoming a mother can be a difficult experience. When her child is born, the poet experiences doubts and uncertainties about her role as a mother:

- She does not seem to know how to respond to the birth of her child. She and her husband 'stand around blankly as walls', not knowing what to do.
- She feels less secure now that the child has come into her life. She says that the child's 'nakedness/ Shadows' her own safety. Before the child was born, she only had to worry about herself. Now, however, her own sense of security has been overshadowed by the child's vulnerability.
- She initially feels distant from the child. She likens herself to a cloud that has shed its rain and no longer bears a connection to that which it once carried.

However, when the poet is at home with the child, she begins to feel more at ease and comfortable about her role as a mother. The description of her rising during the night to feed the child is tender, and suggests that the poet is less troubled by doubt and uncertainty. Her description of herself as 'cow-heavy' introduces a light-heartedness into the poem, as does the mentioning of her 'Victorian' floral nightgown.

Like 'Child', 'Morning Song' suggests that motherhood is not a straightforwardly joyous and natural experience. The responsibilty that comes with the role can be overwhelming, and it can be hard to adjust to the fact that there is now another person in your life that needs your care and protection.

However, unlike 'Child', this poem ends on a positive and rather joyous, uplifting note with the description of the child's 'notes' rising 'like balloons'.

MENTAL ANGUISH

There is a sense in the first half of the poem that the poet does not feel adequate as a mother. Now that her child is born, she no longer feels a bond with it. The child is described as a somewhat alien being, likened initially to a 'statue' and then to a pool of water that exists remotely from the cloud that created it. Both descriptions suggest that the poet is struggling to feel the natural maternal bond that we might expect a mother to feel towards her newborn child. This feeling of inadequacy as a mother is also present in 'Child', where Plath describes the anguish that she feels because she is unable to offer her child the kind of joyful experiences that a child ought to have.

When the poet's child is born, both she and her husband struggle with their response to the birth. The description of them standing 'round blankly as walls' suggests that they are somewhat numb and feel no strong emotion about the arrival of their child. That their 'voices echo, magnifying' the arrival suggests that they feel the need to put on a show of joy in order to mask their lack of natural feeling. Because she does not experience immediate joy, the poet is moved to say that she cannot be called the child's mother. However, the poem eventually shows how, with time, the poet comes to feel a bond with the child, and by the end of the poem we sense that she is no longer feeling neutral about the experience.

TONE

The tone of the first nine lines is rather gloomy, anxious and uncertain. But this changes dramatically in the second half, where the tone is light-hearted and relaxed.

A POET OF STRIKING DESCRIPTIVE POWERS

'Morning Song', like many of Plath's poems, features images of unusual intensity. There are several inventive similes and metaphors scattered throughout this piece:

The poet likens the child to 'a fat gold watch', a reference perhaps to the concept of God as watchmaker. The comparison suggests the complexity of human life. However, it is a rather cold and mechanical comparison, and hints at the poet's struggle to come to terms with her new role as mother. Plath also describes the newborn child as a 'New statue', an especially cold and lifeless comparison to draw with a baby, again suggesting feelings of detachment and uncertainty.

However, the imagery softens and brightens in the second half of the poem, reflecting the poet's growing confidence and acceptance of her role as mother. She likens the opening of the child's mouth as it begins to feed to that of a cat: 'Your mouth opens clean as a cat's'. She compares the sound of the child breathing to the sound of a distant sea, and suggests that it is faint and gentle, like the breathing of a moth.

Mirror

LINE BY LINE

THE MIRROR SPEAKS

Like several of Plath's poems, 'Mirror' gives voice to an inanimate object. The mirror is silver. (This may refer to a silver frame around its reflective surface. Alternatively the reflective surface itself may be made from polished silver.) It is square or rectangular in shape, 'being four-cornered'.

It hangs opposite a pink speckled wall. The mirror claims to stare continuously at this wall, 'meditating' upon it: 'I have looked at it so long'. Every night, it becomes too dark for it to see the wall opposite. Furthermore, people regularly check their reflections in the mirror's surface, blocking its view of the wall: 'faces and darkness separate us over and over'.

The mirror has spent so long 'meditating' in this way that it now believes the pink wall is part of itself: 'I have looked at it so long/ I think it is a part of my heart'. These lines are oddly touching. We get the impression that the mirror has somehow fallen in love with the speckled wall opposite it.

THE MIRROR STRESSES HOW ACCURATE IT IS

The mirror stresses how accurately it reflects anything that is put in front of it. It is 'exact' and 'truthful'. It shows each person and object 'Just as it is'.

The mirror claims to 'swallow' all it sees. This is a metaphor for how mirrors create the illusion of depth. The reflection of a given object seems to be inside a double of the room we're standing in, as if it's been 'swallowed' or taken inside the mirror's world.

The mirror claims to have no feelings whatsoever toward those who examine themselves in its surface. It neither 'loves' nor 'dislikes' them, and has no biases or prejudices toward them: 'I have no preconceptions'. It doesn't blur or alter reflections in order to flatter those it likes or hurt the feelings of those it hates. Everything it shows is 'unmisted by love or dislike'.

Very often, people are disappointed by what they see when they look in the mirror. Most people want to look younger, thinner and sexier. The mirror, however, refuses to be blamed for any dismay or disappointment people might feel when they examine themselves in its surface. It is not 'cruel', having no interest in making them feel bad about themselves. It is simply being 'truthful', doing its job of reflecting the world as it really is: 'I am not cruel, only truthful'.

THE MIRROR AND ITS OWNER

Stanza 2 describes the relationship between the mirror and the woman who owns it. This woman seems to be mentally anguished.

She is regularly gripped by fits of loneliness and despair that involve 'tears and an agitation of hands'. She spends a great deal of time staring in the mirror, gazing at her reflection in an attempt to understand herself.

We get the impression that the mirror looks forward to her daily visits, and would be lonely without them: 'Each morning it is her face that replaces the darkness'. The mirror acts almost like the woman's faithful servant, loyally continuing to reflect her back even when she turns away from it: 'I see her back, and reflect it faithfully'.

The woman also needs the mirror: 'I am important to her'. The mirror is important to the woman in a casual, everyday sense. (How else could she check her appearance before going out?) Yet it is also important to her in a psychological sense. She returns to the mirror again and again, gazing into it in an attempt to reach self-understanding – to find out 'what she really is'.

AN UNEQUAL RELATIONSHIP

We get a sense, however, that the relationship between the mirror and the woman is an unequal one. While the mirror is confined to one place, the woman enjoys the freedom to move around: 'She comes and goes'.

The mirror describes the woman sitting in candlelight or gazing out of her window at the moon: 'Then she turns to those liars, the candles or the moon'. There is a sense in these lines that it is jealous of the candles and the moon, resentful of the fact that the woman is looking at them instead of into its own reflective glass. The mirror, it seems, feels hurt and betrayed when the woman turns away from it. Yet even when she does so, it remains faithful to her, loyally reflecting her back: 'I see her back and reflect it faithfully'.

The mirror depicts itself as a kind of god: 'I am ... the eye of a little god, four-cornered'. This comparison is not as strange as it might first sound — people, after all, pay an almost religious devotion to their reflections.
We spend a great deal of time and energy in an effort to keep ourselves young and beautiful, to make sure the mirror is kind to us when we stare into it.
This description brings to mind the other meaning of the word 'exact', which is to demand payment. The mirror is a kind of god that exacts tribute or payment from those who worship it. The poem suggests that we are willing to pay a high price in sweat and money in order that the mirror will show us what we want to see: 'I am silver and exact'.

MENTAL ANGUISH

The woman in the poem is gripped by a fit of loneliness or despair, examining herself in the looking glass as she cries and wrings her hands: 'She rewards me with tears and an agitation of hand'. We get a sense that much of the woman's turmoil stems from the fact that she has lost her way in life, has lost her sense of her own identity. She gazes into the mirror in an attempt to locate and reconnect with her true self. It's as if staring at her own reflection allows her to explore the depths of her own psyche and discover what really makes her who she is: 'Now I am a lake. A woman bends over me,/ Searching my reaches'.

Feelings of inadequacy and worthlessness are also explored in 'Mirror', where the speaker looks at her reflection with 'tears and an agitation of hands'. She turns away to the soft glow of candles and the moon, as if she does not like what she sees in the mirror. Perhaps she feels inadequate about her appearance, her personality or the way she is living her life.

All the mirror gets in return for this loyalty is the opportunity to witness the woman's distress: 'She rewards me with tears'. According to several critics, the tone here is one of bitterness and sarcasm, as if the mirror feels the sight of the woman's tears isn't much of a 'reward' for its faithful service.

A TERRIBLE FISH

The mirror compares itself to a lake. The comparison between the mirror and a lake is obvious. Like a lake, the mirror has a flat, reflective surface. It is possible, on a calm day, to study one's reflection in a lake just as it is in a mirror.

The mirror has recorded the slow ageing of the woman. When the woman looks at herself in the mirror, she can see traces of the child she once was. Those traces, however, become fainter and fainter as time goes on. The mirror uses a striking metaphor to describe this process, saying that the woman 'has drowned a young girl' in its depths.

Every day, the woman wakes up and looks in the mirror, and every day an older version of herself looks back. With each passing day she sees that the old woman she will one day become is closer and closer. Another powerful metaphor is used to depict this process, the mirror declaring that old age is a fish swimming out of the lake's depths and rising up toward her: 'in me an old woman/ Rises toward her day after day, like a terrible fish'.

The notion of inadequacy brings to mind the depiction of the mirror as something threatening and menacing: as something that swallows all it sees, as an exacting god, or as a lake with treacherous depths. Self-examination, the poem reminds us, can be a dangerous business, leading to all sorts of negative emotions.

POETIC INSPIRATION

Plath felt under pressure to conform to the ideal of the perfect 1950s American young woman: to marry, have children and be a successful mother and housewife. Yet she also harboured the burning ambition to be a great writer. She worried that these two goals were incompatible, writing in her diary: 'Will I be a secretary – a self-rationalising housewife, secretly jealous of my husband's ability to grow intellectually and professionally while I am impeded – will I submerge my embarrassing desires and aspirations, refuse to face myself, and go either mad or become neurotic?'

'Mirror' depicts a situation where the front, or facade, of the perfect housewife is in danger of choking the artist within. The poem's speaker is in danger of forgetting about the artist she really

It is worth pointing out that the mirror itself also seems to feel psychological distress. This stems from its unequal relationship with the woman. As we have seen, the woman can come and go but the mirror cannot. Even when the woman is unfaithful the mirror continues to reflect her back faithfully. When the mirror declares that 'I am important to her', we almost get the feeling that it is trying to convince itself of this fact. 'Elm' is another poem that describes mental anguish arising from a failed relationship.

is, and gazes into the mirror's depths in a desperate attempt to reconnect with her own creativity.

Plath felt that in order to be a true poet, one had to explore one's conscious mind, delving into the darkest depths of the psyche. 'Mirror' explores this theme. The woman looking into the mirror's depths can be taken as a metaphor for this kind of self-exploration.

FEMININITY AND MOTHERHOOD

It is also possible to read 'Mirror' as a comment on the pressure women feel to meet certain standards of beauty, pressure that comes from films, magazines and advertising. (Nowadays, it could be argued that men are also subject to such pressure – unlike when Plath wrote the poem.) We see this in the depiction of the mirror as a kind of god that exacts tribute, or payment. Women, the poem suggests, will pay a high price in order that the mirror will be kind to them. The psychological dangers associated with this pressure are suggested by the description of the mirror having treacherous depths and swallowing all it sees.

TONE

An important feature of this poem is the shifts in tone it contains. At times, the mirror seems confident and assured. It is convinced of its accuracy and truthfulness, and even thinks of itself as a kind of god that swallows all it sees. Yet there are also moments when the mirror's tone is one of need and sorrow. There is something almost pathetic about the way it seems to have fallen in love with the piece of wall opposite it. A similarly needy tone is evident in its jealousy of the candles and the moon and in how it remains faithful to the woman even when she turns away from it, loyally reflecting her back.

PERSONIFICATION

An interesting feature of 'Mirror' is its use of 'personification', where an inanimate object is given human characteristics. The mirror is presented as a 'thinking being', a character with thoughts, ideas and emotions. The poem endows the mirror with human traits such as truthfulness, faithfulness and jealousy. It even has a relationship, of sorts, with its owner, the rather disturbed woman on whose wall it hangs.

FORM

The fact that the poem has two nine-line stanzas seems to reflect its title. There is a sense in which each stanza reflects, or mirrors, the other. Several critics have pointed out how the poem's opening stanza is like a child's riddle. If the poem was stripped of its title, it would be a challenge to work out what object was speaking.

A POET OF STRIKING DESCRIPTIVE POWERS

There are several metaphors and similes in this poem that exhibit Plath's customary invention. Using a fine metaphor, the mirror compares itself to the 'eye of a little god'. The mirror compares itself to a lake and the woman to someone on the lake shore staring into the water's murky depths.

The mirror uses a striking metaphor to describe the process of getting older, saying that the woman 'has drowned a young girl' in its depths. Another powerful metaphor is used to depict this process, the mirror declaring that an old woman is swimming out of the lake's depths and rising up toward her: 'in me an old woman/ Rises toward her day after day'. In a final striking simile, this swimming old woman is compared to a 'terrible fish'.

Finisterre

BACKGROUND

Finisterre, which means land's end, is the westernmost tip of Brittany, in north-west France. Plath visited Finisterre in 1960 with her husband, the poet Ted Hughes. Finisterre is a bleak and rugged headland frequently battered by high winds and stormy seas. The treacherous waters below it have caused so many shipwrecks and drownings that it is known as the bay of the dead.

LINE BY LINE

THE LAND

Finisterre is depicted as a 'gloomy' place: it is a headland of grim, black cliffs. These cliffs are described as 'admonitory', meaning they seem to warn those who see them to stay away. All that grows on them are weak and withering 'trefoils', little three-leaved plants that are 'close to death'.

Rocky outcrops protrude from the water. They are worn and brittle, like the 'knuckled and rheumatic' fingers of an old man. Other large rocks lurk threateningly beneath the water's surface: they 'hide their grudges under the water'. Furthermore, many smaller rocks seem to have been 'dumped' into the ocean. These, too, contribute to the bay's gloominess: 'Now it is only gloomy, a dump of rocks'.

THE SEA

The ocean is presented as menacing and aggressive. It seems terrifyingly vast: 'With no bottom, or anything on the other side of it'. It is an 'exploding' force that 'cannons' into the coastline. It makes an endless and oppressive roaring sound – what Plath describes as a 'doom-noise'.

Its erosion of the land is depicted as a military campaign. It slowly reduces the cliffs to little rocks that litter the seascape like corpses, casualties of its endless assault on the coastline: 'Leftover soldiers from old, messy wars'. The description of the sea 'cannoning' and 'exploding' reinforces our sense of it as a hostile military force.

The poem's opening statement, 'This was the land's end', can be read in two ways. On one level it refers to the fact that Finisterre is one of continental Europe's westernmost points. On another level, however, it can be read as stating that this was the end of the land's existence. The sea seems filled with such apocalyptic fury that it threatens to swallow the entire coastline.

THE SOULS OF THE DROWNED

Plath is reminded of all the people who drowned off the coast of Finisterre. She imagines that the souls of these poor people remain somehow trapped in the bay long after their bodies have passed away:

- She imagines their souls being imprisoned forever in these bleak waters, bobbing and tossing on its raging waves: 'rolled in the doom-noise of the sea'.

- She imagines that patches of white surf on the ocean's surface are the faces of these drowned people: 'whitened by the faces of the drowned'.
- She imagines that the mist rising from the ocean is composed of these drowned souls.
- She imagines this mist of ghosts drifting sorrowfully, aimlessly and hopelessly around the bay: 'They go up without hope, like sighs'.
- When the speaker walks into the mist, she imagines the ghosts wrapping themselves around her in a kind of cocoon and penetrating her mouth: 'they stuff my mouth with cotton'.
- When she walks out of the mist, she imagines the ghosts release her again: 'they free me'.

The Virgin Mary is sometimes referred to as 'Our Lady of the Shipwrecked' because she is believed to help sailors and those who have been lost at sea. However, Plath presents her as being more interested in admiring the ocean before her than in listening to the prayers of sailors and their families: 'She is in love with the beautiful formlessness of the sea'.

When she leaves the fog there are beads of water on her cheeks: 'I am beaded with tears'. This may simply be mist that has condensed on her face. However, it is also possible that the speaker is actually crying, weeping out of pity for those who have drowned over the years off Finisterre's deadly coast.

OUR LADY OF THE SHIPWRECKED

There are a pair of large marble statues near the cliff side. One depicts the Virgin Mary. She has a serene and holy smile on her face: 'Her lips sweet with divinity'. She is depicted wearing a wind-blown pink dress, and walking purposefully in the direction of the ocean: 'striding toward the horizon'.

The other statue depicts a sailor: 'A marble sailor kneels at her foot'. He is depicted kneeling before the Virgin and praying to her in a 'distracted' manner. In this instance, 'distractedly' means desperately and despairingly rather than casually and inattentively. A local woman has come to pray at the statues. However, she seems to focus her prayers more on the statue of the sailor than on the statue of the Virgin herself: 'A peasant woman in black/ Is praying to the monument of the sailor praying'.

Plath personifies the statues of the Virgin and the sailor, depicting them as real people capable of praying and answering prayers. The sailor prays to the Virgin. The Virgin, however, does not pay any attention to his prayers or to the prayers of the peasant woman: 'She does not hear what the sailor or the peasant is saying'.

GIFTS AND POSTCARDS

The local peasants have stalls in the vicinity of the Finisterre headland, where they sell postcards and crêpes to tourists. They urge the poet to eat some freshly prepared crêpes before the sea wind cools them too much: 'These are our crêpes. Eat them before they blow cold'. It is not clear whether the locals are attempting to sell the poet crêpes or are offering them for free.

They also sell little trinkets, which are made by beading seashells onto lengths of lace: 'pretty trinkets … necklaces and toy ladies'. These shell-and-lace trinkets 'flap' in the stiff sea breeze and have to be weighed down with conches to stop them blowing away: 'Gull-coloured laces flap in the sea drafts … The peasants anchor them with conches'.

The peasants tell Plath about the shells used to manufacture these trinkets. They are found 'hidden' in the sea around Finisterre. However, they originate in a faraway, tropical sea: they come 'from another place, tropical and blue,/ We have never been to'. The poet marvels at the thought of the ocean carrying the shells thousands of miles from some tropical paradise to the bleak shores of western Brittany.

THEMES

MENTAL ANGUISH

In 'Finisterre', the sea's violent fury is often taken to represent Plath's tumultuous mental state. The ocean is presented as a terrifyingly vast 'exploding' force that 'cannons' into the coastline, making an endless and oppressive roaring sound; a 'doom-noise'. As we have seen, the images associating it with an invading army reinforce our sense of its violence. It is also possible that the description of the peasants' trinkets in the final stanza suggest this mental turmoil. The speaker's mind is battered by gales of emotion just as the 'toy ladies' made by the peasants are blown about by the sea drafts from Finisterre.

Some readers feel that 'Finisterre' expresses feelings of numbness rather than turmoil. The poem describes the ghosts of the drowned drifting eternally around the bay of the dead. They float endlessly and hopelessly: 'They go up without hope, like sighs'. Their grey, limbo-like existence suggests the mental limbo and emotional deadness that Plath so dreaded.

There are also several instances in Plath's poetry where the speaker expresses what might be described as self-destructive thoughts or desires. Such desires are arguably expressed in 'Finisterre' when the speaker describes herself walking into the sea-mist. She describes how this mist 'erases' the rocks and yet she enters it. It's as if on some level she herself desires to be erased from existence. She imagines the mist being composed of dead souls and yet she enters it, as if on some level she desires to join them in death. Many readers feel that the description of the souls almost choking the speaker also reflects her self-destructive desires: 'They stuff my mouth with cotton'.

THEMES

There is only a slight note of hope in 'Finisterre'. The peasants mention a peaceful place 'tropical and blue' far from the furious waters of the bay where they live. This suggests that the speaker believes an end to her mental turmoil is possible, that she can enter a new and tranquil mental space. Yet as the poem concludes, we are left with the impression that such inner peace is a distant prospect, as distant as the faraway waters to which the peasants have 'never been'.

PSYCHIC LANDSCAPES

There are many poems where Plath creates what she described as 'psychic landscapes'. She uses a scene from nature or an element of the natural world in order to convey an inner state of mind. As we have seen, this tendency is evident in 'Finisterre'. The description of the bay can be taken to suggest a storm of emotional turmoil, a state of complete mental numbness, or perhaps even both.

ORDER AND CHAOS

Many of Plath's poems deal with the notion of order and chaos. In this poem, the sea is associated with chaos. Perhaps its key feature is its 'formlessness'. It is presented as a vast, shapeless void churning chaotically. Order, on the other hand, is represented by the solidity and stability of the coastline.

The poem shows chaos slowly encroaching on order as the sea reduces the coastline to nothing. It breaks down the mighty cliffs of Finisterre until they are worn, rheumatic fingers, then little rocks, then only part of its formless drifting. Human beings, too, are reduced to nothing – or next to nothing – by the ocean. Those it drowns are left as wisps of fog, like lost, pathetic ghosts.

In a sense, this process is presented in a negative light. The speaker seems horrified by the violence and menace of the raging sea's assault upon the land. Yet there is also a sense in which the speaker finds the chaos represented by the ocean attractive and intoxicating. Its formlessness, after all, is described as a 'beautiful' formlessness. To Plath, then, chaos is simultaneously both horrific and attractive.

FEMININITY AND MOTHERHOOD

Many of Plath's poems deal with the difficulties of motherhood and touch upon the idea of mothers failing their children. It is present in 'Finisterre' through the depiction of Our Lady of the Shipwrecked.

Our Lady is often thought of as the 'mother' of the human race. Yet in this poem she is depicted as having failed her children. Despite her serene and beautiful smile, 'her lips sweet with

TONE

The poem's first three stanzas employ heightened, dramatic phrases and violent imagery. They conjure a powerfully grim atmosphere of black cliffs, raging waves and sorrowful mists. The final stanza, however, is more relaxed in tone and reveals a different aspect of the ocean. It is also a storehouse of beautiful shells, which can be made into harmless souvenirs.

A POET OF STRIKING DESCRIPTIVE POWERS

'Finisterre' lives up to Plath's reputation as a poet of violent and memorable imagery. The white surf on the sea's surface is compared to the faces of people who have drowned: 'whitened by the faces of the drowned'. Rocky outcrops protruding from the water are described as fingers: 'the last fingers, knuckled and rheumatic,/ Cramped on nothing'. Smaller rocks are described as dead or wounded soldiers: 'Leftover soldiers from old messy wars'. The mist the speaker walks into is compared to cotton: 'They stuff my mouth with cotton'.

In line 4, Plath describes how the ocean has 'no bottom, or anything on the other side of it'. Of course, she isn't suggesting

that the sea is literally bottomless or endless – rather, she uses hyperbole, or poetic exaggeration, to convey its enormity.

Plath depicts the land and sea as being involved in an endless and brutal conflict: 'old messy wars'. The sea slowly reduces the cliffs to little rocks that litter the seascape like dead or wounded bodies, casualties of its endless assault on the coastline. The rocks that have been submerged by the ocean's advance bear 'grudges', like warriors who have suffered a bitter and humiliating defeat. The description of the sea 'cannoning' and 'exploding' reinforces our sense of it as a hostile military force.

PERSONIFICATION

There are several instances of personification in the poem. Personification occurs when we apply human qualities to inanimate objects or natural phenomena. In this poem, large rocks are described as having 'grudges'. The mists are depicted as human souls drifting mournfully around the bay. The description of the cliffs as 'admonitory', as issuing a warning, is arguably another instance of personification.

divinity', she is cold, distant and uncaring. She no longer hears the pleas of those who pray to her, either of the despairing sailor or of the peasant woman. She is unmoved by the plight of the lost souls that drift around the place like mists (unlike the speaker, who emerges from their fog 'beaded in tears').

POETIC INSPIRATION

To write poetry, Plath believed, it was necessary to explore the darkest recesses of the mind, to explore the deepest reaches of the soul. Plath felt probing the unconscious mind was a risky business, for it risked disturbing all kinds of inner demons. In this poem, the ocean is often taken as a metaphor for the unconscious mind. It is presented as a place of great danger, furious and treacherous, with 'no bottom, or anything on the other side of it'.

Yet just as the peasants venture into the ocean and extract little shells from it, so the true poet must venture into the depths of his or her own psyche. Just as the peasants produce little toys from the fruit of their explorations, so the poet might create a 'pretty trinket' from her own mental explorations – a trinket that would, of course, take the form of a poem.

Personification also occurs in the depiction of the statues. The Virgin is depicted as a real person. She strides toward the ocean. She is capable of ignoring and of answering prayers. She is enthralled by the sea's formlessness. The statue of the sailor, too, is personified: it is depicted as praying 'distractedly' to the Virgin.

VERBAL MUSIC

The opening stanzas of this poem feature several instances of cacophony. Phrases such as 'Knuckled and rheumatic/ Cramped on nothing', 'Whitened by the faces of the drowned', 'a dump of rocks' and 'Leftover soldiers from old messy wars' all feature hard clashing consonants that produce a jarring and unpleasant verbal music. The rhyme between budge and grudges produces a similar effect. Plath uses this cacophony to suggest the furious sound of the raging sea. ☒

Pheasant

LINE BY LINE

A pheasant has settled in the poet's garden. She watches it. It is up on the hill by the house, where the elm tree grows: 'on the elm's hill'. The grass is long ('the uncut grass') but the poet is able to see the pheasant's head as it passes back and forth. She describes how the bird's head juts out above the grass. Its head is 'odd' and 'dark' and it 'startles' the poet: 'It startles me still,/ The jut of that odd, dark, head, pacing'.

The word 'still' suggests that the pheasant has been around for some time. In fact, this is not the first time that the bird has appeared in their garden. The poet recalls seeing it 'last winter' when there was snow on the ground. She could see the 'print of its big foot' in the snow, the 'trail-track' of its movements across the garden. This 'trail-track' ran through the trail left by other smaller birds. Plath describes the criss-crossing pattern in the snow from all these bird tracks: 'crosshatch of sparrow and starling'.

The poet's husband has made up his mind to kill the pheasant: 'You said you would kill it this morning'. We might imagine that he is thinking of killing the bird in order to eat it. But the poet does not wish the bird to be killed. It fascinates and excites her to watch this odd creature move through the garden: 'Do not kill it. It startles me still'.

The poet analyses what it is about the bird that makes it special:
• There is it's appearance. Plath describes how the 'jut of that odd, dark head' still 'startles her'. She also says that it is 'such a good shape'. The pheasant's size and the many 'vivid', bright colours of its feathers make it stand out in a spectacular fashion, especially when seen against the pale white of the snow in winter: 'The wonder of it, in that pallor'. Such is the pleasing nature of the bird's appearance that the poet imagines what a wonderful sight it would be to behold 'a dozen' or a 'hundred, on that hill – green and red,/ Crossing and recrossing'.

- It is 'rare'. It is not often that such a bird is spotted in the garden and even less rare for it to stay as it has done. Plath considers how it 'is something to own a pheasant,/ Or just to be visited at all'.

The poet considers that the bird has a right to be in the garden. It is very much at home there: 'It is simply in its element'. The garden seems made for it and it for the garden. This gives the bird some kind of natural 'right' to be where it is. Plath speaks of 'a kingliness' that the bird possesses, a majesty or regal quality . The pheasant's footprint is also like a royal stamp, validating it's right to be there: 'The print of its big foot last winter'.

The poet does not believe that the pheasant has a 'spirit'. She says that she is not a 'mystical' person.   Her reasons for wishing to preserve the bird have to do with her own pleasure and the fact that the bird seems to be at home where it is.

The fact that it is in 'its element' in the garden is demonstrated again when the bird flies up and settles on one of the branches of the elm tree: 'Settles in the elm, and is easy'. Plath describes how it unfolds or 'unclaps' its wings to take flight. The feathers on the pheasant's wings are 'as brown as a leaf' and the noise of them beating is 'loud'.

It was the poet who disturbed the pheasant, causing it to fly up into the tree. It had been sitting peacefully in the sun amongst the white and yellow flowers: 'It was sunning in the narcissi'. The poet feels clumsy and out of place in the garden. This space seems to rightly belong to the pheasant and she feels like an intruder or trespasser: 'I trespass stupidly'.

The final words of the poem can be read both as an appeal to her husband to let the pheasant live and also as a remark to herself to keep her distance and not interfere with the bird's enjoyment of the garden: 'Let be, let be'.

THEMES

NATURE

The poem is a celebration of the beauty and wonder of the natural world. The poet describes the many wonderful features of a pheasant that has come to live in her garden. She focuses on the beauty of the bird, from the 'odd' shape of its head to the stunning colours of its feathers. The poet's excitement and pleasure is evident throughout the poem and she imagines at one point how spectacular it would be to have a 'hundred' pheasants marching across the hill.

Like 'The Arrival of the Bee Box', this poem deals with the power that humans sometimes wield over the natural world. The poet's husband has threatened to kill the bird, and it is now up to her to convince him that the pheasant's life is worth preserving. There is a sense, however, that the bird will only survive as long as it continues to 'startle' or amuse the poet. She admits that she is 'not mystical' and does not believe that the bird should be preserved for any ethical reasons. That said, the poet does argue that the bird has a 'right' to be where it is because it is 'in its element'. Although the garden belongs to the poet, there is a sense in which it more rightfully or naturally belongs to the pheasant. It is the poet who ends up feeling like a trespasser on her own property when she sees how 'easy' and at home the pheasant is.

POETIC INSPIRATION

This poem suggests that the natural world is a rich source of inspiration to the poet. The pheasant's odd movements and 'vivid' colours startle her and make her imagine how wonderful it would be to have a hundred such birds 'Crossing and recrossing' on the hill. The pheasant is described as 'a little cornucopia', a rich and abundant source of inspiration.

TONE

The poem opens with a somewhat dramatic and tense tone, with the poet pleading with her husband not to kill the pheasant. But this urgent tone quickly gives way to a more contemplative and bemused tone as the poet runs through the reasons why she values the bird. By the close of the poem, the urgency has all but vanished and the poet makes a calm request for the pheasant's life to be preserved.

A POET OF STRIKING DESCRIPTIVE POWERS

The poem features a number of vivid and memorable images. Plath describes the different bird tracks in the snow, how they criss-cross and create an interesting pattern: 'crosshatch of sparrow and starling'. In a wonderful flight of fancy she imagines what a 'dozen' or a 'hundred' pheasants would look like 'Crossing and recrossing' the hill next to her house.

The poet uses a simile when she compares the colour of the pheasant's wings to autumn leaves: 'brown as a leaf'. She also uses a metaphor when conveying what a rich source of pleasure the bird is to her, comparing it to a 'cornucopia', a mythical horn, perpetually full of flowers and fruit.

Elm

LINE BY LINE

INTRODUCTION

This poem focuses on the relationship between two characters or personae: a large old wych-elm tree and a woman who lives nearby. This poem personifies an elm tree; it is depicted as being capable of thought, language and emotion. Personification, we remember, occurs when a non-human object is presented as possessing human qualities.

A strange 'psychic link' seems to exist between the tree and the woman in the house. Both, for instance, are depicted as female. The elm can sense the woman's thoughts and dreams. It can somehow silently communicate with her: 'I know the bottom, she says'. But this weird mental connection goes both ways. For the woman's thoughts and dreams enter and 'possess' the elm, affecting its state of mind.

The woman appears to be in a state of great mental agitation. According to the elm, she

> This poem was inspired by a period Plath spent living in the Devon countryside. There was a large elm tree on a little hill in the garden of her house. At this time Plath's marriage had broken down and she was suffering great emotional and psychological distress.

fears the 'bottom', by which is meant 'rock bottom', a mental state of complete desperation and loneliness: 'It is what you fear'. The elm herself has no fear of this mental desolation, having already experienced and survived it: 'I do not fear it: I have been there'. It has experienced the darkest depths of the mind just as its main or 'tap' root has experienced the darkest depths of the soil, reaching the bedrock itself: 'I know the bottom, she says, I know it with my great tap root'.

THE ELM TORMENTS THE WOMAN

The elm appears keen to torment the woman with the different noises it makes. The wind in its branches, for instance, will remind the woman of the sea. We can imagine how the wind whistling against the elm's leaves might resemble the sound of waves going in and out. This will upset the woman because she associates the sea with sorrow, longing and need: 'Is it the sea you hear in me,/ Its dissatisfactions?'

The woman, it appears, has previously endured episodes of madness that involved the 'voice of nothing'. We might imagine here a state of catatonia, of complete blankness and emptiness where the woman's inner voice and mental life was simply switched off. The elm wonders – or maybe hopes – that the wind passing through its branches will also remind the speaker of these episodes. The wind in its branches might resemble a blank and relentless 'static hiss', putting the woman in mind of that terrible mental emptiness.

The woman seems to have suffered a failed relationship, having been abandoned by her lover. She lies on her bed weeping. The elm, however, is not sympathetic: 'Love', it declares, 'is a shadow' – a worthless and insubstantial illusion. The elm mocks the speaker's need for this illusion, and her distress at being abandoned by it: 'How you lie and cry after it'. It cruelly declares that the woman's love has disappeared, has bolted like a prize horse that will never be seen again.

The elm will allow its branches to knock together in the wind so that the sound they make resembles that of a racing horse: 'All night I shall gallop thus, impetuously'. We can imagine how this repetitive and percussive sound will torture the woman in her agitated mental state. It will also remind her of how her love 'has gone off, like a horse'. But the elm urges the woman to 'Listen'. It wants this noise to fill her consciousness all night long until her mind is numb, until her head feels like the stone struck by a horse's hooves, her pillow like the turf it gallops over: 'Till your head is a stone, your pillow a little turf'.

THE ELM DESCRIBES THE TORMENTS IT HAS ENDURED

The elm claims to have been tortured by some kind of acid rain. The noise it makes is 'the sound of poisons'. These toxic showers make a horrible shushing or hushing sound when they fall upon the elm's leaves: 'This is rain now, this big hush'. They cause the elm to bear strange, almost mutant fruit: 'this is the fruit of it: tin-white like arsenic'. We can imagine the elm sprouting tiny poisonous berries that are a weird metallic white in colour.

The elm has endured sunsets that give off an unbearable and unnatural heat. She describes these sunsets as an 'atrocity', suggesting they are occasions of terrible and unimaginable suffering. Such sunsets 'scorch' the elm's trunk and boughs, burning even its roots that lie buried in the ground. They bake its branches until they resemble 'filaments' or wires, until they're left red, dry and lifeless.

The elm has experienced winds of extraordinary force and violence. These terrible gales break off pieces of the elm's branches and send them flying dangerously through the air: 'Now I break up in pieces that fly about like clubs'. In response to such an onslaught, the elm has no choice but to cry out in agony: 'A wind of such violence/ Will tolerate no bystanding: I must shriek.'

The moon is another of the elm's tormenters. It gets caught in the elm's branches as it drifts through the sky, pulling and dragging them. As it does so it burns the elm with its brightness: 'Her radiance scathes me'. The elm suggests that the moon tortures it out of jealousy: 'She would drag me most cruelly/ Being barren'. We are presented, then, with the image of an infertile female enviously attacking a fertile one. The moon, after all, is traditionally depicted as feminine. It is a barren and infertile place while the elm retains some degree of fertility and fruitfulness.

Or perhaps the elm is responsible for its own discomfort, having accidentally snared the moon in its branches: 'perhaps I have caught her'. Indeed, this seems to be the case: 'I let her go, I let her go'. The moon is caught by the elm tree and is released in a 'flat' and 'diminished' state, like a woman who has undergone 'radical surgery' on her breasts.

These lines are full of strange and perhaps even disturbing imagery: the elm is blasted by acid rain, produces bizarre poisonous fruit, suffers scalding sunsets and even manages to catch the moon in its branches. Such images are not meant to be taken literally. Rather they have the surreal and unpredictable quality of a nightmare, one that powerfully conveys Plath's troubled mental state at the time of the poem's composition.

At the time of this poem's composition, Plath, along with the rest of the world, was very much concerned about the possibility of a nuclear conflict between the USSR and the United States. The intense, blazing heat and the unstoppably violent wind endured by the elm suggests the force of a nuclear explosion. The poisonous rain that falls on it suggests the aftermath of a nuclear disaster or of a comparable environmental catastrophe.

THE PRESENCE IN THE ELM'S BRANCHES

The elm is terrified by a 'dark' presence that dwells within its branches: 'I am terrified by this dark thing'. In many respects, this creature resembles a bird, possessing feathers and 'hooks' or talons. The elm associates it with evil or 'malignity'. It sleeps all day and the elm seems horrified by the sensation of this feathery being turning over in its slumber: 'All day I feel its soft feathery turnings, its malignity'.

Each night this terrible predator 'flaps out' of the elm to hunt, crying or shrieking as it does so. Yet surprisingly it doesn't seek something to kill or eat. Instead it goes 'Looking, with its hooks, for something to love'. There is something sad or pitiful about how each night this lonely predator roams through the surrounding countryside desperately looking for companionship or affection.

But it is not to be pitied. The elm describes how dangerous it is as it lurks in a 'strangle', or tangle, of the elm's branches. Its face bears a 'murderous' expression. Acid comes sizzling and hissing from its mouth: 'Its snaky acids hiss'.

This being seems to be a product of the psychic link that exists between the elm and the woman in the house. The woman's thoughts and dreams 'possess' the elm, causing this nightmarish being to manifest or appear in its branches: 'How your bad dreams possess and endow me'. She gifts or 'endows' the elm with this sad monster that embodies not only all her fears but also all her inadequacies and needs – especially, perhaps, the need for love.

THEMES

MENTAL ANGUISH

'Elm' is a great poem of mental turmoil. The woman in the poem is in an intensely agitated and tumultuous state of mind. She has previously experienced bouts of madness that involved a completely blank or catatonic mental state. She suffers from 'bad dreams' and fears that she might hit rock 'bottom' – complete and total mental desolation. Much of her mental anguish seems to stem from the failure of a relationship. The elm mockingly describes how she lies there weeping over lost love: 'How you lie and cry after it'.

As we've seen, the elm suffers different torments. It is lashed by poisonous rain, burned by the sun, whipped by the wind, then

The elm contemplates the clouds forming and dissolving different shapes in the sky above her: they 'pass and disperse'. Once a given cloud formation breaks up, it is 'irretrievable', it will never reconstitute itself. The elm wonders if love and relationships are as fleeting and transitory as these cloud shapes: 'Are those the faces of love, those pale irretrievables?' We are reminded of the earlier declaration that love is no more than 'a shadow', an insubstantial illusion.

Previously, the elm mocked the speaker for caring about love, for allowing a failed relationship to distress her. Now, however, the elm admits that it, too, allows love to trouble it: 'Is it for such I agitate my heart?' It has allowed love, something no more substantial than a cloud or shadow, to 'agitate its heart'. We sense that this, too, is a product of the 'psychic link' between the woman and the elm, that the woman's need for love has somehow entered or infected the previously indifferent tree.

'dragged' and 'scathed' by the moon. These torments serve as powerful metaphors for Plath's own mental ordeals, reflecting the tortured state of mind she experienced around the time of the poem's composition.

Perhaps the most disturbing aspect of 'Elm' is the way it suggests that there is no limit or extreme to human suffering. The elm claims to have known the 'bottom'. It has experienced the most intense possible degree of mental anguish. It is 'incapable of more knowledge', of dealing with any more mental suffering. However, we are left with the impression that more knowledge must be borne, that more suffering must yet be undergone.

The murderous, bird-like creature in the elm's branches is an incarnation of all the woman's 'isolate' or individual failings. The woman is inhabited by these feelings just as the elm is inhabited by the creature. The woman is disgusted by these faults and failings just as the elm is disgusted by the 'soft feathery turnings' of the creature. The creature flies out each night looking for love, suggesting that Plath associated her need for love with weakness and failure.

According to the elm, the faults embodied by this creature of evil or 'malignity' will slowly but inevitably cause the woman's death: 'These are the isolate slow faults/ That kill, that kill, that kill.' The acid that drips from the creature's mouth suggests how the woman's obsession with her own failings slowly corrodes her mental health. Its gaze 'petrifies' the will to survive, suggesting how the woman's awareness of her own faults almost freezes her desire to go on living.

THEMES

PSYCHIC LANDSCAPES

There are many poems where Plath creates what she described as 'psychic landscapes'. She uses a scene from nature or an element of the natural world in order to convey an inner state of mind. As we have seen, this tendency is particularly evident in 'Elm'. The elm undergoes various tortures, which serve as metaphors for Plath's turmoil-filled mental state. The elm is inhabited by a dark creature, which serves as a metaphor for Plath's feelings of inadequacy or the dark side of her personality.

POETIC INSPIRATION

The elm reaches into the soil with its 'great tap root'. It claims to know the 'bottom', to have reached into the earth's very foundations. This can be taken as a metaphor for the work of the poet. Plath believed that the true poet needed to probe the depths of his or her own psyche. Just as the elm delves into the soil, so the poet must explore the recesses of his or her unconscious mind. Plath was simultaneously fascinated by this type of mental exploration and afraid of what dark thoughts and feelings she might find lurking in her unconscious. In this regard, 'Elm' echoes 'The Arrival of the Bee Box', another poem where Plath touches on the topic of the unconscious mind and the demons that might wait there.

FEMININITY AND MOTHERHOOD

This poem has been described as a study of feminine suffering. It features three female presences, each of which suffers. The female speaker, as we have seen, endures mental turmoil. The elm is depicted as female and suffers all kinds of outlandish tortures. The third female presence that suffers is the moon, which is traditionally portrayed as female.

TONE

At the beginning of the poem, the elm's tone is cold and confident. She addresses the speaker in a cruel and mocking fashion, chiding her need for love. By the end of the poem, however, the elm's coldness and confidence seem to have vanished. Her tone becomes one of fear and agitation. She even admits that she, too, has a need for love: 'Is it for such that I agitate my heart?'.

PERSONIFICATION

Perhaps the stand-out feature of this poem is that the elm is personified, or given human characteristics. It is portrayed as being capable of emotion, speech and suffering. It is even capable of love. As noted above, Plath uses this speaking elm to describe her own mental anguish. The elm's tortures represent Plath's own mental sufferings. The dark creature that inhabits its branches represents the negative and corrosive aspects of her personality: what she saw as her faults, failings and inadequacies.

A POET OF STRIKING DESCRIPTIVE POWERS

It nearly goes without saying that 'Elm' is not a realistic or logical poem. The elm suffers a number of terrible tortures one after the other: poisonous rains, raging storms, a scorching sun. A bizarre bird-like being inhabits its branches and torments it. It even somehow snags the moon in its branches. The narrative of the poem follows its own crazed and surreal path, fading from one grim image to the next with the logic of a nightmare.

Plath uses a wonderful metaphor to depict the withering of the elm's branches, describing their parched, shrivelled forms as 'a hand of wires'. Using a simile, Plath compares the flying branches to weapons ('clubs'), suggesting the wind's violence. We see metonymy in line 28 (metonymy occurs when a thing or concept is not called by its own name but by the name of something intimately associated with that thing or concept). Instead of declaring 'I am inhabited by a creature', the elm declares that 'I am inhabited by a cry', the cry being something intimately associated with the creature. There is a great deal of cacophony throughout this poem. The harsh clashing sounds in phrases like 'My red filaments burn and stand' are appropriate to the torments they describe. ◻

The Arrival of the Bee Box

LINE BY LINE

A DESCRIPTION OF THE BOX

In this poem, the speaker has just received a 'clean wood box' that is full of bees. Tomorrow, she will release the bees into the hive she has prepared for them. Tonight, however, she must keep the box in her house: 'I have to live with it overnight'. The box has the following features:

• It is square in shape: 'square as a chair'.
• It is heavy: 'almost too heavy to lift'.
• It is 'locked', and its only opening is a small grid, or grille, for ventilation: 'There are no windows … no exit'.
• The bees inside it produce a loud buzzing 'din'.

THE SPEAKER'S REACTION TO THE BOX

The speaker reacts to the box with a feeling of dread and horror. She thinks of it as 'dangerous'. She seems to associate it with death, referring to it as a 'coffin'. We get a sense in the opening line that she is regretful or even somehow surprised that she purchased the bees in the first place.

Though the box horrifies the speaker, it also fascinates her. She feels compelled to stay near it: 'I can't keep away from it'. She puts her 'eye to the grid', or grille, and attempts to peer into it. She lays her ear on its surface and listens to the bees buzzing within. The speaker's reaction to the box, then, is complex and contradictory. It seems to repulse her and attract her at the same time.

During the summer of 1962, while she lived with her husband in the Devon countryside, Plath experimented with bee-keeping. This experience provided her with the inspiration for a number of poems about bees, one of which is 'The Arrival of the Bee Box'.

THE SPEAKER'S REACTION TO THE BEES

The speaker reacts to the bees inside the box with what can only be described as fear and horror:

• Though the box's interior is 'dark, dark', when she looks through the grille she can just make out the bees scrambling and 'clambering' around within it. According to the speaker, the bees look like the tiny shrunken hands of dead Africans.
• She finds the sound they make even more horrifying and upsetting than their appearance: 'It is the noise that appals me most of all'. She compares their buzzing to a strange language full of 'unintelligible syllables'.
• She associates the bees with rage and anger, thinking of them 'as a box of maniacs'. They clamber 'angrily' and the sound they make is 'furious'.

The speaker is highly conscious that a swarm of bees can pose a threat to a human being. In this regard, she compares the bees to a rioting crowd in ancient Roman times: 'It is like a Roman mob'. On his own, each member of a Roman mob was powerless; as a rioting group, however, they could threaten the stability of the entire city. Similarly, a single bee can do little harm to a human being. An entire swarm, however, could easily sting a person to death: 'Small, taken one by one, but my god together!'.

The speaker fears that once released, the bees will turn on her and overwhelm her: 'How can I let them out?' It took a powerful ruler like Caesar to master the mobs of Rome. Similarly, it will take a skilled and confident bee-keeper to control the bees once they have been released from the box. The speaker, however, feels she does not possess the qualities necessary to tame or control this raging swarm: 'I am no Caesar'.

WHAT WILL THE SPEAKER DO WITH THE BEES?

The speaker considers her options with regard to the bees. Firstly, she could return them to the shop she bought them from: 'They can be sent back'. Secondly, she could starve them and let them perish in their clean wood box: 'They can die, I need feed them nothing, I am the owner'. Finally, she could overcome her fear of the bees and release them in the morning as she had originally planned. She wonders if the bees are hungry enough to attack her should she decide to release them: 'I wonder how

hungry they are'. She feels there is little real chance of this attack occurring: 'I am no source of honey/ So why should they turn on me?'. The bees, in fact, will probably just ignore her if sets them free: 'They might ignore me immediately'.

The speaker has a god-like power over the bees – the power of life and death. She decides that tomorrow she will act like a 'sweet' or benevolent god. Instead of sending the bees back or letting them die, she will set them free. Having concluded that they pose little threat to her, she will release them into the garden: 'Tomorrow I will be sweet God, I will set them free.// The box is only temporary'.

THEMES

MENTAL ANGUISH

Like many of Plath's poems, 'The Arrival of the Bee Box' depicts mental turmoil. The sight and sound of the locked box fills the speaker with dread: 'The box is locked, it is dangerous'. Her dread is exacerbated by the fact that she can't see into it. On one level, of course, the speaker is simply afraid that the bees might escape and sting her. Yet her intense reaction to the box seems to stem from more than this practical concern. She is 'appalled' by the noise of their buzzing and disgusted by what she can see of them through the grille. She associates them with rage, thinking of them as 'furious' maniacs 'angrily clambering' in the darkness. The dread she experiences seems to reflect her inner turmoil. She has such a strong reaction to the box because of the troubled and tumultuous mental state she is in when they arrive.

Such mental turmoil is also a feature of 'Elm', 'Finisterre' and, arguably, of 'Child'. Unlike those poems, however, 'The Arrival of the Bee Box' features a note of hope. The speaker can overcome her fear of the bees by releasing them, rather like someone who is afraid of flying stepping onto a plane. At present, the speaker is controlled by her terror of the bees. By releasing them, however, she will conquer her fear and empower herself. She will go from being powerless ('no Caesar') to being powerful ('sweet God'). If the speaker can overcome this seemingly irrational fear of the bee box, perhaps she can also overcome the deeper mental turmoil that affects her.

There are several instances in Plath's poetry where the speaker expresses what might be described as self-destructive thoughts or desires. Many readers feel that these desires surface in 'The Arrival of the Bee Box'. When the speaker imagines herself wearing the protective garments of a bee-keeper, she describes

the face covering as a 'funeral veil'. There is a sense here that she is anticipating her own demise, or on some level even desiring it. This tendency is perhaps also evident when she imagines herself being transformed into a tree:

I wonder would they just forget me
If I just undid the locks and stood back and turned into a tree.
There is the laburnum, its blond colonnades,
And the petticoats of the cherry

There is a sense in which the speaker seems to desire this transformation, to leave behind the human condition, with all its trials and tribulations. She wants to give up human consciousness and become an unthinking but beautiful piece of plant life. A similar desire to be released from human consciousness is also present in 'Finisterre' and in 'Poppies in July'.

Many of Plath's poems express what can only be described as feelings of inadequacy and worthlessness. Such feelings of failure are evident in 'Morning Song', where the speaker doubts her ability to be a good mother, and in 'Child', where the speaker laments that she can only give her child the 'agitated wringing of hands'. It is also present in this poem when the speaker doubts her ability to control the swarm of bees once she releases them: 'I am no Caesar'.

POETIC INSPIRATION

'The Arrival of the Bee Box' is often regarded as dealing with the theme of poetry and the unconscious. To write poetry, Plath believed, it was necessary to explore the darkest recesses of the mind, to explore the deepest reaches of the soul. Yet this, she felt, was a dangerous business, for it risked disturbing all kinds of inner demons: various traumas and negative emotions the mind has covered up.

The bee box, according to many readers, represents the hidden aspect of mind, the dark and mysterious parts the true poet must explore:

- Like the bee box, our unconscious mind is almost completely sealed: we cannot know what it contains until we begin to explore it.
- Just as the speaker is terrified and disgusted by the bee box, so Plath was nervous about exploring her unconscious mind, and horrified by the demons that might lurk there.
- By opening up her unconscious, she will unleash her inner demons, just as the speaker will release the bees.

Yet just as the speaker can't stay away from the bee box, so Plath was drawn back again and again to probe around the edges of her unconscious, for she felt that only by exploring this hidden aspect of herself could she create great poetry.

PSYCHIC LANDSCAPES

There are many poems where Plath creates what she described as 'psychic landscapes'. She uses a scene from nature or an element of the natural world in order to convey an inner state of mind. This tendency is also evident in 'The Arrival of the Bee Box'. The box serves as a metaphor for Plath's turmoil-filled mind. The box seethes with furious black bees 'angrily clambering' over one another in a chaotic fashion. Similarly, her mind seethes with dark, angry and negative emotions. 'Finisterre', 'Elm' and 'Poppies in July' are other poems where the natural world is used to convey troubled mental states.

ORDER AND CHAOS

Many of Plath's poems focus on the distinction between order and chaos. In this poem, the bees are a chaotic force, swarming hectically and frenziedly within their box. They are like a wild and disorderly mob. Only the box imposes order on them, containing their fury. Tellingly, the poem's opening lines associate the box with order: 'I ordered this, this clean wood box'. However, once the box is opened, order will be removed. The chaos represented by the bees will be free to make its way into the world.

The speaker finds this an unpleasant and perhaps even frightening prospect: 'How can I let them go?'. In this poem, as in 'Finisterre', Plath seems to regard chaos with what can only be described as fear and horror. Yet also as in 'Finisterre', there is a sense in which chaos is presented as something alluring and attractive. We see this in the way the speaker 'can't stay away' from the bees' frenzy, and in her decision at the end of the poem to release this 'box of maniacs' into the world.

A POET OF STRIKING DESCRIPTIVE POWERS

This poem features the rich and unusual imagery that is typical of Plath's poetry. We see this in her description of the box as 'the coffin of a midget/ Or a square baby'. On one level, of course, this description is outlandish and perhaps even slightly amusing. Yet there is also something unpleasant and unsettling about it. The description of the box as a coffin introduces the notion of death, and suggests the speaker's desire for oblivion.

Metaphor also features in line 31, where Plath compares a bee-keeper's protective clothing to an astronaut's space suit. She also compares a bee-keeper's protective face mesh to a veil worn by a dead woman at her funeral: 'in my moon suit and funeral veil'. These lines also feature a Classical reference, where the speaker imagines herself as Daphne, a doomed character from Greek myth who was transformed by the gods into a tree.

She uses a bizarre and somewhat unsettling metaphor to describe the bees, comparing them to the hands of dead African people that have been cut off, shrunken and exported back to Europe as souvenirs of the 'dark continent': 'African hands/ Minute and shrunk for export'. The image of thousands of tiny hands clambering around the box's dark interior is truly a disturbing one.

Plath uses a conceit or extended metaphor to describe the bees, comparing the swarm to a rioting mob in Roman times: 'It is like a Roman mob'. The sound of the bees' buzzing is likened to Latin, the now 'unintelligible' language spoken in Roman times. Just as it took a powerful ruler like Caesar to master the mobs of Rome, so it will take a skilled and confident bee-keeper to control the bees once they have been released from the box.

VERBAL MUSIC

We see cacophony in lines 13 to 15, where the repetition of hard 'b', 'r' and 't' sounds creates a harsh musical effect appropriate to the disturbing image the lines describe. Euphony occurs in lines 32 to 36: the repeated broad-vowel sounds in 'source of honey', 'moon suit', 'funeral veil' and 'box is only' create a pleasant musical effect. So, too, do the repeated internal and external rhymes between 'honey', 'me', 'sweet', 'free', 'only' and 'temporary'. This pleasant verbal music is appropriate as the speaker imagines herself overcoming her fear and releasing the bees.

Poppies in July

poet wonders where these 'opiates' are and seems to have the various drugs or medicine which are made from these in mind when she speaks of 'nauseous capsules'. Perhaps she is thinking here about how some pain-killers and sleeping pills can make the user feel sick or 'nauseous'.

The poet imagines that she is living in a 'glass capsule' – or, at least, this is how she feels. The image suggests a detachment from the world, an inability to feel or be touched by anything. (Perhaps this capsule is a reference to the fairy tale of Snow White. In that story, Snow White is given a poisoned apple. When she eats the apple, she falls into a death-like sleep. The dwarves with whom she lives place her in a glass capsule and here she remains until a prince wakes her with a kiss.) The poet imagines how the opiates from the poppies might 'seep' or flow into this capsule and put her into a deep sleep. Such 'liquors' would dull her senses and still her agitated mind and body: 'Dulling and stilling'.

The poem's might be a reference to the 'liquors' mentioned in line 13. The poet desires that these be 'colorless'. Or perhaps it is a reference to the world that she would like to enter in her drug-induced sleep. The poppies' vivid and rich colours disturb and agitate her. She would prefer a more neutral environment where she would not have to feel anything at all.

LINE BY LINE

The speaker is looking at a field of poppies in the summer. She is in an extremely agitated state of mind. She uses several violent and disturbing comparisons to describe the poppies:
- The poppies' intense redness reminds her of the fires of hell. The poppies are 'little hell flames'.
- The poppies remind her of mouths that are wounded and bleeding. They are 'wrinkly and clear red, like the skin of a mouth.// A mouth just bloodied.'
- She also compares them to skirts that are covered in blood: 'Little bloody skirts'.

The poet is worn out and exhausted: 'it exhausts me to watch you'. She is gripped by feelings of numbness and emptiness. She longs to escape this numbness by experiencing physical pain. She wants the flames of the poppies to burn her: 'I put my hand among the flames'. She also longs to be brutally punched in the mouth: 'If my mouth could marry a hurt like that'. Her bleeding mouth would resemble the blood-red poppies.

The opium poppy is the species of plant from which opium and poppy seeds are derived. Opium is the source of many narcotics, including morphine (and its derivative heroin). The

FORM
The poem features short, choppy lines, skilfully suggesting the agitated mental state of someone in deep depression.

TONE
The tone is alarmingly agitated and disturbed. It begins with the poet addressing the poppies in an accusatory, irritated and perplexed manner. However, by the end of the poem the poet seems to have lost the strength to challenge the flowers and the tone is one of exhaustion.

A POET OF STRIKING DESCRIPTIVE POWERS
This poem is marked by its vivid, nightmarish imagery. Plath compares the brightly coloured flowers to 'little hell flames', suggesting perhaps the way that the flowers are shimmering or dancing in the breeze. She also compares the shape and the redness of the poppies to 'Little bloody skirts'. The flowers' vivid redness is once again evoked with the disturbing image of a 'mouth just bloodied'.

Child

MENTAL ANGUISH

The speaker of the poem is exhausted and gripped by numbness and emptiness. The fact that she feels nothing causes her great mental anguish. She longs for some form of extreme physical sensation to cut through this numbness. She reaches out to the poppies in the hope that they might 'harm' her, but she is incapable of feeling them, let alone being burnt by the 'flames' that she imagines them to be: 'I cannot touch you./ I put my hands among the flames. Nothing burns'.

The speaker is obviously in a very distressed state of mind. She longs to either feel intense pain or to slip into some drug-induced sleep: 'If I could bleed, or sleep!' She is desperate to escape from her numbed and neutral existence. The poem closes with the poet imagining herself within a 'glass capsule' into which she longs for opiates to 'seep'. These 'liquors' will dull and still her until total oblivion is reached and the world fades away.

PSYCHIC LANDSCAPES

The landscapes that feature in Plath's poems are often representations of her own inner mental state. She referred to such landscapes as 'psychic landscapes'. In 'Poppies in July', the description of the field of poppies corresponds with and illustrates the mental turmoil that the poet is experiencing:

- She is in a hellish place and describes the flowers as 'little hell flames'.
- Because her anguish stems from her neutrality and numbness, the flowers are incapable of being touched or of harming her in any way: 'I cannot touch you'.
- Her longing to experience pain as a means of escaping her neutrality is reflected in the description of the red petals as 'the skin of a mouth ... just bloodied'.
- Her self-disgust is evident in the description of the flowers as 'bloody skirts', a possible reference to menstruation. ⊠

The poet admires the beauty of her child's eye. Her child's eye is 'the one absolutely beautiful thing'. She considers it to be something pure and untainted. It is 'clear', just like a pool of water. She sees her child as something perfect, someone yet untarnished by experience: 'Little// Stalk without wrinkle'.

The child is hungry to learn about the world. The poet describes the child meditating upon new words, possibly those of animals and flowers in a book. The poet mentions some exotic flowers that the child might be looking at: 'April snowdrop, Indian pipe'.

The poet wants to present her child with images that are fun and colourful: 'I want to fill it with color and ducks'. She also wishes to offer the child 'grand and classical images'. Such experiences will nourish the child's mind, allowing it to blossom and grow.

However, the poet seems to be suffering from some form of anguish or depression. She describes the 'troublous/ Wringing' of her hands. The world in which she exists appears to be dark and confined: 'this dark/ Ceiling without a star'. The last line may describe an actual room or it may be a metaphor for the way the poet views her own life. Ultimately, it suggests a terrible lack of hope and despair.

FEMININITY AND MOTHERHOOD

Like 'Morning Song', this poem illustrates how being a mother can be a very difficult and troubling experience. It suggests

THEMES

that a mother should fill her child's world with wonder and joy. The poet is conscious of the fact that her child is hungry for experience and knowledge. She wishes to give her child experiences that will nourish and preserve its beauty and innocence. That she cannot, makes her feel that she is failing in her role as mother, and this leads to feelings of greater anguish and despair.

MENTAL ANGUISH

This is ultimately a stark poem about mental anguish. To the poet, the world seems a terribly dark place: 'dark/ Ceiling without a star'. Her description of the 'troublous/ Wringing' of her hands illustrates her mental suffering. Her child's innocence and her inability to provide it with bright and happy moments only heightens her sense of suffering. She is left feeling inadequate as a mother.

In this regard, the poem can be compared to 'Morning Song' where the birth of the poet's child leaves her feeling numb and uncertain. However, in 'Morning Song' there is a sense in which the poet overcomes her feelings of inadequacy and doubt and relaxes into the role of being a mother. In 'Child' there is no suggestion that her feelings of inadequacy and despair are set to end.

TONE

The poem begins with a loving and hopeful tone but it ends on a terribly dejected and tragic note of despair.

A POET OF STRIKING DESCRIPTIVE POWERS

The flowers that the poet mentions are interesting: 'April snowdrop, Indian pipe'. It is quite possible that Plath meant them to represent something. The April snowdrop is a particularly beautiful flower, pure white in colour. Perhaps Plath meant this flower to represent the child who she considers perfectly beautiful and innocent.

The Indian pipe, on the other hand, is a less beautiful flower. It is said to exist in darkened forests and feeds on the decaying matter of other dead flowers. It may, therefore, represent the mother in the poem. She feels that she is living in a world without light, beneath a 'dark/ Ceiling without stars'. And perhaps she feels that in her despair and her inability to offer the child grand and beautiful images she is sucking the goodness out of it.

Plath compares her child to a 'Little// Stalk without wrinkles'. She also compares the child's eye to a 'Pool'. Both metaphors suggest the child's purity and innocence.

How to Answer the Poetry Questions

I've been asked to write an essay in response to the following statement: 'I like (or do not like) to read the poetry of Sylvia Plath.'

STAGE 1: PLANNING YOUR ANSWER

ESTABLISH A POINT OF VIEW

Firstly, I'm going to decide what my point of view is. I'm going to declare that I like the poetry of Sylvia Plath for the following reasons:

- It is emotionally intense, and it deals with the darker aspects of the human psyche.
- Her vivid and violent imagery lingers in the mind long after we have read the poems.

This is one of the most important steps in the whole process. I have decided on a point of view. I will not be rambling on vaguely about my attitude to Plath's poetry. Everything in my answer will now relate to this point of view.

DECIDE WHICH POEMS TO TALK ABOUT

I am now going to decide which poems to talk about. It's good to talk about four to six poems in an answer. I'm going to talk about six: 'Elm', 'Poppies in July', 'The Arrival of the Bee Box', 'Morning Song', 'Black Rook in Rainy Weather' and 'Child'. I'm going to quickly jot down the titles of these poems along with a couple of quotations from each poem that will relate to my point of view.

STRUCTURE THE ESSAY

Now I'm going to structure my essay. I'm going to write six paragraphs.

- The first paragraph, the introduction, will clearly state my point of view.
- The second paragraph will deal with 'Elm' and 'The Arrival of the Bee Box'. I will be discussing Plath's inner turmoil as exhibited in these poems.
- The third paragraph will discuss 'Black Rook in Rainy Weather' and 'Poppies in July'. I will discuss feelings of numbness or mental neutrality as exhibited in these poems.
- My fourth paragraph will discuss 'Child' and 'Morning Song'. I will discuss the feelings of inadequacy as a mother exhibited in these poems.
- My fifth paragraph will discuss vivid and memorable images in Plath's poetry. I will refer to a number of the poems mentioned above.
- The final paragraph will be the conclusion.

STAGE 2: WRITING THE ESSAY

WRITING THE INTRODUCTION

I'm going to write my introduction. The first one or two sentences of my introduction will simply state the point of view I came up with in the planning stage:

> I really admire the poetry of Sylvia Plath because it is emotionally intense and it deals with the darker aspects of the human psyche. I also like how her vivid and violent imagery linger in the mind long after we have read the poems.

I am now going to flesh this out in a few more sentences. It is good to make these sentences personal, if possible, to describe the impact the work had on you. In this instance, I am going to emphasise the impact Plath had on me by contrasting her with the other poets I have studied:

> I really admire the poetry of Sylvia Plath because it is emotionally intense and it deals with the darker aspects of the human psyche. I also like how the vivid and violent imagery she uses lingers in the mind long after we have read the poems. Throughout my life I have always found poetry to be dull, boring and intellectual. The poets I read never really connected with me. However, this was definitely not the case with Sylvia Plath. This is poetry that came from the heart as much as from the head. Her work spoke to me immediately due to its raw and intense emotional content and its unforgettably violent imagery.

It's obvious that the five sentences I have added here flesh out my point of view. The sentences are personal and show that I have really engaged with the work of the poet.

WRITING THE BODY PARAGRAPHS

I see from my plan that my first body paragraph will deal with the inner turmoil expressed in 'Elm' and 'The Arrival of the Bee Box'. So I'm going to start the paragraph with a topic sentence, declaring what the paragraph is going to be about:

> In 'Elm' and 'The Arrival of the Bee Box' we see Plath expressing intense inner turmoil.

Every other sentence in this paragraph is going to relate to or expand on this topic sentence. If I find myself writing something that does not relate directly to this topic sentence, I know I've gone wrong.

To complete this paragraph I am going to write a couple of sentences about 'Elm' and 'The Arrival of the Bee Box':

In 'Elm' and 'The Arrival of the Bee Box' we see Plath expressing intense inner turmoil. 'Elm' depicts a mind at the end of its tether. The poet is tormented by the dark emotions that dwell within her psyche: 'I'm terrified by this dark thing/ That sleeps in me'. The elm tree has been 'scorched' by the 'atrocity' of 'sunsets', has been lashed by poisonous rain and blasted by 'wind of such violence'. Yet we feel that these terrible sufferings are a metaphor for the mental turmoil the poet endures. 'The Arrival of the Bee Box' is another poem that deals with mental turmoil. The bee box has thrown the poet into a state of confusion and distress. She is both frightened and fascinated by this object: 'The box is locked, it is dangerous./ I have to live with it overnight/ and I can't keep away from it'. She is disgusted by the sight of the bees through the box's grill: 'Black on black, angrily clambering'. She is even more upset by the sounds that are coming from the box: 'it is noise that appals me most of all'. As in 'Elm', we feel that there is an element of metaphor to this poem. The box serves as a symbol for the darker side of the poet's psyche, for the feelings of fear and inadequacy that she keeps locked inside her and that she fears will destroy her should she set them free.

Note how every sentence I have written relates to my topic sentence. I don't wander off the point by talking about Plath's marriage or about life in the 1950s when she wrote the poem.

Note also how I don't fall into the trap of paraphrasing the poems, of telling the examiner everything that happened in each of them. I simply take two or three aspects that are relevant to my topic sentence.

Note also how I back up every point with a quote. The golden rule here is 'Always be quoting'!

Finally, note how at the end of my paragraph I link the two poems it discusses. This is a skill that can be acquired with practice.

I see that my next paragraph is going to deal with feelings of numbness or mental neutrality as exhibited in 'Black Rook in Rainy Weather' and 'Poppies in July'. Once again, I start off with a simple topic sentence:

'Black Rook in Rainy Weather' and 'Poppies in July' display a desperate state of mental neutrality and numbness.

Once again I am going to write a number of sentences that relate to this topic sentence. I'm going to make sure that nothing I write strays away from this topic.

'Black Rook in Rainy Weather' and 'Poppies in July' display a desperate state of mental neutrality and numbness. In 'Black Rook in Rainy Weather', the poet expresses her 'fear/ of total neutrality'. In one sense, this suggests her fear of writer's block, the fear that she will never again be visited by 'the angel' of inspiration, by that 'rare, random descent'. However, the mention of 'total neutrality' calls to mind the intense numbness or emptiness experienced by those suffering from depression. The grey, desolate landscape in which the poem is set serves as a metaphor for this state of 'total neutrality'. The 'desultory weather' and the 'season/ of fatigue' calls to mind the dead inner emptiness the poet fears. In 'Poppies in July', this fear seems to have been realised. The poet is gripped by a feeling of numbness and emptiness. She longs for physical pain just so she can feel something: 'if I could bleed, or sleep! –/ if my mouth could marry a hurt like that'. She wishes the 'flames' of the poppies could burn her in order to return some sensation of feeling to her life.

Note again how every sentence I have written relates to my topic sentence.

I don't fall into the trap of paraphrasing the poems, of telling the examiner everything that happened in each of them. I simply take two or three aspects that are relevant to my topic sentence.

I back up every point with a quote.

Note how the two poems are linked in the middle of the paragraph. Again, this is a skill that comes with practice.

The remainder of the body paragraphs will follow the same format outlined above.

WRITING THE CONCLUSION

The idea here is to sum up what I have said in the essay without repeating myself too much. I am going to bring the point of view I established in the introduction. I am going to try and get personal. The first thing I am going to do is rewrite my point of view in slightly different language.

For me, then, Plath's poetry stands out because of its sheer emotional power.

Now I am going to add a sentence that contains a phrase like 'In the poems discussed above' or 'As I have outlined above' or 'As I have discussed'. This sentence will refer back to the essay I have just written.

If you are good at English, it can be good to finish with a flourish. This might involve using a memorable phrase, a quote from a famous writer or the poet under discussion, or some poetic sentence of your own.

THE SEVEN GOLDEN RULES

1. **Read the question carefully.** This sounds obvious but I can't stress how important it is.

2. **Establish a point of view.** Do this at the beginning of your planning stage. Remember that every sentence in your essay will relate to this point of view.

3. **Structure the essay carefully.** Determine what every paragraph is going to be about before you commence writing.

4. **Begin each paragraph with a topic sentence.** Every other sentence in the paragraph will relate to this sentence.

5. **Don't paraphrase.** Don't retell the story or the action of the poem – the examiner already knows this. Just identify the two or three elements of the poem that relate to your topic.

6. **Always be quoting.**

7. **Be aware of genre.** Are you being asked to write a straightforward essay or are you being asked to do something else like write a letter or give a short talk? If you are being asked to write a letter or a short talk, then the introduction and the conclusion of your piece will need to reflect this.

> For me, then, Plath's poetry stands out because of its sheer emotional power. In poems like those discussed above, there is an emotional intensity like nothing else I have come across in poetry.

Now I am going to add two or three more sentences that flesh out this point. I am going to try to make these as personal as possible.

> For me, then, Plath's poetry stands out because of its sheer emotional power. In poems like those discussed above, there is an emotional intensity like nothing else I have come across in poetry. Reading Plath's poetry, I felt she was really talking to me, that she was describing dark emotional states that I and every other human being will experience at some point. The powerful imagery, like that of the elm, the bee box and the disturbing field of poppies, will remain with me for the rest of my life.

Note how the conclusion is short and does not ramble on and on repeating the points made in the essay. Also note how the conclusion describes a personal response. Finally, note how the conclusion is tied into the point of view established at the start of the essay.

ELIZABETH BISHOP	Moments of Awareness	Love and Respect for Natural World	Childhood	Addiction	Exile and Homelessness
THE FISH	Poet suddenly realises that the fish, like her, is a survivor. It has been caught previously but has managed to escape. She realises that survival is a form of 'victory'.	No detail of the fish's appearance is considered ugly or banal.			
THE BIGHT		Love and respect for natural world comes across in poet's detailed description of the birds in the bay.			
FISHHOUSES	The sea is presented as a symbol of the unconscious, with all the traumatic self-lknowedge it contains.	The poet's fasciation with the natural world comes across in her lovingly detailed description of the sea, the fir tress and the seal.			Great Village is presented as a 'home'and point of origin for the poet, but its community is changing and declining.
THE PRODIGAL	At night the prodigal realises with a shudder the true horror of his existence in the farmyard.			Moving and honest portrayal of addiction. Emphasises how difficult it is for addict to leave addiction behind.	Prodigal's self-imposed exile – feels he does not really have a home to go to anymore.
QUESTIONS OF TRAVEL				Travel is considered as compulsive, restless behaviour.	Poet uncertain where home really is or what the concept even means. Many people travel because they do not know where home is.
THE ARMADILLO		The poet shows a keen awareness of her environmnent. Laments man's careless attitude towards nature.		Compulsive behaviour of the locals – they know fire balloons are dangerous and illegal but insist on releasing them.	
SESTINA	Describes the child's dawning awareness of the tragedy that has befallen her family.		Wonderfully captures childhood mentality. Skilfully evokes a child's point of view.		
FIRST DEATH	Poem documents the child-speaker's dawning awareness of the reality of death.		Wonderfully captures childhood mentality. Skilfully evokes a child's point of view.		
FILLING STATION	Poet realises that even the lowliest people and places have someone who loves them..				
IN THE WAITING ROOM	The poet is stunned and disorientated as she realises the limits of her individuality.		Wonderfully captures childhood mentality. Skilfully evokes a child's point of view.		

EAVAN BOLAND	Ireland: Myth History	Writing in a Time of Violence	Love & Marriage	Family: Myth and History	Motherhood	The Subjugation of Women
THE WAR HORSE	The poet experiences a sense of the wrongs of Irish history stirring within her: 'my blood is still// With atavism'.	The horse represents the war and violence that is taking place beyond the poet's comfortable surroundings. We choose to ignore such violence but the poem suggests that it can happen anywhere.				
THE FAMINE ROAD	The poet's description of the Famine highlights the poet's intense awareness of the wrongs of Irish history.				Focuses on plight of women who are unable to bear children.	Shows how women are oppressed, humiliated and misunderstood by a male-dominated society.
CHILD OF OUR TIME		Emotional response to an innocent victim of violence. We have created a violent world that makes victims of our children. We must learn from our mistakes and create a new order.				
THE BLACK LACE FAN			Portrays the positives and negatives of a long-term marriage. Captures the tensions and uncertainties of early love.	The poet laments how past events – even those involving our immediate family – can never be fully known or recreated.		
THE SHADOW DOLL			Presents an extremely negative view of marriage, suggesting it robs women of their freedom and independence.			Shows how women are silenced and controlled by a male-dominated society.
WHITE HAWTHORN IN THE WEST OF IRELAND				Poet attempts to connect with her heritage as an Irish woman, and to rediscover the countryside and its traditions. But can she?		
OUTSIDE HISTORY	The poet is suddenly aware of all those who have suffered and died throughout history. The poet is determined to remember and speak for all of history's forgotten victims.					
THIS MOMENT					Celebrates the constent, unseen work that mothers do.	
LOVE			Realistic view of long-term relationships. The poet celebrates the lasting bond but is nostalgic for the relationship's early passion.	The poet laments that we can never revisit or recreate the most intense and happiest periods in our lives.		
POMEGRANATE					Highlights the stresses and anxieties that mothers experience, including those associated with sending one's child out into the world.	Poem highlights the particular risks and dangers experienced by women.

PAUL DURCAN	Romantic Love	Marriage	Family	Ireland and Irish History	Mental Suffering	Religion	The Strength and Power of Women
NESSA	Highlights the heady excitement at the beginning of a new relationship. But he feels like his life's spinning dangerously out of control.				Anguish that sometimes accompanies being in love.		This vivacious, spontaneous young woman is portrayed almost as a force of nature.
GIRL WITH KEYS	Captures the intensity and passion of teenage infatuation. The poet is clearly smitten by the striking young Cáit.			Cottage as a metaphor for Ireland in 1960, a time when the country was poor and undeveloped.			
THE DIFFICULTY THAT IS MARRIAGE		Realistic view of marriage: the couple argue a lot but deep down he would refuse heaven to live with this woman forever here on earth.				Heaven is imagined as a 'changeless kingdom', a place of unfaltering bliss where all our earthly troubles are left behind.	
WIFE WHO SMASHED TELEVISION		Depicts a highly dysfunctional marriage where all communication as broken down.	Highlights negative impact of technology on family life.	This poem presents Ireland as an oppressive and repressive place – especially toward women.			This is a woman not afraid to rebel. She has been ignored in favour of the television for long enough.
PARENTS			Our loved ones seem far away while they're sleeping. Perhaps highlights the anxiety felt by parents of sick child.				
EN FAMILLE					Hints at uncomfortable childhood experiences.		

PAUL DURCAN	Romantic Love	Marriage	Family	Ireland and Irish History	Mental Suffering	Religion	The Strength and Power of Women
MADMAN			Touches on the difficult and negative relationship Durcan had with his father.				
'WINDFALL'		Highlights the intimacy and contentment of married life.	Celebration of shared family experiences. Documents just how painful it is to lose one's family.	Criticises the unequal nature of Irish society at the time.			
SIX NUNS						Highlights both the positive and negative aspects of faith and religion.	The nun demonstrates enormous strength and resilience.
SPORT			Highlights the difficult and negative relationship Durcan had with his father.				
FATHER'S DAY		Paints a frank and sorrowful picture of a couple who have fallen a little out of love.	Highlights loneliness that arises when children grow up and leave home.		Sadness and guilt upon realising that relationship with wife has changed.		Wife presented as a cool, calm and competent woman who knows her own mind.
ARNOLFINI MARRIAGE		Suggests that marriage confers great power and authority.					
IRELAND 2002				Captures mindset of country at a particular moment.			
ROSIE JOYCE			Families stretch across the generations, providing a sense of support, meaning and belonging.	Highlights the economic differences between Ireland's eastern and western halves.	Describes poet's struggles with depression over the previous three years.	Poem is like one long prayer of thanks to God for Rosie's birth.	
MACBRIDE DYNASTY		Marriage is not a fairy-tale union but a journey full of difficulty, conflict and betrayal.	Families stretch across the generations, providing a sense of support, meaning and belonging.	The poet highlights his own membership of an important dynasty in Irish life.			Maud is a strong and powerful woman who achieved prominence and influence.

ROBERT FROST	Nature	Childhood	Sorrow And Despair	Transience and Brevity	A Cold Universe	Isolation and Community
THE TUFT OF FLOWERS	Poet inspired and consoled by the sight of the flowers. Nature helps him to overcome feelings of loneliness.		Poet feels dejected when he realises he must work alone. The dead flower that the butterfly circles is also a symbol of sorrow.	Description of the butterfly searching for the flower it had enjoyed suggests the transience and brevity of life.		Speaker initially believes that people work in isolation but the flowers that the mower spared suggest that we work together.
MENDING WALL	Suggestion that there is a sinister force operating in nature. Nature resists our efforts to impose order on the world.					Considers how work unites people. Poem acknowledges that boundaries are needed for community to work.
AFTER APPLE PICKING	Celebrates the beauty of the late autumn season.		Speaker is exhausted with life and seems to desire a long break or sleep.	Sense of the transience of time as the harvest and year comes to its end and the winter sets in.		Speaker has left the other workers on the farm as he needs to be alone to sleep.
BIRCHES	Celebrates beauty and wonder of natural world. Nature offers the poet a means of escape from everyday worries.	Presents childhood as an innocent time of play. Poet longs to return to this time.	Describes poet's weariness with life and his desire to escape his troubles for a brief moment.			Celebrates the pleasures of being alone. Poet longs to be like the young boy playing alone in the woods.
'OUT, OUT –'	Poem contains beautiful descriptions of the Vermont landscape.	Captures the mentality of childhood. Describes the need to allow children to play	Suggestion that those working with the boy fail to demonstrate sorrow at his tragic fate. Sense that life must go on.	Reminds us how quickly life can be snatched away. Urges us not to take life for granted.	Seems to suggest that there is no meaning or point to life – things happen randomly and without reason.	
THE ROAD NOT TAKEN			Sense of sorrow at only being able to take one path in life and not experience others .	Poet hopes to return some day to the other road, but knows that life is too short for this.		
SPRING POOLS	Vivid portrayal of nature's fragile beauty. Flowers and trees used to illustrate the cyclical nature of life.			The pools and the flowers only exist for the briefest spell. Transient beauty of natural world.		
ACQUAINTED WITH THE NIGHT			Moving portrayal of a mind in the grip of depression. Speaker seems trapped in a loop of despair.		Examines the chilling possibility that God does not exist, that universe is uncaring and life meaningless.	Speaker spends his nights cut off from friends and family, alone on the city streets.
DESIGN	Reminds us that natural world can be bloody and unpleasant as often as beautiful and serene.				Frost explores the idea that the universe might be governed by evil forces or that there is no design or meaning to life	
PROVIDE, PROVIDE			.	Highlights transience of beauty, youth and fame.	Suggests that world is cold and uncaring and we should look out for ourselves.	Presents us with a bleak image of isolation in old age. Warns us to avoid this fate.

SEAMUS HEANEY	Art & Craft and Creativity	Love	Crediting Marvels	Conflict and Violence	Process of memory
THE FORGE	Celebrates blacksmith's craft. Blacksmith serves as a metaphor for poetry		This unpromising, functional space is depicted as something marvellous		
BOGLAND	The bog serves as a metaphor for the poet's creative mind		The Irish is depicted as a marvellous and haunting landscape		The bog is a physical embodiment of the nation's memory
THE TOLLUND MAN				Religiously inspired violence of Ireland is compared to human sacrifices carried out in ancient Jutland	
SUNLIGHT	Celebrates the aunt's craft in the kitchen	Celebrates the poet's aunt as a loving and nurturing figure		Depicts a safe space, utterly devoid of this conflict and violence	Depicts composite memories from many different childhood afternoons
A CONSTABLE CALLS				The constable's presence is invasive and alien – hints at the sectarian conflict that would later bedevil Northern Ireland	
THE SKUNK		Celebrate the joys of married life and a resilient long-standing relationship	This everyday animal is considered fascinating		The process of memory is presented as multi-layered and complex, one memory invariably leading onto the next.
THE HARVEST BOW	Celebrates the father's craft in creating the bows.	Examines the complex but ultimately loving relationship between the poet and his father			The bow triggers an intense recollection of the poet's childhood, its loops compared to a screen on which events from the past can be viewed
THE UNDERGROUND		Presents two very different pictures of romantic love, one positive and the other negative			
THE PITCHFORK	Imagines a spontaneous and exuberant form of creativity.		Considers basic, everyday implement to be something wonderful. The farmer's playful imagination and child-like wonder		
LIGHTENINGS VIII			Describes how the ordinary to one person is the marvellous to another		
A CALL	Celebrates the care and craft the father brings to his garden	Examines the complex but ultimately loving relationship between the poet and his father			
TATE'S AVENUE		Celebrate the joys of married life and a resilient long-standing relationship. Different rugs suggest different phases			Presents the process of memory as a kind of internal Instagram

GERARD MANLEY HOPKINS	The Beauty of Nature	God's Presence in Nature	Environmentalism	Sin and Redemption	Doubting God's Goodness	Mental Suffering
GOD'S GRANDEUR	Poet celebrates the beauty of the sunrise.	Senses God's energy flowing through all living things, sustaining the natural world.	Man has lost contact with the natural world and spoils it with his industry.	Man goes against God's will, polluting the beautiful world he has given us.		
SPRING	Poet delights in the newness, freshness and energy of springtime.	Thoughts of nature lead to thoughts of Jesus and his role as our saviour.		Hopkins is keenly aware that childhood innocence will be 'soured with sinning'. Calls on Christ to preserve the innocence of each child.		
AS KINGFISHERS CATCH FIREWINDHOVER	Poet delights in nature's sounds, colour and variety: kingfishers, dragonflies, even stones.	Senses God's presence in all living things. Nature's variety leads him to think of the 'just man' and of living in grace with God.		Calls on us to behave in a 'just' manner and turn away from sin.		
THE WINDHOVER	Poet is exhilarated by the sight of the falcon wheeling masterfully around the sky. It 'stirs' his heart, which had previously been in hiding.	The falcon's strength, beauty and courage inspires the poet to think of Christ's sacrifice on the cross.		Falcon's bravery reminds of Christ's sacrifice on the cross, which redeemed mankind from original sin, giving us the opportunity to be right with God.		
PIED BEAUTY	Poet delights in the beauty of 'dappled things'.	Senses God's presence in the natural world as He 'father's forth' each living thing. Nature's beauty should lead us to praise God.				
FELIX RANDAL				Christ, through communion, is our 'reprieve and ransom', saving us from sin.	Felix curses God for allowing him to become ill.	Felix in physical pain. Felix in mental torment – his mind wanders as his sanity begins to give way.
INVERSNAID	Poet delights in the sights and sounds of a 'burn' or brook.		The poet hopes that wild places like the burn will survive human development. Calls for them to be left alone.			The black whirlpool of despair suggests the poet's unhappiness.
I WAKE AND FEEL THE FELL OF DARK					Poet's prayers are like unanswered 'dead letters'. Jesus seems far away. It seems God has 'decreed' him to suffer.	Poet suffers through long 'black hours' of mental suffering each night. Physical suffering: his body is a tormenting prison of 'gall' and 'heartburn'.
NO WORST THERE IS NONE					Poet feels abandoned by both Jesus and Mary in his hour of greatest need.	Poet 'pitched past pitch of grief' – experiences intense mental suffering.
THOU ART INDEED JUST, LORD					Why does God allow evil men to thrive? Why do those who live holy lives suffer?	Desperate and 'straining' attempts to make something of his life. Feels intense disappointment when these efforts come to nothing.

JOHN KEATS	Nature	Love	Celebrating Artworks	Artistic Creativity	Death	Change and Changelessness
CITY PENT	Country offers much needed break from stresses of modern city life.		Celebrates the joy and pleasure of reading.			
CHAPMAN'S HOMER			Celebrates the joy and pleasure of reading Celebrates the incredible excitement of discovering a great new author.	Celebrates the scope of Homer's unique creative imagination.		
WHEN I HAVE FEARS	Expresses a desire to capture the natural world in his verse.	The poet celebrates his beloved's beauty and longs to be beside this 'fair creature'. But is love and desire a treacherous 'faery power' that can lead to suffering?		Highlights the fertility of his own creative mind and his desire to 'trace' the world – but will he have time?	The poet is terrified that death could claim him before he has reached his potential.	The poet's concerns sink to nothingness when he contemplates eternity – each human life is nothing in the greater scheme of things.
LA BELLE DAME		Sometimes taken to be an allegory of how desire can enslave and torment us.				
NIGHTINGALE	Poet's ecstatic and overwhelming response to the nightingale's song.		The nightingale's singing is celebrated as an extraordinary and moving work of art.	Celebrates the 'wings of poesy', the power of the poetic imagination to transport us. He imagines the entire world of the woodland.	Laments how everyone must age and die. Poet also in love with death.	The nightingale and its song are presented as un-ageing and immortal.
GRECIAN URN		Poem describes how desire can often lead to heartache and misery: 'leaves a heart high-sorrowful and cloy'd'.	Celebrates the beauty of this object that can still enchant after so many centuries.	Highlights the power of the poetic imagination as the poet conjures up an entire world.	Laments how every generation must pass away. The society depicted on the urn suggests a more authentic way of life that embraces death.	Thinks of the characters depicted on the urn as real people – envies the fact they are frozen in time.
AUTUMN	Poet's ecstatic and overwhelming response to autumn's melancholy beauty.				Is the poet's fascination with death evident as he celebrates this this time of year?	Celebrates how the natural world is in a constant state of flux.
BRIGHT STAR		Poet celebrates his beloved's beauty and desires to be with her forever.			Again we see the poet's infatuation with death. He would be happy enough to die if he could do so in his lover's arms.	Poet envies the star because it never changes.

SYLVIA PLATH	Psychic Landscape	Order and Chaos	Mental Anguish	Femininity and Motherhood	Poetic Inspiration	Nature
BLACK ROOK IN RAINY WEATHER	Speaker's dull, uninspired state of mind is mirrored in 'dull, ruinous landscape'.	World presented as a random and chaotic place. No purpose to the natural world.	Fears a numb mental state of neutrality that comes with a lack of inspiration.		A spiritual view of inspiration. Inspiration is random and unpredictable. Highlights artistic insecurity.	
THE TIMES ARE TIDY		Describes a perfectly ordered environment, where the same things happen over and over again in a perfectly regular and predictable fashion.			Plath views this ordered, tidy world as somehow deeply uncreative.	
MORNING SONG			A sense that the poet does not feel adequate as a mother. Parents are somewhat numb and feel no strong emotion about the arrival of their child.	Suggests that motherhood is not a straightforwardly joyous and natural experience. It can be hard to adjust to this new and overwhelming responsibility.		
FINISTERRE	The description of the bay can be taken to suggest either a storm of emotional turmoil or a state of complete mental numbness or perhaps even both.	Sea = chaos Land = order Chaos attracts and repulses.	Inner turmoil. Mental neutrality. Self-destructive urges.	Our Lady is often thought of as the 'mother' of the human race. Yet in this poem she is certainly depicted as having failed her children.		
MIRROR			The woman in the poem is gripped by a fit of loneliness or despair, examining herself in the looking glass as she cries and wrings her hands.	Comment on the pressure women feel to meet unattainable standards of beauty.	Is the front, or facade, of the perfect housewife is in danger of choking the artist within?	
PHEASANT					The colour and movement of the natural world is a rich source of inspiration to the poet.	A celebration of natural world. Life in the poet's hands (the pheasant).
ELM	Elm undergoes various tortures that serve as metaphors for Plath's turmoil-filled mind.		Inner turmoil: elm's sufferings. Suggests how the woman's awareness of her own faults freezes her desire to go on living.	This poem is a study of feminine suffering.	Just as the elm delves into the soil, so the poet must explore the recesses of his or her unconscious mind.	
POPPIES IN JULY	Field of poppies illustrates the mental turmoil of poet.		The speaker of the poem is exhausted and gripped by numbness and emptiness.			
THE ARRIVAL OF THE BEE BOX	The box serves as a metaphor for Plath's turmoil-filled mind.	The bees represent chaos. The box imposes order on them. Chaos both attracts and repulses the poet.	Depicts inner turmoil. Self-destructive thoughts or desires. Inadequacy: the speaker doubts her ability to control the swarm of bees once she releases them.		The bee box, represents the hidden aspect of mind, the dark and mysterious parts the true poet must explore.	
CHILD			Captures the poet's anguish and inner turmoil. A sense of inadequacy in relation to her child.	Illustrates how being a mother can be a difficult and overwhelming experience.		